Hollywood Surf and Beach Movies

The First Wave, 1959–1969

THOMAS LISANTI

Foreword by
ARON KINCAID

McFarland & Company, Inc., Publishers
Jefferson, North Carolina, and London

LIBRARY OF CONGRESS CATALOGUING-IN-PUBLICATION DATA

Lisanti, Thomas, 1961–
Hollywood surf and beach movies : the first wave, 1959–1969 /
Thomas Lisanti ; foreword by Aron Kincaid.
p.   cm.
Includes bibliographical references and index.

ISBN 0-7864-2104-5 (illustrated case binding : 50# alkaline paper) ∞

1. Beach party films—United States—History and criticism.   I. Title.
PN1995.9.B38L57   2005   791.43'657—dc22   2004029518

British Library cataloguing data are available

Cover photograph: Aron Kincaid and Chris Noel in a publicity
shot for the 1965 film *Beach Ball*. Background image ©2005 PhotoSpin.

Manufactured in the United States of America

McFarland & Company, Inc., Publishers
Box 611, Jefferson, North Carolina 28640
www.mcfarlandpub.com

For all the unsung 1960s beach movie actors and
actresses who have brought joy to millions

Acknowledgments

First I would like to express my sincerest thanks to the following wonderful people who took the time to talk with me: Louis Arkoff, Peter Brown, Jackie DeShannon, Dave Draper, Don Edmonds, Shelley Fabares, Edward Garner, Gail Gerber, Susan Hart, Aron Kincaid, Kathy Kohner Zuckerman, Arnold Lessing, Leslie H. Martinson, Jody McCrea, Ted V. Mikels, Chris Noel, Quinn O'Hara, Bart Patton, Bob Pickett, Robert Pine, Frankie Randall, Darlene Tompkins and William Wellman, Jr. Without their insights and anecdotes, this book would have been just another average film compendium.

Special thanks must go to Aron Kincaid, who went beyond the call of duty in helping me bringing this book to life. I will be forever grateful to him for leading me to some of the people interviewed here, supplying photographs from his private collection and for taking the time to write the foreword. Quinn O'Hara described Aron as being "one of the nicest people you ever want to meet." I couldn't agree more. A special "thank you" to the wonderful Quinn, who's still a "red-haired gasser," for her valuable input and for supplying me with numerous photos from her collection. Also a special thanks to Bart Patton and William Wellman, Jr., for also graciously providing the use of their personal photos, to Susan Hart for speaking kindly about me to Frankie Randall and his manager Melinda Read, and to Laree Draper for being a very sweet go-between with her husband, Dave Draper.

Thanks to Sharyn Peacocke from Down Under for allowing me to quote from her interview with Deborah Walley on her website *The Lively Set* and to fellow McFarland author Tom Weaver for putting me in contact with Arnold Lessing and for his superior copyediting skills. I would like to express my gratitude to the staff at The New York Public Library where I work. Thanks to photographers Peter Riesett and Michael Moreno for their expert scanning capabilities, and to Jeremy Megraw, Karen Nickeson and Bob Taylor of the Billy Rose Theatre Collection. I also would like to acknowledge the helpful staff at the Margaret Herrick Library of the Academy of Motion Pictures Arts and Sciences, and Bill Schurk at the Music Library and Sound Recording Archives, Bowling Green State University.

A great big "thank you" to Ernie DeLia for his patience, encouragement and editing prowess. Also thanks go to my friends Louis Paul (who co-authored *Film Fatales* with me) and Shaun Chang for their suggestions and help in organizing this book. A special nod to Jim McGann, my innovative web master, and to my family and friends for their continued support: Diane Bonfanti, James Campbell, Joe and Barbara Casamento, Donna and Michael Cates, John Covelli, Jim Cullen and David Gabriel, Rose DeFeo, Teresa DeTurris, Matt Fletcher, Scott Hannibal, Bill Hay, Pete Kaiser, Tom Kazar, Judy and Rick Keifer, John Kelly, Jeannie and Tony Koproski, Phil Lindow, Joan Lisanti, Joseph and Beth Lisanti, Lorraine and Richie Nicolo, Peter Nunziato, Alan Pally, Shawn Peacock, Al and Barbara Reisinger, Lori Ann Reisinger, Paul Reisinger and Marta Skorynkiewicz, John Rowell, Mark Tolleson, Kevin Winkler and David Youse.

Table of Contents

Part II: The Players

Foreword

by Aron Kincaid

Every once in a while at a social gathering I'm asked by someone what I do for a living. I gleefully answer, "Absolutely nothing! I'm retired." Not the truth, as I've been an artist since I could hold a crayon and I'll probably go to my "final reward" with a brush in my hand and oil paint under my nails.

"Well, what did you do before retirement?" the inquisitive stranger asks.

"I was an actor in motion pictures and television—but that was probably before you were born," I reply. This sort of questioning makes me feel like I was on stage with John Wilkes Booth!

"Cool," my new acquaintance approves. "What films were you in—anything I might have heard of?"

"Did you ever see *Spartacus*? I was Sir Laurence Olivier's standard bearer. I was 17½ years old at the time and...." I reply before being cut off.

"No, I mean ... I think I heard of it. Was Russell Crowe in that one?"

"Well, then, how about the surf and beach movies of the sixties?" I ask. My curious new acquaintance then reacts the way countless others have—their faces light up with smiles of instant recognition. They become like little kids at Grandpa's knee begging to hear the stories of olden days of blue skies, warm sun, lively music (with lyrics in which *every* word could be understood) and a bygone innocence that this old world will never see the likes of again. The fact that I was a part of the various interpretations put on film in an effort to capture this unique era of American pop culture gives me satisfaction and a sense of accomplishment, however misguided that may be perceived by those who look down their noses at such entertainment. The only message these films had was "Enjoy life!" And, boy, did we!

By the early 1930s, sound had become part of the magic of motion pictures. When World War II ended, Hollywood was *the* film capital of the world with blazing Technicolor, world class conductors creating wondrous sounds in lavish musicals and camerawork that was the equivalent of the visions of master artists such as Rembrandt, Goya and Sargent. The finest writers in the world were writing screenplays whose lines are quoted verbatim over a half-century later.

The fifties brought the end of the "studio system" as it was called. The major filmmakers had been forced to relinquish their theaters. They had depended upon

1

these outlets for their film product. No more! It was all over and done! Stars were released from their secure ("restrictive" some might say) exclusive contracts and became (choke! gasp!) freelance players. The lucky ones secured picture deals while those performers less fortunate used what remaining clout they still possessed to become television personalities, often earning far more in this new medium (it had actually been around for 30 years) than they had in films. Performers such as Lucille Ball, Dick Powell, Red Skelton, Gale Storm, Dennis O'Keefe and Robert Cummings became household names who were celebrated and beloved far beyond their fame as motion picture contract players.

CinemaScope, VistaVision, 3-D and lavish spectacles were utilized by the studios to bolster their sagging revenues and by 1962 there were very few surprises on the movie screen. I had been a glorified extra in a couple of movies and since 1960 I'd done a fair amount of television before I enlisted in the United States Coast Guard Reserve during the Vietnam War in 1963. Work in Hollywood for a young actor in those days usually consisted of playing the callow youth whose "big moment" came when he'd say, "Can I have the car tonight, Dad? I have a date with Betty Jane." One of my earliest television roles actually had me bounding into a family gathering and asking, "Tennis, anyone? We've got a half-hour before dinner."

Toward the end of my three-month boot camp (on Government Island near San Francisco) I was given a 12-hour liberty pass. My parents (who lived near the

Aron Kincaid today is a distinguished artist and voice-over actor *(courtesy Aron Kincaid)*.

base) picked me up and took me for lunch with *real food*! I had survived on nothing but salads and fruit for two and a half months due to the fact that "military nourishment" was abominable to my elitist taste buds. After gorging on filet mignon, chicken breasts, French fries with sauce Bernaise and coconut cake, I begged to be taken to a movie— *any* movie! I was as starved for film as I had been for food.

Our neighborhood theater was playing a movie with Robert Cummings and Dorothy Malone. A young actress I had dated was in it, too. She'd made quite a name for herself at Disney Studios. Standing in front of the Piedmont Theatre, I looked at the photo of Annette Funicello on the poster and received quite a jolt! Was it possible in less than a year she had gone from a virginal senorita on *Zorro* to a teen version of Gina Lollobrigida in a white fishnet-topped swimsuit? *Beach Party*, the film we were there to see, held the answer—yes!

When we stepped out into the blinding sunlight after the screening, my mom was the first to speak. "I loved it! Honey, you'd be a natural in a film like that. It's just like the life you led in Los Angeles," she said. I had thought the film silly and a bit empty. The storyline with Cummings and Malone was actually embarrassing. I had sort of liked the parts with the kids on the beach and I had made a mental note that the color orange looked great with a sun tan. Little did I realize that what I had just seen was to shape my life for the next three years!

Being stationed in Southern California after boot camp couldn't have been timed more favorably. Still in uniform, I auditioned for *The Girls on the Beach* thanks to a friend, Bart Patton, from my days at the UCLA film school. I got the part (a lead and starring billing no less!) and we shot the thing in less than a month. My friend Bart was producing another surf and sand "epic" titled *Beach Ball* and once again I played one of the leads. In just two films I'd worked with Lesley Gore, Diana Ross and the Supremes, the Beach Boys, the Righteous Brothers, Frankie Valli and the Four Seasons, The Walker Brothers, and Buddy Holly's backup group, The Crickets! All this and getting a nice paycheck for kissing and hugging some of Hollywood's most gorgeous young actresses.

When filming wrapped for the day, our nights were spent at the clubs in Beverly Hills and along the Sunset Strip. Life was like one big, bright red T-bird convertible with a pulsating soundtrack of surf music and rock 'n' roll.

Sometimes after a day of shooting we'd just stay on location in Malibu where there'd be a bonfire on the beach, the waves washing in, hamburgers on the grill and sing-a-longs with guitars. We'd curl up with a blanket on the sand and when the sun rose we were ready to go. I never needed makeup as I was in the sun all day and was tanned even between my toes. Ah yes, the days of slathering on baby oil (with a few drops of iodine in it), squeezing the juice from lemons in our hair, and dying shirts all shades of orange.

A third film followed immediately for me. *Ski Party* had me further down in the credits but it was my favorite role. We filmed in Sun Valley, Idaho, and finished up on the beach at Santa Monica with The Hondells pounding out a tune. Boy, was I having fun! American International Pictures, producers of *Ski Party*, offered me a seven-year contract. I grabbed it. For me it was like "Old Hollywood Rides Again." I was put in two more films—*Dr. Goldfoot and the Bikini Machine* and *The Ghost in the Invisible Bikini*. Norman Taurog directed the former. He had helmed *Skippy* with Jackie Cooper in 1931 and had guided Dean Martin and Jerry Lewis in their highly successful comedies in the fifties. The latter film boasted the impressive cinematography of Stanley Cortez, who was responsible for the brilliant camerawork in Orson Welles' *The Magnificent Ambersons*. The cast of *The Ghost in the Invisible Bikini* was a Who's Who of Hollywood history—Francis X. Bushman (Messala in the great silent epic *Ben-Hur*), Basil Rathbone (Sherlock Holmes and the nemesis of Errol Flynn in *The Adventures of Robin Hood*), comedienne Patsy Kelly, Benny Rubin, Jesse White and the original monster of Dr. Frankenstein, Boris Karloff. Whatta time!

The demand for photos and stories on the *Beach Party* gang (as we were referred to by the press in the U.S. and Europe) was so great that we were sent in groups of three all over America to do interviews, photo layouts and television shows. My "trio" consisted of statuesque Mary Hughes, the willowy Salli Sachse and me. Off we went to Colorado (where we experienced a tornado, a flash flood and an earthquake all in one day!), Wisconsin, Michigan, Indiana and New York. Meeting The Beatles, recording records, television shows such as *Shindig* and *The Dating Game* (I went barefoot on that one), cocktail parties, receptions, screenings, more photos and a zillion interviews with fan magazines and newspapers—all just part of a normal working week in the magical mid-sixties.

But all good things must come to an end. By 1967 the waves would crash on the silver white beaches of the screen no more. Now it was a time of LSD, marijuana, biker gangs, hot rodders, date rape and lousy photography. But while the surf-and-turf period lasted, it was truly a wondrous time. Now, through his talent and dedicated pursuit of facts and minute details, Tom Lisanti brings back the crazy, carefree mid-sixties world of the Hollywood surf movie. Were it not for Mr. Lisanti's skills in capturing a unique space of time in history of motion pictures, I sincerely doubt that many would find it possible to believe that such a film cycle had ever existed. But as Lisanti presents the films, we see that it did indeed flourish and thrive for a brief period of time … a contemporary Camelot.

Somebody once said, "If you remember the sixties, then you weren't there." But I'm here to tell you I remember it well and I've got the proof on film—I was most *definitely* there!

Aron Kincaid
Beverly Hills, California
December 2004

Preface

Hollywood Surf and Beach Movies: The First Wave, 1959–1969 is a straightforward look at films that were aimed at the teenage audiences. The book does not contain in-depth analyses about the films in terms of their cultural importance or non-importance to surfing or their perception today as being cult, camp, nostalgic or just plain bad movies. There have been many journal articles and chapters in other movie books written about that aspect of these films; some of them are listed in the bibliography. This book, a reference compendium of surf and beach party movies, is, I believe, one of a very few of its kind.

The book is broken up into three parts. The Introduction gives an overview of the Hollywood surf and beach movie genre, from its start with *Gidget* in 1959 through 1969, how it got started, and how it morphed into beach party movies. Also discussed are the reasons for the rise and fall of surf cinema during this period of time.

The main part of the book contains entries on 32 Hollywood surf and beach party movies that were released between 1959 and 1969. Each entry (excluding *Daytona Beach Weekend* and *One Way Wahine*, which I could not locate) contains a brief review by the author and a rating in six categories: overall fun and entertainment value, boy watching, girl watching, surfing footage, music and scenery. Nowadays, fans view these movies for the nostalgic appeal of innocent fun from bygone days. People don't look to these movies for Academy Award–winning performances or insightful writing. They watch to ogle scantily clad sixties actors dancing on the shore or to see their favorite sixties rock group on celluloid or to check out the surfing feats of such hot doggers as Mickey Dora or Johnny Fain or just to marvel at the beauty of the California coastline. These ratings are geared to be helpful to viewers in selecting a film to watch based on their interests.

Each movie entry also includes as complete a list of cast and crew as possible, a plot synopsis, DVD availability, memorable lines from the script and a list of awards and nominations. Actors are listed in billing order from the opening credits. Actors not included in the opening are added as listed in closing credits. Crew members are recorded with job title as listed in credits. Cast and crew members not credited but contained in sources such as the Internet Movie Database or *The American Film Institute Catalog of Motion Pictures: Feature Films 1961–1970* are only included when their presence could be verified. A release date is given but, unlike today where a film usually opens nationally on the same day, during the sixties some of these low-budget films were released regionally and then over a period of time opened in the bigger cities. Most release dates are culled from *The American Film Institute Catalog of Motion Pictures.*

Reviews from the time of the films' original release are included to demonstrate that there were a few critics who did understand that these surf and beach movies were produced for the enjoyment of the discerning teenager. Of course, most reviewers did not and some of their more outrageous and humorous comments are included. Movie grosses gleaned from *Variety* are included wherever possible. Unfortunately, box office tallies were not published as routinely in the sixties as they are today. DVD release information is given but VHS availability is not because most videos are of the bootleg kind or are from companies that are now defunct.

What I hope will make this book more entertaining than the typical film genre compendium is the Behind-the-Scenes sections, with little-known or forgotten facts about these movies and interviews with some of the cast and crew about the making of the films.

Most of the awards and nominations listed are from annual polls in motion picture trade publications such as *The Film Daily* ("Famous Fives"), *Motion Picture Exhibitor* ("Golden Laurel Awards"), *Boxoffice* ("Stars of the Future"), *Screen World* ("Most Promising Personalities"), *Motion Picture Herald* ("Stars of Tomorrow") and the dreaded *Harvard Lampoon* ("Movie Worst Awards"). From these publications, there were no actual awards given to the actors named. But some publications such as *Photoplay* and *Teen Screen* did hand out trophies to the winners, as did the Hollywood Foreign Press with their annual Golden Globe Awards.

The second part of the book, "The Players," contains profiles on a select number of actresses* and actors who made their marks in the surf and beach movie genre. Some include comments from the actors and actresses recently interviewed specifically for this publication.

I've tried to be as specific as possible in terms of crediting sources in the bibliography. A number of magazine articles and reviews came from clipping files from The New York Public Library for the Performing Arts and the Margaret Herrick Library of the Academy of Motion Picture Arts and Sciences. Hence, sometimes exact dates and page numbers were missing. Online sources have also been referenced when pertinent information was found to include in the profiles. A general listing of web sites that were consulted is contained at the end of the bibliography.

For interviews and profiles on beach girls Joy Harmon, Karen Jensen, Deanna Lund, Julie Parrish, Salli Sachse and Lana Wood, consult Fantasy Femmes of Sixties Cinema: Interviews with 20 Actresses from Biker, Beach, and Elvis Movies. *The book* Drive-in Dream Girls: A Galaxy of B-Movie Actresses of the Sixties *features profiles (some with interviews) on Brenda Benet, Diane Bond, Patti Chandler, Nancy Czar, Jackie DeShannon, Gail Gilmore, Luree Holmes, Mary Hughes, Mikki Jamison, Candy Johnson, Suzie Kaye, Marta Kristen, Donna Loren, Meredith MacRae, Claudia Martin, Jenny Maxwell, Mary Mitchel, Valora Noland, Bobbi Shaw, Ulla Stromstedt, Darlene Tompkins, Wende Wagner, Lori Williams and Venita Wolf. Lastly,* Film Fatales: Women in Espionage Films and Television, 1962–1973 *contains profiles on Anna Capri, Yvonne Craig, Donna Michelle, Nancy Sinatra, Maggie Thrett and Raquel Welch.*

Introduction

Surfers loathed them, teenagers flocked to them, critics dismissed them, and producers laughed all the way to the bank. They are surf and beach movies, which were Hollywood's interpretation of the surf culture that for a short period in the sixties became one of *the* most popular genres.

Gidget (1959), a fictionalized look at teenager Kathy Kohner's surfing escapades in Malibu during the mid-fifties, was the first official Hollywood surf movie. It was groundbreaking, as the movie contributed to the mass dissention of surfers on the beach in Malibu and started a series of surf-theme films such as *Gidget Goes Hawaiian* (1961) and *Ride the Wild Surf* (1964). The surf movie soon morphed into the beach party film, whose heyday was from 1963 through 1965. In these films, surfing was only used as a backdrop to fanciful teenage beach adventures. *Beach Party* from American International Pictures (AIP), starring Frankie Avalon and Annette Funicello, launched four sequels—*Muscle Beach Party, Bikini Beach, Beach Blanket Bingo* and *How to Stuff a Wild Bikini*—and a few offshoots such as *Pajama Party* and *Ski Party*. These movies for the most part followed a successful simple formula—start with attractive swimsuit-clad teenagers twisting on the sand, add a dash of surfing footage, mix in romantic misunderstandings, stir in popular musical performers, add aging comedians for comic relief, and whisk in villainous bikers or predatory adults.

Soon other companies were releasing their own *Beach Party* rivals such as *Surf Party, The Girls on the Beach* and *Beach Ball*. Some of these films varied from the formula by shifting the locale to a lake (*A Swingin' Summer*) or the ski slopes (*Winter a-Go-Go, Wild Wild Winter*). Finally there were the hybrids that combined the beach party movie with other genres such as horror (*The Beach Girls and the Monster, The Ghost in the Invisible Bikini*) and spy spoofs (*Out of Sight*).

Before there were Hollywood surf and beach party movies, there were independent 16mm documentaries called "surf movies" produced by surfers mainly for other surfers. Bud Browne is credited with producing the first one, *Hawaiian Surfing Movies* (1953), which was first screened for an audience in the auditorium of a Santa Monica junior high school. By the late fifties and early sixties, Browne was joined by filmmakers John Severson (*Surf, Surf Safari, Surf Fever*), Bruce Brown (*Slippery When Wet, Surf Crazy*) and Greg Noll (*Search for Surf*). At first, these films were made without sound and shown with live narration in rented school auditoriums and legion halls in beach communities up and down the Southern California coast. According to Matt Warshaw, author of *The Encyclopedia of Surfing*, the

7

similar format of surf movies consisted of "two or three dozen surf-action montages interrupted periodically by a comedy sketch or an on-the-road vignette; later movies often had brief surfer interviews, an animated short, an alternative sport (skiing, hang gliding, skateboarding), or an environmental-message sequence."

Original music scores and pre-recorded narration were soon added to these surf movies in the early sixties as other filmmakers such as Dale Davis (*Strictly Hot, Inside Out*), Jim Freeman (*Let There Be Surf*) and Greg MacGillivray (*A Cool Wave of Color, The Performers*) hopped on the surf movie bandwagon. Freeman and MacGillivray would team up in 1966 and their first co-feature was *Free and Easy* (1967). In the seventies they produced one of the most popular surf movies, *Five Summer Stories* (1972). Besides the rad surfing footage, what made these movies popular with the surfing crowd was the camaraderie that developed amongst the surfing enthusiasts in the audience. According to Matt Warshaw, the rowdy surfers who came to watch these movies did not sit there in silence but would "whistle, shout, cheer, boo, hiss, stomp their feet, roll beer bottles down the aisles, throw paper airplanes, and occasionally sprint onstage to moon the audience." In 1966, Bruce Brown was able to get his surf movie *The Endless Summer* blown up to 35mm and distributed to the mainstream moviegoing public. The result was an enormous hit and Brown showed Hollywood that a movie about surfing didn't need to include singing and goofy surfers to make money.

The Hollywood surf movie craze began with a little novel called *Gidget* by Frederick Kohner. This was a fictionalized account of his daughter Kathy's involvement with the Malibu surfing crowd during the summers of 1956 and 1957. The pretty Jewish tenth grader from Brentwood was prodded by her mother to go to the beach on the weekend because she did not want her daughter sitting in the house all day. Mrs. Kohner would drive some of the local neighborhood boys in her Model-T to the shore. Kathy tagged along and became "the group mascot" to the regular crowd of surfers who hung out in Malibu. The guys had nicknames such as Mysto George, Golden Boy, Scooter, Meat Loaf and Tubesteak. Trying to fit in and learn to surf, Kohner, nicknamed "Gidget" (from girl-midget due to her being only five feet tall and weighing 95 pounds), ingratiated herself with the surfers by bringing a steady supply of homemade sandwiches to the beach in exchange for the use of the guys' surfboards.

As she began to master the sport, Kathy became so exhilarated with surfing that she would enthusiastically share her escapades with her parents and voiced a desire to write a book about it as she was keeping a journal on her exploits. Her father, an Academy Award–nominated screenwriter, took on the idea and the novel *Gidget* was released by G. P. Putnam in 1957. The book sold a half million copies and Kathy Kohner was featured in a *Life* magazine article entitled "Gidget Makes the Grade."

The character of Kahoona in the novel was loosely based on Terry-Michael "Tubesteak" Tracey, who lived in a shack on the beach. He got his nickname from the steakhouse where he worked. Tracey claims to have coined the nickname Gidget for young Kathy. Kohner and others think it was surfer Jerry Hurst. Of all the original Malibu surfers at the time, he is the only one who still holds a grudge against the Gidget phenomenon. He remarked in the *Los Angeles Times*, "We didn't know she [Kathy] was taking all those photographs. She was on a covert mission

Poster art for *Beach Party* (AIP, 1963) featuring Frankie Avalon and Annette Funicello in the film that launched the mid-sixties beach movie craze.

at the age of 15. Then suddenly they've got *Life* magazine out there doing a promotion for the book." Tracey said he and his fellow surfers were "idiots" for going along for the ride but he does confess that he got work in Hollywood due to the publicity surrounding the book and the movie. Kathy Kohner dismisses Tracey's suggestion that she had a predetermined plan and says she only took "a few pictures."

Kohner bought her first surfboard from teenager Mike Doyle. The board was blue and decorated with a totem pole design. Her real-life crush was on Bill Jensen, a blonde, blue-eyed 20-year-old surfer. According to Kathy, he was the only surfer who did not have a nickname. "I've re-read my diaries from that time and I only refer to him as Bill throughout," says Kathy. In the novel, Gidget's love is Jeff Matthews, who is nicknamed Moondoggie. Some 50 years later it is understandable that the surfers of the time disagree if there really was a Moondoggie. Jensen thinks it was clipped from a surfer nicknamed Boondoggie while Kathy and Tracey claim that it was the real nickname for Malibu surfer and artist Billy Al Bengston. He received his moniker due to his resemblance to Louis "Moondog" Hardin, a blind New York jazz and poetry artist who wore a beard and had long hair.

Columbia Pictures bought the film rights to *Gidget* and the dark-haired Jewish surfer morphed into a blonde WASP played by Sandra Dee. Veteran actor Cliff Robertson played Kahoona while James Darren essayed the role of Moondoggie. The producers wanted to film at the actual locations where the novel took place but Malibu had become overrun by an influx of new surfers so shooting was relocated approximately 20 miles north. The novel had brought so much attention to the sport that its popularity skyrocketed. Everybody "east of the 405" wanted to surf, crowding out a number of veteran surfers who let their displeasure be known in the surf magazines of the day. It is estimated that the number of surfers in the U.S. went from approximately 2,000 to hundreds of thousands due to the success of *Gidget*. It sparked the surfing phenomenon due to its glamorization of the bohemian Malibu surfers' lifestyle, making it alluring to teenagers all over the country. Surfing would forever become a mainstay of pop culture.

Kohner's novel proved so popular that he authored a sequel *Gidget Goes Hawaiian* in 1961. This was followed by *Gidget Goes to Rome* (1962), *The Affairs of Gidget* (1963), *Gidget in Love* (1965), *Gidget Goes Parisian* (1966) and *Gidget Goes New York* (1969). As the novels progressed, surfing took a backseat to the romantic adventures of our heroine as she traveled the globe. The same held true for the movie sequels. Deborah Walley took over for Sandra Dee as Gidget in *Gidget Goes Hawaiian* (1961). Though Walley, unlike Dee, actually gets on a surfboard in the ocean, there is far less surfing and more romantic problems as Gidget is torn between James Darren's Moondoggie and Michael Callan's television star. In the last theatrical Gidget movie, *Gidget Goes to Rome* (1963), our heroine, now played by Cindy Carol, doesn't even touch her surfboard as she quickly abandons the shores of Malibu for a Roman holiday.

In late 1960, MGM released the beach movie *Where the Boys Are* (1960) starring Dolores Hart, George Hamilton and Yvette Mimieux. It was the story of four Chicago coeds who join thousands of other college students for spring break in Fort Lauderdale where they hit the beach and local nightclubs as they try to trap themselves some husbands. Along with the landlocked *Palm Springs Weekend* (1963) starring Troy Donahue, Connie Stevens and Ty Hardin, *Where the Boys Are* was the start of the teenage spring break film genre. Elvis Presley even got in on the act with the popular *Girl Happy* (1965), playing a band leader secretly chaperoning his boss' 20-year-old daughter Shelley Fabares and her friends Chris Noel and Lyn Edgington while on vacation in Fort Lauderdale. As the years passed, spring break films such as *Malibu Beach* (1978), *Beach House* (1982), *Spring Break* (1983), *Where the Boys Are '84* (1984) and *The Real Cancun* (2003) got wilder and raunchier, featuring lots of foul language, sex, drinking, fighting, wet T-shirt contests and brief male and female nudity.

In 1961, Gidget wasn't the only one to ride the waves in Hawaii. Elvis Presley played a returning G.I. who'd rather surf with his Hawaiian buddies than work on his father's pineapple plantation in *Blue Hawaii*. Surfing vanished from the screen for a while though a few quasi-beach movies appeared here and there, such as *Love in a Goldfish Bowl* (1961), starring Tommy Sands and Fabian, and *Bachelor Flat* (1962), starring Tuesday Weld and Richard Beymer.

During this time, surf music began permeating the airwaves. In 1960, the Ventures followed by Dick Dale introduced instrumental surf music with reverb-sounding guitars that were designed to sound like crashing waves. Dale, who was nicknamed the "King of the Surf Guitar," charted with the regional hit "Let's Go Trippin'" in 1961 followed by "Miserlou" the following year. But it was the Surfaris with "Wipeout" in 1962 and the Chantays with "Pipeline" in 1963 who scored Top Five national hits.

By the time *Beach Party* (1963) went into production, the second wave of surf music began climbing the charts. These were pop songs about surfing or the Southern California lifestyle sung in three- or four-part harmony. The Beach Boys from Southern California had a regional hit with "Surfin'" and then cracked the Top 20 with "Surfin' Safari" in 1962. And in early 1963, Jan and Dean climbed the charts with "Honolulu Lulu," the Queen of the surfer girls, before hitting the top of the charts with "Surf City." These songs inspired the surfing dreams of young people across the country (some of whom had never seen the ocean) and turned the pastime into a national craze.

Beach Party producers James H. Nicholson and Samuel Z. Arkoff of AIP had the foresight to gamble on a new formula suggested by director William Asher, an avid surfer and denizen of Malibu. He convinced the producers to make their first pop musical film about clean-cut, beach-loving surfers just looking for a good time. Screenwriter Lou Rusoff set up an interesting premise in *Beach Party* as it combined aspects of *Gidget* and *Where the Boys Are*. Surfer gets mad at girl for inviting his buddies on their romantic holiday at the beach so he decides to make her jealous. Throw in an older professor studying the sex habits of teenagers, an inept motorcycle gang, the best stock surfing sequences in the entire series and a buxom Hungarian vixen, and you have the makings for an entertaining beach party. In between some of this foolishness, the subculture of surfing is explored. Surfer slang peppers the script; surf culture is off limits to the adults, biker gang and "kooks." Yes, we know that real hot doggers don't break into song, and they are not as dumb as Bonehead, but not since *Gidget* does a film, amid the slapstick, try to explain the appeal of shooting the curl.

Signed to star in *Beach Party* (1963) were singing sensation Frankie Avalon and Mouseketeer cast-off Annette Funicello. Neither actor would be considered an obvious choice to play the typical Southern California beach dweller. The dark-haired Avalon, slight at five-foot-seven, grew up in the inner city of Philadelphia. Annette was a buxom Italian-Catholic brunette who had never donned a bikini and never would. Nevertheless, the chemistry between Frankie and Annette immediately struck a chord with the teenage moviegoing public as they sang, surfed, bickered and fell in love under the California sun. Also contributing to the movie's immense popularity was the gorgeous Malibu shoreline, ample surfing footage, shirtless surfer boys and bikini-clad beauties, Harvey Lembeck as a fumbling motorcycle gang leader, and authentic surf rhythms provided by Dick Dale and His Del-Tones. The adult guest stars, including Bob Cummings, Dorothy Malone and Morey Amsterdam, made it appealing to older audiences as well.

Independent producer-director Maury Dexter was the first to ape AIP's *Beach Party*. He quickly rushed into production *Surf Party* (1964), starring vocalist Bobby Vinton, Pat Morrow and Jackie DeShannon. In his film, three young girls head to Malibu looking for Morrow's wayward brother and get involved with the surfing crowd. Though there was plenty of surfing and songs, this was a serious film featuring youthful characters with problems. 20th Century–Fox released the movie.

Though popular with teenagers, real surfers loathed the beach party movies because of characters such as Jody McCrea's dumb surfer Bonehead, seen here with Salli Sachse (left) and Patti Chandler.

Though it was filmed in black-and-white, the teenage audience's thirst for surfing was strong and *Surf Party* turned a profit. Fox also picked up the distribution rights to *The Horror of Party Beach* (1964), an extremely low-budget black-and-white programmer that was the first to combine the horror and beach movie genres. Filmed in Connecticut on the Long Island Sound, there is not a surfer or a wave in sight as mutant sea monsters from the deep terrorize a beach community's residents (played by a cast of unknowns).

AIP meanwhile followed up *Beach Party* with two immediate sequels re-teaming Frankie and Annette. While the first film showed the surfers smoking cigarettes and drinking beer, these activities slowly disappeared in all the subsequent films so as not to rile the parents of the teenagers for whom these films were intended. In *Muscle Beach Party* (1964), the surfers battle a group of bodybuilders led by the hysterical Don Rickles for their turf on the beach while Annette has competition with Luciana Paluzzi (as an Italian countess) for the charms of Frankie. *Bikini Beach* (1964) was the first AIP movie to introduce another sport as drag racing replaced surfing as the focal point. It also lampooned the Beatles, with Avalon playing the dual role of Frankie the surfer and the Potato Bug, a British pop singer who flips for Annette.

Musically, Dick Dale and His Del-Tones returned for *Muscle Beach Party* and were joined by Donna Loren and Little Stevie Wonder. Dale refrained from appearing in *Bikini Beach* and "house band" duties were assumed by surf band the Pyramids, who had a Top 20 hit with "Penetration" in early 1964. Subsequent performers in the AIP beach party movies included the Nooney Rickett Four, the Hondells, the Kingsmen and the Bobby Fuller Four. As the movies shifted away from surfing, so did the music. Also by 1965, the British Invasion had pretty much knocked surf music off the charts save for the pop songs by the Beach Boys.

To the chagrin of the surfing community, the Hollywood surf and beach movies were extremely popular as they struck a chord with the teenage psyche. AIP was probably the first company to realize that roughly two-thirds of the movie ticket buying public were between the ages of 15 and 25. The beach party movies were tailored squarely for that audience, combining their love of rock music with their hormonal thirst for titillation (e.g., scantily clad boys and girls twitching and singing about love and heartache on the shores of Malibu) without straying from the moral attitudes of the time. The surf and beach party movies created a carefree environment where good kids don't have a care in the world and enjoy an easygoing, parentless lifestyle of surfing, dancing, rock 'n' roll and romance, which was unconnected with reality. It was an escapist fantasy look at the American youth culture— an innocent ideal that most teenagers of the time embraced.

Regarding the popularity of the AIP beach party movies in particular, William Asher commented in *The New York Times*, "The key to these pictures is lots of flesh but no sex. It's all good clean fun. No hearts are broken and virginity prevails." The films may have been innocent and the kids chaste but they were also very sexy with all the curvaceous bikini-clad girls and the shirtless surfer boys frolicking on the sand. According to Donna McCrohan, author of *Prime Time, Our Time*, these films were also reassuring to parents because with girls like Annette and Chris Noel as the defenders of virtue they showed that "it's possible to spend the whole summer on the sand in practically no clothes, fall in love with another terrific-looking nearly naked person and still not 'go all the way.'" It was this wholesomeness, real or imagined, that attracted the kids and their approving parents. It is this same wholesomeness and naïveté that make these movies popular to this day. Their innocence has a nostalgic aspect to them as a sort of "pop mythology" as noted by Andrew J. Edelstein in *The Pop Sixties*.

While young people across the nation went gaga over these Hollywood surf and beach party movies, real-life surfers felt maligned by them ("Real surfers don't sing to their chicks!"). They were annoyed that they were being portrayed as silly, crooning wave riders who danced on the sand or as moronic imbeciles, as in the case of the character Bonehead in *Beach Party*. According to Dominic Priore (writing in *Hollywood Rock*), during that film's premiere real surfers turned away or walked out in disgust with what was transpiring on screen; surf stunt man Mickey Dora released a jar of moths, which quickly covered the screen, in protest. Surfers wouldn't have been caught dead waiting in line to see *Muscle Beach Party* or *The Girls on the Beach*. They considered these movies to be "lame." Forty years later, surfers such as Mickey Munoz and Greg Noll are still disdainful of these movies. In interviews regarding director Stacy Peralta's documentary *Riding Giants* (2004), Noll vehemently dismisses *Gidget* and *Ride the Wild Surf*, calling them "stupid" and the actors "dorks." Peralta, a self-described "surf rat" since the early seventies, remarked in *The New York Times* and *Surfer* that he directed *Riding Giants* to help debunk the sixties Hollywood myth of guitar-strumming surfers, played by "actors paddling around in a fish bowl" pretending to surf.

Some surfers-turned-actors such as Don Edmonds of *Gidget Goes Hawaiian* and *Beach Ball* also did not like the image these movies were projecting. Edmonds remarked, "Those films absolutely did make us look dumb." The surfing press also reviled these movies even though the presence of top surfers such as Mickey Dora, Johnny Fain and Butch Van Artsdalen surf-doubling gave the movies some credence.

Not all surfers felt this way. Malibu surfer and AIP regular Ed Garner opines, "I think what you hear from a lot of surfers is sour grapes. A number of them were left out of the loop and not asked to appear in these films; or the products they created or were pitching, such as surfboards or swim trunks, were not used. The beach party films fantasized a lifestyle that existed in Southern California. This ideal was marketed to the masses. James Nicholson was a promotional genius in that regard. In the process, the films did exploit the surfing craze, but so what?"

Sam Arkoff's son Louis was a teenager and a surfer back then. He remarks, "In the fifties and early sixties, surfing existed mostly in the beach towns of Southern California and Hawaii. You had this small group of surfers who really dug the sport and created their own subculture. Then for a movie like *Beach Party* to come along with guys yelling 'cowabunga' and characters like Eric Von Zipper, the real surfers watching this thought what a crock of shit. This movie helped popularize surfing, which was a sport to the rest of the country. I began surfing and there weren't that many good places. You'd get to a spot where there was a crowd and they would beat you up." It is this influx of newcomers to the sport that riled surfers the most about *Gidget* and *Beach Party,* as the exploitation of surfing expanded the sport's popularity from a small cult to a commercialized million-dollar industry complete with surfing competitions and paid endorsements.

The creators of the beach party movies in particular defend their product and claimed they never set out to make true surfing movies. Producer Sam Arkoff remarked in *People*, "They weren't about surfing; that was just a nice background. They were about kids." Director William Asher, a surfer himself, concurs and firmly stated in *Filmfax* magazine, "These films are not about surfing.... It was background,

Aron Kincaid, star of *The Girls on the Beach* and *Beach Ball*, signs autographs for a mob of pubescent admirers, ca. 1965 *(courtesy Aron Kincaid)*.

and you build a story around it." However, to the naïve teenager living in Kansas who never set foot out of his home state, it is understandable why he would think that kids his age living in Southern California were goofy cut-ups who partied and danced on the beach all summer long when not riding the waves.

The beach party movies were fantasies exporting the glamorous myth of the Southern California beach culture, which was being touted in songs by the Beach

Boys and Jan and Dean, to the millions of young people who didn't live there. Sam Arkoff emphatically remarked in *Cult Movies* that they were building a dream world for teenagers from the slums and cities where they could visualize themselves at the beach with pretty bikini-clad girls and riding the waves. Chris Noel, star of *Beach Ball*, adds, "These beach movies were an escape from reality. They were innocent fun. Life is rough enough without having to watch it on the movie screen. I should know as I went to Vietnam a number of times during the war." Her *Beach Ball* co-star, Aron Kincaid, gets annoyed when these movies are criticized for representing a false look at an idealized America that never existed. "Well, it did exist," exclaims Kincaid. "It just depended on where you lived. Sometimes when shooting wrapped for the day, some of the actors would hang out on the beach for awhile and then we'd go to dinner and hang out just like in the films we were making."

As the debate about surf and beach party movies continued and Hollywood kept churning them out one after another in 1964 and 1965, life for surfers went on. Expert Leonard Lueras, author of *Surfing: The Ultimate Pleasure*, wrote, "Throughout and despite all that big screen embarrassment, California's surfing society continued to develop a character all its own. It evolved into an aloof cult ... and established a sense of 'surfer style' and ritual that endures to this day."

Despite the criticisms from real-life surfers for the misrepresentation of their sport and lifestyle, and reviewers for the juvenile plots, amateur acting and inane dialogue, these surf, sand and sex epics became a staple of American pop culture. Besides Frankie Avalon and Annette Funicello, actors James Darren, Sandra Dee, Deborah Walley, Don Edmonds, John Ashley, Jody McCrea, Jackie DeShannon, Pamela Tiffin, Peter Brown, Tommy Kirk, Susan Hart, William Wellman, Jr., Chris Noel, Aron Kincaid and Michael Blodgett, among others, became extremely popular with the teenage set due to their beach movie appearances. DeShannon defends these films and comments enthusiastically, "Beach movies were the forerunners to the popular films that we have now. People should know that those films are a lot more important than what they are given credit for. They should be studied in college film curriculums for their place in film history and what they were for that period of time and for what they spawned."

While Frankie and Annette were already famous, the AIP beach party movies' supporting players found fleeting fame as well. John Ashley, who portrayed Frankie's loyal friend Johnny, and Jody McCrea, who played the moronic surfer Bonehead, both had a small following of fans before appearing in *Beach Party*. Teenagers clamored for articles in their favorite fan magazines such as *Teen Screen* and *Teen Magazine* about them as well as newcomers Donna Loren, dancer Candy Johnson, cute surfer boys Mike Nader, Ed Garner and Johnny Fain, and sexy beach girls Mary Hughes, Patti Chandler, Luree Holmes and Salli Sachse.

In 1964, *Look* magazine produced a multi-page spread on AIP's roster of stars and its new movie *Pajama Party*. The following year, *The Saturday Evening Post* also did a multi-page feature on the beach party phenomenon. To keep the momentum going, AIP sent their stable of actors, who were later joined by Deborah Walley, Susan Hart, Bobbi Shaw, Aron Kincaid and Sue Hamilton, on press tours around the country to promote the movies. In each city they were treated like Hollywood royalty as they posed for pictures, gave television and radio interviews and hosted contests in conjunction with the film that they were promoting. Their popularity proved amazing. Richard Warren Lewis reported in *The Saturday Evening Post* that teenagers trampled an airport fence to get a glimpse of *Beach Blanket Bingo* stars Avalon and Deborah Walley. The police needed to escort Annette away from over-zealous fans while promoting *Muscle Beach Party* while fans at a Connecticut drive-in mobbed John Ashley. Aron Kincaid recalled in *The Los Angeles Times*, "We would go to drive-ins where they would show these movies. They would introduce us from the stage, and the parents would be yawning and their young children would be screaming and clawing for us. It was really a remarkable time."

Muscle Beach Party and *Bikini Beach* both were box office hits. One reason director William Asher feels they were so popular was because of the titles. He explained in *The Saturday Evening Post*, "It's like a television series, these sequels. You can't call each one the same. But the similarity of titles identifies the product, and the teenagers go and see it." Also giving these movies a familiar feel were that the same set of characters are put in slightly different situations in each movie. The thin plots may vary but the faces remained the same, as these teenagers were free of the parental interference which vexed the *Gidget* films and some of the other beach movies, and were just out to have a good time surfing, dancing and romancing.

It's not surprising then that other film companies entered this new booming genre and began releasing their own surf and beach party movie copycats, pairing different young and upcoming stars. United Artists released *For Those Who Think Young* (1964) with handsome James Darren and sultry Pamela Tiffin as the new Frankie and Annette. However, they were let down by the producers, who were not paying attention to the formula that made the AIP films successful; the film is peppered with parents, teachers and way too many old fogies. Still, the movie made money as it rode the crest of the *Beach Party* wave and Darren and Tiffin were re-teamed in the teenage hot rod flick *The Lively Set* (1964).

Much better than *For Those Who Think Young* and the best Hollywood surf movie of the sixties was *Ride the Wild Surf* (1964) from Columbia Pictures. This was an earnest and ambitious attempt by Hollywood to capture the surf culture and what attracted young men to the sport. Fabian, Tab Hunter and Peter Brown play surfers who travel to Hawaii to conquer the big waves at Waimea Bay and in the process take a step to becoming more mature adults. They also find romance with, respectively, a blonde Shelley Fabares (as a vacationing coed), Susan Hart (as a local beauty with an overprotective mother) and Barbara Eden (as an auburn-haired tomboy). *Ride the Wild Surf* features spectacular on-location photography and the most awesome big wave surfing footage with the top surfers of the day. However, the film grossed less than the AIP movies and *For Those Who Think Young*. Its disappointing box office receipts may have shown Hollywood that the mainstream audience did not want true surfing movies but the fantasy fun-in-the-sun, twisting-on-the-sand epics that AIP was producing. Real surfers were not overjoyed with the film and cringed whenever the pretty boy actors got in front of the waves with the romantic subplots. Even so, *Ride the Wild Surf* set the standard as it was the first surf movie to feature the "test of manhood" ending as the surfers must face their fears as they ride the big waves during the finale. This "rite of passage" would become a cliché as it would be repeated often in future Hollywood surf

In *Ride the Wild Surf* (Columbia, 1964), Jim Mitchum (left) and Fabian played rival surfers out to win the King of the Mountain competition at Waimea Bay *(courtesy the Billy Rose Theatre Collection, The New York Public Library for the Performing Arts, Astor, Lenox and Tilden Foundations).*

movies such as *Big Wednesday* (1978), *North Shore* (1987), *Point Break* (1991) and *Blue Crush* (2002).

The last beach film to be released in 1964 was *Pajama Party* from AIP, which decided to cash in on the success of its beach party films by offering a twist on the series. Annette Funicello was back, *sans* Frankie Avalon, with new leading man Tommy Kirk as a Martian who crashes the beach party in this movie with a sci-fi bent. All the AIP regulars including Harvey Lembeck are here along with musical production numbers choreographed by David Winters. New faces included hip-swiveling Susan Hart, buxom blonde Bobbi Shaw and veteran comic Buster Keaton. Despite the ridiculous plot, a poolside setting and a shift from surfing to beach volleyball as the sport of choice, *Pajama Party* was still a box office hit.

The Hollywood surf and beach movies that were released in 1965 strictly followed the formula laid out by the Frankie and Annette beach party movies. Hence, surfing was used just as filler or background to the various shenanigans of the youthful casts and the musical performers. In most of these films it was the same: a bunch of actors grabbing surfboards at the call "surf's up," then paddling out into a perfectly flat ocean, followed by stock footage of real surfers doubling for them riding huge waves. It wasn't surfing or the young actors that was the main attraction of these films but the lineup of rock acts. In the days before MTV and music videos, the only places where fans could see their favorite music groups were on television shows such as *American Bandstand* and *Shindig* or occasionally on the big screen. These beach movies were really pop musicals that tried to appeal to every teenager's taste by featuring everything from surf music to Motown to the British Invasion to garage rock. Guest stars ranged from extremely popular groups such as the Beach Boys, the Supremes, James Brown and the Famous Flames and Freddie and the Dreamers to less well-known acts or one-hit wonders including the Astronauts, the Hondells, the Castaways and Jackie and Gayle. Even a then-unknown duo called Sonny and Cher shows up. The lineup of musical guest stars is the one area where most of the beach party knockoffs excelled over the Frankie and Annette films. Also unlike most of the AIP movies, the others except *Beach Ball* had companion soundtrack LPs to capitalize on the music.

A Swingin' Summer was the first beach movie to be released in 1965. Producers knew that they needed to offer something new to attract the teenage audience. William Wellman, Jr., and Quinn O'Hara stood in for Frankie and Annette as the action shifted from the beaches of Malibu to Lake Arrowhead. The change of locale, some hot bikini-clad babes including gyrating blonde Lori Williams of *Faster, Pussycat! Kill! Kill!* fame and a newcomer named Raquel Welch, and popular rock acts the Righteous Brothers, the Rip Chords and Gary Lewis and the Playboys raised the film a few notches above par. However, poor production values and limited distribution prevented it from becoming a big hit.

Paramount Pictures picked up the distribution rights to the Roger Corman–financed film *The Girls on the Beach*. The plot (a group of bikini-clad coeds led by Noreen Corcoran, trying to raise money to save their sorority house, get tricked by surfer boys Martin West, Aron Kincaid and Steve Rogers into believing that the Beatles will perform a benefit concert for them) was incidental. There were a limited number of beach scenes and one brief shot of the guys sitting on their surfboards, but fans flocked to the movie anyway, mainly to see the Beach Boys in their sole beach movie appearance. They perform three songs including the title tune and most memorably "Little Honda" in a nightclub setting.

Hollywood kept churning out the beach movies in 1965 as the genre reached an apex. Fox once again went to Lippert (producer of *Surf Party*) for another low-budget black-and-white film, *Wild on the Beach*, starring Frankie Avalon look-a-like Frankie Randall and Sherry Jackson. Surfing footage was added sporadically to a claustrophobic plot that had a group of college boys vying with some coeds for a beach house where most of the action took place. The main attraction was the debut of the singing duo Sonny and Cher. *One Way Wahine*, a caper film set in Hawaii, focussed on four beach denizens (including buxom blonde Joy Harmon) who get involved with stolen money and the mob. The film had nothing to do with surfing but the sport had become so popular it was used in the ad campaign to entice viewers into the theaters. *The Beach Girls and the Monster* was exactly as its title suggests as a supposed creature from the sea begins killing off nubile beach girls and surfer boys. This black-and-white film featured about ten minutes of first-rate color surfing footage shot in Hawaii by co-star Dale Davis and a stinging portrayal by Sue Casey as an acid-tongued stepmother on the make.

With the over-saturation of beach movies in the marketplace, the innovative

American International Pictures needed other hooks to lure the fickle teenage ticket buyers into the drive-ins. They began the year hitting the bulls-eye with *Beach Blanket Bingo*, arguably the best of the Frankie and Annette beach party movies. It threw in everything from mermaids to sky diving and came out a winner thanks to the attractive cast of regulars, newcomers to the genre Linda Evans and Marta Kristen, and hilarious bits from Don Rickles, Harvey Lembeck and especially Paul Lynde. But AIP ended the year with a thud. Though *How to Stuff a Wild Bikini* featured a pleasant musical score warbled by the cast, the film was weakened by unconvincing leading man Dwayne Hickman, a preoccupied and pregnant Funicello and a hammy Mickey Rooney.

In between films, AIP released the handsomely produced *Ski Party*. It relocated the beach bash to the slopes where Hickman, Deborah Walley, Yvonne Craig and Aron Kincaid joined Frankie Avalon for a frolic in the snow. This was not the first ski musical from this time period as Sam Katzman produced *Get Yourself a College Girl* (1964) starring Mary Ann Mobley and Chad Everett. Not quite part of the beach party movie genre, the film followed in the wake of Katzman's other teenage musicals such as *Don't Knock the Rock* (1956), *Twist Around the Clock* (1961), *Hootenanny Hoot* (1963) and *When the Boys Meet the Girls* (1965). In *Ski Party*, though the regular troupe of beach boys and girls were clothed, they were clad in some tight, form-fitting ski pants and briefly in swim suits for the mandatory poolside dance number and beach setting finale. One of the film's highlights is the sudden appearance of James Brown and the Famous Flames who come in out of the cold to sing "I Got You (I Feel Good)." AIP also used the beach party crowd in the military service comedy *Sergeant Deadhead* (1965) starring Avalon and

Bruce Johnston, Al Jardine, Dennis Wilson and Brian Wilson of the Beach Boys, one of the many rock groups that appeared in beach movies, relax with a game of volleyball *(courtesy the Billy Rose Theatre Collection, The New York Public Library for the Performing Arts, Astor, Lenox and Tilden Foundations).*

Walley, and the spy spoof *Dr. Goldfoot and the Bikini Machine* (1965) with Vincent Price, Avalon, Hickman and Susan Hart.

The popularity of the beach gang continued to hold in 1965. *Photoplay* commissioned a special fashion layout shot on the sands of Malibu with Jody McCrea, Ed Garner, Aron Kincaid and Peter Sachse attired in tuxedoes and Donna Loren, Mary Hughes, Patti Chandler and Salli Sachse modeling exquisite evening gowns. There were also two magazines published, one focusing on the AIP beach movie actors and the other (devoted to the actresses) called *The Beach Girls*, which featured on the cover Annette Funicello, Deborah Walley, Bobbi Shaw, Salli Sachse and Aron Kincaid. Soon, however, the bubble would burst and most of the beach party gang would fade into obscurity.

Beach Ball was the last beach movie to be released in 1965 and it was one of the best. The producing-directing team of Bart Patton and Lennie Weinrib adapted the AIP formula to good effect. Four college dropouts, including Edd Byrnes, Aron Kincaid and Don Edmonds, living at the beach, secure a student loan for tribal music studies when in fact they need the money to pay for their rock group's instruments. When the brainy girls at the college union led by Chris Noel realize that they have been bamboozled, they rip up the check, remove their eyeglasses, tease their hair and head for the beach to try to entice the guys to return to school. A la *Beach Blanket Bingo*, the movie mixed surfing with a little bit of everything and a great lineup of musical talent—the Supremes, the Four Seasons and the Righteous Brothers, among others—to attract the youth market.

Meanwhile, the success of *Ski Party* begat *Winter a-Go-Go* (1965) from Columbia Pictures. Those *Swingin' Summer* boys, William Wellman, Jr., and James Stacy, put on some clothes and head for Sun Valley to open a ski resort that one of them has inherited. They take along some nubile dishes including Julie Parrish, Linda Rogers and Nancy Czar to help out. These enterprising babes even pack bikinis despite the fact that the temperature does not go above 40 degrees.

What is especially interesting about *Winter a-Go-Go* and makes it an undiscovered camp classic is that it arguably introduces the first ambiguous gay character to appear in a beach party–type movie. The role of Roger that screenwriter Bob Kanter created for himself is the asexual best friend of socialite Janine (Jill Donohue). Though he travels with her and her friend Dori (Judy Parker), there is no evidence of any current or past romance with either gal. During the course of the film, Janine sets her sights on Danny (Stacy) and Jeff (Wellman, Jr.) but winds up reuniting with Burt (Anthony Hayes). Dori makes goo-goo eyes at Frankie (Tom Nardini) throughout the film. Poor Roger—if he is not running to Jeff and Danny for protection from the bullying Burt, he just sits there drinking his Cokes making catty comments about the proceedings.

Gay subtext had crept into a few of the beach movies before this, giving these films camp appeal today. Discounting the obvious fact that these movies were titillation for homosexual men of the time, as good-looking shirtless movie hunks frolic on the sand in swim trunks or the slopes in tight ski pants, or that gay actors such as Tab Hunter, Tommy Kirk and Paul Lynde appeared in these movies, there were other factors that probably were not obvious back in the sixties. Either a director or screenwriter may have tried to slip in with a wink and a nudge to the homosexual community in an unassuming way that got it past the oblivious producers and censors.

The most obvious example is *Muscle Beach Party* (1964) featuring a clean-cut group of surfers versus a cult of bodybuilders headed by Don Rickles' Jack Fanny. During the fifties and sixties, the public automatically associated bodybuilding with homosexuality because musclemen of the time appeared as objects of desire wearing posing briefs (or sometimes nothing at all) in physique magazines whose readers were mostly gay men. Film historian Joan Ormond wrote in her article for *Scope: An Online Journal of Film Studies*, "Homosexuality in this era was regarded as potentially more damaging to society than the wild antics of surfers." Hence, the bodybuilders of *Muscle Beach Party* are seen as the bad guys along the lines of Eric Von Zipper's motorcycle gang of *Beach Party* as they are out to corrupt the youth of America.

Though handsome Fabian, Tab Hunter and Peter Brown pursue beach babes when not in the water in *Ride the Wild Surf*, there is a strong homo-erotic undercurrent throughout. The scenes of these shirtless surfers bonding or comforting each other while tackling the huge waves of Waimea Bay have become gay porn staples. Supposed swinging bachelors Paul Lynde and Woody Woodbury in *For Those Who Think Young* come off like two bickering old queens rather than swinging playboys. There's even a beach scene with Paul Lynde holding two large-sized hot dogs. Keeping with the hot dog symbolism, the scene of boyish surfer boy Mike Nader inserting a wiener into the mouth of equally cute Johnny Fain in *Beach Blanket Bingo* while Donna Loren sings about an unrequited love is certainly an eyebrow raiser. In *The Ghost in the Invisible Bikini*, while Deborah Walley's Lili sleeps alone in a twin bed, Tommy Kirk's Chuck shares his with Aron Kincaid as Bobby.

Scenes of guys dressed in drag dominated three beach movies. In *The Girls on the Beach*, Martin West, Aron Kincaid and Steve Rogers make glamorous college girls complete with lip gloss, false eyelashes and mascara as they don women's clothes to sneak out of a sorority house. In *Ski Party*, Frankie Avalon and Dwayne Hickman disguise themselves as British lasses "Jane" and "Nora," respectively, to infiltrate the opposite sex and learn what women are looking for in a man. In the process, suave Aron Kincaid as ladies' man Freddie falls for Hickman's female persona. At first Hickman finds it annoying but when his girlfriend keeps giving him grief, he decides to turn back into "Nora" and go out with Freddie because he knows "how to treat a girl." In *Beach Ball*, Kincaid was back to wearing a dress along with the rest of the male leads as they try to avoid the police at a music fair.

In 1964, surfing began invading primetime television beginning with episodes of *Burke's Law*, starring Gene Barry, and *Dr. Kildare*, starring Richard Chamberlain. The latter featured the especially memorable "Tyger, Tyger" two-part episode with angelic blonde Yvette Mimieux of *Where the Boys Are* as an avid surfer who is diagnosed with epilepsy but refuses to give up the sport she loves, with tragic results. That same year saw the debuts of local California television interview programs *Surf's Up* on KHJ and *Let's Go Surfing* on KTTV. In 1965, KTLA got into the act with *Surfing World*.

The television sitcom *Gidget* starring Sally Field as the precocious wave rider was the first weekly series to feature surfing footage on a regular basis. Debuting in September 1965, *Gidget* returned Francie Lawrence to high school and put her back on the beach where she belonged. Co-starring with Field were Lynette Winter as Larue, Gidget's beach-hating best friend, and Don Porter as Gidget's father, now a widower. Mike Nader, from the *Beach Party* movies, had a recurring role as a surfer nicknamed Siddo. *Gidget* was the typical mid-sixties comedy series featuring silly teenage misunderstandings buoyed by the perky, effervescent Sally Field. She pumped whatever life there was into this but it never caught on with an audience beyond adolescent girls. When the series premiered, the real Gidget, Kathy Kohner, was now a housewife and young mother. "I wish the series had more surfing

Aron Kincaid as ladies' man Freddie Carter and Dwayne Hickman in drag as Nora were the most romantic couple in *Ski Party* **(AIP, 1965)** *(courtesy Aron Kincaid).*

in it," remarks Kathy. "I remember I was nursing my first child in 1965 and I'd be watching the program and thinking, 'Gosh, where's the surfing?' I wanted to see more of that."

After the cancellation of *Gidget* in the spring of 1966, surfing was relegated to weekends with the occasional televised surfing competition. In 1967, ABC-TV introduced the short-lived variety show *Malibu U* hosted by Ricky Nelson. That same year, Miss Clairol's Summer Blonde model (and actress) Andrea Dromm hosted the primetime special *Hit the Surf*, which took a look at the surfing boom. The show followed the lovely Dromm learning to surf in Huntington Beach, visiting a surfboard factory and watching some of the world's top surfers challenge the huge waves at Hawaii's Banzai Pipeline.

Back on the big screen, all this sand, surf and sex hoopla began to wind down in 1966, but beach movies were still popular enough to be parodied in *Lord Love a Duck* (1966) starring Tuesday Weld. Universal signed Bart Patton and Lennie Weinrib to a contract and the first result was the disappointing *Wild Wild Winter*. Frustrated Alpine College guys Don Edmonds and Steve Rogers recruit Malibu surfer Gary Clarke, who masquerades as a top skier to melt the icy demeanor of head sorority girl Chris Noel so they can score with her fellow coeds.

Seeing how poorly *How to Stuff a Wild Bikini* was received, AIP decided to shake up the formula. The lavish though trouble-plagued production *Bikini Party in a Haunted House* was re-edited and re-named *The Ghost in the Invisible Bikini* (1966); Susan Hart played the title character while Tommy Kirk and Deborah Walley replaced Frankie and Annette as the leads. The beach was nowhere in sight as the action shifted to a spooky mansion with a large in-ground swimming pool. Kirk, Walley and Patsy Kelly are heirs to a fortune but must survive a night in the house. Kelly invites her nephew Aron Kincaid along and he brings his surfer buddies and their girlfriends. The Bobby Fuller Four, Nancy Sinatra, Quinn O'Hara and "Italian Sensation" Piccola Pupa provided the musical numbers. Suffice it to say the film was not a hit and AIP, knowing when a good thing was over, abandoned the beach movie genre. AIP then teamed Frankie and Annette in the race-car action drama *Fireball 500* (1966).

Following suit, producer Bart Patton combined the beach and spy genres for the spoof *Out of Sight* (1966) starring Jonathan Daly as a novice secret agent and Karen Jensen as the beach babe who needs his help to thwart a madman's plan to destroy rock 'n' roll. Again, not much surfing is shown as the musical guest stars including Gary Lewis and the Playboys, Freddie and the Dreamers, the Turtles and the Knickerbockers dominate the film.

With Hollywood floundering surf movie–wise, it was up to independent filmmaker Bruce Brown to teach the major studios the lesson that a great film about the sport could be produced and could find a wide audience. The movie was *The Endless Summer* (1966). It was filmed in late 1963 and early 1964 in locations around the world, showing two surfers who traipse the globe following the summer season, searching for the perfect wave. Brown made the film with a bigger audience than the typical surf movie in mind. However, Hollywood rejected his final product, fearing it wouldn't play east of the 405 Freeway in California.

Determined to prove "the suits" wrong, Brown rented a theater in land-locked Kansas City during the late fall of 1965 and broke attendance records. However, he still could not land a distributor for his film. He then gambled and did the same in New York City. *The Endless Summer* opened in one theater on June 15, 1966, and by the end of the year it was still running. The critics raved and the audience came. Cinema V picked up the distribution rights and the little surf movie became a national and worldwide hit. The movie succeeds because Brown's witty and light-

Surfer Lance Carson catches a big wave in *The Endless Summer* (Cinema V, 1966).

hearted narration doesn't talk down to the non-surfing audience and doesn't make fun of surfers. Plus it features some of the finest surfing footage of the decade and finally shows surfers in a positive image.

Surprisingly, the success of *The Endless Summer* did not start a new wave of surf movies. *The Golden Breed* (1968) was the only film to make an impact beyond its core surfer audience by 1969. Produced and directed by Dale Davis, it was similar to Bruce Brown's movie as it trailed a group of surfers, including Jock Southerland, Ricky Grigg, Nat Young, Mickey Dora, Greg Noll and Butch Van Artsdalen searching for that perfect wave in Hawaii, Mexico and California.

Possibly due to the success of *The Endless Summer,* two beach movies that were filmed in the latter half of 1965 and had been sitting on the shelf were given limited release in the spring of 1967. Coincidentally, both starred Tommy Kirk. *Catalina Caper* shifted the action from Malibu to Santa Catalina and from surfing to scuba diving. Though the film is nicely photographed, a hackneyed plot revolving around a stolen Chinese scroll sinks the film. *It's a Bikini World* is a bit better, though Kirk is miscast as a lothario who is challenged by early women's libber and beach girl Deborah Walley to a series of athletic competitions. Surprisingly, surfing is not one of them though "sidewalk surfing" (better known as skateboarding) is. As with other beach party knockoffs, the musical guest performers (including the Animals, the Castaways and the Gentrys) make it worth viewing.

The times they were a-changin' in late 1966 and early 1967, so it is no surprise that young people began abandoning the innocent carefree beach movies, which had become passé. The Civil Rights movement was marching on. The counterculture was in full swing with hippies and flower children. College students were turning on, tuning in and dropping out. They fought the establishment in every way—from protesting the U.S. presence in Vietnam to taking LSD to practicing free love. During the Age of Aquarius, teenagers weren't buying the beach films because there was nothing meaningful in them. Their plots about clean-cut all–American lily-white teenagers whose only problems seemed to be trying to get their virginal girlfriends to put out or worrying when the next big wave would roll in seemed outdated amid the problems in the world. The innocence of the early sixties was being replaced by the cynicism of the late sixties. AIP sensed this change first and began catering to this new, hipper audience with biker films and "alienated youth" movies.

Two additional adult-oriented surf movies were produced before Hollywood totally abandoned surfing. *Don't Make Waves* (1967) starring Tony Curtis, Claudia Cardinale and Sharon Tate, was a satire on the Southern California lifestyle including surfing and bodybuilding. The film succeeded best when poking fun at the beach culture, which had previously been packaged as the ultimate in fantasy living to the rest of the country and the world. *Don't Make Waves* featured shallow and materialistic adults, vapid young people, mud slides and every other negative component of Southern California living it could find.

In *The Sweet Ride* (1968), an aimless surfer, an aging tennis bum and an offbeat jazz musician share a Malibu beach house where they get involved with a young television actress who ends up beaten and left for dead on the side of the road. The movie is a melodramatic look at the youth culture who want the beach party to last forever so they do not have to deal with the pressures of adulthood. An attractive cast including Michael Sarrazin, Jacqueline Bisset, Tony Franciosa, Bob Denver and Michele Carey buoy the film.

Neither *Don't Make Waves* or *The Sweet Ride* were box office hits. Realizing that they had milked surfing and the beach movies for all they could, Hollywood moved on to other topics to make a fast buck. What it left behind was not a definitive look at surfers or the surf culture but an innocent moment in history for teenagers before they had to start worrying about war, social unrest and drugs.

Surfing didn't make a comeback onto the big screen until 1978 with the release of John Milius' ambitious *Big Wednesday*. This was the start of Hollywood's second wave of surf movies, which wanted to dash the myth that started in the beach party films that all surfers were dumb, fun-loving people, and to portray a more realistic look at surfers and their lifestyle, with an emphasis on the thrill of surfing.

PART I

The Movies

★ 1 ★

Gidget (1959)

Watch out Brigitte.... Here comes Gidget!

Fun: ★★★★
Surfing: ★★★
Boy watching: ★★★★
Girl watching: ★★
Music: ★★
Scenery: ★★★

Release in April 1959. *Running time:* 95m. *Box office gross:* $1.5 million.
DVD release: Triple bill with *Gidget Goes Hawaiian* and *Gidget Goes to Rome,* Columbia Tri Star Home Video (August 4, 2004). [Beware: All three movies are in the pan-and-scan format rather than wide screen.]

Sandra Dee (*Francie*), James Darren (*Moondoggie*), Cliff Robertson (*Kahoona*), Arthur O'Connell (*Russell Lawrence*), The Four Preps (*Themselves*), Mary LaRoche (*Dorothy Lawrence*), Joby Baker (*Stinky*), Tom Laughlin (*Loverboy*), Sue George (*B.L.*), Robert Ellis (*Hot Shot*), Jo Morrow (*Mary Lou*), Yvonne Craig (*Nan*), Patti Kane (*Patty*), Doug McClure (*Waikiki*), Burt Metcalfe (*Lord Byron*), Richard Newton, Ed Hinton (*Cops*). *Not credited:* Linda Benson, Mickey Dora, Johnny Fain, Mickey Munoz.

Columbia Pictures. *Produced by:* Lewis J. Rachmil. *Directed by:* Paul Wendkos. *Screenplay by:* Gabrielle Upton. From the novel by Frederick Kohner. *Director of Photography:* Burnett Guffey, A.S.C. *Color Consultant:* Henri Jaffa. *Music Supervised and Conducted by:* Morris Stoloff. *Orchestrator:* Arthur Morton, John Williams, Jr. *Art Director:* Ross Bellah. *Film Editor:* William A. Lyon, A.C.E. *Set Decorator:* William Kiernan. *Assistant Director:* Milton Feldman. *Makeup Supervisor:* Clay Campbell. *Hair Styles by:* Helen Hunt. *Recording Supervisor:* John Livadary. *Sound:* Josh Westmoreland. Filmed in CinemaScope and Columbia Color.

"Gidget" by Patti Washington and Fred Karger, performed by the Four Preps over the opening credits and by James Darren on screen. "The Next Best Thing to Love" by Stanley Styne and Fred Karger, performed by James Darren. "Cinderella" by Glen Larson and Bruce Belland, performed by the Four Preps.

Gidget remains one of the best Hollywood surf movies of all time. The story of a teenage tomboy who doesn't fit in with her female friends and who just wants to surf with the guys is extremely entertaining. It makes a sincere effort to capture the surfer culture of the time albeit toned down for movie audiences. The film has lots of exciting surfing footage, beautiful Malibu scenery and a wonderful cast headed by the sweet Sandra Dee as the "girl-midget" nicknamed Gidget and Cliff Robertson as the manly surf bum Kahoona.

29

Sandra Dee as Gidget with James Darren as Moondoggie and Cliff Robertson as Kahoona in *Gidget* **(Columbia, 1959).**

As hoped for from the first official Hollywood surf movie, there is lots of surfing action, excellently photographed, featuring some of Malibu's real-life surfers such as Mickey Dora and Johnny Fain. However, a minor drawback is the main stars' lack of athletic ability. The only hindrance about Sandra Dee is that she looks like she can barely hold a surfboard let alone surf on one. The constant filming of her and James Darren in a tank on the studio lot or in front of the blue screen pretending to be riding the waves is a detriment to this movie, especially to fans reared on Kate Bosworth in *Blue Crush*. Unfortunately, using the blue screen would become standard practice in most surf movies to follow during the sixties.

Surfing is not the only thing that is plentiful in *Gidget*, so is the beefcake. It is a boy watcher's dream. Numerous scenes of the shirtless young men riding the waves are featured. So much flesh is on display that there is a boy for every taste from rugged and virile Cliff Robertson to boyish and smooth James Darren.

If bikini-clad beauties are your cup of tea, you are out of luck. There are some early shots of shapely Yvonne Craig and Jo Morrow in two-piece bathing suits but the best *Gidget* offers up is the flat-chested, skinny 14-year-old Dee, who was never popular with the girl-watching crowd even when she matured into adulthood. Sue George is a fright with her short-cropped haircut and looks totally out of place for 1959.

Musically, *Gidget* features the Southern California–based Four Preps. They and later James Darren (who sings the catchy title tune) perform well but the other two songs included are schmaltzy ballads, which unfortunately would become the norm in beach party movies to come. Despite the minor flaws, *Gidget* exudes a wonderful Southern California fun-in-the-sun feeling, and aided by the attractive cast, remains a memorable first look at the cult of surfing and the throngs who are attracted to it.

The Story

Sixteen-year-old Francie Lawrence goes to the beach with her three boy-chasing friends who have set their sights on a group of surfers. The girls' obvious methods strike out and they blame the ocean-loving Francie, describing her as more "fish than dish." Ignoring their catty remark, the petite blonde dons her double-snorkel mask to go swimming and gets caught in an undertow. She is saved by a surfer who pulls her out of the water and onto his surfboard. Fascinated with her hero (nicknamed Moondoggie) and with surfing, the young girl is determined to buy a board so she can learn.

After cajoling the money from her parents ("gilt-edge guarantee for a summer of sheer happiness"), Francie goes to make her purchase and meets the Kahoona, the leader of the group of young surfers and a self-admitted surf bum. Francie is only able to afford a used, somewhat battered and extremely waterlogged surfboard. Deciding to let her hang around, Kahoona regales the young girl with tales of his worldwide adventures and officially introduces her to the surfers who dub her Gidget. As one of the surfers explains, "It's arrived at by osmosis: girl and midget." At first the guys don't take Gidget seriously. They use her to make food runs to the snack bar while ladies' man Lover Boy pulls some lecherous moves on the naïve girl on the pretense of teaching her how to surf. Moondoggie once again comes to the smitten girl's rescue but then sends her home to Mommy.

Gidget heads back to the beach the next day, where during a faux surfer's initiation she becomes entangled in kelp and is saved from drowning by Moondoggie. After spending two weeks in bed with tonsillitis, Gidget returns to the shore where Kahoona begins teaching her to surf. Days go by before she is finally able to ride a wave in formation with the other guys. The petite surfer thinks she is part of the group only to learn that she is not invited to their upcoming luau and that Moondoggie is bringing a date. Desperate, Gidget offers Hot Shot $20 to escort her to the bash and is able to persuade Kahoona to let her attend with a promise to bring lots of steaks.

Gidget's plan goes awry when her parents discover the food is missing, and learn the reason why. Her father demands that she stay home, but Gidget storms out. She is shocked to learn that she will be spending the evening with Moondoggie, paid by Hot Shot to take his place. Confused about whom Gidget wants to make jealous, the two grow closer as the surfer croons a love song to Gidget on the sand. They kiss but the magical moment is spoiled by Hot Shot. Embarrassed, Gidget flees down the beach, not hearing Moondoggie's call for her to wait. She winds up in a beach house with Kahoona, whom the confused girl is resolved to seduce. But he is on to her games and tells her to scram. A jealous Moondoggie misunderstands the situation and the two get into a fistfight while Gidget is hauled off to jail for driving without a license.

Grounded from surfing, Gidget is forced to go on a date with the son of her father's friend whom she was avoiding all summer. When she bounds down the stairs to meet Jeffrey Matthews, she is stunned to see that he is Moondoggie. The two pretend to have just met and drive to the beach. They run into Kahoona, who is leaving not to travel the world surfing but to become an airline pilot. Moondoggie then asks Gidget to wear his college pin and she ecstatically accepts as they consummate their relationship with a kiss.

Behind-the-Scenes

The novel *Gidget* by Frederick Kohner about the fictional surfing exploits of his daughter, nicknamed Gidget by her surfing buddies, was well-received by critics and readers in 1957. *Life* magazine even did a cover story on the real Gidget, Kathy Kohner, and her friends at Malibu Point. Seeing this surfing phenomenon beginning to grow by leaps and bounds, Columbia Pictures purchased the screen rights to the book for $50,000. Kohner gave five percent of it to his daughter. Surprisingly, Kohner (a prolific screenwriter who received an Academy Award nomination for *Mad About Music* in 1938) was not asked to adapt his novel for the big screen. Instead, the assignment was given to first-time screenwriter Gabrielle Upton, who had written for television and was the head writer for the daytime soap opera *The Secret Storm.*

A number of actresses were considered for the role of Gidget including Tuesday Weld and Carol Lynley. But a petite 14-year-old named Sandra Dee got the part. At the time, the film industry thought Dee was 16 as she lied about her age to get movie work. The real Gidget, Kathy Kohner-Zuckerman, says, "I had never heard of Sandra Dee. I met her in the summer of 1959 when she graduated from University High School though she really wasn't a student there. She was very sweet to me but there wasn't a lot of interaction between us."

Ross Hunter had previously signed Dee to a contract at Universal, where she appeared in *The Restless Years* (1958) and *Imitation of Life* (1959). He thought loaning her out to Columbia for *Gidget* was a good career move for his rising star because he believed *Gidget* was going to become a big hit with younger audiences. His hunch proved right and *Gidget* (along with *A Summer Place*) propelled Dee to the top of the Teen Queen heap for 1959.

The role of Moondoggie was cast with Columbia contract player James Darren despite the fact that he not only couldn't surf but he was a weak swimmer as well. But the studio had high hopes for this strikingly handsome actor. The only problem was that the Moondoggie character in *Gidget* had to sing and Columbia did not have faith that the newcomer could pull it off. Darren recalled in the *Los Angeles Herald-Examiner,* "I told the studio that I could do it. When the soundtrack got attention, I made a deal with the studio's record division to do it as a single." Though the title tune from *Gidget* just failed to crack the Top 40, Darren's prior single "Angel Face" was a Top 10 hit. His biggest seller came in 1961 with "Goodbye Cruel World," which peaked at No. 3 on the charts.

The roles of Moondoggie's surfing buddies were cast with Tom Laughlin (who had just played one of the shirtless seafaring navy men in 1958's *South Pacific*), Doug

McClure and a newcomer named Joby Baker. Dark-haired, gray-eyed and tall, comedian-turned-actor Baker never became a bona fide movie star but that was fine by him. As early as 1959, he was telling columnists, "I'll never be a leading man–hero type, but let's face it, I don't want to be." A protégé of Jerry Lewis, Baker was signed to a contract with Columbia Pictures and is the only actor, other than James Darren, to have appeared in all three Gidget movies—*Gidget, Gidget Goes Hawaiian* (1961) and *Gidget Goes to Rome* (1963).

Among the actresses hired to play Gidget's friends were Jo Morrow and former ballerina Yvonne Craig. Morrow was a Texas native who won a "Be a Star" contest that led to a contract with 20th Century–Fox where she played a waitress in *Ten North Frederick* (1958). After Fox did not renew her option, Morrow signed with Columbia and landed a lead role in the low-budget rock 'n' roll musical *Juke Box Rhythm* (1959). *Gidget* was her second film for the studio. Yvonne Craig also had two previous films to her credit—*Eighteen and Anxious* (1957) and *The Young Land* (1959). Though she was happy to be appearing in *Gidget,* she revealed in her autobiography *From Ballet to the Batcave and Beyond* that she was dismayed that she had to wear a white bikini because she felt her bottom would look too large on the big screen. As for Sandra Dee, Craig described her as "a sweet, frail, waif-like little girl" whose mother was always on the set. Dee revealed to Craig and the other girls that as a model she "used vomiting and laxatives as a weight control device."

Johnny Fain was the first Malibu surfer hired for the movie. He was only 5'5" but he was blonde, cute and personable so it is no wonder he impressed the producers of *Gidget.* He then introduced the legendary Mickey Dora to them. Dora had surfed with the real Gidget, Kathy Kohner, during her time hanging out at Malibu.

Gidget was filmed on location in California at Arroyo Seco, north of Trancas. The surfing scenes were filmed at Leo Carillo Beach, about 20 miles north of Malibu. It was too crowded to film on location in Malibu because of the influx of surfers. The newfound popularity of the sport was due in part to the release of the novel.

Sandra Dee made an attempt to film her surfing scenes in the ocean. Columnist Mike Connolly was present for Dee's venture into the water and reported in *Screen Stories*: "The first day's shooting took place at famous Paradise Cove near Malibu with the company working from a barge that lay a half-mile offshore. The shots were mainly close-ups of Sandra and Jimmy Darren paddling on their surfboards. The husky young Darren could take it, but Sandra turned blue, and then bluer."

Years later, Dee recounted to *Celebrity Collector Magazine*, "I went out in the ocean with Jimmy Darren and a [professional] surfer. It was March. We had on wet suits. I was paddling in the water and asked if I could catch a wave. The surfer said to wait. I thought that, finally, this was going to be fun! Well, at 5:30 A.M., we had a shooting call.... The director asked if we were ready. I was out of my wet suit and jumped into the ocean with my two-piece bathing suit on—and froze! I was purple! They couldn't get me out fast enough."

Dee refused to do any more ocean work so the shots of her on a surfboard were filmed in a tank filled with warm water on the studio back lot. At 5'4" and weighing 130 pounds, Mickey "Mongoose" Muñoz (wearing a one-piece bathing suit and blonde wig) surf-doubled for Dee. Munoz was part of that original Malibu surfing crew and purportedly dated the real Gidget, Kathy Kohner. Pre-*Gidget*, Munoz was one of the first California surfers to ride the waves at Waimea Bay in 1957 and was featured in the surf flick *Search for Surf* (1958). Johnny Fain donned the suit and wig for Dee in the scene where Gidget almost drowns in the kelp beds. According to Kathy Kohner, Diane Kibborn also doubled for Dee in some of the surfing scenes.

Mickey Munoz was also hired to act as lifeguard in the water and to teach Dee the basics of surfing including how to grasp a surfboard and walk to the shoreline and how to paddle out into the waves. In interviews that Munoz has given over the years, he admitted he was not impressed in the least with Dee, who was not athletic. He described as being "a skinny little Hollywood blonde."

Doug McClure was the only actor in the movie who could actually surf but Terry "Tubesteak" Tracey doubled most of the time for him. Though Cliff Robertson took surfing lessons and hung out with real surfers to learn more about their lifestyle to get the feel for his role as the Kahoona, he never surfed in front of the cameras. Instead, surfer Pete Peterson stepped in to ride the waves for him while Mickey Dora doubled for James Darren.

Despite her dislike of the ocean, Sandra Dee calls *Gidget* the film she had the most fun working on. *Gidget* gave Dee the opportunity to work with a large group of young people who made the shoot a very pleasant experience for her. However, according to a 1963 interview in *The Saturday Evening Post*, she fell asleep watching the movie and despised watching herself on screen. She remarked, "I get sick at rushes, sicker at previews."

Dee was a perfect choice to bring the character to life on the big screen despite her lack of surfing knowledge and physical strength. She received outstanding notices from most of the critics of the day. The petite actress had just the right combination of innocence, perkiness and personality for the audience to believe in her love for the sport of surfing. Producer Ross Hunter, commenting on Dee's success as Gidget, said in Dodd Darin's book *Dream Lovers* that teenagers fell in love with her because it was her first role where "she was one of the kids."

When *Gidget* opened in 1959, Kathy Kohner had abandoned the shores of Malibu for the ivory halls of Oregon State College. "I kept a journal at that time," remembers Kathy. "I wrote in it that I thought it was quite funny seeing Sandra Dee and these other people acting in a movie that some of us lived. I think Miss Dee did an outstanding, memorable job and captured a moment in time that has now lasted 45 years. I am a real person. I am shorter than Dee and have dark hair. I was a bit tenacious and a bit fearless. Miss Dee was afraid of the water so I heard that they built a tank for her to swim in. But the sweetness was the wonderful characteristic about the character Gidget in the movie. Certainly, I had a different personality but of all the actresses that played Gidget, Sandra Dee came closest in capturing my experiences from surfing to wishing my breasts would grow bigger to my relationship with my parents. There was nothing not to like about the way that she played the character."

Gidget received flak and criticism from the surfing press and real surfers at the time for not presenting a true picture of the sport and their community. Kathy

In *Gidget* (Columbia, 1959), Sandra Dee (*center*) shares the thrill of catching a wave with Sue George as her best friend and Mary LaRoche as her baffled mother.

Kohner opines, "I think the film captured the imagination enough of that Southern California surf culture for everybody that there still is *Gidget* week every summer on television. It certainly captured the fancy of everybody east of the 405 Freeway." This is a bit of an understatement as the surfing craze exploded in Malibu. The one area of the film that Kathy does fault is the actors who couldn't surf, hired to play surfers; "If the movie was remade today it probably would be more realistic with the surfers."

The movie version of *Gidget* proved to be such a hit that it spawned two sequels, *Gidget Goes Hawaiian* (1961) with Deborah Walley and *Gidget Goes to Rome* (1963) with Cindy Carol. In the fall of 1965, a half-hour situation comedy called (what else?) *Gidget* starring Sally Field debuted but it lasted only one season. Gidget was then relegated to the small screen with the television movies *Gidget Grows Up* (1969) with Karen Valentine and *Gidget Gets Married* (1972) with Monie Eillis. By 1973, Gidget had finally run her course and remained off the screens of America until the 1985 television movie *Gidget's Summer Reunion* with Caryn Richman, who was probably closer physically to Kathy Kohner than any of her predecessors. A ratings winner, it launched a syndicated television series called *The New Gidget* with most of the cast from the film. After two seasons, the show was cancelled. In

1999, the character of Gidget was parodied in the film *Psycho Beach Party* starring Lauren Ambrose (of *Six Feet Under* fame) as a psychotic surfer named Chiclet. Columbia Pictures announced in 2004 that screenwriter Erica Beeney had been commissioned to pen a remake of the original *Gidget* for release in 2005.

Over the years, Gidget invaded other forms of entertainment including a comic book series beginning in 1966, a darkly comedic novel by Fred Reiss called *Gidget Must Die: A Killer Surf Novel* (released in 1995) and a theatrical production entitled *Gidget: The Musical*, co-written by Francis Ford Coppola. A rock band called The Suburban Lawns released a song called "Gidget Goes to Hell," the Chihuahua from the Taco Bell commercials is named Gidget and a sandwich on the menu at Malibu Chicken is called The Gidget.

When asked if she thinks that Gidget's long-lasting popularity is because it was about a determined girl who conquers adversity and reaches her goal of becoming a surfer when there weren't any female surfers, Kathy Kohner replies modestly, "There were always girl surfers. I was just the one that got famous. I never saw myself in a gender role but just wanting to belong. I very much wanted a family outside my own family. Having lived it, I never felt that I had to do this to prove to them that a girl could surf. I wanted to be accepted and I want them to see that I could do it. It was not so much that I was a girl but that I was determined to be part of this group."

James Darren and Joby Baker were the only actors from *Gidget* to appear in the sequel *Gidget Goes Hawaiian*. Due to studio commitments, Sandra Dee gave up playing Gidget and took over for Debbie Reynolds as the cornpone Tammy in *Tammy Tell Me True* (1961) and *Tammy and the Doctor* (1963).

Of the supporting players, Yvonne Craig was the sole female cast member to appear in another beach party movie. In 1965, she joined Frankie Avalon and Deborah Walley in Sun Valley for a *Ski Party* before finding lasting fame as television's Batgirl on the last season of *Batman* (1967-68). Doug McClure found television success playing Trampas on the hit Western series *The Virginian* while Tom Laughlin went on to introduce his popular Billy Jack character in *The Born Losers* (1967).

As for Kathy Kohner, she stopped surfing in 1960. "Malibu got very crowded. The novel and the movie created this surfing boom. I got a bit frightened by all the surfboards in the water. Some of the fellows I had hung out with in the mid-fifties had gone off to serve in the military. For me, it was sort of the in-between years. I drifted away to other activities. I never talked much about being Gidget." Kathy married Marvin Zuckerman, now the dean at Los Angeles Valley College, and had two sons, David and Phillip. She started to become reacquainted and more comfortable with her Gidget persona when the syndicated series *The New Gidget* hit the airwaves in 1986. Gidget was a travel agent in the show so Kathy decided to emulate her and also became one. In 1999, *Wahine* magazine did a cover story on Kathy Kohner in celebration of the fortieth anniversary of the *Gidget* movie, which was the impetus that propelled her to re-issue the original novel. Published by Berkley Books, it included a foreword by Kathy, a new introduction by Deanne Stillman plus photos of Gidget during her surfing days. That same year, *Surfer* magazine voted her the seventh most influential surfer of the twentieth century. Today, Kathy Kohner Zuckerman works part-time as a restaurant hostess and has ventured back into the surf at her old stomping grounds in Malibu.

Memorable Lines

GIDGET (on surfing): Honest to goodness, it's the absolute ultimate!

GIDGET: Surfing is out of this world! You can't imagine the thrill of shooting the curl. It positively surpasses every living emotion I've ever had.

Selected Reviews

The Hollywood Reporter—"*Gidget* ... deals compassionately and humorously with the growing pains of young people who are neither criminal nor delinquent. The locations at Carillo Beach are invigorating with a feeling of sun and salt spray and the action sequences concerning surf boarding are novel and exciting."

Edwin Miller, *Seventeen*—"*Gidget* is a delightful lightweight comedy about a shy teenager who longs for a boy she can call her steady. Locations scenes shot at California's Carillo Beach are stunning."

Philip J. Scheuer, *Los Angeles Times*—"*Gidget* is invigorating. Sandra Dee is a lot of fun, and so are her companions—most of them surf bums."

Howard Thompson, *The New York Times*—"*Gidget* is enough to make anybody leave one of the neighborhood theatres and light out for the Long Island Sound. As a surf portrait of adolescent America, the film has a relaxed air befitting its nice young people and some random, knowing observations about growing up."

Variety—"*Gidget* is a class teen-age comedy in which the kids are, for once, healthy and attractive young people instead of in some phase of juvenile depravity. Burnett Guffey's sun-washed photography effectively captures the summer spirit and has some exciting shots of surfing."

Awards and Nominations

Golden Laurel Award: "Top Female Comedy Performance"—Sandra Dee, fifth place

Golden Laurel Award: "Top Male New Personality"—James Darren, ninth place

Photoplay Gold Medal Award nomination: "Favorite Male Star"—James Darren

Photoplay Gold Medal Award nomination: "Favorite Male Star"—Cliff Robertson

Photoplay Gold Medal Award nomination: "Most Promising New Star—Male"—Joby Baker

★ 2 ★

Where the Boys Are (1960)

The hilarious INSIDE STORY of those rip-roaring spring vacations.

Fun: ★★★
Surfing: ★
Boy watching: ★★
Girl watching: ★★★
Music: ★★
Scenery: ★★★

Released in December 1960. 96m. *Box office gross*: $3.5 million.
DVD release: Warner Home Video (January 6, 2004).
Dolores Hart (*Merritt Andrews*), George Hamilton (*Ryder Smith*), Yvette Mimieux (*Melanie*), Jim Hutton (*TV Thompson*), Barbara Nichols (*Lola*), Paula Prentiss (*Tuggle Carpenter*), Connie Francis (*Angie*), Chill Wills (*Police Captain*), Frank Gorshin (*Basil*), Rory Harrity (*Franklin*), Ted Berger (*Stout Man*), John Brennan (*Dill*), Vito Scotti (*Maitre D'*). Not credited: Maggie Pierce (*Jody*), Bess Flowers (*Annoyed Patron at Nightclub*), Paul Frees (*Narrator*), Percy Helton (*Fairview Motel Manager*), Jack Kruschen (*Café Counterman*), Jon Lormer (*Cheap Motel Manager*), Sean Flynn (*Boy Throwing Football on Beach*), Robert Woods (*College Boy*).
An Euterpe production, MGM release. *Produced by*: Joe Pasternak. *Directed by*: Henry Levin. *Screenplay by*: George Wells. Based on the Novel by Glendon Swarthout. *Director of Photography*: Robert Bronner, A.S.C. *Music*: George Stoll. *Original Dialectic Jazz by*: Pete Rugolo. *Choreographer*: Robert Sidney. *Art Directors*: George W. Davis, Preston Ames. *Set Decorators*: Henry Grace, Hugh Hunt. *Color Consultant*: Charles K. Hagedon. *Special Effects*: Lee LeBlanc. *Film Editor*: Fredric Steinkamp. *Recording Supervisor*: Franklin Milton. *Women's Costumes*: Kitty Mager. *Assistant Director*: Al Jennings. *Assistant to the Producer*: Irving Aaronson. *Hair Styles by*: Mary Keats. *Makeup by*: William Tuttle. Photographic Lenses by Panavision. Filmed in CinemaScope and MetroColor.
Songs: "Where the Boys Are" and "Turn on the Sunshine" by Howard Greenfield and Neil Sedaka, performed by Connie Francis. "Have You Met Miss Fandango?" by Stella Unger and Victor Young, performed by Barbara Nichols.

Despite its uneven mixture of slapstick comedy and melodrama and its heavy-handed moralizing about the evils of premarital sex, *Where the Boys Are* is so handsomely produced and charmingly acted that it can't help but be entertaining. When the gals drop their guard and party hearty, the film is top drawer but when they get in that mindset to trap a husband the film falls flat. As for the boys, they are all portrayed as having only one thing on their mind—sex!

Where the Boys Are is probably one of the first movies to suggest that it is okay for young women to have sex before marriage. This was very outlandishly daring for 1960. However, to counteract this novel idea, good girl Merritt doesn't practice what she preaches and the audience is hit over the head by Prentiss' character, who is out to land a husband while holding on to her virginity. The film is so dated that Prentiss' Tuggle boasts that girls like her "are not built to be educated but to become a walking-talking baby factor." It is lines like this that will have even the most hardened male chauvinist pig rolling his eyes in disbelief. Yvette Mimieux is the easy girl out to reel in an Ivy Leaguer using her feminine wiles but of course she has to pay for her wanton ways. Not only does she get raped, the poor thing gets hit by a car to boot. Mimieux is just another popular starlet in a long line of late fifties–early sixties fair-haired good girls gone bad who had to suffer for going all the way. For instance, unwed high schooler Carol Lynley gets pregnant and is sent away in *Blue Denim* (1959) while Diane McBain meets a nasty end as a Southern tramp shot dead in her bedroom in *Claudelle Inglish* (1961).

The movie captures the craziness of Fort Lauderdale wonderfully from the crowded beaches to the packed sidewalks and traffic-laden streets. The on-location photography elevates the film immensely. However, the scenes with the principals on the sand were obviously filmed on the MGM back lot and none of the actors wade into the water on screen. Some of writer George Wells' hip dialogue was square back in 1960 but a number of his lines do retain their humor, especially when delivered by deft comic actors Jim Hutton and Paula Prentiss.

The cast for the most part is first-rate and very attractive. The fresh-faced Dolores Hart with her big expressive blue eyes makes a charming leading lady and is always one step ahead of George Hamilton, who makes a super suave though wooden Ryder Smith who is out to seduce her. Paula Prentiss proves to be a delightful comedienne in the vein of Rosalind Russell or Eve Arden and delivers some funny wisecracks as Tuggle though her determination to remain chaste wears thin. She is matched every step of the way by the equally good Jim Hutton as her goofy love interest who is "queer for hats." Connie Francis is too pretty to be cast as the "unattractive one" but she is surprisingly humorous playing the role in a ditzy manner. The only one who comes off maudlin is the beautiful Yvette Mimieux but to be fair she is saddled with the weak role of the doomed ingenue. Of course, as the "bad" girl she is the only one who sports two-piece swimsuits. Hamilton bares his chest briefly while Hutton remains covered up, leaving those cads Rory Harrity and John Brennan to spice up the film in the beefcake department.

The title song, belted out by Connie Francis at the beginning and end of the movie, is one of the most memorable songs of sixties Hollywood as it totally captures the essence of the movie. Suffice it to say the fact that the snooty music branch of the Academy failed to nominate it for Best Song is not surprising considering some of their other misguided nominations from the past. Composer George Stoll also incorporates the haunting melody into his musical score. Pete Rugolo contributes some cool dialectic jazz pieces to heighten the mood.

All in all, *Where the Boys Are* is a good introduction to sixties beach movies and what was yet to come.

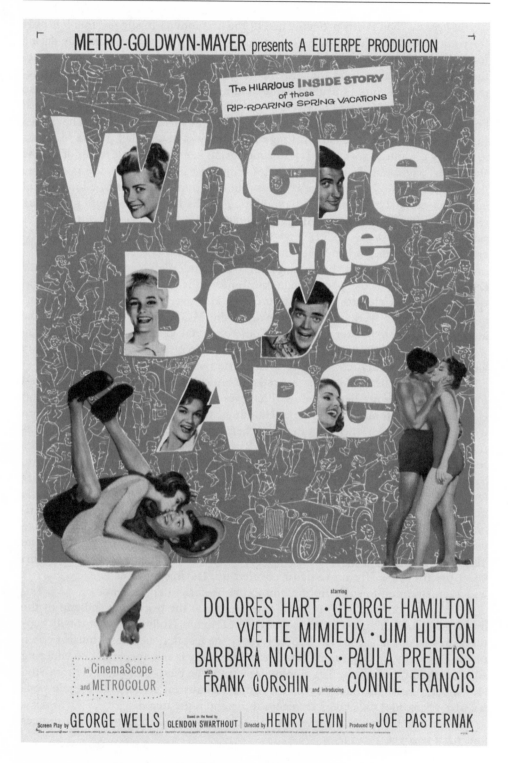

Poster art for *Where the Boys Are* (MGM, 1960).

The Story

The movie opens with narration extolling the peacefulness and beauty of Fort Lauderdale, Florida, one week before "the annual invasion" of college kids from across the country. Meanwhile, during a blizzard in the Midwest, college coeds Melanie and Tuggle try to convince their friend Merritt Andrews to leave the cold and snow to accompany them on their spring break vacation in Fort Lauderdale. Merritt, suffering from a head cold, feels too ill to travel and needs the time to catch up on her schoolwork. In her class about courtship and marriage, a cranky Merritt blurts out that she thinks it is okay for a girl to have sex before marriage, shocking her classmates and outraging her professor. Melanie, however, takes Merritt's words to heart. The dean doesn't and, also citing her poor grades, puts Merritt on notice. Not wanting to face her parents, the outspoken girl decides to join her friends on their trek south.

Man-hungry though insecure Angie joins wisecracking statuesque Tuggle, determined blonde Melanie (who is overeager to land an Ivy Leaguer) and the forthright Merritt on their jaunt. As they are driving through northern Florida they spot a hitchhiker. Deciding that he looks harmless, the gals pick him up. He introduces himself as TV Thompson from Michigan State; the gawky, amiable lad is attracted to Tuggle despite her 5'10½" frame.

The girls check into their small room at the Fairview Apartment Motel and let two coeds from Ohio State, Jody and Jill, crash on their floor since they cannot afford a room ($22 a night). Meanwhile, the town's police captain is giving his officers a pep talk regarding the imminent insurgence of over 20,000 rowdy college students. The next morning, while Merritt, Tuggle and Angie try to ration their money, Melanie frolics in the motel's swimming pool with two college guys from Yale, Dill and Franklin.

Tuggle is excited to get her first look at a Florida beach as she and the other gals brave the crowds to get to the sand. However, before they step foot on it, TV hijacks Tuggle to have a beer at the Elbo Room where the underage Tuggle uses a fake ID to drink. On the beach, Angie and Jody notice a handsome dark-haired college guy who smiles at them but keeps walking. Melanie gets close with Dill, who entices her away from her friends to find a spot on the beach where they can be alone. Tuggle gets to know TV better as they pound the beers but every time he brings up sex she changes the subject.

When a disappointed Tuggle bemoans that she didn't get a chance to go swimming, TV (who hates the water) escorts her to the town's swankiest hotel to use the pool. Later as they get more romantic poolside back at the Fairview Motel, Tuggle reveals that she is a "good girl" and a frustrated TV heads home for the night. Melanie returns with Dill and makes him promise not to tell anyone that she went all the way with him.

Merritt awakens the next morning to find a new girl sleeping on the floor and Melanie smoking a cigarette. She is gushing over a girl who married a boy that she met there during last year's spring break. Merritt bursts her bubble and informs her that the gal got pregnant. Tuggle chimes in that she is going to find a boy the chaste way.

The next day, Dill stands Melanie up and the handsome dark-haired college boy shows up again on the beach and introduces himself to Merritt. They go for a drink and he reveals that his name is Ryder Smith and that he attends Brown University. He takes her to his grandfather's estate and they have dinner on the family yacht. Ryder intrigues Merritt as he does not fit into any of three categories she has for the boys she has dated.

The next day the gals join the throngs headed for the beach and are almost run down by a truck driven by near-sighted jazz musician Basil. He invites the girls to hear his combo play some cool dialectic jazz music at the Elbo Room. While Tuggle and Merritt dig the beat, Angie is not impressed in the least. She does agree to go on a date with the hipster after he strikes out with her two friends.

That night the gals get dolled up for their dates. When Angie bemoans that Basil doesn't even know that she is alive, Jody suggests that maybe another musician would spark his interest, giving the little gal an idea. During his performance she breaks into song, impressing him. Meanwhile, Merritt and Ryder are getting too close and the coed pulls back, saying she is not ready to have sex. She goes home early and is there with Tuggle when an inebriated Melanie arrives, exclaiming that she and Franklin are in love. The next day she admits to Merritt that she went all the way with Franklin. When her friend voices her disapproval, Melanie calls her a hypocrite. When Franklin stands Melanie up, Merritt invites her on her date with Ryder.

The next day on the beach, the gang realizes that they only have two more days left in Fort Lauderdale. They decide to get dressed up and go to a fancy nightclub. Melanie remains behind hoping Franklin will call. A tipsy TV becomes so infatuated with showgirl Lola (who performs her act in a water tank) that he jumps in. Knowing he can't swim, the gang tries to come to his rescue and they all wind up in the water. After they explain their story to the police captain, he lets them go. On the beach, Lola makes a play for TV, who cruelly rejects Tuggle. The heartbroken gal returns to the motel and is there when a desperate Melanie (who was just raped by Dill) phones from some cheap motel. Ryder drives Merritt and Tuggle to her rescue and arrives just as a car hits the despondent Melanie, who in a state of shock has wandered onto the highway.

The doctor assures the girls that their friend will recover nicely. Hating all men, Merritt sends Ryder away while Tuggle and a contrite TV reconcile. The next day he drives Tuggle, Angie and Basil back to school, leaving Merritt in Florida with a recuperating Melanie. While strolling along the deserted beach, Merritt is surprised to see Ryder and she apologizes for her rude behavior. He accepts and offers to give her and Melanie a lift back to the university when the blonde is released from the hospital.

Behind-the-Scenes

MGM bought the film rights to Glendon Swarthout's novel *Where the Boys Are* and tapped veteran producer Joe Pasternak to produce. He was given a fairly big budget of $2 million and decided to cast the film with newcomers rather than any big stars. Pasternak commented in *Variety* that he wanted novice actors because "no one tells you that the 'dialogue stinks' or that the 'cameraman is not photographing me from the right angle.'"

Not all the actors hired were unknowns, however. Receiving top billing was the beautiful Dolores Hart. Discovered by producer Hal B. Wallis, Hart made her film debut playing Elvis Presley's love interest in *Loving You* (1957) and starred opposite him again in *King Creole* (1958). She had just come off a successful run on Broadway in *The Pleasure of His Company* for which she received a Tony Award nomination for Best Featured Actress in a Play when Pasternak cast her as the sensible gal of the bunch, Merritt. Even though she found the novel to be "trashy," Hart grabbed the role.

Dark-haired George Hamilton, looking every bit a movie star, also was familiar to movie audiences. He won a Golden Globe for his film debut in *Crime and Punishment, USA* (1959). He followed this up with an excellent performance as the brooding son of macho Robert Mitchum in *Home from the Hill* (1960) but he bombed in the dreary dud *All the Fine Young Cannibals* (1960) starring Natalie Wood and Robert Wagner. In *Vanity Fair* he described his role in *Where the Boys Are* as being "a watered-down Rock Hudson *Pillow Talk* replica" that typed him as "the perfect playboy."

New MGM contract player Yvette Mimiuex was given the ingenue role of Melanie, the good girl who has to suffer for her wanton ways. She had just made a fetching girl from Earth's far future in George Pal's sci-fi tale *The Time Machine* (1960). Mimieux told the *Newark Sunday News* that she was thrilled to get the part in *Where the Boys Are* because "Dolores Hart and George Hamilton are going to star in it."

Producer Pasternak saw Connie Francis performing at a club in Hollywood and asked her to appear in the movie. He was impressed with the petite singer's stage presence and noticed that she had comedic talent. Francis, who was enjoying worldwide success as a vocalist, was adamant that she did not want to act in movies, but Pasternak was persistent in his quest to cast her as Angie. After discovering that the producer had discovered such luminaries as Elizabeth Taylor, Deanna Durbin, Kathryn Grayson and Jane Powell, Francis finally agreed. However, she was disillusioned with the role of the unattractive Angie and told *Seventeen* in 1961 that she asked the producers to beef up the part to give her "some character." This wasn't Francis' first encounter with the film industry. She dubbed Tuesday Weld's singing voice in *Rock, Rock, Rock* (1956) and made a cameo appearance as herself in *Jamboree* (1957).

Pasternak sent MGM talent scouts around the country to find new actors. Paula Prentiss, then Paula Ragusa, was a student at Northwestern University. She and her husband, actor Richard Benjamin, tested doing a scene from *A Hatful of Rain*. Impressing the talent scout, he asked for a picture to take back to Hollywood. Just as she was to appear in summer stock before starting graduate school, Paula was asked to come to New York to read and then to Hollywood to screen test at MGM for *Where the Boys Are*. She auditioned with Jim Hutton, another MGM contract player who had been discovered by director Douglas Sirk. The gangly young actor had two films to his credit including his film debut as a Nazi repulsed by his assignment to a firing squad in *A Time to Love and a Time to Die* (1958). The pair performed the love scene where their characters first kiss while lounging around the hotel's swimming pool. Pasternak was impressed with their chemistry and the fact that at 6' 2" Hutton was the perfect height for the 5' 10" Prentiss. The statuesque brunette won the role of Tuggle and a seven-year contract with the studio but the producer insisted that Paula change her Sicilian last name to something less ethnic-sounding. Since he renamed Deanna Durbin and Doris Day, he also gave Paula a name with alliteration.

Marilyn Monroe wannabe and former exotic dancer Barbara Nichols gets star billing as Lola though she doesn't come on screen until the last half-hour. She was usually cast as bumbling dumb blondes, tough gun molls or grasping goldiggers in such films as *The King and Four Queens* (1956), *Pal Joey* (1957), *The Pajama Game* (1957), *Sweet Smell of Success* (1957) and *The George Raft Story* (1961).

Others cast in minor roles included busy television starlet Maggie Pierce (whom Paula Prentiss describes in the DVD commentary as being "adorable") as Jody and Harvard graduate Rory Harrity, the handsome son of playwright Richard Harrity, as one of Yvette Mimieux's abusers. Rory was a stage-trained actor who co-starred on Broadway in *A Visit to a Small Planet* and the Noël Coward comedy *Look After Lulu* with Roddy McDowall and Tammy Grimes. Harrity headed west to Hollywood in 1959 and made his film debut in a minor role in *From the Terrace* (1960).

Another offspring in the movie was Sean Flynn, the son of Errol Flynn and former actress Lili Damita. If you blink you'll miss Sean throwing a football on the beach in Fort Lauderdale while Connie Francis and Maggie Pierce ogle passerby George Hamilton. Tall and handsome, Sean not only inherited his father's good looks, charisma and athletic prowess but also his adventurous streak and risk-taking ways. Actor Aron Kincaid spoke with Sean briefly a few times at various Hollywood social events and remarked, "Sean Flynn was physically the most handsome guy I think I ever met. I was so jealous when he got the starring role in *Son of Captain Blood*. That was a part I would have killed to play. Though Sean looked great, he was not an actor in the least."

Veteran director Henry Levin (whom Prentiss described as being "very patient") was hired to helm *Where the Boys Are*. Levin made his directorial debut with *Cry of the Werewolf* (1944). As he was directing novice actors, some of whom had never been in front of the camera before, his technique of working with them at a leisurely pace paid off. He also was responsible for introducing Paula Prentiss to her agent, Phil Gersh, with whom she remained for over 40 years.

The exteriors and some of the interiors featuring long shots of the cast were shot on location in Fort Lauderdale, purportedly the first time the city was used for motion picture location filming. The real places in Fort Lauderdale were recreated on the soundstages on the back lot at MGM to shoot the actors' closeups. The cast was in Florida for approximately three weeks. Prentiss was particularly excited about going to Fort Lauderdale because while a student she remained behind at school while her friends traveled to the beach oasis for spring break.

According to the film's pressbook, the scene where Sean Flynn tosses a football high in the air was filmed on the beach in Fort Lauderdale but the shot of the guy catching it was filmed on a local beach in California. Approximately a thousand local boys and girls aspired to be background players in the movie. Only 300 were chosen to participate.

Connie Francis enjoyed shooting at MGM much more than filming in Florida. She commented in *Seventeen*, "It was awful. We were miles out on a country road and the bugs! Ugh! We had those trailers to change clothes in—it was hotter inside than out. I was happy to get back to the studio."

Barbara Nichols is featured in one of the film's funniest bits when Jim Hutton's TV dives into a water tank to admire the underwater dancer's "lungs." The rest of the gang (trying to rescue the smitten lad who can't swim) soon follows him. While all this commotion is going on around her, Nichols' character has to keep performing her ballet. The buxom blonde admitted in the film's pressbook that she "has always been a little afraid of water" and had to spend several nights a week submerged in water at a local health club pool to become accustomed to it before filming. The scene took three days to shoot with the principals spending four hours a day underwater.

According to Paula Prentiss, the cast got along wonderfully and she became close with some of them over the years. While filming, Prentiss got sick and Dolores Hart would bring her soup to help her get her strength back. George Hamilton was the only one of the cast to act "the movie star." According to Prentiss, each day he came to the studio by limousine and sat in the sun with an aluminum shield to maintain his golden tan. Connie Francis called him "a card" because he was always pulling practical jokes on her.

Joe Pasternak had some of Hollywood's top songwriters on consignment to compose the title song, which Connie had her choice of. However, she asked Pasternak if he would give her friends Howard Greenfield and Neil Sedaka first crack at it since they wrote all of her previous records that became top hits. He agreed, giving them one week to come up with something. Greenfield and Sedaka submitted two versions—one that they and Connie loved and a second that they all hated. Pasternak of course chose the song Francis despised and she had to tell the duo back in Brooklyn the good news that their song would be included in the movie and the bad news that it was the version that they disliked immensely. Though the songwriters and Connie didn't like this version, "Where the Boys Are" became one of Francis' most enduring hit records, reaching No. 4 on *Billboard*'s Pop Charts.

According to a Francis interview in *Seventeen*, Joe Pasternak was unhappy with her for having too many projects going at once. Besides making the movie, Connie was recording songs for two upcoming albums, giving interviews to promote them and preparing to leave for a European tour. He insisted that if she ever worked for him again, her contract would specifically limit her to acting only. Nevertheless, she and the producer had a wonderful relationship. She remarked, "I would call Mr. Pasternak and he would give me advice about everything. 'Don't become mixed up in the Hollywood world,' he said. 'You'll see a lot of things here that will surprise and shock you. Don't get involved.'"

To help boost interest in the movie, MGM sent the stars on a six-week promotion tour across the U.S. Demanding that their contract players uphold their movie star personas for the public, the studio supplied them with a wardrobe befitting their stature. Paula Prentiss was excited to be wearing a coat that Elizabeth Taylor wore in *BUtterfield 8*.

Where the Boys Are was released during the Christmas holidays in 1960 and opened at Radio City Music Hall in New York City. It became an immediate sensation and according to *Variety* was the 27th highest grossing film of 1961. By the time spring break rolled around that April, over 300,000 college kids descended upon Fort Lauderdale due to the popularity of the movie.

Over 20 years later, the movie was remade as *Where the Boys Are '84* (1984) starring Lisa Hartman, Wendy Schaal, Lynn Holly Johnson, Lorna Luft, Russell Todd and Howard McGillin. In homage to the original, George Hamilton makes a cameo appearance. Vulgar, crass and unfunny, the film was a box office dud and deservedly sunk the movie careers of most of the cast.

Post–*Where the Boys Are,* two of its actors had dramatic career changes. The first was Dolores Hart, who abandoned a blossoming acting career in 1963 to become a cloistered nun. Suffice it to say, they don't ask Mother Dolores where the boys are any longer. In 2001, Paula Prentiss visited her dear friend at the Abbey of St. Regina in Bethlehem, Connecticut, and the duo went for a drive in Prentiss' convertible just like they did in the movie.

George Hamilton built a solid career playing the urbane sophisticate in such films as *Two Weeks in Another Town* (1962), *That Man George* (1966), *Doctor, You've Got to Be Kidding!* (1967) and *Jack of Diamonds* (1967). But he enjoyed his greatest success when cast against type as Hank Williams in *Your Cheatin' Heart* (1964) or parodying his screen persona in *Love at First Bite* (1979) and *Zorro the Gay Blade* (1981). He is still very active in show business today.

Because they were the tallest contract players at the studio and had such screen chemistry, MGM teamed Hutton and Prentiss in three additional comedies, *The Honeymoon Machine, Bachelor in Paradise* (both 1961) and *The Horizontal Lieutenant* (1962). Regarding her late co-star Jim Hutton, Prentiss commented on the film's DVD, "We had a wonderful working relationship and a friendship too."

Connie Francis continued recording and reunited with Prentiss for an unofficial sequel to *Where the Boys Are,* entitled *Follow the Boys* (1963), where they played tourists trying to find romance on the French Riviera. She followed this with the musicals *Looking for Love* (1964) and *When the Boys Meet the Girls* (1965).

The second dramatic career change involved Sean Flynn. His minor bit in *Where the Boys Are* went unnoticed by most critics but Robert C. Roman of *Films in Review* commented that Sean "has many of the attractive physical attributes of his father. In fact, he seemed to me to have

The girls can be found where the boys are when they look as strikingly handsome as Sean Flynn.

more star-potential and virile sex appeal than George Hamilton, Jim Hutton and Rory Harrity." After being wooed to Europe to star in *Son of Captain Blood* (1962), Sean made a few low-budget espionage and adventure films including *Mission to Venice* (1963), *Duel at the Rio Grande* (1963) and *Stop Train 349* (1964). However, he never fully felt at ease in front of the camera and headed for Vietnam in January 1966, working as a photojournalist for the magazine *Paris Match* though he continued making intermittent film appearances until 1968. Flynn developed a very close friendship with renowned photographer Tim Page and remained in Vietnam until February 1967. He came back to the war-torn country in 1968, and left once again this time for a photo assignment that led him to New Guinea and Indonesia. However, Vietnam had a strong hold on Flynn and he returned in March 1970 working freelance for *Time* and teaming up with photographer Dana Stone. The pair was nicknamed the Easy Riders as the hippie-looking duo sporting long hair traveled the landscape by motorcycle. On April 6, 1970, against the advice of colleagues, they headed for a roadblock on the Cambodia border to snap pictures of the North Vietnamese operating in that country—and disappeared. Despite the persistent efforts of many people, including Sean's grief-stricken mother, to get them released, Flynn and Stone's capture was never confirmed nor denied by the North Vietnamese. People who knew Sean were positive that he was strong enough in mind and body to survive in the jungle and would emerge alive. However, Sean and Stone were never heard from again.

After years of speculation and rumor, Sean's fate was finally discovered according to author Jeffrey Meyers. Flynn survived for 14 months as a prisoner, first of the Vietcong and then the Khmer Rouge. In June 1971 he contracted a severe case of malaria and was given a lethal injection. He died a few weeks after his thirtieth birthday.

Memorable Lines

(The bartender at the Elbo Room cards Tuggle, who gives him a fake ID courtesy of TV.)

TUGGLE (laying on a thick Southern accent): My name is Kitty Gruder. I'm 21 years old and I live in Macon, Georgia.

BARTENDER: And you're five-foot-three and your hair is red. Only *you* aren't and *it* isn't.

TUGGLE: Well, I'm still *growing* and I *dyed* it.

(TV and Tuggle are getting close and kissing while lying on a chaise lounge poolside.)

TV (eagerly): Are you a good girl, Tuggle?

TUGGLE: Mmm-hmmm.

TV (disappointedly): Oh.

TUGGLE: *I knew it.* Well, so long, TV.

Reviews

Roger Angell, *The New Yorker*—"[A] deplorable tale."

Christian Science Monitor—"*Where the Boys Are* is sometimes funny and occasionally touching. Unfortunately, the total effect is spoiled by a kind of cheapness, a sophomoric sex obsession by elders who should know better."

Janet Graves, *Photoplay*—"You'll have a ball with the girl-hunting guys and husband-hunting girls who invade Fort Lauderdale. The whole picture's a terrific showcase for young talent and whatever type you go for."

Edwin Miller, *Seventeen*—"*Where the Boys Are* will make any date sit up and shudder as he watches its four college heroines ... descend on a Florida resort to hunt boys for marriage with a single-mindedness that would make Little Red Riding Hood's wolf yelp for mercy."

Sidney Rechetnik, *Motion Picture Daily*—"Light, frothy, romantic comedy, marred somewhat by a corny melodramatic climax, and elegantly produced by Joe Pasternak with a bevy of attractive young players."

Time—"*Where the Boys Are* is one of those pictures every intelligent moviegoer will loathe himself for liking—corny, phony raucous outburst of fraternity humor, sorority sex talk and house-mother homilies that nevertheless warms two hours of winter with a travel-poster tanorama of fresh young faces, firm young bodies and good old Florida sunshine."

Variety—"Unusually strong appeal for young people [although] the more studious collegian may cringe in horror at this adult eye-view of modern undergrads at play.... It's a long way from Andy Hardy."

Awards and Nominations

Film Daily's Famous Fives: "Best Performance by a Supporting Actress"—Paula Prentiss

Film Daily's Famous Fives: "Finds of the Year"—Paula Prentiss

Golden Laurel Award: "Top Comedy"—second place

Golden Laurel Award: "Top Female Comedy Performance"—Paula Prentiss, third place

Golden Laurel Award: "Top Female New Personality"—Dolores Hart, third place

Golden Laurel Award: "Top Female New Personality"—Connie Francis, fourth place

Golden Laurel Award: "Top Female New Personality"—Paula Prentiss, ninth place

Golden Laurel Award: "Top Male New Personality"—Jim Hutton, third place

Motion Picture Herald's Star of Tomorrow—Dolores Hart, fifth place

Motion Picture Herald's Star of Tomorrow—Paula Prentiss, sixth place

Motion Picture Herald's Star of Tomorrow—Jim Hutton, eighth place

Photoplay Gold Medal Award: "Favorite Female Newcomer"—Paula Prentiss

Photoplay Gold Medal Nomination: "Favorite Actor"—George Hamilton

Photoplay Gold Medal Nomination: "Favorite Actress"—Dolores Hart

Photoplay Gold Medal Nomination: "Favorite Female Newcomer"—Connie Francis

Photoplay Gold Medal Nomination: "Favorite Male Newcomer"—Jim Hutton

Screen World Award: "Most Promising Personalities"—George Hamilton

Screen World Award: "Most Promising Personalities"—Jim Hutton

Screen World Award: "Most Promising Personalities"—Yvette Mimieux

★ 3 ★

Blue Hawaii (1961)

Ecstatic Romance ... Exotic Dances ...
Exciting Music in the World's Lushest Paradise of Song!

Overall Rating: ★★★
Surfing: ★
Boy watching: ★★
Girl watching: ★★★
Music: ★★★
Scenery: ★★★★

Release date: November 22, 1961. Running time: 101m. Box office gross: $4.2 million. DVD release: Paramount Studios (December 12, 2003).

Elvis Presley (*Chad Gates*), Joan Blackman (*Maile Duval*), Nancy Walters (*Abigail Prentace*), Roland Winters (*Fred Gates*), Angela Lansbury (*Sarah Lee Gates*), John Archer (*Jack Kelman*), Howard McNear (*Mr. Chapman*), Flora Hayes (*Mrs. Manaka*), Gregory Gay (*Mr. Duval*), Steve Brodie (*Mr. Garvey*), Iris Adrian (*Mrs. Garvey*), Darlene Tompkins (*Patsy*), Pamela Kirk (*Sandy*), Christian Kay (*Beverly*), Jenny Maxwell (*Ellie*), Frank Atienza (*Ito O'Hara*), Lani Kai (*Carl*), Jose De Varga (*Ernie*), Ralph Hanalie (*Wes*). Not credited: Anglina Bauer (*Hula Girl*), Pat Fackenthall (*Airline Stewardess*), Lenmana Guerin (*Hula Girl*), Hilo Hattie (*Lei Seller*), Flora Hayes (*Mrs. Maneka*), 'Lucky' Luck (*Airline Passenger*).

Paramount Pictures. *Produced by*: Hal B. Wallis. *Directed by*: Norman Taurog. *Screenplay by*: Hal Kanter. *Story by*: Allan Weiss. *Associate Producer*: Paul Nathan. *Music Scored and Conducted by*: Joseph L. Lilley. *Vocal Accompaniment by*: The Jordaniares. *Technical Advisor*: Col. Tom Parker. *Musical Numbers Staged by*: Charles O'Curran. *Director of Photography*: Charles Lang, Jr., A.S.C. *Art Directors*: Hal Pereira, Walter Tyler. *Special Photographic Effects*: John P. Fulton, A.S.C. *Process Photography*: Farciot Edouart, A.S.C. *Set Decorators*: Sam Comer, Frank McKelvy. *Assistant Director*: D. Michael Moore. *Editorial Supervisor*: Warren Low, A.C.E. *Film Editor*: Terry Morse, A.C.E. *Costumes*: Edith Head. *Technicolor Color Consultant*: Richard Mueller. *Second Unit Photography*: W. Wallace Kelley, A.S.C. *Dialogue Coach*: Jack Mintz. *Makeup Supervisor*: Wally Westmore. *Hair Style Supervisor*: Nellie Manley. *Sound Recorders*: Philip Mitchell, Charles Grenzbach. Filmed in Panavision and Technicolor.

All songs sung by Elvis Presley. "No More" by Don Robertson, Hal Blair. "I Can't Help Falling in Love" and "Ku-U-I-Po" by Hugo Peretti, Luigi Creatore and George David Weiss. "Rock-a-Hula Baby" by Fred Wise, Ben Weisman and Dolores Fuller. "Moonlight Swim" by Sylvia Dee and Ben Weisman. "Ito Eats," Slicin' Sand," "Hawaiian Sunset," "Beach Boy Blues" and "Hawaiian Wedding Song" by Charles E. King, Al Hoffman and Dick Manning.

Blue Hawaii is arguably Elvis Presley's best post–Army musical—even more entertaining than the overrated *Viva Las Vegas*. It excellently blends comedy, romance, music, lush locations and a bit of surfing to make it a beach movie well worth viewing. The film unfolds like a beautiful travelogue—one where you don't mind when the actors get in front of the scenery. Elvis is very good as a returning G.I. who'd rather surf and work as a tour guide than accept a job on his dad's pineapple plantation. Most of the laughs come from Roland Winters as Elvis' droll father and Angela Lansbury as his bewildered Southern belle mother.

After recently returning from military duty, Elvis is handsome and slim and sports a fit physique for his many shirtless scenes. He is the only Caucasian boy around though he is surrounded by bare-chested, beefy Hawaiians. But this is a film more for girl watchers.

Curvaceous Joan Blackman is charming, pretty and pleasant, and she makes a fetching leading lady for the King. Despite the rumors of Elvis' dislike for Joan off-camera, the two definitely have on-screen chemistry. All the girls, except Christian Kay who resembles Big Ethel from the Archie comic books, are extremely attractive. Though they are clad in modest one- or two-piece swimsuits, their luscious curves are fully on display. Jenny Maxwell makes a sexy teenage temptress but she is so annoying and bitchy that you are rooting for Elvis to ditch her in some pineapple grove. However, one would never guess that he'd take the little witch over his knee and give her a spanking instead, making *Blue Hawaii* a fetishist lover's dream come true.

Unlike Elvis musicals to follow, here at least the songs mesh into the plot. Standing out are "Rock-a-Hula Baby" and the poignant "Can't Help Falling in Love," which was touted for an Academy Award nomination. However, at that time the stuffy "old guard" members of the Academy's music branch ignored the song in favor of such "classics" as "Bachelor in Paradise" from the movie of the same name and "Love Theme from *El Cid* (The Falcon and the Dove)."

Publicity photos to the contrary, there are no shots of Elvis or a stunt double surfing. Presley is seen only lying on his board in the bay or coming out of the surf carrying it. Another small strike against the film is that the beach party scene is so obviously filmed on a soundstage. This is truly disappointing considering so many of the other scenes were filmed on-location. Elvis' obligatory fight scene is well-staged and the lush color photography of Hawaii is superb. *Blue Hawaii* remains a spectacular travelogue come to life with pleasant songs, pretty girls and Elvis at his peak.

The Story

Chad Gates returns home to Honolulu after a two-year hitch in the Army determined not to do what his parents want, which is to take a job on the family pineapple business, settle down and marry a girl of his own social position. He is greeted at the airport by his French-Hawaiian sweetheart Maile and instructs her to take him to his surf shack on Hanauma Bay where he presents her with a two-piece bathing suit from France. While swimming, Maile loses her top but a dog comes to her rescue and brings her a sarong. Chad decides to crash at the beach. Hiding out from his parents, Chad surfs the days away with his native pals.

Poster art for *Blue Hawaii* (Paramount, 1961).

Realizing that he can't avoid them forever, the forthright young man faces his folks after coaxing from Maile, who reveals that his father knows he has returned. Chad's reunion with his parents quickly goes sour when his mother Sarah Lee insists that he stop hanging out with his native beach boy friends, drop Maile and accept a position with his father's company. He storms out and heads over to Maile's family home, where they are celebrating her grandmother's birthday.

He rejects his father's offer to work at his pineapple plantation and accepts a job offer as a tour guide in the agency where Maile works. The girl is thrilled until she gets a glimpse of his first assignment. Chad is scheduled to escort a beautiful, sophisticated schoolteacher named Abigail Prentice and her four high school students.

After making arrangements to start the tour the next day, Chad takes Maile to his parents' house for a "Welcome Home" party. His father and Jack Kelman, a family friend and Mr. Gates' boss, greet Maile cordially but Sarah Lee openly resents her presence. The party is a drag so Chad asks his pals who are supplying the music to kick up the tempo. Soon Chad has the place jumping as he and Maile perform a number with the band. Outraged, Sarah Lee suffers a near-collapse.

Chad meets Miss Prentace and her charges Patsy, Sandy, Beverly and Ellie the following morning. He takes the group on a scenic drive to the pineapple fields. Three of the girls are friendly and pleasant, but Ellie is self-centered and rude to Chad. During the next few days, Chad takes the group sailing, canoeing and gives them surfing lessons. At a Hookie Lau, Ellie changes tactics and kisses Chad. Taken aback, he tells her that "he doesn't rob cradles," which infuriates the nubile teen.

Though his parents are disappointed in his new job, Jack Kelman admires Chad's gumption and accompanies him to a luau where he is introduced to Miss Prentace. Troublemaking Ellie flirts with a tipsy tourist. When he starts to respond, Chad breaks it up, a fight ensues and Chad winds up in jail. After his father bails him out, the tourist agency's owner, Mr. Chapman, fires him. Standing up for her man, Maile quits in protest. Blaming the incident on Maile and the Hawaiian surfers, Chad's parents insist that he give Maile up. Chad refuses and leaves home.

The newly unemployed Chad and Maile spend their days at the beach surfing. When Maile informs Chad that Abigail cancelled her tour with the agency in protest of Chad's firing, he gets an idea and convinces Abigail to hire him as a freelance tour guide. With Maile's help they book the girls in a hotel for three days on Kauai. On the first night, Ellie (dressed in a revealing peignoir) comes to Chad's room and tries to seduce him. Just then he gets a phone call from Maile, who is in the lobby with Jack Kelman. Chad tells her to stay put and that he'll meet her there. But before he can get rid of Ellie, Patsy and Sandy show up looking for the wayward youth. Ellie greets them with a "so what" look. A showdown is postponed by Abigail's rap on the door. The schoolteacher is ecstatic, confessing that she came to Hawaii seeking romance and that she has found it. Believing that she means him, Chad tries to get her to lower her voice by moving closer to her. Ellie, watching from a back window, misinterprets the scene and runs away sobbing. Maile too has witnessed this and she flees to her room.

Patsy and Sandy return to Chad's room and tell him that Ellie has driven off in a Jeep. He follows her to the beach and pulls her out of the ocean. After making sure that she is not hurt, he gives her a lecture and then an old-fashioned spanking.

The next morning, Maile avoids Chad, who is evading Abigail. But the teacher finally corners him and finishes what she tried to tell him the night before—she's in love with Jack Kelman. Chad happily tells Maile, who doesn't believe him until she sees Jack and Abigail strolling together hand-in-hand.

To help Chad, Kelman gets Fred Gates to come to Kauai where Chad presents his plan for the company to hold its conventions in Hawaii with all the arrangements being handled by Chad and Maile's new agency. Kelman and Gates think Chad's idea is wonderful. So does Maile, who accepts his impromptu marriage proposal. The couple is then married in a beautiful boat ceremony set in a tropical paradise of a park.

Behind-the-Scenes

When Elvis Presley returned home from the Army, his first movie was for producer Hal B. Wallis and Paramount Pictures. *G.I. Blues* (1960) cast Elvis as an Army private stationed in Germany whose friends bet him that he cannot score with a sexy entertainer (Juliet Prowse). The film featured European locales, beautiful women and lots of songs, making it a hit with Elvis fans. The King had returned but he quickly fell from grace with his next two movies produced by 20th Century–Fox. The critics praised his performances as a half-breed caught in a war between the whites and Indians in the Western *Flaming Star* (1960) and as a juvenile delinquent with writing aspirations in the turgid soap opera *Wild in the Country* (1961). However, reviewers don't buy tickets and both films underscored at the box office. Determined to return Elvis to his former box office glory, and knowing that his fans wanted to see Elvis singing to pretty girls with lush scenery in the background, Hal Wallis gave them what would become the standard Elvis Presley picture.

Blue Hawaii (1961) began production as *Hawaii Beach Boy*. The screenplay by Hal Kanter was based on Allan Weiss' original story "Beach Boy." Veteran Academy Award–winning director Norman Taurog was hired to direct. He had first worked with Elvis on *G.I. Blues*. It has been reported that he was Presley's favorite and would go on to work with the King on *Girls! Girls! Girls!* (1962), *It Happened at the World's Fair* (1963), *Tickle Me* (1965), *Spinout* (1966), *Double Trouble* (1967), *Speedway* (1968) and *Live a Little, Love a Little* (1969).

Trying to repeat the on-screen chemistry of Elvis and Juliet Prowse in *G.I. Blues*, Hal Wallis arranged a loan-out of the actress, who was under contract to 20th Century–Fox. The two had hit it off on *G.I. Blues* and even became romantically involved despite Prowse's highly publicized love affair with Frank Sinatra. Though Juliet only had two films in the can, she decided to play "movie star" and would only appear if certain conditions were met. She insisted that her own makeup man be hired, that passage to Hawaii be paid for her secretary and that her billing be changed. Defending herself in the tabloids, Prowse explained to the Associated Press, "I have a face that is difficult to make up; I wanted someone who knew me." As for her secretary, "I wanted a companion. I didn't know anyone else in the company except Elvis, and he's always surrounded by a dozen buddies." When Wallis wouldn't concede to any of her demands, Prowse walked off the film and was suspended by Fox.

A new leading lady was needed fast so Wallis offered the film to his recent discovery Pamela Tiffin. She had signed a contract with the producer after making her film debut in *Summer and Smoke* (1961). Astonishingly, the newcomer turned it down! Tiffin explained in *Fantasy Femmes of Sixties Cinema* that she was advised by many people in the industry not to do an Elvis Presley movie as it could hurt her fledgling career. She abided by their advice but years later regretted it.

Wallis then cast Joan Blackman in the part. The dark-haired beauty had been lunching with friends at the Paramount commissary when Wallis noticed her. A singer and dancer, she was given a screen test and signed to a contract though her roles up to this point had all been dramatic. She received excellent notices as the neglected wife of aspiring actor Tony Franciosa in *Career* (1959) before she went on to co-star with Jerry Lewis in *Visit to a Small Planet* (1960).

Actress Dolores Fuller, who was a friend of producer Hal Wallis, campaigned heavily for the role of the schoolteacher. Fuller was the ex-girlfriend of cult director Ed Wood, Jr., and the star of his films *Glen or Glenda?* (1953) and *Jailbait* (1954). However, Wallis was more impressed with her songwriting skills than with her acting prowess. Fuller recalled in *Outré* magazine, "I said, 'Aw, come on, Hal! I want to go to Hawaii with Elvis!' He said, 'No, Dolores! Tomorrow morning at nine o'clock, you be at Hill and Range, and I'm going to introduce you to Freddy Bienstock, who publishes all the songs that go into Elvis' films.'" Fuller didn't get the part but she co-wrote the hit song "Rock-a-Hula Baby" for *Blue Hawaii* and went on to contribute tunes for other Elvis musicals including "Do the Clam" in *Girl Happy* (1965).

The part Dolores Fuller craved went instead to Nancy Walters, a former model, whose most notable credit was the horror film *Monster on the Campus* (1958). She was borrowed from MGM, where she played a minor role in *Bells Are Ringing* (1960) and the female lead in the British racing car drama *The Green Helmet* (1961).

Angela Lansbury had been appearing in the dramatic play *A Taste of Honey* on Broadway when she was offered the role of Southern-fried Sarah Lee, the mother of Elvis' Chad Gates. The British-born actress jumped at the chance to play this comical character even though she was only ten years older than Presley. It was a trend that would continue with more sixties roles for Lansbury. In *The Manchurian Candidate* (1962) she was three years older than Laurence Harvey (her on-screen son) and in *Harlow* (1965) her Mama Jean had only six years on Carroll Baker. Over the years, Lansbury has stated in interviews that her family tried to talk her out of accepting this role. It was not so much due to the age difference but the stigma of being in an "Elvis Presley movie," which they felt could harm her career.

Kewpie-doll blonde Pamela Kirk, better known as Pamela Austin, and lanky brunette Christian Kay both made their film debuts in *Blue Hawaii* as two of the four schoolgirls. The most coveted part of the bratty Ellie went to Jenny Maxwell, a cute blonde similar in looks to Tuesday Weld and Carol Lynley. She previously played the latter's school chum in *Blue Denim* (1959). The fourth actress cast was Darlene Tompkins, who had just starred in the low-budget science fiction adventure *Beyond the Time Barrier* (1960). According to Tompkins, hundreds of young actresses vied for these roles. "My favorite memory of this is the day my agent called me and told me I got the part," comments Darlene. "I remember jumping up and down and screaming. I was so excited and afraid at the same time. I was sure that if I saw Elvis and he spoke to me that I would faint.

"Well, I met Elvis and he spoke to me and I didn't faint," continues Tompkins with a laugh. "Now, after all these years knowing how much he impacted my life and how much I miss him, I should have fainted."

Blue Hawaii opens with Elvis' return from a two-year Army hitch. A number of Presley's movies that followed would begin this way including *Paradise, Hawaiian Style* (1966), the most obvious rip-off. *Blue Hawaii* was filmed on location in the islands of Oahu and Kauai. The film's wedding scene was shot at the Polynesian Cultural Center on Oahu. Other locations used included Mt. Tantalus, Waikiki Beach, Ala Wai Yacht Club, Honolulu Airport, Hanauma Bay, Ala Moana Park, Wailo Tea Room, Lydgate Park, Wailua River, Coco Palms and Anahola Bay. Some scenes such as the luau on the beach were shot on a soundstage at Paramount Studios. Filming lasted four weeks.

Angela Lansbury respected Elvis and commented in the book *Elvis Up Close*, "He liked to get his scenes in one take. It wasn't the kind of material that allowed him to show signs of unusual talent. During free time on the set, he broke bricks with his hand."

Remembering her co-stars, Darlene says, "Elvis was just so handsome and extraordinarily polite. I adored Nancy Walters, who had a glow about her. I never saw her without a smile on her face. She was one of the easiest people to talk to that I ever met. Joan Blackman, however, was very full of herself. I had heard of her and thought she was a star so I wasn't surprised. A week after I started, I felt that Jenny Maxwell was a much better actress and more down-to-earth."

Over the years there has been scuttlebutt that Blackman was Presley's least favorite leading lady. Joan has refuted this by claiming she had a love affair with him, and the fact that she worked with him a second time. She remarked in the book *Down at the End of Lonely Street*, "We had rooms next to each other in the hotel, and for weeks we just about lived together." Darlene Tompkins can't verify or deny these claims but she remarks, "When Elvis had some down time he'd like to sit with me or one of the other girls but I never saw him walk over to Joan. Elvis invited some of us to have dinner with him and I never saw Joan there. Of course that was dinner—*I don't know about later in the evening.*"

Though Darlene Tompkins did not personally care for Blackman, she admired her work ethic. She also was fascinated by a technique Joan used for the exterior shots. Tompkins revealed in *Drive-in Dream Girls* that Joan would look directly into the sunlight so she could practice not blinking when looking at the production lights.

When *Blue Hawaii* opened it received mostly positive reviews, but no one expected it to be such a huge hit. It grossed $4.2 million, becoming the eighteenth highest grossing film of 1962 per *Variety*. "The movie's success really, really surprised me because it was done so light-hearted," admits Tompkins. "We had so much fun just filming it nobody expected it to as big as it was. You'd think if a movie were going to be such a hit you'd put your blood, sweat and tears into it. But on *Blue Hawaii* we just had fun."

The soundtrack album contained 14 songs—the most ever for an Elvis movie. It was also his biggest-selling LP (over six million copies). It hit No. 1 on the *Bill-*

board charts in the fall of 1961 and remained there for a record-breaking 20 weeks in a row. Two songs were released as singles. The poignant "Can't Help Falling in Love Again" reached No. 2 on the *Billboard* Pop charts while "Rock-a-Hula Baby" peaked at No. 23.

As for Elvis, the film's success had a negative effect on his acting career in that his manager Col. Parker steered him away from anything different and challenging. Darlene Tomkins reveals, "Elvis told me that he was going to be remembered for being a dramatic actor—it was his fondest dream. It seems surprising to me that someone as talented and dedicated as he was never able to fulfill his dream. If the Colonel [Tom Parker] hadn't held him back from doing *A Star Is Born* and the other dramatic movies offered to him, I know Elvis would have gotten an Academy Award." The majority of Presley's remaining movies followed *Blue Hawaii*'s formula—pretty scenery, beautiful gals, a fistfight or two and lots of songs. Not that these films were bad (okay, there were a few stinkers such as *Harum Scarum* and *Double Trouble*) but the logic was that all Elvis needed to do was follow that format and the fans would flock to the theaters—and flock they did.

Blue Hawaii was also a hit with television viewers when it first aired on November 29, 1966. It received a 27.3 rating and a 45 share, making it the second highest watched sixties beach movie behind *Gidget Goes Hawaiian*.

Joan Blackman would co-star opposite Elvis one more time in *Kid Galahad* (1962). The remainder of her career was erratic. She played the love interest of Richard Chamberlain in his first starring film *Twilight of Honor* (1963) but by the mid-sixties she was only able to land roles in such B-movies as *Intimacy* (1966) and *The Destructors* (1968). Her most noteworthy project was her year-long stint on television's *Peyton Place* where as Marian Fowler she was responsible for the hit-and-run that left Mia Farrow's Alison in a coma. Blackman disappeared from Hollywood and returned in the mid-seventies playing the wife of sheriff Max Baer, Jr., in the drive-in hit *Macon County Line* (1974) and another wife role, this time of the philandering kind, in *The Moonrunners* (1975). In 1985, Joan surprisingly turned up playing the mother in Ray Davies' mini-rock opera *Return to Waterloo*. Today, Blackman resides in Northern California and in 2003 was one of the guests of honor at an Elvis Presley convention in Memphis. However, it has been reported on the Elvis Presley News website that the former actress was rude, complained about the fans, overcharged for photocopies of chapters from her unpublished autobiography and berated the staff member assigned to her for the event.

Jenny Maxwell received excellent notices for her performance in *Blue Hawaii*. "Emotes with youthful relish and spirit" (*Variety*), "a standout" (*The Hollywood Reporter*) and "shows promise" (*Motion Picture Herald*) were just some of the raves she received from the critics. Stardom should have come her way but after losing out on *Lolita* to Sue Lyon, Maxwell was only able to rustle up the role of a boy-chasing coed in support of Sandra Dee in *Take Her, She's Mine* (1963). She finally did get to play a nymphet on the big screen but it was in the grade–Z production *Shotgun Wedding* (1963). Movies never beckoned again for the sexy blonde but she continued being cast as teenagers on television in such series as *Death Valley Days*, *The F.B.I.*, *My Three Sons* and *Judd for the Defense* through the late sixties. Sadly, she was gunned down in front of her Los Angeles home in a botched robbery attempt in 1981.

Elvis Presley played a returning G.I. who'd rather surf than work in *Blue Hawaii* (Paramount, 1961).

Pamela Kirk changed her name to Pamela Austin and signed a contract with Warner Bros. She did television and played a minor role in *Rome Adventure* (1962) before joining the ranks at MGM. The perky blonde landed leading roles in the teenage cornpone musicals *Hootenanny Hoot* (1963) and *Kissin' Cousins* (1964) where she reunited with Presley. She is probably best remembered for her series of television commercials as the Dodge Rebellion Girl. Austin was the original dumb blonde on *Rowan and Martin's Laugh-In* but her handlers never let her sign a contract and instead pushed her into playing Pauline in three unsold *Perils of Pauline* pilots. A newcomer named Goldie Hawn than replaced her on the hit variety show. Today, it is believed that Pamela Austin resides in Palm Springs.

Her screen presence in *Blue Hawaii* impressed the executives at Paramount so much that Darlene Tompkins was signed to a contract and was chosen as the studio's Hollywood Deb Star for 1962. However, Tompkins was newly married and her young husband was jealous of the attention his wife was receiving. Darlene played a bitchy aspiring actress in the Debbie Reynolds comedy *My Six Loves* (1963) and then did some television before calling it quits to devote her time to her family. After her divorce in the mid-seventies, she tried to revive her acting career but nobody remembered her. She began doing stand-in work and doubled for Cheryl Ladd on *Charlie's Angels* and some of her movie projects. Today, the effervescent Tompkins can be found working at the Elvis Presley Museum in Las Vegas where she and another Elvis co-star, Cynthia Pepper, rotate speaking with visitors about the King and the making of the movies they worked with him on.

Memorable Lines

(Potential client Abigail Prentice questions Chad to see if he would make an appropriate tour guide.)

ABIGAIL: Mr. Gates, do you think you can satisfy a schoolteacher and four teenage girls?

CHAD: Well, uh, I'll sure try, ma'am. I'll do all I can.

(Chad announces to his parents that he will not work in the family business and will not give up his girlfriend Maile.)

SARAH LEE: Oh, Daddy, what'd we do wrong?

FRED: Offhand, I'd say we got married.

Reviews

Robin Bean, *Films and Filming*—"Hal Wallis is going to find the value of his multi-million dollar investment quickly deteriorate if he thinks up any more absurd starring vehicles like *Blue Hawaii* for Presley. This is little more than a travelogue of the Hawaiian Islands...."

Dorothy Masters, *New York Daily News*—"Nobody bothered with a plot, nobody cared that the players are generally incompetent or that the comedy is atrocious. Aside from the cameraman, only the man in charge of the sound track has any real concern for Elvis."

Edwin Miller, *Seventeen*—"Elvis Presley goes Hawaiian in this entertaining new movie, playing an enthusiastic citizen of the fiftieth state complete with ukulele, a smile for a pretty wahine (Joan Blackman) and a song on his lips."

Newsweek—"*Blue Hawaii* was obviously made by malihinis; it is luausy."

Show Business Illustrated—"Palms, pineapple plantations, lavish luaus, dazzling whitecaps. Hawaii never looked so good. It also never had it so bad. The cad responsible for tarnishing the glitter of this tropical paradise is Elvis Presley ... the hillbilly hipster."

Howard Thompson, *The New York Times*—"Nothing could be prettier or emptier than *Blue Hawaii* starring the pride of Memphis: yeah, man, Elvis Presley. And if ever the word 'balmy' applied to a film, it encircles the Presley frolic like a blossom lei."

Variety—"*Blue Hawaii* restores Elvis Presley to his natural screen element—the romantic, non-cerebral filmusical.... It is this sort of vehicle, which the singing star seems to enjoy his greatest popularity...."

Awards and Nominations

Golden Laurel Award: "Top Musical"—fourth place

Grammy Award nomination: "Best Sound Track Album or Recording of Original Cast from Motion Picture or Television"

Photoplay Gold Medal Award nomination: "Favorite Male Star"—Elvis Presley

Photoplay Gold Medal Award nomination: "Favorite Female Star"—Joan Blackman

Writers Guild Award nomination: "Best Written American Musical"—Hal Kanter

★ 4 ★

Gidget Goes Hawaiian (1961)

What happens when kids go Waikiki-wacky under that
great big romantic tropical moon? P.S. It should happen to you.

Fun: **
Surfing: **
Boy watching: ***
Girl watching: **
Music: *
Scenery: **

Release date: June 2, 1961. Running time: 102m. Box office gross: $2.2 million.

DVD release: Triple-bill with *Gidget* and *Gidget Goes to Rome*, Columbia Tri Star Home Video (August 4, 2004). [Beware: All three movies are in the pan-and-scan format rather than wide screen.]

James Darren (*Jeff Mather*), Michael Callan (*Eddie Horner*), Deborah Walley (*Gidget Lawrence*), Carl Reiner (*Russ Lawrence*), Peggy Cass (*Mitzi Stewart*), Eddie Foy, Jr. (*Monty Stewart*), Jeff Donnell (*Dorothy Lawrence*), Vicki Trickett (*Abby Stewart*), Joby Baker (*Judge Hamilton*), Don Edmonds (*Larry Neal*), Bart Patton (*Wally Hodges*), Jan Conaway (*Barbara Jo*), Robin Lory (*Dee Dee*), Arnold Merritt (*Clay Anderson*), Terry Huntingdon (*Stewardess*), Jerardo de Cordovier (*Waiter*), Vivian Marshall (*Lucy*), Guy Lee (*Bellboy*), Johnny Gilbert (*Johnny Spring*), Y. Chang (*Mr. Matsu*).

Columbia Pictures. *Produced by*: Jerry Bresler. *Directed by*: Paul Wendkos. *Written by*: Ruth Brooks Flippen. Based upon the characters created by Frederick Kohner. *Director of Photography*: Robert J. Bronner, A.S.C. *Choreography*: Roland Dupree. *Music*: George Duning. *Art Director*: Walter Holscher. *Film Editor*: William A. Lyon, A.C.E. *Set Decorator*: Darrell Silvera. *Makeup Supervisor*: Ben Lane, S.M.A. *Assistant Director*: Jerrold Bernstein. *Sound Supervisor*: Charles J. Rice. *Sound*: Lambert Day. *Orchestration*: Arthur Morton. Eastman Color by Pathé.

"Wild About That Girl" by Fred Karger and Stanley Styne, performed by James Darren over the opening credits. "Gidget Goes Hawaiian" by Fred Karger and Stanley Styne, performed by James Darren.

Surfing takes a backseat to romance in *Gidget Goes Hawaiian*, an inferior sequel to *Gidget*. The movie comes off as a puppy love story aimed at adolescent girls rather than a look into the surfing subculture like the original. Gidget jets off for a family vacation in the Hawaiian Islands where she and her surfing sweetheart Moondoggie try to make each other jealous by getting romantically involved with, respectively, a handsome television performer and a spoiled vixen. In an obvious

61

ploy to pump up the box office by attracting adults to the movie as well as youths, the older actors as parents hog way too much screen time. However, the Hawaiian beach scenes, a few surfing sequences and some of the attractive younger performers save it from being a total wipeout.

Though *Gidget Goes Hawaiian* was filmed in Hawaii and the locations are pretty, it doesn't come near to the breathtaking photography of *Blue Hawaii*. It also doesn't take advantage of some of the hot surfing spots of the area and stays put in Waikiki. Hence, Gidget and her pals only hit the surf twice here but at least the actors are filmed surfing in the actual ocean. Kudos must be given to Deborah Walley. Though the attractive redhead lacks the tenderness of Sandra Dee and comes across more often as whiny and irksome, Walley proves more athletic and daring than her predecessor, and scores points for braving the one- to two-foot waves of Waikiki for her surfing sequences. Of course, the main actors are shot in front of the obligatory blue screen for their surfing close-ups.

As with *Gidget*, the boys dominate in the flesh department. Dark-haired James Darren returns as Moondoggie and he has some serious competition in the looks department from equally handsome Michael Callan, sporting an impressive physique in his tight swim trunks. Both guys have nice torsos and are not afraid to exploit them. Don Edmonds, Joby Baker and boyish Bart Patton add to the beefcake on display. There are lots of beach and water scenes so the boys are shirtless a number of times. Girl watchers fare a little bit better here than in the original. Deborah Walley is older and more curvaceous than Sandra Dee and gets some competition lookswise from sultry brunette Vicki Trickett. Alas, both beauties are clad in one-piece bathing suits. The other two gals, a tall, lanky blonde and a short, squat brunette, are very homely and thankfully stay covered up.

There are only two songs in *Gidget Goes Hawaiian*, both warbled by James Darren. Neither is very memorable though "Gidget Goes Hawaiian," sung in the middle of the movie, is catchy. Overall, this is not one of the best entries of the genre and makes for only a passable diversion.

The Story

On the beach, Moondoggie has just asked Gidget to wear his pin and the elated girl accepts. However, Gidget's euphoria soon evaporates when she learns her family has planned a two-week vacation in Hawaii. Gidget refuses to leave her boyfriend for that long a period but when Moondoggie thinks she is passing up an opportunity of a lifetime, the miffed teenager throws his pin back at him and heads off on her Hawaiian holiday. On the plane, while Gidget's parents Russ and Dorothy Lawrence mingle with restauranteur Monty Stewart and his ditzy wife Mitzi, Gidget unloads her tale of woe onto the couple's beautiful spoiled daughter Abby, who misinterprets her "relationship" with Moondoggie.

Gidget's sour mood continues once they land, making her the drag of Waikiki. This is just fine by Abby, who is the belle of the beach surrounded by television dancer Eddie Horner and college guys Judge Hamilton, Wally Hodges and Larry Neal. Abby half-heartedly tries to persuade Gidget to come to dinner with her but the lovelorn gal just wants to sulk in her room. Satisfied that Gidget is staying put,

Deborah Walley as Gidget and Michael Callan as her prospective love interest strike a pose on the beach in *Gidget Goes Hawaiian* **(Columbia, 1961).**

Abby puts on a big show, telling the guys how she begged her "best friend for life" to leave her room but she is too heartbroken. Realizing that she is ruining her parents' vacation, Gidget decides to enjoy her time in Hawaii. All dolled up, she attends dinner and quickly becomes the life of the party, dancing center stage with suave Eddie—much to Abby's dismay.

Meanwhile, Russ Lawrence has wired the funds for Jeff to come to Hawaii, but has not told his daughter. Moondoggie arrives just as Eddie is about to kiss Gidget on the sand after a surfing lesson. "At least you stick to one ocean," says a miffed Jeff, who turns and walks away. He begins seeing Abby while Gidget tries to make Jeff jealous by dating Eddie and paying attention to the rest of the boys. She then tries water ski jumping and wipes out but is rescued by Jeff. Trying to hide her true feelings, Gidget continues trying to make him jealous.

Fed up with Gidget's antics, Abby "slips" and tells her mother that Gidget went all the way with a boy named Moondoggie back home. Mitzi immediately informs Dorothy, who refuses to believe it. However, she and Russ confront their daughter, who is sickened that her parents would swallow such nonsense. As the tension between the adults escalates, Gidget goes off to a luau where Eddie professes his love to her. Though flattered, she rebuffs him. Crestfallen, she wanders off down the beach while Abby reveals to Jeff that on the plane Gidget told her that she got carried away with somebody named Moondoggie. After revealing his nickname to Abby, he leaves the dumbfounded troublemaker to find his girl. The duo reconciles and heads back to the hotel where further complications ensue when Gidget suspects her parents of having extramarital affairs. The series of misunderstandings is cleared up and the film concludes with prima donna Abby getting her comeuppance as she is forced to go for a surfboard ride with Gidget.

Behind-the-Scenes

Seeing the box office receipts for *Gidget* were high, and noting the surge in popularity of surfing around the country, Columbia Pictures decided to produce a sequel to the popular comedy. Frederick Kohner's follow-up to *Gidget* entitled *Gidget Goes Hawaiian* was just published and Columbia immediately bought the screen rights.

Though the novel is based on fiction, Kathy Kohner reveals that she went to Hawaii in the summer of 1959. "I went because one of my first boyfriends was Hawaiian," recalls Kathy. "I remember my mother and father went there shortly after I did." Most likely their visits must have inspired Frederick Kohner to set the follow-up in that island paradise.

Columbia wanted Sandra Dee to reprise her role as Gidget but she was under contract to Universal Pictures, who refused to loan her out this time as she was chosen to replace Debbie Reynolds as Tammy in *Tammy Tell Me True* (1961). With great fanfare, a search was on for the big screen's new surfing sweetheart. A petite redhead named Deborah Walley was selected over 150 aspiring actresses, including blonde Mary Mitchel, to play Gidget. Columbia talent agent Joyce Selznick discovered Walley in New York appearing in an off–Broadway production of *Three Sisters* by Chekhov. Among her acting credits were two small roles on the television series *Naked City*.

Most actresses would have been thrilled to land a starring role in a motion picture but Walley was not. While riding the Sixth Avenue bus in Manhattan, she even contemplated ways to extricate herself from the movie. Shortly before she passed away, Walley revealed to writer Sharyn Peacocke, "I was this kind of snobby New

York actress, involved with the Actors' Studio, and I felt all my friends would think I was selling out. I had a very low opinion of Hollywood at the time—which I admit now was a totally distorted picture—but it wasn't what I wanted. And I guess I had a premonition—although I couldn't have verbalized it at the time—that this was going to really mark my career, and take it in a direction that I was really not wanting to go. But, of course, I couldn't get out of it. I came up with an idea to tell them that I had leukemia but of course to pull it off I'd need a doctor's note."

While Walley was sulking in New York City, young actor Don Edmonds was jumping for joy in Hollywood after being cast as Larry in *Gidget Goes Hawaiian*. He had been knocking around Hollywood since the mid-fifties landing minor roles on television, most notably five episodes of *Playhouse 90*. Don recalls, "Somehow I bullied my way onto the Columbia lot and I got an interview with Jerry Bresler who was the producer. I was scared out of my mind. I'm a kid and I don't know what I am doing. It was a very small casting process—*they only saw about 9,000 guys!* When I got to meet Jerry, they had already cast the other roles with Michael Callan, Joby Baker and Bart Patton. They had one part open. When I got in there I told him that I was a surfer. I grew up in Long Beach, California, and I could really surf. None of those other guys could. It was a stupid interview and I remember saying, 'I, uh, would really love to be in, uh, your movie, Mr. Bresler.' And I'll be damned—he cast me. He looked at me and said, 'Go to wardrobe.' I was like 'Whoa!' There were all these other guys waiting in the hallway to interview. It was as simple as that, really.

"Jerry Bresler was a terrific man but he was like a real serious old-line producer," continues Edmonds. "He scared the crap out of you when you were called into his office. I thought he came from the Harry Cohn school of producing. There is nobody like him anymore."

Under contract to Columbia, James Darren had to reprise his role of Moondoggie. Michael Callan, who had started on Broadway playing Riff in *West Side Story*, played Darren's rival for Gidget. Also a Columbia Pictures contract player, his previous films included *They Came to Cordura* (1959), *Because They're Young* and *Pepe* (both 1960).

The only other actor from *Gidget* to appear in the sequel was Joby Baker, now playing a college guy named Judge. Carl Reiner and Jeff Donnell were cast as Russ and Dorothy Lawrence (replacing Arthur O'Connell and Mary LaRoche, who played Gidget's parents in the original). All the other roles were new to the series including Bart Patton as college boy Wally Hodges and Gidget's rival Abby played by Vicki Trickett. The sultry brunette was Omaha, Nebraska's top model and had appeared in numerous television commercials when actor Tab Hunter spotted her at a horse show and brought her to the attention of Columbia. She made her film debut in *Pepe*. *Gidget Goes Hawaiian* was her second feature.

Deborah Walley proved more adept in the water than Sandra Dee and actually did most of her own surfing and water skiing, except the ski jump, in the film. She arrived in Hawaii two weeks before the rest of the cast so she could learn to surf. An ice skater and dancer, the flexible Walley took to the sport fairly quickly. However, surf champ Linda Benson doubled for Walley in the more intricate surfing sequences. At that time, the pretty blonde San Diego native with the page-boy haircut was considered to be the top woman surfer in the world and one of the first women, if not *the* first, to ride the big waves at Waimea Bay. In 1959, Benson at age 15 placed first at the West Coast Surfing Championships (she repeated the win in 1960) and the Makaha International.

The actors in the film all needed doubles for the surfing sequences except for Don Edmonds, who had been surfing since he was a kid in the early fifties. Edmonds says, "We only did a little bit of surfing out on the water. The other actors were lumps and couldn't surf. I was the only one out there with the surfing doubles. But that movie had a lot of process shots of James Darren, Deborah Walley and Michael Callan standing on a box on a soundstage for the closeups. They intercut those shots with the shots of us actually out on the water. Michael Callan is a great dancer but he did not take to surfing at all!"

Bart Patton adds that James Darren was even more helpless. "He didn't know how to swim," reveals Bart. "It was ridiculous seeing him in the water. I was not a surfer before I was hired but I learned how while we were in Hawaii. It was easier than I expected. There's not much waves to the Waikiki surf."

Though Deborah Walley was reluctant to do *Gidget Goes Hawaiian*, once she arrived in Hawaii she got into the spirit of it and enjoyed her time there. She commented, "I ended up working with some wonderful people like Carl Reiner and Peggy Cass and Jeff Donnell and a lot of people coming from theater backgrounds, like Michael Callan. And everyone was really wonderful to me and I realized that all Hollywood actors hadn't sold out—there were really some good actors, and it was just a totally different medium that was new to me."

Don Edmonds concurs, "Deborah had fun. We became friends and stayed friendly after that for a long time. She married John Ashley and they lived nearby. I know she wanted more substantial parts but, c'mon, whom did she want to play— Lady Macbeth? She was just a boop-boop-e-doop ingenue. She was the next Sandra Dee for a while and made a good living playing those type roles for Walt Disney and then AIP. She may not have wanted to play Gidget due to whatever was in her head but I'll tell you she had a great time."

"I agree with Don," says Bart Patton emphatically. "Deborah was really together. She worked hard and never blew a line. She seemed very happy to me. James Darren on the other hand was a loner. Vicki Trickett couldn't act her way out of a paper bag. It was sad. She had this great personality off-camera but I think the pressure of being on screen got to her and she would be so nervous before doing a scene. She fell to pieces and none of her real pizzazz came through."

By all accounts the *Gidget Goes Hawaiian* shoot went extremely smoothly and the cast, old and young, got along wonderfully. Nobody brought their egos to the set unlike in other beach movies that followed. Don Edmonds says fondly, "Paul Wendkos [the director] was a lovely man. He was a pro and knew what he was doing. He took good care of us. I loved Mickey Callan. He was a sweet guy. So was Jimmy Darren. Bart Patton and I go back a long way. I was very friendly with him and his wife at the time, Mary Mitchel. They were part of that UCLA crowd that included Tony Bill and Francis Coppola. Bart was terrific.

"There were so many great people on this movie like Carl Reiner, Peggy Cass, Jeff Donnell, and Eddie Foy," continues Edmonds. "They were seasoned pros. Peggy was a doll. One night Carl called the cast and invited us all up to his room. We were eating and drinking when Carl said, 'This is something that I've done but nobody has ever heard it. I was just hoping to get your reaction to it.' He puts on this big bomber of a tape recorder and played for us two hours of *The Two Thousand Year Old Man.* I thought I was going to die. I had never heard anything so funny. I didn't know who Mel Brooks was and most of the others didn't know either. They recorded this in a club where they ad-libbed on stage. It was edited down and they released the album, which just blew the doors off."

Coming from television where all the filming is done on a sound stage, Edmonds was surprised with the crowds of people that would flock around to watch the making of the movie. One instance in particular stands out in his mind. He recalls, "Two grips were digging a hole in the sand to put the camera in for a low-angle shot. It was about five o'clock in the morning. The cast showed up an hour or so later. It was a scene where Deborah and Mickey had to run down the beach towards their towels where the rest of us were sitting. There were only a few lines of dialogue. There was nobody on the beach when we started but by the time when we shot it there must have been thousands of people standing around watching. I was amazed. But people find a camera anywhere. You put up a 35mm camera on a tripod and you'll draw a crowd."

Summing up his experience working on *Gidget Goes Hawaiian,* Edmonds exclaims, "It was a dream. To be staying at the Royal Hawaiian on location in Waikiki for my first feature picture? I couldn't believe it. It was the single best experience I ever had in my life!"

James Darren, Vicki Trickett, Michael Callan, Bart Patton, Deborah Walley, Jan Conaway, Robin Lory, Don Edmonds and Joby Baker as visitors to the island paradise in *Gidget Goes Hawaiian* (Columbia, 1961).

"I really had a great time working on this too," adds Bart Patton. "Don and I roomed together and had a fun time in Hawaii."

Gidget Goes Hawaiian was a hit with the public and made more money than the original but the critics were split over Walley. "Deborah Walley is not as flexible an actress as her predecessor, Sandra Dee" (*New York Herald Tribune*). "Deborah Walley ... is cute as a button and displays a versatility not matched by the equally attractive Miss Dee in the original" (*Variety*). "Frankly, we'll take Miss Dee's direct sweetness to Miss Walley's squealing, calliope innocence any day" (*The New York Times*). "Miss Walley, as the cutest scatterbrain alive, seems definitely here to stay" (*Los Angeles Herald-Examiner*). "Deborah Walley is pert and plumpish but is just passable in the role of the precocious heroine" (*Boxoffice*). "Deborah Walley does not measure up to the creator of the role, Sandra Dee, in pert personality but she is a fresh talent who can be developed" (*Motion Picture Herald*).

Despite her mixed reviews, Walley became a favorite of the ticket-buying public, especially the teenage kind, so Columbia commissioned another sequel, *Gidget Goes to Rome*. But the sprightly redhead's pregnancy prevented her from reprising the role. A young actress named Carol Sydes, a regular on the television series *The New Loretta Young Show*, won the part. The studio lightened her hair and changed her name to Cindy Carol. James Darren continued on as Moondoggie and Joby Baker was cast as yet another college guy. Bart Patton and Don Edmonds were not asked to participate. "Man, I would have loved to gone to Rome," remarks a disappointed Don. "But that was Jerry Bresler's call."

Commenting on the *Gidget* movies, James Darren told the *Los Angeles Herald-Examiner*, "*Gidget* was a pretty good motion picture. What followed—the sequels and the other beach films—weren't very good. It was just a nice, wholesome, happy thing." He also preferred Sandra Dee to Deborah Walley and Cindy Carol, and described her as being "adorable."

Kathy Kohner adds, "*Gidget Goes Hawaiian* is the most popular of the *Gidget* movies. I was impressed that Deborah Walley actually got on a surfboard in Hawaii. She was a very lovely lady and told me that of all the things she did, people remembered her most for *Gidget Goes Hawaiian*. In retrospect, looking back I wish this had more surfing sequences. Basically, the premise of *Gidget* is about surfing and pursuing that endless summer along the Pacific Coast Highway in Southern California."

Gidget Goes Hawaiian also holds the distinction of being the highest-rated sixties beach movie when first televised. Airing on March 31, 1966, it pulled a 29.6 rating and a 49 share of the audience.

Michael Callan's popularity as a leading man lasted for a couple of more years as he starred in such films as *Bon Voyage!* (1962), *The Interns* (1962) and *The New Interns* (1964). After playing a supporting role in the hit comedy Western *Cat Ballou* (1965), Columbia dropped Callan and the once-promising actor turned to television and starred in his own sitcom, *Occasional Wife* (1966–67). The seventies and eighties found him relegated to television guest spots and made-for-television movies. Recently, his career had a resurgence and he turned up in the Matt Damon–Greg Kinnear comedy *Stuck on You* (2003).

After appearing in *Gidget Goes to Rome*, Joby Baker left Columbia and signed with MGM, where he became a regular in their energetic teenage musical romps including *Hootenanny Hoot* (1963), *Looking for Love* (1964) and the beach movie *Girl Happy* (1965).

Vicki Trickett went on to co-star in *The Three Stooges Meet Hercules* (1962) and *The Cabinet of Caligari* (1962). According to Don Edmonds, "Columbia wanted to groom Vicki for major stardom. She was a very pretty girl. But she said, 'no this isn't for me.'" Trickett abruptly abandoned Hollywood and her promising career to return to Omaha in 1963 after divorcing Richard Herre, her husband of three years, and obtaining custody of their daughter Symea.

Women's surfing champion Linda Benson would go on to surf double and do background work in the AIP beach party movies including *Muscle Beach Party* (1964), *Bikini Beach* (1964), *Pajama Party* (1964) and *Beach Blanket Bingo* (1965). She remarked in *Girl in the Curl*, "In 1963, the movie company paid each stunt surfer $350 a week, plus I got an extra hundred each time I went in the water, which was sometimes three or four times a day. I felt rich!" Surfing-wise, Benson would go on to win the West Coast Championships in 1960 and 1961 and the United States Championships in 1964 and 1968. In the mid-sixties, she became a flight attendant for United Airlines. Today, Linda is still flying the friendly skies but she is also a successful avocado and commercial flower farmer. Surfing is still her favorite pastime and she catches the waves at Cardiff and Moonlight Beach.

Memorable Lines

(Abby introduces her date Jeff to her friends at dinner.)

ABBY: This is Larry, Barbara Jo, Dee Dee, Judge, Wally, Eddie Horner and Gidget.

JEFF: Midget?

GIDGET: *Gidget.*

Reviews

Sara Hamilton, *Los Angeles Herald-Examiner*—"*Gidget Goes Hawaiian* is a bright, young, sassy movie with three handsome young people, James Darren, Deborah Walley and Michael Callan, living it up with songs, dance and crazy romances."

James Powers, *The Hollywood Reporter*—"*Gidget Goes Hawaiian* is a frothy summer concoction, purposely light in texture and bland to the taste. It is an animated travel poster, full of romantic notions in gaudy hues, but very animated...."

Bob Salmaggi, *New York Herald Tribune*—"*Gidget Goes Hawaiian* seems to have been dipped in a huge vat of syrup and honey. The film's light-headed, frothy approach strongly reminds you of those vapid family situation comedies, but for what the part demands there's no great cause for concern."

John L. Scott, *Los Angeles Times*—"A light, relaxing production with songs and dances, the story of surfboards and puppy love will appeal to teen-agers...."

Howard Thompson, *The New York Times*—"Gidget is back in a sequel—a broad but bouncy one—with some pretty Hawaiian scenery for armchair travelers."

Variety—"Sporadically amusing sequel.... Some of the youthful effervescence of *Gidget* has vanished in this sequel, but the combination of extremely handsome young players in the foreground and seasoned comedy veterans in the background ... should bail it out."

Awards and Nominations

Golden Laurel Award: "Top Female New Personality"—Deborah Walley, sixth place

Golden Laurel Award: "Top Female New Personality"—Vicki Trickett, seventh place

Photoplay Gold Medal Award: "Most Promising New Star—Female"—Deborah Walley

Photoplay Gold Medal Award nomination: "Favorite Male Star"—James Darren

Photoplay Gold Medal Award nomination: "Favorite Male Star"—Michael Callan

★ 5 ★

Beach Party (1963)

It's what happens when 10,000 kids meet on 5,000 Beach Blankets!

Fun: ★★★½
Surfing: ★★★
Boy watching: ★★★★
Girl watching: ★★★
Music: ★★★★
Scenery: ★★★

Release date: August 7, 1963. Running time: 101m. Box office gross: $2.3 million. DVD release: MGM Home Entertainment (December 18, 2001).

Bob Cummings (*Prof. Robert O. Sutwell*), Dorothy Malone (*Marianne*), Frankie Avalon (*Frankie*), Annette Funicello (*Dolores*), Harvey Lembeck (*Eric Von Zipper*), John Ashley (*Ken*), Jody McCrea (*Deadhead*), Dick Dale and His Del-Tones (*Themselves*), Morey Amsterdam (*Cappy*), Eva Six (*Ava*), Andy Romano (*J.D.*), Jerry Brutsche, Bob Harvey, John Macchia, Alberta Nelson, Linda Rogers (*The Ratz and Mice*), David Landfield (*Ed*), Valora Noland (*Rhonda*), Bobby Pane (*Tom*), Delores Wells (*Sue*), Duane Ament (*Big Boy*), Meredith MacRae, Lorie Sommers, Luree Nicholson, Laura Nicholson, Donna Russell, Pam Colbert (*Beach Girls*), John Fain, John Beach, Roger Bacon, Mike Nader, Mickey Dora, Eddie Garner (*Beach Boys*), Candy Johnson (*Perpetual Motion Dancer*), Not credited: Roger Bacon (*Tour Guide*), Yvette Vickers, Sharon Garrett (*Yogi Girls*), Vincent Price (*Big Daddy*), Paulette Rapp, Marlo Baers, Bill Slosky, Brent Battin, Roger Christian, Gary Usher, Bill Parker (*Beach Girls and Boys*).

American International Pictures. *Produced by*: James H. Nicholson and Lou Rusoff. *Directed by*: William Asher. *Written by*: Lou Rusoff. *Executive Producer*: Samuel Z. Arkoff. *Associate Producer*: Robert Dillon. *Production Supervisor*: Bartlett A. Carré. *Photographed by*: Kay Norton. *Music Coordinator*: Al Simms. *Music Score by*: Les Baxter. *Art Director*: Daniel Haller. *Film Editor*: Homer Powell. *Music Editor*: Eve Newman. *Sound Editor*: Al Bird. *Costumes by*: Marjorie Corso. *Titles and Photographic Special Effects*: Butler-Glouner, Inc. *Unit Manager*: Robert Agnew. *Assistant Director*: Clark Paylow. *Properties*: Karl Brainard. *Sound*: Don Rush. *Assistant to the Director*: Lois O'Connor. *Makeup*: Carlie Taylor. *Hairdresser*: Scotty Rackin. *Set Decorator*: Harry Reif. *Second Construction Coordinator*: Ross Hahn. *Production Assistant*: Jack Cash. Filmed in Panavision and Pathecolor.

"Beach Party" by Gary Usher and Roger Christian, performed by Frankie Avalon and Annette Funicello, and by Frankie Avalon over closing credits. "Secret Surfin' Spot" and "Surfin' and A-Swingin'" by Gary Usher and Roger Christian, performed by Dick Dale and His Del-Tones. "Promise Me Anything (Give Me Love)" by Guy Hemric and Jerry Styner performed by Annette Funicello off-screen. "Treat Him Nicely" by Guy Hemric and Jerry Styner performed by Annette Funicello. "Don't Stop Now" by Bob Marcucci and Russ Faith, performed by Frankie Avalon.

Beach Party combined the Malibu surfing scenes of *Gidget* with the beachgoing teenage vacationers of *Where the Boys Are,* added a number of songs, a hilarious comedy bit from Harvey Lembeck as an inept motorcycle gang leader and started a whole new genre. During spring break, Frankie, his girlfriend Dolores and their friends share a beach shack where their main concerns are surfin', dancin' and romancin'. Unbeknownst to them, they are being spied on by an anthropologist and his pretty assistant, doing a research paper comparing teenage culture to that of primitive natives. Though *Beach Party* is not *the* best of the Frankie-and-Annette beach capers, it is enjoyable, colorful, fast-moving fun as the skies are blue, the boys are shirtless, the girls are attractive, the surfing plentiful and the parents are nowhere in sight. It is also the most earnest attempt of all the AIP beach party films in trying to convey the Southern California surfing subculture, even having the kids drink beer at the local hangout. In later films their beverage of choice is Coke.

Director William Asher was a Malibu denizen and a surfer so he does his best to add realism in the beach and surfing scenes. He hired real-life surfers including Mickey Dora, Johnny Fain, Mike Nader and Ed Garner to surf-double. Malibu is not known for big waves but Asher sprinkles the film with lots of exciting group surfing shots. Though this footage is not that spectacular, compared to what came after in the sequels it is the best of the series. As for the surfing abilities of the lead actors, save for Jody McCrea, they did not surf or attempt to learn to surf so it was off to the blue screen for Avalon, Funicello and John Ashley.

Frankie and Annette have immediate chemistry and make an extremely attractive pair of swimsuit-clad young lovers who try to make each other jealous. Lots more flesh is on display here with shirtless surfer boys traipsing over the sand or riding the waves. The standouts are sexy dark-haired John Ashley, tall and slim Mike Nader and bushy-blonde, lean Ed Garner. Beefy Jody McCrea surprisingly dons a Speedo bathing suit in a number of scenes, ratcheting up the beefcake meter. Unfortunately, in future movies he is clad in swim trunks like the rest of the guys.

Though Annette is committed to wearing only one-piece bathing suits, it doesn't matter as her bountiful bosom is clearly on display. The former Mouseketeer truly blossomed into a beautiful young woman. As for the other girls, wild-haired blonde Valora Noland makes a curvaceous and sexy Rhonda and will have every boy's heart beating faster as she does her morning stretches clad in a bikini. Candy Johnson with her big blonde bouffant hairdo is forever gyrating—straight through to the end credits. Voluptuous Eva Six as "the Hungarian goulash" comes across as a combination of Marilyn Monroe and Eva Gabor, dahling. The rest of the beach girls (including handsome blonde Meredith MacRae) are surprisingly demurely clad in modest swimsuits. Thankfully, in future beach party films the suits get skimpier and the girls sexier.

Musically, the standouts are Dick Dale and His Del-Tones who perform two Gary Usher–Roger Christian surf tunes. The earring-clad Dale definitely brings an edge to the movie and especially rocks out on "Swingin' and Surfin'" while the beach gang does the Frug. Unfortunately, Dale does not perform any of his own surfing instrumentals, which would have given the film a jolt of authenticity. Like

Annette Funicello and Frankie Avalon were the unofficial queen and king of the beach party.

the subsequent beach party films, this one also features a maudlin ballad warbled by Annette. Here it is "Treat Him Nicely." Much better is "Promise Him Anything," which has a bouncy sixties lounge feel to it. Les Baxter's musical score is sprightly and the dancing on the shores of Malibu and in the teenage nightclub vigorous.

The Story

Frankie and his girlfriend Dolores excitedly drive in his souped-up yellow jalopy complete with two surfboards on back. Their destination is a Malibu beach house where Frankie believes he and Dee Dee will spend a romantic and idyllic two-week vacation alone together. When he carries his girl into the dark house, he trips over a body and discovers their friends including Deadhead, Ken, Rhonda and Sue sleeping on the floor. They were all invited by Dolores to join them on their vacation—much to Frankie's obvious dismay and anger.

In an adjoining beach house, Professor Robert Sutwell and his attractive, long-suffering assistant Marianne are observing the surfing and beach play antics of the young couples next door. Sutwell, a famous anthropologist, is gathering data for a research book on the sex play and other habits of the youngsters with a view to comparing them with primitive South Seas island tribes. Marianne vainly tries to convince him that they are normal kids.

Frankie and his friends hit the waves to shoot the curl. Dolores remains on the sand and explains to the bewildered Rhonda that she sabotaged Frankie's romantic plans because she wants something more to come of their relationship—marriage. Continuing his secret monitoring of the beach kids, Sutwell is intrigued when Dick Dale and his group perform a song while the beach gang twists along. At the same time, Frankie concocts a plan with his surfing buddies to get back at Dolores by feigning interest in a buxom Hungarian blonde named Ava. She works as a waitress at Big Daddy's, a local dance and drinking establishment (owned by resident poet Cappy) that caters to the young crowd.

That night at Big Daddy's, after the youngsters are treated to another song from Dick Dale, Frankie sings and dances with Ava, Candy and some of the other girls while Dolores jealously looks on. Rat Pack leader Eric Von Zipper and his leather-jacketed motorcycle gang suddenly invade the joint. Von Zipper makes a play for the dejected Dolores and, when he tries to kiss her against her wishes, Prof. Sutwell comes to the girl's rescue. He uses some Zen Judo tactics on the biker, putting him into time suspension. The gang carries their leader out while Sutwell offers to escort Dolores home, much to Frankie's chagrin. Sutwell is only looking for friendship with Dolores and her help in his research project but his actions are misinterpreted as romance by the smitten girl and an eavesdropping Frankie, Deadhead and Ken.

The next day, Sutwell confides to Marianne that he made contact with Dolores but she and her friends have made him feel that he's missed out on having fun during his lifetime. On the beach, Ava gets cozy with Frankie in front of Dolores and the guys. When Dolores storms off to see Sutwell, Frankie abandons Ava. The professor, wearing an outdated bathing suit from the twenties, accompanies Dolores to the beach where Ken and Deadhead label him a square and cajole him to try surfing. Despite his careful planning and calculating, Sutwell is a flop and continually wipes out. Frustrated, he realizes his mistake and after correcting a minor error in his mathematical formula ("I forgot to carry the two"), he masters the art of surfing.

Sutwell pays a visit to Cappy to acquire more insight about the youngsters that he is studying. Cappy suggests that they need a cause since all their energies are directed toward each other. Frankie finds Sutwell and tells "the over-aged fuzzy-face" that he loves Dolores and will fight to keep her.

That night at the beach bonfire, the surfer finds Dolores and admits his love for her. The two reconcile but only briefly. A jealous Ava shows up and informs a miffed Dolores that Frankie professed his love to her earlier on the beach. Dolores tries to get romantic with Sutwell, who arrives wearing a hideous straw hat which Ken sets afire. Frankie fights off an amorous Ava; love-starved Rhonda pouts while her beau Deadhead eats. After Dolores convinces "Old Pig Bristles" to shave his beard off, the girl goes gaga over the new Sutwell. She agrees to fly off with him in his private plane while Marianne overhears their entire conversation.

Von Zipper and his gang return to the beach seeking revenge against Sutwell. After flirting with Ava, the inept motorcycle leader picks the wrong house to enter and awakens Dolores. Her screaming brings Sutwell to her rescue once again. Von Zipper's gang deserts him ("The Finger!") and leaves their fearless leader to the mercy of Sutwell, who sends him on his way. Frankie and the gang arrive and are stunned to find Dolores in the professor's arms on her bed.

Dolores sneaks off for her airplane ride with the professor, who is still upset that the youngsters misconstrued the situation they came upon in Dolores' bedroom. While in flight, it finally dawns on Sutwell that Dolores thinks she is in love with him. Back at his beach house, he coaxes Marianne to kiss him as Dolores arrives. She tells the old coot off. Seeing how upset she is, Frankie and the guys confront the two-timer and discover his recording equipment and research notes. While the lads are engrossed in the report, Sutwell and Marianne slip out and head over to Big Daddy's.

The youngsters and then Von Zipper's gang discover him there. Though Frankie and his friends dislike Sutwell, they detest Von Zipper even more and try to protect the professor from the bikers. A wild melee breaks out with punches thrown and chairs broken. Cream pies are flung in all directions after Dolores nails Ava in the face with one. After the Rat Pack makes a hasty retreat, all the misunderstandings are cleared up. Frankie and Dolores pledge their love to each other and Marianne agrees to accompany Sutwell on his next research venture.

Behind-the-Scenes

Over the years there have been a number of conflicting stories reported in regards to how *Beach Party* came about. The late Sam Arkoff, director William Asher and James H. Nicholson's daughter and beach party regular Luree Nicholson have presented contradictory versions of the events in various publications.

Writing in his autobiography, Sam Arkoff states that he and Jim Nicholson were in Italy in 1962 screening movies for possible distribution by AIP in the U.S. One of the films was about an older man involved with a 20–something girl and her friends, set on a beach. They found the film inappropriate for their teenage target audience but Arkoff boasted that he thought the idea of a beach setting with scantily clad teenagers dancing on the shores would be a big moneymaker. He reportedly commissioned his brother-in-law Lou Rusoff to spend time on local Southern California beaches observing the teenage set and to write a script around it.

Luree Nicholson tells a different version. She commented in *Drive-in Dream Girls*, "Sam Arkoff didn't want *Beach Party* to be made. He thought that it would be a complete loser. Of course that is not the story he told afterwards." She claims that Arkoff wanted to begin another series of films about rebellious teenagers similar to AIP's juvenile delinquent movies of the mid-to-late fifties but her father had the idea about doing a movie about clean-cut teenagers on the beach. This differs from reports that both Nicholson and Arkoff were interested in more films about restless youths but it was William Asher who suggested a story about good clean-cut kids.

According to an Asher interview in *Filmfax* magazine, Jim Nicholson was more receptive to his idea and he had to convince Arkoff otherwise. The producer couldn't fathom a film about all–American teenagers having fun surfing at the beach rather than getting into trouble. Asher was insistent that he didn't want any schools or parents in the movie either so the screenplay needed to be revamped. The director envisioned the opening shot being that of the kids tasting freedom on the first day of spring vacation. Though skeptical, Arkoff gave in. Asher remarked in *Filmfax*, "He [Arkoff] was pretty shaky on it. I know he had no trouble later on, claiming it was his idea from the beginning."

Sam Arkoff's son Louis, who has followed in his father's footsteps and is currently remaking two AIP monster movies as theatrical releases, was only 12 years old at the time but he puts the events into perspective as he recollects. "The impetus for *Beach Party* was a *Life* magazine cover on surfing," reveals Louis. "It was extolling the popularity of The Beach Boys and this Southern California sport. Somewhere around this time, Jim and Sam had a discussion about this and brought in Lou Rusoff, my uncle on my mother's side, who was sort of the idea guy in the company. He had written many of the teenage juvenile delinquent movies [*Shake, Rattle, and Rock!* (1956), *Runaway Daughters* (1956), *Dragstrip Girl* (1957) and *Motorcycle Gang* (1957), among others] and a couple of the monster movies. He would come up with the scripts. With *Beach Party* that was what kind of what went on.

"It is very possible that William Asher brought the *Life* article to their attention," continues Louis. "The beauty of AIP was that this family-like situation. They had this 'open door' creative policy. Ideas were exchangeable and you'd throw suggestions around like a real creative community. Jim was a genius with titles. In some cases he would match the title with the story idea and other times he would create the title and they would write a story around it. My father kept a very good gauge of what was going on with teenagers. We had a screening room in our house and he would welcome as many friends that I wanted to watch these movies to study their reactions to it."

The one area where everyone seems to agree is about Lou Rusoff's major contributions to *Beach Party*. Luree added that Rusoff studied his teenage sons and their friends on the beach from afar. However, Louis Arkoff refutes this as he hung around with Rusoff's sons and firmly states "my cousin Gary was never on a surfboard in his life." He thinks Rusoff just watched a variety of young beachgoers and surfers. In any event, Rusoff incorporated "his spying" into the screenplay for *Beach Party* with the Prof. Robert Sutwell character.

"The interesting thing about *Beach Party* is that *Beach Party* was not a kid's movie," comments Louis Arkoff. "It was a story about an anthropologist in his mid-forties who is doing a paper on the mating habits of teenagers. The movie is told from the point of view of the older man, which by the way is what Jim, Sam and Bill Asher were at the time."

Whatever his initial involvement, William Asher was the perfect director for *Beach Party*, his first motion picture. He had won an Emmy for producing *The Dinah Shore Chevy Show* and directed a number of television sitcoms including *I Love Lucy, Our Miss Brooks, Make Room for Daddy* and *December Bride.* He was adept with slapstick (which is found in abundance in *Beach Party*) from his TV forays, and living on the beach he was water-savvy and knew about surfing. By the time he was hired, the main characters had been cast.

There hasn't been much reported how the studio settled on Bob Cummings and Dorothy Malone for the adult roles but it is known that Jim Nicholson liked to recruit TV performers (since they usually came with a loyal fan base) and actors whose movie careers needed a boost. Cummings starred in the popular comedy series *The Bob Cummings Show* (1955–59) and the short-lived *The New Bob Cummings Show* (1961–62). Dorothy Malone saw her movie career slide downhill after winning the Academy Award for Best Supporting Actress in 1956 for *Written on the Wind.* Despite a few good roles such as James Cagney's disturbed wife in *Man of a Thousand Faces* (1957) and alcoholic Diana Barrymore in *Too Much, Too Soon* (1958), she was relegated to the mediocre films *Quantez* (1957), *Tip on a Dead Jockey* (1957) and *The Last Sunset* (1961).

More important to the success of *Beach Party* was who was going to play the film's young lovers. Luree Nicholson says that, although Sam Arkoff takes credit for casting Annette Funicello in *Beach Party*, he and Bill Asher actually wanted Sandra Dee or another blonde of that ilk. It was Lou Rusoff who suggested Annette, a choice James Nicholson agreed with. Her agent and future husband Jack Gilardi began working with AIP and mentioned his client for the female lead. Annette wrote in her autobiography, "When offered the part, I thought, *Why not?* I knew *Beach Party* probably was not going to win anyone an armload of Oscars, but that was okay. The story was imaginative and the cast was great."

By this time Funicello had blossomed into a voluptuous young woman, leaving her *Mickey Mouse Club* days far behind. But Walt Disney was still misusing her in films aimed at ten-year-olds. Funicello's contract with Disney contained a clause that she needed approval by the studio's attorneys before she could do a movie for another company. According to Arkoff, they would give their consent to let her appear in *Beach Party* as long as she did not don a bikini. It was agreed to by AIP (though it did not stop them from putting Annette in two-piece swimsuits) and the contract signed. Arkoff went on to write that Walt Disney hit the roof when he learned of the deal. He called AIP and pleaded to have her dropped from the project. He was over-protective of her image and labeled the 20-year-old Funicello his "little girl." Asher backs this up and states the only time he was ever on the Disney lot was to meet with Walt, who said that if Annette donned a bikini or revealed her navel he'd pull her off the picture.

Louis Arkoff was witness to one of these phone calls between his father and Walt Disney negotiating the loan-out of Annette. "The entire conversation was about an anti–belly button clause," says Louis with a laugh. "It was a very funny discussion. But you have to understand that Annette was like Disney's golden girl and my dad had made these outrageous teenage movies like *The Cool and the Crazy*, which was about drugs. To be honest, I was always surprised that Walt Disney let AIP have her at all. But *Beach Party* was a clean-cut movie and it gave her perhaps the opportunity to grow up, which made her useful for Walt; otherwise he certainly wouldn't have done it."

Funicello in her autobiography claims that Disney approved of *Beach Party*, calling it "good clean fun" and only proposed that she not wear a bikini in order to be different and to stand out from the other girls in the movie. If this is true, it proves what a shrewd and astute businessman Disney was, as he wanted to protect his investment in Annette's "pure" image and used some reverse psychology on the young starlet (though there is no doubt that he had paternal feelings for her as well). Annette agreed to Disney's "suggestion"; however this caused problems down the road as she was constantly pressured into wearing skimpier swimsuits. "I stood my ground, politely but firmly answering, 'No, I do not have to follow "boss's orders."' This is something I chose to do and will do."

AIP originally wanted Fabian for the male lead but he was under contract to 20th Century–Fox. Singer Bobby Vinton's managers pushed mightily for their client to get the part but the studio instead chose Philadelphia native Frankie Avalon, a singer who had worked for AIP previously in *Panic in Year Zero!* (1962) and *Operation Bikini* (1963); they felt he was a better match with Annette.

The supporting roles were cast with a combination of TV actors, former AIP players, newcomers, offspring of famous movie stars and kids plucked directly from the beaches of Malibu. Harvey Lembeck was known for being a wiseguy comic most notably from the hit TV comedy series *The Phil Silvers Show* and such movies as *Stalag 17* (1953). He also taught comedy to aspiring actors and, when he was cast as inept motorcycle leader Eric Von Zipper, he surrounded himself with an ensemble of actors he personally chose to play his leather-jacketed followers.

John Ashley was a personal favorite of Jim Nicholson's daughters Luree and Laura. Lou Rusoff discovered the handsome dark-haired young actor while he was waiting for his girlfriend to audition for a role in *Dragstrip Girl* (1957). Ashley won the male lead and went on to star in *Motorcycle Gang* (1957) and *Hot Rod Gang* (1958), among others, for AIP. According to Luree, her father always had hopes of Ashley finding major movie stardom and this may be the reason that he was the lone actor from this crop of JD films to cross over into the surf movie genre.

Chosen to play Annette's girlfriends were newcomers Valora Noland, Delores Wells and Candy Johnson. Pretty blonde Noland had a few TV credits under her belt plus a minor role in *Five Finger Exercise* (1962), her film debut. She came close to winning the role of Billie Jo Bradley in TV's *Petticoat Junction* but her disappointment was short-lived as she learned she won the role of Rhonda shortly thereafter. Curvy and petite, dark-haired Delores Wells was a Playboy Playmate for the month of June 1960. *Beach Party* was her first movie. It was also the debut of "Perpetual Motion Machine" Candy Johnson. The dancer with the big blonde bouffant was the toast of Palm Springs, California, with her stage revue "The Candy Johnson Show." Her expert wiggling won her scads of press. Purportedly Jim Nicholson caught her stage act. Though she was older than most of the other beach girls, he thought her wild gyrations would still be a great addition to the movie.

Scions of famous actors in *Beach Party* included cute Meredith MacRae, the daughter of Gordon and Sheila MacRae, in her film debut and Joel McCrea and Frances Dee's boy, Jody McCrea. He had the same singing teacher as Frankie Avalon and Fabian. They were friendly and made the California boy an honorary citizen of South Philly. Frankie also hooked him up with his agent Jack Gilardi, who brought McCrea to the attention of Jim Nicholson and Sam Arkoff. They liked the strapping young actor and cast him as a seaman in *Operation Bikini* with Avalon. One of the reasons he got the role of Deadhead in *Beach Party* was because he could actually surf (unlike Avalon and John Ashley). "I had been surfing since the fifties and I loved to go dancing at night," says Jody McCrea. "It helped me stay in shape. These beach movies were right up my alley. My surfing buddy was Richard Zanuck. He was quite a surfer in those days. When he came back from the Army, he stopped surfing because he always set a high standard for himself and he couldn't keep up with the sport so he quit."

With two leading actors who looked as far removed from the beach as possible, director William Asher knew that he needed to recruit young beach denizens to back them up. He literally scoured the beaches of Southern California from San Diego to Malibu looking for boys who looked good and could surf, and girls who were pretty and could nicely fill a bikini. After awhile, Asher felt like a letch approaching pretty beach bunnies and asking them if they would like to audition to be in his new movie, and decided to take a different path.

In *Beach Party* (AIP, 1963), Annette Funicello (center) as Dolores and her friends (including Meredith MacRae, left) eye the boys on the beach. Pictured in the background are surfers Johnny Fain (*left*) and Mike Nader (*second from right*).

Enter blonde 20-year-old surfer Ed Garner. "I knew this gentleman named Bill Howard who was an agent for the Louis Shurr Agency," recalls the actor. "They represented Dorothy Lamour, who was Bill's stepmother. Bill knew that I surfed. He had received a script for *Beach Party* from William Asher and arranged a meeting between Asher and me at his office. Bill asked me if I knew any surfers that I could recommend. I told him that I knew Mickey Dora, Johnny Fain, Mike Nader, Duane King, Mike Doyle, Mike Hynson and Dewey Webber. All of these guys were surfing at Malibu in the early sixties.

"Asher asked me if I would do a casting call," continues Garner. "About eight or nine of my buddies showed up for the audition. He interviewed us all and chose Mickey Dora as sort of the point person. Mickey and I hired eight of the original surfers to do the doubling in *Beach Party*. My childhood friend Brian Wilson [not of the Beach Boys] rode for Jody McCrea, Johnny Fain doubled for Frankie Avalon and John Ashley, and the rest of us just filled in." Asher bucked SAG rules by not going through Central Casting to fill these background roles but AIP eventually had to make them actors, which was an expensive proposition as the studio paid all the fees to get these kids into the union.

Among the beach girls hired for the film were Jim Nicholson's daughters Luree and Laura. According to Luree, her father had given them the opportunity to be in his pictures beginning in the late fifties. The girls were never pressured and the option to do the movies was left up to them. Luree graduated from doing background work without credit in *I Was a Teenage Werewolf* (1957) to a minor supporting role in *Diary of a High School Bride* (1959). However, Luree's familial connections did create a bit of a backlash for her from some actors. She ignored the petty comments and was the first to admit that the only reason she was cast in the beach movies was because of her father and that she had no desire to pursue an acting career. Psychology was her bag.

Sam Arkoff's kids were not given permission to appear in *Beach Party*. "I asked my dad if I could be in the beach movies and he told me he'd rather that I be a pimp than an actor," laughs Louis. "So that took care of my acting career."

To give *Beach Party* some authentic surf music, Dick Dale and His Del-Tones were hired as the house band. In 1960, Dick and his band were playing at an ice cream parlor in Balboa when they were discovered by the local surfers, who dug "the combo's clangy brand of rock 'n' roll." They quickly became the rage of Southern California's teenage set and Dale was dubbed the "King of the Surf Guitar." Before long, due to Dale, the Beach Boys and Jan and Dean, surf music became the new national fad. Dale, an expert surfer, remarked in *Newsweek*, "I'm the only one with the real surf guitar sound. The others just sing surf words to rock 'n' roll." Describing his authentic surf sound, Dale calls it "a heavy staccato sound on the low-key guitar strings, with a heavy, throbbing beat-like thunder, or waves breaking over you."

Beach Party began filming in March 1963 with a budget of approximately $300,000. The shoot lasted three weeks. Annette Funicello commented, "When we filmed on the beach, it was early in the morning and always shivering cold, especially after they'd hosed us down so we'd look like we'd just come out of the surf." According to Jody McCrea and Ed Garner, *Beach Party* was a smooth shoot and everybody was professional and got along. "I was totally in awe of having the opportunity to be in a movie," exclaims Garner. "It was remarkably pleasing that every actor in *Beach Party* was exceedingly gracious, humble, nice and human. There were no airs or pretenses on this set. It was just a happy family."

Credit must go to director Bill Asher, who juggled the various personalities of the cast. The one actor who gave him trouble was Bob Cummings. He wanted to discuss practically every scene and was not satisfied with his dialogue. Asher was spending so much time with Cummings that he was giving the other actors short shrift. Pressured to deliver his film on time and within budget, Asher finally refused to give in to another of Cummings' demands. The irked actor stormed off the set. Bill shot around him for the rest of the day but then had to approach his unhappy star. In *Filmfax*, Asher recalls that he said to Cummings, "What's wrong here is that you'd like Willie Wyler as your director, and I'd like Cary Grant as my star, but I have you and you have me and let's just stop this fooling around and go make a movie." And that's just what they did.

Regarding Bill Asher, Jody McCrea says, "Bill liked all the things I brought to the part like ingenuity and new lines. Deadhead was originally just a small part, but I created a lot of it myself. Bill was impressed so the part grew and got bigger in each movie culminating with *Beach Blanket Bingo*, which was written all for me.

"Asher had the ability to take someone like Mike Nader and make an actor out of him," continues McCrea. "Mike would go on to star opposite Joan Collins on *Dynasty*. It took him a while to get there but he made it."

Of all the Frankie and Annette beach movies, *Beach Party* concentrated the most on surfing with many scenes of the surfers shooting the curl. The only problem was that their lead actor Frankie Avalon was a non-surfer. Ed Garner reveals that the Philadelphia native had no desire whatsoever to learn to surf as he had other interests. In *Filmfax*, Asher disclosed that he had a bit of a problem with Frankie, who couldn't handle carrying his heavy nine-foot redwood surfboard. In one shot, the slight actor was barely able to lift the board let alone snatch it from its A-frame and carry it while running to the shore. Encouragement from Asher enabled Avalon to pull off the scene.

Recalling the surfing sequences in *Beach Party*, Ed Garner reveals, "They weren't choreographed as people sometimes think. Bill Asher would figure out who was doing the doubling for which actors. Mickey Dora was doubling occasionally for Frankie Avalon but Johnny Fain did most of the surfing for him. If we were fortunate enough to be shooting on a day with great waves, Asher would shoot a lot of stock footage and archive it. We really didn't have tremendous swells at any of the locations such as Zuma Beach and Paradise Cove where we shot the actual movies. Most of those areas were not known for waves."

Jody McCrea adds, "I did most of my own surfing and had the ability to do it all but sometimes they were shooting two units at once and I had to be with the first unit. A guy named Brian Wilson would then double for me in the surfing sequences. In *Beach Party*, Dick Dale and I surfed in tandem with two girls on our shoulders and we had Mike Nader fall off his board, wiping out the other surfers. Unfortunately, something happened with the film and the second unit wasn't able to shoot it. I was so disappointed because I had never surfed with someone on me before."

Among the surfers who toiled on the beach movies, Mickey Dora was the most skilled and infamous. He had previously appeared in *Gidget* with his good buddy Johnny Fain. "Mickey was actually nicknamed 'The King of Malibu,'" remarks Garner. "He was so graceful and so beautiful to watch. He was such an innovative surfer that everybody was in awe of him. He basically created a whole ballet. Prior to him, no one really understood how to manipulate a board the way Mickey could. Once he got on his surfboard, he could just feel the wave in a way that nobody else could feel it. You manipulate your board by the way you walk on it. He basically invented the technique of getting into the curl of a wave and either gain a momentum of the wave or slow it up. He was one of the first surfers to really start using the back of the board to swing it either to the right or left to be able to get the top of the wave or be able to drop down to the bottom of the wave."

Dora was always goofing off on the sets of the beach movies. He had no interest in acting and would be forever in the background cracking jokes or trying to distract the actors so they'd blow their lines. Ed Garner states, "Mickey got along very well with the cast. He had a very graceful rapport with everybody he meant. He was just a total character—everything about him was unique." Jody McCrea concurs: "Mickey Dora was a good guy and such a tremendous surfer. Watching him surf was like watching ballet on a board. He was a cut-up on the set but he didn't bother me in the least. I was a bit of a clown off-camera as well."

Interestingly, director Asher did not mind his antics since he was such a phenomenal surfer. Garner says, "Bill Asher just adored Mickey because he was such a flamboyant character with a dynamic personality. Those were the types of people Asher especially liked." This is especially true as the folks who displeased the director (like Garner and Luree Holmes) were constantly pushed to the background only to emerge when another director such as Don Weis or Alan Rafkin took the reins.

One bit of trouble that occurred on the set involved Jody McCrea. Big and jovial, he would playfully roughhouse with some of the beach girls on the sand. After the AIP executives lectured him, he curtailed his antics but they threatened to fire him when it was reported that he had made a pass at co-star Dorothy Malone. John Ashley commented to Richard Warren Lewis of *The Saturday Evening Post*, "She was too much of a lady to say anything. It got so bad I threatened to punch him out." McCrea learned his lesson the hard way and in future films made sure to stay clear of his female cast members.

To enhance the movie, AIP wisely incorporated the surf music sound that was beginning to hit the airwaves in 1963. They turned to songwriter-producer Gary Usher to contribute some surf rhythms. Usher co-wrote with Brian Wilson a number of early Beach Boys songs including "In My Room" and "409." He had become a partner with LA disc jockey Roger Christian, who also had collaborated with Wilson. Their output included "Don't Worry Baby" and "Little Deuce Coup." Usher was contracted to Capitol Records when he was approached by AIP to write some songs for the film.

Another wise decision by AIP was hiring Dick Dale and His Del-Tones to appear. Dale and his group were extremely popular with Southern California teenagers and he was one of the pioneers of surf music. Though he was known for his instrumentals, he and his group sang two tunes by Usher and Christian, who also penned the title tune. Guy Hemric and Jerry Styner contributed all but one of the remaining songs and would eventually take over head songwriting duties at AIP from Usher and Christian.

There was a seventh song in *Beach Party* but it was not credited. Jody McCrea reveals, "I used to be a disc jockey and I wrote music. They couldn't get permission to use the song they wanted so I offered up mine. It was called "The Looney Gooney Bird." I sang just a portion of it *a cappella* and later cut it as a record [on Canjo Records] but it never charted."

When "The End Almost" appeared at the film's finale, it segued into a barefoot Candy Johnson wearing a green tasseled dress shimmying and shaking to Frankie Avalon's solo version of "Beach Party" as the end credits began. This was to become a standard practice in the AIP beach party movies, to keep the kids in their sits until the last credit rolled.

After *Beach Party* wrapped, things became stressful around AIP. Sadly, Lou Rusoff had been diagnosed with brain cancer and died while the film was in the editing stage. Also, according to Sam Arkoff, "When *Beach Party* was ready for distribution, there was no tidal wave of confidence around the AIP offices."

AIP hosted a gala premiere for *Beach Party* in San Diego, flying down from Los Angeles members of the press for a weekend of fun. Cast members who attended included Annette Funicello, Harvey Lembeck, Eva Six and Dick Dale. Frankie Avalon had a previous engagement in New York while Jody McCrea was on an around-the-world tour with his mother, Frances Dee. AIP head James Nicholson was there as well as Milton Moritz, AIP's director of advertising and publicity, who pulled out all the stops to attract attention to *Beach Party*. Moritz arranged for 30 winners from KLAC's contest "Why I'd like to attend 'The Beach Party'" to be flown down along with shapely contestants competing for the title of "Miss San Diego Beach Party." When the contingent arrived in San Diego, they were met by a group of shirtless surfers who transported the guests to their hotels in their jalopies. Various critics were chosen to judge the beauty contest. AIP had also arranged for its guests to go sailing or to just relax at the hotel where sumptuous meals were plentiful. When the group returned to LA, AIP arranged for its bikini girls from the film to chauffeur the press home.

Despite the reception the film received by the critics and fans in San Diego, the producers weren't sure teenagers in the Midwest would relate to beachgoing Southern California adolescents so AIP released *Beach Party* in only three cities. When they realized that had a huge hit, they rolled it out across the country. However, according to an interview Sam Arkoff gave to Mark Voger for *Filmfax* magazine, AIP received flak from puritanical groups all over the country due to their ad campaign showing a girl in a bikini with her navel revealed. Close to 200 newspapers had to airbrush out the belly button to appease their readers. Arkoff exclaimed, "Can you *believe* that! I mean, it's really amazing. Just as though some evil lurked in the belly button!"

AIP did not issue a soundtrack LP despite all the musical talent connected to *Beach Party*. There were a few reasons for this. AIP didn't make the necessary plans, this was their first "comedy with music," and once the film took off at the box office, AIP was more interested in producing a sequel rather than an album. Also, all the participants were contracted to different labels. This situation vexed AIP for most of their beach movies to come.

Though AIP didn't capitalize on the music in *Beach Party*, the stars' recording companies did. Buena Vista released *Annette's Beach Party* featuring Funicello's original solos from the soundtrack and re-recordings of the four other songs from the movie. Avalon re-did "Beach Party," which was released as a single with the B-side "Don't Stop Now." The song failed to crack *Billboard*'s Top 100.

Though the film's music didn't make a dent in the charts, *Beach Party* was a smash at the box office, striking a chord with teenagers across the country. Being savvy producers, Jim Nicholson and Sam Arkoff knew it was time for a sequel or two. The fun in the sun had just begun.

Memorable Lines

(Frankie and Dolores are embracing on the beach as they arrive for their weeklong vacation.)

FRANKIE: You know the only thing I've studied this semester is you!

DOLORES: Well, I hope you don't flunk.

FRANKIE: Well, there's always summer school you know!

(Some of Eric Von Zipper's catchphrases that would become staples of the *Beach Party* series:)

VON ZIPPER: Eric Von Zipper likes you. And when Eric Von Zipper likes someone, they stayed liked.

VON ZIPPER: You stupids!

VON ZIPPER: He is my idol.

Reviews

Lee Atwell, *Film Quarterly*—"Released during the snows of the year, this film offers cold comfort. The promise of vacation, the beach, warm flesh ('surfin' all day, swingin' all night') is so simperingly advanced that we are not released from the discontent of our winter."

Greater Amusement—"Summertime fun, romance and music are replete for the tired anybody in this American International's first musical comedy spectacular. The songs are melodious and catchy, the story easy on the brain cells and the cast beyond wonderful."

Dorothy Masters, *New York Daily News*—"Everything is overworked—too many variations on the twist, too much slapstick, too many inanities."

Motion Picture Herald—"The film is just what the title says it is, a beach party on the Pacific, with surf-boarding the order of the day with the bikini the costume of the moment, and summer fun the first and apparently the only order of business. It all adds up to bright, cheerful and lively musical entertainment."

New York Post—"*Beach Party* ... gets by with a serviceable plot, and fizzles out before there is any question of higher citations. The two outstanding items are the surfing ... here well photographed and demonstrated—and the twisting which is presented in pleasing variety, coming to a climax in the furious gyrations of one Candy Johnson."

James Powers, *The Hollywood Reporter*—"*Beach Party* ... directed with humor and intelligence by William Asher, takes a fairly routine teenage situation and elevates it by handling things with class and taste. The cast is well balanced between young and old. Frankie Avalon and Annette Funicello ... make an appealing couple."

Howard Thompson, *The New York Times*—"Doom-daddle, doom-daddle, doom-daddle. That's the swingin' beat, the dialogue flavor and just about the sum and substance of *Beach Party*."

Time—"An anthropological documentary with songs. As a study of primitive behavior patterns, *Beach Party* is more unoriginal than aboriginal. In comparison, it makes Gidget's Roman misadventures look like a scene from *Tosca*."

Variety—"It's a bouncy bit of lightweight fluff, attractively cast (Annette Funicello, Frankie Avalon et al.), beautifully set (Malibu Beach), and scored throughout (by Les Baxter) with a big twist beat."

Jesse Zunser, *Cue*—"A sappy bit of seashore nonsense in which an abundance of twisty turns and wriggles are set to puerile jungle rhythms and a foolish plot."

Awards and Nominations

Golden Laurel Award: "Sleeper of the Year"

Harvard Lampoon Movie Worst Awards: "The Uncrossed Heart" (for the least promising young performer) – Annette Funicello

Photoplay Gold Medal Award nomination: "Favorite Male Star"—Frankie Avalon

Photoplay Gold Medal Award nomination: "Favorite Female Star"—Annette Funicello

★ 6 ★

Bikini Beach (1964)

It's where the girls are BARE-ing ... the guys are DARE-ing ... and the surf's RARE-ing to GO GO GO!

Fun: ★★½
Surfing: ★★
Boy watching: ★★
Girl watching: ★★★
Music: ★★
Scenery: ★★

Release date: July 22, 1964. Running time: 100m. Box office gross: $4.5 million.
DVD release: MGM Home entertainment (December 18, 2001).

Frankie Avalon (*Frankie/The Potato Bug*), Annette Funicello (*Dee Dee*), Martha Hyer (*Vivien Clements*), Don Rickles (*Big Drag*), Harvey Lembeck (*Eric Von Zipper*), John Ashley (*Johnny*), Candy Johnson (*Candy*), Jody McCrea (*Deadhead*), Meredith MacRae (*Animal*), Donna Loren (*Donna*), Keenan Wynn (*Harvey Huntington Honeywagon*), Danielle Aubry (*Lady Bug*), Delores Wells (*Sniffles*), Paul Smith (*Officer #1*), James Westerfield (*Officer #2*), Janos Prohaska (*Clyde*), Val Warren (*The Teenage Werewolf Monster*), Timothy Carey (*South Dakota Slim*), Mary Kovacs (*Old Lady #1*), Renie Riano (*Old Lady #2*), Sheila Stephenson (*Miss Simms*), Ronnie Dayton (*Avalon's Double*), Alberta Nelson, Linda Rogers, John Macchia, Bob Harvey, Andy Romano, Jerry Brutsche, Allen Fife (*Rat Pack*), Guy Hemric, Gary Usher, Roger Christian, Frank Alesia, Johnny Fain, Mickey Dora, Duane King, Mike Nader, Ned Wynn, Ed Garner, Bud Kemp, Jay Mullin (*Surfers*), Luree Holmes, Darlene Lucht, Mary Hughes, Salli Sachse, Linda Benson, Nancy Long, Linda Bent, Patti Chandler, Julie O'Connor (*Beach Girls*), Boris Karloff (*The Art Dealer*). Guest stars: Little Stevie Wonder, The Pyramids, The Exciters Band.

American International Pictures. *Produced by*: James H. Nicholson and Samuel Z. Arkoff. *Co-Producer*: Anthony Carras. *Directed by*: William Asher. *Screenplay by*: William Asher, Leo Townsend and Robert Dillon. *Technical Advisers*: Tommy Ivo, Von Deming ("West Coast Go-kart Champion"). The producers wish to thank the following for their cooperation: Dean Jeffries (Designer of the "Manta Ray"), Keith Black and Don Prudhomme (Designers of the "Frieda"), Larry Stallings (Designer of the "Britannica"), Stan Adams (Publicity Director, The Pomona Drags), Chuck Griffith (Business Manager, The Pomona Drags), Lt. Ron Root (Secretary, The Pomona Drags Board of Directors), The Pomona Valley Timing Association and The Pomona Police Department. *Production Supervisor*: Joe Wonder. *Photography by*: Floyd Crosby, A.S.C. *Music Score by*: Les Baxter. *Music Coordinator*: Al Simms. *Choreography by*: Tom Mahoney. *Second Unit Director*: Anthony Carras. *Art Director*: Daniel Haller. *Film Editors*: Fred Feitshans, A.C.E., Eve Newman. *Music Editor*: Milton Lustig. *Sound Editor*: Kathleen Rose. *Costumes by*: Marjorie Corso. *Surfboards by*: Phil of

Downey, California. *Beachwear and Women's Sportswear Clothing by:* Sun Fashions of Hawaii, Ltd. *Ah Men's Sportswear, Hollywood, Designed by:* Jerry Furlow. *Titles and Photographic Special Effects:* Butler-Glouner. *Special Effects by:* Roger George, Joe Zonar. *Assistant Director:* Clark Paylow. *Properties:* Karl Brainard. *Sound:* Don Rush. *Makeup:* Ted Coodley. *Hairdresser:* Eve Newing. *Set Decorator:* Harry Reif. *Production Assistant:* Jack Cash. Filmed in Panavision and Pathecolor.

Songs by Guy Hemric and Jerry Styner: "Bikini Beach" performed by Frankie Avalon, Annette Funicello and the cast. "Love's a Secret Weapon" performed by Donna Loren. "Gimme Your Love, Yeah, Yeah, Yeah" and "How About That" performed by Frankie Avalon. "Because You're You" performed by Frankie Avalon and Annette Funicello. "This Time It's Love" performed by Annette Funicello. "Happy Feelin', Dance and Shout" performed by Little Stevie Wonder. "Record Run" and "Bikini Drag" by Gary Usher and Roger Christian, performed by the Pyramids. "Gotcha Where I Want You" by Jack Merrill and Red Gilson, performed by the Exciters Band.

The third film of the series, *Bikini Beach* opens with a rousing title song sung by Frankie, Annette and the cast but the movie quickly goes downhill from there. Annette's Dee Dee falls for a hot rod racing British pop star, the Potato Bug, making Frankie jealous and determined to beat the Brit in a drag race. Meanwhile, an old stuffy real estate developer is determined to drive the surfers off the beach by proving that his chimp is more intelligent than they are. Despite it being the highest-grossing AIP beach party film, *Bikini Beach* is definitely one of the lesser efforts. The story is moronic and unfunny, the surfing scenes are uninspired and the obligatory drawn-out car chase sequence is sillier than usual.

The best thing about *Bikini Beach* is Frankie Avalon's performance playing Frankie the surfer and the Potato Bug. His over-the-top mannerisms and mimicking of the Beatles is the film's highlight. Coincidentally, Mike Myers' Austin Powers character is a bit reminiscent of the Potato Bug complete with bad teeth. Could it be that Myers is a *Bikini Beach* fan?

This is the first beach party film where surfing takes a back seat to another sport—drag racing. Though the scenes at the drag strip are well-done and look authentic, the spectacle of cars racing at top speeds is not as visually stimulating as the sight of surfers shooting the curl with the sun glistening off the water.

Avalon, Ashley, McCrea and the rest of the surfers are all present and shirtless, but as there are less beach and surfing scenes and more on the drag strip, the guys are clothed more. Girl watchers fare better mainly due to the introduction of cute sandy-haired beach girl Patti Chandler. The curvaceous lass with the wicked smile quickly became one of the most popular stars at AIP. Here she joins beach beauties Mary Hughes, Salli Sachse and Linda Opie. Throw in Annette, Meredith MacRae, twisting Candy Johnson and wholesome Donna Loren and you have a girl watcher's feast.

Musically the movie succeeds with some great surf tunes rendered by garage surf band the Pyramids. They even perform an amusing gag as they come on stage in Beatles wigs only to have them pulled off to reveal their shaved heads. The Exciters Band lets loose with a swingin' Watusi number that gets the whole joint jumping. Donna Loren gets to rock on "Love's a Secret Weapon" early in the film while Candy Johnson and the beach crowd dance around her. Little Stevie Wonder returns but his number is cut off midway as the end credits begin to roll. Avalon has one good song in the tradition of the British Invasion, but his duet with Annette and her solo numbers are weak. That coupled with the unfunny subplot with Wynn and the chimp should have made *Bikini Beach* the worst in the series but its saving grace is Avalon's amusing performance.

The Story

Frankie, Dee Dee, handsome Johnny, laconic Deadhead, hip-shaking Candy, man-hungry Animal, pixyish Sniffles and the rest of the gang head to Bikini Beach for more fun, surfing, music and dancing. Candy awakens the gang the next morning after discovering a large tent compound on the beach. They think it belongs to an Arabian Prince but it is the headquarters of British singing sensation the Potato Bug. The vocalist is protected by a bodyguard named Yvonne a.k.a. Lady Bug, who wards off an amorous Deadhead with French foot-fighting tactics.

When the youngsters return to surfing, a new menace to their beach fun rears its head as Harvey Huntington Honeywagon reveals that he intends to have the surfers thrown off Bikini Beach so he can expand his senior citizens' retirement community. Accompanying the millionaire is a chimpanzee named Clyde who he uses to prove his allegation that young people have sunk to animal levels by demonstrating that his monkey can surf just as well as the youths.

Despite this new threat to their summer fun, the gals are more interested in the Potato Bug. Sniffles and Animal convince him to sing a song and the girls go gaga over him. The jealous boys challenge the British singer to come surfing. But he prefers drag racing at speeds up to 200 miles per hour rather than the "tame" sport of surfing. When Frankie announces that he wants to take up the dangerous sport, an angry Dee Dee gets cozy with the Potato Bug.

Honeywagon begins his campaign against the surfers in his newspaper and arouses the ire of a beautiful teacher named Vivien Clements. She barges into the millionaire's office to personally challenge his views and agrees to give him a chance to prove his allegations. They visit the surfers' hangout, Big Drag's Pit Stop, but Big Drag (who also owns the Bikini Beach Drag Strip and is an avant-garde artist) refuses to cooperate with Honeywagon. Motorcyclist Eric Von Zipper and his Rat Pack crash the joint and Von Zipper dubs Honeywagon his idol due to his crusade to rid the beach of surfers—the cyclists' arch-enemies. Honeywagon doesn't want their support, especially when they begin to rough up Big Drag. They retreat when the inept Von Zipper gives himself the "Himalayan Suspenders treatment," freezing himself in suspended animation. His Rat Pack carry him off, vowing to return.

Meanwhile, Frankie and the guys learn more about drag racing and the souped-up "rails" at the drag strip. Frankie stews while the Potato Bug gets all the adoration from the fans after breaking the world's record. Honeywagon and Vivien show up and Clyde bests the Potato Bug's time as part of the millionaire's campaign to prove that youngsters operate at a chimp's level. Later Frankie, Johnny and Deadhead ask Big Drag to show them some rails that he has for sale. They pool their money to buy one so Frankie can race against the Potato Bug.

Back at Big Drag's, while The Pyramids jam and the kids shimmy, Harvey continues putting them down to Vivien's displeasure. Von Zipper shows up pledging his support to Honeywagon while the Potato Bug is coaxed to sing a song. Dee

Dee dances along with him to make Frankie jealous. The Exciters perform a Watusi number and Honeywagon takes advantage and snaps a picture of Clyde dancing with Candy to run in the next day's newspaper. Meanwhile, Frankie and Dee Dee go for a stroll along the shore and make up. However, when Dee Dee insists that Frankie abandon drag racing, it only strengthens his resolve to beat the Potato Bug.

Due to Vivien's influence, Honeywagon tempers his hostility towards the surfers and retracts his views. This angers Von Zipper and his gang, who vow revenge. Frankie disguises himself as the Potato Bug to derail Dee Dee from convincing the pop star to call off their race. His creative ruse goes awry when the real Potato Bug happens on the pair. Dee Dee storms off after both fellows stubbornly refuse to back down. After cooling off, Dee Dee finds Frankie at Big Drag's with the guys readying his rail and she pledges to support him.

At the drag strip, Von Zipper sabotages the Potato Bug's dragster, hoping Frankie will be blamed for the nefarious deed. However, he mistakenly tampered with Frankie's roadster and the surfer narrowly escapes injury when the car crashes after the race ends in a dead heat. After the flustered Von Zipper inadvertently reveals that he was the culprit, the surfers chase him back to Big Drag's. After a wild melee with surfers versus cyclists, the Rat Pack hightails it out of there after Von Zipper once again gives himself "the Finger." Potato Bug announces his engagement to Lady Bug; Frankie and Dee Dee reconcile; and Vivien and Honeywagon become firm friends.

Behind-the-Scenes

The third of the Frankie and Annette beach party films, *Bikini Beach*'s budget was $600,000—double the amount expended on *Beach Party*. It was money well-spent as the movie brought in $4.5 million at the box office, making *Bikini Beach* one of the biggest hits of 1964. However, it probably would have even grossed lots more if AIP's first rock group choice appeared in the movie—the Beatles.

According to William Asher, Jim Nicholson had seen the Beatles perform in London before anyone in the U.S. had ever heard of them. Asher was once again slated to direct and he was co-writing the screenplay with Robert Dillon (who worked in producer capacities on *Beach Party* and *Muscle Beach Party*) and Leo Townsend. The writer of numerous television scripts including many for *My Three Sons*, Townsend also authored the screenplays for such movies as *It Started with Eve* (1941), *Vicki* (1953), *Running Wild* (1955) and *Four Boys and a Gun* (1957). He would go on to collaborate on the screenplays for *Beach Blanket Bingo, How to Stuff a Wild Bikini* (both 1965) and *Fireball 500* (1966).

A script was written where the British pop group comes to the sunny shores of Malibu to see what it is like to live on the beach. The story had the boys camped alongside the surfers, and one of them would find romance with Annette. Before filming began, the Beatles appeared on *The Ed Sullivan Show,* their careers took off like a rocket and their managers refused to let them appear in the movie for the small fee that was offered. Asher then had to quickly rewrite the script and, instead of four British longhaired singers, there was now only one called the Potato Bug. It was decided that Avalon would play this part complete with "blond Beatle hairdo,

In *Bikini Beach* (AIP, 1964), Donna Loren sings, Candy Johnson shimmies and the surfers (including Mike Nader, right) are having a ball.

brush mustache, round spectacles and front tooth gap." The movie is also the first beach party film to shift away from surfing. Samuel Z. Arkoff commented in *Look* magazine that when AIP learned that paid admissions to car races ranked with baseball, they had Asher incorporate drag strip racing in the story.

Among the crew members assembled for the third installment in the beach party series was Floyd Crosby (the father of singer David Crosby), who was brought in as the new director of photography. He would go on to shoot the remaining AIP beach movies as well as *Beach Ball*. He already worked for AIP on such films as *The Young Racers, The Haunted Palace* and *The Comedy of Terrors*. Gary Usher and Roger Christian, who wrote most of the songs to the first two movies, only contributed a pair of tunes performed by the Pyramids. Guy Hemric and Jerry Styner penned the remaining songs except one. Usher, Christian and Hemric also appear in the movie as Avalon's surfing buddies.

Gary Usher remarked to author Stephen McParland that the reason his songwriting output declined at AIP was that he and partner Roger Christian had become too busy with other projects. As a team they became a major influence in surf rock, co-writing songs for the Surfaris, Dick Dale, Jan and Dean, the Astronauts and the Hondells. Usher produced the latter group, which was actually a rotating roster of session players. He later produced two LPs for the Byrds.

Most of the main cast from *Beach Party* and *Muscle Beach Party* returned for *Bikini Beach* including Frankie Avalon, Annette Funicello, John Ashley, Jody McCrea, Candy Johnson, Delores Wells and Don Rickles, who morphed from Jack Fanny into Big Drag. Both Gary Usher and Al Simms shared stories with author Stephen McParland regarding Don Rickles' clowning and hilarious ad-libs that would send the production into overtime due to re-shoots. A lot of the delays had to do with Rickles' interaction with a bird named Felicia. One scene had the feathered creature perched on his head. According to Gary Usher in McParland's *It's Party Time*, Rickles quipped, "So help me, if you shit on my head I'll have you for dinner."

Among the missing actors from the first two movies was Valora Noland, who played boy-crazy Animal in the previous film. Meredith MacRae, who had played a beach girl in *Beach Party*, assumed the role. Dick Dale and His Del-Tones were conspicuously absent and the new house band was the garage-surf group the Pyramids, who were riding high on the pop charts with their hit instrumental called "Penetration." The five members were from Long Beach, California, and were friends from high school. As a counterpoint to the shaggy-haired Beatles, the guys sported shaved heads. Harvey Lembeck and his Rat Pack returned as the surfers' main antagonists after being replaced by a group of well-formed bodybuilders in *Muscle Beach Party*.

Harvey Lembeck's co-stars welcomed his return to the beach party. "I didn't have a lot of interplay with Harvey," says Jody McCrea. "But I liked to watch him work. He had an ensemble playing his gang members and he led that whole group. Harvey rehearsed their scenes and would present it to the director. I knew some of the actors that worked with Harvey and they were nice guys."

"Harvey Lembeck was a hell of a nice man," exclaims Ed Garner. "I had absolutely no passion for acting whatsoever. But anybody that did, such as Mike Nader, would be taken underneath Harvey Lembeck's wing. He spent literally hours with Mike going over lines and talking about different philosophies of acting. He suggested various schools Mike should attend." Surprisingly, the shy Annette Funicello liked him too and described him in her autobiography as being "kind and gregarious." He and his wife became Annette's lifelong friends.

Lembeck was proud of his portrayal of bungling motorcycle leader Eric Von

Zipper and was even prouder of the teenage audience who got the joke of his character. He commented, "Young people all over the nation tell me that they understand and appreciate what Eric Von Zipper means in terms of satirization of the tough-sounding but really weak bully who is common to all neighborhoods. It's a tribute to our American youth that they see Von Zipper as a weapon against juvenile delinquency as I intended him to be the first time he appeared in *Beach Party*."

Making her film debut as one of the beach girls in *Bikini Beach* was pretty Patti Chandler. According to *Look* magazine, "She saw an advertisement in the paper for a Bikini-girl contest at American International. An hour later, she had been selected from over 100 contestants for *Bikini Beach*, which was starting production that day in Pomona, California. In another hour, she was on location, and an hour later, she was in front of the cameras." Chandler had no outstanding acting ability (who *did* in the beach party movies?) but she was beautiful girl with shoulder-length honey-brown hair, an infectious smile and a curvaceous figure that looked striking in a bikini. "I'll never forget seeing Patti Chandler for the first time," remarks Jody McCrea with a laugh. "She walked by me and quickly caught my attention! Alas, she started dating Lee Majors shortly thereafter and helped get him discovered."

Aron Kincaid, who would work with Chandler in *Ski Party* and *The Ghost in the Invisible Bikini*, described her as being "like a kid sister—half brat and half angel. She had this horrible little Yorkshire Terrier that was just covered with fleas. She always brought it to work and it was in her trailer. Patti was always coming up with some new plan or idea for everybody to do. She was just a slaphappy little kid racing about the set dating and crying and pouting. One minute she was angry and then she'd be happy. I enjoyed her and always had a good relationship with her but at the same time I was smart enough to keep my distance."

The surprise guest star in *Bikini Beach* was Boris Karloff. He played an art collector who is constantly rebuffed by Rickles' Big Drag. The audience only sees the back of his head until the film's finale where he flips over a painting done by Clyde the chimp and says, "I must tell Vincent Price about this place" (Price was a serious and respected art collector). Karloff had appeared in a number of prior AIP films *The Raven*, *The Terror* (both 1963) and *The Comedy of Terrors* (1964). *Bikini Beach* would be his only beach party appearance until he shot additional scenes with Susan Hart that were added to *The Ghost in the Invisible Bikini* (1966).

The film also features an appearance by Val Warren, a *Famous Monsters of Filmland* makeup contest winner. His prize was a cameo as the Teenage Werewolf in the pool hall scene.

Bikini Beach was filmed on location in Paradise Cove, Malibu, California, and at the Pomona Drags. No expense was spared to make the drag racing scenes as authentic as possible. Racecar driver Tommy Ivo was hired as a technical advisor and some of the West Coast's top rails were used in the drag races. The film also introduced to movie audiences the sport of Karting with West Coast champion Von Deming and boat wake surfing demonstrated by Mickey Munoz, Linda Benson and Bing Copeland.

Credit must go to producers James H. Nicholson and Samuel Z. Arkoff for taking the time and money to try to get these scenes right. "They were very much on the level and didn't talk down to you," comments Jody McCrea. "They treated

Frankie Avalon as the Potato Bug belts out a tune while Annette Funicello as Dee Dee dances along in *Bikini Beach* (AIP, 1964) *(courtesy the Billy Rose Theatre Collection, The New York Public Library for the Performing Arts, Astos, Lenox and Tilden Foundations)*.

the actors as being part of a team. It was a good partnership in a way. We each helped each other." Despite liking the duo, McCrea never signed a contract with AIP, operating on a picture-by-picture deal.

Ed Garner, however, was under contract to AIP. "We saw quite a bit of Jim Nicholson," recalls Garner. "He would invite us out on his boat with his then-wife prior to marrying Susan Hart. His daughters Luree Holmes and Laura Nicholson appeared in the beach movies. I didn't get to know them very well. They weren't really beach girls but they were very nice and polite. On the sets of the movies, we were sort of segregated. The stars were one group, the surfers and beach girls hung as another group, and Harvery Lembeck and his crew were the third."

Recalling the camaraderie between Frankie and Annette and their co-stars, Jody McCrea reveals that there wasn't any. "I got along very well with Frankie and Annette because I left them alone. They always had many lines to memorize or songs to sing. I just concentrated on my part and didn't fraternize with either of them at all."

Ed Garner opines, "I don't think Frankie and Annette were aloof but I think they both started having other agendas. Frankie began playing Vegas more and Annette began seriously dating her agent Jack Gilardi. Frankie even once rented a bus for all of us to come see his show at one of the Las Vegas hotels. Don Rickles wound up introducing us on stage and ripping into all of us."

McCrea also discloses that Avalon's height, or lack of height, was also an issue in these films. "I had known that taller guys were fired from the early movies," says Jody. "I always tried to stand burrowed in the sand so I wouldn't tower over Frankie or John Ashley, who was about the same height. After we did a few movies, I said to Frankie, 'Thanks for not having me fired on *Beach Party*.' He replied, 'Well, the little guy gets all the sympathy anyway.'"

While surfer Mickey Dora continued to retreat to the background, his good friend Johnny Fain was getting more and more screen time. Despite his lack of stature, the cute blonde-haired surfer photographed well, had a nice physique and could twist with the best of them. "Johnny wanted to be an actor," Ed Garner says matter-of-factly. "He really made it known to everybody that he'd like to have as much of an opportunity as possible to get involved in that field of endeavor. He tried to learn to act and Harvey Lembeck helped him a lot. It was like with Mike Nader. Mike fell in love with acting and so did Johnny Fain.

"Johnny tried to emulate everything that Mickey Dora did," continues Garner. "He just didn't have the personality that Mickey had. But nobody could compare to Mickey. He was in a class of his own. He basically had his own lingo and his own hand language, which kind of emulated his speech. Everybody tried to ape the way Mickey Dora acted because he utilized his hands in such an exaggerated way. It was almost like what rap artists do now. Mickey had a hand signal for practically everything he said."

However, Mickey Dora's schtick did not go over with everybody. Aron Kincaid, who would go on to work with Dora in *Ski Party*, found the surfer to be "uncouth. I remember that Alan Rafkin could never find him during the day's shoot." Gary Usher described Dora to writer Stephan McParland as being "quite strange." Dora could also be very outspoken and conceited. Ned Wynn wrote in his autobiography that Dora boasted to him, "I'm the best [surfer]. The rest are primitives. They're nothing. They ruin the waves. Cavemen on logs. I won't share a wave with a Cro-Magnon."

According to a press release by Ruth Pologe, *Bikini Beach* was given a pre-release publicity buildup by AIP that sent Frankie, Annette, Harvey Lembeck and Buddy Hackett to the New York World's Fair. At the Hollywood Pavilion, an actual set from the movie (flown in from California) was displayed at the premiere party at the Better Living Center's Beech-Nut Theatre. Afterwards, Frankie and Annette placed their handprints and footprints in cement outside the Pavilion, which was a replica of the famed Grauman's Chinese Theater in Hollywood.

When *Bikini Beach* was released nationwide, it became the biggest box office hit of the Frankie and Annette films. Whereas Annette received most of the kudos in their previous picture *Muscle Beach Party*, Avalon got the praise this time for his dual role and would go on to win a few accolades for the movie.

As she did with *Beach Party* and *Muscle Beach Party*, Annette released an album from Buena Vista featuring some of the songs from the film. Titled *Annette at Bikini Beach*, it included new recordings of "Bikini Beach," "Love's a Secret Weapon," "Because You're You," "How About That" and "Happy Feeling." The only song that was the original recording from the film was Annette's solo "This Time It's Love."

Annette once again had competition on the charts but this time it wasn't Frankie Avalon—it was Candy Johnson! Her LP was titled *The Candy Johnson Show at Bikini Beach* and featured all the songs from the movie except the two by Gary Usher and Roger Christian. Johnson performed the material backed by the Exciters Band. Her album, released on Canjo (a record label named for Candy and formed by her manager and soon-to-be-husband Red Gilson), also included all-new recordings and one original from the movie. In this case it was the Exciters Band's "Gotcha Where I Want You," which was released as a single under the group name The Candy Johnson Show with Candy Johnson's Exciters. Neither Annette's or Candy's album made the charts and the latter sold so few copies that today it is a collector's item selling up to $550.

Though the pairing of Frankie and Annette proved extremely profitable, AIP's next beach venture, *Pajama Party*, was an experiment to see if Annette *sans* Frankie could score at the box office.

Bikini Beach was the end of the party for Playboy Playmate Delores Wells and Meredith MacRae. Wells would go on to play Reena in the cult sci-fi flick *The Time Travelers* (1964) before her movie career sunk into the ocean. MacRae would find much more success. When her role of Sally was written off of *My Three Sons* in 1965, she assumed the role of Billie Jo Bradley from Gunilla Hutton on *Petticoat Junction* in 1966. The third actress to play the part, she quickly made it her own and enjoyed immense popularity. When the sitcom was cancelled in 1969, MacRae returned to the big screen in the Glen Campbell–Joe Namath road movie *Norwood* (1970) and never lacked for work. She continued acting mostly on television and in low-budget movies, appearing on the top game and talk shows, and even co-hosting the daytime chat show *Mid-Morning LA*, that netted her an Emmy Award in the eighties. The lovely Meredith MacRae passed away from a brain cancer on July 14, 2000.

Memorable Lines

(Deadhead thinks he recognizes Big Drag.)

BIG DRAG: I used to be Jack Fanny. I had a string of musclemen whose muscles were mainly in their heads. But I got out of the fanny business—that's all behind me now.

Reviews

Eugene Archer, *The New York Times*—"A horrible juvenile comedy in which surfers fight cyclists and convert their elders to the pleasures of the bronzed physique."

Janet Graves, *Photoplay*—"Fans of popular beach series could almost write the scripts themselves by now. In fact, it looks as if they've done just that."

Mandel Herbstman, *The Film Daily*—"Fun and frolic, music, dancing and surfing are the ingredients of the latest beach-inspired picture from American International. It rolls along merrily, churning up complications, romantic and otherwise. A spirited cast ... go through their assignments with bounce and zest."

Robert Salmaggi, *New York Herald Tribune*—"It's all quite corny, quite juvenile, but the surfing's nice to watch, as are the drag-racing sequences, and like wow, the way those kids do dance! Their groovy twitchings are by far the best part of the picture."

Kevin Thomas, *Los Angeles Times*—"*Bikini Beach* bounces along the same successful path the box office as it predecessors. A couple of truckloads of good-looking healthy kids, plenty of singing and dancing, and solid comedy from old pros add up to two hours of mindless relaxation...."

Variety—"Same mixture as before.... Introduction of some first-rate satire is so overloaded with coatings of slapstick that the satire will be lost on the great mass of youngsters who will provide the film's greatest support...."

Awards and Nominations

Film Daily's Famous Fives: "Best Performance by a Juvenile Actor"—Frankie Avalon, fifth place

★ 7 ★

For Those Who
Think Young (1964)

*Here come those Ho-daddies and Beach-dollies in
the swingin'est young people's picture of the year!*

Fun: **
Surfing: **
Boy watching: **
Girl watching: ***
Music: **
Scenery: *

Release date: June 3, 1964. Running time: 96m. Box office gross: $1.6 million.
DVD release: Not as of August 2004.

James Darren (*Gardner "Ding" Pruitt, III*), Pamela Tiffin (*Sandy Palmer*), Paul Lynde (*Sid Hoyt*), Tina Louise (*Topaz McQueen*), Bob Denver (*Kelp*), Robert Middleton (*Edgar J. Cronin*), Nancy Sinatra (*Karen Cross*), Claudia Martin (*Sue Lewis*), Ellen McRae (*Dr. Pauline Swenson*), Woody Woodbury (*Himself*), Louis Quinn (*Gus Kestler*), Sammee Tong (*Clyde*), Addison Richards (*Dean Watkins*), Mousie Garner (*Mousie*), Benny Baker (*Lou*), Anna Lee (*Mrs. Pruitt*), Sheila Bromley (*Mrs. Harkness*), Jack LaRue, Allen Jenkins, Robert Armstrong (*Mr. Cronin's Business Associates*), Edie Baskin, Laurie Burton, John Christopher, Pam Colbert, Mickey Dora, Lada Edmund, Marie Edmund, Linda Feldman, Byron Garner, Laura Hale, Susan Hart, Jan March, Mike Nader, Maureen O'Hanlon, Leslie Perkins, Donna Russell, Don Voyne, Gordon Westcourt, Larry Weston, Maria White (*College Girls and Boys*), George Raft, Roger Smith (*Detectives*), Amedee Chabot (*Blonde on the Beach*), Alberto Morin (*Butler*), Byron Kane (*Reporter*), Harry Antrim, Eleanor Audley (*45th Anniversary Couple*), Anthony Eustrel (*Faculty Member*). Also: Jimmy Griffin.

A Schenck-Koch Production, a United Artists release. *Executive Producer*: Howard W. Koch. *Producer*: Hugh Benson. *Director*: Leslie H. Martinson. *Screenplay*: James O'Hanlon, George O'Hanlon and Dan Beaumont. *Story*: Dan Beaumont. *Assistant to the Producer*: Red Doff. *Edited By*: Frank P. Keller, A.C.E. *Musical Numbers Choreographed and Staged By*: Robert Tucker. *Music Composed and Conducted By*: Jerry Fielding. *Director of Photography*: Harold E. Stine, A.S.C. *Production Manager*: Frank Caffey. *Art Directors*: Hal Pereira, Arthur Lonergan. *Set Decorators*: Sam Comer, James Payne. *Assistant Director*: Arthur Jacobson. *Men's Costumer*: Bud Clark. *Women's Costumer*: Grace Harris. *Makeup Artists*: Sydney Perell, John Stone. *Hair Stylist*: Maryce Jane Bates. *Sound Recorders*: Hugo Grenzbach, John Wilkinson. *Titles By*: Pacific Title. *Fashions By*: Jax. *Bathing Suits By*: Peter Pan Swimwear International. *Beach Hats By*: Leon Bennett. Filmed in Technicolor-Techniscope.

"For Those Who Think Love" by Mack David and Jerry Livingston, performed by James Darren over the opening credits. Not credited: "Ho Daddy, Surf's Up" performed by Bob Denver. "I'm Gonna Walk All Over This Land" performed by unidentified vocalist with Paul Johnson of the Bel-Airs, and Glen Grey and Richard Delvy of the Challengers.

For Those Who Think Young was the second major studio film aping AIP's beach movie formula. Despite his grandfather's protestations, a rich playboy romantically pursues a proud but poor coed whose guardians work in a nightclub catering to the swinging college crowd, with the action flitting from the shores of Malibu to the college campus. The film is a perfect example of just how the majors didn't understand what made the Frankie and Annette pictures so successful. Instead of rock groups, there are parents! Rather than lots of beach scenes and surfing footage, there is comedian Woody Woodbury! Also note to producers: peppering the film with character actors from the 1930s does not a beach party make.

There are not enough outdoor scenes for a beach movie in this studio-bound production, so the flesh factor is low. The film's young leads, James Darren and Pamela Tiffin, look great in swimsuits and make a fetching couple. Darren is perfectly cast as the suave, rich ladies' man while Tiffin is truly one of the most beautiful actresses to set foot on a Hollywood soundstage. It is a bit surreal to see Tina Louise and Bob Denver together shortly before they became stranded on *Gilligan's Island*. Louise is a knockout as a sexy stripper with a high I.Q. but has little to do. Nancy Sinatra is still in her dark-haired good girl phase so no bikinis or tight clothing for her.

The film features one above-average surfing sequence that is nicely scored and excellently photographed. It could have used more of that and less of the nightclub scenes with Woody Woodbury, whose routine is dated and unfunny. What is unintentionally funny are the scenes of roommates Woodbury and Paul Lynde acting like two bickering old queens when they are supposed to be swinging bachelors.

Musically, *For Those Who Think Young* does not have much going for it except for one standout number. Darren does fine belting out the bouncy opening song "For Those Who Think Love." But it is Bob Denver who steals the show performing the tribal surf stomp "Ho Daddy, Surf's Up" while buried in the sand with only his inverted mouth showing with a cartoon face painted on it upside down with beach boys and girls dancing around him. This scene and the film's attractive young players make it an okay time waster.

The Story

Rich playboy Gardner "Ding" Pruitt III is driving back to school with his friend and assistant, the beatnikish Kelp, after a day of surfing. He calls gorgeous coed Sandy Palmer from his car phone to make a date, but the girl turns him down to the shock of her sorority sisters, Karen and Sue. Determined to go out with her, Ding sneaks into her sorority house after stealing a parking space from Woody Woodbury. Hiding behind a surfboard, he makes it to the upstairs bedroom hallway when the housemother, Mrs. Harkness, walks by. Sandy emerges from her room just in time to sneak Ding in before he is seen by the ditzy woman. Desperate to get him to leave, she agrees to go on a date with him. While sneaking back down the stairs, Ding trips and crashes into Woody, who turns out to be Sandy's uncle and guardian.

Sandy asks Ding to take her to the Silver Palms, a dive bar where Woody and her Uncle Sid perform their tired vaudeville act. The two are practically booed off the stage by a ragtag audience that wants to see red-haired stripper Topaz McQueen. Spotting Sandy in the audience, Woody has the manager throw them out for being under 21. When Woody kisses Sandy goodbye, Ding gets infuriated until the cunning girl admits that he is her uncle. The playboy then tries to entice her to his fabulous apartment, Ding-a-Ling's hideaway, but the headstrong gal declines.

The next day on the beach, Woody makes a pass at attractive college professor Pauline Swenson, but she rebuffs him. That night Woody and Sid learn it is going to be their final show. Sid backs out so Woody goes it alone and is a hit with some college students in the audience. Soon he is packing them in with his new routine at Surf's Up, a renovated Silver Palms. Back on the sands of Southern California, Kelp is making time with Karen, while Ding is trying to get another date with Sandy. He almost succeeds when a beautiful blonde strolls up and thanks him for the bathing suit he sent her. A jealous Sandy flees. Ding chases after her as, the big waves start rolling in. While buried in the sand, Kelp leads the beach crowd singing a tribal surf song. Afterwards, they grab their boards to go surfing.

Unbeknownst to Ding, his controlling grandfather, Edgar J. Cronin, has his employee Clyde tailing him. Thinking that Sandy is a golddigger and not good enough for his grandson, Cronin plots to break them up. At the local Baskin-Robbins ice cream shop, Ding fakes a surfing injury to gain sympathy from Sandy, but the bright coed sees through his ruse.

With Woody now the big draw at Surf's Up, Topaz rehearses her new act with Sid. She goes off to her dressing room with a college boy after Ding's grandfather shows up. He tries to buy off Woody by paying for Sandy's education at a college of her choosing. When Woody refuses to meddle in his niece's life, Cronin vows that he'll ruin him and the club. At a meeting of the college deans, Cronin's donation hinges on the closing of Surf's Up. The staid Dr. Swenson volunteers to go undercover to get the goods on the joint for serving liquor to minors. The manager recognizes her and spikes her fruit juice drink. The inebriated professor is taken home by Woody and sleeps on his couch. She shows up at the club the next day where Woody proves to her that the club identifies all underage club goers and that Topaz moonlights as a math tutor. Feeling foolish, Pauline apologizes and accepts Woody's dinner invitation.

Back on the beach, Sandy agrees to go to Ding's twenty-first birthday party. When Karen informs her that she is the only guest, Sandy admits that she already knows that. The wily girl plays along with Ding's charade and surprises the lothario by putting the moves on him. Guilt-ridden, Ding admits to the love-trap that he set for her. But Sandy takes his heartfelt confession as a sign that he truly loves her and they kiss. The mood is interrupted when Sandy catches Clyde photographing them and gets the wrong impression. After his houseman confesses that Ding's grandfather has been paying him to spy, Ding takes Sandy to confront the old man. Admitting to everything, Cronin insults Sandy and her lineage. In front of his grandfather and mother, Ding proposes to the dumbstruck girl, who accepts.

James Darren and Pamela Tiffin emerge from the surf in *For Those Who Think Young* (United Artists, 1964).

The next night, Cronin gets his cronies to work at Surf's Up to make sure the place is closed down for serving alcohol to minors. Ding shows up with Sandy and recognizes his grandfather's friends. He informs Woody and Gus, but before they can react the club is raided by the police and closed down. Sandy is ready to give up Ding to get Cronin to drop the charges against Woody but he will not hear of it. Watching television, Sid views an old newsreel clip that reveals B. S. Cronin as former mobster Nifty Cronin during Prohibition. He wants to use this information to blackmail Cronin into dropping the charges but Woody refuses. Sid, the college kids and the dean converge on Cronin's house after seeing the clip about the former gangster. Pressured, Cronin has a change of heart and withdraws the charges while welcoming Sandy into his family.

Behind-the-Scenes

For Those Who Think Young was developed by Frank Sinatra's Essex Company. Warner Bros. executive Bill Orr had built a dynasty for the studio's television division and at the height of its success they had eight series on the viewing schedule. Orr and his assistant Hugh Benson eventually left Warner Bros. to work on feature films with Howard W. Koch at Essex.

James Darren, who had built up a large fanbase due to the *Gidget* movies and his recording success, was tapped to play the male lead. Producers seemed to only consider Darren for teenage movies, frustrating the young actor. He remarked in *Seventeen,* "The *Gidget* pictures hurt me because whenever anyone would think of me for a role, they would say, well, he falls into that *Gidget* category, and they would dismiss me. Actually, the *Gidget* pictures were fairly big pictures in that they were expensive, but a lot of people in the movie business didn't think of them that way."

Pretty Pamela Tiffin was cast as Darren's surfing sweetie. The stunning, soft-spoken brunette from Oklahoma made her film debut co-starring with the esteemed Geraldine Page in *Summer and Smoke* (1961) and then acted with James Cagney in Billy Wilder's frenetic comedy *One, Two Three* (1961). Not just another ingenue, Tiffin brought a flair for comedy to her pristine girl-next-door roles in such films as *State Fair* (1962), *Come Fly with Me* (1963) and *The Pleasure Seekers* (1964). The studios however, were always trying to change her appearance. Tiffin commented in *Fantasy Femmes of Sixties Cinema,* "In Hollywood, they always asked me to be blonde and I always said no because in the Midwest nice girls didn't dye their hair."

Though she was not forced to change her hair color, Tiffin, who had just married New York–based publisher Clay Felker, was pressured into doing *For Those Who Think Young* despite her objections. Contracts with Hal Wallis, the Mirisch Brothers and 20th Century–Fox kept the starlet busy.

The supporting cast of *For Those Who Think Young* was filled with recognizable names and aspiring newcomers. Bob Denver was fresh off the cancellation of the successful sitcom *The Many Loves of Dobie Gillis* while film star Tina Louise had been living in New York studying Method acting after having exiled herself in Italy trying to obtain better roles. Commenting in the film's pressbook on her role as a stripper with a high I.Q, she said, "I didn't have much trouble convincing myself I was a striptease artist. But I assure you the year at the Actors Studio certainly came in handy when I tried to think of myself as a mathematical genius."

Comedian Paul Lynde had a banner 1963 appearing in the hit films *Bye Bye Birdie* and *Under the Yum Yum Tree.* New faces included Ellen McRae in her first movie after working steadily on television in such series as *Maverick, 77 Sunset Strip, The Real McCoys* and *Gunsmoke,* and comedian Woody Woodbury, who replaced Johnny Carson as host of *Who Do You Trust?* after Carson was hired for *The Tonight Show.* Since *For Those Who Think Young* was produced by Frank Sinatra's production company, it is no surprise that his daughter Nancy and family friend Claudia Martin (Dean's daughter) both make their film debuts in this. Nepotism was alive and well in Hollywood.

To give *For Those Who Think Young* that *Beach Party* feel, producer Howard W. Koch was able to convince James H. Nicholson of American International to loan out some of his contract players. Mickey Dora, Mike Nader, Ed Garner (inexplicably listed as "Byron Garner" in the credits) and Pam Colbert appeared as part of the beach and college crowd. Comparing this shoot to the making of an AIP movie, Garner exclaims, "*For Those Who Think Young* was done on a much grander scale! Everybody had his or her own private dressing room. You were treated a lot differently."

With casting complete, a director was needed to complete the movie in 21 days and within budget. Recalling how he got the assignment, Leslie H. Martinson says,

"I was under contract at the time to Warner Bros. I'd been there for about seven and a half years. Howard Koch was the executive producer and of course he knew my work. There is only one Howard Koch and I can't say enough good things about him. I was a script supervisor when he was an assistant director at MGM in the forties. He suggested me to Frank Sinatra, who knew me from when we worked together on the movie *Take Me Out to the Ball Game*. Frank told Howard to get me for the film so I went on loanout from Warner Bros."

Martinson was a perfect choice to bring *For Those Who Think Young* to the screen. He directed a number of features in the mid-fifties including his first movie entitled *The Atomic Kid* (1954) with Mickey Rooney, which was shot in 12½ days. After joining the ranks of Warner Bros., Martinson built up a solid reputation as a proficient director who was able to deliver professionally shot television episodes on time. He worked on all the top series including *Cheyenne, Maverick, Lawman, 77 Sunset Strip, Hawaiian Eye, SurfSide Six*, etc. On the big screen, he had just completed directing *PT 109* (1963) starring Cliff Robertson as John F. Kennedy. "*For Those Who Think Young* was a big movie with a 21-day shooting schedule with all kinds of musical numbers and exterior location shootings," says Martinson. "I was used to shooting fast so I think that was one of the reasons why they hired me.

"When I first read the script, I was a bit leery because it was very fluffy," continues Leslie with a laugh. "But I thought it would be challenging to pull off. There was just a potpourri of characters being thrown at the audience. A couple of days before I was ready to shoot, they cut the schedule to 18 days. This movie with its big cast, production numbers and location shots was done in that short amount of time. It was a fun experience for me but I was a little concerned about the schedule. We got through it and there were no problems with any of the cast. They did a good job and the relationships between the characters worked."

For Those Who Think Young was a typical shoot in the sense that scenes were filmed on location at Malibu Beach and Occidental College as well as on a soundstage. It was an unusual shoot in that producers usually barred the public from the set but fans were *encouraged* to watch the filming as Hugh Benson welcomed visitors to spur word of mouth about the movie. Art Seidenbaum reported in the *Los Angeles Times*, "Hundreds of invited guests have dropped into this most open of open sets. On a make-believe beach inside stage eight it was impossible to tell the players from the passerby. Visitors swarmed over the sands like ants at a picnic." According to Benson, there were a total of 6,774 visitors who watched some portion of the movie being filmed. The only closed set was Tina Louise's striptease number, which was staged by Robert Tucker (who worked with Natalie Wood on 1962's *Gypsy*). Louise reportedly rehearsed for two straight weeks and when it came time to film her dance routine she had lost so much weight—13 pounds— that her costumes needed major altering.

The film also had a number of product tie-ins including clothiers Jax, Peter Pan Swimwear and Wembley; food chains International House of Pancakes and Baskin-Robbins; sunscreen maker Coppertone; and car manufacturers Honda and Buick. The most expensive prop used for the film was a Buick Riviera that was custom-made at a cost of $18,000. Barrie Kustoms fitted the automobile with a "Congo alligator leather top, removable front half of top (to accommodate the surfboards, of course), aerodynamic-styled front end, auto-stereo and two radio telephones." In return for their product placement, these companies were contracted to promote the movie in their ad campaigns.

The most blatant product endorsement was from Pepsi-Cola, whose slogan was used as the title of the film. A huge Pepsi dispensing machine is featured prominently in several scenes. In her second movie *One, Two Three* Pamela Tiffin played the daughter of a Coca-Cola executive and here the equal-opportunity actress was pushing Pepsi. To this day, Leslie Martinson has no knowledge of the deal between the soft drink company and the producers. "I never knew what the connection to Pepsi-Cola was," admits Leslie. "The company was not at all involved in the making of the film. That just came out of Frank Sinatra's office. He never got personally involved with the making of the film. Howard Koch would report back to him and show him the dailies. He was very happy with what he saw."

To keep the anticipation level for the movie high, the cast would pose for numerous publicity stills and grant interviews for all the movie fan magazines. In between scenes, they were required to participate in a television making-of featurette being produced in hopes of getting viewers off their couches and into the theaters. Nancy Sinatra and Claudia Martin were featured prominently. According to Art Seidenbaum, "Dean's girl is introspective, inclined to think a couple of times before answering foolish questions—more self-searching than self-assured. Frank's daughter, who has had to parry the press for nearly 20 years, is quick on the up-take, alert to the putdown and the more ebullient of the two."

Trying to juggle the publicity machine buildup and the shortening of the shooting schedule kept director Leslie Martinson on his toes. He discovered that he had only a day to shoot all the scenes at the beach. He recalls, "In that one day, I shot about 18 minutes of cut film with the 'Surf's Up' number and two or three surfing scenes. I saved the dialogue scenes for nightfall and shot them as day-for-night. Nancy Sinatra and Bob Denver in particular were in most of these scenes. Nancy was just a delight and she still is. We stayed friendly through the years. Working with her was one of the most enjoyable experiences I ever had working with an actress. She is talented and bright and made some nice contributions to the movie." Ed Garner concurs, "Nancy Sinatra was great! I knew her socially so it was a lot of fun working with her. She was married to Tommy Sands at the time so he would visit the set often."

One of the film's highlights, shot that day on the beach, is Bob Denver's singing the surfer lament "Ho Daddy, Surf's Up." According to Denver, nobody informed him that he was going to sing. While walking on the soundstage, the assistant director told him that music director Jerry Fielding was waiting for him with a full orchestra to record his song. Denver thought he was joking until he was handed the sheet music that was never delivered to him and was told to go to the scoring stage where Fielding was waiting with baton in hand, musicians in place and backup singers. After explaining to Fielding the situation, the patient composer suggested that they record the song a little at a time.

Harder for Denver was lip-synching the song buried in the sand with his chin and mouth sticking out and two eyes and a nose drawn upside down on his chin. Bob remarked in his autobiography, "It was photographed upside down so my goatee became the little face's hair and my mustache the goatee. Sound confusing? How about lying with your head wrapped in towels, in a hole, covered with sand,

For Those Who Think Young (United Artists, 1964) featured Nancy Sinatra and Bob Denver as a pair of kooky, beach-loving college students.

and trying to lip-synch a song? I remember a muffled voice telling me I was off and I thought, 'Everything's upside down. How can you tell if my lips match or not!' After many takes we got the song." Martinson praised Denver for his patience while filming this. "Bob just dug in there and had a talent for it," says Leslie. "He didn't cause any delays."

James Darren was juggling filming *For Those Who Think Young* while performing twice a night at a Las Vegas nightclub. According to an interview he gave in *Seventeen*, the busy actor would hop a flight at 4:30 P.M. to Vegas, perform his two shows, then take a sleeping pill and be chauffeured via ambulance back to the studio.

Not apparent to the cast and crew was the unhappiness of leading lady Pamela Tiffin. Not only was the beautiful newlywed missing her husband, but she also had to contend with an overly friendly co-star. Tiffin remarked, "James Darren was very jazzy and flirty. He was married at the time. I didn't know anything about his singing career. Another actress warned me about singers and that made me jumpy. I was very circumspect around him."

Darren liked Pamela (maybe too much?) and told *Seventeen* in 1964 that they "get along really well; it's fun working with her." Co-star Ed Garner remembers it that way also. "James Darren was a really nice guy," says Garner. "It seemed to me that he and Pamela Tiffin were enamored equally with each other." Nancy Sinatra concurred and remarked in *TV Guide,* "Show-business people aren't real people any more. Something happens to the ego. But with Jimmy there are never any pretenses, facades, ever."

Regarding Pamela's unhappiness, Leslie Martinson remarks, "I wasn't aware of any of this. Whatever was going on was kept between the two of them. I found James Darren to be a very pleasant fellow, but I can't say enough about Pamela Tiffin. In fact, my wife Connie and I became very friendly with Pamela. We had dinner at my home with her a number of times. She was a just a delightful, beautiful young woman—one of the prettiest of her day. In fact, I was driving her back from the studio to have dinner with Connie and me one early evening. The harsh setting sun coming through the windshield could be very tough on the loveliest of ladies, but it made Pamela look even more beautiful. I never told her that. She was like spring rain. But as gorgeous as she was, Pamela was terribly bright. Connie was very impressed with her."

Despite the combination of newcomers and seasoned pros, Martinson was able to keep the filming on an even keel and balanced the distinct personalities. "Strangely enough, I have a wonderful relationship with Tina Louise," says Leslie with a laugh. "Tina had her own way of working and was very smart but she could be considered a bit difficult at times. She had her own ideas but somehow we were on the same beat. Paul Lynde could get a little nervous but other than that he was fine to work with. I don't know who discovered Woody Woodbury but what a pleasant guy! He was very big-time in Florida—but that's kind of local in terms of what we think of. He came off quite well in the film. What you see on screen is Woody. I've talked with him on the phone through the years and he is still doing his nightclub gigs in Florida."

Martinson was used to working with new talent. He read and hired acting novice Frank Gorshin for the second lead in *Hot Rod Girl* (1956). While directing episodes of television's *Bourbon Street Beat,* he cast Mary Tyler Moore in her first big role and gave Richard Chamberlain (who had no credits) a part as well. Asked if it was difficult directing first-time actors on such a rushed schedule, Martinson comments, "I was raised on 'what you see is what you got.' After directing a number of episodes of *The Roy Rogers and Dale Evans Show,* I went over to MCA when they first started producing these two half-hour series, *Chevron Theatre* and *City Detective.* We'd shoot each episode in two days. A number of directors came and went who couldn't meet this schedule. I always enjoyed it because we had the luxury of one day of rehearsal. Just that one day to work with actors where you can lay out all your shots was paradise.

"In these short shoots, a director has to rely on the actors to help pull it off," continues Leslie. "Sometimes actors don't like to hear it but an expression directors use often is that 'he or she is a real pro to work with.' A pro encompasses more than just knowing your lines and hitting your marks. It involves the actor and director relating and interacting with each other in a professional manner. It is smooth sailing with actors who are pros."

Looking back on the shoot, Martinson remarks, "I sound like a Pollyanna but it was a delightful experience. Take it from me—it doesn't always work out this way. But this cast had a lot of respect for me since I had done a lot of television so that always helps the director too. The set was always comfortable. The crew was excellent—very fast and professional. People don't understand that if you have 30 to 35 set-ups a day and you have a cinematographer who takes one minute longer in a light, that is an extra half-hour. The cinematographer could put you in the toilet and cause delays—he's *the* man. Some of them would start to paint a little but you can't afford it if you are on a strict schedule. Many a poor director has gone down the drain because their cinematographers were just slow.

"The director's first cut is the most important thing of all," Leslie continues. "I always said to film editors, 'I am going to try to make this script 10 or 20 percent better than what is on the page.' At Paramount where I worked on numerous episodes of *Mission: Impossible, Mannix* and *Love, American Style* in the late sixties and early seventies, the editors gave out a yearly award to the director they most preferred to cut. I won it two years in a row. I was very proud of this though it doesn't really mean anything to anybody."

Regarding the final product, Martinson says, "I thought *For Those Who Think Young* was well-received. The press was kind to it considering that it was very light entertainment. It all came together and I understand it was the one film that made money for Essex Productions. Sometime after it was released, Red Doff, the assistant to the producer, received a residual check for $10,000 based on the financial success of the movie."

According to an item in *Variety*, after the movie was released ventriloquist Paul Winchell sued the producers, the studio and Bob Denver. The suit alleged that Denver's character was a rip-off of Winchell's "Mr. Goody-Good" and Winchell was asking the defendants to "be enjoined from using the dispute characterization."

Martinson continued directing non-stop through the eighties. After directing the feature films *Batman* (1966) for which he won the Italian Giffoni Film Festival Award and *Fathom* (1967) with Raquel Welch, he returned to television. Among the hundreds of television shows that he lent his talents to in the seventies were *Room 222, The Brady Bunch, Alias Smith and Jones, Cannon, Longstreet, Ghost Story, The Magician, The Six Million Dollar Man, Wonder Woman, Quincy* and *Eight Is Enough*. He reunited with Bob Denver and should have reunited with Tina Louise when he was hired to direct the long-anticipated tele-movie *Rescue from Gilligan's Island* (1978). "This was the second-highest-rated program for the entire year," boasts the director. "Two generations of Americans wanted to see how they got off that island! I had never worked on the series. Tina declined to do the movie because of her dissatisfaction with the money offered and her problems with the cast. They apparently had a little trouble accepting—what I call—the uniqueness of Tina Louise. I worked with her again on the series *Dallas* soon after this. We have stayed very close."

The eighties found the versatile director working on *Buck Rogers in the 25th Century, Young Maverick, Harper Valley P.T.A., Manimal* and *Airwolf*. He directed Gary Coleman in two television-movies, *The Kid with the Broken Halo* (1982) and *The Kid with the 200 I.Q.* (1983). Martinson's last directing gig was on the sitcom *Small Wonder* in the late eighties. Today, he is retired and living with his wife Connie, the hostess of the long-running cable show *Connie Martinson Talks Books*, in Beverly Hills, where he still enjoys a good game of tennis.

Bob Denver and Tina Louise would get stranded for three years on *Gilligan's*

Island soon after this. According to Denver, he never met Louise while working on *For Those Who Think Young* as they didn't have any scenes together. Denver would also pop up in the last surf movie of the sixties, *The Sweet Ride* (1968).

Nancy Sinatra and Claudia Martin co-starred again in AIP's *The Ghost in the Invisible Bikini* (1966). Ellen McRae would eventually change her name to Ellen Burstyn and go on to win an Academy Award for Best Actress in *Alice Doesn't Live Here Anymore* (1974). Sheila Bromley went on to play another sorority mother in *The Girls on the Beach* (1965).

Memorable Lines

(Ding tries to entice Sandy to go out with him again.)

DING: Tell me you feel something for me.

SANDY: Yes, I do. I'm not immune. I've caught the Pruitt infection.

DING: Then why don't we run a temperature together.

Reviews

Judith Crist, *TV Guide*—"*For Those Who Think Young* are for those who think stupid."

Allen Eyles, *Films and Filming*—"Quite a jolly picture ... *For Those Who Think Young* doesn't try to amount to anything more."

Wanda Hale, *New York Daily News*—"If *For Those Who Think Young* has an audience it would be for those who are too young to think. Extra-curricular activities on a college campus by the sea are noisy and agitated, the story is tasteless, the actors talentless."

Margaret Harford, *Los Angeles Times*—"*For Those Who Think Young* hardly holds me that long but teenagers don't give a hoot what the middle-aged think of them, so there!"

Howard Thompson, *The New York Times*—"For those who think young? There's nothing particularly youthful about this 'swingin'-surfin'' color frolic. It's strictly summery, light-headed fare, pretty to look at but about as obvious and empty as a breeze."

Time—"Surf bore! *For Those Who Think Young* borrows a popular soft-drink slogan, but carelessly omits the fizz. Probably it never should have been put in the can."

Archer Winsten, *New York Post*—"*For Those Who Think Young* gives an assist to older brains by using high visibility girl, Tina Louise, as a mathematician doubling as nightclub stripper and Pamela Tiffin as catnip to all male eyes. Suffice it to say it jumps, it wiggles good like a young torso should, and those surf-riders start high in the curl and end up still standing ear-deep in foam."

William Wolf, *Cue*—"You have to think very young to dig this picture, or better, not think at all."

Awards and Nominations

Golden Laurel Award: "Top New Faces, Female"—Nancy Sinatra, tenth place

Motion Picture Herald's Star of Tomorrow—Nancy Sinatra, ninth place

★ 8 ★

The Horror of Party Beach (1964)

*Out of the Sea They Came ... Transforming a Carefree Twisting
and Frolic-Filled Teenage Beach Party Into a Nightmare!*

Fun: ★
Surfing: ★
Boy watching: ★★★
Girl watching: ★★
Music: ★★
Scenery: ★

Release date: April 1, 1964. Running time: 82m. Box office gross: Not available.
DVD release: Not as of August 2004.

John Scott (*Hank Green*), Alice Lyon (*Elaine Gavin*), Allan Laurel (*Dr. Gavin*), Eulabelle Moore (*Eulabelle*), Marilyn Clarke (*Tina*), Agustin Mayer (*Mike*), Damon Kebroyd (*Lt. Wells*), Munroe Wade (*Television Announcer*), Carol Grubman, Dina Harris, Emily Laurel (*Girls in Car*), Sharon Murphy, Diane Prizio (*Girls*), Charter Oaks M.C. Riverside, Conn. (*Motorcycle Gang*). Guest Stars: The Del-Aires. Not credited: Robin Boston Barron (*Biker*), Del Tenney (*Gas Station Attendant*).

An Iselin-Tenney Production, a 20th Century–Fox release. *Producer and Director*: Del Tenney. *Associate Producer*: Alan V. Iselin. *Screenplay*: Richard L. Hilliard. *Additional Dialogue*: Ronald Gianettino and Lou Binder. *Director of Photography*: Richard L. Hilliard. *Art Direction*: Robert Verberkmoes. *Costumes*: Dina Harris. *Supervising Editor*: Gary Youngman. *Editors*: Leonard De Munde, Richard L. Hilliard, David Simpson. *Assistant Editors*: Robert Rose, Mary Ann Miles. *Cameraman*: Leonard De Munde. *Second Unit Photography*: David Simpson. *Assistant Directors*: Daniel Walker, Wayne Tippet. *Sound Recorder*: Daniel Aldridge. *Boomman*: Roland Streeter. *Production Coordinator*: Ruth Freedman. *Still Photographer*: Mary Ann Miles. *Re-recording*: Albert Gramaglia. *Musical Director*: Bill Holcombe. *Stunts*: Robin Boston Barron. Filmed in b/w.

All songs performed by the Del-Aires. "Drag" by Ronnie Linares, Gary Robert Jones and Wildrid Holcombe. "Joyride," "The Zombie Stomp" and "You Are Not a Summer Love" by Wilfrid Holcombe and Edward Earl. "Wigglin' and Wobblin'" by Garry Robert Jones. "Elaine" by Ronnie Linares.

The Horror of Party Beach is by far the worst of the sixties beach films. Though production-wise it is on par with *The Beach Girls and the Monster,* at least that film is campy fun. Radioactive waste dumped into the ocean turns human skeletons into flesh-eating monsters that terrorize a Long Island beach community. *Party Beach* treats its subject matter far too seriously and the film falls flat in every department, from the amateurish performances to the comical-looking monsters to the ridiculous screenplay, which tries to be funny but fails. Yes, the film was made for less than $50,000 and was aimed for the undiscriminating sixties teenage drive-in audience. However, that cannot excuse the film's many shortcomings in the acting, script and camera departments. Filmed in grainy black-and-white (a major no-no for surf movies), some scenes are lit so darkly that it would seem that Del Tenney wanted to spare the audience from watching the silliness on the screen. The real horror of party beach is trying to sit through this mess!

The film's few bright spots are the early beach scenes featuring some scantily clad beach boys (some in Speedo bathing suits, a rare treat for 1964) and bikini-clad girls dancing up a storm on the sands to the music of the Del-Aires. The director also throws in a brief but titillating playful wrestling match between a guy and girl, and some bare-chested beach boys fighting leather-clad bikers.

John Scott (resembling James Franciscus) provides the beefcake as the film's hero but he lacks charisma. An anorexic-looking blonde named Alice Lyon is the film's heroine. She is not particularly attractive and displays not an iota of emotion making Elaine Du Pont of *Beach Girls and the Monster* look like Meryl Streep. Marilyn Clark is okay as the sexy femme fatale but she checks out of the film far too early.

Surfing scenes are nil as this was filmed on a beach off the flat Long Island Sound. The only music is provided by the Del-Aires, a rock group from New Jersey compromised of five young men, none looking a day over 16, wearing crisp striped shirts. They are not bad rocking on a handful of songs and look like they are enjoying themselves. Too bad the viewer can't say the same.

The Story

While driving to the beach, beer-guzzling party gal Tina spurs a drag race between her boyfriend Hank and a motorcycle gang. It culminates on the beach where a wild rock 'n' roll party is going on. As the teenagers twist and shout on the shore to the rhythms of the Del-Aires, a barrel containing radioactive waste is dumped from a passing ship. It sinks to the bottom of the ocean and splits open on a jagged rock. An ominous-looking black liquid oozes out, covering a human skull which suddenly starts to move. It morphs into an encrusted vicious monster which slowly comes to life. Soon there are others—all craving human blood to survive.

Tina has told off her "square" boyfriend for berating her behavior and begins dancing with the leader of the biker gang. Hank, meanwhile, runs into pretty blonde Elaine Gavin and he asks her to dance. They are interrupted by a lot of hooting and hollering. The inebriated Tina has begun to do a striptease. A shirtless Hank rushes in to stop her and gets into a fistfight with the biker. A bored Tina goes off to sunbathe on the rocks and is attacked by the monsters from the ocean floor who have crashed the beach party. Her screams stop the dancing. When the teenagers come upon her lacerated body, they call the police who enlist the aid of Elaine's father, Dr. Gavin, a science professor.

Tina's murder has unnerved Elaine and she won't leave the house. Hank wants to take her to the dance at the beach but she is hesitant. After prodding from her father and the family maid, Eulabelle, she decides to accept Hank's invitation. At the party, two girls leave to catch the bus home and are attacked by the monsters. The next night Elaine is invited to her sorority slumber party but the smart gal declines to attend. As the girls sit around waiting for the boys to crash, they hear mysterious noises. They presume it is the fraternity guys but it is the hideous monsters from the deep, who slaughter the coeds.

While Dr. Gavin and Hank work together to find a solution, the monsters kill a girl who moronically decides to go swimming alone. Three female motorists passing through town get a flat tire out in the woods. As they attempt to change it, the monsters emerge from the forest and feast on their flesh. During another assault, one of the monsters loses an arm. Dr. Gavin examines it. When it moves by itself, a startled Eulabelle accidentally spills a beaker of sodium on it. The appendage bursts into flames and Gavin realizes that pure salt will destroy the monsters, whose composition is largely water.

Hank begins to gather all the sodium available in the area for a last-ditch defense against the rampaging monsters. He leaves for New York City to get a supply. Meanwhile, Dr. Gavin, Elaine and the police test the lakes and ponds for radioactivity. Elaine stumbles upon the monsters' lair. In the distance, the scared girl can hear the menacing noises of the creatures in search of blood. She sprains her ankle while trying to flee. Her father tries to come to her rescue but is attacked by one of the creatures. Hank arrives in the nick of time with the extra sodium and destroys all the monsters. Dr. Gavin recovers from his wounds while Hank pledges his love to Elaine.

Behind-the-Scenes

The Horror of Party Beach is all the fault of producer-director Del Tenney. He was born in Iowa but at age 12 he relocated with his family to California. He began acting when he enrolled in the drama school of Los Angeles State College. Only able to land extra work in such films as *Stalag 17* (1953) and *The Wild One* (1954), he moved to New York in the late fifties to try his luck in theater. He was cast in a number of Off-Broadway and summer stock productions. Around this time he married actress Margot Hartman and they founded the Harvest Theatre in Stamford, Connecticut. In the early sixties he gravitated to film, working behind the camera as assistant director on such low-budget exploitation pictures as *Orgy at Lil's House* and *Satan in High Heels* (1962) also acting in the latter (playing a homosexual). The following year, Tenny produced and wrote the axe-murder thriller *Psychomania* starring Lee Philips, Shepperd Strudwick, James Farentino, Jean Hale and Sylvia Miles. Made on a budget of $42,000 in Stamford, the movie became a grind house hit.

Tenney quickly went to work on his next two films, *The Curse of the Living Corpse* and *The Horror of Party Beach,* which were filmed back-to-back in two weeks on location in Stamford with a combined initial budget of $100,000. Fill-in shots were added later. Tenney used the old Gutzon Borglum Studio for interiors. Borglum

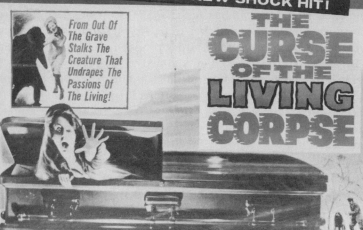

was the renowned sculptor who had designed Mount Rushmore. Tenney's father-in-law bought Borglum's estate and kept the studio while developing the land around it.

The success of *Psychomania* and the fact that associate producer Alan V. Iselin owned a drive-in theater chain in upstate New York may have been what initially caught the attention of 20th Century–Fox. The studio was looking for product to release to drive-ins across the country in the summer of 1964. Studio executives screened *The Curse of the Living Corpse* and offered to release it on a double bill with Tenney's second feature but only after they got a chance to preview it. *The Horror of Party Beach* was actually titled *Invasion of the Zombies* at this point. Del Tenney told writer Tom Weaver in *Fangoria*, "[It] started as an evolutionary story about atomic waste speeding up evolution, changing a fish into a man who becomes a monster. Then Alan [Iselin] and I tried to work the music into it, the Del-Aires and all that stuff, and tie in some kind of a beach-blanket beat." The movie was going to then be called *The First Monster Musical* before the title *The Horror of Party Beach* prevailed. Though the screenplay is credited solely to Richard Hilliard, Del Tenney and Margot Hartman contributed greatly to it.

While Tenney was able to get some well-known actors to appear in his other films, *The Horror of Party Beach* was populated with unknowns. John Scott, a good-looking strapping blonde hunk, was cast as the male lead while Alice Lyon, the college roommate of Tenney's wife, played the heroine. Dark-haired, curvaceous Marilyn Clark was cast as the bad girl while some of the crew popped into the film in minor roles. Tenney played a gas station attendant; assistant editor and sound boom man Rhoden Streeter was one of the monsters; and costume designer Dina Harris played one of the ill-fated victims in the car.

To give the movie a swinging beat, a New Jersey garage rock band called the Del-Aires was hired to perform in the movie. The quartet consisted of lead singer Ronny Linares, Bob Osborne, Garry Jones and John Becker. Ronny was even given lines and interacts with the film's two leads. Popular on the East Coast, the Del-Aires released an album featuring songs from the movie including "The Zombie Stomp" and "You Are Not a Summer Love."

The Horror of Party Beach was a problem-plagued shoot according to interviews given by Del Tenney. He had hired members of the Charter Oaks Motorcycle Club to play bikers. During the film's motorcycle and car race, one of the members decided he did not want to be in the back of the pack so he sped up to the front, clipping the handlebars of the actor hired to play the gang's leader. He fell and his motorcycle landed on top of him while other cyclists crashed into him or each other trying to avoid the pile-up. The police were notified and, on the way to the incident, they got into an auto accident. A handful of bikers were hospitalized including the actor, who suffered extensive injuries which caused a delay in production. Smartly, Tenney had all the bikers sign a release form before filming began releasing him and the production of all liability if any of the bikers suffered injury or their motorcycles were damaged during the course of the shoot. Tenney

Opposite: Trade ad for the 20th Century–Fox 1964 double feature of *The Horror of Party Beach* and *The Curse of the Living Corpse.*

was not as lucky with the town's officials, who strongly recommended that he not shoot any more movies in Stamford.

Tenney's troubles with the bikers continued when they paid him a late night visit while he was editing their footage. Tenney thought they were going to harm him, but all they wanted was to see the scene that they appeared in. It was photographed from three different angles so Tenney spent the entire night showing them the same footage over and over.

Various crew members donned the rubber monster suits that had sponges sewed onto them. A special mask was created for closeup shots of the creatures with hot dogs for teeth. The monster costumes were designed by theater set designer Bob Verberkmoes. The heads of the monsters were actually above the heads of the men wearing the costumes so holes were made in the neck so they could see.

The movie went over-budget by $20,000, bringing the total spent on *The Curse of the Living Corpse* and *The Horror of Party Beach* to $120,000. Thinking his second feature was "a piece of crap" and that Fox would pass on it, Tenney had a guy don the monster costume and hide in the men's room during the screening on the Fox lot to distract the Fox decision makers from the film. When the head of distribution of 20th Century–Fox excused himself to go to the restroom, Tenney's guy jumped out, startling him but sending his colleagues into hysterics. These theatrics were not necessary as Fox was impressed with the horror movies and were confident that they would make money. They tested the films at drive-ins in Fort Worth and Dallas, Texas, over a weekend. Surprisingly, Tenney's low-budget double-feature out-grossed the competition including *Move Over, Darling* and *PT 109*.

Fox gave the double bill a big promotion. Adding to the popularity was Iselin's gimmick that audiences had to sign a Fright Release "absolving the theater of all responsibility for death by fright during the showing of *The Horror of Party Beach*." And as a tie-in for the movie, Warren Publishing released the publication *The Horror of Party Beach*, which was touted as "A new kind of magazine! A photo story of teenage excitement, romance and mystery!" Actual stills from the movie were used as comic book style panels with blurbs.

Hailing itself as "the first horror monster musical," the movie has the dubious distinction of being crowned one of the worst movies of all time in a book by Harry and Michael Medved. In his horror treatise *Danse Macabre*, novelist Stephen King called *The Horror of Party Beach* "an abysmal little wet fart of a film."

Post–*The Horror of Party Beach*, Del Tenney's association with Alan Iselin broke up when Iselin wanted to hire him to direct *Frankenstein Meets the Spacemonster* rather than be his partner on it. Instead, Tenney produced and directed *Voodoo Blood Bath*, which was shot on location in Florida. Distribution problems kept this zombie thriller on the shelf until 1970 when producer Jerry Gross bought the rights to it. He re-titled it *I Eat Your Skin* and released it on the bottom half of a double-bill with *I Drink Your Blood*. Tenney left the movie business to concentrate on real estate. He stayed away from filmmaking until 1999 when he and his wife Margot produced and played small roles in the drama *Clean and Sober* starring William Katt and *Do You Wanna Know a Secret?* (2001) starring Joey Lawrence.

Though *The Horror of Party Beach* was a hit with the drive-in crowd, its success did nothing for the careers of its stars, which is not too surprising, as most of

Cover of *The Horror of Party Beach* tie-in magazine.

them never acted again. The only one to find a bit of notoriety was Alice Lyon, who went on to marry Jacqueline Kennedy's brother.

Reviews

Eugene Archer, *The New York Times*—"The question in *The Horror of Party Beach* is, which is more horrible—the monsters or the rock 'n' roll? The most curious aspect of the film is why, after the first couple of homicides, the rest of the victims linger around the disaster area, waiting for the worst. Audiences lured into the theater may ask themselves the same thing."

Raymond Durgnat, *Films and Filming*—"Initially this promises to be quite jolly. The opening car drive is neatly edited and ... almost persuaded me that in Del Tenney we had as cool a customer as Roger Corman. Disillusionment occurred when the monster appeared. This cross between a kipper and a Triffid has electric light bulbs for eyes and a mouth filled with what looked to me like a bunch of bananas. Thereafter boredom is abject and total."

Frances Herridge, *New York Post*—"This one is set for good measure on one of those beaches where bikini-clad youngsters romp and jive to a special jazz combo. The monsters, born underwater of atomic waste, are really not as frightening as some of those gum-chewing teenagers on the make."

Dale Munroe, *The Citizen-News*—"Undistinguished acting and uninspired rock 'n' roll numbers highlight what is otherwise an almost consistently uninteresting movie—direction-wise, script-wise and any other wise."

Newsweek—"A radioactive vampire-zombie-sex-maniac would be disturbing enough, but musical numbers like 'The Zombie Stomp' by the Del-Aires push this 20th Century–Fox release over the bottom as the worst movie of the last twelve months."

James O'Neill, *Terror on Tape* [Video Review]—"A classic of ineptitude combining a Frankie-and-Annette beach party movie with a monster cautionary tale on the horrors of atomic waste."

Robert Salmaggi, *New York Herald Tribune*—"*The Horror of Party Beach* has a dozen of the most ridiculous-looking 'monsters' we've ever seen. Wait 'til you encounter the unbelievably amateurish acting and direction of 'the first horror musical ever made.' The dancing's the best part of the film."

⋆ **9** ⋆

Muscle Beach Party (1964)

*When 10,000 Biceps meet 5,000 Bikinis
... you KNOW what's gonna happen!*

Fun: ***
Surfing: ***
Boy watching: ****
Girl watching: ***
Music: ***
Scenery: **

Release date: March 25, 1964. Running time: 94m. Box office gross: Not available.

DVD release: Double bill with *Ski Party*, MGM Home Entertainment (April 15, 2003).

Frankie Avalon (*Frankie*), Annette Funicello (*Dee Dee*), Luciana Paluzzi (*Julie*), John Ashley (*Johnny*), Don Rickles (*Jack Fanny*), Peter Turgeon (*Theodore*), Jody McCrea (*Deadhead*), Dick Dale and His Del-Tones (*Themselves*), Candy Johnson (*Candy*), Rock Stevens (*Flex Martian*), Delores Wells (*Sniffles*), Valora Noland (*Animal*), Donna Loren (*Donna*), Morey Amsterdam (*Cappy*), Buddy Hackett (*S. Z. Matts*), Alberta Nelson (*Lisa*), Amedee Chabot (*Floe*), Larry Scott (*Biff*), Bob Seven (*Rock*), Steve Merjanian (*Tug*), Dan Haggerty (*Riff*), Chester Yorton (*Sulk*), Gene Shuey (*Mash*), Gordon Cohn (*Clod*), Luree Holmes, Laura Nicholson, Lorie Summers, Darlene Lucht (*Beach Girls*), Duane Ament, Gary Usher, Roger Christian, Guy Hemric (*Beach Boys*), Mary Hughes, Kathy Kessler, Salli Sachse, Linda Opie, Linda Benson, Patricia Rane (*Surfer Girls*), Charles Van Artsdalen, Mike Diffenderfer, Bill Graham, Charles Hasley, Larry Shaw, Duane King, Mike Nader, Ed Garner, John Fain, Mickey Dora (*Surfer Boys*). Introducing: Little Stevie Wonder. Uncredited: Peter Lorre as Mr. Strangdour.

American International Pictures. *Produced by*: James H. Nicholson and Robert Dillon. *Executive Producer*: Samuel Z. Arkoff. *Directed by*: William Asher. *Screenplay by*: Robert Dillon. *Story by*: Robert Dillon and William Asher. *Production Supervisor*: Joe Wonder. *Second Unit Director*: Anthony Carras. *Photographed by*: Harold Wellman, A.S.C. *Music Coordinator*: Al Simms. *Music by*: Les Baxter. *Surfboards by*: Phil of Downey, California. *Muscle Man Dance Sequence Choreographed by*: John Monte (National Dance Instructor, Fred Astaire Studios). *Swim Suits by*: Rose Marie Reid. *Ah Men's Designs by*: Jerry Furlow. *Women's Sportswear by*: Phil Rose of California. *Mr. Hackett's Wardrobe by*: Mr. Guy of Los Angeles. *Film Editors*: Eve Newman, Fred Feitshans, A.C.E. *Sound Editor*: Kathleen Rose. *Music Editor*: Lloyd Young. *Costumes by*: Marjorie Corso. *Titles and Photographic Special Effects*: Butler-Glouner, Inc. *Assistant Director*: Clark Paylow. *Properties*: Karl Brainard. *Sound*: Don Rush. *Makeup*: Ted Coodley. *Hairdresser*: Betty Pedretti. *Special Effects*: Pat Dinga. *Set Decorator*: Harry Reif. *Construction Coordinator*: Ross Hahn. *Art Director*: Lucius Croxton. *Production Assistant*: Jack Cash. Filmed in Panavision and Pathecolor.

Songs by Gary Usher, Roger Christian and Brian Wilson: "Surfer's Holiday" performed by Frankie Avalon, Annette Funicello and Dick Dale. "My First Love" and "Muscle Beach Party" performed by Dick Dale and His Del-Tones. "Runnin' Wild" performed by Frankie Avalon. "Muscle Bustle" performed by Dick Dale and Donna Loren. "Surfin' Woodie" performed by the Cast (a cappella) and Dick Dale. "A Boy Needs a Girl/A Girl Needs a Boy" by Guy Hemric and Jerry Styner, performed by Frankie Avalon and Annette Funicello. "Happy Street" by Guy Hemric and Jerry Styner, performed by Little Stevie Wonder.

The first sequel to *Beach Party*, *Muscle Beach Party* is one of the best, though fans are divided. It's surfers versus bodybuilders for control of the beach while Frankie is romanced by an Italian countess, which throws Dee Dee into a tizzy. Frankie and Annette hit their stride as the beach-loving couple, surfing is still the main sport, and the conflict between the surfers and musclemen is a nice change of pace from the surfers' usual outlandish clashes with Eric Von Zipper's motorcycle gang. The movie is also very funny thanks to a surprisingly subdued Buddy Hackett as a business manager and the hysterical Don Rickles playing the leader of the body beautiful. The serious film student may try to read between the lines regarding the film's gender issues while the rest of the audience can just sit back and wallow in the acres of near-naked flesh on display.

Avalon and Funicello both give good performances and prove that their successful pairing in *Beach Party* was not a fluke. Here Annette is the standout giving a feisty performance and her verbal sparring, trading catty quips with Luciana Paluzzi, is a highlight. Avalon seems to have pumped some iron since *Beach Party* and he looks especially fine in his tight striped swim trunks. But he, Ashley and McCrea pale next to Rock Stevens a.k.a. Peter Lupus and the other bodybuilders who flex throughout the film in their posing briefs. If chiseled muscle boys are not your cup of tea, don't fret as lean Mike Nader, compact Johnny Fain and baby-face Ed Garner are still shirtless and present for ogling.

Girl watchers can rejoice with *Muscle Beach Party* as Annette squeezes her amble bosom into a two-piece bathing suit and even unintentionally exposes her navel! Back from *Beach Party* are sexy blonde Valora Noland and hip-shaking Candy Johnson, who gets an extended dance number, backed by her group the Exciters. Clad in a tasseled mid-riff, her bumps and grinds send the surfers off their boards and the male audience members into a frenzied state. Luciana Paluzzi (or, as Bond fans know her, Fatima Blush from *Thunderball*) still manages to look luscious even when costumed in ridiculous waif-like outfits that not even Sandra Dee would have been caught dead in. The film also introduces three more soon-to-be bikini-clad regulars, statuesque Mary Hughes, a Brigitte Bardot lookalike, and Linda Opie and Salli Sachse, who with their long brown hair worn in a swirl were nicknamed "the bookends."

For surfing enthusiasts, lots of big and small wave action is nicely photographed (though on the murky side). There are lots of surfing scenes and Annette even gets her hair wet. It is probably the last movie where she makes an effort to pretend to be surfing. Based on the size of some of the waves, a few scenes looked like perhaps it was stock footage filmed in Hawaii.

Les Baxter's musical score is okay but not one of his best. It's up to Dick Dale and His Del-Tones to provide some authentic surf rhythms but Dale was once again prevented from playing his own music. But that doesn't hamper him from giving, along with Little Stevie Wonder, the best musical performance in the movie. As for the rest of the songs, the romantic ballads sung by Frankie and Annette are sappy but the opening number "Surfer's Holiday" (co-written by Brian Wilson of the Beach Boys) is the standout.

The Story

Sweethearts Frankie and Dee Dee head to Malibu with their surfer friends and their girls and rent a beach house. The teenagers have a special spot on the beach as their own but things become tense when gym owner Jack Fanny appears on the sand with Flex Martian, the reigning Mr. Galaxy, and his troop of muscle men. The surfers make fun of the well-muscled bunch but things get tense when Fanny keeps traipsing over Johnny's towel. He and Deadhead confront the group and Jack Fanny makes it very clear that both groups need to stay on their own side of the beach.

Directly offshore, a yacht belonging to Contessa Juliana Gioto-Borgini is anchored. Accompanying Julie are her business manager S. Z. Matts and her attorney Theodore. The spoiled Italian beauty has fallen in love with a picture of Flex that she saw in a magazine and it is up to S. Z. and Theodore to introduce her to the bodybuilder. Julie's helicopter sets down on the beach and, after being introduced to all the musclemen, Julie lays claim to a stunned Flex over the objections of Jack Fanny. To make up for his loss, S. Z. offers to set up a string of Jack Fanny gyms all over the world. Julie and S. Z. fly back to her yacht with Flex for a quiet lunch.

That night, Frankie and Dee Dee take a moonlight walk and Dee Dee brings up the subject of marriage with Frankie. The surfer is not interested in "chains" and just wants to be free to catch the next big wave. The couple quarrels and Frankie puts on his wetsuit to go night surfing. Julie comes across a lovelorn Frankie singing on the beach. The fickle Italian vixen switches her affections to the surfer boy—angering Dee Dee, antagonizing Flex and increasing the hostility between the musclemen and the surfers.

At Cappy's nightclub, Frankie is trying to make up with his hurt girlfriend. As the couple slow-dances, Julie and S. Z. arrive with a crew to record Frankie, which angers Dee Dee. When Frankie finishes singing, Julie beguiles him with talk of going on a worldwide singing tour with her. An irate Dee Dee confronts Julie and threatens to punch her unless she goes somewhere else to "peddle her pasta." The Italian sexpot is saved by Flex, who scoops her up into his arms. When Julie chooses Frankie (or, as Jack Fanny describes him, that "scrawny mouse") over Flex, the bodybuilders declare war on the surfers. The boys band together but when Deadhead arrives yelling "surf's up," the wave riders vacate Cappy's, leaving Frankie behind. Luckily, the wiry lad is able to shake the lumbering Flex and make his escape.

At the beach, huge swells roll in and the gang hits the surf. Later that night, Julie promises to sail with Frankie to the top surfing spots around the world. Overhearing the surfers dancing to "Muscle Bustle," an irate Fanny formulates a plan to crush them once and for all. When Frankie brags to his friends about his future

Trade ad for *Muscle Beach Party* (AIP, 1964) (*courtesy the Billy Rose Theatre Collection, The New York Public Library for the Performing Arts, Astor, Lenox and Tilden Foundations*).

life with Julie and his big-time recording career, they turn a deaf ear. Liking Frankie and Dee Dee, S. Z. fills him in on Julie's numerous ill-fated love affairs and the sorry fate of her other boyfriends. Frankie finally sees the light and heads over to Cappy's to make up with Dee Dee. Julie and S. Z. arrive and Frankie tenderly tells the smitten young woman that they are just not right for each other. As the kids hit the dance floor, their good fun is ruined when the musclemen invade the club to recapture Julie for Flex. A melee breaks out between the bodybuilders and the surfers. The mysterious benefactor Mr. Strangdour then arrives and stops the free-for-all. Telling Flex he's too young to look at girls, Strangdour takes him by the ear and leads him away. Frankie promises Dee Dee that he'll never stray again while Julie realizes that the man for her has been in front of her eyes all the time— S. Z.

Behind-the-Scenes

Beach Party was the surprise sleeper hit of 1963. Realizing that there was more money to be made with their fun-in-the-sun epics, AIP commissioned a sequel with the working title *Muscle Beach*. But conflict with other pictures already made or contemplated resulted in the name change to *Muscle Beach Party*. The movie was filmed on location in Paradise Cove, Malibu, California. The story was basically the same as in *Beach Party*—surfer boy loves beach girl, surfer boy loses beach girl after being vamped by a foreign beauty, surfer boy and beach girl are reunited. Capitalizing on the growing bodybuilding scene at Malibu Beach, the surfers tangle with gym owner Jack Fanny and his group of arrogant musclemen (replacing Eric Von Zipper and his motorcycle gang as the film's chief antagonists). Beach boy Ed Garner opines, "I think *Muscle Beach Party* was great because there was just such a contrast between the bodybuilders—they were really nice guys—and the surfers."

Jody McCrea reprised his role of Deadhead in *Muscle Beach Party* but he almost missed the opportunity. "After doing *Beach Party*, I left the country for Europe traveling the long way via Hawaii and Asia with my mother and Dr. Norman Vincent Peale," recalls McCrea. "One of the highlights of the trip for me was meeting Nehru in India. It was wonderful. I had no idea while I was traveling that *Beach Party* had become a big hit. For me it was just a one-shot movie that I appeared in. They called me while I was overseas and asked me to come back to be in *Muscle Beach Party*. I was working on a movie deal with the son of Arthur Rank in England. He saw a few of the movies I was in and Peter Sellers' agent arranged a two-picture deal for me with Rank but it didn't work out. It is too long a story why but I was supposed to star in *Temple of the White Elephants*. Sean Flynn later did it. Instead I flew back home and made *Muscle Beach Party*."

Also returning from *Beach Party* to keep things familiar for the audience was most of the supporting cast including John Ashley, hip-swiveling Candy Johnson, Delores Wells and Dick Dale and His Del-Tones. Blonde Valora Noland, who played Rhonda previously, was now cast as a man-hungry beach girl named Animal. This part would be played by a string of actresses in the upcoming series of films. "My relationship with Valora Noland was completely professional," says McCrea with a trace of disappointment in his voice. "She was what we used to call 'a good girl.' We did a commercial together for New Dawn Hairspray that was filmed in Colorado Springs. She is sleeping and instead of waking her with a kiss I rouse her with the hairspray."

Surfers Mickey Dora, Johnny Fain, Mike Nader and Ed Garner returned for the film and a new crop of beach girls were recruited. Statuesque blonde Mary Hughes was discovered on the beach in Malibu. Salli Sachse, Linda Opie and a few others came from Windansea Beach in San Diego. They were friends of cartoonists Mike Dormer and Lee Teacher, who were in Hollywood to market their cartoon strip hero "Hot Curl." With his shaggy hair, knobby knees and a can of beer in his hand, Hot Curl was a caricature of the thousands of Southern California surfers at the time. Dormer and Teacher eventually found their way to AIP, who hired them to design the opening credits and to use their cartoon character as a backdrop in a nightclub scene. Looking for new faces to populate the background of the beach scenes, they were asked if they knew any beach girls or surfer boys. Salli Sachse recounted in *Fantasy Femmes of Sixties Cinema*, "About 10 or 15 of us piled into a couple of Woodys and drove up to Los Angeles. We met Sam Arkoff and Jim Nicholson at their offices. They asked us to line up in our bathing suits. They literally went right down the line pointing and saying, 'You. You. You.' When they were done choosing, they told us, 'This is Jack Gilardi. He'll be your agent.' That's how it started."

Duane King was a new surfer boy on the scene and he quickly became a favorite of William Asher. However, unlike Mickey Dora, King did not have a dynamic personality to warrant much attention from the director. Ed Garner says, "Duane was an extremely good-looking kid but he was a little bashful in front of the camera. Even though Bill Asher tried to give him a couple of opportunities to be more engaged as an actor, for some reason he was a little timid once the director yelled action. But he got a really incredible modeling career out of doing a few beach movies. He resembled Montgomery Clift and became one of the country's top male models for several years during the sixties."

Some of the country's top bodybuilders were recruited to appear in *Muscle Beach Party*. Peter Lupus played the lead role of Flex Martian. A world class bodybuilder, Lupus held the titles Mr. Indianapolis 1954, Mr. Indiana 1960 and Mr. International Health Physique. He signed a contract with AIP and they changed his name to Rock Stevens, which they felt was more fitting for an actor with his chiseled physique. The other musclemen included Chester "Chet" Yorton, who would go on to win the Mr. America contest in 1966, and Larry Scott, a Mr. California 1960 and Mr. America 1962 before he was named the first Mr. Olympia in 1965. "They were all great guys," remarks Jody McCrea. "I worked out with them a little bit during the shoot. I had been an athlete all my life. I was a javelin thrower at UCLA and in 1956 we won the national championship that year. Peter Lupus became a really good friend of mine. We hit it off really well. He was using a stage name and went off to Rome to do those muscle movies. He is a wonderful guy and a good businessman. His wife took good care of him and he did well."

Alberta Nelson, who appeared in *Beach Party* as part of Eric Von Zipper's biker gang, and Amedee Chabot, a former Miss California, played the female fitness nuts in the film. Chabot's luscious body was also on display in *For Those Who Think Young*.

Fun in the sun with the cast of *Muscle Beach Party* (AIP, 1964): Jody McCrea, Annette Funicello, Delores Wells, John Ashley and (lying down) Frankie Avalon.

Muscle Beach Party also introduced comedian Don Rickles to the beach crowd. Known for his insults and putdowns, Rickles was always performing even off-camera. "He was the most hysterical guy in the world," exclaims Ed Garner. "The first time he walked on the set, I thought he was an electrician or a grip. Then he started poking fun at everybody. I had no idea who he was. He made it just a totally incredible environment to work in." Jody McCrea agrees even though the comedian intimidated the burly actor. "I hid from Don because he would always tear into you with the insults," says McCrea. "I avoided him for quite awhile until I thought I could take him. He was 'on' all the time, keeping people laughing on the set. It was a joy to work with him. When he'd see me, he'd make a horse sound and tell me my mare was waiting. He was a funny guy."

Beach girl Luree Holmes, the daughter of AIP founder James H. Nicholson, revealed that she and Annette Funicello were not favorites of director William Asher. In fact, her good friend Annette revealed to Luree that she did not like the director. But being the professional that she was, Annette kept working with him anyway and never went on record regarding her dislike for Asher. But she was quoted a number of times about her distaste for swimming and surfing. In 1965 she told Richard Warren Lewis's in *Look* magazine, "The only part I don't like about filming them is at the beach. I don't really enjoy that." Odd that the queen of the beach party would reveal to the world how she hated the sand and the surf.

As for Luree Holmes' relationship with the director, she remarked, "William Asher handpicked a lot of the girls to be in the beach movies. He favored girls like Salli Sachse and Linda Opie because they had the best figures. I definitely understood that. Since I was tall—5' 7"—he was always telling me to stand in the back. In a lot of the scenes you had to be really upbeat and because I wasn't very outgoing it was difficult for me."

Another "favorite," Jody McCrea, remarks, "William Asher was best suited for directing the beach movies. He was always smiling. You would see his grin from behind the camera and it would just lift you up. He would get your confidence so high that as an actor you would try different things with your role. Most of it would work because of his faith in you. And yes, he favored some of the young guys like Mike Nader that he discovered on the beach. Mike had a lot of natural ability and Asher had a great talent for making you feel good while working with him. I think I was one of his favorites also because I had a lot of training. He liked all the things I brought to the part."

Vocalist Donna Loren, who was the Dr. Pepper Girl, was not originally supposed to sing in the movie. The soda company had invested in the film in return

In *Muscle Beach Party* (AIP, 1964) surfers Jody McCrea, Dick Dale, John Ashley, Frankie Avalon and Annette Funicello (egad, with her navel showing!) watch the musclemen pose.

for product placement and Loren was just supposed to make a cameo, possibly seen drinking a Dr. Pepper. The producers or someone connected to the production invited her to duet on the song "Muscle Bustle" with Dick Dale. Impressed with her look and talent, AIP signed her to a contract. In every one of her appearances, the underage singer's father was present on the set keeping a close eye on her. "He was very protective of her," remarks Ed Garner. "I don't think it was anything other than the fact that he thought he had a major star on his hands. But a lot of it started because Jody McCrea apparently had this terrible reputation of wanting to grope everything in sight. But he was just a big flirt and this was sometimes taken the wrong way."

Muscle Beach Party was Dick Dale's final beach party appearance. It is only speculation but it is believed that he became frustrated with the musical material and was never allowed to perform any of his own compositions. Cast member Ed Garner comments fondly, "Dick Dale was great. I turned 21 right after this picture wrapped and I threw a birthday party at my little apartment on Doheny. There were about 60 or 70 people squeezed into my place. Dick Dale came and played out on my patio. I'll never forget that."

To keep the audience guessing about the identity of Mr. Strangdour, AIP kept Peter Lorre's name off the opening credits and publicity material. However, during the end credits the following was inserted: "The producers extend special thanks to Mr. Peter Lorre for his contribution to this film as Mr. Strangdour. Soon to be seen in *Bikini Beach*." Unfortunately, Lorre passed away before production began on the new movie. Candy Johnson in her signature tasseled go-go dress was chosen once again to shake and shimmy during the film's end credits accompanied by Little Stevie Wonder singing "Happy Street" as her bumps and grinds blast the titles off the screen.

Brian Wilson of the Beach Boys, collaborating with Gary Usher and Roger Christian, contributed six songs to the movie. "Surfer's Holiday" and "Runnin' Wild" are considered two of the series' best. AIP was still not savvy enough to release a soundtrack LP. Instead, Buena Vista Records released an Annette Funicello album called *Muscle Beach Party* where she recorded new versions of five songs from the film combined with five additional Gary Usher–Roger Christian songs, and two from her Walt Disney feature *The Misadventures of Merlin Jones*.

Not to be outdone, Frankie Avalon, recording for United Artists, released an LP entitled *Muscle Beach Party and Other Movie Songs*. Featured on this album were new versions of two songs ("Beach Party" and "Don't Stop Now") from *Beach Party* and four songs (including "Surfer's Holiday" and "Runnin' Wild") from *Muscle Beach Party*. The remainder of the album was filled with other movie tunes re-recorded by Avalon. Neither Annette nor Avalon's LP sold enough copies to chart on *Billboard*'s Top 100 Albums.

Though *Muscle Beach Party* was a hit and made money, the producers realized that the musclemen were a one-shot gimmick. Harvey Lembeck and his motorcycle crew were brought back for the next beach movie, *Bikini Beach* (1964).

After appearing in *Muscle Beach Party*, Lupus, still using the moniker of Rock Stevens, journeyed to Italy to appear in a string of peplum films for AIP including *Hercules and the Tyrants of Babylon* (1964) and *Goliath at the Conquest of Damascus*

(1964). Using his real name, Lupus played the popular role of IMF agent Willy Armitage in the Emmy Award–winning spy series *Mission: Impossible* from 1966 to 1973. When the series came to an end, Lupus disrobed for the pages of *Playgirl* magazine as its Man of the Month for April 1974. He still is active in show business today.

Chet Yorton would go on to play another muscle man in the Southern California satire, *Don't Make Waves* (1967) while Dan Haggerty subsequently appeared in a number of biker movies including *Angels Die Hard* (1970), the gay-themed *The Pink Angels* (1971), and *Bury Me an Angel* (1971). He found fame on television as the lead in *The Life and Times of Grizzly Adams* (1977–78). Haggerty has worked nonstop ever since and his most recent films include *An Ordinary Killer* (2002) and *Wild Michigan* (2004).

While in Hollywood, sexy Amedee Chabot was cast in only minor roles such as a Slaygirl in *Murderers' Row* (1966) starring Dean Martin. She then was lured to Mexico where she starred in over 20 films between 1966 and 1969 usually cast as the sexy, dumb American blonde. Despite the fact that her dialogue was dubbed into Spanish, Chabot reigned briefly as one of Mexico's most popular actresses. In the late sixties, Chabot returned to the U.S. and today she is a very successful real estate agent in Southern California.

Memorable Lines

(Jack Fanny signs the contract prepared by S. Z. Matts giving Julie ownership of his musclemen in exchange for a series of gyms to bear his name.)

S.Z. MATTS: "Jack, it's a pleasure doing business with a Fanny like you."

(Dee Dee catches Julie kissing Frankie.)

DEE DEE: "What's the matter, did you run out of musclemen?"

JULIE: "Oh no! It's just that he looks so sad, like a lost pup."

DEE DEE: "Then maybe you didn't notice his license."

JULIE: "I didn't even notice his leash."

Reviews

Boxoffice—"The two singing stars of *Beach Party* ... romp, sing, surf and twist through another entertaining comedy with music which is made-to-order for the teenage trade and family audiences."

Janet Graves, *Photoplay*—"Faster and livelier than *Beach Party*, it's a similar romp through cheerful nonsense, plentiful songs and youthful romantic carrying-on."

Edwin Miller, *Seventeen*—"Those lighthearted teen-agers of *Beach Party* are still twisting in the sand in this diverting sequel, which adds some zany complications."

New York Post—"*Muscle Beach Party* is the formula of before, plus a bevy of muscle men or beefcake boys. The IQ level of this entertainment is abysmal, being far below that of its predecessor. The true excitements of surfing, the valid beat of the new dances, and the intrinsic marvel of musculature brought to fantasy are so incredibly vulgarized in this picture that it can't miss with millions of morons."

James Powers, *The Hollywood Reporter*—"American International has a box-office weight-lifter, a Hercules hit, in *Muscle Beach Party*. The key ... is the script by Robert Dillon. His attitude is mildly satirical, sharp enough for the kids—who are very sharp—yet retaining a romantic flavor which the immature cynics want even though they may knock it."

Robert Salmaggi, *New York Herald Tribune*—"Well, strictly for teen-aged cats and jammers comes *Muscle Beach Party*, son of *Beach Party*. Throw in three or four songs by Avalon and Annette, a couple more by Dick Dale and Little Stevie Wonder, some frenetic shimmies by Candy Johnson and those attractive swimsuit babes, a few faked-in shots of some expert surfing and you've about got the picture."

Howard Thompson, *The New York Times*—"A twist-and-twitch musical film which stars Frankie Avalon and a tangle of vigorous young people with beautiful bodies and empty heads. If you can last through this you're a double-dyed stoic."

Awards and Nominations

Golden Laurel Award: "Top Female Musical Performance"—Annette Funicello, fifth place

Harvard Lampoon Movie Worst Award: "Worst Movie"—tenth place

Harvard Lampoon Movie Worst Award: "The Uncrossed Heart" (for the least promising young performer)—Annette Funicello

⋆ **10** ⋆

Pajama Party (1964)

When the Pajama Tops Meet the Pajama
Bottoms someone's gonna have a Fit!

Fun: ⋆⋆⋆½
Surfing: ⋆
Boy watching: ⋆⋆⋆
Girl watching: ⋆⋆⋆⋆
Music: ⋆⋆⋆⋆
Scenery: ⋆⋆⋆

Release date: November 11, 1964. Running time: 85m. Box office gross: Not available. DVD release: MGM Home Entertainment (December 18, 2001).

Tommy Kirk (*Go-Go*), Annette Funicello (*Connie*), Elsa Lanchester (*Aunt Wendy*), Harvey Lembeck (*Eric Von Zipper*), Jesse White (*J. Sinister Hulk*), Jody McCrea (*Big Lunk*), Ben Lessy (*Fleegle*), Donna Loren (*Vikki*), Susan Hart (*Jilda*), Bobbi Shaw (*Helga*), Cheryl Sweeten (*Francine*), Candy Johnson (*Candy*), Luree Holmes (*Perfume Girl*), Buster Keaton (*Chief Rotten Eagle*), Dorothy Lamour (*Head Saleslady*), Andy Romano, Linda Rogers, Alan Fife, Alberta Nelson, Jerry Brutsche, Bob Harvey (*Rat Pack*), Renie Riano (*Maid*), Joi Holmes (*Topless Bathing Suit Model*), Kerry Kollmar (*Little Boy*). Joan Neel, Patricia O'Reilly, Marion Kildany, Linda Opie, Mary Hughes, Patti Chandler, Laura Nicholson, Linda Benson, Carey Foster, Stacey Maxwell, Teri Hope, Margo Mehling, Diane Bond, Keva Page, Toni Basil, Kay Sutton, Connie Ducharme, Joyce Nizzari, Jeri Blender, Leslie Wenner (*The Pajama Girls*), Ray Atkinson, Frank Alesia, Ned Wynn, Ronnie Rondell, Howard Curtis, Johnny Fain, Mike Nader, Rick Newton, Guy Hemric, Ed Garner, Frank Montiforte, Ronnie David, Gus Trikonis, Bob Payne, Roger Bacon, Ronnie Dayton (*The Pajama Boys*). Guest stars: The Nooney Rickett 4. Not credited: Don Rickles (*Big Bang*), Frankie Avalon (*Socum*), Teri Garr, Dorothy Kilgallen and Lori Williams.

American-International Pictures. *Producers*: James H. Nicholson and Samuel Z. Arkoff. *Co-Producer*: Anthony Carras. *Directed by*: Don Weis. *Written by*: Louis M. Heyward. *Production Supervisor*: Joe Wonder. *Director of Photography*: Floyd Crosby, A.S.C. *Music Score by*: Les Baxter. *Musical Supervisor*: Al Simms. *Choreography by*: David Winters. *Art Director*: Daniel Haller. *Film Editors*: Fred Feitshans, A.C.E., Eve Newman. *Music Editor*: Milton Lustig. *Sound Editor*: James Nelson. *Costuming and Designing by*: Marjorie Corso. *Custom Tailoring by*: Maurice Langer of Beverly Hills. *Swimsuits by*: DeWeese Designs of California. Ah Men's Sportswear, Hollywood, *Designed by*: Jerry Furlow. *Men's and Women's Pajamas by*: Weldon. *Titles and Photographic Special Effects*: Butler-Glouner. *Special Effects*: Roger George, Joe Zonar. *Assistant Director*: Clark Paylow. *Properties*: Karl Brainard. *Sound*: Philip Mitchell. *Makeup*: Bob Dawn. *Hairdresser*: Eve Newing. *Set Decorator*: Harry Reif. *Costruction Coordinator*: Russ Hahn. *Production Assistant*: Jack Cash.

Motorcycle Coordinator: George Dockstader. *Stunts:* Jesse Wayne. Filmed in Panavision and Pathecolor.

Songs by Guy Hemric and Jerry Styner: "Pajama Party" performed by Annette Funicello. "Beach Ball" performed by the Nooney Rickett 4. "It's That Kind of Day" performed by Annette Funicello. "There Has to Be a Reason" performed by Annette Funicello and Tommy Kirk. "Where Did I Go Wrong?" performed by Dorothy Lamour. "Among the Young" performed by Donna Loren. "Stuffed Animal" performed by Annette Funicello.

The first offshoot in the *Beach Party* series, *Pajama Party* is, despite Frankie Avalon's absence, arguably the second best of the AIP productions after *Beach Blanket Bingo.* A Martian is sent to Earth to pave the way for an invasion. He mixes with the beach crowd and winds up tangling with a biker gang, an Indian, a Swedish bombshell and some con artists while wooing Annette. Admittedly, the plot is inane, but *Pajama Party* is handsomely produced and features the most energetic production numbers of the series thanks to choreographer David Winters. Surfing fans should stay away, though—there's nary a surfboard in sight.

Pajama Party greatly differs from the previous beach party movies as most of the outdoor action moves poolside, volleyball replaces surfing as the teenagers' sport of choice and Tommy Kirk takes over from Frankie as Annette's love interest. Along with *How to Stuff a Wild Bikini,* it comes closest to being a musical in the truest sense of the word as most of the songs move the plot along and are not just interjected without any apparent reason. Composer Les Baxter's bouncy score is perhaps his best in the series. Also David Winters' choreography enhances the musical numbers, especially the beach volleyball dance scene in the sand with a bikini-clad Toni Basil gyrating front and center. Annette proves she has all the right moves with the *Hullabaloo*-inspired poolside dance number "Pajama Party" where PJ–clad boys and girls surround her. Donna Loren delivers the best vocal performance as she belts out "Among the Young" backed by the Nooney Rickett 4 on a stage with a wiggling Susan Hart and gyrating Candy Johnson adding to the scene. The one wrong note is the maudlin ballad "Stuffed Animal" performed by Annette wearing a nightgown, as she cuddles a teddy bear, explaining about why she'd choose her stuffed friend over a boy.

Lots of poolside and beach scenes equal more flesh, making this film a treat for girl watchers but a letdown for fans of the male physique. Knockouts Susan Hart and Bobbi Shaw make their AIP debuts and are worth the price of admission alone. Sultry Hart does a slow shimmy (in contrast to Candy Johnson's frenetic shaking), making volcanoes erupt and flowers wilt. Shaw's cleavage is on display throughout, especially in her fur-trimmed bikini. Annette is back with a fancy hairdo but the same demure swimsuits though they are much more attractive than the ridiculous ones donned by Donna Loren. The vocalist does have a figure but you wouldn't know it from these movies. The film is also peppered with shots of such bikini-clad lovelies as Mary Hughes, Patti Chandler, Linda Opie and Teri Garr. For boy watchers there is the usual cadre of lean surfers and some handsome new faces as background dancers, particularly the dark-haired Speedo-clad boy who dances with Toni Basil in the sand. Tommy Kirk is boyishly cute and is a good contrast to manly Jody McCrea.

Brisk direction, lush photography, Annette at her peak, perky performances, Don Rickles' wisecracks, Buster Keaton's clowning and some rockin' songs makes this *Pajama Party* well worth crashing.

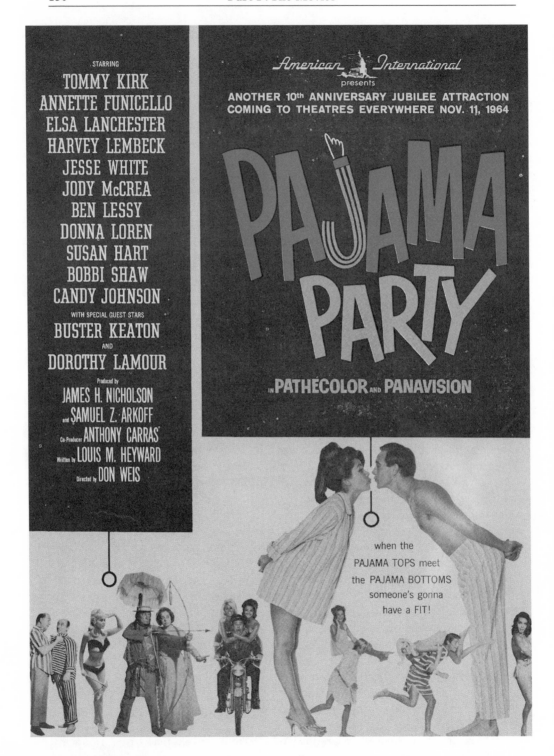

Trade ad for *Pajama Party* (AIP, 1964) starring Tommy Kirk and Annette Funicello.

The Story

Strapping Big Lunk, his fetching girlfriend Connie and a gaggle of beach boys and bikini girls crash his Aunt Wendy's Malibu pad for a pool party. Unbeknownst to them, they are being observed by two Martian leaders, Socum and Big Bang, who are planning to take over Earth. To facilitate their plot, they intend to send Go Go, "a big goof off," to prepare the way for the invasion. As the kids dance and swim, Connie tries to get romantic with her dumb boyfriend. But the lug only has volleyball on his mind. Meanwhile, in the house next door, J. Sinister Hulk and his accident-prone associate Fleegle are hatching a plot to steal Aunt Wendy's fortune, hidden somewhere in her home. Hulk plans to use Swedish blonde bombshell Helga to find the location of the loot by enticing Wendy's nephew Big Lunk to reveal it. The only catch is that Helga does not speak English; a bumbling Indian named Chief Rotten Eagle is the only person who can communicate with her.

Go Go arrives and makes contact with Aunt Wendy but she doesn't believe that he is a Martian. She allows him to stay in the house and Go Go tries various ways to convince her that he is telling the truth. Thinking he is a daft magician, she nicknames him George and gives him a pair of swim trunks so she can intro-duce him to her teenage friends. While Big Lunk and the gang are playing beach volleyball, they are watched intently by Eric Von Zipper and his motorcycle gang. Irked that they are getting "footprints all over my sand," Von Zipper leads his gang to chase them off. However, the inept gang leader rides straight into the volleyball net and is hurled into the ocean. The Rats and Mice vow revenge.

Before heading to the beach, George walks into the bathroom and finds Helga bathing as Chief Rotten Eagle has brought the buxom blonde into the wrong house. This leads to a wild chase between the three. Wendy comes across a forlorn Con-nie on the sand. To get Big Lunk's attention, Wendy introduces her to George and suggests that the young man accompany Connie to her dress shop later. Connie accepts even though she thinks he is a kook with his claims of being from Mars and being pursued by an Indian and a Swede. Back at the house, Connie uses George to try to make Big Lunk jealous, but the dumb boy is oblivious. When George takes a shine to Big Lunk's red baseball cap, the miffed Connie takes it from his head and gives it to her escort.

There is a fashion show in progress at the dress shop as Chief Rotten Eagle arrives with Helga and gets into a perfume fight with a salesgirl. Go Go enters with Connie and is spotted by Chief Rotten Eagle (whose orders were to find the nephew wearing a "goofy broad-billed red baseball cap"), mistaking him for Big Lunk. Von Zipper has followed them and he too thinks Go Go is Big Lunk. He swipes his cap as Helga emerges from the dressing room in her fur bikini and begins kissing Von Zipper. The mixups end when Big Lunk arrives to retrieve his baseball cap and car. As he gets into his convertible, the Indian and an amorous Helga jump in. They drive off with Von Zipper and his gang in pursuit. Big Lunk is able to shake the ragtag group of cyclists.

That night Big Lunk goes out on a date with Helga, unaware that J. Sinister Hulk has wired the girl and instructed her to find out where his Aunt Wendy's money is hidden. But the clueless beach boy has no idea. Hulk comes up with one last scheme. He decides to throw a pajama party at his house and asks Aunt Wendy to help chaperone. Then with her house deserted, they can search for her fortune. The Nooney Rickett 4 gets the party swinging and then Connie sings with the band before getting dunked into the pool. Fleegle goofs up Hulk's plot when he invites Von Zipper and his gang to pretend to be Hulk's clean-cut all–American nieces and nephews. The pajama party turns into a melee with punches being thrown and bodies pushed into the water. Von Zipper and gang have the upper hand until Go Go intervenes with his laser wand, sending the motorcycle delinquents fleeing. He then rounds up Big Lunk to go to Aunt Wendy's after Helga telepathically reveals Hulk's plan to fleece the rich widow. Following a chase through the house, the inept bandits hide in the closet where Go Go teleports the trio to Mars. Aunt Wendy's money is saved, Big Lunk gets Helga and Go Go decides to remain on Earth with Connie.

Behind-the-Scenes

Pajama Party was AIP's first offshoot from the *Beach Party* series. Not only was there a new leading man in Tommy Kirk but Don Weis was brought in as director and the renowned David Winters was hired to choreograph the musical numbers. The film introduced some new faces to AIP who would become part of its stable of actors. A press release was issued in June of 1964 that new AIP contract player Deborah Walley had been signed for a role in *Pajama Party* but she did not appear in it.

When the movie began production on August 10, 1964, at Producers Studio (location footage was shot in Malibu), the working title of the film was *The Maid and the Martian*. A title song by Guy Hemric and Jerry Styner was penned and recorded by Annette. When the film's name was changed to *Pajama Party*, the song was dropped.

Producers James H. Nicholson and Samuel Z. Arkoff hired Tommy Kirk, a Walt Disney contractee, to take over leading man duties from Frankie Avalon, who cameos as a Martian leader. Kirk had previously worked with Annette Funicello on *The Mickey Mouse Club* and co-starred with her in *The Shaggy Dog* (1959) and *The Misadventures of Merlin Jones* (1964). It was their successful on-screen chemistry which probably caught Nicholson and Arkoff's eye. It was also known that Annette liked working with Tommy Kirk very much so the producers knew their leading lady would feel comfortable with him. Co-star Jody McCrea found Kirk to be "a real good guy with a nice personality."

With much hype, pretty blonde Cheryl Sweeten, a former Miss Teenage Colorado in 1962 and Miss Colorado in 1963, made her film debut in *Pajama Party* along with ten year-old Kerry Kollmar, the youngest son of columnist Dorothy Kilgallen and Richard Kollmar. *Pajama Party* was the first AIP movie for soon-to-be regulars Buster Keaton, Susan Hart and buxom-blonde Bobbi Shaw, who became Keaton's comic foil. James H. Nicholson discovered Hart who was co-starring in the Columbia Pictures beach movie *Ride the Wild Surf*. He had noticed her while screening the film's dailies. He wanted to sign the brunette beauty to a contract but Mike Frankovitch, who was the head of Columbia at that time, had high hopes for her as well and had Hart under a six-month option. During about the fifth month of her term with Columbia, Susan went over to AIP to meet with Nicholson. Not only did she land a contract with AIP, she eventually would wed the boss.

Nicholson liked populating the beach movies with movie veterans such as Vincent Price, Peter Lorre and Keenan Wynn. *Pajama Party* employed the talents of comedian Jesse White, Elsa Lanchester of *Bride of Frankenstein* fame and silent film star Buster Keaton, whose career had long been in decline due to his alcoholism. However, film buffs in the sixties had rediscovered his genius and Nicholson offered the comic a chance to prove to the world that he still had the gift. Keaton rose to the occasion and stole the show. His silent perfume fight with Nicholson's daughter Luree Holmes was particularly hilarious and he is perhaps the first screen actor to use the phrase "cowabunga."

Though film historians feel that Keaton was working well beneath his talents in *Pajama Party* and the other beach movies to follow, this was the only work offered him. Not even television had approached him. According to Sam Arkoff in *Filmfax* magazine, Keaton was forever grateful to have the chance to work in feature films again after being "kind of laid aside." Director Don Weis dubbed Keaton "a genius" in *Filmfax* and revealed that Keaton created all his physical gags himself. Weis remarked, "Here was a 65-year-old man doing all these things he shouldn't be doing. He couldn't use a stunt man because they were all funny gags that only he could do—the falls and things that were his kind of style."

Surprisingly, most of the young cast did not know anything about Buster Keaton but the few who did were in awe. Jody McCrea exclaims, "It was a privilege and honor to work with Buster Keaton. He had over 60 years in the business by then. I didn't talk to him much off-camera because I wanted to give him his space." Tommy Kirk had a different perspective on the comic and opined in *Scarlet Street* magazine, "Well, I remember feeling embarrassed because this great, great star was running around in an Indian suit doing low-comedy in this schlock 'B' film."

Recalling Keaton's on-screen partner Bobbi Shaw, Jody McCrea says, "I remember that nobody introduced us. Our first scene together was a kissing scene. They just told me to get into this rumble seat of this car with her. We kissed a lot before I officially met her. That was quite an experience since Bobbi was built like every girl would have liked to be. They put her in this mink bikini and physically she was a super girl. Just looking at her made me feel good."

Don Weis was an excellent choice to helm *Pajama Party*. He directed a number of movies during the early fifties, including the musical *I Love Melvin* (1953) with Donald O'Connor and Debbie Reynolds, and segued to television by mid-decade. Concentrating on directing in episodic television, he was able to slip in a few features including *The Gene Krupa Story* (1959) and *Looking for Love* (1964), both featuring young cast members and musical numbers. He had the perfect combination of musical experience and fast-paced shooting skills to bring *Pajama Party* to the big screen. Jody McCrea remarks, "Don was a good director. He was fun to work with as well. We shot the pool scenes up at this house in Holmby Hills. He liked having the cast get wet."

To give the dance sequences a fresh look, David Winters was recruited as choreographer. Acting, singing and dancing since he was a child, Winters found fame on Broadway playing Baby John in *West Side Story* in 1957. When the acclaimed musical became a motion picture, Winters was hired to play A-Rab. During the sixties he accepted intermittent acting roles but concentrated on choreography, most notably in a number of Elvis movies and television's *Hullabaloo*. He also toiled as a dance instructor and would hire his students for the films he was working on. Among the dance troupe of Pajama Boys and Girls was Gus Trikonis who played a Shark in *West Side Story*, became a film director and was once married to Goldie Hawn; Lori Williams, who would go on to star in Russ Meyer's *Faster, Pussycat! Kill! Kill!* (1966); Teri Garr, who became a regular on *The Sonny and Cher Comedy Hour* in the seventies and received an Academy Award nomination in the eighties for *Tootsie*; and Toni Basil, who had a No. 1 hit record in 1982 with "Mickey."

The producers requested that Winters incorporate into the film a cleaned-up version of a new dance called the Swim, which an AIP executive had seen being performed in a San Francisco club. In *Drive-in Dream Girls* Lori Williams remarked that Winters and she were friends and spent time together. "Professionally, he was very proficient and very tough. He didn't want the dance sequences in the movies he was working on to look choreographed. All the dancing and gyrating was choreographed loosely to give it a natural style."

With Winters' professional dancers front-and-center in *Pajama Party*, the usual roster of AIP beach boys and girls (including twisting machine Candy Johnson) were pushed farther into the background than usual. Susan Hart, a newcomer to AIP at that time, remarks, "I remember that David Winters was a real fun guy and he was very talented but I think he told me to just do what I did in *Ride the Wild Surf*. Toni Basil was double-jointed and just a fabulous, creative dancer."

Winters' dance sequences greatly enlivened *Pajama Party*'s musical numbers, especially Dorothy Lamour's song "Where Did I Go Wrong?" written especially for her. As young women emerge to model the latest fashions in sleep wear, casual wear (that's Teri Garr in the tennis outfit), formal wear and swim wear, they start gyrating wildly as the tempo picks up, horrifying Lamour, who sings about the old days.

Director Weis credits the film's success and the fact that it stands a cut above some of the other beach movies to David Winters, whom he described to Robert Nott in *Filmfax* as being "a marvelous choreographer." Weis added, "He upgraded the dancing so that it wasn't just tits and ass."

The house band hired for *Pajama Party* was a Los Angeles–based combo called the Nooney Rickett 4, consisting of Rickett, Kent Dunbar, Tommy Funks and Tommy Poole. Of all the rock groups that appeared in the AIP beach movies, none got as much screen time as the Nooney Rickett 4. With their sun-bleached blonde hair, the guys had the perfect look for a beach movie but musically they never had a hit record to warrant such exposure.

By the time *Pajama Party* was released in late 1964, the beach party movies had become such a phenomenon that *Look* magazine did a cover story with a six-page spread on the movie and the series' popularity. It wasn't surprising to see Annette Funicello interviewed but the feature focused on the supporting players, particularly Jody McCrea, Patti Chandler, Mary Hughes, Meredith MacRae and Ed Garner (despite his lack of speaking lines in the movies). "I really didn't request to be a part of this," admits Garner matter-of-factly. "I had the opportunity but it just

Susan Hart as Jilda is the sexiest volleyball player on the beach in *Pajama Party* (AIP, 1964).

wasn't something I wanted. I did all the publicity as I was told to do but I never fought for lines because I felt somebody who really cared about it should have them. The studio mandated that all the contract players attend acting, speech and dance classes. I never really went to any of them. I know most of the gang did and were getting sold into the industry."

Jim Nicholson remarked in the *Look* piece that the formula of "comedy and music, lots of young people, plus established old-time performers" is what kept the audience coming back for more. He went on to comment, "We have without question the happiest company in Hollywood." However, outward appearances may have been deceiving.

After singing only in *Muscle Beach Party* and *Bikini Beach*, Donna Loren had her first speaking role as Vikki but was not that thrilled with working in the beach movies. She griped in *The Saturday Evening Post*, "It's always the same sort of dialogue, never anything fresh or new. I go for something more grabbing, more significant." Background beach boy Ned Wynn, the grandson of Keenan Wynn, too wasn't very happy working in *Pajama Party* due to the bullying of Jody McCrea. Wynn remarked in his autobiography, "Jody was a barely conscious individual, a young giant whose repertoire of jokes consisted mainly of walking up behind people, grabbing their ear, twisting it and then standing there with their ear gripped in his hand." According to Wynn, McCrea then would lead his victim (usually

Wynn) around the set by the ear. McCrea responds, "I felt a kind of kinship with Ned because he was a third generation actor. I didn't know that's how he perceived me. It could be that he was envious because I had a much bigger role than he."

Tommy Kirk also had his problems working on *Pajama Party*, all due to Elsa Lanchester. He remarked in *Scarlet Street*, "She was a bitch to me. I don't know; I guess I rubbed her the wrong way and she rubbed me the wrong way. I don't know why it happened."

Kirk had better luck with co-star Annette Funicello, whom he had known for years. They worked well together and got along nicely. Kirk described his co-star, the consummate professional, in *Filmfax* magazine as being "a perfect lady, perfect manners, very careful about her career." Annette proved her professionalism, as she was not particularly fond of the beach because "the sea air made my hair frizzy." But she never let her disdain affect her job.

Pajama Party is one of the rare occasions where Annette actually gets her bouffant wet after being tossed into the pool during the closing number. On the set, Annette stayed to herself and didn't mingle much with the beach boys and girls. She had a close-knit group of friends including Shelley Fabares, Donna Corcoran and Luree Holmes. Tommy Kirk said in *Filmfax*, "We've always been friendly, but never been friends." Susan Hart recalls, "Annette Funicello was very quiet. She was very close to Frankie Avalon and his double, an extremely personable guy by the name of Ronnie Dayton. I remain friends with Ronnie to this day. Annette had a small group of people that she was friendly and close to, as most of us do. I remember her being upbeat and courteous, not unfriendly."

"I didn't fraternize with Annette at all," says Jody McCrea. "She always had many lines to memorize or songs to sing that I just watched her. If she said hello, I'd reply hello back. I knew my place and stayed in it. I was a featured performer— a little star. Annette and Frankie were the *big* stars. On *Pajama Party* we did relate to each other a bit more but it still wasn't what I'd call friends. Annette was about to wed our agent Jack Gilardi at this time so she was preoccupied."

Salli Sachse remarked in *Fantasy Femmes of Sixties Cinema*, "Annette was such a straight girl—a good Italian Catholic. Because we grew up on the beach, a lot of us thought we were so cool compared to Frankie and Annette. I remember that on one movie we were filming some beach scenes late in the afternoon. It was really chilly and we were fighting the light. Wrapped in terry cloth robes, a group of us huddled together to keep warm. Karl the prop man handed us a bottle of brandy. We were surprised when Annette took a couple of swigs. She got a bit tipsy and was clowning around. It was the only time I ever saw her let herself go wild."

Aron Kincaid remembers fondly, "I had taken Annette out a couple of times before I did *Ski Party*. I took her to a Hollywood premiere and some other thing. She was just the most natural, shy, sweet girl you could imagine. I'm sure she has been all along. But I didn't have any contact with Annette the entire time I was at AIP. We appeared in two movies but we were never in a single scene together. She had her two best girlfriends, Luree Holmes and Shelley Fabares, and she had her family. Annette didn't fit in with the beach girls. Salli Sachse, Patti Chandler and the rest of them were part of that beach and Hollywood crowd. Annette wasn't that way. She was more evening Vespers and confession."

Continuing with its trend to keep the audience in its seats for the film's end credits, *Pajama Party* featured Susan Hart wearing tasseled bikinis of various colors, a nightgown-clad Elsa Lanchester and Buster Keaton in his Indian costume dancing around to an instrumental version of "It's That Kind of Day."

After three movies, AIP finally was able to get matters in hand and produce a soundtrack album released through Buena Vista Records. However, it was not an easy task. Since Annette Funicello was under contract to Buena Vista, all the songs, including Donna Loren's "Among the Young," were re-recorded by Annette except "Where Did I Go Wrong" sung by Dorothy Lamour, which was included on the LP. All the background music played by the Nooney Rickett 4 in the film was replaced by Tutti Camarata's versions. Though the album charted, it did not produce any hit singles.

Tommy Kirk would go on to co-star with Annette Funicello one more time but not for AIP. Walt Disney reunited them in *The Monkey's Uncle* (1965), the sequel to *The Misadventures of Merlin Jones.*

While *Pajama Party* introduced a crop of new young stars to the teenage audience, this was the swan song for "Perpetual Motion Girl" Candy Johnson and Rat Pack member Linda Rogers, who was replaced in later movies by Myrna Ross. Johnson never appeared in another movie again, abandoned her lounge act and is rumored to be residing in Palm Springs married to a golf pro. Titian-haired Linda Rogers turned up in the *Beach Party* clones *Winter a-Go-Go* (1965) and *Wild Wild Winter* (1965) as well as the Elvis Presley musical *Tickle Me* (1966) before her film career sputtered to an end.

Great things were expected from Cheryl Sweeten as theater owners named her one of the Stars of Tomorrow of 1964. Alas, tomorrow never came for Sweeten, at least acting-wise, as this was her sole movie. The fragile-looking beauty returned to college where she earned a Masters Degree in Psychology. *Pajama Party* was Kerry Kollmar's only film appearance as well. Today he holds a Black Belt in karate and is the founder of Martial Hearts, Inc., an organization committed to stopping violence against women and children.

Pajama Party was another hit for AIP and, according to *Boxoffice* magazine, was the top box office attraction in Chicago, Hartford, Memphis and Minneapolis the week it opened. It proved that if the movie stuck to the AIP patented formula, even without the combination of Frankie and Annette, it could still draw the teenagers to the theaters. *Pajama Party* paved the way for other AIP offshoots such as *Ski Party, Sergeant Deadhead* and *Dr. Goldfoot and the Bikini Machine.*

Memorable Lines

(Martian leader Socum summons Go-Go to lead the Martian invasion of Earth and his First Officer, Big Bang, requests permission to leave before the inept Martian arrives.)

BIG BANG: It's not that I don't like him, *it's just I can't stand him!*

(Go-Go, introduced to Connie by Aunt Wendy on the beach, explains that he is holding a scrub brush because he walked in on a blonde woman in the bathtub and then was chased by an Indian while trying to return it to her.)

CONNIE (to Aunt Wendy): This kid is a kook!

AUNT WENDY: No, dear not a kook—a Martian.

CONNIE: *A Martian*!

AUNT WENDY: From Mars.

CONNIE: Both you birds belong in a clock.

Reviews

Boxoffice—"Lively, song-and-danced filled, light entertainment."

Mandel Herbstman, *The Film Daily*—"This one brims with youthful vitality, glows with trim young bodies and resounds to song and dance."

Dale Munroe, *The Citizen-News*—"Tasteless and lacking in originality."

James Powers, *The Hollywood Reporter*—"It is frantic and it is often rather brainless, but it is fun and it is the kind of thing youngsters want. The dance numbers are in some ways the best things about this particular film."

John L. Scott, *Los Angeles Times*—"AIP's stock company puts on a frantic, funny show."

Variety—"As before there's strong accent on pulchritude and near-nudity via brief attire. Miss Funicello ... displays an engaging presence and registers solidly. Kirk likewise shows class and Miss Lanchester projects a rather zany character nicely. Bobbi Shaw ... is a standout as the sexy lure White uses to learn where the money is secreted, and Donna Loren, Susan Hart and Candy Johnson romp through for further distaff interest."

⋆ 11 ⋆

Ride the Wild Surf (1964)

*Ride the wild surf in Hawaii with the world's "wild water" champs
... who ride and romance Waimea Bay ... the Big Surf Daddy of them all!*

Fun: ⋆⋆⋆⋆
Surfing: ⋆⋆⋆⋆
Boy watching: ⋆⋆⋆⋆
Girl watching: ⋆⋆⋆
Music: ⋆⋆
Scenery: ⋆⋆⋆⋆

Release date: August 5, 1964. Running time: 101m. Box office gross: $1.4 million.
DVD release: Columbia TriStar Home Video (January 4, 2005).

Fabian (*Jody Wallis*), Shelley Fabares (*Brie Matthews*), Tab Hunter (*Steamer Lane*), Barbara Eden (*Augie Poole*), Peter Brown (*Chase Colton*), Anthony Hayes (*Frank Decker*), Susan Hart (*Lily*), James Mitchum (*Eskimo*), Catherine McLeod (*Mrs. Kilua*), Murray Rose (*Swag*), Roger Davis (*Charlie*), Robert Kenneally (*Russ*), Paul Tremaine (*Vic*), Alan LeBuse (*Phil*), John Kennell (*TV Commentator*), David Cadiente (*Ally*), Yanqui Chang (*Mr. Chin*).

A Jana Film Enterprise Picture. A Columbia Pictures release. *Written and Produced by*: Jo and Art Napoleon. *Directed by*: Don Taylor. *Music*: Stu Phillips. *Director of Photography*: Joseph Biroc, A.S.C. *Art Director*: Edward S. Haworth. *Film Editors*: Eda Warren, A.C.E., Howard A. Smith, A.C.E. *Surfboards by*: Phil. *Hawaiian Fashions by*: Sun Fashions of Hawaii, Ltd. *Sports and Swimwear by*: Catalina. *Assistant Director*: R. Robert Rosenbaum. *Makeup Supervisor*: Ben Lane. *Hair Styles by*: Virginia Jones. *Sound Supervisor*: Charles J. Rice. *Sound*: Don R. Rush. Eastman Color by Pathe.

"Ride the Wild Surf" by Jan Berry, Brian Wilson and Roger Christian, performed by Jan and Dean over the closing credits.

Ride the Wild Surf stands head and shoulders above all the sixties beach party movies. Three California surfers come to Hawaii to surf the huge waves of the North Shore and in the process mature and find romance. It makes an honorable effort to portray surfers and the sport of surfing sincerely and to showcase the big waves of the North Shore of Hawaii. There are no singing surfers or goofy motorcycle gang members in this film as it opens with a narrator explaining why young men from all over the world come to Hawaii to surf. Then the wave action takes over and never lets up, making *Ride the Wild Surf* the best Hollywood surf movie of the sixties. Kudos to an excellent cast, stunning photography by Joseph Biroc and one of the all-time best pop surf songs "Ride the Wild Surf," sung by Jan and Dean over the closing credits.

The incredible surfing action is draped around a storyline that is thin, but peppered with some sharp and hip dialogue, and all the actors play their roles believably. Peter Brown and Barbara Eden are the most interesting couple as Eden's perky lovelorn tomboy tries to melt the veneer off of Brown's uptight college boy. Susan Hart and Tab Hunter make the most handsome duo though Shelley Fabares with her blonde hair and the usually shirtless Fabian give them a run for the money. Jim Mitchum, who is the splitting image of his dad, makes a quietly menacing heavy. The movie is a smorgasbord of flesh as the boys are all tanned and muscled and the girls are curvaceous and bikini-clad. There's someone for every taste—from dark and adorable Fabian to blonde and lean Peter Brown, from sultry and curvaceous Susan Hart to perky and buxom Barbara Eden.

Ride the Wild Surf really excels showing what it takes to be a top-notch surfer and to challenge the big waves of Hawaii. Joseph Biroc expertly filmed real surfers (including Mickey Dora, Greg Noll and Butch Van Artsdalen) challenging the big waves at Banzai Pipeline, Sunset Beach and Haleiwa. This footage is spread generously throughout the film, climaxing with big wave thrills at the "King of the Mountain" contest at Waimea Bay. It is by far the most exciting and best surfing sequences in any Hollywood surf movie of the sixties. However, some of the scenes of the actors on their boards were obviously filmed in a studio tank where one minute the water is like a sheet of glass and then all of a sudden it cuts to huge swells that come out of nowhere.

The shots around the island of Oahu are stunningly picturesque, especially the scenes at Waimea Falls. The movie captures the beauty of the islands almost as spectacularly as *Blue Hawaii*. Trying to distance itself from the AIP beach films, *Ride the Wild Surf* has no musical guest acts—only Jan and Dean singing the title song over the end credits but surfing is the film's major attraction.

The Story

Pretty boy Jody Wallis, handsome Steamer Lane and staid blue-blood Chase Colton travel from Southern California to the palm-fringed north shore of Oahu to surf the world's biggest waves in the King of the Mountain competition. As the guys hit the beach at Haleiwa, Jody and Chase run into fellow Malibu surfer Russ and his friends Swag and Ally. Steamer meanwhile catches the eye of a beautiful half–Hawaiian girl on horseback but she quickly gallops away. Later that night, at a luau thrown by Ally, a chestnut-haired Black Belt named Augie Poole entertains the crowd by grappling with a bigger Hawaiian and then Chase. Defeated by the pretty girl, the stodgy surfer skulks off in embarrassment. While Augie tries to make amends with Chase, Jody's enthusiasm and cockiness riles current King of the Mountain champion Eskimo, who challenges him to a harpoon-shooting contest. Jody catches the eye of a disapproving blonde named Brie who turns out to be a friend of Augie's. Brie reluctantly agrees to go for a walk with Jody. She becomes even more disenchanted with him when she learns that he is a college dropout and surf bum.

The next day, Jody does especially well surfing the big waves, impressing surfboard shaper Phil and some surf photographers. Steamer finds out that the girl on the horse is named Lily Kilua and pays her a visit. Lily is pleased to see Steamer and leads her mother to believe that he is from the local mechanic's garage, sent to repair their tractor. The sultry girl agrees to meet him later but wants to keep it a secret from her overprotective mother, who despises surfers ever since her husband left to ride the waves in Bora Bora and never came back.

While Chase accompanies Augie to Mr. Chin's House of Everythin' to collect her fireworks order for New Year's Eve, Jody and Brie are caught in a downpour while exploring Waimea Falls. They take shelter in a hut where the disillusioned Jody shares with Brie the story of his dysfunctional family. With Brie's words of encouragement, he agrees to give school another try when he returns to the States. But for now his concentration is on surfing. He and the others hit all the hot spots like the Banzai Pipeline and Makaha in preparation for the big waves of Waimea Bay. The surf is rough and there are numerous wipeouts. It is clear that Jody is going to be Eskimo's fiercest competitor for the King of the Mountain title but a severe wipeout rattles the young surfer.

Lily accompanies Steamer to the New Year's Eve party. Chase's over-protectiveness gets the best of him and he empties the gunpowder from Augie's gigantic rocket. He feels foolish after an enraged Augie tells him that the rocket was supposed to spell out their initials in a heart for all of Hawaii to see. A drunken Chase then heads up to Waimea Falls where, according to Hawaiian legend, the big waves at Waimea Bay will commence after an 80-foot dive into the rocky pool by a surfer. Jody, Brie and Augie plead with Chase not to risk his life. As the crowd spurs him on, the surf horn goes off announcing the start of the big swells. Augie is relieved but Chase takes the dive anyway to prove to her that he can be impulsive too. Back at the luau, Steamer proposes to Lily and she accepts. They then share the news with Mrs. Kilua, who refuses to accept the marriage.

The surfers hit the ocean as the huge waves (some 20 to 30 feet high) come rolling in at Waimea Bay. While the rest of the surfers test their abilities against the mammoth waves, Jody just sits in the lineup too nervous to surf. But when Chase wipes out due to a cracked rib he sustained from his jump, Jody takes off to rescue his friend. The injured Chase drops out of the contest but Jody regains his confidence and returns to the lineup. Steamer's surfboard splits in half, knocking him out of the competition, but his disappointment quickly turns to happiness when Lily runs up to him with her mother, who is prepared to condone the marriage and Steamer's love of surfing. Jody rides the wild surf against the taciturn Eskimo as the last remaining surfers. They each keep wiping out and Eskimo tries to convince Jody to call it a draw. The determined youth refuses. Eskimo quits and returns to the shore. Alone, Jody finds the strength and courage within to ride a 40-foot wave, winning the title of King of the Mountain and Brie as well.

Behind-the-Scenes

During late 1963 into early 1964, producers Art and Jo Napoleon traveled to Hawaii with cinematographer Joseph Biroc to film a group of surfers riding the waves at Haleiwa, Sunset Beach, Pipeline and Waimea Bay for a two-and-a-half-month period. Hired to ride the big waves were many of the top surfers at that time, including Phil Edwards, Mike Hynson, Rusty Miller, Butch Van Artsdalen and Mickey Dora. This was Malibu surfer Dora's first encounter with the giant waves of Hawaii's North Shore of Oahu. He was used as the surf riding double for the film's main character, Jody.

Greg "Da Bull" Noll, a staple at the North Shore, was surfing at the same time the Napoleons were shooting. Since he was captured on film catching so many waves wearing his signature black and white striped trunks, the character of Eskimo was created around him. He was invited to audition for the role back in Hollywood but lost out to Jim Mitchum. However, his surfing footage remained in the film. Many years later, Noll bemoaned in the surfing documentary *Riding Giants* (2004) that the film "wanted to make me puke."

A number of the surfers who participated in *Ride the Wild Surf* say that winter had some of

Fabian and Peter Brown as California surfing buddies out to test the big waves on Hawaii's North Shore in *Ride the Wild Surf* (Columbia, 1964) (*courtesy the Billy Rose Theatre Collection, The New York Public Library for the Performing Arts, Astor, Lenox and Tilden Foundations*).

the biggest waves and best sets they ever encountered in Waimea and Sunset Beach. Joseph Biroc caught all the impressive surfing action using top-of-the line 35mm camera equipment placed on the shoreline. There were no cameramen positioned in the ocean. This hampered the production from shooting close-ups of the surfers shooting the curl or wiping out, as most of this footage is filmed in long shots. Also, from that distance the danger of surfing big waves was not conveyed. But this may have also been done purposely so the audience would not readily notice the surfers doubling for the actors hired for the movie.

Regarding *Ride the Wild Surf*, Mickey Dora commented in *Surf Guide*, "We did something that had never been done before. Big-wave riding was filmed in 35mm. They were good people and really wanted to understand surfing ... to capture the atmosphere surrounding the many surfers who make the annual winter trip to the Islands to ride big waves." Used to the four-foot waves at Malibu, Dora admitted to being "psyched out" by the huge waves he had to surf on the North Shore. He began losing his hair and developed a stomach ulcer. Persevering, he conquered the waves for the camera—some of the best surfing scenes contained in a Hollywood surf movie at that time.

Returning to Hollywood, the Napoleons wrote the script around the surfing sequences, actually matching the bathing trunks worn by the actors to the surfers in the footage that they had. They pitched the idea to Columbia Pictures, which wanted to cash in on AIP's successful beach party movies. The couple was hired to produce the movie and Art was slated to direct. He had previously directed *Man on the Prowl* (1958) and *Too Much, Too Soon* (1958), the latter starring Dorothy Malone as Diana Barrymore. *The Hollywood Reporter* ran an item in January of 1964 that the film was going to be called *Surfing Wild* and that actor Glenn Corbett would headline the cast. But that never came to be.

To assure box office success, Columbia borrowed Fabian, a friendly rival of Frankie Avalon, from 20th Century–Fox to play Jody and hired the singing duo of Jan and Dean to make their film debuts as, respectively, Steamer and Chase. Fabian was one of a group of young crooners who found chart success in the late fifties while Elvis Presley was serving time in the military. He did not have much of a singing voice (which he readily admitted) but with his dark hair and eyes he projected a brooding quality that drove teenage girls crazy. His persona easily transferred to the big screen and Fabian was surprisingly good in his early films, most notably *Hound-Dog Man* (1959) with Carol Lynley and *North to Alaska* (1960) with John Wayne. He gave a mesmerizing performance as a psychotic teenager in a controversial episode of television's *Bus Stop*. Fabian had been AIP's first choice for *Beach Party* but the studio did not have the budget to pay Fox to loan him out. Columbia Pictures, however, did and worked out an agreement to have the heartthrob play the film's lead surfer.

Singing duo Jan and Dean had just hit the top of the charts with "Surf City," the first surf song to go to No. 1. Riding high, Columbia Pictures thought to capitalize on their popularity by casting the handsome pair as surfers in *Ride the Wild Surf*. However, before filming began it was revealed that Dean Torrence had been lending money to school chum Barry Keenan, who used it to finance the botched kidnapping of Frank Sinatra, Jr. Due to the notoriety and bad press, Columbia pressured the singing duo to withdraw from the movie. However, Jan and Dean were still able to record the title tune, which was sung over the end credits. "Ride the Wild Surf" was released as a single and climbed to No. 16 on the pop charts. Fifties teen heartthrob Tab Hunter, whose career was in decline in 1963, and popular television star Peter Brown, who had just wrapped up four seasons on the western *Lawman*, were then recruited to take over the roles vacated by the popular singing duo.

Record producer Lou Adler had arranged for Jan and Dean to be part of *Ride the Wild Surf*. He was also instrumental in getting his new bride Shelley Fabares the female lead. The pretty brunette had just exited the hit sitcom *The Donna Reed Show*, which made her a star amongst the teenage set. "Leaving *The Donna Reed Show* was one of the most difficult decisions I ever made in my life," confessed Fabares in *Outré* magazine. "We really were like a family on the show. It took me a year to make up my mind because I was so happy there. But I decided to leave the show mainly because I had been working all of my life. I was 19 and I was about to get married in real life to Lou Adler. And I felt I needed some time to be sort of myself. It was incredibly painful but I felt it was the right thing to do at that time."

When Shelley showed up on the Columbia lot for her interview for *Ride the Wild Surf*, she was now sporting platinum blonde hair to try to change her teen queen image and to give her a sexier look. The studio loved it, which was a good thing for Fabares, but not for co-star Barbara Eden as the roundelay of hair coloring continued with Eden being forced to dye her hair an auburn-brown. Always the trouper, Eden proved to be a good sport about it even though at this point in time, the former 20th Century–Fox blonde contract player had appeared in far more movies than Fabares. Among her film credits were *From the Terrace* (1960), *All Hands on Deck*, *Voyage to the Bottom of the Sea* (both 1961) and *7 Faces of Dr. Lao* (1963).

The third female in the cast was dark-haired Susan Hart, who auditioned and won the role of half-Hawaiian Lily. Her only film credits prior to this were the female lead in the B-monster movie *The Slime People* (1963) and minor roles in *A Global Affair* (1964) and *For Those Who Think Young* (1964). Susan had to darken her hair for this role to look more like a native of the island. Tab Hunter's hair was also darkened while Peter Brown had to lighten his. "The reason I had to go blonde was to match up with the guy who surfed as my character," says Brown. "I not only had to match him with the hair color but with the swim trunks he had on."

Others in the cast included handsome Australian Olympic champion swimmer Murray Rose and, as the film's heavy, Jim Mitchum, the son of actor Robert Mitchum. The spitting image of his father, Jim inherited his rugged looks but not his versatile acting prowess. Hence, Jim was usually cast as a military man, cowboy, villain or hard-boiled detective. Mitchum made his official film debut playing his father's younger brother in *Thunder Road* (1958). Other supporting roles followed in two 1959 Mamie Van Doren films, *The Beat Generation* and *Girls' Town*, and the Western *Young Guns of Texas* (1963).

Before filming officially began, Susan Hart, Peter Brown and Mitchum went over to Hawaii three to six weeks before the rest of the cast and crew. Hart recalls, "The producers sent me to Hawaii to learn to ride a horse. First I was trained on a pony and then I worked my way up to a decent-size horse. Every day the trainer had me out practicing in the cane fields learning to ride. Eventually, I became fairly competent. When we finally were ready to film the scene, they brought in this huge horse that Charlton Heston rode in the film *Diamond Head*. They dressed me in white shark-skinned pants and they oiled the horse down pretty good to make him look beautiful. But there was no way I could stay on the horse. I kept sliding right off. They ended up taping me onto the horse with double-face tape. To get me off, they actually had to peel me off of it."

Brown and Mitchum went to Hawaii early for other reasons. Though they were hired to play surfers, neither one of them knew a thing about the sport. "They took Jim and me out to Malibu to teach us to surf," recalls Brown. "I had done a little bit of surfing—mostly body surfing but not board surfing. I remember we were out there in February and it was freezing. Jim and I just could not stay in the water so we called the studio and asked when they were going to go to Hawaii. We were told in about a month and that they already had rented houses on the North Shore for the cast and crew. I told them, 'Jim and I want to go over now so we can hire a Hawaiian surf instructor. I've already researched it and the guy I want is named Rabbit Kekai.* We'll occupy one of the houses so we can learn to surf and we'll be ready when you get there.' That's what we did. By the time the company got to Hawaii, Jim and I could surf. We started in Honolulu, then worked our way to Sunset Beach, Waimea and then Pipeline. I'm not saying we surfed 30-foot waves—we did not. But we were certainly capable of picking up a wave outside and riding it in."

Fabian and Hunter were not so skilled. According to Brown, "I don't think they became as proficient with it as we did. I really liked Fabian as a person but he couldn't comb his hair and walk at the same time. He was the most uncoordinated guy. I think he went through about five rental cars while we were over there."

When filming of *Ride the Wild Surf* began, the cast and crew were housed in specially built homes situated on knolls overlooking the shore. Mishaps and delays quickly began happening. Shelley Fabares notes that this may have been avoided if the producers had listened to one of the locals. "He told somebody in our company that we should get the whole production blessed because we were filming on sacred burial grounds. Somebody thought it was a joke and let it go but some terrible things wound up happening on this movie. We shut down for a few weeks after Art Napoleon was let go from the film along with his wife. Then a little girl who was the daughter of someone connected to the film died. While production was halted until the new director came aboard, a high priest was brought in to bless the grounds and things went fairly smoothly after that."

Studio politics may have lent a hand in Art Napoleon's termination from *Ride the Wild Surf* but a very unhappy cast and crew were the catalyst for his being let go. Peter Brown comments, "I don't really like to badmouth anyone in the industry but there was bad stuff happening on the set all the way down to the food that they were providing for us, which you wouldn't give to your dog. It got to a point that Jim Mitchum and I would drive into the city on our lunch break. They'd asked where we were going and we'd reply, 'We're getting something to eat.' The AD would say that there were box lunches but we'd tell him, 'You eat it.' Sometimes we'd be late getting back and they would piss and moan. I was the star of my own television show at that point and I didn't have to take their bullshit. They just weren't treating us well. There were so many complaints from so many people in every echelon that it got back to the studio. Columbia sent some executives to investigate and they wound up firing Art. I don't know if it was Columbia's pinching pennies or whose responsibility that was but it shouldn't have been the director's to feed the cast and crew. But you never know how those things work."

Without a director, Columbia closed the movie down for a few weeks but kept the cast and crew on payroll until a replacement was found for Napoleon. The actors were not bothered in the least, especially Peter Brown. "You don't mind sitting around in Hawaii," he exclaims. "I had a girlfriend in town and I had Barbara Eden hanging around. She was delightful to work with. We'd go surfing and swimming. A friend of mine lived in Honolulu and she was in Hong Kong so she said I could use her place. I had a house on the North Shore and an apartment in Honolulu. I was doing just fine!"

*A protégé of Duke Kahanamoku, Kekai, now in his eighties, still teaches surfing on Waikiki Beach today.

Actor-turned-director Don Taylor was hired to take over for Napoleon. As an actor, Taylor appeared in a number of impressive films such as *The Human Comedy* (1943), *Winged Victory* (1944), *The Naked City* (1948), *Battleground* (1949) and *Father of the Bride* (1950) before going behind the camera in the mid-fifties. Though he directed many television shows including *Alfred Hitchcock Presents, M-Squad, Dr. Kildare* and *The Dick Powell Theatre,* his only film credit was the comedy *Everything's Ducky* (1961) starring Buddy Hackett and Mickey Rooney. Despite his inexperience in moviemaking, Taylor did an excellent job injecting his own ideas and vision into this film, which was created by someone else. Peter Brown opines, "I think the fact that the story holds up well had a lot to do with Don Taylor coming in and making those scenes work. He was great to have as a director because he was once an actor. But it didn't seem to me that he had any surfing experience."

With Taylor in place as the new director, *Ride the Wild Surf* resumed production only to close down for a short period yet again. Shelley Fabares recalls, "We were told when we first arrived that if a siren went off, it meant there was a tsunami approaching. They said it was just like your air raid sirens on the mainland. One day I was in the makeup hut getting my hair bleached and we got a phone call that said we would have to evacuate because there was a tidal wave on the way. I had all this purple bleach all over my head and the hair stylist quickly rinsed it off. I then called out to Barbara Eden and Susan Hart—we shared a house together—and told them to pack our things because we had to evacuate. We loaded up this car and raced out of there but the sirens still had not gone off. We went in to what was our commissary and the three of us were shocked that nobody was doing anything. Some guys on the crew said, 'Oh, nothing is going to happen.' All of a sudden the siren went off and, literally, people were jumping out of the windows—we were on ground level—trying to get back to their places. We all evacuated up to this huge mountain. One of the locals came over to me where I was standing which was very high up and said, 'See how the mountain goes straight down from here? This is where the tidal wave of 1944 stopped.' It washed everything below away. It turned out that this was the huge earthquake of 1964 that almost split Alaska in half. This tidal wave was heading straight for Hawaii but somewhere around the Aleutian Islands it split and went around the backside. We all ended up okay but it was very scary."

With all the false starts and delays, it was a good thing the actors enjoyed working with each other. Fabares remarked, "It was my first time working with Fabian and he was very nice—just a sweet fellow. All the guys were terrific. I had a great time with Barbara Eden and Susan Hart, whom I shared a house with. They were fun." Susan Hart returns the compliment and says, "I had a wonderful time working and living with Shelley Fabares and Barbara Eden during the course of the shoot. Tab Hunter, Catherine McLeod and I used to play chess a lot between takes on the beach. We spent quite a bit of time together. Tab was one of those special people you meet in your lifetime and never forget. There is a real sweetness about him and I had a great time working with him. I think Tab and I liked each other as people, and it showed on the screen—at least, this is what I prefer to remember."

The guys seemed to get along as well but the camaraderie that developed between the actresses for the most part did not evolve amongst the actors. Peter

Brown comments, "There was a friendship and a mutual respect between Fabian, Tab Hunter and myself, which is always helpful. I admired their professionalism. They came to work on time, knew their lines and knew how to hit their marks. Working with actors that don't cause you any grief is always a pleasure. I became friendlier with Jim Mitchum. He played an asshole in the movie but he is a sweetheart of a guy. I know his brother also. They are terrific people."

With all the major surfing sequences already filmed by Art Napoleon, director Don Taylor was responsible for the scenes on land and for the shots of the actors on their boards in the ocean before catching a wave. Unfortunately for the film, a lot of this was not shot in the ocean but a studio tank back on the Columbia lot, which is why the water is so flat. Most of the closeups of the actors surfing were shot in front of the blue screen at the studio. Peter Brown observes,

In *Ride the Wild Surf* (Columbia, 1964), opposites attract as Barbara Eden's impetuous tomboy is drawn to Peter Brown's uptight blue-blood surfer.

"I don't think the editing process was very good, in particular where they matched the surfing footage with the actors in the water. I think they could have done a lot better with the footage that they had at their disposal. But I don't know how much time Don Taylor had to look at the existing footage that Art Napoleon shot of the surfers and then try to set up shots."

However, per Peter Brown, there were a few scenes where the actors had to do some real surfing and had some scary moments in the surf. "I pearled a couple of times," says Peter. "That's what they call it when you get too far forward on the nose of the board and it dips into the water, throwing you off. You have to stay under long enough to make sure that board hasn't flipped up and is not going to come down on top of your head when you surface." Another mishap involved Murray Rose. While trying to ride the big waves in Haleiwa, he wiped out and lost two teeth when his board struck him in the mouth.

Peter Brown's most harrowing moment was when he had to climb up the cliff at Waimea Falls and jump into the lagoon. He recounts, "I made the climb up there and that was severe enough. It was easier for me to jump off than to climb down. I actually did, but they did not use that shot." Nobody seems to remember who actually took the dive for Brown but it was most likely one of the surfers hired by Art Napoleon who hung around to watch the filming of the movie.

Ride the Wild Surf was released to most of the U.S. in August of 1964 but for some unknown reason did not play theaters in New York City until that December. Most of the reviews were positive because it tried to take a serious look at surfers and the sport. Also, the surfing footage was far superior to the surfing scenes in the AIP beach party movies. The surfing press, always critical of Hollywood's surf and beach movies, still found fault with *Ride the Wild Surf.* For instance, *Surfing* magazine asked, "How is it that whenever the stars are wiped out and come to the surface, the board is always there?" But they all agreed that the stunt surfing by some of the world's top surfers was excellent.

In an unusual move, ads for *Ride the Wild Surf* included a testimonial from pro football player Frank Gifford about the film's authenticity. In these spots, Gifford exclaims, "See the spills and thrills the champ surfers take in *Ride the Wild Surf.* It packs as big a wallop as anything I've ever run across on the football field!" Not using a top surfer to appeal to the surfing community was more proof that Hollywood didn't understand or just didn't care to get approval from surfers whose lifestyles they were exploiting for profit.

Shelley Fabares would go on to star opposite Elvis Presley in three musicals, including *Girl Happy* (1965). Barbara Eden of course found fame in a bottle on television's *I Dream of Jeannie.* Susan Hart would sign a contract with AIP and appear in a few of their beach films.

Fabian played one more teen heartthrob part in the comedy *Dear Brigitte* (1965) opposite Gidget #3, Cindy Carol, before trying to toughen up his screen image. He tackled racecar driver and hardened criminal roles in such exploitation fare as *Fireball 500* (1966), *Thunder Alley* (1967), *The Wild Racers* (1968), *The Devil's 8* (1969) and *A Bullet for Pretty Boy* (1971). Actress Quinn O'Hara, who had a relationship with Fabian in 1963, opines, "Fabian was never appreciated as an actor. He gave some very good dramatic performances. Unfortunately, that was against his 'image' at the time and I feel ultimately that was what did him in." To reenergize his acting career Fabian posed nude in the pages of *Playgirl* magazine and made one last attempt for big screen stardom with the awful *Bonnie and Clyde*–inspired gangster film *Little Laura and Big John* (1973). The rest of the seventies and eighties found Fabian, now Fabian Forte, working in episodic television and made-for-television movies. Still active today, Fabian tours the country with fellow fifties crooners Frankie Avalon and Bobby Rydell as the Golden Boys.

Tab Hunter's career floundered after starring in *Ride the Wild Surf.* The likes of *War-Gods of the Deep* (1965) and the awful comedy *Birds Do It* (1966), playing second fiddle to Soupy Sales, drove the sexy actor to Spain and Italy for Westerns of dubious merit. He made a comeback in the U.S. during the mid-seventies when he replaced Philip Burns as George Shumway on television's *Mary Hartman, Mary Hartman.* A favorite of filmmaker John Waters, Hunter starred opposite 300-pound female impersonator Divine in *Polyester* (1981) and in Paul Bartel's *Lust in the Dust* (1985). In between, due to the nostalgia craze for the fifties and sixties, Hunter was cast as a high school teacher in *Grease 2* (1982). Most of these later roles had Hunter parodying his former movie star image. Tab made his last appearance on the big screen in *Dark Horse* (1992) with Ed Begley, Jr., and Mimi Rogers.

Perennial supporting actor Jim Mitchum was able to graduate to lead roles in the late sixties but it was in a slew of low-budget European productions. In between, he appeared in *Two-Lane Blacktop* (1971), *Moonrunners* (1975), *Code Name: Zebra* (1984) and *Hollywood Cop* (1988). His last known credit was playing a major in *Fatal Mission* (1990) starring Peter Fonda.

Columbia gave Murray Rose the big press build-up and called him "one of the best bets for stardom in a long time." Rose, however, chose to concentrate on working as a television sports commentator for NBC over acting though he did play a supporting role in *Ice Station Zebra* (1968). In 2003, he returned to the big screen in a cameo role as a reporter in *Swimming Upstream*, the inspirational true story of Australian swimming champion Tony Fingleton.

Memorable Lines

(A drunken Chase has just announced to the crowd that he is going to jump off the cliff at Waimea Falls.)

FRIEND OF AUGIE'S: He's not really going to do it, is he, Augie?

AUGIE: Of course not! He's got too much sense. *I think*!?!

Reviews

Kathleen Carroll, *New York Daily News*—"That certain madness, which pits bronzed young men and their flimsy-looking boards against the mightiest waves, has been an endless source of teen movies lately. *Ride the Wild Surf* ... does more justice to the sport of surfing than most of these efforts."

Motion Picture Exhibitor—"This entry offers action on the high surf, romance on the beach, colorful atmosphere, a yarn that holds interest fairly well, neat performances by attractive youngsters, and good direction and production."

Dale Munroe, *The Citizen-News*—"The lovely scenic vistas coupled with some of the most spectacular surfing photography ever put on celluloid makes *Wild Surf* an excellent outdoor family film."

James Powers, *The Hollywood Reporter*—"The Jo and Art Napoleon production has a good cast for marquee value, and some of the best surfing footage ever seen in a commercial film. The story is weak; it lacks variety and development."

Robert Salmaggi, *New York Herald Tribune*—"*Ride the Wild Surf* is, in a seashell, an adult variation on those 'beach party' clambakes that have brought another studio merry moolah. The surf sequences are dandy, well photographed, and easily provide the film's most absorbing moments."

Kevin Thomas, *Los Angeles Times*—"*Ride the Wild Surf* skims along fine at sea but is snagged by script clichés on shore. It has an attractive, healthy-looking cast, some exciting shots of expert surfing and a lot of lush Hawaiian scenery in color."

Variety—"A new background is provided for this latest youth market entry, the high waves of Hawaii and the wild surf riders. In a sense, the Jo and Art Napoleon production, lushly and sometimes sensationally filmed in the Islands, is a sports subject with a thin story line woven around its core. Surfing scenes are adroitly handled and furnish a new slant on a sport, which will be new to most inland audiences."

Awards and Nominations

Golden Laurel Award: "New Faces, Female"—Shelley Fabares, eighth place

Photoplay Gold Medal Award nomination: "Favorite Female Star"—Shelley Fabares

Photoplay Gold Medal Award nomination: "Favorite Male Star"—Peter Brown

Photoplay Gold Medal Award nomination: "Most Promising New Star—Female"—Susan Hart

⋆ 12 ⋆

Surf Party (1964)

*It's what happens when boys take to
the sea ... and the girls take to the boys!!!*

Fun: ⋆⋆
Surfing: ⋆⋆⋆
Boy watching: ⋆
Girl watching: ⋆⋆
Music: ⋆⋆⋆
Scenery: ⋆⋆

Release date: March 1964. Running time: 68m. Box office gross: Not available.
DVD release: Not as of January 2005.

Bobby Vinton (*Len Marshal*), Patricia Morrow (*Terry Wells*), Jackie DeShannon (*Junior Griffith*), Kenny Miller (*Milo Talbot*), Lory Patrick (*Sylvia Dempster*), Richard Crane (*Sgt. Wayne Neal*), Jerry Summers (*Skeet Wells*), The Astronauts (*Themselves*), The Routers (*Themselves*), Martha Stewart (*Pauline Lowell*), Lloyd Kino, Mickey Dora, Johnny Fain, Pam Colbert, Donna Russell (*Beach Boys and Girls*).

An Associated Producers, Inc., production. A 20th Century–Fox release. *Produced and Directed by*: Maury Dexter. *Associate Producer*: "By" Dunham. *Written by*: Harry Spalding. *Music*: Jimmie Haskell. *Director of Photography*: Kay Norton. *Supervising Film Editor*: Jodie Copelan, A.C.E. *Production Manager*: Harold E. Knox. *Assistant Director*: Harold E. Knox. *Property Master*: Jockey Liebgold. *Set Decorator*: Harry Reif. *Wardrobe*: George Herrington. *Makeup*: Ted Coodley. *Sound*: William Bernds. *Script Supervisor*: Dixie McCoy. Filmed in b/w.

"If I Were an Artist" by "By" Dunham and Bobby Beverly, performed by Bobby Vinton. "Glory Wave" by "By" Dunham and Jimmie Haskell, performed by Jackie DeShannon. "Never Comin' Back" by "By" Dunham and Jimmie Haskell, performed by Jackie DeShannon, Patricia Morrow and Lory Patrick. "Pearly Shells" by Loni Kai, "By" Dunham and Jericho Brown, performed by Kenny Miller. "That's What Love Is" by "By" Dunham and Bobby Beverly, performed by Patricia Morrow. "Fire Water" by "By" Dunham and Jimmie Haskell, performed by the Astronauts. "Crack Up" by "By" Dunham and Jimmie Haskell, performed by the Routers. "Surf Party" by "By" Dunham and Bobby Beverly, performed by the Astronauts. "Great White Water" by "By" Dunham and Jimmie Haskell.

Surf Party is a melodramatic look at the surfing craze and Malibu surfers in particular. It is also an obvious rip-off of *Beach Party* without the zaniness. There is some neat surfing footage featuring pros like Mickey Dora and Johnny Fain but the flat black-and-white photography doesn't do it justice. The female leads all do well but Bobby Vinton and Kenny Miller fail miserably trying to pass themselves off as surfers.

Harry Spalding's script about three gals who come to Malibu to learn to surf and to locate the brother of one of the girls is a bit overwrought at times, but he gets praise for injecting surfer slang and tips on how to surf. Too bad producer-director Maury Dexter couldn't get anybody other than Bobby Vinton to deliver the lines. If AIP had hired him for *Beach Party*, there wouldn't have been a series of films. Worse than Vinton is the pudgy Kenny Miller, who was way too long in the tooth to be playing a 20-year-old. However, Miller has a pleasant singing voice and does well with his solo. Only Jerry Summers as the leader of the renegade surfing crew makes an impression though we never once see him shoot the curl but just hit the sheets first with his older woman benefactor and then with his sister's girlfriend.

Dexter had better luck with his female cast. Patricia Morrow sports a bitchin' flip hairdo and makes a nice heroine. Unlike Annette, she even gets her bathing suit wet! Jackie DeShannon plays the dippy blonde to good effect while dark-haired Lory Patrick gives a sympathetic performance as the good girl who goes all the way only to regret her actions. The only downside with these gals is that they wear one-piece or very modest two-piece swimsuits. There's not a bikini wearer in the bunch!

The music in *Surf Party* is a mixed lot because it throws in different styles (even Gospel!) to try to please everyone. The best songs are the ones delivered by the Astronauts, who aggressively try to attain a surf reverb sound, and the Routers with "Crack Up." Maury Dexter gets kudos for his surfing footage and actually gets shots of the actors out in the ocean on their boards. Rather than use the dreaded blue screen for close-ups, Dexter put Kenny Miller and the others on a speedboat and filmed them as if they were surfing. Though this approach isn't always convincing, it is more creative than putting the actors in a tank with a fake backdrop. Dexter also gets praise for getting Mickey Dora out of the water and giving the surfer more screen time than in any of his other pictures.

With a bigger budget and more convincing male leads, *Surf Party* could have been considered one of the best Hollywood surf movies of the time, instead of just a middling cheap knockoff of *Beach Party*.

The Story

Three Arizona coeds load up a trailer and drive to Malibu Beach for summer vacation. Terry Wells is a pretty, straightforward brunette who is looking for her brother Skeet, once a promising football player who now resides on the Coast. A head injury curtailed his career and Terry has only heard from him once since he moved away a few years ago. The two friends that accompany her on her search are rich girl Sylvia Dempster and naive blonde tomboy Junior Griffith.

The girls arrive at the house where Terry thinks Skeet lives but he is with an older woman and doesn't answer the door. Seeing a letter addressed to him in the mailbox, they camp on the beach and sing about never leaving Southern California. The next morning, Len Marshall, who owns a surf shop, awakes the girls and informs them that it is illegal to park on the beach and that they should leave before the police come by. However, Sgt. Wayne Neal of the Beach Patrol arrives before they have a chance to depart and orders them off the beach. After moving to a trailer park, the girls head to Len's surf shop to rent surfboards and to inquire about surfing lessons. Len personally takes the trio to the beach to instruct them in the sport. In the process, he becomes interested in Terry. While teaching the girls the basics, Len literally drags his friend Milo out of the ocean when he notices that he is attempting to surf through the pilings of a nearby pier. The young surfer is angry because that is his initiation to become a member of the surfing group called the Lodge. Milo's rage abates when he notices Junior. While chatting with him, the kooky blonde learns where Skeet hangs out.

That night, Milo takes the girls to a beer joint where the members of the Lodge are meeting. The bartender won't let Milo in but seats the girls when he learns that Terry is Skeet's sister. Her wayward brother finally arrives and promptly falls for Sylvia. The next day he takes the smitten girl surfing. Determined to join Skeet's group, Milo tries to surf the pier but suffers a terrible wipeout. Len pulls him from the water and sends for an ambulance.

Sgt. Neal drops in at Len's shop and tells him that it is likely that the beach will be off-limits to surfers because of the unruly antics of Lodge members. Enraged that he may lose his business, Len goes to Skeet's house, where a party is in progress, and gets into a fight with him. The fisticuffs come to a halt when Terry screams that Skeet still suffers from a head injury. Embarrassed, Skeet throws everyone but Sylvia out. Len and Terry argue about Skeet. Terry leaves in a huff and heads back to the trailer alone. Sylvia doesn't come home until five in the morning after spending the night with Skeet. Terry announces to Sylvia and Junior that they are returning to Arizona the next day. Both girls refuse to go. Sylvia is in love with Skeet and Junior wants to be there for Milo when he is released from the hospital.

The following night, Skeet throws another party. It is interrupted by Pauline Lowell, a fortysomething redhead who finds Skeet in his bedroom with Sylvia. She reveals to everyone that she has been keeping Skeet and tells him to get out. Skeet is once again shamed in front of his surfer friends and Sylvia. The next day, Terry comes and helps her crestfallen brother pack. After she leaves, Skeet says goodbye to Sylvia and goes to the beach to watch the girls surf. Sgt. Neal offers to give him a lift to the bus depot since his sports car belonged to Pauline. Down on the shore, Terry, Len, Junior and Milo, with his arm in a sling, are enjoying themselves. Even a heartbroken Sylvia manages a weak smile. The girls then pack up their trailer and return to Arizona with their memories of summer in the land of the surf.

Behind-the-Scenes

Producer-director Maury Dexter was a former actor who turned to producing and directing in the late fifties. He worked mainly for producer Bob Lippert, who signed a deal with 20th Century–Fox to provide low-budget second features through Associated Producers, Inc., to be paired with Fox's bigger films. Dexter began assisting API head Bill Magginetti and took over from him in 1961. The company churned out a number of low-budget Westerns, war films, horror flicks and

Lobby card for *Surf Party* (20th Century–Fox, 1964) featuring Patricia Morrow, Bobby Vinton, Jackie DeShannon and Kenny Miller.

teenage musicals between 1960 and 1965 including *Walk Tall* (1960), *Air Patrol* (1962), *Young Guns of Texas* (1963) and *The Young Swingers* (1964).

The first actor cast in *Surf Party* was blonde Kenny Miller, even though he was 32 years old at the time! Miller had known Maury Dexter since 1952 when Kenny was drafted into the Army and Dexter turned out to be a sergeant at his basic training camp. The two developed a close friendship when Dexter learned that the new recruit was an actor. A few years later, Dexter offered Miller featured roles in *Rockabilly Baby* (1957) and *The Little Shepherd of Kingdom Come* (1959). *Surf Party* was their third and final film together.

Because of his kinship with Dexter, Miller had no qualms about introducing his friend, singer Jackie DeShannon, to the producer in hopes that he would cast her opposite him. The pretty blonde singer and songwriter had just toured the U.S. as one of the opening acts for the Beatles. The savvy producer knew talent when he saw it and immediately hired the perky blonde to play the tomboyish Junior Griffith. "I was very excited to get the role because it was an *acting* job," says Jackie. "It may have not been Bergman or Truffaut—I saw every film they ever made because foreign films were my high at that time—but I was hungry to learn everything about acting and you do learn from everybody that you work with."

It was well-known through Hollywood that singer Bobby Vinton wanted to act. The "Polish Prince," as his loyal fans fondly dubbed him, had two huge hits,

"Roses Are Red (My Love)" and "Blue Velvet," prior to his acting debut. Vinton's agent pushed mightily for the crooner to star in *Beach Party* at AIP. When he did not get that part (the producer felt that, being of Italian heritage, Frankie Avalon was a better match for Annette Funicello), Dexter swooped in to offer him the lead in *Surf Party* at a salary of $750 per week. Though his screen persona was lacking, Vinton turned out to be very agreeable on the set. "He was great to work with," exclaims DeShannon. "Bobby was a very funny guy. We all got along well." Surprisingly, despite his success as a vocalist compared to the rest of the cast, Vinton only sings one song (to his surfboards) in the movie.

Former child actress Patricia Morrow was hired to make her film debut playing opposite Vinton. The role of the jilted rich girl went to actress Lory Patrick, who was a regular on the Western series *Tales of Wells Fargo* (1961–62) and had appeared on many other television shows. Jerry Summers, who had worked with Maury Dexter previously on two other movies (including *The Little Shepherd of Kingdom Come*) and starred in the syndicated series *The Beachcomber*, was cast as Morrow's missing brother, the catalyst for the movie's plot.

Aping AIP, the producers hired the cinematographer and set decorator from *Beach Party* and peppered the film with rock acts. *Surf Party* was the first film appearance of the Astronauts, a Midwestern surf group that performed two instrumentals. The Routers were made up of mostly black studio musicians. However, the members seen on screen were white extras hired to fake playing the instruments and lip-synch the songs.

Because Fox wanted to make as accurate a surfing movie as possible, expert surfers Mickey Dora and Johnny Fain, who worked at AIP, were hired to double for the non-surfing cast. But the game actors on the movie tried as best they could. *Surf Party* was Jackie DeShannon's first time on a surfboard. "It was hysterical," says Jackie, laughing. "I went to get up on the board during the shoot and my top fell down!"

Rather than use a blue screen for Kenny Miller's surfing scenes, the actor was filmed standing on the back of a speedboat since he could not surf. Writing in his autobiography, Miller recounted, "They didn't photograph my feet in those scenes because I was spread-legged on the back of the speedboat, trying desperately not to fall off. The cameraman and lighting guy were in front, and I was on the back with the pier in the background and the wind and the spray whipping me around. I fell off about 20 times while shooting those scenes because I didn't have anything on which to balance."

Not expecting to fill the role of Junior with a bona fide singer, Dexter commissioned his composer and co-producer "By" Dunham to write a song for Jackie DeShannon. She remarks, "The song 'Glory Wave' was great for me because I am from Kentucky and have gospel roots. There were a few lyric changes but the music was the same. It was like being in the church choir for me."

The budget for *Surf Party* was so minuscule that the movie was shot in black-and-white as compared to the splashy Pathecolor opuses coming from AIP. To some beach movie fans this is a turn-off, but not to Jackie DeShannon. "In a way, *Surf Party* stands out because it *was* shot in black-and-white. When you think how these movies were produced with so little money, I was so proud that it was done in black-and-white. For me that was the best thing about the movie. I'm not into slick—I never have been. A lot of the other beach movies were done cheaply in color but they had much more of a budget for marketing. But that doesn't necessarily mean that they were better."

Unlike AIP, 20th Century–Fox was savvy enough to capitalize on *Surf Party* by releasing a soundtrack LP featuring the songs from the movie. Unfortunately, Bobby Vinton was signed to Epic Records, which forbade him from participating, so his song was re-recorded by Kenny Miller.

Fox was very happy with *Surf Party* since the film made money at the box office and its soundtrack album sold decently. The studio then commissioned Dexter to begin production immediately on a second low-budget beach movie to be called *Wild on the Beach*.

Regarding *Surf Party*, Bobby Vinton remarked in *Seventeen*, "It's not great but at least I have an idea of what it's like to be in front of the camera." He continued recording after the release of this beach movie but an acting career never materialized for this vocalist. Vinton didn't have the screen presence of Frankie Avalon (or even that of Fabian) to sustain a movie career in B-movies, let alone major films. According to a 1965 article in *Life* magazine, the frustrated actor-wannabe sued his manager for $300,000 "for failing to deliver on a promise to make him a movie star." Vinton remained off the big screen for the rest of the decade. Surprisingly, he popped up in two John Wayne Westerns, *Big Jake* (1971) and *The Train Robbers* (1973). In 1975, he hosted his own syndicated variety series for a season. Wisely, the velvety-voiced crooner has concentrated solely on singing live on stage and still tours internationally today.

Patricia Morrow found semi-fame as good girl Rita Jacks, who snares rich Norman Harrington on television's *Peyton Place* (1965 to 1969). She reprised her popular role on the daytime soap *Return to Peyton Place* from 1972 to 1974 and in the television-movie *Peyton Place: The Next Generation* (1985).

In 1965, Jackie DeShannon had a Top Ten hit record with the Burt Bacharach–Hal David–penned song "What the World Needs Now Is Love." Her recording of it was so popular that she received the Teen Screen Award for Favorite Female Vocalist for 1965–66. Though DeShannon never returned to the beach party, she made one more film appearance in a teenage movie, the college campus musical *C'mon, Let's Live a Little* (1968) co-starring Bobby Vee. DeShannon scored another hit record in 1969 with "Put a Little Love in Your Heart." She continued recording in the seventies but never achieved the level of success she had in the previous decade. Still a prolific songwriter, her tunes were recorded by many artists, most memorably Kim Carnes, who went to No. 1 on the pop charts in 1981 with "Bette Davis Eyes," which won DeShannon a Grammy Award for Song of the Year. In 2000, DeShannon returned to the recording studio and released the CD *You Know Me* to critical acclaim.

Extremely popular with teenagers in the late fifties, Kenny Miller's career ran out of steam after the release of *Surf Party*. He made a comeback in the seventies with the awful crime film *Little Laura and Big John* (1973) with Fabian and Karen Black and the cheap horror movie *The Night Daniel Died* (1978), playing a lounge singer who meets a gruesome end. Today Miller, who is good buddies with Burt Reynolds, resides in Florida and recently co-authored his autobiography detailing his exploits in show business, *Kenny Miller: Surviving Teenage Werewolves, Puppet People and Hollywood*.

Memorable Lines

(Milo reveals to Junior that he knows Terry's brother Skeet, who is a member of the Lodge, a clan of surfers.)

JUNIOR: Do you belong?

MILO: One of the things you have to do is run the pier. But I'm practicing.

JUNIOR: Kind of messy if you miss.

Reviews

Boxoffice—"Mislabeled a comedy, this light drama with music is geared to the teenage craze for surfboard riding, with numerous musical numbers of jukebox caliber to add interest. Surfing scenes are interspersed with romantic ones...."

Kathleen Carroll, *New York Daily News*—"Even for the young of heart, the picture flounders, not in the surf, but in the silly affairs of its trite characters. Bobby Vinton plays the harmless hero who sings to his surfboard."

New York Post—"The surfing is strictly minor league, but then so are plot and characterizations. The leading girl, played by Patricia Morrow, is very pert. She looks at home on a beach, and so do the surfboards, and the fellows who stand on them. Mostly it's the music and dancers that swing."

David Rider, *Films and Filming*—"Want to see something sick? Go and see this and watch a lad with a fractured shoulder in a cast singing a pop song—and twisting too. That is about as low as this film sinks but it doesn't get very much higher either."

Robert Salmaggi, *New York Herald Tribune*—"*Surf Party* is another of those harmless little teen-time crackerjacks insisting that youth will be surfed, providing there's a big, wide wonderful ocean and lots of rocking, rolling music. There's the usual wide-eyed amateur-level acting, piddling plot, and babes in bikinis, all of which serves as window dressing for some half dozen songs served up in uninspired style."

Allen M. Widem, *Motion Picture Herald*—"Some of America's best known-and-respected young recording artists—Bobby Vinton et al.—move with suitable spiritedness against the background of California's sunshine splashed Malibu Beach during the competently-guided course of this latest Maury Dexter produced-and-directed effort...."

★ 13 ★

Beach Ball (1965)

Nothing bounces like Beach Ball!

Fun: ★★★½
Surfing: ★★
Boy watching: ★★★
Girl watching: ★★★★
Music: ★★★★
Scenery: ★★★

Release date: September 29, 1965. Running time: 83m. Box office gross: $1 million. DVD release: Not as of January 2005.

Edd Byrnes (*Dick Martin*), Chris Noel (*Susan*), Robert Logan (*Bango*), Aron Kincaid (*Jack*), Mikki Jamison (*Augusta*), Don Edmonds (*Bob*), Brenda Benet (*Samantha*), Gail Gilmore (*Deborah*), James Wellman (*Bernard Wolf*), Anna Lavelle (*Polly*), Dick Miller (*Police Officer #1*), Jack Bernardi (*Mr. Wilk*), Bill Sampson (*Announcer*), John Hyden (*Police Officer #2*), Rita D'Amico (*Wendy*). Also: Lee Krieger. Guest Stars: The Supremes, The Four Seasons, The Righteous Brothers, The Hondells and The Walker Brothers. Not credited: Bart Patton, Sid Haig, Ron Russell and Brian Cutler.

The Patton Co.–La Honda Service Production. A Paramount Pictures release. *Produced by*: Bart Patton. *Directed by*: Lennie Weinrib. *Screenplay by*: David Malcolm. *Associate Producer*: Stephanie Rothman. *Production Manager*: Peter Broadrick. *Assistant Director*: Gary Kurtz. *Production Coordinator*: Sharon Compton. *Director of Photography*: Floyd Crosby. *Film Editor*: Jack Woods. *Makeup*: Ted Coodley. *Sound*: Ryder Sound Services. *Girls' Beach Wear*: Rose Marie Reed. *Surfboards*: Phil of Downey. *Production Designer and Art Director*: Ray Storey. *Assistant Art Director*: Tracey Green. *Music*: Frank Wilson. Filmed in Technicolor.

"I Feel So Good," "Surfin' Shindig" and "Wigglin' Like You Tickled" by Chester Pipkin and Frank Wilson, lip-synced by the Wigglers. "We've Got Money" by Al Capps, lip-synced by the Wigglers. "Come On to the Beach Ball with Me" and "Surfer Boy" by Eddie Holland, Brian Holland and Lamonte Dozier, performed by the Supremes. "Dawn (Go Away)" by Bob Gaudio and Sandy Linzer, performed by the Four Seasons. "My Buddy Seat" by Gary Usher and Roger Christian, performed by the Hondells. "Baby, What You Want Me to Do" by Joe Reed, performed by the Righteous Brothers. "Doin' the Jerk" by Scott Engel, performed by the Walker Brothers. Uncredited: "Cycle Chase" by Mike Curb and Davie Allen, instrumental heard as background score.

Despite the drubbing it got from the critics and some beach movie fans, *Beach Ball* is arguably the breeziest and most enjoyable of the *Beach Party* clones. It is also the most blatant ripoff, throwing in everything from surfing, sky diving and hot

158

rodding to a battle-of-the-bands contest and the guys in drag to match the zaniness of the AIP beach movies. Four college dropouts try to con some nerdy girls at the student union to give them a student loan for tuition but in fact the money is needed to pay for their musical instruments. The gals get wise to their scheme and try to trick the guys into returning to school. The film works well because it is fast-paced, nicely photographed in color and has some funny moments, lots of beach scenes, a healthy-looking cast and an excellent roster of musical performers (most notably the Supremes, the Righteous Brothers and the Four Seasons) who are interspersed throughout the movie.

As for the cast, unlike Annette Funicello in the *Beach Party* movies or Noreen Corcoran in *The Girls on the Beach*, perky Chris Noel and the other gals are not afraid to show off their shapely figures in very revealing bikinis. Pretty blonde Anna Lavelle in particular dons the skimpiest swimsuits and has some funny moments as the guys' addled-brained beach groupie Polly. The movie boasts perhaps the most curvaceous set of lead actresses in any surf movie from the decade. For boy watchers, the guys sport nice physiques, particularly handsome Robert Logan and blonde Aron Kincaid, who gives a droll performance as ladies' man Jack. Edd Byrnes is

Beach Ball (Paramount, 1965) featured (*left to right*) Aron Kincaid, Don Edmonds and Robert Logan as the Wigglers with Edd Byrnes as their manager (*courtesy Aron Kincaid*).

definitely too long in the tooth to make a believable college guy but he does look good in his swim trunks.

Surfing is limited to the opening stock footage of surfers riding huge swells. (As with most beach party movies when the actors emerge from the ocean it is calm without a big wave in sight.) There are, however, plenty of scenes of the gang frolicking on the beach. A scene with the kids playing "Keep Away" with a football on the shore is nicely photographed and scored. The film's major asset is the music, from the catchy instrumental entitled "Cycle Chase" heard throughout to the songs lip-synched by Kincaid and the others (as the Wigglers) to all of the numbers performed by the rock acts. The standout is definitely seeing the Supremes singing "Come to the Beach Ball with Me" and "Surfer Boy." Though the Motown songwriters did not come close to capturing the authentic surf sound (hell, they were from Detroit and what did they know about surfing anyway?), the girls sing the catchy tunes well. Florence Ballard and Mary Wilson look great but Diana Ross is a fright with her chipped tooth and big beehive wig. Her close-ups are truly scarier than anything found in *The Horror of Party Beach*—another reason why *Beach Ball* is a must-see.

The Story

Four college dropouts live at the beach and have formed a musical group called the Wigglers. Surfer Dick is their manager. When payment is due on their musical instruments, he formulates a scheme to keep proprietor Mr. Wolf from retrieving his property so that guitarist Jack, drummer Bango and sax player Bob can win the upcoming music contest. Not believing the guys can raise the money in two days, Wolf decides to wait for it at their house. Jack enters a drag race while Bob and Bango try to borrow some cash from their scuba diving and sky diving friends. When they all come up empty, Dick cons brainy coed Susan into giving him a college loan to study tribal chants.

Impressed by Dick, the uptight blonde decides to deliver the good news and the check in person, accompanied by her equally square friends Augusta, Samantha and Deborah. Arriving at Dick's beach pad, the gals are appalled to come upon a wild party. Learning that she was deceived, Susan rips up the check and leaves in a huff with her friends in tow. Dick now has to come up with a new plan to get some dough. To keep Wolf at bay, Dick unleashes bikini girl Polly to distract the old geezer.

As members of the Dropout Rescue Squad, Susan and her friends decide to formulate a plan to convince the guys to return to school. To reach their goal, they take off their glasses, tease up their hair and don some hip clothes. As the guys deposit a sleeping pajama-clad Wolf onto the back of a convertible parked down the street, the gals drive by. The guys don't recognize them and invite the babes to the beach. The girls get more than they bargained for as Polly offers to loan them some bikinis. Dick quickly pairs up with Susan, Bango with Deborah, Bob with Samantha and Jack with Augusta. After much frolicking on the sandy shores of Santa Monica, the guys get down to business to win the contest. Susan gets Dick to contemplate using the remainder of their anticipated winnings to return to college.

While the guys try impressing the girls with tales of skydiving, undersea scuba diving and auto racing, an irate Mr. Wolf returns after being arrested for indecent exposure. To distract him, the guys begin singing and the bikini-clad Susan and the other gals start dancing. The next day, clad in his nightshirt, he once again is awakened and arrested by two police officers. The girls have by now fallen for their respective guys and formulate a plan to keep Wolf at bay and to get the guys accepted into the contest. They gas Wolf with nitrous oxide and bribe the promoter to let the Wigglers compete for the top prize.

When the boys find out what the gals did, they balk. Bango and Bob split before Dick finds out from Polly that the promoter was so impressed with the band that he ripped up the girls' check. With one hour to spare, Dick and Jack then race around town in a hot rod to round up their missing buddies to perform at the show. Their speeding attracts the police and a chase ensues. To avoid being spotted by the police at the auditorium, the guys dress in drag. They perform donned in women's clothes, win the contest, get the girls and decide to return to college.

Behind-the-Scenes

After appearing in *Dementia 13* (1963), directed by his college friend Francis Coppola, actor Bart Patton began a professional relationship with producer/director Roger Corman. "After I worked in that movie, Roger would call me to produce additional footage for films that he bought to expand the running time so he could sell them to television," recalls Patton. "I got to the point where I was doing more production work than acting. One morning he phoned me and said, 'Bart, come down to Kantor's Deli, I want to talk to you about producing a movie.' I sat down with him and he said, 'Bart, there are several things that I want you to be in charge of.' He went on to list everything in a movie from the cast to props to makeup. Roger added that I had $100,000 and that he already committed $25,000 to Edd Byrnes to star in it. He said, 'I'll deposit the difference into your checking account and basically you've never heard of me. It is a totally independent film.'

"I asked Roger if I could direct the movie because I had those aspirations," continues Patton. "He replied, 'No, because I hired a comic who has never directed before but I think he is funny so here's your partner, Lennie Weinrib.' That's how Patton-Weinrib got started."

Before the rest of the cast had been set or production begun, Patton and Weinrib needed to photograph the picture's wild chase finale at a real auto show. "Roger told us that we had to go shoot because it was 'free production value for nothing,'" recalls Bart with a laugh. "I don't know how we got clearance to film but we did *or maybe we didn't*." Patton rounded up four friends (including actors Don Edmonds and Aron Kincaid) and shuttled them to the Long Beach Civic Center. Kincaid remembers, "They told us, 'We're going to send the cops after you and you are to run from them.' That was all the direction that we received. The people there thought we had really done something wrong. The crowds are grabbing us and yelling, 'We've got 'em!' The cameras were all out of sight. One camera was hidden in a giant straw purse up on a little tower shooting with a zoom lens. Then they did a lot of close-up shots where our faces actually showed."

Don Edmonds says, "Edd Byrnes wasn't there. They had to put one of the other guys in a wet suit hood to pretend to be Edd's character. It was mostly long shots so it didn't matter. There was a script but they had to film this because the car show was going to end before the film went into production. So we went down there and ran around for a couple of days."

Though Edmonds knew he was going to be cast in the movie, Kincaid did not. "They offered me 50 bucks a day," says Kincaid. "Here I just finished this starring role in a movie [*The Girls on the Beach*] but I thought, 'Nobody is going to know it's me if my face doesn't show. I could pick up some extra money.' I had a feeling at that time that they were conducting a screen test that would amount to footage they would be able to use without having to pay me an actor's rate. I was right because four days later they called my agent and offered me one of the leads in the picture."

The footage was eventually used in the end and it is evident that Kincaid and Edmonds had no makeup on. Kincaid's five o'clock shadow and pasty white skin is especially noticeable when he is pretending to be a corpse lying in front of a tombstone. The cast returned to the now vacant Long Beach Civic Auditorium about a month later for insert shots. This fake auto show was made up of just a bunch of extras and the Supremes, who sang to about a dozen people.

Bart Patton describes Kincaid as "a sweetheart of a guy. We'd hang out together and had a lot of fun. I remember one time when he brought Sue Lyon of *Lolita* fame to my beach house for a barbecue." The only other actor recruited by Patton from *The Girls on the Beach* to appear in *Beach Ball* was Gail Gerber (now being billed as Gail Gilmore). "She was a comedy relief cutie," remarks Bart. Regarding her name change, Gail said it was due to her agent, Sam Armstrong, who felt Gerber was too German sounding for Hollywood, which he called "a Jewish town." She stole "Gilmore" from a friend and dance partner, Glen Gilmore.

Taking the lead roles in *Beach Ball* were Edd Byrnes and shapely blonde Chris Noel. Byrnes had become an immediate teenage idol with his role as Kookie on television's hit detective series *77 Sunset Strip* in 1958. He left the series in 1962 and tried unsuccessfully to shake that teenybopper image. Though he turned down a number of beach movies, he accepted the part in *Beach Ball* purportedly due to the large salary offered to him. Byrnes remarked in his autobiography, "Beach pictures often came with a stigma, and I vowed to only do it this one time, not wanting to become another Frankie Avalon."

Noel had been a contract player at MGM where she essayed supporting roles in such films as *Get Yourself a College Girl* (1964), *Girl Happy* and *Joy in the Morning* (both 1965). According to Bart Patton, "Chris was suggested by Roger Corman. We checked her out and she was great." It is speculation but Corman must have seen Noel in some of her other film roles. Noel jokes with a laugh, "Maybe— *I was on my way up!*"

Though Bart Patton was friendly with most of the actors hired for *Beach Ball*, that did not preclude them from auditioning. He jokes, "You'd think we were making *Hamlet!*" Other lead roles were filled by former Warner Bros. contract player Mikki Jamison, newcomer Brenda Benet (who had only one minor role in the 1964 Bob Hope comedy *A Global Affair* to her credit) and actor Robert Logan, who had worked previously with Edd Byrnes on *77 Sunset Strip*. When Byrnes' character

Coeds Gail Gilmore, Mikki Jamison, Chris Noel and Brenda Benet plot their next move to convince their guys to return to college in *Beach Ball* (Paramount, 1965) (*courtesy of Aron Kincaid*).

Kookie was upgraded from parking lot attendant to full partner in the detective agency in 1961, Logan was brought in as J. R. to fill the void of the jive-talking hipster.

Missing from the cast list was Patton's beautiful wife Mary Mitchel. In fact, he never hired her for any of his subsequent movies either. "It never occurred to me," laughs Bart. "We had a child in 1963. When she did *A Swingin' Summer* I was babysitting our son and when it came time for *Beach Ball* it was her turn to watch him."

Beach Ball began production with a three-week shooting schedule. The screenplay was by Sam Locke (who wrote *The Girls on the Beach*), still using the pseudonym of David Malcolm. "We shot on a stage about the size of a bathroom," says Bart jokingly. "During production Roger Corman had insisted that we change the title of the film to *Bikini Party*. We were getting threats from AIP that we couldn't use that name. Lennie and I didn't like it. We preferred *Beach Ball*."

Unlike most actors who checked their ego at the door at the beginning of a film shoot, Edd Byrnes brought his right onto the set. Chris Noel in particular had many problems working with him. After he tried to ram his tongue down her throat one too many times during a kissing scene, she warned director Lennie Weinrib that if he didn't get Byrnes to stop, she was walking off the picture. It is most certain Noel was not at all interested in being lent Kookie's comb.

"She never complained to me about this," remarks Bart. "I don't recall this at all. I'm surprised because Edd was a dream to work with. It was a silly part, but he had an angle for it and he was funny. I thought he was extremely cooperative. I had worked with him on *77 Sunset Strip* so I felt very relaxed with him. Frankly, I thought he and Chris got along great. Chris seemed like a very sheltered girl. She kept to herself a lot."

When asked why she didn't inform Patton of Byrnes' behavior, Chris replies, "I thought Bart was a nice guy. Lennie handled my problem with Edd so that was the end of it."

Commenting on the Edd Byrnes–Chris Noel situation, Aron Kincaid says, "Chris Noel was a sweetheart. She was very conscientious about what she was doing. Though we had a lot of scenes together, all of Chris Noel's energies and focus were on her part and avoiding Edd Byrnes' lecherous advances towards her. He was a bit pompous but I liked him anyway. I was not a fan of *77 Sunset Strip* but I admired his performance in *Yellowstone Kelly* and told him so. I think he liked the fact that I never mentioned the Kookie character. He was a little tired of that and was trying to go elsewhere with his career." Gail Gerber adds with a laugh, "Edd Byrnes was a big star at that time and I remember thinking, 'What the hell is he doing in this crummy movie?'"

"All the negative comments about Edd Byrnes were theoretically true," admits Don Edmonds. "But I've known Edd since then and I have found him to be a really okay guy. But on *Beach Ball* he walked in with a bit of an attitude and we weren't doing Shakespeare. He also wasn't really suited for physical comedy and wasn't used to putting on flippers and slapping around. It just wasn't his style."

Chris Noel also encountered Byrnes after the making of *Beach Ball* and agrees with Don. "Edd turned into a great guy," remarks his former co-star. "I like him now. But on *Beach Ball* he was a jerk. He had all the girls gaga over him when he was a star. He tried to be what he thought people wanted him to be. I have to say Edd today is funny and honest. He told the truth about his past in his autobiography, which I think is remarkable. He certainly didn't need to do that."

While Noel had to contend with Byrnes, Aron Kincaid was getting grief from Robert Logan. "It seemed that he wanted to be elsewhere and he let everybody know it. He had very little interest in what he was doing unless it involved action or stunts. One day, he came in early and took my clothes and put them on. I came in and found his ratty clothes over in the corner of the wardrobe room where my things were. I noticed he had my slacks on and my orange vest. I asked him why and he said, 'I had a case of the crabs yesterday and I don't want to get it again.' I yelled, '*But it is okay for me to get it!*' He was just horrible."

Bart Patton concurs up to a point, "Robert Logan always wanted to go off sailing. He wasn't much of an actor. He was playing the drummer in the group and he wasn't much of a drummer either. I think his disinterest was due to his being uncomfortable acting. He could do takes and shticks but that was it." Chris Noel recalls with a laugh, "Robert Logan was a pretty boy and had an ego. But he never bothered me. *It must have been a guy thing!*"

Don Edmonds only has the fondest memories of working on *Beach Ball.* "This movie was a goof. I had known Lennie Weinrib for awhile. He and Bart Patton were cool. I got along well with all the guys—and the girls too. Gail Gerber was hot. She was sweet, very smart and had a lot going for her. Chris Noel later did some really good work with the GIs in Vietnam. She has a good heart. But I have never been in love more than with Brenda Benet. She was the love of my life. I brought Brenda to Hollywood [from the Valley] and got her situated in a place called the Studio Club, which was a place for young actresses to live. My dad signed for her first car. I was with her when her son died [of complications from an emergency tracheotomy] and at the end [a distraught Benet committed suicide in 1982]. She was the single greatest human being that I ever knew."

Aron Kincaid has cherished memories of his leading lady Mikki Jamison as well. "Mikki was great," exclaims Kincaid. "At the age of 16, she was under contract to Warner Brothers. That is when I first met her. We have gone through a lot together including the Cuban Missile Crisis. We've had some fun times and some sad times."

According to Kincaid, the actresses improvised the scene in their dorm room. The way they took their positions on the bed was very comedic but Lennie Weinrib did not orchestrate it, they came up with it on their own. Aron opines, "I think all four of them, because they were so attractive, really enjoyed the fact that they were playing these little mousy characters with the glasses and prim proper clothes. I thought they were better in these scenes then when they become glamorous. But I did think the scene where they get dragged off to the beach house was the funniest. They come out in their bikinis and act like they are naked."

Bart Patton opines, "The whole ensemble was great. The guys and the gals really had chemistry. I think they helped make this the best of the three pictures I produced." And unlike the petty jealousies and rivalries between the actresses on *The Girls on the Beach,* the gals on *Beach Ball* got along nicely. "Why not?" asks Chris. "I'm not a bitch so there is no reason for someone years later to attack my behavior. *I* never gave anyone any problems. I would come to the set to do my work and never got into people's personalities very much. I thought Gail Gerber and Mikki Jamison were nice but Brenda Benet was my favorite. She was such a sweet girl. I liked her a lot."

Patton was lucky that his leading ladies were all comfortable enough to don bikinis—very skimpy ones at that. Unlike other actresses such as Annette, Donna Loren, Noreen Corcoran and Linda Marshall who signed to star in beach movies and then refused to wear bikinis, Chris Noel and the other gals in *Beach Ball* were not at all shy in displaying their curvy figures. "This was never an issue with me," asserts Chris. "Wearing bikinis on film didn't bother me. I grew up in Florida and lived on the beach. To my knowledge, none of the other girls had a problem with it either."

When *Beach Ball* was filmed in 1964, the Supremes did not have a Top 20 record and the biggest draw was thought to be the Four Seasons. Roger Corman polled local disc jockeys and record storeowners asking them whom they felt would be the new hot singing group. The Supremes were mentioned the most and they were signed to sing two songs in the movie. Corman's choice proved correct. By the time the movie was released in September 1965, Diana Ross, Mary Wilson and

Florence Ballard had five number one records and received top billing over the other musical performers. "Roger had the Supremes and the rest of the groups already lined up before our meeting at Kantor's," says Patton. "He found them through a guy named Nick Venet."

It is a good thing that the Supremes hit it big before *Beach Ball* was released because Diana Ross seems out of place and uncomfortable singing two surf tunes written by Motown songwriters. "I preferred hearing the Supremes sing rather than watching them," says Aron with a laugh. "Florence Ballard was cute and a real sweetheart. But Diana Ross was terrifying to look at. She had a missing back tooth that showed up in the film very prominently, one big eyebrow going across her face and that sprayed hair. With her eyes rolling, she was a long way from playing Billie Holiday [in *Lady Sings the Blues*]." Don Edmonds concurs. "They had them singing 'C'mon, c'mon to the beach ball with me.' Ooh. It was like—get them out of here! But hey, Berry Gordy was standing out in the audience and he wanted them on the screen."

"When we shot the Supremes, we had them up on this little stage doing playback," says Patton. "When Nick Venet pre-recorded the Supremes the lyrics went 'C'mon, c'mon, bikini party with me.' When we finally convinced Roger that *Beach Ball* was a better title, we had to go back to over-dub 'beach ball.' Their mouths say 'bikini party' but the lyrics say 'beach ball.'"

According to *The Hollywood Reporter*, the Supremes commanded a fee of $2,500 to appear in the movie, the same as headliners the Four Seasons. The Righteous Brothers received $500 while the Hondells were paid scale ($100 per member, which totaled $400). "The Four Seasons showed up without their drummer so in the picture I am playing drums," reveals Patton. "I put myself in cameo parts in *Wild Wild Winter* and *Out of Sight* as well."

More soon-to-be famous names that worked on *Beach Ball* were Stephanie Rothman and actor Sid Haig. Roger Corman asked his protégé Rothman to work second-unit, filming the car chase scenes with Aron Kincaid. "I think Stephanie did a great job with that footage she shot," comments Patton. "She incorporated those Keystone Cops gags to give it a classic movie feel."

Character actor Sid Haig worked on the crew as "a gaffer, grip and boom man." He also sat in as the drummer while the Righteous Brothers performed. Aron Kincaid says laughing, "I remember Sid being such a cut-up. I said, 'This guy is nuts. He should definitely be in front of the camera instead of behind it.'"

Commenting on the beach party movie craze at that time, director Lennie Weinrib told *The Saturday Evening Post*, "There's a great danger that too many of these films are being made. Over-saturation makes you nervous, but it's also very good for your creativity. It makes you ingenious. You have to find a new way to say something that's been said over and over."

"Lennie Weinrib was a fine director," remarks Patton. "We actually became a great team because I was hip to how to shoot and cut film and he was really a theater guy. He'd lay out his plan and we'd work together on how to shoot scenes. We had a great time and were an excellent pair. We formed Patton-Weinrib Productions, average age 30. I was 27 and he was 33." Regarding his directorial debut, Weinrib commented in the *Los Angeles Times*, "The fun of being a director is that you get to play all the parts. I did 14 or 15 parts in the [*Billy Barnes*] revue. But

Sheldon Leonard once said that a comedy movie is just an elongated joke. He's right."

Before *Beach Ball* was released, a friend of Weinrib's arranged a meeting between the duo and Lew Wasserman, the head of Universal Studios. The ingenious pair "borrowed" the black-and-white rough-cut of *Beach Ball*, inserted seven minutes' worth of color footage that they shot in one take and screened it for executives at Universal. They then spliced out the color insert and sneaked it back into Roger Corman's editing offices. Their daring antic cost them $43 for the color print but won them a seven-year non-exclusive contract. First up for the creative pair was *Wild Wild Winter* co-starring *Beach Ball* actors Chris Noel, Don Edmonds, and Anna Lavelle whom Patton says Lennie Weinrib had fallen in love with.

Handsome Aron Kincaid in a typical Hollywood surfer boy pose (*courtesy Aron Kincaid*).

To generate interest in the soon-to-be-released *Beach Ball*, Chris Noel and Brenda Benet participated in a swimsuit fashion shoot in *Photoplay*. Along with Jody McCrea from the *Beach Party* movies, Tony Dow from the teenage soap opera *Never Too Young* and other young actors including Chad Everett and his future wife Shelby Grant, they modeled bikinis and swim trunks by some of the top designers of the day. Noel wore a two-piece bathing suit by Rose Marie Reid while Benet was clad in a nylon suit by Cole of California.

According to Bart Patton, *Beach Ball* came in at approximately $125,000 and Roger Corman had pre-sold the distribution rights to Paramount for $350,000. The film went on to gross $1 million at the box office.

After appearing in *Harum Scarum* (1965) with Elvis Presley and *Village of the Giants* (1965), Gail Gerber stopped acting to be with writer Terry Southern, whom she met on the set of *The Loved One* (1965). The relationship lasted until his death in 1995.

Robert Logan worked for Bart Patton again in the seventies. Bart recalls, "I began my relationship with my current wife Judy Ponder when she was the makeup artist and wardrobe mistress on *The Further Adventures of the Wilderness Family* starring Robert Logan. [Logan had starred in the very successful *The Adventures of the Wilderness Family* (1975).] I was the producer and my good friend from UCLA Frank Zuniga directed it. By that time, Logan was pretty good. He's a great type. He reads just like John Wayne reads on camera. He really looks like he is a wilderness kind of guy and did a nice job in that film."

Logan and Mikki Jamison reunited on the big screen in *The Sea Gypsies* (1978), a family drama about a man, his two children and a female reporter who get stranded on an island during an around-the-world sailing adventure.

Memorable Lines

(The girls retire to their dorm after almost being duped into giving a student loan to Dick and his friends to pay off the money owed on their musical instruments.)

AUGUSTA: If you ask me, we ought to tell the police about those horrible dropouts.

DEBORAH: *The police!* For heaven's sake, Augusta, nobody *murdered* anybody.

AUGUSTA: *No!?!* That boy *murdered* Susan's faith in human nature.

(The bikini-clad girls hesitantly emerge from the beach shack trying to cover parts of their exposed anatomies.)

DICK: Those candy bars look good without the wrappers on.

Reviews

Stan Bernstein, *Los Angeles Times*—"The beach-based, bikini-filled fillip has a plot that fails to intrude on the singing of such favorites as the Supremes, the Righteous Brothers, the Hondells, the Walker Brothers and the Four Seasons."

Boxoffice—"A lively, entertaining and completely inconsequential college-type musical...."

Loren G. Buchanan, *Motion Picture Herald*—"It is definitely against tradition to let the surfboards and bathing suits get wet in a beach picture, but this swinging color production ... stands a better-than-even chance to end up a box office smash despite the breach."

Kathleen Carroll, *New York Daily News*—"*Beach Ball* bounces as much as a bowling ball. It's been done before—with imagination. This effort does nothing more than follow the formula."

Mandel Herbstman, *The Film Daily*—"Pop tunes rattle and roll in a frenzy of melody.... The story is a featherweight farce that vibrates with action and enthusiasm."

John Molleson, *New York Herald Tribune*—"*Beach Ball* takes us back to the earliest days of film—to Mack Sennett, the bathing beauties, the sight gags, speed-ups and the chase. The formula is a good one and it has lost nothing now that the girls are twisting, surfing and tossing beach balls in bikinis, and the sight-gags rely on skin-diving and sky-diving...."

Dale Munroe, *Citizen-News*—"*Beach Ball* ... is neither the best nor the worst of the 'beach party' style musicals. Let it simply be said that 'Beach' will be a 'Ball' for the younger members of the jet-set, but anything *but* a 'ball' for the average parent."

David Rider, *Films and Filming*—"This movie is amazingly indigenous. It includes great all–American activities like surfing, hot-rodding, sky-diving, skin-diving, dancing and a liberal helping of pop music ... the main interest for most of its British audience."

Awards and Nominations

Photoplay Gold Medal Award nomination: "Favorite Male Star"—Edd Byrnes

★ **14** ★

Beach Blanket Bingo (1965)

It's the game that separates the girls and the boys ... into groups of two!

Fun: ★★★★
Surfing: ★★
Boy watching: ★★★
Girl watching: ★★★★
Music: ★★★★
Scenery: ★★★

Release date: April 14, 1965. Running time: 98m. Box office gross: Not available.
DVD release: MGM Home Entertainment (June 5, 2001).

Frankie Avalon (*Frankie*), Annette Funicello (*Dee Dee*), Deborah Walley (*Bonnie Graham*), Harvey Lembeck (*Eric Von Zipper*), John Ashley (*Steve Gordon*), Jody McCrea (*Bonehead*), Donna Loren (*Donna*), Marta Kristen (*Lorelei*), Linda Evans (*Sugar Kane*), Timothy Carey (*South Dakota Slim*), Don Rickles (*Big Drop*), Paul Lynde (*Bullets*), Buster Keaton (*Himself*), Earl Wilson (*Himself*), Bobbi Shaw (*Bobbi*), Donna Michelle (*Animal*), Mike Nader (*Butch*), Patti Chandler (*Patti*), Andy Romano, Alan Fife, Jerry Brutsche, John Macchia, Bob Harvey, Alberta Nelson, Myrna Ross (*Rat Pack*), Ed Garner, Guy Hemric, Duane Ament, Ray Atkinson, Brian Wilson, Mickey Dora, Ned Wynn, Frank Alesia, Phil Henderson, Johnny Fain, Ronnie Dayton (*Beach Boys*), Linda Benson, Mary Hughes, Salli Sachse, Linda Merrill, Luree Holmes, Laura Nicholson, Linda Bent, Chris Cranston, Mary Sturdevant, Judy Lescher, Pat Bryton, Pam Colbert, Dessica Giles, Stephanie Nader, Jo Ann Zerfas (*Beach Girls*). Guest stars: The Hondells.

American International Pictures. *Producers*: James H. Nicholson and Samuel Z. Arkoff. *Co-Producer*: Anthony Carras. *Director*: William Asher. *Written by*: William Asher and Leo Townsend. *Production Supervisor*: Jack Bohrer. *Director of Photography*: Floyd Crosby, A.S.C. *Music Supervisor*: Al Simms. *Musical Score by*: Les Baxter. *Choreography by*: Jack Baker. *Art Director*: Howard Campbell. *Film Editors*: Fred Feitshans, A.C.E., Eve Newman. *Music Editor*: Milton Lustig. *Sound Editor*: James Nelson. *Costuming and Designing by*: Marjorie Corso. *All Men's Sportswear, Hollywood, Designed by*: Jerry Furlow. *Swimsuits by*: DeWeese Designs of California. *Titles and Photographic Special Effects*: Butler-Glouner. *Special Effects by*: Roger George, Joe Zomar. *Assistant Director*: Dale Hutchinson. *Sound*: Bob Post. *Makeup*: Bob Dawn. *Hairdresser*: Eve Newing. *Set Decorator*: Harry Reif. *Production Assistant*: Jack Cash. *Motorcycle Coordinator*: George Dockstader. Filmed in Panavision and Pathecolor.

Songs by Guy Hemric and Jerry Styner: "Beach Blanket Bingo" and "I Think, You Think" performed by Frankie Avalon and Annette Funicello. "It Only Hurts When I Cry" performed by Donna Loren. "I Am My Ideal" performed by Harvey Lembeck. "New Love" and "Fly Boy" performed by Jackie Ward, lip-synced by Linda Evans. "These Are the Good

Times" performed by Frankie Avalon. "The Cycle Set" by Guy Hemric and Roger Christian, performed by the Hondells.

In the immortal words of Eric Von Zipper, *Beach Blanket Bingo* is "nifty." It is the best, the zaniest, the quirkiest and most fondly remembered of the Frankie and Annette epics. Admittedly, the story centering around Dee Dee proving to Frankie that girls can sky dive as well as boys, Bonehead falling in love with a mermaid and a beautiful singer kidnapped by Von Zipper's biker gang is far-fetched. But it contains some very funny lines mostly delivered by Don Rickles as Big Drop and Paul Lynde as an acid-tongued press agent whose verbal sparring with Avalon is one of the movie's highlights. Lots of colorful beach scenes are intermingled with stock sky diving shots. All your AIP favorite stars are here, the songs are bouncy and light, an array of guest comics provide some of the series' funniest moments and a bevy of beautiful blondes (including Linda Evans of *Dynasty* fame) enhance the action.

Frankie, looking especially cute here, delivers one of his best performances but poor Annette, who proved she could act in *Muscle Beach Party*, really has nothing much to do, as her character seems resigned to the fact that her boyfriend has a roving eye. Jody McCrea finally gets to stretch his acting muscle and his scenes with the stunning Marta Kristen as a mermaid are touching and bittersweet. Linda Evans is darling as the naïve Sugar Kane and stands out whenever she dons a bikini. It is these two hot blondes along with *Playboy* Playmate Donna Michelle as Animal and the rest of the bikini-clad beach girls that make *Beach Blanket Bingo* a winner with girl watchers. For boy watchers it is the same old crew but at least surfer boys Mike Nader and Johnny Fain get lots more screen time.

Another big plus for *Beach Blanket Bingo* is the music score. The songs are some of the best from the series beginning with the title song—the grandest opening number of all the beach party movies. The up tempo tune is sung in such a light and bouncy manner by Frankie and Annette that you can't but help want to jump to your feet and dance along. They also do well with their second duet, the popular "I Think, You Think." Pretty Donna Loren turns up early to expertly belt out the heart-wrenching "It Only Hurts When I Cry." Jackie Ward delivers the Linda Evans lip-synced songs in fine style but it is the Hondells who stand out with "The Cycle Set." Every beach party movie has one clunker and in *Beach Blanket Bingo* it is "These Are the Good Times" crooned by Avalon as if he was still living in the fifties. He also sang this song on *The Patty Duke Show* during a guest appearance, which may explain why his handlers wanted it included in the movie.

On the down side, as with most of the beach party movies, *Beach Blanket Bingo* does not do surfers any justice and doesn't even bother to insert any stock surfing footage. The other wrong note in the film is John Ashley. After playing Frankie's buddy Johnny in *Beach Party*, *Muscle Beach Party* and *Bikini Beach*, his being cast as Avalon's jealous rival Steve throws off the continuity of the series. But despite its minor flaws, *Beach Blanket Bingo* is the apex of the beach movie genre. Little did anyone know at the time that this would be the last beach pairing of Frankie and Annette and that the films to follow would go straight downhill.

The Story

Frankie, Dee Dee, Bonehead and the rest of the gang are hanging out on the beach surfing and dancing when they notice a girl in a candy-striped jump suit, with a candy-striped parachute, sky dive from a plane. Seeing a yacht where she landed, the kids think it is a publicity stunt but when the boat does not pick her up the guys grab their surfboards to rescue her. But in fact it *was* a publicity stunt as skydiver Bonnie took the fall for aspiring singer Sugar Kane, who is left floundering in the ocean. When the guys led by Frankie bring her to shore, her press agent, Bullets Durham, is waiting there with columnist Earl Wilson and a photographer. They snap a picture of Frankie, the hero surfer, and Sugar, the damsel in distress. When the surfers begin bombarding Sugar with questions about sky diving, she stammers nervously that she took lessons at Big Drop's Sky Diving Club.

Up on a hill, motorcycle gang leader Eric Von Zipper has eyed the whole incident. He announces to his gang that Sugar Kane needs rescuing from the surfer bums. "I think I adore her," he says. "She's nifty." Knowing they have gone down this route before, Puss and Boots exchange exasperated glances.

At the beach house, Frankie announces he wants to learn to sky dive but when Dee Dee also expresses interest, the chauvinist chides her, claiming a girl's place is in the kitchen. The whole gang except Bonehead heads to Big Drop's the next day to sign up for lessons. Sexy redhead Bonnie immediately begins flirting with Frankie to the consternation of her pilot boyfriend Steve and Dee Dee.

Bonehead is surfing alone when a wave knocks his board into the air and it hits him on the head, rendering him unconscious. He comes to briefly, just in time to glimpse a mysterious beautiful blonde pulling him towards shore. Sugar Kane sees him in trouble from the deck of her house and runs out to help him. When Bonehead awakes on the sand, Sugar is being heralded a heroine by Bullets but the dazed surfer suspects there was someone else in the ocean.

The story is in the next day's paper, angering Von Zipper. He decides to crash the party Bullets has organized that night in celebration of Sugar's heroic actions. The Hondells and Sugar Kane perform for the beach crowd when Von Zipper and his gang enter. Von Zipper professes his love for the beautiful vocalist before being thrown out. Dee Dee notices that Bonehead has slipped out as well and voices her concern to Frankie. Bonehead swims out to the spot where he had the accident, and the beautiful blonde reappears. He is confused as to why she didn't come to shore until she reveals that she is a mermaid named Lorelei. They agree to meet the next night at a nearby cove.

When Bonehead announces to Frankie and Dee Dee that he has fallen in love with a mermaid, a worried Frankie brings Sugar Kane over and reminds the dazed surfer that he promised to escort her to the dance at the Pavilion. At the beach club, Bonnie stares dreamily at Frankie. Tired of her games, Steve cuts in on Frankie to dance with Dee Dee while Bonnie sidles up to Frankie. Sugar and Bonehead take a walk along the beach. The surfer suddenly hears soft music. Sugar doesn't hear it but then screams after getting bit on the ankle. When she claims it is a "people bite," Bonehead realizes that he is late for his date with Lorelei and abandons Sugar. Back at the dance, Frankie sings a song. Fed up with Bonnie's mooning over the surfer, Steve goads him into taking his first free fall the next day.

Lorelei, clad only in a bikini that she made from a parachute, tells Bonehead that mermaids are permitted to use legs only a few times in their life for a short period of time. Bonehead tries to determine her dress size to get the beautiful "fish out of water" some clothes to wear. At Big Drop's, Frankie makes a successful jump, inspiring Dee Dee to do the same. He tries to talk her out of it and when that fails he accompanies her up in the plane piloted by Bonnie. After she safely jumps, Bonnie puts the plane on automatic pilot and makes a pass at Frankie, who rejects her. Furious, she tears her blouse and, when they land, she goes running into Steve's arms. Seeing through Bonnie's charade, he slaps her. Frankie berates both Steve and Bonnie and advises the pilot to let his girlfriend know that he cares about her so she doesn't have to play games to get his attention.

Excited about his date with Lorelei, Bonehead gets Frankie and Dee Dee to double date with him before heading to a ladies' clothing store. Lorelei looks stunning in the beautiful blue dress Bonehead has picked out for her. Later at the pavilion, Lorelei is unable to do any of the wild dances so Bonehead gets the band to play a waltz. At midnight, the sullen surfer escorts Lorelei back to the cove where they profess their love for each other. Knowing they can never be together, they kiss goodbye as Lorelei returns to the sea. With a tear in his eye, Bonehead buries her clothes in the sand, not realizing that he is being watched by some of his surfing buddies.

The next morning, the guys report what they saw to Frankie just as Bullets arrives, accusing Bonehead of drowning Sugar. Bonehead swears he hasn't seen her. Frankie leads the press agent to think it is a publicity stunt set up by Sugar and Bonehead, who once again hears the call of the mermaids. In a trance he heads for the beach where in the sand Lorelei has scrawled "Von Zipper." The mermaid also comes to Frankie's aid after his chute fails to open in time after doing a free fall. Dazed, he sees that Lorelei has helped him. When she goes to swim away, he grabs a medallion from around her neck.

Bonehead informs the gang that Von Zipper has kidnapped Sugar and that she is at the pool hall. The motorcycle leader admits to his nefarious deed but claims he only wanted to teach her to play pool. They learn that South Dakota Slim has tied Sugar to some railroad tracks. The surfers and cyclists team up to rescue the pretty vocalist. Puss and Boots try to help Sugar escape but are thwarted by Slim, who carries her to a tower. Frankie bursts in and saves Sugar by knocking out Slim with one punch. But it is Bonehead who is proclaimed the hero by the grateful blonde.

That night on the beach, Frankie gives Bonehead the medallion he took from Lorelei. Dee Dee questions if Lorelei really was a mermaid. Bonehead reunites with Sugar and the couple leaves Bullets to his publicity stunts as they gaze out onto the ocean. Sugar suggests that they were brought together by some mystery of the sea. Holding the medallion in his hand, the surfer puts it into his pocket and puts his arm around his new girl.

Behind-the-Scenes

After being paired with Tommy Kirk in *Pajama Party*, Annette Funicello was reunited with Frankie Avalon for the fourth film in the beach party series, *Beach Blan-*

It's the game that separates the girls and the boys...into groups of two!

BEACH BLANKET BiNGO

Lobby card for *Beach Blanket Bingo* (AIP, 1965) featuring *Playboy* Playmate Donna Michelle as Animal vexing the local surfers including Johnny Fain (*second from left*) and Mike Nader (*with hands outstretched*).

ket Bingo. After having tackled surfing, musclemen, drag racing and Martians, screenwriters William Asher and Leo Townsend came up with the gimmicks of sky diving and mermaids to coax teenagers off their couches and into the drive-ins across the country.

The popular cast of AIP regulars was rounded up to support the film's leads. Donna Loren and Harvey Lembeck returned as well as the usual crop of beach boys and girls including Mike Nader, Ed Garner, Mickey Dora, Johnny Fain, Bobbi Shaw, Patti Chandler, Mary Hughes, Salli Sachse and Luree Holmes. Jody McCrea was given a bigger part than usual, probably due to his success in *Pajama Party*, and had not one but two love interests. "This is my favorite because it was written specifically for my character," boasts Jody McCrea proudly. "It is considered to be the most popular of all the beach movies."

John Ashley also appears but instead of playing Frankie's loyal friend Johnny, he assumes the role of his arrogant rival while Ashley's then-wife Deborah Walley joined the AIP fold as his flirtatious girlfriend. Regarding their first on-screen pairing, Walley commented in *Screen Stories*, "We've been married for three wonderfully happy years and now we have to start battling from the opening scene, to the end of the picture. It will be a true acting test, because John and I never allow petty jealousies to affect us. The only thing that bothers me are his kissing scenes with other girls. I refuse to watch them and always cover my eyes."

Ashley responded, "I'm only bothered when my wife kisses another guy in a scene. But if it didn't bother either one of us that's when we'd *really* be in trouble!"

New faces to the beach party included *Playboy* centerfold Donna Michelle (Miss December 1963 and Playmate of the Year for 1964), who assumed the role of Animal last played by Meredith MacRae in *Bikini Beach* (1964). Commenting on the sexy gals decorating these beach epics, Jody McCrea says, "In the later movies, AIP began using *Playboy* Playmates in the movies. But the girls like Salli Sachse and Patti Chandler were more adept at playing beach girls since they were discovered right on the beaches of Southern California. They were the best looking girls of their type in the world."

The role of Sugar Kane was intended for Nancy Sinatra. AIP touted the signing of the vocalist in all the trades. However, she dropped out of the movie when friends of singers Jan and Dean kidnapped her brother Frank Sinatra, Jr. Though he returned home safely to his family, Sinatra's managers thought the role hit too close to home as Sugar is snatched from her bed during the course of the film. Scrambling to fill the part, the wily producers once again raided Walt Disney's stables and signed Linda Evans. She had just finished making *Those Calloways* (1964) for Disney. Evans was a sleek, pretty blonde and filled her bikini nicely but she wasn't a singer. Jackie Ward (who had a Top 20 hit in 1963 with "Wonderful Summer" under the name of Robin Ward) was brought in to dub the two songs lip-synced by Evans in the movie.

Another Disney cast-off was Marta Kristen, who had just appeared in *Savage Sam* (1963) for the studio. She was signed to play the mermaid Lorelei. Commenting on his two beautiful co-stars, Jody McCrea exclaims, "You can't do better than romancing on screen Marta Kristen and Linda Evans! When I first saw Marta I thought, 'That's a girl I could fall in love with.' But she was married at the time so that idea was shot down. We'd drive over together to the location and practice lines in the car. I only had contact with Linda Evans on the set. I would have liked to been more familiar with her and the other girls but I stayed away."

"I remember when Linda Evans had her first kissing scene with Frankie Avalon," says Ed Garner with a laugh. "You could not help but notice the spark. Even with 'Lights! Camera! Action!' something goes on in all of us that you just can't stop."

No AIP beach party flick would be complete without a handful of adult actors and comedians. *Beach Blanket Bingo* boasted Earl Wilson, Don Rickles, Paul Lynde and Buster Keaton, who remarked in *Screen Stories*, "They wanted us in the picture just in case audiences tire of looking at the surf and sand muscle boys and beach bunnies' wild bikinis."

Regarding the renowned silent film star, William Asher commented in *Video* magazine, "I always loved Buster Keaton. I thought, what a wonderful person to look on and react to these young kids and to view them as the audience might, to shake his head at their crazy antics. He would bring me bits and routines. He'd say, 'How about this?' and it would just be this wonderful, inventive stuff."

The only guest musical act in the film was the Hondells. Though seen on screen, they actually only lip-synched one of the series' best dance numbers, "The Cycle Set." According to Gary Usher (the driving force behind the group), the song was recorded with Chuck Girard singing lead vocals and Usher hitting the high falsettos. Seen in the movie, however, was the same line-up of guys who appeared in *Beach Ball*—Dick Burns, Wayne Edwards, Randy Thomas and Jerry LeMire. Though not seen on-screen, Darlene Love and the Blossoms provided background vocals to a number of the songs that were heard in the movie.

As with most of the beach party films, *Beach Blanket Bingo* was shot during the colder months so the film could be released in the spring. The shooting schedule was 18 days and the beach scenes were filmed in Paradise Cove in Malibu. According to *Screen Stories*, "The entire company of 150 performers and technicians ate together and there was no special menu for Annette, Frankie and the other stars. To the contrary, the ravenously hungry group lined up at that inevitable old chuck wagon belonging to a belabored catering service. It was all part of the noon-day chore to dish out 150 pounds of mashed potatoes, 10 gallons of vegetables, 200 pounds of pork chops, 90 gallons of coffee and 200 pints of ice cream."

Recalling the shoot, Jody McCrea says, "The scenes with Marta Kristen were actually filmed in the ocean. Marta nearly turned blue one day because the second unit guy took a lot longer than he should have to set up the shot. We all had to pretend how warm it was and it really wasn't. Since I surfed during the winter because the waves were bigger, it didn't bother me as much." Kristen mentions on her website that she couldn't comprehend all of director William Asher's instructions from the shore. She had to "pop up from under the surface of the water" and dive back under while trying to avoid crashing into nearby rocks and wearing pasties in rough 55-degree water.

Since this was the fourth or fifth time the cast had worked together, fans have imagined that it was a party off-camera as well. But for the most part the stars kept their distance. "My relationship with Frankie was closer back in the East than when I was working with him on the beach movies," reveals McCrea. "I considered ourselves buddies but we didn't have each other's phone number. He was very private. Even by this movie I still didn't talk to Annette much. I barely got a 'Hello, how are you?' out of her. That was it for our conversations."

"I used to stay alone myself," continues McCrea. "I would lie down and think about my part. They thought I slept a lot but I mostly did what Gary Cooper, James Dean and my dad did. Instead of talking with the cast, which would have been wasted energy, I would rest and visualize my character. I was concentrating mentally on it."

As for any potential romances on the set, McCrea says with a sigh, "The beach girls were more protected than nuns were. I just learned to be very careful around them. They were constantly telling the guys not to lay a hand on the girls. It was as if they were a bunch of porcelain dolls. You would have had a better chance of putting your hand on a nun's shoulder than trying anything with the beach girls. I found out the hard way."

When asked which of the beach girls he found most attractive, Jody replies, "It's hard to choose. But I would say Salli Sachse, from afar, was my favorite. I would have been interested in starting up with her but she was married. I tried to hire her for *Cry Blood, Apache* but it didn't work out. There was nothing she was really suited for."

The one guy who seemed to get lucky often was bushy blonde-haired Ed Garner, *the* ladies' man of Paradise Cove. "Ed Garner came from a very wealthy family in Beverly Hills," remarks McCrea. "He was a good guy and he got a lot of the girls. They loved Ed because he was an upstanding guy."

McCrea's success playing a dim-witted surfer had its plusses and minuses for the serious actor. "These movies made me very popular for a time," admits McCrea. "Frankie told me when he'd go to openings, people would ask him, 'Where is Bonehead?' or 'Where is Deadhead.' My dad would get a kick when young people would ask him, 'Are you Jody's dad?' He thought, 'The kid's starting to make it.' However, these parts were endangering me of being typecast.

"My character was designed to be made fun of," continues Jody. "If people laughed at me, then I did my job. Fans would chuckle when I came on the screen because I would always be wearing a funny hat and would act dumb. The way I would approach these roles is by diminishing about half my intelligence and playing the part as a slow Southern guy."

Just before *Beach Blanket Bingo* was to be released, the song "I'll Never Change Him" by Guy Hemric and Jerry Styner, and sung by Annette Funicello was excised from the picture. It has been reported that the tune was deleted because Deborah Walley had cut a somewhat different version of it for *Ski Party* and the producers thought it would work better in that movie. When *Beach Blanket Bingo* was sold to cable television in the nineties, the scene was restored in the print shown on American Movie Classics. Unfortunately, the DVD version released in 2001 does not contain this song.

After *Beach Blanket Bingo* began playing at theaters across the country, AIP received flack from Walt Disney. According to Sam Arkoff, Disney was so protective of Annette Funicello that he would monitor the studio's promotional ads. The one that infuriated him the most from *Beach Blanket Bingo* had the tagline, "When 10,000 Bodies Hit 5,000 Bikinis." He called Arkoff in a rage, chastising the producer for degrading the wholesome Annette. Arkoff tried to calm him down and suggested that he actually see the movie, which did not contain anything offensive. Disney wouldn't hear of it and accused AIP of corrupting the young people of America. Arkoff opined in his autobiography, "It seemed to me that Disney never recognized that teenagers had different interests—and were attracted to different types of movies—than grade school kids. *The Mickey Mouse Club* was fine for young kids, but by adolescence, youngsters had outgrown *Old Yeller* and *Son of Flubber.*"

The film's end credits feature the bikini-clad Bobbi Shaw, Patti Chandler and Mary Hughes dancing and clowning around with Buster Keaton as the title tune sung by Frankie and Annette is repeated. There is also an announcement that proclaimed, "Get ready for the next beach blast ... *How to Stuff a Wild Bikini.*"

As it did with all its beach pictures, AIP sent their contract players on tour to promote the film. The actors were usually paired off or grouped in threes and traveled all over the United States and Canada doing junkets and personal appearances signing autographs. Ed Garner says with a laugh, "Luckily, we all got along extremely well. Eventually there were about nine of us signed to a contract including Donna Loren, Bobbi Shaw and Susan Hart. I never saw any friction. To pro-

Surfer hunk Jody McCrea shows off his muscular body to Patti Chandler in a promotional photograph for *Beach Blanket Bingo* (AIP, 1965).

mote *Beach Blanket Bingo* and *Ski Party* we appeared on *The Tonight Show Starring Johnny Carson,* which was an incredible experience. Johnny was very impressed with Bobbi Shaw and *Playboy* Playmate Jo Collins and bantered with them. Afterwards, he took us all out for dinner. He and Ed McMahon were just as delightful as could be."

Beach Blanket Bingo was another big hit for AIP but the company still did not capitalize on the music from its movies. Capitol Records issued the soundtrack album *Beach Blanket Bingo* with all the songs re-recorded by Donna Loren. The tie-in LP was produced by David Axelrod and arranged and conducted by H. B. Barnum. Loren cut all the tracks in 14 hours for her sole album. Axelrod and songwriter Guy Hemric thought "The Cycle Set" (originally sung by the Hondells in the film) was the album's best record and tried pushing it as a single. Loren sang it on *Shindig* and other televised teenage music shows but the song never charted. She followed this up with the single "New Love" but that too failed. As for the album, though Loren's voice is in top form, the LP sold a disappointing 20,000 copies despite Capitol's big push. In 2000, Collectable Records issued *The Very Best of Donna Loren* on CD. It featured all the songs from her *Beach Blanket Bingo* LP plus nine others. Unfortunately, none of the additional songs were from any of the other beach movies Loren performed in.

Loren would appear in one more movie for AIP, the comedy *Sergeant Deadhead* (1965), before her film career sputtered to an end. In between beach party films, Loren was a recurring regular on the popular dance show *Shindig*. Her popularity was so huge that even though she never had a hit record she received the Teen Screen Award for Favorite Female Vocalist in 1965. At that time Loren began acting more by appearing in a number of television shows such as *Ben Casey*, *Batman* and *The Monkees*. With her career red hot, she shocked her young fans by completely dropping out of show business in 1968 after she married Lenny Waronker, the then-president of Warner Bros. Records. A fashion designer, the remarried Donna Loren currently resides in Hawaii and owns her own clothing company, Adasa Hawaii.

Marta Kristen and Linda Evans both found fleeting fame on television right after *Beach Blanket Bingo* was released. Kristen co-starred for three seasons as Judy Robinson on Irwin Allen's hit sci-fi series *Lost in Space* while Linda Evans (who was married to actor John Derek from 1968 to 1974) hit the Western trail for four seasons as Audra Barclay on *The Big Valley*. Of course, Evans found superstardom as Krystle Carrington on *Dynasty* in the eighties. Disappointingly, she trashed *Beach Blanket Bingo*, calling it "embarrassing," during a 2004 appearance on CNN's *Larry King Live*.

Ex–*Playboy* Playmate Donna Michelle was not as lucky as Kristen and Evans. Marianne Gaba replaced her as Animal in the following beach party movie, *How to Stuff a Wild Bikini*. Michelle went on to appear in two episodes of *The Man from U.N.C.L.E.*, which were expanded into the features *The Spy with My Face* (1965) and *One Spy Too Many* (1966). After appearing in a few movies in France where her luscious uncovered body was on display, Michelle quit the acting business to concentrate on photography. In the early seventies, she was back at *Playboy*, this time working behind the camera.

Memorable Lines

(After pulling Sugar Kane out of the ocean, Frankie is hailed as a hero by the singer's press agent Bullets and columnist Earl Wilson.)

BULLETS: I didn't catch your name, boy.

FRANKIE: I didn't throw it.

BULLETS: That's pretty tacky, boy.

FRANKIE: I didn't want us to have a language barrier.

(Eric Von Zipper plots his next move with the Rat Pack by his side.)

VON ZIPPER: I'm thinkin' until I get it thunk.

Reviews

Katherine Carroll, *New York Daily News*—"The *Beach Party* gang returns for a new romp every time someone thinks up a new title. A funny thing about all this silliness, it's funny."

Margaret Harford, *Los Angeles Times*—"Some of it is pretty silly but there are a lot of attractive bikini beauties to look at while trying to sort out the plot and subplots. The film ... is best when it is giving the kids a sly drubbing."

Mandel Herbstman, *The Film Daily*—"The latest in the 'Beach' series ... alternates from gay surfing to sky diving for its kicks. Although the action, splash, comedy, songs and color are fairly good the story is routine, with some of the dialogue trite."

Frances Herridge, *New York Post*—"Beach Blanket Bingo ... is another of those Frankie Avalon party capers, with more gimmicks than usual. For the audiences that go for them—and judging by their box office success, their fans are legion—this should be more of a ball than ever."

John G. Houser, *Los Angeles Herald-Examiner*—"For their fourth 'Beach' picture, American International decided to play 'Bingo' and they have come up with a surefire winner.... *Bingo* is fun for anyone who likes mild movie diversion that is well-made."

Robert Salmaggi, *New York Herald Tribune*—"It's beach party time again, you lucky people.... The movie follows the usual 'beach' formula—lots of bikini-clad dancing dolls, songs, puppy love, and spoof slapstick."

Variety—"If tunes with a beat, sloppy story lines with action and sentimental young romance and a bevy of half clad boys and girls with delicious looks are the points that satisfy, James H. Nicholson and Samuel Z. Arkoff will probably be again coining on a picture that strictly caters to the inanities of youth."

Awards and Nominations

Harvard Lampoon's Movie Worst Award: "The Elsa Maxwell Kudo" (for the most unattractive social event of the season)—*Beach Blanket Bingo*

★ 15 ★

The Beach Girls and the Monster (1965)

Call It a Bash! Call It a Ball! Call It a Blast!

Fun: ★★½
Surfing: ★★★
Boy watching: ★★
Girl watching: ★★
Music: ★★★
Scenery: ★★

Release date: September 15, 1965. Running time: 70m. Box office gross: Not available. DVD release: Image Entertainment (May 7, 2002).

Jon Hall (*Dr. Otto Lindsay*), Sue Casey (*Vicky Lindsay*), Walker Edmiston (*Mark*), Elaine Du Pont (*Jane*), Arnold Lessing (*Richard Lindsay*), Read Morgan (*Sheriff Michaels*), Carolyn Williamson (*Sue*), Gloria Neal (*Bunny*), Tony Roberts (*Brad*), Clyde Adler (*Deputy Scott*), Dale Davis (*Tom*), Kingsley the Lion (*Himself*).

U.S. Films, Inc. *Produced by*: Edward Janis. *Directed by*: Jon Hall. *Screenplay by*: Joan Gardner. *Original Story by*: Joan Gardner. *Additional Dialogue*: Robert Siliphant and Don Marquis. Music: Frank Sinatra, Jr. Music Arranged and Conducted by: Chuck Sagle. *Assistant Director*: William Larkin. *Director of Photography*: Jon Hall. *Assistant Cameraman*: Walker Mitchell. *Supervising Editor*: Dolf Rudeen. *Art Director*: Shirley Rose. *Special Effects*: Bob Hansard. *Sound*: Emery Cohen. *Production Manager*: Henry Rose. *Hair Stylist*: Adelade Halpern. *Makeup*: Joan Howard. *Women's Wardrobe*: Bonnie Cole. *Statues by*: Walker Edmiston. *Surf Films by*: Dale Davis. *Sound Recorded by*: Glen Glenn Recording System. *Titles by*: Cinema Research Corporation, Steve Gross. Filmed in b/w.

"Dance Baby Dance" by Frank Sinatra, Jr., and Joan Janis, performed by unknown group. "More Than Wanting You" written and performed by Arnold Lessing. "There's a Monster in the Surf" by Walker Edmiston and Elaine Du Pont, performed by Elaine Du Pont and Kingsley the Lion.

Noted for being one of the worst movies of all time, *The Beach Girls and the Monster* gets a bad rap and is actually entertaining. Is the creature that is killing off bikini girls and beach boys a monster from the depths or a man in a rubber suit? A teenage surfer with a domineering father and a salacious stepmother (the zesty Sue Casey) tries to figure it out. Though the film is admittedly chock full of amateurish acting, grade-Z production values, a less-than-menacing monster that looks

181

straight out of Saturday morning television, unconvincing rear-projection driving scenes and one of the most God-awful songs ever to be warbled on the big screen, it is fun unadulterated camp. Credit must go to the wooden Jon Hall who directed, photographed and starred as the mad doctor in this wonderful mess.

Surf movie filmmaker and co-star Dale Davis impressively photographed the colorful surfing footage that appears in the middle of this black-and-white movie and for surfing fans it is worth the wait. But its inclusion has no significance to the plot. Frank Sinatra, Jr., of all people, supplies the musical score and his compositions surprisingly feature excellent deep-reverb surf instrumentals, which hold up well and add much-needed flavor to the movie. Less successful are the original songs. Arnold Lessing does okay with his solo while Elaine Du Pont's atrocious duet with a puppet lion has to go down in the annals of B-movie history as one of the worst numbers ever performed on the big screen.

As with a number of the Hollywood surf movies, the actors hired are just too old for their roles. Handsome and virile, Lessing tries as the confused surfer and looks quite beefy in swim trunks. He is also better cast in his role than his co-star Walker Edmiston, who looks thirtysomething; their "friendship" is never fully explained. Shapely Elaine Du Pont returned to the big screen after a six-year absence to portray Jane and acts like the biggest ninny on the sand. Didn't the producers realize that there was a reason why Du Pont, with the annoying kewpie-doll

In this publicity photo from *The Beach Girls and the Monster* (U.S. Films, 1965), surfer Arnold Lessing sings while the girls from the Whiskey A-Go-Go shake their bodies.

persona, hadn't landed a movie role in awhile? The "actors" and "actresses" hired to surround the young leads are the most unattractive bunch ever to don a swimsuit. If you are going to make a cheap beach movie, at least stock it with pretty, nubile beach babes and hunky surfer boys. These are just some of the missteps that make *The Beach Girls and the Monster* a must-see.

The Story

A trio of surfers and their girls are enjoying a day at the shore when one of the beach bunnies runs away from her boyfriend. The girl is soon found dead in a cave after being attacked by a seaweed-covered lizard creature. The murder occurs below the home of troubled surfer Richard Lindsay, who has to deal with an overbearing father who wants him to work at his oceanography lab. But the lad is only interested in surfing and hanging out with his girlfriend Jane. The other residents of the dysfunctional Lindsay household are Richard's sexy, acid-tongued stepmother, Vicky, whose hobbies are boozing and sexually taunting Richard's friend Mark, a sculptor, who was injured in a car accident due to Richard's negligence and lives in a connected guest house on the property.

Mark advises his friend to try to get along with his stepmother and father. He then shows Richard a surfing film some friends sent to them from Hawaii. The next day, while Richard and Jane avoid the beach and swim in his pool, Vicky braves the sand and sea where she almost becomes the next victim of the creature. She then models for Mark and taunts the frustrated sculptor who is attracted to her.

The sheriff finds a mysterious footprint left in the sand and brings it to Dr. Lindsay's lab. The scientist wants his son to help him investigate but the surfer has plans to attend a nighttime beach party despite a creature on the loose. Dr. Lindsay gets even more perturbed when he returns home and his bored wife callously informs him that she is leaving him. The brazen hussy then makes a date with another man.

The creature attacks during the beach bash, leaving a surfer named Tom dead on the sand. Later he strikes again and kills an inebriated Vicky, leaving a hideous scar across her face. Mark enters the house and stumbles upon the creature in the kitchen. After a struggle he rips off the mask, revealing Dr. Otto Lindsay, as Richard and Jane enter the residence. Mark dies from his wounds while Richard contacts the police. A chase is on and the doctor loses control of his car and perishes in a fiery crash. While a stunned Richard looks on, the sheriff theorizes that the scientist snapped and wanted to rid the beach of "loafers" and "little tramps" (as Dr. Lindsay described them) so Richard would return to work at the lab.

Behind-the-Scenes

The Beach Girls and the Monster, whose working title was *Surf Terror*, was produced by Edward Janis and written by his wife Joan. Edward was a former magazine cartoonist who created his own television cartoon *Spunky and Tadpole*. Actor

Jon Hall, best remembered as the star of *The Hurricane* (1937) and other colorful tropical programmers (usually co-starring Maria Montez), was hired to direct, photograph and star as Dr. Otto Lindsay. He had retired from acting in 1958 to work behind the camera.

When it came time to cast the film, the Janises went to their friends first. Actress Sue Casey had known Joan Janis since high school and ran into her while doing a commercial. The beautiful, sleek brunette was a former Goldwyn Girl in the late forties and played minor and bit roles in over 30 movies including, *Annie Get Your Gun* (1950), *An American in Paris* (1951) and *Rear Window* (1954). She took a respite from acting in the mid-fifties to raise a family but returned to films in the early sixties. Janis invited Casey to come audition for her husband and Jon Hall for the part of the acerbic stepmother, which she got.

Walker Edmiston was another friend of the couple's who was cast as the crippled sculptor. Edmiston then recommended cute Elaine Du Pont for the part of the ingenue. He had worked with the starlet on his local television kiddie series *The Walker Edmiston Show* in the LA area. Du Pont began playing minor roles in such films as *From Here to Eternity* (1953) and *There's No Business Like Show Business* (1954). Later she garnered bit roles in teenage exploitation films such as *Rock Around the Clock* (1956) and *I Was a Teenage Werewolf* (1957). After playing a wild youth involved with a car club and a haunted house in *Ghost of Dragstrip Hollow* (1959), Du Pont landed a co-hosting gig on the late night discussion program *The Tom Duggan Show* and a recurring role on *The Adventures of Ozzie and Harriet*. Because of her looks and talent, Du Pont was hired for *The Beach Girls and the Monster*.

The youthful male lead went to a handsome 28-year-old actor named Arnold Lessing. "I didn't have to audition to get this role," says Lessing. "Ed Janis saw me in the play *Take Her, She's Mine* and offered me the part."

No one is quite sure how Hall became involved with *The Beach Girls and the Monster*. Sue Casey theorized in *Drive-in Dream Girls* that Jon Hall owned a lot of stock footage like the scene of the Mercedes crashing used at the end of the movie and was offered a package deal to direct and star in exchange for using the footage. Lessing opines, "I would say he probably had a profit participation in the film."

The Beach Girls and the Monster was filmed in April of 1964 in Los Angeles on an extremely low budget. The exterior beach scenes were shot without permits near Will Rogers State Beach, usually in the early morning or nighttime hours. The scenes outside the Lindsay home were shot near the abode of Mexican film star Raquel Torres, who was Jon Hall's ex-wife. The interiors and the pool scenes were filmed at a spacious house in upscale Brentwood while one outdoor night shot was photographed at Jon Hall's Malibu beach pad.

Sue Casey remarked, "There was no money in this film to do anything. I did my own hair, my own makeup and supplied all the clothes I wore." Co-star Elaine Du Pont, however, in a *Fangoria* magazine interview with Tom Weaver, claimed it took three weeks to film and was not as low budget as people think. Arnold Lessing agrees with Casey and refutes Du Pont. He says, "It was due to budgetary constraints why Jon Hall wore so many hats on this. Who knows how little it cost to produce this movie? Half of it was filmed in somebody's house. The cost of developing the film probably was most of the budget."

Working with Hall was a unique experience for both actresses. Sue Casey commented, "I tried to not have a lot of interaction with him because he was not kind. We'd do a take and he would never get it right. He'd finally get it by (say) the eighth take but I'd do something wrong and he would save that one. It was not much fun working with him." Elaine Du Pont commented in *Fangoria* that Hall "enjoyed directing. Occasionally he didn't like a shot we did and he'd pop off, but most of the time we were pretty good."

Arnold Lessing recalls, "There were times where Jon Hall took an excessive amount of time to make Sue Casey look good like when she enters the house, goes to the bar to make a drink and staggers down the hall just before she gets murdered. He spent about half a day shooting that sequence. For my scenes, everything was one take. Jon Hall didn't do anything to make me look good. He gave me no advice or direction. *I felt that he wanted my part!*"

The body of the rubber monster costume came from Western Costume but the head could not be found. Walker Edmiston had designed the puppets for his children's show so he was recruited to create the monster head. Coming from Saturday morning television, it is no wonder his creature looked more sweet than monstrous. It has always been speculated that Hall donned the rubber suit himself to play the creature. Sue Casey could not confirm that but Elaine Du Pont is adamant that he alone wore the suit. Arnold Lessing insists some "big, husky young kid" wore it except "for the last scene when you see him [Hall] in the suit."

Frank Sinatra, Jr., yet another friend of the Janises, composed the jazzy musical score, reportedly in only two days. It features some highly original surf music rhythms. He co-wrote with Joan Janis the exciting main title theme, "Dance Baby Dance."

Besides contributing sculptures of Sue Casey and a mermaid to the film, jack-of-all-trades Edmiston was enlisted to pen a song. He co-wrote with Elaine Du Pont "There's a Monster in the Surf" 15 minutes before the cameras rolled. Du Pont, Edmiston (wearing dark glasses and a beard so he would not be recognized) and a hand puppet sang this ditty in a nighttime beach scene around the bonfire. However, a shoot that lasted all night on the beach into the dawn strained the electric generators, which in turn sabotaged the recording equipment, affecting the speed and pitch of Edmiston and Du Pont's voices. It also altered the song Arnold Lessing contributed. He says, "I actually sang the song on the beach. Rhino Records contacted me recently to obtain the original recording from the movie because it was so kooky they wanted to include in a CD containing the best music from the worst movies. I offered to go in to re-record the song but they weren't interested. They wanted the original."

Inserted into the middle of the film was about ten minutes' worth of color surfing footage shot by co-star Dale Davis. The only conceivable reason it was included was to pad the film's running time. "I grew up surfing and knew half the guys in the footage," reveals Lessing. "They were all Santa Monica surfers. Mickey Dora and I ran around together in 1955 and 1956. We met at Santa Monica College. Years later I did an Oldsmobile television commercial with him and Johnny Fain."

While working on the movie, Lessing landed a small role playing Linda Saunders' boyfriend in *The Girls on the Beach*. He appeared in both films simultane-

A beach girl recoils in terror (or is that laughter), from the pathetic-looking creature in this promotional still from *The Beach Girls and the Monster* (U.S. Films, 1965).

ously. "This was a funny thing," remarks Arnold. "The day we stayed up all night into the early morning hours on *Beach Girls* I had to be at the Santa Monica Pier to do *Girls on the Beach*. I drove home to my place, took a quick shower and then headed over to the pier. I had been up all night at Zuma Beach where it was really, really cold pretending it was a hot summer night. On the other one, I'm on the pier, the sun is coming up and it is warm. Everybody was standing around chilled but to me it felt wonderful."

When asked about working with Sue Casey and Elaine Du Pont, Lessing says with a laugh, "They were both fine but Elaine gave me a migraine headache when she screamed after finding the body in the kitchen. She had such a shrill voice and in that confined area I felt something snap at the base of my skull. I got sick and almost vomited."

Though filmed in April of 1964, *The Beach Girls and the Monster* did not see the light of day until September 1965. This didn't bother Arnold Lessing who "didn't give it a thought." It was released on a double-bill with the Italian horror film *War of the Zombies*. "I remember going to the opening at a drive-in up north," says Lessing. "The producer gave me a cigar, which was the first time I ever smoked one. The movie played the top of the bill and was even reviewed by *The New York*

Times. I got a good review but they mixed me up with Walker Edmiston. I didn't have a PR guy to have them write a retraction." He also received positive notices from *Boxoffice,* whose reviewer commented, "Lessing, a personable young man, does well in a musical number."

In the late sixties, the rights to *The Beach Girls and the Monster* were sold to television and the film was re-titled *Monster from the Surf* for no apparent reason. The producers were able to recoup some of their losses, which helped the actors because, according to Sue Casey, "we never got paid for it. When the producers sold it to television they came to us with these contracts to approve and paid us a little bit of what they owed us but we had to sign our lives away so that it could play on television forever without the actors getting any more money." Elaine Du Pont remembers getting paid "above scale—way above scale."

Over the years *The Beach Girls and the Monster* has gained cult status for many reasons, from the bad acting to the not-very-terrifying monster to the many gaffes in the movie. These begin with the opening scene of surfers riding some big waves. However, when the actors come on shore, the water is as smooth as glass. When the monster murders his first victim he heads away from the ocean, but his footprints in the sand point in the direction of the water. And at the end of the film, Otto flees his house in a white M.G. but the car seen going over the cliff is another make and model.

This monster from the surf not only killed nubile beachgoers but it also ended the film careers of Jon Hall, Arnold Lessing and Elaine Du Pont. Hall never acted or directed again although according to actress Celeste Yarnall she was hired to appear in a film entitled *Arielle* but Hall could not raise funding to complete the filming and the movie was shelved. The once popular actor committed suicide on December 13, 1979, due to his suffering from cancer of the bladder. After appearing on such television shows as *I Spy* and *Star Trek,* Lessing abandoned show business in the late sixties when he married. Today, he is an instructor at Santa Monica Community College. Du Pont lingered in Hollywood and currently hosts a celebrity chat show on access cable.

Actor and puppeteer Walker Edmiston went on to a long career playing minor roles on primetime television and in films. But he was most active in children's television as a voiceover artist for such programs as *H.R. Pufnstuf, Sigmund and the Sea Monsters, Land of the Lost, Spiderman, The Smurfs* and *Transformers.*

Sue Casey followed this with *Swamp Country* (1966) and her second beach movie, *Catalina Caper* (1967). Other films include *Camelot* (1967), *Paint Your Wagon* (1969), *The Happy Ending* (1969), *The Main Event* (1979), *Hysterical* (1983) and *American Beauty* (1999). The hardworking Casey is still active today but now juggles acting with a highly successful real estate career.

Dale Davis was the producer and director of such highly regarded surfing documentaries as *Walk on the Wet Side* (1963), *Strictly Hot* (1964) and *Inside Out* (1965), which had critics dubbing him "the king of surfing films." Branching out from surfing documentaries, Davis produced and directed the 1963 television pilot *Surf Scene* starring the singing sensation Jan and Dean; it highlighted the pair's humor and featured a video format in the style of MTV almost 20 years before that network was launched. Though that series didn't sell, his pilot *Never Too Young* did. Debuting on September 27, 1965, it was the first afternoon soap opera geared to teenagers. A Malibu backdrop set the romances and problems of various adolescent characters (played by such actors as Cindy Carol, Tony Dow, Dack Rambo, Mike Blodgett and Joy Harmon) apart from other daytime dramas, but it only lasted nine months. After accepting an acting role in *The Beach Girls and the Monster*, Davis went behind the camera again and scored his biggest hit with his film *Golden Breed* (1968), which has often been compared to *The Endless Summer* as the ultimate sixties surf documentary. Davis slipped from a helicopter while filming high above Waimea Bay for the movie and luckily survived though he broke his back. In the seventies, a recovered Davis produced and directed *Liquid Space* (1973) and lent guidance to John Milius, who was directing the Hollywood surf movie *Big Wednesday*. Davis continued promoting the sport of surfing tirelessly until he suffered a stroke in 2001. He passed away two months later on September 13, 2001, at the age of 61.

Memorable Lines

(Vicky comes across Richard kissing his girlfriend Jane in the driveway.)

VICKY: My, my—what a touching little scene.

RICHARD: Hi, Vicky.

VICKY: I see you brought one of your little mermaids home—*how nice*. Mmm. Well, I'm going down to the beach before I play model for Mark so you'll have the house all to yourself. *Have fun, children.*

Reviews

Nadine M. Edwards, *The Citizen-News*—"Reading the telephone directory would probably prove much more entertaining and exciting and suspenseful and satisfying and psychologically rewarding than does this Edward Janis production...."

James O'Neill, *Terror on Tape* [video review]—"Laugh riot tale of the terrible consequences of adolescent sloth. With plenty of surfing scenes (some of them in color), a swingin' Frank Sinatra, Jr., score, and a monster that looks like an escapee from *Sesame Street*, this is one turkey you don't have to wait until Thanksgiving to enjoy."

Kevin Thomas, *Los Angeles Times*—"Movie for morons.... This mindlessness is glossed over with polished photography ... a good jazz score ... and deft editing that provides a rapid pace. A slick job despite amateurish acting and a script devoid of even simple cause-and-effect logic."

Variety—"A surfside murder a go-go, this uneven quickie attempts to break into the Beach pix market, but black and white photography, small name cast, and skimpy production will make it hard going."

★ 16 ★

Daytona Beach Weekend (1965)

It's a blast! 60,000 fun-hungry kids blow off steam in one big beach rumble!

Released on April 14, 1965. 87m. Box office gross: Not available.
DVD release: Not as of January 2005.
Don Jackson (*Bill*), Rayna (*Jill*), Steve Harkins (*Mike*), Linda Poland (*Liz*), Joyce Pruitt (*Gloria*). Guest Stars: Del Shannon, The Offbeets, Houston and Dorsey, and Sue Skeen— Miss New York State.
A 60th Arts production. A Dominant Films release. *Produced and Directed by*: Bob Welborn. *Musical Director*: Bob Quimby. *Director of Photography*: Joseph Squires. *Location Production Manager*: Joe Barone. *Film Editor*: Ralph Bevins. *Wardrobe*: "Wickline." *Makeup*: Dixie Craft. *Hair Styling*: Vicki Hageman. *Shuffleboards*: "Kahuna." *Sound Editor*: George Yarborough. *Script Girl*: Jessie Brown. Filmed in Ansco Color.
"Runaway" and "Stranger in Town" performed by Del Shannon. "Double Trouble," "She Lied" and "Hey Little Girl" performed by the Offbeets. "Hopelessly" and "You're the Boy for Me" performed by Rayna. "Wreck on the John B." and "Hootenanny Annie" performed by Houston and Dorsey.

Very little is known about the plot of *Daytona Beach Weekend*, an obscure beach movie that is very hard to find if it even exists at all on video. Don Jackson and Rayna played college students who fall in love amid the beachgoing, partying and rioting while on spring break in Daytona Beach. In between romantic clinches and scenes on the beach, musical guest stars including Del Shannon and the Offbeets perform making the movie more akin to *Beach Party* than *Where the Boys Are*.

Behind-the-Scenes

Daytona Beach Weekend was shot on location in Daytona Beach, Florida, in 16mm and then blown up to 35mm for a limited release to mostly drive-ins in the Southeast. According to the film's pressbook, the movie was shot over a nine-month period on a $2.5 million budget, which seems preposterous considering the no-name cast and crew. Purportedly, real footage of a riot that broke out on Daytona Beach during spring break of 1964 was included in the film. Though a number of online sources credit Robert Welby as producer and director, the *Daytona Beach Weekend* pressbook credits Bob Welborn. Despite profiles on the cast and musical performers, no information on Welborn was included.

Trade ad for *Daytona Beach Weekend* (Dominant, 1965).

Boyish and slim, Don Jackson, who was discovered by Bob Welborn, played the film's lead. According to the pressbook, he and his co-star Rayna had a real-life romance while shooting the movie. Jackson was hyped to the heavens as he was called another James Dean who "will win the hearts of female moviegoers the world over, as well as the respect and admiration of the men." Welborn predicted that the newcomer would become "a full-fledged Hollywood star" and "1965's biggest new-comer." Jackson was slated to star in Welborn's upcoming movies *Dona Evita, Caribou* and *Blast at Play College* but none of these ever came to fruition, probably because *Daytona Beach Weekend* did not become a hit.

Described as a "Southern belle, with an extremely great talent in the vocalist department," pretty Rayna had a recording contract with Carellen Records. She sings two songs in *Daytona Beach Weekend,* one of which ("Hopelessly") director Welborn filmed outdoors while over 2,500 people looked on.

Daytona Beach Weekend also featured two beauty queens. Blonde Linda Poland won a number of local contests. A college student, she was appearing in a production of *The Diary of Anne Frank* at Stetson University in Deland, Florida, when Welborn discovered her. Reportedly, she was offered a role in a movie called *Hi Ho Jamaica* but turned it down to co-star in *Daytona Beach Weekend.* Dark-haired Sue Skeen, who resembled Nancy Sinatra, was Miss New York State of 1964. She acted previously mostly in television commercials for National Airlines and Gillette Right Guard.

Musical director Bob Quimby was the owner of a central Florida recording studio, which was the home of the Tropical and Carellen labels whose artists included the Surftones, the Earthmen and the Fastbacks.

Of the musical guest stars, only singer Del Shannon was internationally known. He had a No. 1 record with "Runaway" in 1961, which he sings in *Daytona Beach Weekend,* and had Top Ten hits with "Hats Off to Larry" and "Little Town Flirt." Never fitting the typical teen idol role a la Frankie Avalon or Fabian due to his harder rocking musical style, Shannon was more popular in Europe than in the U.S. and toured with the Beatles before appearing in *Daytona Beach Weekend.*

The Offbeets were hyped as "America's answer to the Beatles." The handsome quartet, which performed wearing matching sports coat and ties, consisted of lead singer Tom Wynn on drums, Jim Robertson on bass guitar, David Messimer on lead guitar and David Duff on rhythm guitar. At the time of filming *Daytona Beach Weekend,* Messimer was the oldest band member at 20 years of age while the other three were all teenagers. The group, managed by Ron Dillman, purportedly had a recording contract with Canadian American Records and their first release was the 45 "Double Trouble" and "She Lied," which they sang in the movie. Needless to say, the Offbeets didn't come close to becoming Freddie and the Dreamers let alone the Beatles. In fact, the group disbanded soon after the movie was released. Tom Wynn and David Duff together with castoffs of Dillman's other act, the Trade-marks, formed a new group called We the People. A versatile garage rock band that could easily switch from playing raucous party rock to melodic ballads, We the People are highly regarded today for their "depth and diversity" though they only found regional success during the sixties. Wynn left the band in 1966 after recording their first single while Duff remained until the group folded in 1970.

Houston and Dorsey were an older comedy-musical duo who performed in

Don Jackson and Rayna dance on the shore in *Daytona Beach Weekend* **(Dominant, 1965).**

nightclubs throughout Florida. They were described in the pressbook as "free flowing comics who are also excellent instrumentalists." The duo joined forces in the late forties and toured with Steve Allen, Ray Anthony and Gene Autry. They made their film debut in *We Shall Return* (1962) with Cesar Romero. Producer-director Welborn caught Houston and Dorsey's act at the Castaway Beach Motel in Daytona Beach and signed them for the film.

Despite all the hyperbole, *Daytona Beach Weekend* did not reach a national audience so it is not too surprising that its future "stars of tomorrow" never came close to stardom or appeared in a movie again.

★ 17 ★

Girl Happy (1965)

Elvis jumps with the campus crowd to make the beach "ball" bounce!

Fun: ★★½
Surfing: ★
Boy watching: ★★
Girl watching: ★★★★
Music: ★★★
Scenery: ★★

Released in April 14, 1965. 96m. Box office gross: $3.25 million.

DVD release: Not as of January 2005.

Elvis Presley (*Rusty Wells*), Shelley Fabares (*Valerie*), Harold J. Stone (*Big Frank*), Gary Crosby (*Andy*), Joby Baker (*Wilbur*), Nita Talbot (*Sunny Daze*), Mary Ann Mobley (*Deena*), Fabrizio Mioni (*Romano*), Jimmy Hawkins (*Doc*), Jackie Coogan (*Sgt. Benson*), Peter Brooks (*Brentwood Von Durgenfeld*), John Fiedler (*Mr. Penchill*), Chris Noel (*Betsy*), Lyn Edgington (*Laurie*), Gail Gilmore (*Nancy*), Pamela Curran (*Bobbie*), Rusty Allen (*Linda*), George Cisar (*Bartender at the Kit Kat Club*), Nancy Czar (*Blonde on the Beach*), Jim Dawson (*Muscle Boy*), Mike De Anda (*Burt*), Darren Dublin (*Driver*), Tommy Farrell (*Louie*), Ted Fish (*Garbage Man*), Milton Frome (*Police Captain*), Norman Grabowski (*"Wolf Call" O'Brien*), Dan Haggerty (*Charlie*), Alan Hanley (*Waiter #1*), Ralph Lee (*Officer Jones*), Richard Reeves (*Officer Wilkins*), Olan Soule (*Waiter #2*). Not credited: Lori Williams, Beverly Adams, Theresa Cooper, Stasa Damascus, Hank Jones, Kent McCord, Julie Payne (*College Boys and Girls*)

An Euterpe production. An MGM release. *Produced by*: Joe Pasternak. *Directed by*: Boris Sagal. *Written by*: Harvey Bullock and R. S. Allen. *Director of Photography*: Philip H. Lathrop, A.S.C. *Music*: George Stoll. *Vocal Backgrounds*: The Jordanaires. *Art Directors*: George W. Davis, Addison Hehr. *Set Decorators*: Henry Grace, Hugh Hunt. *Film Editor*: Rita Roland. *Assistant Director*: Jack Aldworth. *Technical Advisor*: Col. Tom Parker. *Makeup Supervisor*: William Tuttle. *Hairstyles by*: Sydney Guilaroff. *Recording Supervisor*: Franklin Milton. *Camera Operator*: William Lloyd Norton. *Choreographer*: David Winters. *Sound Mixer*: Larry Jost. *Sound*: Bruce Wright. *Unit Production Manager*: Al Shenberg. *Wardrobe*: Lambert Marks, Elva Martien. *Makeup*: Ron Berkeley. *Dialogue Coach*: Jack Mintz. Filmed in Panavision and Metrocolor.

All songs sung by Elvis Presley except where indicated. "Girl Happy" by Doc Pomus and Norman Meade. "Cross My Heart and Hope to Die" by Ben Weisman and Sid Wayne. "Spring Fever" by Bill Giant, Bernie Baum and Florence Kaye, performed by Elvis Presley and Shelley Fabares. "Do Not Disturb" and "Wolf Call" by Bill Giant, Bernie Baum and Florence Kaye. "Do the Clam" by Ben Weisman, Sid Wayne and Dolores Fuller. "Fort Lauderdale Chamber of Commerce" and "Puppet on a String" by Sid Tepper and Roy C. Bennett.

"I've Got to Find My Baby" and "The Meanest Girl in Town" by Joy Byers. "Startin' Tonight" by Lenore Rosenblatt.

Girl Happy was Elvis Presley's attempt to capitalize on the beach movie craze. However, compared to other films of this genre, *Girl Happy* is severely landlocked. Despite the ad campaign, there aren't many scenes on the beach. In fact, Elvis is seen on the seashore only briefly, in a montage sequence and a nighttime production number where he sings on a makeshift sand dune.

On its own, however, *Girl Happy* is pleasant fare and one Elvis' better post–*Viva Las Vegas* movies despite its wafer-thin plot. Though filmed mainly on the back lot, the colorful production is first-rate, the action never lets up, and the film has that glossy, vibrant MGM sheen to it. Director Boris Sagal keeps the story moving briskly and surrounds Elvis with a perky, talented supporting cast including standouts Jimmy Hawkins as naïve Doc and Mary Ann Mobley as a frustrated vixen. Presley seems comfortable with his role and plays it breezily. He and Shelley Fabares make a charming couple and have a few tender scenes together.

Though this is a supposed beach movie, Elvis (sporting a fit and trim physique) is never seen in shorts or a bathing suit! The film features a number of handsome actors, all of whom remain covered up. Not so for the gals, though. *Girl Happy* lives up to its title in the flesh department. There is an array of swimsuit-clad cuties on display from the leads Shelley Fabares and Mary Ann Mobley to the featured performers Chris Noel and Lyn Edgington to bit players Nancy Czar, a knockout in a leopard print bikini, and Gail Gilmore a.k.a. Gerber.

The popular soundtrack is one of the King's most varied and best from this time period. From the touching "Puppet on a String" to the swinging "Do the Clam" to the romantic "Do Not Disturb," the songs help buoy the movie and make it fun for Elvis' core audience. But despite the enjoyable soundtrack, Elvis at his peak, energetic dancing choreographed by David Winters and a bevy of bikini-clad gals, beach party fans may still want to skip this one.

The Story

Girl Happy opens with a narrator contrasting a beautiful bikini-clad girl with the measurements 36-24-36 in sunny warm Fort Lauderdale with a beautiful parka-clad girl with the same measurements in snowy cold Chicago as Rusty Wells and His Combo begin singing the title tune. The guys finish their set and celebrate their upcoming road trip to Fort Lauderdale but the Six Hundred Club's owner, the tough, steely-eyed Mr. Frank, decides to extend their contract another six weeks since they have been playing to sell-out crowds. Andy, Wilbur and Doc are resigned to the fact that they won't be going to sunny Florida but Rusty chooses to stand up to Big Frank.

Rusty overhears him mumbling about his daughter Valerie who has decided to accompany her two college friends, Betsy and Laurie, to Fort Lauderdale for spring break. Rusty coyly suggests that she'd need chaperoning since the town is filled with "30,000 sex-starved boys" and that Big Frank would want him and his friends to keep an eye on her. Big Frank agrees and sends the combo to Florida with a threat that if his daughter gets into any trouble they are fired.

Poster art for *Girl Happy* (MGM, 1965).

Arriving at the motel, Rusty's easy task of chaperoning Valerie hits a snag when the nerdy coed turns out to be a knockout. He decides to invite her to the Sandbar Club where he and his combo will be performing. She declines after catching Rusty making eye contact with the shapely Deena. Later, on stage, the guys notice Valerie, who has come to the club with bookworm Brentwood Von Durgenfeld, BVD for short. After the set, the guys rendezvous with their newfound girlfriends at the motel. Rusty is making time with Deena on his patio when he notices BVD, who reveals that Valerie went off with Italian exchange student Romano Rossi to his boat at Coral Pier.

Rusty deserts Deena and rounds up the guys to rescue the naïve coed. As the Latin lover is plying Valerie with champagne, the guys notice the boat is still tethered to a winch on the trailer truck that transported it. They activate the winch, safely bringing the boat onto the trailer. After propping the cabin door shut, the guys race home, depositing the cruiser into the motel's pool. An inebriated Valerie is back in time to take her father's nightly phone call. The guys' satisfaction quickly turns sour when their deserted dates Bobbie, Nancy and Linda tell them off. Rusty goes to his room to be with Deena but she is gone and has written "Drop dead" in lipstick on his mirror.

The next day, Valerie and her friends go to the beach. Andy takes first watch but is distracted when he notices a curvaceous blonde in a leopard bikini on the sand. Romano shows up and escorts Valerie back to her room. Panicked, the guys interrupt Rusty, who is making time with the placated Deena in a park. He abandons the girl once again. At the motel he gets the manager, Mr. Penchill, to go to the room where they find Valerie and Romano playing bridge with Betsy and Laurie. Penchill wants to throw them out for having a boy in their room but Rusty convinces him not to.

Back in Valerie's good graces, Rusty invites her to perform with his combo. After they finish, the guys draw straws and Doc loses so he has to follow Valerie for the night. Just as Rusty settles in with an appeased Deena, a frantic Doc contacts him with news that Valerie has slipped off with Romano. Forsaking their frustrated women once again, the guys try to track the couple down. With no luck, Rusty gets an idea and starts singing on the beach and the kids come flocking to do "The Clam." Andy and Wilbur spot Romano, roll him into a beach blanket and dump him onto a passing truck. Rusty walks the confused Val back to the motel and she confesses that she had a date with Romano but is glad that he ran off. She then thanks him for making her time in Florida wonderful and gives him a sweet, gentle kiss on the lips for being such a special guy.

Feeling like a heel, Rusty tells his elated buddies that he is going to take over chaperone duties full-time so they can be with Nancy, Bobbie and Linda. While Rusty and Valerie are having a grand time water-skiing and exploring the city on motor scooters, the guys are feeling sorry for Rusty. They decide to make it up to him and convince Deena that Rusty has been pining for her. To surprise him, Deena sets up a romantic dinner for two in his room. But Rusty already has dinner plans with Valerie. Keeping Val outside in front, he juggles the two women until Valerie has to leave to take her father's phone call. When the elated girl blurts out to Big Frank that she has met a wonderful boy named Rusty Wells, he laughs and tells his daughter that he is paying him to keep an eye on her. Hurt and furious, Valerie calls Romano and makes a date to ensure that Rusty earns his money.

At the Kit Kat Club, Valerie gets sloshed and jumps on stage to perform a strip tease to the amusement of Romano and stripper Sunny Daze. While trying to stop her, Rusty gets into a fistfight with some drunken students and all hell breaks lose. The would-be hero is knocked unconscious and dumped into a flower-pot. When he awakes, the club is in a shambles and everyone is gone. Wilbur and Andy inform him that Valerie and her friends are in jail. Rusty tries everything to get the girl sprung to no avail. He then gets some guys to dig a tunnel to her cell. Dressed as a woman, he finally reaches the cell where he finds Sunny but no Valerie. The dancer informs him that her father bailed her out.

As Valerie is packing her bags, she berates Big Frank for paying a boy to take her out, sing for her and to kiss her. Her contrite father admits he only paid Rusty to keep an eye on her and suggests that Rusty did those other things on his own. When Betsy and Laurie come in with news of the dramatic way Rusty broke into the jail cell, Valerie realizes that he really does care for her. At the Sandbar Club, Rusty and his combo are playing their last number. As Rusty sings he spots Deena and as he begins to approach her, Valerie steps in front of him with Big Frank behind her. After getting Big Frank's permission, Rusty takes Valerie into his arms.

Behind-the-Scenes

Seeing the success of the surf and beach party films during 1963 and 1964, MGM decided to go back to the well that started it all. *Girl Happy* was a combination of the studio's *Where the Boys Are* and AIP's *Beach Party* from Joe Pasternak, the producer of the former. Elvis on spring break in Fort Lauderdale surrounded by bikini-clad beauties and a trio of comic actors as friends while belting out song after song must have sounded perfect on paper. This was Elvis' first movie since *G.I. Blues* (1960) where he played the leader of a combo and his first and only appearance in drag.

Boris Sagal was brought in to direct and the fact that he had never worked with Elvis before may have given the film a freshness and vitality that were lacking in some of Elvis' other films that were directed by stalwart Norman Taurog during this time. Sagal had been working in television since 1955. *Dime with a Halo* (1963) starring Barbara Luna was his debut feature before directing Richard Chamberlain in his first starring movie role, as a smalltime lawyer in *Twilight of Honor* (1963).

Recalling how she got to play Presley's leading lady, Shelley Fabares said in *Outré* magazine, "My agents had negotiated a three-picture deal with MGM and the first one was to be with Elvis Presley. I was a fan of his but I was not a rabid fan. I remember—and always will remember—the first day that I met him on the set. We were getting ready to rehearse our first scene and all of a sudden he was walking across the soundstage and I suddenly thought, '*Oh my God. It's Elvis Presley!*' You're always nervous when starting a film but until I saw him that's when I *really* got nervous. It wasn't because he was beautiful—though he looked great on film, he was much more gorgeous in person—but he was like a god walking across that stage. And it really sort of took my breath away. But happily after we met we clicked right away. It was like we had known each other for a long time. Thankfully I quickly got over the nervousness because you can't act with someone if he awes you."

MGM peppered the remaining roles with other contract players. Though it was released after *Get Yourself a College Girl* (1964), this was Mary Ann Mobley's first movie as she landed the second lead of Deena, the sexy girl Elvis keeps deserting to rescue Fabares' character. Comic actor Joby Baker played the wisecracking combo member Wilbur and won the best notices of the supporting cast. "A good actor who always delivers when he has some comedy to work with" (*The Hollywood Reporter*) and "gives strong support" (*Variety*) were some of the compliments thrown his way. Fabrizio Mioni played the suave Italian playboy while the nerdy bookworm role went to tall blonde Peter Brooks.

Pretty, flaxen-haired Chris Noel portrayed one of Fabares' college friends on vacation with her. Noel noted in *Fantasy Femmes of Sixties Cinema* that Fabares and Mobley had received flowers from Elvis but she and Lyn Edgington did not. She pointed this out to the King and the next day their trailer was full of flowers.

The cast was rounded out with an assortment of young actors mostly familiar to younger audiences. Bing's oldest son Gary Crosby, who while under contract to 20th Century–Fox had appeared in such breezy teenage fare as *Mardi Gras* (1958), *Holiday for Lovers* (1959) and *Two Tickets to Paris* (1962), played the girl-crazy Andy. Cast as naïve innocent Doc was busy television actor Jimmy Hawkins, who was juggling recurring roles on *The Donna Reed Show* and *The Adventures of Ozzie and Harriet*. Comedienne Nita Talbot was cast an exotic dancer, a role similar to the one played by Barbara Nichols in *Where the Boys Are*. Gail Gerber, a former ballet dancer trained in classical and jazz music, played the minor role of Doc's spring fling. Elvis took a shine to the pretty blonde but she kept turning down his invitations to parties at his home. It wasn't until she began dating author Terry Southern that she learned of Presley's importance to popular music.

Girl Happy was filmed in June and July of 1964. Though the movie is set in Fort Lauderdale, there are not many beach scenes in *Girl Happy* because, according to Chris Noel, "We shot this in California on the same beaches they used for the other surf and beach movies." To keep the mountains from appearing on screen, lots of close-ups and tight shots are used in the few outdoor scenes. The penny pinchers at MGM probably figured they could to save money and get away with substituting Santa Monica for Fort Lauderdale without the unsophisticated audience members noticing—especially since there were only three scenes set on the sand. The rest of the movie was filmed on the studio's soundstages.

Despite her No. 1 record "Johnny Angel" in 1962, Shelley Fabares was very disappointed that she had to sing a duet with Elvis. A number of his previous leading ladies such as Joan O'Brien and Cynthia Pepper were talented vocalists who did not get the opportunity to sing with Presley but wished they did. Fabares explains, "Recording 'Johnny Angel' was a devastatingly difficult experience because I'm not a singer and don't like singing. But I am very proud of the song and how it has brought joy to many people. So when I got this role they said I would be singing. I said, 'I don't think I could do this.' And they said, 'Sure you can.' Of course by that time I had cut two albums so I didn't have much of a leg to stand on.

"In the scene, Chris Noel, Lyn Edgington and I are bopping along singing the song 'Spring Fever' and it's intercut with Elvis and the guys singing as we're all driving down to Fort Lauderdale," continues Fabares. "I sound like Minnie Mouse my voice is so high! I think they had to do that so Elvis could sing in his key and I guess I could sing in that higher key, such as it was."

According to the cast interviewed, *Girl Happy* was a smooth shoot. Fabares especially has fond memories. "It was wonderful. Those sets were a lot of fun. Everybody worked hard because the films were shot very quickly. There were always a lot of dance routines and production numbers. I've known Jimmy Hawkins all of my life so it was like old home week. Gary Crosby was very nice. Fabrizio Mioni was very charming and sweet. Mary Ann Mobley is exactly like you'd think she would be—an incredibly beautiful, gentle, strong Southern belle. She is just a lovely woman. And Chris Noel was darling to work with. We all got along great!"

Mary Ann Mobley remarked in *Elvis Up Close*, "Elvis had a great sense of humor, a good attitude, and he was a perfect gentleman. I never dated him, but I did two movies with him, and we became friends. Elvis and Shelley Fabares got along well, too. She's a lovely lady as well as being a good actress. She didn't have any hidden agendas with Elvis, either."

Surprisingly, Chris Noel liked everyone except Mary Ann Mobley, with whom she co-starred in *Get Yourself a College Girl* (1964) and *For Singles Only* (1968). "Mary Ann was a phony," remarks Chris with a laugh. "She was the only person I worked with that I would say that about. She was saccharine, sweet and *phony!*" Dancer Lori Williams remarked in *Drive-in Dream Girls* that she too had "a problem" working with Mobley, whom she described as "a prima donna."

During the course of the shoot, Fabares was dreading the scene where her character gets drunk and jumps on stage at a nightclub and begins singing while stripping her clothes off. "It was one of the times that I was going to get out of the business. I was terrified and just thought there was no way I could sing, dance and act drunk and hopefully be funny all at the same time. But I remembered a story Donna Reed told me when I was nervous about doing a tap dance routine on her show. She said to me, 'Early in my career I had to do three things in this movie— sing, dance the jitterbug and fall over backwards into a pool. I really thought about bowing out of the film because those three things scared me so much. But I had to do it. One of the things you'll find in life is that the things that scare us the most are the things we should go forward and do.' The movie she was talking about was *It's a Wonderful Life*. It was a great pep talk and has stayed with me all of my life."

Though she didn't feel comfortable singing, Fabares also felt awkward sitting or standing there while being serenaded by Elvis. It was a problem faced by all his leading ladies. What do you do while this guy is singing to you? Most would just stare at him with a dreamy look in their eyes. Fabares opines, "Those scenes were difficult for him—I'm sure—and they were certainly hard for me. He pre-recorded all the songs and would sing along with the recordings. I think his movies were very constricting to him. He wasn't allowed to do what he could really do on a performance level. Most of time when he would sing to the girl, he'd be on the beach or in a sailboat and he would have a guitar and suddenly start singing. For the actress in the role you had to hopefully not look like too much of a simpleton sitting there adoringly. But you also had to try to keep it live and remember who your charac-

Elvis Presley surrounded by his lovely co-stars Chris Noel, Shelley Fabares and Mary Ann Mobley in a publicity photo from *Girl Happy* (MGM, 1965).

ter was and what she was supposed to be feeling at the time. What was actually the hardest thing for us is that we just laughed all the time. So trying to do these scenes with serious songs was very difficult.

"I've made it a policy to say just a few things about Elvis and how I felt about him," Fabares continues. "I've just always felt that since he never talked about himself when he was here it wouldn't be right for me to discuss him now. I will say that he was a wonderful person—kind, sweet and funny. Doing those pictures with him were some of the happiest experiences I ever had professionally or personally." Gail Gerber also found him to be "intelligent, quiet and very sweet." But he also seemed to her "like a young man in turmoil—sort of like a *'who do I have to fuck to get off this picture'* kind of thing. Elvis was a tortured guy who obviously hoped for something better."

"I loved Elvis," exclaimed Chris Noel. "He was wonderful. However, I had a problem with him one day when he stuck his tongue in my ear. I was sitting in a chair on the set watching them film a scene. Suddenly, in my right ear is this wet tongue. I automatically yelled, 'Lay off!' I turned to my right and there was Elvis. I was flabbergasted. Of course, when I look back I think, 'Oh my God! I should have said, *Elvis do it again and again and again!* But I must have really stood out because a lot of his friends throughout the years have come up to me at times and told me that Elvis always said good things about me. He respected and liked me, and always said I was one of the top girls in Hollywood. I thought that was really, really nice."

Girl Happy was one of Presley's biggest hits of the mid-sixties. The combination of the King singin' and romancin' on spring break surrounded by a bevy of bikini-clad lovelies attracted not only his core group of fans but beach movie lovers as well. Though it was not shot on location in Florida, the production values were first-rate, raising *Girl Happy* a cut above some of his other movies at the time such as *Kissin' Cousins* and *Tickle Me*. Fabares remarks, "I think it was the best movie Elvis and I made together. It is also my favorite because it is a good movie. Maybe one of Elvis' best films too. It had a strong, wonderful director in Boris Sagal, a good script, tuneful songs and a talented cast. All those ingredients that went into an Elvis film worked particularly well in *Girl Happy*."

Presley also had another hit soundtrack LP with *Girl Happy*, which hit No. 8 on *Billboard*'s Pop Album charts. Two songs, "Do the Clam" and "Puppet on a String," were released as singles and both cracked the Top 25 Pop Singles.

Some of the actors in *Girl Happy* went on to work with Elvis again. Reportedly his favorite leading lady, Fabares starred with Elvis in *Spinout* (1966) as a spoiled heiress and *Clambake* (1967) as a young woman out to trap herself a rich husband. Mary Ann Mobley graduated to the female lead as an Arabian princess in *Harum Scarum* (1965), which also featured Gail Gerber in a supporting role as a dancing gypsy. Jimmy Hawkins was once again cast as one of Presley's band mates in *Spinout*.

Gary Crosby, who of all Bing's children resembled Bing the most, never found super stardom as did his father but he was a competent actor who kept working through the early nineties, mostly on television. His most remembered role was that of Officer Ed Wells on the hit police series *Adam-12*. However, Crosby lived a tortured life in his father's shadow and turned to alcohol. This was a hereditary condition as his mother singer Dixie Lee died from causes related to acute alcoholism. His brothers Dennis and Lindsay also were also affected and both committed suicide. Gary was able to get sober in the early eighties and wrote a scathing account of life with his abusive father in *Going My Own Way*, which was published in 1984. He passed away of lung cancer on August 24, 1995.

Always the funny second banana, Joby Baker finally got a chance to play a lead role on the sitcom *Good Morning, World* (1967–68) co-starring Julie Parrish. Created and produced by the revered Carl Reiner and Sheldon Leonard, the show about two morning radio disc jockeys was not a hit despite positive reviews from the critics. Baker continued playing supporting roles on television and in films through the early eighties. His last known credit was playing a police detective on the acclaimed drama series *The Paper Chase* in 1984.

Frustrated with only getting supporting roles, Chris Noel left MGM to go freelance, landing lead roles in the beach party flicks *Beach Ball* (1965) and *Wild Wild Winter* (1966).

Peter Brooks seemed to always be cast as the bespectacled nerd beginning in *Gidget Goes to Rome* (1963) followed by *Girl Happy* and *The Girls on the Beach* (1965), his final movie appearance. Fabrizio Mioni on the other hand was typecast as the Latin lover and went on to appear in *The Venetian Affair* (1966) and *The Secret War of Harry Figg* (1967). He worked in Hollywood until the early seventies, when his last known credit was the appropriately titled episode "Love and the Latin Lover" on *Love, American Style* (1972).

Memorable Lines

(Rusty tries to save Valerie and her friends from being evicted from their motel room after he summons the manager on her because he mistakenly thinks she is alone with Romano.)

RUSTY: What's the trouble?

VALERIE: All we were doing was playing bridge!

RUSTY: Yeah, what's wrong with that?

MR. PENCHILL: They've broken the rules—article 3, subparagraph B—"Thou shall not have a boy in the room."

RUSTY: You don't listen. They were playing bridge. That wasn't a boy—it was a fourth.

Reviews

Janet Graves, *Photoplay*—"Yep, here we are … back 'Where the Boys Are.' Elvis' visit hasn't the wild pace of that memorable riot, but it's an entertaining musical romp on its own terms."

Margaret Harford, *Los Angeles Times*—"Another 'beach musical' that looks livelier and fresher than most. Elvis sings a batch of swinging tunes … and romances the Misses Mobley and Fabares in his own, wooden Indian style. It gets 'em, though."

Mandel Herbstman, *The Film Daily*—"An assortment of pretty girls, lovely outdoor scenery centering around Fort Lauderdale, Fla., and songs galore by Elvis Presley put Joe Pasternak's production *Girl Happy* … in the popular category. The story rolls along its carefree way without making the slightest demand of concentration. It is fashioned for fun and frolic in the formula way."

Frances Herridge, *New York Post*—"Elvis Presley has gone in for one of those teenage beach parties in *Girl Happy*…. He's getting a bit old for that kind of kid stuff, which may be a good thing. His smooth, more mature manner keeps the craziness under control…."

John G. Houser, *Los Angeles Herald-Examiner*—"*Girl Happy* … does insult an adult intelligence with a trite story and cliché-ridden scenes and dialogue."

James Powers, *The Hollywood Reporter*—"*Girl Happy* is … a picture with a sharp trim and bright decoration, lively action and some good jokes, as well as the usual blend of song and romance."

Howard Thompson, *The New York Times*—"Even with a large throng of clean-cut youngsters and some fetching Fort Lauderdale backgrounds woven in for travel-poster picturesque-ness, the picture meanders familiarly. The saving grace is the steady stream of tunes, as rhythmical as they are unoriginal…."

William R. Weaver, *Motion Picture Herald*—"Presley ... never seemed freer or happier in any picture than here. He's got the undertaking comfortably under control from start to finish and seems to enjoy it as much as his audiences will."

Awards and Nominations

Golden Laurel Award: "Best Musical" fourth place

Golden Laurel Award: "Top New Faces—Female"—Mary Ann Mobley, seventh place

Photoplay Gold Medal Award nomination: "Favorite Male Star"—Elvis Presley

Photoplay Gold Medal Award nomination: "Favorite Female Star"—Shelley Fabares

★ **18** ★

The Girls on the Beach (1965)

It takes off where the others leave off!

Fun: ★★★
Surfing: ★
Boy watching: ★★★
Girl watching: ★★★★
Music: ★★★★
Scenery: ★★

Release date: May 12, 1965. Running time: 80m. Box office gross: Not available. DVD release: Not as of January 2005.

Noreen Corcoran (*Selma*), Martin West (*Duke*), Linda Marshall (*Cynthia*), Steven Rogers (*Brian*), Anna Capri (*Arlene*), Aron Kincaid (*Wayne*), Nancy Spry "Miss Teen USA" (*Betty*), Sheila Bromley (*Mrs. Winters*), Lana Wood (*Bonnie*), Mary Mitchel (*Emily*), Gail Gerber (*Georgia*), Peter Brooks (*Stu*), Linda Saunders (*Patricia*), the Crickets (*Themselves*), Arnold Lessing (*Frank*), Mary Kate Denny (*Janine*), Nan Morris (*First Sorority Sister*), Pat Deming, Michele Corcoran, Larry Merrill (*Dancers*), Dennis Jones (*Guy I*), Bill Sampson (*Guy II*), Carol Jean Lewis (*Dancer*), Joan Conrath (*Second Sorority Sister*), Rick Newton (*Parking Lot Attendant*), Ron Kennedy (*M.C.*), Bruno Ve Sota (*Pops*), Lynn Cartwright (*Waitress*), Richard Miller (*First Waiter*), Leo Gordon (*Waiter No. 2*), Helen Kay Stephens (*Contestant and Dancer*). Guest Stars: The Beach Boys and Lesley Gore.

Paramount Pictures. *Produced by*: Harvey Jacobson. *Associate Producer*: Paul Rapp. *Executive Producer*: Gene Corman. *Directed by*: William N. Witney. *Screenplay by*: David Malcolm. *Music*: Gary Usher. *Music under the Supervision of*: Nick Venet. *Director of Photography*: Arch Dalzell. *Production Manager*: Jack Bohrer. *Film Editor*: Morton Tubor. *Music Editor*: Edwin Norton. *Sound Effects Editor*: Gene Corso. *Sound*: John Bury, Jr. *Swim and Sun Fashions by*: DeWeese Designs. Eastman Color by Pathé.

"Girls on the Beach" and "Little Honda" by Brian Wilson and Mike Love, performed by the Beach Boys. "Lonely Sea" by Gary Usher and Brian Wilson, performed by the Beach Boys. "Leave Me Alone" by and performed by Lesley Gore. "It's Gotta Be You" by Claus Ogerman and Mark Barkan, performed by Lesley Gore. "I Don't Wanna Be a Loser" by Ben Raleigh and Mark Barkan, performed by Lesley Gore. "Why Do I Love You So" by Gary Usher and Roger Christian, vocals by Carol Connors, lip-synced by Gail Gerber, Linda Marshall, Lana Wood and Noreen Corcoran. "We Want to Marry a Beatle" by Carol Connors and Richard Taugman, vocals by Carol Connors, lip-synced by Gail Gerber, Linda Marshall, Lana Wood and Noreen Corcoran. "(They Call Her) La Bamba" arranged and adapted by Jerry Allison and Buzz Cason, performed by the Crickets.

The Girls on the Beach is one of the better *Beach Party* clones enhanced by witty dialogue, a pleasant, wholesome cast and outstanding musical performances by the

204

Beach Boys and Lesley Gore. A gaggle of coeds are trying to raise funds to save their sorority house when three surfer dudes who want to score with them trick the gals into thinking that they are tight with the Beatles. The girls then announce a fundraiser with the Fab Four as headliners, much to the chagrin of the guys. When they learn that they have been duped, the coeds don longhaired wigs and impersonate the Beatles.

As expected from the title, there are lots of girls on the beach. A wisecracking little blonde named Gail Gerber stands out as the ditzy, man-hungry Georgia. Gail is a knockout in her skimpy swimsuit but has stiff competition from Natalie's younger, sexier sister Lana Wood as the girl in the gold lame bikini and Anna Capri as the curvaceous, busty Arlene. The female lead, Noreen Corcoran, is cute with dyed blonde hair, but she comes across stilted and uncomfortable clad in some of the ugliest swimsuits to ever appear on the California coast. Linda Marshall as Cynthia spends most of the movie ridiculously draped in a towel that she carries around with her. She's the female Linus Van Pelt of the beach set. As the trio of lothario surfers, hunky Martin West is fine as the leader, handsome blonde Aron Kincaid shows comedic promise, and pretty boy Steve Rogers with his striking dark features and penetrating crystal blue eyes has a disarming charm about him. It's a pity that the guys aren't shirtless more often.

As with the latter crop of low-budget Hollywood surf movies, surfing scenes are minimal though the guys are actually filmed out in the ocean sitting on their surfboards rather than in a tank in front of a blue screen on the studio lot. Despite the limited number of scenes filmed at the seashore, the movie is strongly enhanced by the presence of the Crickets, Lesley Gore and especially the Beach Boys, who perform three songs. Their performance of "Little Honda" is classic and that clip has been broadcast on music video outlets and used in practically every Beach Boys documentary. The Crickets wail on a speeded-up version of "La Bamba" while Lesley Gore delivers two of her hits, "Leave Me Alone" and "I Don't Wanna Be a Loser." Unfortunately, the viewing audience has to sit through two numbers of the girls masquerading badly as the Beatles while the crowd on screen goes wild in appreciation at the film's climax. Disregarding this ending, *The Girls on the Beach*, though short on surfing scenes, is still one of the better copycat *Beach Party* movies.

The Story

At the local college hangout, the Sip 'n' Surf, the Beach Boys are performing on stage while a trio of surfer boys (Duke, Brian and Wayne) eye pretty blonde Selma and her Alpha Beta sorority sisters Cynthia, Georgia and Bonnie. But before the guys can introduce themselves, the girls are called away by their housemother, Mrs. Winters. At the sorority beach house, the doting old woman nervously explains to the girls that a "$10,000 balloon payment" is due on the mortgage and that they do not have the money to pay it since she squandered the sorority's "nest egg" helping other less fortunate friends. With foreclosure eminent, the girls head for the beach (where else?) to meet up with their fellow sorority sisters with a scheme to enter them into various contests to win prize money to help save Alpha Beta. Cooking expert Janine is paired with ace chemistry student Emily to enter a bake-off.

Patricia, a statuesque brunette engaged to domineering Frank, is chosen to represent the sorority house in a local beauty pageant. Sexy blonde Arlene is tapped to use her feminine wiles on nerdy intellectual Stu to solve a newspaper puzzle contest.

Unbeknownst to the girls, Duke and the guys have been spying on them from their surfboards. Thinking they are star-struck due to their perusing of movie fan magazines, the guys finally are able to get dates with Selma, Cynthia and Georgia by pretending that they know a lot of Hollywood show people as the girls are desperate to hire a headliner for their fundraiser. Listening to the Beach Boys again at the Sip 'n' Surf, Selma announces she wants to hire them for their show. Duke laughs and boasts to Selma and her friends that he knows the Beatles. He then concocts an elaborate ruse to prove it, by sneaking out to the parking lot and pretending to be Ringo calling from London. His telephone gag goes awry when Selma asks "Ringo" to be the star of their show and, taken aback, he (Duke) agrees.

All hopes are pinned on the Beatles as the other girls are not faring so well with their contests with exploding cakes and malfunctioning computers. Only the belly dancing Patricia achieves success. The guys meanwhile intercept a Western Union messenger who reveals that Selma and Alpha Beta are being sued for fraudulent misrepresentation by the Beatles' management. After reading Duke the riot act, Brian and Wayne agree to sneak into the sorority house with him to steal the telegram from Selma's room. The girls return home and the guys dress in drag and dance with some college boys to slip by Mrs. Winters and the coeds.

At the sold-out benefit concert, the crowd starts to get unruly after listening to the Crickets and Lesley Gore and start chanting that they want the Beatles. The surfers show up and finally confess to the girls that they have conned them. Furious, they throw the guys out. Selma, Cynthia, Georgia and Bonnie then come up with a scheme to don Beatles wigs and impersonate the Fab Four. Selma sends Georgia and Emily to purchase the costumes and sends belly dancing Patricia out to stall the crowd. Wearing a veil, her betrothed doesn't recognize her as he ogles and makes a pass at her. She then clobbers Frank over the head. Dressed in men's suits and wearing wigs, the girls perform as the Beatles. The audience goes wild but demands their money back when they realize they've been had. Duke steps in to save the day, the girls perform an encore *sans* wigs and enough money is raised to save the sorority homestead.

Behind-the-Scenes

The Girls on the Beach was backed by producer Roger Corman though his name does not appear on the credits. He enlisted his brother Gene Corman to act as executive producer to watch over his investment during production. Roger had just signed an exclusive contract with Columbia Pictures, which forbade him from directing movies for any other studio. Besides *The Girls on the Beach*, Corman produced *Beach Ball*, two Monte Hellman–directed Westerns (*The Shooting* and *Ride in the Whirlwind*) and the sci-fi flick, *Queen of Blood* during this time. He and Columbia dissolved their agreement with Corman never directing a film for the studio. Paramount, wanting to get in on the money being made on teenage beach

Linda Marshall, Gail Gerber, Lana Wood and Noreen Corcoran as enterprising college students out to save their sorority house in *The Girls on the Beach* (Paramount, 1965) (*courtesy Aron Kincaid*).

and surf movies, purchased the distribution rights to *The Girls on the Beach*, which was originally entitled *Beach Girls*.

Actor Bart Patton was working for Roger Corman at the time and invited a number of his friends to come down to Corman's office to interview for roles in the movie. Aron Kincaid recalls, "I knew Bart from UCLA. He had done a lot of other things and was one of the stars of Francis Ford Coppola's *Dementia 13*. His wife was Mary Mitchel, who I also knew from UCLA. We all seemed to be connected one way or another—it was like one degree of separation. He called me to come down and audition. I had only been out of the Coast Guard for about a week or two so I was in the best physical shape I had been in, which is not to say that it was anything great! In those days people didn't have the bodies like they do today. Just not having a tire around your middle was considered a great physique. I went on the interview and got one of the starring roles in *The Girls on the Beach*."

Martin West and Noreen Corcoran headlined the movie. West had appeared in such features as *Freckles* (1960), *The Sergeant Was a Lady* (1961) and *Captain Newman, M.D.* (1963) but was not a star by any means. Corcoran had a following from the six years she co-starred on the popular comedy series *Bachelor Father* and had just appeared in the movie *Gidget Goes to Rome* (1963). Seeing the wonderful transition that ex-sitcom star Shelley Fabares of *The Donna Reed Show* went from being a brunette to a sexy blonde in *Ride the Wild Surf* (1964), the producers of *The Girls on the Beach* required that Corcoran do the same. However, the results were not nearly as successful.

The third male lead was cast with Steve Rogers, a Robert Wagner lookalike, making his film debut. This was also the first movie for Gail Gerber, Linda Marshall and Linda Saunders. Natalie Wood's younger sister Lana Wood acted for a short time as a child. Her most notable screen credit was the John Ford–directed Western *The Searchers* (1956) starring John Wayne and her sister. Anna Capri began acting as a young teenager and co-starred in the television series *Room for One More* in 1962. Patton's then-wife Mary Mitchel was a veteran compared to some of her co-stars and appeared in such films as *Twist Around the Clock* (1961) and *Dementia 13* (1963). Despite her co-star billing, Miss Teen USA Nancy Spry has only two lines of dialogue.

Roger Corman put the movie in the hands of veteran director William N. Witney. He had experience directing numerous television shows and a few low-budget exploitation movies of the fifties such as *Young and Wild, Juvenile Jungle* and *The Cool and the Crazy* (all 1958). *The Girls on the Beach* had a three-week shooting schedule with interiors shot at Occidental Studios on Pico Boulevard and only two days filming on the beach in Santa Monica rather than Malibu, the usual locale for the beach movies, which would have been too costly for this low-budget production. Describing Witney's directing style, Aron Kincaid remarks, "He encouraged everybody to improvise, I think because he thought of us just a bunch of dumb young kids. But we were all professional and dead serious about our work. It's funny regarding these beach movies. You'd think it was just a bunch of kids slapping around and having a good time. But everybody analyzed every scene that they did.

"For instance, in the opening scene Martin West is telling Steve Rogers and me what we got to do to pick up these girls at the next table," continues Kincaid. "While he is talking he is playing with a straw. Witney yelled cut because they had to set up a light differently so I stepped over to the side. Steve Rogers said, 'Do you notice what Martin is doing with the straw?' I said, 'Yeah, he's playing with it. He didn't do that in rehearsal.' Steve then said, 'He's doing this to draw all the attention and eyes to him on the screen.' I said, '*We've got to fight back!*'"

Though he enjoyed working with William Witney and thought he was a fun guy, there was one scene in the film where Witney gave Kincaid direction that the young actor truly didn't like. It was just one instance of Witney's style of improvising that did not pan out well. The scene is near the beginning of the movie where the girls are talking into the phone thinking it is Ringo Starr of the Beatles on the other end and Kincaid is standing behind them smirking. Aron remembers, "As we were doing this, Witney yelled *cut* and I thought 'Oh God, what now?' Witney said, 'Aron, smell the perfume in the girls' hair and get carried away with it.' I said, '*What?*' He said, 'Sniff their hair and go from one to another like you're smelling flowers.' He was the director so what do you do? It's your first movie so you shut up and do what you're told. I did it and I knew it was wrong. When I saw it on the screen, I knew more than *ever* that it was wrong. I looked like a total ass.

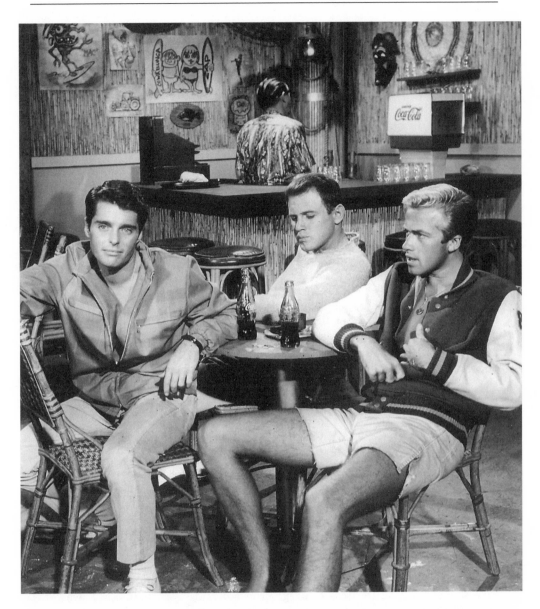

In *The Girls on the Beach* (Paramount, 1965), Steve Rogers, Martin West and Aron Kincaid play surfers who pretend to know the Beatles to impress a gaggle of coeds (*courtesy Aron Kincaid*).

It made no sense and it looked like I was hamming it up trying to take the scene away from the girls."

Corman knew what he was doing by hiring Witney. Working on a short production schedule, the veteran director worked his young cast mercilessly. Kincaid remembers that at one point they just finished a scene that took a number of takes and Witney only gave them a five-minute break before the next set-up. As the young actors and actresses plopped down in their chairs, there was a lot of grumbling from the cast. "Gail Gerber was this little tough blonde," says Aron. "I remember she was puffing on a cigarette and she shouted in frustration, '*Who do you have to fuck to get off this picture?*' A crew guy yelled back, '*The same guy you fucked to get on it!*' Gail laughed as hard as the rest of us."

To assure that teenagers would flood the theatres, the film was peppered with musical guest stars Lesley Gore, the Crickets and the Beach Boys (who perform three tunes). Brian Wilson wrote the songs "The Girls on the Beach" and "Little Honda" especially for the movie and the recordings appeared on the Beach Boys' LP *All Summer Long*. When Gary Usher discovered that the Beach Boys were not going to release "Little Honda" as a single, he recorded a version with Chuck Girard on lead vocals and released it under the Hondells. The song was a big hit, peaking at No. 9 on the *Billboard* charts.

"I knew some of the Beach Boys before we even did the film," says Aron Kincaid. "Dennis Wilson lived up the street. I'd be out in front of my house watering the lawn and he'd always wander by with the girl-of-the-moment that he was dating. I didn't know Mike Love or Al Jardine but I did know Brian and Carl Wilson. When we did the musical number 'Little Honda' with them in a nightclub scene, I didn't think, 'Oh God, the Beach Boys!' I just thought of Dennis as being the guy from around the corner and that we were all being paid to do some crazy work. On the set they were very friendly and did their job."

Gail Gerber (who changed her name to Gail Gilmore for her next movie appearance) had a different experience working with them. She recalled in *Drive-in Dream Girls* that she was instructed to twist and frug to the Beach Boys' song but found the song to be extremely boring. "Thirty years later I am reading about the leader of the Beach Boys [Brian Wilson] describing this scene in his early youth, which he said was his lowest moment because there was this girl gyrating out in front during his very important song. I am sorry I caused him so much grief. If only we were able to read each other's mind."

The Beach Boys' third number, "The Lonely Sea," was shot on the beach. According to Aron Kincaid, "It was supposed to be a night scene but it was filmed during the afternoon as a day-for-night shot. It was about 97 degrees and we are all bundled up with sweat pouring down our backs."

The *Girls on the Beach* screenplay was by David Malcolm, a pseudonym for television comedy scribe Sam Locke, who went on to author the screenplay for *Beach Ball*. The one common thread that can be found in both movies is that in each the actors have to dress in drag. Aron Kincaid says laughing, "It was only years afterwards that I realized that the same man wrote them. I don't know but he must have liked to see all of us in dresses or something!"

In *The Girls on the Beach*, West, Rogers and Kincaid get trapped in the girls' sorority house and the only way they can sneak out is by donning the girls' clothes and wigs. Of course, they could have hung out the window and dropped to the ground but that would not have been as much fun. Though he didn't mind dressing up, Kincaid did not think the scene was very realistic. "If three guys did have to do such a thing, they would hardly be putting on false eyelashes and lip gloss with a lipstick brush, which is what the makeup man did to us. Everybody said that I looked like Lana Wood. I swore that Steve Rogers looked like Lizabeth Scott and Martin West resembled Rose Marie of *The Dick Van Dyke Show*. In *Beach Ball*, when the guys were in drag it was more like what guys would do. They put a blob of red rouge on, the lipstick was all smeared and the hair was hanging down. Our feet were over hanging our high-heeled shoes and the dresses weren't buttoned up."

With a number of aspiring actresses in the film, you'd expect the fur to fly and it did, according to Aron Kincaid, once the buxom Lana Wood hit the sound stage. "None of us had seen Lana other than in *The Searchers* when she was eight or nine years old," recalls Aron. "She came on the set the first day and it was like Jayne Mansfield's entrance in *The Girl Can't Help It*. There was everything but a drum going bump, bump, a-bump, bump, a-bump. She was in this gold lame bathing suit and I guess she was only 18 at the time. She was built far beyond the other girls. Most of the others huddled with towels around them to hide false and imagined flaws. Linda Marshall carried a big white towel with red flowers on it and always had it draped around her because she was terrified that her thighs were going to look too big on the screen. But Lana—the brave soul that she was—just came on with this *well here I am, take it or leave it* attitude. Well, *everybody* wanted to take it. She was a knockout. I think the other girls in their little two-piece cotton polka-dot numbers felt sort of showed-up but nobody could compete with a gold bikini.

Actors Martin West and Aron Kincaid as surfers actually hit the ocean rather than a tank in front of a blue screen on the studio lot in *The Girls on the Beach* (Paramount, 1965).

"The other gal in it who was a pretty hot number was Anna Capri," continues Aron. "To say that the other girls on the picture ostracized Anna and Lana is an understatement. You think guys are competitive and scheming—you should see the women! They realized that they had some rough competition in Lana and Anna. Happily, it didn't show on the screen. Though Anna's character was sort of ostracized in the movie too."

According to Aron, Gail, Linda and Noreen Corcoran were the only ones who didn't feel threatened by Lana and Anna. "The girls were in awe of Linda because she was already married and the mother of children. None of the other girls were even engaged and here Linda was out there doing the bumps and grinds. She was so nice.

"Noreen doesn't have a jealous bone in her body," continues Aron. "She was an actress from the word go and had been performing since she was six years old in films. They had bleached her hair blonde for this, which drove her mad because she didn't feel like herself. All the girls had a can of hairspray apiece on them. Noreen didn't like that and she felt very self-conscious wearing the bathing suits, so they gave her more feminine flowing ones like the one with a veiled cape over the top and things like that. She really photographed beautifully. I was amazed that people did not jump on her bandwagon and immediately put her in three or four other films. But everything acting-wise more or less came to an end for Noreen after this."

According to a short piece in *Variety*, *The Girls on the Beach* was shown throughout the Sam Levin theater chain in Ohio during early July 1964 in negotiations for a distributor. Paramount Pictures picked up the rights and released it nationally the following spring.

Post–*Girls on the Beach*, Gail Gerber changed her name to Gail Gilmore for her next movie, *Beach Ball*. Arnold Lessing would get bumped up to leading man status in *The Beach Girls and the Monster*. Linda Saunders, who played Lessing's girlfriend, became Lori Saunders later that year when she took over the role of Bobbi Jo Bradley from Pat Woodell on *Petticoat Junction*. The producers didn't want fans to get her confused with co-star Linda Kaye Henning.

Lana Wood found fame on television playing trashy waitress Sandy Webster for two years on *Peyton Place*. She reunited with co-star Aron Kincaid playing a scuba bum in the television movie *Black Water Gold* (1970) filmed on location in Jamaica. But it was her role as the amply endowed Plenty O'Toole in *Diamonds Are Forever* (1971) that she is best known for. Lana continued acting through the early eighties before getting work behind the camera. Most recently, she co-produced and appeared as herself in the made-for-television movie *The Mystery of Natalie Wood* (2004), about the life of her sister.

Aron Kincaid and Steve Rogers went on to work together again in *Ski Party*. Martin West had a successful career in the soaps playing Dr. Phil Brewer on *General Hospital* (1967–75) and Donald Hughes on *As the World Turns* (1977–78). His film appearances include *Lord Love a Duck* (1966), *Harper* (1966), *Soldier Blue* (1970), *Family Plot* (1976) and *Assault on Precinct 13* (1976). He remained active on television in guest roles and television movies until the late eighties.

Bart Patton progressed to producer and with his partner, director Lennie Weinrib, turned out *Beach Ball* (1965), *Wild, Wild Winter* (1966) and *Out of Sight* (1966).

Mary Mitchel appeared in one more beach movie, *A Swingin' Summer* (1965), before retiring from acting to raise her son Tyler Patton. She eventually would return to show business, working behind the scenes.

For years *The Girls on the Beach* played on television, yet the cast failed to get residuals. Aron Kincaid constantly complained to the Screen Actors Guild but no one was able to help. Some 20-odd years passed before a helpful employee solved the mystery. According to Aron, "A woman at SAG discovered that the film was listed under the working title *Beach Girls* and not *The Girls on the Beach* so that is why none of us received any money from it. When Paramount was notified, they had a fit that they owed thousands of dollars on it. SAG caved in and made a special deal and we received a pittance."

Memorable Lines

(As the guys sit around the table eyeing Selma and her shapely sorority sisters, Duke stops his impetuous buddies from making their move.)

DUKE: This is the battle of the sexes. If we are gonna capture the enemy, we gotta fight 'em smart.

BRIAN: Yeah, but I don't wanna fight 'em—I want to *fraternize.*

(Sitting on a beach blanket surrounded by all the sorority sisters, Selma explains to a reluctant Patricia why she should be the one to represent Alpha Beta in a beauty pageant.)

SELMA: You're the prettiest girl in the sorority. Everybody admits that.

ARLENE: Well, now, *I* wouldn't say that.

GEORGIA: Sit down, darling! It's a beauty contest, not a stag party!

Reviews

Margaret Harford, *Los Angeles Times*—"These beach bashes are getting bolder and bolder and closer to the edge of bad taste. A couple of words to the producers of teen-age movies: Watch it!"

Mandel Herbstman, *The Film Daily*—"This Harvey Jacobson production is pleasant to the eye, provocative to the ear and no strain on the mind."

James Powers, *The Hollywood Reporter*—"With considerable promotion it might stir up some reaction, but it doesn't have the style, humor and bounce of the AIP pictures in the same vein."

Lowell E. Redelings, *Los Angeles Herald-Examiner*—"The Beach Boys, babes in bikinis, Beatles talk—and a "B" plot comprise the elements of a merry melange making up the structure of *The Girls on the Beach.*"

Robert Salmaggi, *New York Herald Tribune*—"With the box-office success of the string of "Beach Party" flicks (you know—sun, sand, surf, song, bikini'd babes and romping Romeos), it was inevitable that carbon copies would follow in the foaming wake. Though the girls can't act, girl-watchers will doubtless enjoy the sight of curve-some cuties...."

Variety—"Pleasant teenager entry with rock 'n' roll action and plenty of pretty girls to assure nice reception in its particular market."

★ 19 ★

How to Stuff a Wild Bikini (1965)

*For Beginners and Experts ... an interesting
course in The Birds ... The Bees and Bikinis*

Fun: **
Surfing: *
Boy watching: **
Girl watching: ***
Music: ***
Scenery: **

Release date: July 14, 1965. Running time: 93m. Box office gross: Not available.
DVD release: MGM Home entertainment (May 1, 2001).

Annette Funicello (*Dee Dee*), Dwayne Hickman (*Ricky*), Brian Donlevy (*B. D.*), Harvey Lembeck (*Eric Von Zipper*), Beverly Adams (*Cassandra*), John Ashley (*Johnny*), Jody McCrea (*Bonehead*), Len Lesser (*North Dakota Pete*), Bobbi Shaw (*Khola Koku*), Marianne Gaba (*Animal*), Irene Tsu (*Native Girl*), Buster Keaton (*Bwana*), Mickey Rooney (*Peachy Keane*), Arthur Julian (*Dr. Melamed*), Alberta Nelson (*Puss*), Andy Romano (*J. D.*), John Macchia, Jerry Brutsche, Bob Harvey, Myrna Ross, Alan Fife (*Rat Pack*), Alan Frohlich, Tom Quine, Hollis Morrison, Guy Hemric, George Boyce, Charles Reed (*Ad Men*), Patti Chandler (*Patti*), Mike Nader (*Mike*), Luree Holmes, Jo Collins, Mary Hughes, Stephanie Nader, Jeannine White, Janice Levinson (*Beach Girls*) Ed Garner, John Fain, Mickey Dora, Brian Wilson, Bruce Baker, Ned Wynn, Kerry Berry, Dick Jones, Ray Atkinson, Ronnie Dayton (*Beach Boys*), Salli Sachse, Linda Bent (*Bookends*), Marianne Gordon (*Chickie*), Sheila Stephenson (*Secretary*), Rosemary Williams (*English Girl*), Sue Williams [Hamilton] (*Peanuts*), Tonia Van Deter (*Italian Girl*), Uta Stone (*German Girl*), Toni Harper (*Barberette*), Michelle Barton (*Manicurist*), Victoria Carroll (*Shoe Shine Girl*). Uncredited: Frankie Avalon (*Frankie*), Elizabeth Montgomery (*Bwana's Daughter*). Guest Stars: The Kingsmen

American International Pictures. *Produced by*: James H. Nicholson and Samuel Z. Arkoff. *Co-Producer*: Anthony Carras. *Directed by*: William Asher. *Written by*: William Asher and Leo Townsend. *Production Supervisor*: Jack Bohrer. *Director of Photography*: Floyd Crosby, A.S.C. *Music Supervisor*: Al Simms. *Musical Score by*: Les Baxter. *Choreography by*: Jack Baker. *Art Director*: Howard Campbell. *Film Editors*: Fred Feitshans, A.C.E., Eve Newman. *Music Editor*: Milton Lustig. *Sound Editors*: James Nelson, Gene Corso. *Costume Supervisor*: Richard Bruno. *Surfboards Furnished by*: Malibu Plastics. *Motorcycles Courtesy of*: Yamaha International. *Opening Titles by*: Art Clokey. *Photographic Effects by*: Butler-Glouner. *Special Effects by*: Roger George, Bill Ferrier. *Animation by*: Jack Kinney. *Special Interior Decorator*: Ian Phillips, LA Difference. *Assistant Director*: Dale Hutchinson. *Properties*: Karl R. Brainard, Richard M. Rubin. *Sound*: Don Rush. *Makeup*: Ted Coodley. *Hair Stylist*: Ray Forman. *Set Decorator*: George Nelson. *Construction Coordinator*: Ross Hahn. *Production Assistant*: Jack

Cash. *Motorcycle Coordinator*: George Dockstader. *Motorcycle Stunts*: Bud Ekins. Filmed in Panavision and Pathecolor.

Songs by Guy Hemric and Jerry Styner: "How to Stuff a Wild Bikini" performed by John Ashley and the cast. "How About Us" performed by Mickey Rooney and the beach girls. "That's What I Call a Healthy Girl" and "After the Party" performed by the cast. "The Boy Next Door" and "Follow Your Leader" performed by Harvey Lembeck. "Better Be Ready" and "The Perfect Boy" performed by Annette Funicello. "If It's Gonna Happen" performed by Lu Ann Simms (lip-synced by Irene Tsu), Annette Funicello, Frankie Avalon and Dwayne Hickman. "Madison Avenue" performed by Brian Donlevy and Mickey Rooney. "Give Her Lovin'" by Lyn Easton, performed by the Kingsmen.

How to Stuff a Wild Bikini is the least entertaining of the AIP beach party movies even though it tries to ape *Pajama Party*, one of the series' best. Frankie is on naval reserve duty and pays a native witch doctor to conjure up a beautiful red-head in a bikini to distract the beach boys away from his girl, Dee Dee, who is nevertheless romantically pursued by a motorcycle-riding ad man. The film is structured as a traditional musical (such as *My Fair Lady*), which were quite popular around this time. With surfing pushed aside once again, this time for motorcycle racing, AIP may have thought musical production numbers would lure the kids back into the theaters. They should have been concentrating on a decent story instead.

The movie is jam-packed with 11 songs, more than in any other AIP beach movie. Except for an instrumental by the Kingsmen and two solo numbers by Annette, all the other songs are performed by the characters usually as part of the

The cast of *How to Stuff a Wild Bikini* (AIP, 1965) featured (*from left to right*) Dwayne Hickman, Annette Funicello, John Ashley, Beverly Adams and Mickey Rooney.

ensemble. Standout numbers are the title tune sung by a guitar-strumming John Ashley, while possibly backed by the Kingsmen, and "How About Us?" sung by the beach girls with aid from Mickey Rooney, who hams it up as Peachy. As the curvy, bikini-clad beauties dance on the sand extolling their charm, looks and brains, and lament, "We're the chicks who know all the tricks, hey what about us?," who could disagree? Harvey Lembeck and crew get two songs and lots of extra screen time here but Lembeck's schtick has grown tiresome and he is more often annoying than funny.

Though there are lots of shots on the beach, there are no surfing scenes in *How to Stuff a Wild Bikini* so this is definitely not recommended for surfing addicts. Girl watchers get four new beauties to ogle—exotic Irene Tsu as a native girl, voluptuous Beverly Adams wearing an unflattering long red wig, sexy blonde Marianne Gaba as man-hungry Animal and petite Sue Williams as Peanuts—plus nice shots of Mary Hughes, Patti Chandler and Salli Sachse. For the boy watchers, Ashley, Jody McCrea and the rest of the crew are shirtless and clad in the obligatory swim trunks.

Of all the various pairings in the AIP beach party films (i.e., Frankie and Annette; Frankie and Deborah Walley; Annette and Tommy Kirk; Kirk and Deborah Walley), *How to Stuff a Wild Bikini*'s Annette and Dwayne Hickman is by far the weakest. The fact that Annette was a few months pregnant and is fully clad even in her beach scenes looking bored to death doesn't help. There is absolutely no chemistry between her and Hickman and their timing seems off. Actually most *everything* is off in this movie as it was a big letdown in terms of quality and box office receipts after being released on the heels of the far superior *Beach Blanket Bingo.* The times they were a-changing in late 1965 and AIP knew they had to try something new to attract teenagers to the movie theaters. Deciding that the beach party genre still had some life in it, they planned to revamp the formula with the next movie, *Bikini Party in a Haunted House.*

The Story

Frankie is on naval reserve duty stationed on a Pacific island called Goona, Goona. Lounging under a palm tree with a beautiful native girl, the sailor boy wants to know if his girlfriend back home Dee Dee is remaining faithful. Witch doctor Bwana mixes up a special potion from which he conjures a pelican to keep tabs on Dee Dee and creates a beautiful curvaceous redhead whom he sends to act as a decoy to keep the surfer boys' attention off Frankie's girl.

On the beach in Southern California, Frankie's friends are stunned as a titian-haired knockout named Cassandra fills a leopard-skin bikini. Two advertising men come to the beach to find the perfect girl-next-door to ride a bikini motorcycle in a new ad campaign and have noticed Cassandra also. The older one, Peachy Keane, thinks she would be a perfect choice but she declines. While Peachy tries to change her mind and fight off the other beach girls who want to take her place, his handsome young partner Ricky is attracted to demure Dee Dee, who is sitting on a blanket reading a book. Cassandra has a change of heart after learning that Ricky is the boy-next-door. Peachy's boss B. D. McPherson is pleased with Cassandra.

However, after getting to know Dee Dee, Ricky thinks she would be a better choice. Flattered, she declines due to her commitment to Frankie but accepts Ricky's invitation to be his partner in an upcoming motorcycle rally.

Cassandra proves to be a klutz so Peachy takes her back to the beach and begs Animal and the rest of the girls to help her. Motorcycle leader Eric Von Zipper is immediately attracted to Cassandra and declares that "she's my idol." Learning of Peachy's campaign, Von Zipper and his crew pay him a visit at his office. Peachy sends Cassandra to see a doctor who theorizes that her clumsiness is due to a fear of the opposite sex. That night Peachy takes Cassandra to the local teen hangout and to Peachy's amazement the girl glides across the floor with Von Zipper. The inept motorcycle leader wants Ricky eliminated and pool shark North Dakota Pete vows to do it for him.

The next day, B. D. orders Peachy to change Von Zipper's image since he seems to be the only boy Cassandra can relate to. On the beach, Animal reads to Dee Dee a letter that Frankie wrote to Mike bragging about the four native girls who are crazy about him. Infuriated, Dee Dee decides two can play that game and tells Ricky "to have my kimono ready at seven." At the pool hall, the Rats and Mice are horrified to see their leader wearing a business suit and bowler hat to enhance his new image as the boy-next-door. The native girl gives Frankie the bad news that Dee Dee is wavering and is all too happy to console him. At the same time, Dee Dee is getting very cozy with Ricky. As they begin to kiss, North Dakota Pete crashes into Ricky's pad to finish him off. As punches are thrown, Dee Dee tries to come to Ricky's aid but winds up cracking a vase over his head by mistake.

Under pressure from B. D., the devious Peachy has paid North Dakota Pete and the Rats and Mice to sabotage the race course to assure Von Zipper and Cassandra's victory. The race gets underway and, despite a series of crashes and wrong turns, Ricky and Dee Dee still manage to win the race thanks to the bungling of the inept Von Zipper, who gets disqualified. A furious B. D. is about to fire Peachy when he notices that Dee Dee is the perfect girl next door. The kids throw a beach bash to celebrate Ricky and Dee Dee's triumph. Dee Dee realizes that Ricky is not the marrying kind and tells him she's going to wait for Frankie. Understanding her position, Ricky hooks up with Cassandra.

With his tour of duty over, Frankie asks Bwana to get him home to his sweetheart fast. He can't do it but his "bewitching" daughter zaps Frankie to Dee Dee at the beach where they are reunited.

Behind-the-Scenes

How to Stuff a Wild Bikini was the fifth and final beach movie directed by William Asher. By this time the series showed that the formula was getting tired and needed a major fix if it was going to continue. With beach party movies' budgets increasing, only the Kingsmen are seen performing. Not helping matters, Frankie Avalon appears only briefly and Annette Funicello has hardly anything to do and seems lost without Avalon.

As with *Pajama Party* (1964), Avalon played a cameo role and appeared only at the beginning and end of the movie. He received a special thank you from the producers during the film's end credits. His cameo appearance was due to the fact that he was starring in the service comedy *Sergeant Deadhead*, which was in production simultaneously. With limited screen time, Avalon sings only one song with Annette accompanied by Dwayne Hickman and Irene Tsu (shot in a split screen process).

Tommy Kirk was announced as Annette's new leading man but before filming began Dwayne Hickman replaced him. Coincidentally, Kirk was arrested for marijuana possession days before the cameras were to begin rolling. Though AIP asserted that this incident had nothing to do with Kirk being dropped, rumors disputed that statement. It is surprising that Hickman accepted the role as a few months prior in an interview in *Seventeen* he made it a point to mention that *Ski Party* was "not one of those beach movies." He went on to remark, "If you take too many of the wrong kind of roles, you ruin yourself in this town. Like Tab Hunter—surf movies, records, stage, where is he now? I don't want to be a perennial juvenile. I'm 30 now and I want to do things that will further my career."

Newcomers to the beach series included beach girls Stephanie Nader (the sister of Mike Nader) and sexy, flaxen-haired Sue Hamilton, a native of Glendale, California. Not much is known about Sue's childhood except that she wished to become a farmer when she grew up. Instead she began modeling using the name Sue Williams. She posed semi-nude in the pages of *Playboy* as Miss April in 1965 where her measurements were touted as 34-20-34. Her ambition was to be a Bunny at the Los Angeles Playboy Club and to attend USC. When asked why she loved being a Playmate, she replied, "Because it gives my life a spark of something new, interesting and different." A talent scout at AIP saw some of her pictures and cast her as one of the background beach girls in *How to Stuff a Wild Bikini*.

The role of Animal was taken over by a pretty blonde named Marianne Gaba, a former Miss Illinois. Like Donna Michelle, who played the part previously in *Beach Blanket Bingo*, Gaba was a former Playboy Playmate, gracing the magazine's centerfold as Miss September 1959. She came to AIP with a background of minor roles in schlock such as *Missile to the Moon* (1958) and *The Choppers* (1962). Gaba joined Hamilton (along with Mary Hughes, Patti Chandler, Deanna Lund and Salli Sachse, among others) as one of the bikini-clad robots in *Dr. Goldfoot and the Bikini Machine* before disappearing from the big screen.

Beverly Adams was cast in the role of sexy Cassandra, but her brunette tresses were hidden under a hideous long red wig in her first major screen role. Under contract to Columbia Pictures since 1963, she played bit parts in *Roustabout* (1964) with Elvis Presley for Paramount and *The New Interns* (1964) before being loaned to AIP to play the shapely conjured vixen. Adams' next movie was the surf 'n' snow flick, *Winter a-Go-Go* (1965).

Another new cast member was a pelican named Pete, the only "acting" pelican on the West Coast at this time. His trainer Ray Berwick had rescued the stranded bird from an oil slick on Malibu Beach four years prior. He nursed Pete back to health and discovered that the bird was talented and could be trained.

Annette Funicello was several months pregnant during filming. In past beach party movies she normally was clad in demure one- or two-piece bathing suits, but in this film to hide her condition she is kept fully clothed, wearing oversize sweaters or very loose blouses even in the beach scenes. Besides being distracted by her new marriage and the baby on the way, Annette was also missing Frankie Avalon terribly (though she found Dwayne Hickman to have "a great sense of humor"). Hickman returned the compliment in his autobiography, describing Funicello as "sweet, shy, quiet, and very ladylike" with "one of the best figures of any of the girls in the movie." One wonders if he noticed that Annette was pregnant at the time. Compliments aside, Annette remarked in her autobiography, "This is one of my least favorite beach party movies." Unfortunately, her distaste shows up on the screen, which is one reason why the Funicello-Hickman pairing is not successful. Not that Hickman did anything wrong, the chemistry just wasn't there. According to co-star Jody McCrea, "Dwayne Hickman was a real nice guy and a total professional."

McCrea was becoming dissatisfied with the beach movies as well but for other reasons. He comments, "After *Beach Blanket Bingo* was a hit I agreed to do *How to Stuff a Wild Bikini*, which Jim Nicholson and Sam Arkoff bought for the title. I didn't mind that my part was smaller in this because I was burnt out on the beach movies by this time. After that picture, I told them I was retiring from the beach movies because I was tired of people talking to me as if I was really Deadhead. I have a high IQ and a college degree so I wanted to improve my screen image. I didn't want to get typecast playing only the dumb surfer. I went on to do the biker movie *The Glory Stompers* and the Western *Cry Blood Apache*, both of which I helped produce."

Continuing with producer James Nicholson's approach of populating the beach party movies with veteran actors to attract older audiences, he was able to get Mickey Rooney, Buster Keaton and Brian Donlevy to agree to appear. Annette found Rooney to be "outgoing, personable, and entertaining," but Hickman had major problems working with him. Though Hickman concurs that Rooney was always engaging the cast and crew, he says the actor also liked to tell his fellow actors how to play their roles. Fed up with his "suggestions," Hickman reported in his autobiography, "I turned to Bill Asher, the director, and said, 'Who's directing this movie, you or Rooney?' After that, Rooney never directed me again. In fact, he never spoke to me for the rest of the film."

Most likely to save money, *How to Stuff a Wild Bikini* is the first AIP beach party film to contain songs in Broadway musical fashion. In the previous movies, Frankie and Annette would either belt out a song together or solo with musical guest stars such as Dick Dale, Donna Loren, Little Stevie Wonder, the Pyramids, etc., popping in to sing a number or two that had nothing to do with the plot. In this film, Guy Hemric tied the lyrics into the story to keep the scenario flowing. With Frankie away on naval reserve duty, singing chores were taken over by John Ashley and Dwayne Hickman. That is actually Ashley singing lead, backed by the beach gang on three songs including the title tune. Hickman however could not sing well and was dubbed (as was Irene Tsu by Lu Ann Simms of *The Arthur Godfrey Show*). Tsu recalled in *Fantasy Femmes of Sixties Cine*ma, "On my first morning of shooting he [William Asher] gave me a tape of a song he wanted me to sing later that day as a duet with Frankie. I said, 'You must be kidding! I have to learn this now?' Asher said, 'Oh, but you have about an hour and a half.' That's how every scene in this film was shot—wham bam bam."

The house band in the movie was the definitive garage band the Kingsmen; Guy Hemric told author Stephen McParland that he really wanted them in the

Annette Funicello can try but she can't hide her pregnancy standing next to former *Playboy* Playmates Marianne Gaba as Animal and Sue Williams a.k.a. Hamilton as Peanuts in *How to Stuff a Wild Bikini* (AIP, 1965).

movie because he liked them a lot. They are best remembered for the 1963 hit song "Louie, Louie." In *How to Stuff a Wild Bikini* they got the chance to perform one of their own songs, "Give Her Lovin'." Hemric also appears in the movie. In past films, he was usually seen on the beach as one of the surfer boys in the background. Now over 30 years old, director William Asher felt Hemric was a bit long in the tooth to play a teenage beach boy so he cast him as one of the ad men who sing the song "Madison Avenue" with Mickey Rooney and Brian Donlevy.

According to some of the cast, the filming of *How to Stuff a Wild Bikini* went smoothly. By now they were used to the cramped dressing rooms, fast-paced shooting schedule and William Asher's favoring of some of the actors over others. According to Luree Holmes, this was the only film were she gave a performance that pleased director Asher. She remarked, "The only time he ever complimented me was when we did the scene in which the girls were on top of the guys' shoulders and we had to knock each other off. I really had a great time doing that. I was part of the last two couples standing. Asher said to me, 'Well, that was great! You finally came alive.' It was a backhanded compliment. Except for that scene, I was never able to put on the show he wanted."

Well before the time *How to Stuff a Wild Bikini* went into production William Asher had relegated Ed Garner to the background as well. Once a favorite of Asher's, Garner quickly fell out of favor with the fickle director. Garner recalls, "It happened when he found out that my grandfather was H. B. Warner who had a son named Bud, my uncle. Apparently he and Asher had several fistfights while going to school together. That's when the tide definitely shifted for me. It was like being the teacher's pet and then you're not. When you were under William Asher's tutelage he embraced you and made you feel like you were a real part of what he was involved in. I think he eventually made better relationships with some of the other people and developed a better rapport with them. He liked to give screen time to his favorites but all in all I think he was very generous with everybody. He sort of adopted Mike Nader and Duane King. And he just loved Salli Sachse, Linda Opie and Mary Hughes."

The petite Sue Williams, a newcomer to AIP, quickly became a favorite of Asher's. Completely taken with the charming diminutive beauty, he gave her lines as the character Peanuts who interacts with Mickey Rooney's ad man. It was an unprecedented move to get a speaking role so quickly considering contract players such as Patti Chandler, Mary Hughes and Salli Sachse still had to jockey to get lines.

The film's opening Claymation credits were designed by Art Clokey, who was responsible for *Gumby*. As with *Ski Party*, the *Wild Bikini* end credits also did not feature any dancing beach girls. Instead the entire chicken fight beach sequence with the gals on the shoulders of the guys trying to knock each other off was repeated with instrumental music playing as the credits unveiled.

Unlike *Pajama Party*'s soundtrack LP featuring new versions of the movie's songs recorded by Annette, the soundtrack release for *How to Stuff a Wild Bikini* included most of the film's original recordings. Scepter/Wand Records of New York released the album. The only track that greatly differed from the movie version was the song "If It's Gonna Happen." In the film, Frankie, Annette, Dwayne Hickman and Lu Ann Simms (dubbing Irene Tsu) sing it. On the soundtrack album, Simms performed it as a solo. The Kingsmen sing the title tune on the LP but it is not known if they dubbed the lyrics for John Ashley and the male cast in the movie. To boost sales, the album was touted with the Kingsmen's name featured prominently on the cover. However, it wasn't enough and the LP never charted.

How to Stuff a Wild Bikini was the last of the beach parties for John Ashley, Jody McCrea and ace surfer Mickey Dora. It was just the beginning for Sue Williams, who changed her billing to Sue Hamilton and went to appear in *Sergeant Deadhead* (1965), *Dr. Goldfoot and the Bikini Machine* (1965) and *The Ghost in the Invisible Bikini* (1966). AIP had high hopes for Sue and sent her on a promotional tour with the cast of *Ski Party*. Aron Kincaid recalls being perplexed why she was with them but found her to be "the sweetest little thing."

Memorable Lines

(On Goona, Goona somewhere in the Pacific, naval reservist Frankie tells his island sweetie that he is certain that his girlfriend Dee Dee has remained faithful to him.)

NATIVE GIRL: You navy boys have funny idea. Okay for boy but not okay for girl. Here in Goona, Goona we have better idea: When you are not with the boy you love, love the boy you're with.

(The surfer boys and beach girls ogle a floating bikini.)

MIKE: Dig that wild bikini!

ANIMAL: It ain't nothin' without the stuffin'.

BONEHEAD: How do we stuff it?

Reviews

Boxoffice—"Packed with entertainment for every age group. Filmed with hummable and toe-tapping songs and dance numbers, plus excitement and romance and side-splitting comedy...."

Mandel Herbstman, *The Film Daily*—"Spirited young bodies splash and frolic against a background of fun and fantasy in the latest American International offering with the 'beach gang.' It offers good production values, many melodic interludes and pleasant, formula-style fun that should especially please the teenager."

Dale Munroe, *The Citizen-News*—"*How to Stuff a Wild Bikini* is relaxing entertainment for teenagers and should provide that spirited age group with an hour and a half of summertime fun."

Reed Porter, *The Hollywood Reporter*—"AIP's latest teen topic ... is far funnier than its kindred 'Beach' and 'Party' series. Emphasis is less on muscles and rock 'n' roll, more on slapstick and sight gags. Straight plot would fit into a peanut shell but most of the gags are marvelously inventive."

Lowell E. Redelings, *Los Angeles Herald-Examiner*—"It should lure out the faithful who follow this sort of thing, but scarcely anyone else. This time the kitchen sink is absent, but everything else is dragged in including Buster Keaton ... and a pelican. [Mickey] Rooney comes off best in the acting department, if you can call it that—but the pelican gives him some stiff competition in the scene-stealing category."

Variety—"American International's latest contender in the youth market ... is a lightweight affair lacking the breeziness and substance of past entries. A nonsensical plot without enough happening and a story line barely skimming the surface are further deterrents. Miss Funicello, usually with a bulk of the footage in these beach romps, has little to do. Avalon, too, has little more than a bit...."

★ 20 ★

One Way Wahine (1965)

She's the Swingin'est Thing on Waikiki!

Release date: October 1965. Running time: 80m. Box office gross: Not available. DVD release: Not as of January 2005.

Joy Harmon (*Kit Williams*), Anthony Eisley (*Chick Lindell*), Adele Claire (*Brandy Saveties*), David M. Whorf (*Lou Talbot*), Edgar Bergen (*Sweeney*), Lee Krieger (*Charley Rossi*), Ken Mayer (*Hugo Sokol*), Harold Fong (*Quong*), Alvy Moore (*Maxwell*), Aime Luce (*Tahitian Dancer*), Ralph Hanalei (*Paulo*).

Continental Pictures Inc., A Cal-Hawaiian Production. United Screen Arts release. *Executive Producer*: Leon E. Whiteman. *In Charge of Production*: Larry Jackson. *Produced and Directed by*: William O. Brown. *Screenplay*: Rod Larson. *Director of Photography*: John Arthur Morrill. *Music Score*: Jo Hansen. *Second Unit Director*: Dan Laifer. *Supervising Editor*: George White. *Music Editor*: Josef Von Stroheim. *Sound Editor*: Bill Keith, M.P.S.E. *Makeup Artist*: Lillian Lawson. *Wardrobe*: Maudine Adair.

"One Way Wahine" performed by Jody Miller over the opening credits. "When the One Way Wahine Does the Bird" written and performed by Ray Peterson. "When I Look at You" performed by Ray Peterson.

One Way Wahine was the next beach movie, after *Ride the Wild Surf*, to be filmed on the sands of Hawaii. It was marketed to the teenage audience as a beach movie but it is a more serious look at the seamy side of Hawaii and the surf bums and one way wahines who go there to make a quick buck. In fact, Anthony Eisley was pushing 40 when he starred in this, definitely giving the film more of a mature feel. The main pleasure of this hard-to-find beach movie is Joy Harmon, the buxom, wide-eyed blonde who can always be counted on to give a bubbly, infectious performance in any part she played.

The Story

Working at a liquor store owned by Quong, Lou Talbot makes a delivery of booze and a Chicago newspaper to a beach house inhabited by Charley Rossi and Hugo Sokol. The two men want to party with some beach babes and enlist the good-looking Lou to find some for them. When Lou declines, one of the men offers him $50 and $100 for each girl. The delivery boy's interest is piqued, especially since the money shown him is still in bank wrappers.

Thinking about the deal later, Lou picks up a copy of the same newspaper to discover a story about two bank clerks from the Windy City who absconded with $100,000. He shares this with his friend Chick Lindell and they formulate a plan to steal the money from the robbers. Lou thinks he can get the cooperation of buxom blonde Kit Williams (newly arrived from the mainland on a one-way ticket to find a better life) and cocktail waitress Brandy Saveties to go to the beach house to distract the men while he and Chick steal the loot. However, what Lou doesn't realize is that the men are gangsters and not bank employees.

Lou returns to the beach house and talks up Kit and Brandy to the men suggesting that they finesse the chicks with a few drinks and music. Back at the beach, Lou tries to enlist Kit and Brandy's help but the girls balk even though they desperately need the money. He then divulges the rest of his plan, where the girls would slip knockout pills into the men's drinks.

Bubbly, naïve Kit is game only if Brandy goes along. The skeptical waitress wants proof of the effectiveness of the pills. Along comes beachcomber Sweeney, who is offered a drugged drink by Lou. Before he can finish it, the old codger is out cold. Convinced, the girls agree to go along with the scheme. That evening things are swinging at the beach house when Brandy offers everyone a second round of drinks. She slips the pills into Charley and Hugo's glasses and then leads Hugo into the bedroom where she thinks the loot is hidden. She tricks him into playing a drinking and kissing game and soon Hugo is sound asleep. Brandy then begins searching for the stolen cash.

Kit is having a harder time with Charley, who has spilled his drink. The amorous Charley grabs Kit and things start to get rough. Brandy, who has found the money, hears Kit's cries and goes to help her friend. Charlie stuns her with a blow to the neck but this gives Kit time to hit her ardent pursuer over the head with a whiskey bottle, knocking him unconscious. Brandy is able to get the sack of money out the window to a waiting scuba gear–clad Chick, who is ready to swim away. But the plastic sack catches on a nail, ripping open and scattering the packets of money all along the beach.

Chick realizes he can't swim with the packets in his arms so he hides the money in a nearby trash can and swims away. Brandy and Kit make a run for the door but are rushed by an irate Charley holding a machine-gun. He begins shooting wildly but a well-placed kick to the chin by Kit stops him. The girls get away and are picked up by Lou in his Jeep.

The following morning the four beach denizens are startled to read the morning newspaper's headline "Gangster Dead in Flaming Gun Battle." Realizing that the two men were not bank embezzlers as they thought, the four head to the trash can to retrieve the money and turn it over to the proper authorities. However, Sweeney has already stumbled upon the money and is showing it to a policeman. He shouts to the gang that they will never believe what's happened. Lou replies, "Y'know, Sweeney, I kinda think we will." The four then head back down the beach, leaving Sweeney and the police with the money.

Behind-the-Scenes

In 1964, Cal-Hawaiian Productions received an investment of $3 million from Argonaut International Corp., headed by Arthur G. Maddigan and Leon E. White-

Poster art for *One Way Wahine* (United Screen Arts, 1965) featuring the voluptuous Joy Harmon.

man, to attract more American companies to film in Hawaii. *One Way Wahine* was the first of five pictures slated to shoot there.

The term "One Way Wahine" was coined by locals for girls from the mainland who arrived on the Hawaiian Islands via a one-way ticket, hoping to earn enough money to pay their transportation back home.

Pretty Joy Harmon was cast as the title character. With her big blue eyes, wild mane of blonde hair and ample bosom, she was one of the most popular pin-ups of the late fifties. While appearing on Broadway in the hit comedy *Make a Million,* Harmon became a favorite as the dumb blonde foil to such television talk show hosts as Steve Allen, Gary Moore and Dave Garroway. Joy was soon posing, though never nude, for all the top men's magazines such as *Rex, Show* and *Nugget,* and made her film debut as a tough-acting chick in *Let's Rock* (1958). She went to Hollywood in the early sixties and landed a regular gig on Groucho Marx's new series *Tell It to Groucho* in 1962. She also began appearing on a number of television sitcoms where her talent for comedy was put to excellent use. *One Way Wahine* was her first starring role.

Harmon's leading men were former Warner Bros. contract player Anthony Eisley, who became popular with teenage audiences due to his role on the hit detective series *Hawaiian Eye* from 1959 to 1962, and David M. Whorf, the son of Richard Whorf, the former actor turned director. David entered show business as a child and made his film debut in *On Our Merry Way* (1948). During the fifties he was able to juggle work in theater and television while becoming a member of the Directors Guild. In 1961, he co-starred in *Twist All Night* with Louis Prima and June Wilkinson and then landed a supporting role in *PT 109* (1963) starring Cliff Robertson as JFK.

Exteriors for *One Way Wahine* were filmed on location at Lanakai Beach, Oahu, Hawaii with interiors shot in California at KTTV Studios. Hovering Marine helicopters with soldiers craning their necks to get a glimpse of buxom Joy Harmon on the beach below reportedly interrupted filming many times. The crew was sure some of the Marines would fall to the beach below.

The film tried to launch a new dance craze called the Wahine Rock, which is performed by Harmon, who commented about her experience in *Fantasy Femmes of Sixties Cinema,* "My sister Gay went with me to Hawaii and she was in the movie too. I was the lead and worked every day all the way through the shoot. I had a really good part—it was a very emotional role. At one point my character almost gets raped. It wasn't like any of my previous roles. The actors in *One Way Wahine* were all fun to work with—especially Edgar Bergen."

Harmon continued playing the lovable ditz on television and in movies, most notably in *Village of the Giants* (1965), loosely based on H.G. Wells' *Food of the Gods.* But her most memorable role was her silent bit as a sexy Southern vamp seductively washing her car knowing the prisoners of a chain gang are ogling her in *Cool Hand Luke* (1967), starring Paul Newman. She stopped acting in 1973 to concentrate on raising her family.

Ruggedly handsome Anthony Eisley was unjustly relegated to lead or second lead roles in B-movies including *The Naked Kiss* (1964), the Elvis musical *Frankie and Johnny* (1966), *The Navy vs. the Night Monsters* (1966), *Journey to the Center of Time* (1967) and *The Witchmaker* (1969). By the seventies his film career sunk even lower, when Eisley stared in Grade Z productions such as *Dracula vs. Frankenstein* (1971) and *The Doll Squad* (1973). Though good movie roles were scarce, Eisley segued into a television character actor, playing tough guys, hard-nosed detectives or crooked cowboys, and worked steadily until the late eighties. His last credit was the Spanish production *Deadly Deception* in 1991. He passed away from heart failure on January 20, 2003.

One Way Wahine was dark-haired David M. Whorf's last acting credit. He switched his focus to working behind the camera in an array of positions from director to assistant director to unit manager on a variety of television shows and films including *Batman* (1966), *Caddyshack* (1980) and *The Right Stuff* (1983). His most recent credit was working as first assistant director on the made-for-television movie *A Secret Life* (2000). He also co-owns a software company called Alnitak Computing Company and co-created the first film production software package, "AD/80."

Reviews

Boxoffice—"The plot has enough action to keep audiences interested, as well as the two girls whose measurements will be enough to attract male viewers. Joy Harmon boasts a 42-22-35 figure.... Adele Claire ... is equally good to look at. Both girls are adept at comedy, and with David Whorf, perform adequately."

Jack Tierney, *Motion Picture Editor*—"What makes *One Way Wahine* refreshing is the approach to a modern story of life in that tropical land. Another is the presence of a young actress named Joy Harmon who fits a bikini with plenty to spare and whose curves and beauty make her, indeed, a Joy to behold. Accompanying all the intrigue are generous scenes of life as it is lived on the beaches of Hawaii, with the bikini battalion out in full force."

Variety—"A slick comedy of errors, this kooky, offbeat production, basking in a Hawaiian locale, presents a frisky plot, workable comedic situations, subtle color and eager acting by unknowns, as well as some nicely photographed ethnic dancing as opposed to ho-hum hula. A surfing pix, this is not. Blonde newcomer Joy Harmon, an American type Brigitte Bardot, carries the weight of the show ... and is irrepressibly alive."

∗ 21 ∗

Ski Party (1965)

*It's where the He's meet the She's on skis
and there's only one way to get warm!*

Fun: ∗∗∗½
Surfing: ∗
Boy watching: ∗∗∗
Girl watching: ∗∗∗∗
Music: ∗∗∗∗
Scenery: ∗∗∗∗

Release date: June 16, 1965. Running time: 90m. Box office gross: Not available.

DVD release: Double bill with *Muscle Beach Party*, MGM Home Entertainment (April 15, 2003).

Frankie Avalon (*Todd Armstrong/Jane*), Dwayne Hickman (*Craig Gamble/Nora*), Deborah Walley (*Linda Hughes*), Yvonne Craig (*Barbara Norris*), Robert Q. Lewis (*Donald Pevney*), Bobbi Shaw (*Nita*), Aron Kincaid (*Freddie Carter*), The Hondells (*Themselves*), Steve Rogers (*Gene*), Patti Chandler (*Janet*), Mike Nader (*Bobby*), Salli Sachse (*Indian*), John Boyer (*Ski Boy*), Mikki Jamison (*Vicki*), Mickey Dora (*Mickey*), Bill Sampson (*Arthur*), Mary Hughes, Luree Holmes (*Ski Girls*), Sigi Engl (*Ski Instructor*). Uncredited: Ronnie Dayton, Jo Collins, Paul Gleason and Annette Funicello (*Prof. Roberts*). Guest Stars: James Brown and the Famous Flames, and Lesley Gore.

A Gene Corman Production. American International Pictures release. *Produced by*: Gene Corman. *Directed by*: Alan Rafkin. *Written by*: Robert Kaufman. *Executive Producers*: James H. Nicholson and Samuel Z. Arkoff. *Director of Photography*: Arthur E. Arling, A.S.C. *Musical Score by*: Gary Usher. *Production Manager*: Jack Bohrer. *Assistant Director*: Dale Hutchinson. *Sound*: Bob Post. *Costume Supervisor*: Richard Bruno. *Makeup*: Ted Coodley. *Property Master*: Ted Cooper. *Script Supervisor*: John Dutton. *Construction Coordinator*: Ross Hahn. *Film Editor*: Morton Tubor. *Art Director*: Howard Campbell. *Set Decorator*: George Nelson. *Sound Editor*: Tom Stevens. *Music Editor*: Edwin Norton. *Musical Supervisor*: Al Simms. *Ski-wear by*: White Stag. *Motorcycles and Skis Courtesy of*: Yamaha International. *Poles Furnished by*: Scott-USA. Filmed in Panavision and Pathecolor.

"Ski Party" by Gary Usher and Roger Christian, performed by Frankie Avalon over the opening credits and by the Hondells on the beach. "The Gasser" by Gary Usher and Roger Christian, performed by the Hondells. "I Got You (I Feel Good)" by Ted Wright, performed by James Brown and the Famous Flames. "Lots, Lots More" by Ritchie Adams and Larry Kusik, performed by Frankie Avalon. "Paintin' the Town" by Bob Gaudio, performed by Frankie Avalon. "Sunshine, Lollipops and Rainbows" by Marvin Hamlisch and Howard Liebling, performed by Lesley Gore. "We'll Never Change Them" by Guy Hemric and Jerry Styner, performed by Deborah Walley.

After its success with the beach milieu, AIP was the first studio to switch the party from the sandy shores of Malibu to the ski sloops of Sun Valley with *Ski Party* (though the movie concludes back on the beach). It was a move that paid off nicely although, as with *Muscle Beach Party*, *Ski Party* is another AIP film that fans are divided upon. Two average college guys, losers when it comes to the ladies, masquerade as English lasses on a ski trip to discover why the coeds dig suave Freddie and what they really want in a guy. Complications ensue when the pompous ladies' man falls in love with one of the guy's female incarnation. The first half of the picture unfolds quite briskly with excellent musical numbers performed by Frankie Avalon, James Brown and Lesley Gore though the second half bogs down a bit with a ludicrous ski jump contest and an overlong chase sequence, standard for these AIP romps.

Ski Party stands out from the rest of the AIP beach party movies not only because of the change in locale but because of the superior production values. Credit must go to producer Gene Corman and his crew. The film is exquisitely filmed on location with some awesome ski shots. Alan Rafkin also does a first-rate job of directing and keeps the action moving. He brings some originality to the musical numbers as well. Having Frankie Avalon, Deborah Walley, Dwayne Hickman and Yvonne Craig sing "Paintin' the Town" while on a sunlit sleigh ride helps elevate the song with the beautiful shots of the foursome traveling through the snow-covered back roads. "Lots Lots More" would just have been a standard song warbled by Frankie Avalon with twistin' beach babes dancing beside him if it were not for Rafkin's unusual camera angles capturing the curvy features of Deborah Walley, Patti Chandler, Mikki Jamison and Jo Collins.

The musical performances by the guest stars are the standouts of any beach party movie. Here it is no exception. Lesley Gore sings the catchy "Sunshine, Lollipops, and Rainbows" on the bus ride to Sun Valley. Following the release of *Ski Party*, the song became a hit and peaked at No. 13 on the *Billboard* charts. The Hondells turn up on the beach and rock on "The Gasser" and the title song. Finally, the appearance of James Brown and the Famous Flames who come in out of the snow to perform their Top 10 record "I Got You (I Feel Good)," is truly one of the greatest musical moments in beach movie history.

Frankie Avalon and Dwayne Hickman are well paired as the wisecracking losers-in-love Todd and Craig and are very believable and amusing as the peppery English lasses Jane and Nora. As the objects of their devotion, Deborah Walley and Yvonne Craig are only okay but they look stunning in Pathecolor, making it perfectly plausible to the audience why the boys would go to so much trouble to win them over. Bobbi Shaw is engaging as a sexy Swede who decides she prefers love, American style. It is nice to see AIP contract players Patti Chandler and Salli Sachse given more to do here than in previous beach movies. They along with Luree Holmes, Mikki Jamison and *Playboy* Playmate Jo Collins look very good in their bathing suits or tight-fitting ski clothes. For beefcake watchers, there's lean, boyish-looking Mike Nader and handsome, chiseled Steve Rogers. But it is the smarmy charm of Aron Kincaid as the pompous Freddie who flips for a guy in drag who steals the movie. Usually clad in dark sweaters and turtlenecks (a perfect contrast to his blonde hair and fair features), Kincaid is striking looking and awes every girl on screen and every girl in the audience (not to mention a boy or two).

The Story

Todd Armstrong and Craig Gamble are average college guys who can't seem to score with pretty coeds Linda and Barbara the way suave ladies' man Freddie Carter can. When they overhear the lothario telling his overly amorous date named Janet that she'll get another chance to be alone with him on the upcoming ski trip, the guys, despite their ignorance of skiing, decide to go along to impress Linda and Barbara.

Arriving at the lodge, the group is met by persnickety hotel manager Mr. Pevney. When curvy blonde ski instructor Nita glides through the throng wearing only a bathing suit, Gene and Bobby lead the charge for the boys to change into swim trunks, abandoning a miffed Linda, Barbara and the rest of the ski bunnies. Janet declares it's time to fight fire with fire as the chicks race to change into bikinis and head for the pool.

Wanting out of the advanced ski lessons arranged for all the guys, novice skiers Todd and Craig come up with the brainstorm to masquerade as English lasses, Jane and Nora, so they can be instructed by Nita. During their first lesson, Jane loses control and careens down the hill with Linda in pursuit. Nora skis into Freddie, who becomes instantly smitten with the feisty lass. After a sleigh ride where Todd and Craig once again strike out with Linda and Barbara, the girls have a slumber party and invite Jane and Nora. The girls sit around trashing their boyfriends with Linda and Barbara particularly making fun of past dates with Todd and Craig. As Jane and Nora get up to leave, a pillow fight breaks out and the boys retaliate, clobbering the girls. "Never have so few done so much for so many," remarks Jane proudly.

On the ski slopes, Todd gets a notion to abandon the plan of becoming ace skiers and instead schemes to make the girls jealous by dating Nita and her friend Helga. Jane heads to the lodge to change back into Todd, leaving Craig-as-Nora who is enticed by Freddie bearing hot cocoa to accompany him on a sleigh ride. Pretending to be a reporter for the school newspaper, Todd interviews Nita within earshot of a jealous Linda. Todd then makes a date with Nita to meet by the fireplace in the lodge. Sitting around the roaring fire, Freddie bemoans a "lost" Nora, Barbara accuses Craig of seeing the English lass behind her back and Linda sulks while Todd plays cards with his Swedish bombshell. After berating Todd and Craig for their lack of skiing ability, Freddie challenges Todd to enter the next day's ski jump contest. Todd balks but Nita persuades him to change his mind with promises of winning her as well.

Todd straps on a helium tank to give him some lift in the jump but it sends him out of control. Craig shoots him down and Todd suffers a broken leg. Despite his injury, a determined Todd wobbles over to Nita's where he is extremely disappointed when the buxom Swede decides that she wants to be treated like her chaste American counterparts with lots of talk and maybe a kiss on the cheek. After being rejected by Barbara, Craig-as-Nora makes a date with Freddie. He returns and announces to Todd that they are pinned. Fearing for the sanity of his pal, Todd is able to convince Craig to return with him to Malibu in a taxi. An enraged Freddie's in pursuit on Pevney's scooter, thinking his "Nora" has run off with Todd. After Craig reveals to a relieved Todd that he was only joking about Freddie, the guys arrive at Todd's family's beach house followed by the busload of their friends. While the kids quickly change into bathing suits and twist on the sand to the sounds of the Hondells, a contrite Linda searches for Todd while Barbara looks for Craig. After Todd confesses to Linda about his charade as "Jane," he and Linda reunite as she is touched that he went through all that trouble to win her love. The same goes for Craig and Barbara, who lead Freddie to believe that Nora has disappeared into the ocean. Determined to save his true love, a frantic Freddie wades into the surf in search of her.

Behind-the-Scenes

When Jim Nicholson and Sam Arkoff decided to take their beach party to the snow, it was determined to bring in a different producer and director. They were impressed with *The Girls on the Beach* and so Gene Corman was hired to produce *Ski Party*. He was given creative control to an extent. Instead of using William Asher or Don Weis to direct, Corman recruited Alan Rafkin to make his feature-directing debut. Rafkin was a respected television comedy director who worked on such sitcoms as *The Donna Reed Show*, *The Dick Van Dyke Show*, *The Farmer's Daughter*, *The Patty Duke Show* and *Gomer Pyle, U.S.M.C.* Prolific television writer Robert Kaufman was hired to author the screenplay.

AIP handed the lead roles to Frankie Avalon and Deborah Walley. As with Frankie in *Pajama Party*, Annette Funicello only appears in a cameo. Dwayne Hickman, the star of television's *The Many Loves of Dobie Gillis* from 1959 to 1964, had just wrapped working on the Western *Cat Ballou* when he was offered the co-starring role of Craig Gamble. He recalled in *Filmfax* magazine, "When I got the offer to do *Ski Party*, I didn't want to do it. I didn't really care for those beach pictures. Then I read the script ... it was very funny." After meeting with Frankie Avalon, Hickman thought they could make a good team a la Bob Hope and Bing Crosby and signed on.

The role of Hickman's love interest Barbara went to Yvonne Craig though it was announced in the trades that Susan Hart was slated to play the role. A former ballerina, the fetching Craig had an interesting career before being cast in *Ski Party*. She did scads of television and made her film debut in *Eighteen and Anxious* (1957). She played one of Sandra Dee's disapproving friends in *Gidget* (1959) and went on to play loose women in *The Gene Krupa Story* (1959) with Sal Mineo and *By Love Possessed* (1961) with George Hamilton. To soften her screen image, she signed a contract with MGM in 1962. Elvis Presley fans remember as the girl the King jilted early on in *It Happened at the World's Fair* (1963) and as the bare-footin' hillbilly Azalea in *Kissin' Cousins* (1964). In her autobiography, Craig wrote that she was impressed with Robert Kaufman's writing ability and was thrilled when he sent a script to her agent. Dwayne Hickman, whom she had worked with a few times on his sitcom, was already signed to play opposite her. Craig remarked, "I told my agent that if Dwayne was in it and Bob had written it, I didn't even need to read it. I was sure it was wonderful. Only too late did I realize that Bob was in the throes of 'writer's block' and that *Ski Party* was the derivative result."

For the role of suave Freddie Carter, AIP was pushing contract player John

Deborah Walley, Aron Kincaid, Mike Nader, Mikki Jamison, Dwayne Hickman and Frankie Avalon as college students out to have a *Ski Party* (AIP, 1965).

Ashley on Gene Corman; the company even ran items in the trades that he was going to co-star in *Ski Party*. But Corman felt Ashley was too short and similar-looking to Frankie Avalon. He envisioned the role with a tall, blonde, Nordic-looking actor. The person he had in mind was Aron Kincaid, who had appeared in Corman's two previous beach movies. Kincaid recalls, "Gene Corman phoned me and asked, 'Hey Aron, do you ski?' I said, 'Oh, yeah!' and he said, 'Good. I have a part here I think you can do. I'll call you later. Bye.' I quickly got on the phone and called my cousin Terry who worked as a ski instructor in Big Bear Lake. I said, 'Terry, I'm coming up there on Friday. You have to teach me how to ski in two days!' Terry said, 'You're not going to be able to *walk* in two days!' I answered, 'I will. I can do it! *I can do it!*'"

Corman put up a fight to get Kincaid in the movie and AIP finally relented. ("The people at the studio didn't know who I was but they knew that Gene wanted me and they felt that it was an unimportant enough role not to have one of their contract players do it.") Corman was also able to hire favorite actors Steve Rogers from *The Girls on the Beach* and Mikki Jamison from *Beach Ball* to play small roles alongside the usual AIP contract players such as Mike Nader, Patti Chandler, Salli

Sachse and Luree Holmes. It is surprising that Jamison would accept such a minor part after playing a leading role in *Beach Ball* and on many television shows. Aron says, "Mikki wanted to go to Sun Valley. The producer knew her work and thought she'd be great. With what little they gave Mikki to do, she made the very most of it. She even stands out in scenes where she has no lines."

Before he left for the shoot, Kincaid decided he was going to make sure the audience noticed him even if he was just in the background of a scene. To that end he concentrated on what his character would be wearing. "I picked out my entire wardrobe for the movie and with the help of the costume coordinator, Richard Bruno, got it all approved," reveals Kincaid. "All the kids are wearing brightly colored clothes and I come on all in black with white collars. I knew that to stand out since this was a big splashy Technicolor film was not to wear colors. That was the way to go."

Ski Party was filmed on location in Sun Valley and Sawtooth National Forest with a three-week schedule. Even though this cast consisted of a number of new faces for AIP including Kincaid, Rogers, Jamison and Jo Collins (*Playboy*'s Playmate of the Year for 1965), off-camera the actors socialized within their groups. According to Luree Holmes, "It was very clear on all of the movies that there were levels of how well known you were. Frankie, Annette, Dwayne Hickman, Deborah Walley, Yvonne Craig, etc., were a group. The beach boys and girls who were contract players were another group. Finally, there were the one-time-only actors who were not part of the AIP stable. This really shook out during *Ski Party*. The four leads pretty much stuck to themselves. Frankie Avalon was very friendly if you approached him but he was not very outgoing. Even with me, I would have to go up to him to start a conversation. Poor Aron Kincaid, who was very nice and liked by everybody, was a newcomer to AIP when he did this movie and he didn't know where he fit in."

Kincaid concurs, "I was very uncomfortable working with the film's leading players. They weren't friendly at all. Frankie Avalon was aloof but not in a hurtful manner. I think he just wanted to do his work and go home to his wife and kids. Dwayne (who I get along great with today) was unfriendly at times but this may have been an effort on his part to make our on-screen 'chemistry' as Nora and Freddie more effective. The rest of them all looked through me like I was invisible. I dated Deborah Walley for a short period after the movie but even then I was treated more like her pool boy or gardener than her escort. Yvonne Craig was polite but she was dating older guys like Mort Sahl so I don't think I had anything to warrant her interest. I didn't hold their aloofness against them but it just would have been fun to have a little more camaraderie.

"Now that almost 40 years have gone by, when I run into them you'd think I was their best friend from outer space or something," continues Kincaid. "Even Dwayne Hickman wrote in his book, *Forever Dobie*, only the most praise-worthy comments about me. [Hickman described Kincaid as "a hunk" with "chiseled good looks."] I couldn't believe it. I thought, '*Was I on a different set?*' Maybe it was just because they were more intensely involved in the motion picture process than I was. For me, making a film was a big vacation. It was serious but it was also fun. I was more a fan than a performer. But I did get along great with the kids who weren't the stars—Salli Sachse, Patti Chandler, Mikki Jamison, Luree Holmes, Mike Nader and Steve Rogers—and the crew."

Though the aloofness of the cast may have perturbed Kincaid, he found some-one else to take his mind off of them. Staying in the hotel room next door to him was one of his favorite actresses, Norma Shearer. Here he was in Sun Valley hav-ing dinner and sipping champagne with one of the screen's all-time goddesses while a tuxedo-clad orchestra entertained the diners. "Things don't get much better than that for a 24-year-old," exclaimed the star struck Kincaid to the Tribune Media Services. Kincaid admits he was embarrassed at the vulgar behavior of surf legend Mickey Dora. "He'd sit there with his napkin tucked into his shirt holding his fork in one fist and his knife in the other waiting impatiently for his dinner to be served."

Technical advisor Sigi Engl was one of the nation's top ski instructors at the time and essentially played himself. He was there to help the actors with their ski-ing but it was to no avail. Avalon and Hickman never learned to ski and there were times that filming on the mountain was delayed because the cold temperatures would freeze the cameras. As all the other skiers would glide down the mountain, the two actors would be the only ones taking the ski lift back. Kincaid never mas-tered the sport either. "When we left to film in Sun Valley I was dreading the day that I was going to have to put the skis on," admits Kincaid with a laugh. "I thought they are all going to know that I could not even walk in them. I never encountered anything so foreign to me in my life—stomping around on these big long pieces of wood with metal edges."

Ski Party stuck to the beach party formula of having the musical performers come out of nowhere to sing a song. However, in no other AIP film was this done more outrageously. First, on the bus to Sun Valley, Lesley Gore materializes standing in the aisle singing her hit song "Sunshine, Lollipops, and Rainbows" and even gets the beach gang to accompany her. She was supposed to also sing "We'll Never Change Them" (a re-working of the tune "You'll Never Change Him," which was sung by Annette Funicello in *Beach Blanket Bingo* but excised from the final print) in the girls' hotel room but backed out. Deborah Walley then had to perform it on short notice.

At the end of the film, the kids hit the beach only to just happen upon the Hondells performing on the sand. Chuck Girard provided lead vocals for the Hon-dells but it is the touring version of the group (Dick Burns, Randy Thomas, Wayne Edwards and Ron Weiser) that is seen lip-synching the songs "Ski Party" and "The Gasser." The most head-scratching scene is when the parka-clad ski patrol returns the frozen body of Mr. Pevney to the hotel as the gang is relaxing around the fireplace. Yvonne Craig's Barbara recognizes them as James Brown and the Famous Flames and persuades them to perform "I Got You (I Feel Good)" before disap-pearing into the cold night whence they came.

As James Brown wails on his song, don't look for Yvonne Craig to be danc-ing with the other kids here or anywhere else for that matter in the movie. Though she was a classically trained ballerina, Craig could not master social dancing despite her determination. During rehearsals of the James Brown number, director Alan Rafkin watched Craig trying to do the Twist. She revealed in her autobiography, "He delicately suggested that I sit on the hearth and clap to the music while the others danced. On viewing the rehearsal (I apparently clap on the off-beat) Al said I could actually sit on the hearth and *sway*." This is probably the reason Craig is nowhere in sight during the poolside dance sequence "Lots, Lots More" and Deb-orah Walley's number.

During the filming of "Paintin' the Town," Frankie Avalon, Deborah Walley, Dwayne Hickman and Yvonne Craig were supposed to lip-synch to the song as they are riding in a horse-drawn sleigh. Avalon shared with the ladies the time he appeared with Hickman on *American Bandstand* and how Dwayne had to lip-synch a song with disastrous results. Every time Hickman opened his mouth to chime in on this song, the others would burst out laughing, delaying the shoot. Avalon and Hickman caused more interruptions for director Alan Rafkin during the scene when they are dressed in drag and riding in a car. As they pulled off their wigs to say their lines, they would both get hysterical with laughter. Hickman remarked in his book, "Unfortunately, Alan Rafkin was not amused. Ten takes later and a lot of lip biting, we finally got through the scene."

Aron Kincaid had trouble working with Alan Rafkin as well. "There are two scenes in particular where we quarreled," states Kincaid. "I gave Frankie a gladiator's salute as he is about to enter the ski competition. Rafkin thought it was a Nazi salute but it wasn't. He didn't understand it and wouldn't listen to reason. I had to then give Frankie an army salute.

"For the end of the film, I had purchased this beautiful very expensive yellow sweater," continues Kincaid. "I wore it as Freddie chased his Nora back to Santa Monica in the middle of the night. Richard Bruno advised me that if I wore my standard black, the audience wouldn't be able to see me. The script called for me to jump into the ocean when I am misled to believe that Nora has tried to drown herself. In rehearsal I began stripping off my clothes before I go in. But Rafkin wanted me to run in—clothes and all. I argued with him that my sweater, *which I paid for myself*, would be ruined. He didn't care and I didn't want to act like a prima donna in front of the cast so I complied. Richard Bruno told me that he would immediately treat the sweater when I came out of the ocean. We shot the scene but the sweater was never the same. I wound up giving it away to the winner of this *Movie Teen* magazine contest, as first prize was a piece of Aron Kincaid's clothing!"

Despite his problems with the cast and director, Kincaid relished making *Ski Party* because "I had played a villain only once before in a *Channing* episode with Peter Fonda and Michael Parks. I never had any fun with a character since that role until I played Freddie Carter. I loved it. I ate, lived and breathed the character of Freddie. I really enjoyed doing the picture."

Yvonne Craig also enjoyed working on *Ski Party* though she was disappointed in the script. She remarked in *Filmfax* magazine, "Working for AIP was great fun. They had no wardrobe department so they went out and bought us all new clothes. And we got to keep them, so I got a whole ski wardrobe. They also took us to Sun Valley and paid for our ski lessons." But Craig's ski instructions came to a quick halt when someone at AIP realized that the actress could break her leg, causing a delay in production.

Despite AIP's precautions, accidents did abound on the slopes of *Ski Party* according to an article in the *Los Angeles Herald Examiner*. Dwayne Hickman suffered back injuries and Deborah Walley strained her ligaments when the pair was thrown off a toboggan during a photo shoot. Hickman's stand-in Corky Fowler broke his leg skiing and cameraman John Stevens fractured two ribs when the snow-rig he was riding on hit a rock.

Frankie Avalon enjoyed making this movie and remarked in *Seventeen,* "*Ski Party* is a lot of fun. It's a take-off on *Some Like It Hot.* I think it will be very funny."

Ski Party's end credits finished inviting the audience to "Turn off your television when it's time to come back and watch 'CRUISE PARTY.'" This movie was never produced by AIP. It is speculated that since the box office receipts of *Ski Party* were not up to *Beach Party* or *Bikini Beach,* it was best to have the action return to the sandy shores of Malibu rather than an ocean liner. The film also did not offer any shimmying bikini-clad girls during the end credits as in the other beach party movies. Instead the Hondells sang "Ski Party" while a number of skiers holding torches skied downhill at night.

Just before *Ski Party* was released to the public, Kincaid learned that his billing was not going to be equal to the size of his role. Being a newcomer at American International he sort of expected it, but was disappointed nevertheless. "American International Pictures had like 20 people under contract. According to the size of my part I should have had third billing. Instead, I was billed sixth after Robert Q. Lewis, who was listed as a guest star. I was the first name listed under co-starring credit. When you throw in James Brown and Lesley Gore my billing dropped to eighth. It was even worse for my friend Mikki Jamison. In *Beach Ball,* she was my leading lady and then in *Ski Party* as my billing was reduced she was reduced even further to featured status." Inexplicably, Mary Hughes is credited as a co-star on the film's poster art though she has much less screen time than Jamison, Steve Rogers, Salli Sachse and Luree Holmes.

Impressed with his performance in the movie, AIP sent Aron Kincaid on a three-week PR tour for *Ski Party* along with Mary Hughes and Salli Sachse. Among the states they visited were Colorado, Wisconsin and Indiana. It ended in New York. Kincaid recalls, "They took us to Shea Stadium to introduce us to all the fans. I remember waiting in the Green Room and the Beatles were appearing that day. We were all having Cokes and talking and laughing with Paul, John, George and Ringo. I should have gotten all their autographs! If it had been Hedy Lamarr and Susan Hayward I would have been killing myself to get them to sign my book. But I thought the Beatles were just young guys my age and I didn't need their autographs."

While on tour, Kincaid found himself in trouble with the public relations men from AIP on more than one occasion. In Hollywood, actresses (especially nubile bikini-clad ones who co-star in surf movies) didn't warrant much respect. Aron came to their defense on more than one occasion. "I always thought of the girls as actresses and not as beach bunnies," remarks Aron. "The studio and PR guys used to call them that and other things like 'bikini girls' and 'pin-ups.' I'd take them aside and say, 'Look, these are young actresses and they are never going to stay in the business if they have to put up with people like you so treat them with a little respect.' That got me grief from AIP more than once. But it was sickening to hear this kind of talk. It made it sound like a machine had cranked them all out. But they were individuals with distinct personalities. Each one had their pluses and each one also had their minuses like we all do. But just lumping them together in one big mass bothered me."

After the release of *Ski Party,* things picked up for Kincaid. He began getting barraged by movie magazines and newspapers for interviews and was selected to

In *Ski Party* (AIP, 1965), Aron Kincaid as lothario Freddie Carter is enticed by beach girls (*left to right*) Patti Chandler, Salli Sachse, Jo Collins, Mary Hughes and Mikki Jamison, but he only has eyes for Dwayne Hickman's Nora.

appear with Patti Chandler on the cover of *Look* magazine. Recalling that photo shoot, Kincaid says, "The only scar on my body came from Salli Sachse when she turned around in her skis and slit my ankle. It felt like a guillotine cutting me all the way to the bone. We were, of all places, on the sand dunes of Palm Springs in the middle of summer, no less. Well, the sand looked like snow."

It was around this time that 14-year-old Louis Arkoff began working in the mailroom at AIP. A self-described "nosy kid," the teenager began opening envelopes and stumbled across many love letters addressed to Aron Kincaid from his adoring female public. Louis recalls, "One night while we were sitting around the dinner table and my dad asked me how it was going in the mailroom. I told him about all these letters Aron Kincaid was receiving." AIP soon offered Kincaid a seven-year contract. James Nicholson and Sam Arkoff released a joint statement that said, "We confidently predict a most promising future as an actor for Kincaid on the basis of his performance in *Ski Party*, the unprecedented flood of fan mail he has received on his debut appearance in that musical comedy, and the unanimously favorable responses we have received from both exhibitors and fans as a result of his brief personal appearance tour of the Midwest last month."

Regarding his bosses at AIP, Kincaid comments, "Jim Nicholson was just a complete, elegant gentleman. He did everything with style. You would never believe that he was a part of exploitation films, teenybopper movies and all the things that he produced. Sam Arkoff, however, was just a complete character with his cigar and street-wise, crude ways. But he meant well underneath it all. He didn't have a lot of friends in this town. The guy would have done anything for a buck and to save money. Jim, on the other hand, was putting us up at the Sun Valley Lodge during *Ski Party*. He lavished limousines and dinners on us at places like 21 and the Stork Club while we were on tour in New York. We were hauled around like prize racehorses to the New York fan magazines. Jim could have easily worked into the hierarchy during the early days of MGM. But Sam was pure Harry Cohn at Columbia. That was the difference between them but I think that was what made them such a successful duo. You had the good and the bad and the black and the white."

AIP was so pleased with the pairing of Frankie Avalon and Dwayne Hickman that they teamed them again in the spy spoof *Dr. Goldfoot and the Bikini Machine* (1965). Yvonne Craig played a mini-skirted scientist opposite Tommy Kirk as an alien in *Mars Needs Women* (1966), one of the many low-budget direct-to-television AIP films directed by Larry Buchanan, before finding fame as Batgirl during the last season of television's *Batman* (1967–68).

Memorable Lines

(Freddie is trying to fight off the advances of an amorous Janet.)

FREDDIE: Janet, *please* let me go. My lips are exhausted. Look, you'll have another date with me again sometime soon I promise—well, before we graduate anyway.

(Jane, Nora, and Nita watch as the coeds gather and chat on the ski slopes.)

JANE (Todd): What's wrong with the American girl?

NITA: You know, it's funny that you ask me that. I was just going to ask you the same thing.

NORA (Craig): Games, games, games. All they do is play games.

JANE (Todd): And talk.

NORA (Craig): Talk, talk all the time.

NITA: In Sweden it's very different. In Stockholm when a boy and girl meet and they like each other—*no* games and *very little* talk.

Reviews

Harry Gilroy, *The New York Times*—"Along come Frankie and Deborah again. The scenery of the Sawtooth National Forest is gorgeous and a busload of girls who agitate their bikinis and ski pants at the camera are willowy."

Margaret Harford, *Los Angeles Times*—"When writer Robert Kaufman puts male stars Dwayne Hickman and Frankie Avalon in drag for three-fourths of the picture, you know ideas are running pretty thin. The female impersonation act is a bore and the dialogue seems awfully childish even for teenagers."

Mandel Herbstman, *The Film Daily*—"Fun, mischief and romance roll along in *Ski Party*.... The picture is put together with the formula elements that assure success especially with teenagers."

Motion Picture Exhibitor—"Teenagers especially should appreciate this comic entry with plenty of the music of the day.... The story is nonsensical and should not be taken seriously...."

Sy Oshinsky, *Motion Picture Herald*—"A light and frothy tale which should appeal to the young set."

Variety—"*Ski Party* is an entertaining teenage comedy romance in snow-country settings, with excellent direction of good satirical script and fine performances by young thesps. Gene Corman production values are standout, and seven tunes enliven pace. Film is sort of snowbound *Some Like It Hot* combined with *Tom Jones* asides to audience."

Awards and Nominations

Golden Laurel Award: "Best Musical" fifth place

Golden Laurel Award: "Best Musical Performance—Male" Frankie Avalon, fourth place

Golden Laurel Award: "New Faces, Male"—Dwayne Hickman, fourth place

Screen World Award: "Most Promising Personalities"—Aron Kincaid

★ 22 ★

A Swingin' Summer (1965)

Spread out the beach towels ... Grab your gals ... And go-go-go bikini!

Fun: ★★★½
Surfing: ★
Boy watching: ★★★
Girl watching: ★★★★★
Music: ★★★★
Scenery: ★★★

Release date: April 1965. Running time: 80m. Box office gross: Not available.
DVD release: Not as of January 2005.

James Stacy (*Mickey*), William A. Wellman, Jr. (*Rick*), Quinn O'Hara (*Cindy*), Martin West (*Turk*), Mary Mitchel (*Shirley*), Raquel Welch (*Jeri*), Allan Jones (*Mr. Johnson*), Lili Kardell (*Sandra*), Robert Blair (*Tony*), Reno Carell (*Mark*), Bucky Holland (*Les*), Glenn Stensel (*Lou*), Mike Blodgett (*Dancer*), Mauree Garett (*Beauty Contestant*), Robert Porter (*Kenny*), Gypsy Boots (*Himself*), Diane Bond (*The Girl in the Pink Polka-Dot Bikini*), Lori Williams, Sherry Nix, Irene Sales, Darlene Hunter, Cathy Frances, Diane Swanson (*The Swingin' Summer Girls*). Guest Stars: The Righteous Brothers, The Rip Chords, Donnie Brooks, and Gary Lewis and the Playboys.

Reno Carell–National Talent Consultants production. United Screen Arts release. *Produced by*: Reno Carell. *Directed by*: Robert Sparr. *Executive Producers*: Kenneth Raphael and Larry Goldblatt. *Associate Producer*: Patrick Curtis. *Screenplay by*: Leigh Chapman. *Original Story by*: Reno Carell. *Music Scored and Conducted by*: Harry Betts. *Production Manager*: Jack C. Lacey. *Director of Photography*: Ray Fernstrom, A.S.C. *Supervising Film Editor*: James T. Heckert. *Film Editor*: William E. Lee. *Assistant Director*: Rusty Meek. *Costumer*: Marjorie Corso. *Choreographer and Lead Dancer*: Mike Blodgett. *Music Coordinator*: Mike Post. *Musical Advisor*: Roger Carroll. *Recording Supervisor*: Earl Snyder. *Sound Editor*: George Emick. *Music Editor*: Helen Sneddon. *Makeup Supervisor*: Danny Greenway. *Hair Stylist*: Eve Newing. *Script Supervisor*: Rita Michaels. *Sound by*: Goldwyn Studios. *Fight Coordinator*: John Indrisano. *Technical Advisor*: Larry Parker. *Title Design by*: Consolidated Film Industries. *Bikinis by*: Peter Pan. *Motorcycles by*: Suzuki. *Cobra by*: Shelby-American. Filmed in Technicolor and Techniscope.

"A Swingin' Summer" by Carol Connors, Roger Christian and Buzz Cason, performed by Jody Miller over the opening credits. "Justine" by Don Harris and Dewey Terry, performed by the Righteous Brothers. "I'm Ready to Groove" performed by Raquel Welch. "Penny the Poo" performed by Donnie Brooks. "Red Hot Roadster" performed by the Rip Chords. "Nitro" and "Out to Lunch" performed by Gary Lewis and the Playboys.

In *A Swingin' Summer*, the beach party moves from the sands of the Pacific to the shores of Lake Arrowhead; water skiing and motorboat racing replace surfing in this teenage saga. Of all the *Beach Party* clones, it has perhaps the most plausible plot. Instead of portraying teenagers on holiday or just hanging out at the beach, these kids are working students out to make a buck. Three college kids take over the Lake Arrowhead Dance Pavilion and a have a week to make money or they lose the gig. Trouble ensues from a jealous lifeguard who wanted the chance and attempts to sabotage the event. Interspersed are a number of musical performances keeping the movie true to the beach party formula. However, the film's strong points (an agreeable cast, great musical numbers and frenzied dancing) are slightly hampered by low production values.

Despite the budget constraints, this film is highly recommended for beach party fans. However, if you are looking for surfing footage, there isn't any but in one head-scratching scene James Stacy inexplicably paddles in from the lake on a surfboard. Director Robert Sparr keeps the story moving briskly and the change of locale to Lake Arrowhead adds to the movie, making it a cut above the rest. William Wellman, Jr., and Quinn O'Hara make a charming couple and handsome James Stacy shows off a great body, a disarming smile and a roguish charm. Mary Mitchel is amusing playing O'Hara's wisecracking friend but aging starlet Lili Kardell is totally miscast as O'Hara's rival for Wellman, Jr.

There is plenty of male and female flesh on display (redheaded Diane Bond, busty blonde Lori Williams and Michael Blodgett sporting tight abs stand out) to keep both boy and girl watchers enthralled. The most famous of the beach babes is curvaceous Raquel Welch, a knockout in her signature yellow bikini. But pretty redhead Quinn O'Hara gives her a run for the money in the sexiness department, especially when she is clad in an outrageous bikini featuring a very tight top (two sizes too small) featuring a turtle neck and long sleeves with matching bikini bottoms. For boy watchers the guys are attired in tight bathing trunks and white tube socks, and there is a fight scene on the beach between Wellman and West that turns into a mud-wrestling match.

The music is hot, from Jody Miller's title tune sung over the opening credits to the Righteous Brother's finale singing "Justine." *A Swingin' Summer* was filmed before Gary Lewis and the Playboys hit it big in 1965 so they do not perform any of their hits and act more like a backup band. But their instrumentals get the teenagers swinging. Donnie Brooks sings the ridiculous song "Penny the Poo" but director Robert Sparr has Michael Blodgett and Lori Williams performing some frenzied dancing to distract from the lyrics. Raquel Welch evens gets a song but her singing and bump-and-grind dance routine is more embarrassing than enticing. All in all, *A Swingin' Summer* is one beach party well worth attending.

The Story

Driving to Lake Arrowhead to begin their summer jobs at a dance pavilion, lothario Mickey, enterprising Rick and Rick's supportive girlfriend Cindy are startled to hear an announcement on the radio that promoters made a last-minute decision to cancel the series of concerts. Cindy reminds Rick that her father's offer to work for him is still open but the proud boy does not want to take charity. He then comes up with an idea to run the pavilion since a friend of his works as an agent

Poster art for *A Swingin' Summer* (United Screen Arts, 1965), one of the many *Beach Party* clones released between 1964 and 1967.

for the National Talent Consultants and could provide the musical acts. The trio heads to Lake Arrowhead to talk to Mr. Johnson, the village manager, and persuade him to give them the chance. They find him sitting poolside with lifeguard Turk. After laying out his plan, Rick is crushed to learn from Johnson that $1,000 is needed up front to cover expenses. The dejected boys head back to the car while Cindy, returning to fetch her sunglasses that she purposely left behind, makes a secret deal with Johnson, assuring him that her wealthy father will back Rick. The pleased girl then tells the fellows that she persuaded Johnson to give them a chance.

With the help of Cindy's friend Shirley, intensive work to get the pavilion ready before the opening weekend gets underway. While Rick lines up the musical guests and Cindy creates signs promoting the event, Mickey posts them in the town and is noticed by Jeri, a brainy brunette in glasses who follows him to the beach. While Mickey enjoys frolicking with a bevy of bikini-clad beauties, Rick is all work and no play—much to Cindy's chagrin. At the local college hangout, Mickey and Rick are ordering food at the counter while lifeguard Turk flirts with Cindy. He and his buddy Tony leave after almost coming to blows with Mickey over an insult thrown Turk's way. Rick and Cindy quarrel again and when Rick accuses the pretty redhead of acting childish she concurs and vows to find a guy who'd appreciate her. He and Mickey head over to the coffee shop where they overhear Cindy making plans with Turk.

Rick learns from Shirley that Cindy is just trying to make him jealous. Jeri, meanwhile, is still tailing Mickey. After psychoanalyzing him, the curvaceous beauty announces that he is going to be her summer romance. A frightened Mickey thinks she is nuts and quickly paddles off on his surfboard. Rick contemplates making up with Cindy until she drives by on another date with Turk. Instead, he heads for the beach and meets the older Sandra, who shamelessly flirts with him and convinces the forlorn boy to escort her to a party. Realizing it is at Cindy's home, Rick protests that they don't belong, but Sandra wants to go. Rick has a run-in with Turk, who accuses Rick of playing "big man" with the money provided by Cindy's father. Despite Cindy's pleading, a verbal showdown between Rick and Turk ensues and quickly progresses into fisticuffs with Rick coming out on top.

The Dance Pavilion finally opens and the event is a hit as the teens pack the dance floor. A pleased Rick leaves followed by a contrite Cindy, who apologizes for her behavior and for going behind Rick's back. When Cindy reveals that her father did not give the money but loaned the funds at 12 percent interest, Rick smiles and declares, "That is illegal. He'll get six percent and not a penny more." The two make up and seal it with a kiss.

At the beach, a jealous Tony challenges Mickey to a game of chicken on water skis to impress Jeri. Cindy and Rick try to dissuade Mickey from being goaded into it, but the headstrong boy doesn't back down. The dangerous race with the boats begins propelling the skiers toward each other at over 50 miles per hour. Mickey finishes the victor while Tony wipes out and is pulled from the lake bruised and defeated.

Seeking revenge on Rick, Turk pays off three hoods to crash the pavilion dance and break up the program. The hired toughs try to crash the gate but are stopped by Rick and Mickey. A fight ensues and the hoods are beaten and leave. The gang's leader Les then forces Turk to help them rob the pavilion. As the house band jams,

Jeri steams as Mickey ogles the hip-swaying dancing Swingin' Summer girls. She then takes off her glasses, lets down her hair, strips down to a tight-fitting leotard and belts out "I'm Ready to Groove," knocking the socks off an astonished Mickey. While she is entertaining the crowd, Turk arrives and persuades Cindy to let him into the box office to make a phone call. Les and his goons then show up and steal the strong box. They clobber Turk and make off through the woods with Rick, Mickey and the rest of the gang in pursuit. The thieves take a motorboat and speed off on the lake. Trying to make amends, Turk jumps into his boat and with Rick pursue the hoods. The kids retrieve the money after a wild boat race. The film concludes with the Righteous Brothers performing "Justine" at the dance pavilion.

Behind-the-Scenes

Executive producers Larry Goldblatt and Kenneth Raphael were the springboard for *A Swingin' Summer*. They were only 24 and 28 years old, respectively, at the time. Goldblatt was running his own advertising agency at 19 in Minneapolis and Raphael was producing college concerts while still in school. The duo met at the beach and formed National Talent Consultants, which represented new musical performers of the day.

Reno Carell knew Goldblatt and Raphael and at the time he was roommates and partners in a production company with William Wellman, Jr. "We had several projects in development and this was one of them," recalls Wellman, Jr. "I had always wanted to star in a movie with Jim Stacy. Reno found a guy to invest in the movie. I was one of the film's producers but in those days nobody thought it was a good idea to take double credit. If you were an actor you were supposed to be only an actor and not a producer or a writer. I didn't take any screen credit but I did a lot of the pre-production work and hired Leigh Chapman [a sometimes actress who made a few appearances on television's *The Man from U.N.C.L.E.*] to author the screenplay. I actually wanted Edward Lakso but he was too busy with his television series *Combat*. He suggested his girlfriend Leigh so we went with her hoping Ed would be looking in on things. Reno did most of the casting and he gets all the merit for hiring Raquel Welch."

Carell also gets the blame for the miscasting of Lili Kardell. According to Bill, "Reno had met Lili Kardell while he was working in Rome with Gordon Scott. Lili was one of their favorites. Reno remembered her and offered her a role in the movie."

Carell also hired Robert Sparr to direct. Like most beach party movie directors Sparr came from television where he worked on a number of series including *Lassie, Bonanza, 77 Sunset Strip* and *Voyage to the Bottom of the Sea*. "I *liked* Robert Sparr," remarks co-star Quinn O'Hara fondly. "He'd been around for a long time and knew what he was doing. He wasn't an outstanding director like Don Weis but he was quite the professional."

William Wellman, Jr., only had one actor in mind to play his friend—James Stacy. Their friendship began in 1956 on location in Santa Maria when they both worked together on *Lafayette Escadrille*. Wellman, Jr., recalls, "We were then cast in *Sayonara* and had the same amount of lines but he was just blowing his so the director, Joshua Logan, kept giving them to me. I was nervous enough working with Marlon Brando. Jim and I became pals and we always wanted to star in a film together. The guy had a great personality. He was trying to be a dramatic actor. When we did *The Young Sinner*, he was showing this wonderful persona that he had."

A Swingin' Summer was shot entirely on location at Lake Arrowhead and Lake Arrowhead Village, located a mile high in the San Bernadino Mountains approximately 85 miles east of Los Angeles. It was decided that Stacy was to play the fun-loving guy doing the comedy relief while Wellman would portray the straight guy who wants to keep everybody working. However, just before shooting began, Stacy went to Wellman, and begged to switch roles with him. "If I had been smarter, I would have done it," says Bill with a laugh. "The guy who's having a good time and cracking the jokes is the guy you like—the straight guy pushing people to go back to work is a pain in the ass!"

Quinn O'Hara agrees, "William Wellman, Jr., and I played two doormats. The best parts were James Stacy and Mary Mitchel's. She was so cute in this. Martin West did a good job as the heavy."

Blonde Linda Evans was signed to play the female lead but bowed out at the last minute when she was cast as Audra Barclay in the television series *The Big Valley*. Titian-haired Quinn O'Hara, who had also tested for Audra and was being considered for the role of Sandra in *A Swingin' Summer*, replaced Evans as Cindy instead. "When I met Reno Carell, Linda Evans had already been cast," recalls Quinn O'Hara. "He interviewed me for the part Lili Kardell played. He said, 'I wish I had met you when we were casting the lead. If this girl can do it, we already have the part cast. If anything happens we'd like to get in touch with you.' A day or so later Linda Evans got *The Big Valley* and dropped out of the movie." Going into the picture at the last minute, O'Hara had only a week to learn her lines. She also had to go out and purchase a wardrobe since the clothes bought for Evans in the movie didn't fit the shapely, shorter redhead.

As for Reno Carell, Quinn describes him as "quite the ladies' man. He was a real skirt-chaser. Thank God there were a lot of girls up there in Lake Arrowhead! But he was fun to be around."

Since executive producers Goldblatt and Raphael were in the music business, they recruited all the musical performers for the film except for one. Though the Righteous Brothers would go on to appear in *Beach Ball* (1965) and Donnie Brooks in *The Love-Ins* (1967), this was the only film appearance of the Rip Chords. The road group members (Phil Stewart, Rich Rotkin and Arnie Marcus) are seen on screen but the song's producer Terry Melcher, Doris Day's son, actually sang lead vocals on their song. The one group hired by William Wellman, Jr., was Gary Lewis and the Playboys. "I signed them as a favor to Gary's dad Jerry. He was a great guy and practically every time he made a film I'd get a call offering me a role. I never knew how to pay him back until *A Swingin' Summer*. I told Reno Carell that Jerry's son had just formed a rock group and that I was hiring them to appear in the film. Soon after the movie was released they hit with their first big record, 'This Diamond Ring.'"

Micheal Blodgett began acting to finance his college tuition at California State. His film debut was playing a minor role in *Take Her, She's Mine* (1963) with James

Stewart and Sandra Dee. In *A Swingin' Summer* (1965) the lean blonde hunk was cast as one of the shirtless college guys hanging around Lake Arrowhead. Though he had no formal training, he was able to convince the producers to hire him as choreographer as well. This allowed him more screen time as he was front and center in many of the dance numbers and gave him a heftier paycheck for school. According to his co-stars, the freewheeling Blodgett would "organize" the dance scenes without giving specific steps or routines to follow. Co-star Lori Williams, who shimmied in such films as *Kissin' Cousins*, *Viva Las Vegas*, *Get Yourself a College Girl* (all 1964), *Girl Happy*, and *Tickle Me* (both 1965), commented in *Drive-in Dream Girls*, "Mike Blodgett was fun to dance with."

Reno Carell's most infamous casting was that of Raquel Welch as Jeri, the bookworm who learns to groove. Hiring Welch was a boost for the movie but also caused many problems on the set. Prior to *A Swingin' Summer*, Welch was the Billboard Girl on the television variety show *The Hollywood Palace* and played bit roles in movies such as *Roustabout* (1964) and *A House Is Not a Home* (1964). She received "and introducing" billing in the credits. Welch showed up with her manager Patrick Curtis. According to William Wellman, Jr., "Patrick Curtis was doing everything for Raquel. He was telling her what she should do, what classes she should take, who she should talk to, who she should stay away from." Curtis became such a presence on the set that he was offered an associate producer credit. "He was a

James Stacy, Mary Mitchel, William Wellman, Jr., and Quinn O'Hara as college kids dancing to a rockin' beat provided by Gary Lewis and the Playboys in *A Swingin' Summer* (United Screen Arts, 1965).

nice guy but a pathological liar," adds Quinn about Curtis. "I think he couldn't help himself. He wanted to manage me but I told him to stick with Raquel."

Welch meanwhile was not endearing herself to some of her female co-stars or the crew. Lori Williams remarked, "Raquel Welch was a problem on this movie and she was a major, major bitch. She wanted to have her signature bikini in the film. I had bought my bikinis before we got to Lake Arrowhead and she wouldn't let me wear any of them. I had to go out and buy new swimsuits. Working with her was not a lot of fun."

Quinn O'Hara adds, "I had no trouble with Raquel. But I heard about that bathing suit incident. I didn't have a hell of a lot of choice of what to wear since I barely had time to get a wardrobe together. I thought 'Raquel is going to have to like it or lump it' because I wasn't getting another swimsuit."

The headstrong Raquel also made enemies of the crew. "She did her own makeup and wouldn't let the body makeup woman touch her," recalls Quinn. "She swatted her hand away. The cameraman told me that she was going to look terrible with those windshield wiper eyelashes because they were so heavy and casting shadows on her face. I don't think it made her look bad at all." Lori Williams recalled, "She kept trying to get people fired. We lost two cameramen who quit because she was just wretched. For me, she was just the worst person I ever met during the time I worked."

Coming from a different perspective, William Wellman, Jr., remarks, "Quinn O'Hara was very nice and a lot of fun to work with. Everybody got along wonderfully with Quinn. I loved Mary Mitchel and thought she was going to be a star. She had this cute voice, was very attractive and had a great way about her. Lori Williams was very friendly also. But I don't think Raquel Welch treated any of them badly, she just didn't pay any attention to them. She kept pretty much to herself throughout the shoot. We shot this on location and a lot of the cast was partying most of the time. Raquel did not want to be a part of that. Her room was next to mine and I could hear her working on her dance routine. She was working all of the time. A lot of people who worked on the beach movies were there just for the good time. Raquel really took it seriously. I was married by this time and I wasn't partying either." Quinn O'Hara concurs with Wellman about Raquel: "Yes, Raquel did stay to herself. You didn't really get to know her."

Just as their characters were different from each other, so were William Wellman, Jr., and James Stacy off the set. According to Quinn O'Hara, both actors reflected the parts they played off-camera. Wellman was reserved while Stacy (despite his marriage to Connie Stevens, who visited the set briefly) had an eye for the ladies. "William Wellman, Jr., was all business but I liked him a lot," states Quinn. "He was great to work with and I had no problems with him. He was the consummate professional and always there if you needed to go over lines with him. I really, really liked Jim Stacy. He was so friendly and outgoing. I thought he was going to become a major star. Jim had everything going for him. He had charisma not to mention good looks with that dark hair and blue eyes. When he had his motorcycle accident a few years later, I was just crushed.

"I remember one funny incident with Jim Stacy," continues Quinn. "I had bought this two-piece bathing suit with a matching skirt and hat. The swimsuit was very skimpy. I am a bit buxom and that is before women starting having boob jobs.

I had a hard time finding one-piece swim suits that fit properly so that is why I wore bikinis. We were doing a scene where they were going to keep cutting from me to Jim. I was wearing the bikini and Jim said to me, 'Quinn, can you put something on to cover yourself up a little bit?' I asked why and he said, "Because I can just hear the guys in the audience yelling, 'Get back to the broad, get back to the broad' every time the camera is going to be on me.'" Unbeknownst to Quinn, Stacy wasn't joking and even went to the producers to convince her to cover up.

One of the things that makes *A Swingin' Summer* a standout beach party movie are the dance scenes. As with *Pajama Party*, a special choreographer was brought in to make the dance moves memorable. Michael Blodgett was a fantastic dancer and also played a part in the movie. "Michael was a lot of fun," comments O'Hara. "He kept everybody's spirits up. Though he organized the dance scenes, I just danced as if I was out at a nightclub. Michael never gave me steps or moves to learn. We danced together for some publicity photos and I enjoyed that. He was very pleasant and charming with a great body. I heard some unkind things about him afterwards as he had a drinking problem too."

Despite Blodgett's talent, he wasn't able to help William Wellman, Jr., overcome his lack of dancing prowess. "I never fancied myself a dancer, though I used to do the Twist like everybody else. But this was a low-budget film. They throw you into everything and you sort of muddle through. When Robert Sparr said to me, 'Bill, I want you to just get up on the stage and start dancing,' I replied, 'I don't really feel right about this.' He said, 'Don't worry. The camera is only going to be on you a little bit.' The camera's on me a lot! Mike Blodgett was a terrific dancer and tried to help me out but I got thrown into the mix while we were shooting. It wasn't like it was planned or I would have practiced. I think of that scene and it makes me cringe to this day." Quinn concurs, "Yes, Bill Wellman was not a great dancer but he looked *so* good in this I don't think it mattered."

Since he was once a boxer, Wellman felt more comfortable with his fight scene with Martin West. But again the film's low budget put restrictions on it. "We had to choreograph this ourselves. There weren't any retakes. The fight could have looked a lot better but the money wasn't there."

One funny mishap on the set involved Quinn O'Hara and Reno Carell, who played one of the heavies in the film. "The first time we shot the scene where he grabs me and I tried to fight him off, I instinctively kneed him you-know-where," says Quinn, chuckling. "Shit happens on a set."

After filming was completed, *A Swingin' Summer* should have been one of the highest grossing beach movies but distribution problems prevented the film from reaching a wide teenage audience. Bill Wellman explains, "The movie was shopped to Warner Bros., Universal and Columbia for distribution rights. Though offers were made, Reno Carell signed a contract with actor Dale Robertson who had just formed United Screen Arts. I was against this since the deal did not give us the right to make an outright sale to a major studio. Robertson wouldn't give up the distribution rights because he didn't have any product and believed that *A Swingin' Summer* was going to be as successful as *Beach Party*." The movie could have been but with Robertson's limited contacts it didn't play in as many theaters as the AIP movies.

A Swingin' Summer was barely in the can when Patrick Curtis contacted the producers. "He called us to get a print of the film before it was released to show the executives of 20th Century–Fox who were interested in Raquel," recalls Bill. "You would never hear this from Raquel though. If you ever mention *A Swingin' Summer* to her, she'll run the other way. We sent the print to Richard Zanuck the head of the studio and he signed her to a contract as a result of *A Swingin' Summer*. She's wonderful in the film—hell, it's not Shakespeare. She looks beautiful, she's dancing, she's singing. Through it all, Patrick Curtis was right there helping her. He doesn't get enough credit for her success even though he eventually married her."

The newly formed Hanna-Barbera Records released the soundtrack LP *A Swingin' Summer* in 1965. However, they could not get the permission to license the songs performed Jody Miller or Gary Lewis and the Playboys from their respective labels. The title song was then re-recorded by Carol Connors (an unbilled extra in the movie) and Gary Lewis and his group's songs were remade by a studio band formed by Harry Betts and called the Swingers.

James Stacy and Quinn O'Hara relax between camera set-ups on *A Swingin' Summer* (United Screen Arts, 1965) (*courtesy Quinn O'Hara*).

Despite William Wellman, Jr.'s, disappointment that *A Swingin' Summer* didn't reach a wider audience, the major studios took notice and Columbia Pictures contracted Reno Carell to do another beach party movie reuniting Wellman, Jr., and James Stacy.

Most of the rest of the cast went on to appear in more beach movies as well. Martin West progressed to the lead (joined by Mary Mitchel) in a featured role in *The Girls on the Beach* (1965) while Quinn O'Hara was recruited by AIP for a starring role in *The Ghost in the Invisible Bikini* (1966). Mike Blodgett went on to choreograph and co-star in *Catalina Caper* (1967).

The film's "The Girl in the Pink Polka-Dot Bikini" Diane Bond worked as a stuntwoman between acting roles. She went on to play a minor role in the Elvis Presley musical *Tickle Me* (1965) before landing the high profile part of one of Derek Flint's assistants in the popular spy spoof *In Like Flint* (1967) starring James Coburn. After acting in a few European movies including *House of 1,000 Dolls* (1968) and *Barbarella* (1968), Bond retired from show business to become a writer on feminist issues.

Post–*Swingin' Summer*, Lori Williams found cult movie fame as the tough-talking, hot rod–racing, go-go–dancing Billie in the Russ Meyer drive-in classic *Faster, Pussycat! Kill! Kill!* (1966) co-starring Tura Satana and Haji.

As for Raquel Welch, she got her contract with 20th Century–Fox. Her first movie for the studio was the hit science-fiction classic *Fantastic Voyage* (1966) playing a surgeon's sexy assistant. But it was the prehistoric adventure film *One Million Years B.C.* (1967) that catapulted Raquel to become arguably the number one international sex symbol of the sixties.

Memorable Lines

(The arrogant Turk factiously admires Cindy and Shirley's dedication to their jobs.)

SHIRLEY: That reminds me. Aren't you the lifeguard around here?

TURK (proudly): Head lifeguard.

SHIRLEY: Remind me not to go swimming.

Reviews

Boxoffice—"A bunch of lovely girls and handsome boys frolicking in a Lake Arrowhead setting, while various singing groups give out with lively song numbers, make this ... a strong entry for the teenage market."

George Martin, *Motion Picture Editor*—"Engagingly performed by a cluster of 'Stars of Tomorrow,' United Screen Arts' lighthearted and tune-filled *A Swingin' Summer* offers delightful entertainment for moviegoers of every age."

James Powers, *The Hollywood Reporter*—"*A Swingin' Summer* is peopled with attractive youngsters, dancing and playing, and there are a good number of musical interludes to spell the slim plot."

Variety—"A breezy bouncing bunch of boys, babes, bosoms, buttocks and bodies bob about in this bucolic beach-bash broth. There is action, some top wax names, and lush Lake Arrowhead settings."

William Weaver, *Motion Picture Herald*—"A tip-top entry in the trade-wide competition for teenage patronage. It rocks and it rolls, jumps and bounces, and carries along with somewhat more story than is par for the beach-bikini course."

Awards and Nominations

Junior Philharmonic Orchestra of California: "Star of Tomorrow"—James Stacy

Photoplay Gold Medal Award nomination: "Most Promising New Star–Female"— Raquel Welch

⋆ *23* ⋆

Wild on the Beach (1965)

*They Rented a Beach House ... and They Rented the
SAME Beach House ... and now it's Wild on the Beach.*

Fun: ⋆⋆
Surfing: ⋆⋆
Boy watching: ⋆⋆
Girl watching: ⋆
Music: ⋆⋆⋆
Scenery: ⋆⋆

Release date: August 25, 1965. Running time: 77m. Box office gross: Not available.
DVD release: Not as of January 2005.

Frankie Randall (*Adam Miller*), Sherry Jackson (*Lee Sullivan*), Jackie Miller (*Toby Carr*),
Gayle Caldwell (*Marsie Lowell*), The Astronauts (*Themselves*), Sonny and Cher (*Themselves*),
Cindy Malone (*Herself*), Sandy Nelson (*Himself*), Russ Bender (*Shep Kirby*), Booth Colman (*Dean Parker*), Justin Smith (*Mort Terwilliger*), Jerry Grayson (*Vern Thompkins*), Marc
Seaton (*Jim Bench*), Robert Golden (*Policeman*), Larry Gust (*Josh*).

A Lippert, Inc., Production. A 20th Century–Fox release. *Produced and Directed by:*
Maury Dexter. *Assistant Producer:* Hank Tani. *Associate Producer:* "By" Dunham. *Written by:*
Harry Spalding. *Original Story by:* Hank Tani. *Director of Photography:* Jack Marquette.
Supervising Film Editor: Jodie Copelan, A.C.E. *Assistant to the Producer:* Hank Tani. *Assistant Director:* Willard Kirkham. *Set Decorator:* Harry Reif. *Script Supervisor:* Billy Vernon.
Wardrobe: Joseph Dimmitt. *Makeup:* Dan Greenway. *Transportation:* Joe Padovich. *Sound:*
John Bury. *Sound Facilities by:* Ryder Sound Service. *Music by:* Jimmie Haskell. Filmed in
b/w.

"The House on the Beach" by "By" Dunham and Bobby Beverly, performed by Frankie
Randall. "Rock This World" by "By" Dunham and Bobby Beverly, performed by the Astronauts. "It's Gonna Rain" by Sonny Bono, performed by Sonny and Cher. "Run Away from
Him" by "By" Dunham and Bobby Beverly, performed by Cindy Malone. "Yellow Haired
Woman" by "By" Dunham and Eddie Davis, performed by Russ Bender. "Drum Dance"
by Joe Saraceno and Frank Warren, performed by Sandy Nelson. "The Gods of Love" by
"By" Dunham and Bobby Beverly, performed by Frankie Randall. "Winter Nocturne" by
"By" Dunham and Eddie Davis, performed by Jackie and Gayle. "Little Speedy Gonzalez"
by Stan Ross and Bobby Beverly, performed by the Astronauts. "Pyramid Stomp" by "By"
Dunham and Jimmie Haskell, performed by the Astronauts. "Snap It" by Jimmie Haskell,
performed by the Astronauts.

The second beach movie from director Maury Dexter, *Wild on the Beach* is a
claustrophobic production not recommended for fans of surfing or beach movies

though the musical lineup includes an eclectic array of talent. Due to a housing shortage on campus, Adam and his buddies must share a beach house with miffed owner Lee and her two girlfriends while keeping their coed habitat a secret from a disapproving college administration. There's nothing wild or beachy about this black-and-white programmer that should have stuck with its working title *Beach House Party* since the actors don't leave their abode much with nary a bikini-clad girl to be found! The only lengthy surfing footage is during the opening credits as Frankie Randall, a dead ringer for Frankie Avalon, nicely croons the catchy "The House on the Beach."

Frankie Randall and Sherry Jackson try valiantly as the feuding couple but the humorless screenplay lets them down. Jackson is wasted as the prim coed while the good-looking Randall, nicely attired in tight chinos, showed a flair for light comedy. Marc Seaton stands out as the aptly named Jim Bench due to his fantastic physique, which he shows off quite frequently to every boy watcher's delight. Too bad there weren't any beach scenes where he could strip down to swim trucks. Seaton was arguably the best-built beach boy to almost traipse the sands of Malibu. The handsome all–American–looking actor boasted rock-hard pecs, thick biceps and washboard abs, which was a rare sight in sixties beach movies.

Girl watchers should skip this altogether. Though Sherry Jackson is a very pretty brunette, she is fully clothed throughout even when she takes a stroll on the

Feuding college students Sherry Jackson and Frankie Randall call a temporary truce in this lobby card scene from *Wild on the Beach* (20th Century–Fox, 1965).

beach! If you want to see more of her, you are better off scrounging up her issue of *Playboy* where she disrobed for their cameras.

Every time someone gazes out the window in this movie, stock surfing footage is inserted to remind viewers that the house is on the beach though the actors rarely step foot on the sand. This is mind-boggling, as there are a few outdoor scenes shot on location at a Malibu beach house. The fact that it didn't occur to anyone working on this that maybe since this was a beach party movie there should be at least one scene with bikini girls and shirtless surfer boys is beyond belief.

The only reason to sit through *Wild on the Beach* is for the musical performances. Forget about third-rate singer Cindy Malone and enjoy the rest of the line-up. Frankie Randall has a pleasant voice and a style reminiscent of Frank Sinatra but for 1965 this must have come off as being square. Sandy Nelson wails on the drums, the Astronauts rock out on three numbers, Jackie and Gayle sweetly harmonize, but the film is stolen by Sonny and Cher performing "It's Gonna Rain" in a nightclub setting. This was their first big screen appearance. With their hippie garb, they stand out from the rest of the conservatively dressed teens and were a harbinger of what was to come.

The Story

The college population of a Southern California university has become so large that only students with a place to live are being accepted. Into town comes sultry brunette Lee Sullivan, who has inherited a beach house from her uncle. She plans to turn it into a dormitory for coeds so that the rent she collects could pay her tuition. When Lee and her friends Marsie and Toby arrive at the house, they discover a party going on. Dark-haired Adam claims that Lee's uncle gave him and his friends Vern and Jim permission to live there through a gentleman's agreement. Unaware that he has already filed for an off-campus housing permit, the gullible coed gives in and lets Adam and his friends stay for the night with the condition that they leave in the morning. While Adam and Lee are negotiating terms, the tone-deaf Vern and pretty blonde Toby bond over their mutual interest in sound effects while nearsighted muscleman Jim is attracted to home economics major Marsie.

The next morning, Lee goes to apply for a permit while Dean Parker sends faculty member Mort Terwilliger to the beach house for inspection. When Mort arrives, all traces of the girls are gone, as Adam has hidden their belongings. Vern and Jim have taken Toby and Marsie to a local hangout, the Wheel, where the Astronauts and Sonny and Cher perform. Despite finding a bra in one of the boys' bedrooms, Terwilliger approves Adam's permit. Meanwhile, next door, Professor Shep Kirby is trying to convince singer Cindy Malone to record a song using his echo machine. Intrigued, the shapely blonde agrees. But when the record is ruined due to Vern's sound effects, an irate Cindy leaves in a huff. Shep then calls the police to complain about the noise from Lee's beach house.

Lee returns home dejected that the university was not accepting new housing applications for another week. Adam reveals his signed application and magnanimously offers to put up Lee and her friends. The coed is furious and becomes more so when a policeman serves her a summons for disturbing the peace. Lee is then forced to share the house with Adam. The "iron curtain" is set up segregating the house between the boys and girls. The Dean sends Terwilliger back to the house to investigate after he realizes that Lee has applied for a permit for the same house that he (Terwilliger) just granted one.

Lee visits Shep to see if he would drop the complaint. Stating that the noise from her house killed his last chance to get back into the record business, the instructor refuses. Desperate, Lee promises that Vern will remove all his tape recorders. Intrigued, since he needs equipment for his recording business, Kirby accompanies Lee back to her house and is impressed with Vern's set-up as they listen to the Astronauts on tape. He agrees to drop the complaint if he could meet the band. As Kirby, Lee, Vern and Jim exit to go to the Wheel, Terwilliger sneaks in the back and finds Marsie baking a cake. They get into a whipped cream fight while Adam races through the house hiding the girls' belongings. Toby arrives home and pretends to be a guy shaving, which fools the school's investigator.

After singing a little ditty with the house band at the Wheel, Kirby and the kids go in search of the Astronauts. Meanwhile, a policeman has delivered complaints against three student residences to the Dean, who learns that Lee Sullivan was issued one as the owner and occupant of the beach house. Seeing that the college's new faculty member Shep Kirby filed the charge, the Dean summons Terwilliger and they go off to meet with him. Not finding him home, the Dean comes up with a plan to raid the beach house at the crack of dawn "commando-style" to find out once and for all if boys and girls are co-habiting.

Returning home, Lee agrees to go for a walk on the beach with Adam, who professes his love to her in a song. He later takes her out to dinner and they share a good-night kiss. Entering her home, Lee finds the living room full of boys. Adam admits that he got Lee out of the house so his homeless friends could bunk there for the night. Lee is furious until she learns that Adam's permit is only temporary. Waking at 6 A.M. the following morning, Lee, Toby and Marsie lock the slumbering boys up in their sleeping bags but as Lee is about to leave the house the Dean enters. Commotion ensues as the Dean sets off the alarm and bumps into a shirtless Jim, who has managed to climb out of his sleeping bag but loses a contact lens in the process. As the muscleman crawls around the floor trying to find his missing lens, the girls chase the Dean and Terwilliger out of the house, unaware who they are.

The next day, the Dean revokes the housing permit and suspends Adam, Lee and the rest of their friends. The dejected bunch begins packing their bags when a jubilant Kirby arrives hyped about the upcoming recording session with the Astronauts. After hearing their tale of woe, he tells the kids to sit tight as he pays a visit to the Dean. Kirby is shocked to find the Dean in his naval uniform and announcing that he has been called up for reserve duty; the Sullivan matter is now in the hands of Terwilliger. Kirby informs the new dean that the boys will be living in his house and the girls in Lee's. He tears up the complaints against the students and convinces Terwilliger to issue two new housing permits. Kirby invites him to bring the permits over the next day during the recording session.

The beach house is packed with college students as Toby and Marsie record a song before the Astronauts perform "Little Speedy Gonzalez." Arriving with the housing permits, Terwilliger enters through the kitchen where Marsie accidentally dumps flour over his head. The two enjoy a laugh as the film ends with Adam and Lee strolling along the beach.

Behind-the-Scenes

Since *Surf Party* made money, 20th Century–Fox requested another beach-party film from Robert Lippert's production company. Originally titled *Beach House Party*, the movie tried to ape AIP's successful *Beach Party* film right down to casting similar looking actors to Frankie and Annette.

Handsome, dark-haired Frankie Randall, born Frank Joseph Lisbona in Clifton, New Jersey, made his film debut as the male lead. A talented crooner, he began taking classical piano lessons at the ripe old age of seven and switched to jazz in his mid-teens. After graduating from Fairleigh Dickinson University, he was discovered while singing at Jilly's, one of New York's top celebrity hangouts in the early sixties. He caught the ear of Frank Sinatra, who had been quoted as saying, "Frankie Randall is my favorite piano player and a marvelous talent who sings great and plays more piano than there are keys." It was praise like this that helped Randall land an exclusive recording contract with RCA and then a starring movie role in *Wild on the Beach*. "I recall that I had to read for the part," says Frankie Randall. "But I don't remember if it was for Bob Lippert or Maury Dexter. Every kid dreams of being an actor and at that point in my life I often thought about it too. It wasn't until my singing career took hold that people began asking me if I was interested in doing any acting. Of course when this opportunity came along, it certainly spurred my interest."

Randall's co-star was sultry brunette Sherry Jackson, but unlike Annette she doesn't warble a note. Jackson was a former child star trying to project a mature, sexier image now that she was in her twenties. She worked steadily from 1949 most notably in the "Ma and Pa Kettle" series, *The Miracle of Our Lady of Fatima* (1952) and *Trouble Along the Way* (1953) starring John Wayne. She landed a star-making role as Danny Thomas's feisty daughter Terry on the television sitcom *Make Room for Daddy* in 1953 but left in 1958 to attend college.

In an unusual move, the singing duo Jackie and Gayle filled the roles of Jackson's two friends. Jackie Miller and Gayle Caldwell were former members of the New Christy Minstrels who left the group to go out on their own. Though they had not scored a hit record or had any acting experience, they were signed to make their film debuts in this movie. Unknowns filled the rest of the supporting roles.

Though Jackie and Gayle were the featured musical talent, they were outshone by another singing duo calling themselves Sonny and Cher. The pair had been recording for such labels as Vault and Reprise under that name and Caesar and Cleo without any luck. It was undecided how they were going to be credited in the movie. The duo then released a single in May 1965 for Atco called "I Got You Babe" under the Sonny and Cher moniker. When the song began climbing the charts, billing as Sonny and Cher prevailed.

According to Frankie Randall, the shoot lasted approximately two weeks and the house used for exteriors was in Malibu. Interiors were shot at the Samuel Goldwyn Studios on Santa Monica Boulevard. Asked if he knew why there were no beach scenes except the one with Randall and Jackson strolling down the shore, Frankie replies, "I really can't answer that. I don't know how the folks from Maury on down decided what they were going to include. There were no beach scenes filmed like in the Frankie Avalon movies nor were any in the script but not shot."

As a novice actor, Randall had no problems with the shoot due to his director and cast mates. "It was kind of edgy for me because I had never acted before and I was working with some seasoned actors," remarks Randall. "Sherry Jackson in particular had been acting for a long time. I was a bit nervous and Maury was very helpful. He gave me some direction in terms of my performance and guided me with blocking and hitting my marks.

"Sherry Jackson was also very helpful to me," continues Randall. "We'd go off sometimes when they were setting up and go over the next scene. She was very good to work with. So was Marc Seaton. He was a real nice guy and very congenial. In fact, everybody in the movie was terrific and easy to work with."

Frankie Randall was no doubt hired due to his resemblance to Frankie Avalon. But the similarities did not stop there. Randall also sang in the same style as Avalon. "I knew Frankie was doing movies and I would be compared to him," remarks Randall. "It is like with reality television today. Something comes on and is a hit so the other networks try to ape it. It was the same back in the sixties with the beach party movies. The Frankie and Annette films were so well received that the other studios just wanted to climb on to that band wagon, so to speak." With his smooth delivery, crooner Randall was the perfect choice to perform the songs written especially for the movie. "I was told what songs I would be singing. They thought the last song I sang, called 'The Gods of Love,' was especially ideal for me."

Of the cast, Randall has the fondest memories of Sonny and Cher, whom he met on the set. "That was my first encounter with them. When they walked out onto the set, I think all of us thought that they were of kind of extraordinary." With their hippie garb, Sonny and Cher unquestionably stood out from the all–American girls with their hemlines below the kneecap and the clean-cut, sweater-wearing boys. "Everybody else in the film was of a different era almost, as compared to Sonny and Cher. They were certainly unique and different for the time. They performed terrifically and the number they sang in the movie was just fine.

"I got to know Sonny very well when I moved to Palm Springs in 1975," continues Randall. "It was on the suggestion of my close friend Frank Sinatra and his whole crew who had wonderful times there. I lived there for about 27 years. During that time Sonny was very active in politics—first as mayor and then as a Congressman. I got very close to him and was involved with his campaign. He used to kid me about *Wild on the Beach* and tell everyone that I gave him his first break in movies. I still see Mary, his widow, every so often. I got to know Cher pretty well and saw her a couple of times after making the movie though we haven't been in touch in years."

Wild on the Beach was not successful at the box office. That is not surprising since the movie is very claustrophobic, cheaply produced and filmed in black-and-white—a big no-no for a Hollywood surf movie. Even so, RCA Victor issued a soundtrack LP featuring all the songs as performed in the movie except "The Yellow Haired Woman." Russ Bender's version was replaced by a new recording by Randall. RCA even released it as a single with "The Gods of Love" as the B-side. It never charted.

FRANKIE RANDALL · SHERRY JACKSON · ... JACKIE & GAYLE · SONNY & CHER · THE ASTRONAUTS · CINDY MALONE · SANDY NELSON

Lobby card for *Wild on the Beach* (20th Century–Fox, 1965) featuring Sonny and Cher in their first movie appearance together.

Looking back on the movie, Randall muses, "I wasn't particularly proud of any particular one thing I did in *Wild on the Beach*. I was just happy to have made a movie and certainly to have been the star of the movie. Is it the greatest movie I have ever seen—definitely not. But it got my feet wet in regards to being in front of the camera. For what it was and when it was done and how old I was at the time, I am very pleased with the way it turned out."

Wild on the Beach was Maury Dexter's swan song at Lippert–20th Century–Fox. He then began directing low-budget exploitation fare for AIP including *Maryjane* (1968), *The Young Animals* (1968) and *Hell's Belles* (1970).

Frankie Randall went on to record seven albums for RCA Records and appeared on numerous television variety and talk shows including *The Tonight Show Starring Johnny Carson, The Dean Martin Show* and *The Ed Sullivan Show*. He was also a regular on *The Dean Martin Summer Show*. Randall let the acting drift because "I decided to redirect myself to what I felt I did best and that was singing." Even so, Randall found the time to make the rare film appearance in such movies as *Day of the Wolves* (1973) starring Richard Egan and Martha Hyer and *Tempest* (1982) starring John Cassavetes and Gena Rowlands. The seventies found Randall touring nightclubs across the country. Booked for a four-week engagement at the Golden Nugget Hotel and Casino in Atlantic City in 1982, he impressed casino magnate Steven Wynn so much that Wynn offered the vocalist a lifetime contract to perform. Randall later progressed to Entertainment Director for the Golden Nugget and then Vice President of Bally's Grand Hotel and Casino. In 1991, Randall resigned to concentrate once again on his singing career. His most recent CDs include *Frankie Randall Sings Steve Allen* and *Then & Now* comprised of 24 of the best songs ever written. He can be found performing in Palm Springs and Las Vegas. Catching one of his recent shows, Susan Hart enjoyed his singing immeasurably and remarked that Randall is "charismatic and has great stage presence."

Post–*Wild on the Beach*, Sherry Jackson tried to shake her goody-goody image by playing a Southern vamp in the hardboiled detective caper *Gunn* (1967) and posing semi-nude for *Playboy* in a layout entitled "Make Room for Sherry." Although Jackson had talent, there was an innocence about her that made it hard for viewers to fully believe her as man-hungry vixens or duplicitous femme fatales. Her film credits include the biker film *The Mini-Skirt Mob* (1968), the Don Edmonds–directed *Bare Knuckles* (1977) and the drive-in hit *Stingray* (1978) playing the violent leader of a drug ring. Episodic television and B-movies kept Jackson gainfully employed until the early eighties when she took a hiatus from show business. In 2001, Jackson returned to the big screen playing a countess in the fantasy feature *In Service to the Dream*.

Jackie and Gayle would go on to appear in only one more film, *Wild Wild Winter* (1966). Though the girls had pleasant voices and were nice to look at, it wasn't enough to carry them to any chart success. Miller, the blonde, became Mrs. John Davidson in 1969. The dark-haired Caldwell did some television for awhile, most notably playing Rebecca in two episodes of *The Beverly Hillbillies* before disappearing from Hollywood.

As for Marc Seaton, a body alone does not an actor make no matter how big and well-formed the muscles. Though Seaton does well playing the appropriately named Jim Bench, whose brains were all in his biceps, his acting career went nowhere, much to every boy watcher's dismay. He played minor roles in *The Chase* (1966) and *What's So Bad About Feeling Good?* (1968) before being cast as a biker in *Angels Hard As They Come* (1971). His last known credit is the violent B movie *Rape Squad* (1974). Seaton was killed on April 10, 1979, without ever achieving a modicum of fame.

Memorable Lines

(While inspecting the beach house where Adam and his friends have applied for a rooming permit, college administrator Terwilliger stumbles upon a girl's black lacey bra.)

ADAM: What's that?

TERWILLIGER: It ain't no hammock. Well, who's got this room? I want his name.

ADAM: Several guys moved in today. I'm not sure which took which.

TERWILLIGER: He's a 36C. That ought to make him stand out in your mind.

Reviews

Boxoffice—"A raucous, swinging teenaged musical ... will please the young audiences for which it is intended but appeal will be strictly limited to these groups."

Kathleen Carroll, *New York Daily News*—"*Wild on the Beach*, that somehow floated into circuit theatres on the wave of surf and sound movies, is a dreary sampling of [Maury] Dexter in action. The word action is used loosely in this instance because there isn't any. The boy-girl-singing duo of Sonny and Cher appear to be having a hair-growing contest and this viewer will not venture a guess which face belongs to which name."

Mandel Herbstman, *The Film Daily*—"A spirited comedy with spirited music. Although the story is no work of art, it does have the bounce and freshness to make it popular with the youngsters."

New York Post—"*Wild on the Beach* is what they slightly and correctly call a 'Teen Musical.' The kids dance the frug, monkey, jerk, etc. Plot doesn't amount to much, which puts it squarely up to the singing and dancing. They aren't so great either."

Robert Salmaggi, *New York Herald Tribune*—"*Wild on the Beach* is a tame, lame attempt to cash in on the current teen craze for those assembly-line fun-in-the-sun beachparty flicks. Alternating with the dull action are some hardly inspiring pop numbers. Producer Maury Dexter is guilty of the wooden direction, but then, he had some wooden talent to work with."

★ 24 ★

Winter a-Go-Go (1965)

Ski Buffs and Ski Babes ... The Go-Go Crowd Goes Ga-Ga on Skis!

Fun: ★★★
Surfing: ★
Boy watching: ★★★
Girl watching: ★★★
Music: ★★★
Scenery: ★★★★

Release date: October 28, 1965. Running time: 88m. Box office gross: Not available. DVD release: Not as of January 2005.

James Stacy (*Danny Frazer*), William Wellman, Jr. (*Jeff Forrester*), Beverly Adams (*Jo Ann Wallace*), Anthony Hayes (*Burt*), Jill Donohue (*Janine*), Tom Nardini (*Frankie*), Duke Hobbie (*Bob*), Julie Parrish (*Dee Dee*), Buck Holland (*Will*), Linda Rogers (*Penny*), Nancy Czar (*Jonesy*), Judy Parker (*Dori*), Bob Kanter (*Roger*), Walter Maslow (*Jordan*), H. T. Tsiang (*Cholly*), Peter Brinkman (*Himself*), Carey Foster, Arlene Charles, Cheryl Hurley, Cherie Foster (*Winter a-Go-Go Girls*). Guest Stars: The Nooney Rickett Four with Joni Lyman, The Reflections.

A Reno Carell Production. A Columbia Pictures release. *Produced by*: Reno Carell. *Directed by*: Richard Benedict. *Screenplay by*: Bob Kanter. *Story by*: Reno Carell. *Music by*: Harry Betts. *Director of Photography*: Jacques Marquette. *Production Manager*: Jack Lacey. *Art Director*: Walter Holscher. *Film Editor*: Irving Berlin, A.C.E. *Set Decorator*: Morris Hoffman. *Assistant to the Producer*: Jan Lloyd. *Assistant Director*: Robert Vreeland. *Choreography*: Kay Carson. *Recording Supervisor*: Earl Snyder. *Costumer*: Joseph Dimmitt. *Makeup Supervisor*: Dan Greenway. *Hair Stylist*: Linda Trainoff. *Ski Clothes by*: Roffe-Rene, Inc. *Sweaters by*: Demetre. *Motorcycles by*: Suzuki. Color by Pathé.

"Winter a-Go-Go" by Howard Greenfield and Jack Keller, performed by the Hondells over the opening and closing credits. "King of the Mountain" by Howard Greenfield and Jack Keller, performed by Joni Lyman. "Ski City" by Howard Greenfield and Jack Keller, performed by the Nooney Rickett Four. "Hip Square Dance" by Steve Venet, Tommy Boyce, Bob Hart and Harry Betts, performed by James Stacy. "Do the Ski (with Me)" by Steve Venet, Tommy Boyce, Bob Hart and Toni Wine, performed by the Nooney Rickett Four with Joni Lyman. "(I'm) Sweet on You" performed by the Reflections.

This is a personal favorite though most critics consider it one of the lesser beach party movies. Unlike *Ski Party* and *Wild Wild Winter*, which incorporated beach scenes into their plots, *Winter a-Go-Go* heads straight for the slopes and remains there the entire time though there is an obligatory bikini scene. Jeff inherits a ski resort and with a pack of friends heads off to turn the lodge into a success, but trouble ensues when the mortgage holder hires two goons to wreak havoc so he can foreclose. Of all the beach party films, this is the campiest with its scantily clad dancing Winter a-Go-Go girls, to James Stacy singing "Hip Square Dance" in his pajamas to the bitchy barbs thrown out by ambiguous gay guy Roger to an impromptu wedding finale.

Jacques Marquette expertly photographs the ski scenes and the outdoor setting in the mountains is sumptuous. Harry Betts provides a sprightly music score. The Hondells begin the film singing the bouncy title tune, which they also perform over the closing credits. Though not major names, the Nooney Rickett Four (also in *Bikini Beach*) and Joni Lyman perform songs that are upbeat and catchy. They do especially well singing together on "Do the Ski (with Me)." The only musical misfire is the Reflections, who come off like a cut-rate version of the Four Seasons and are totally out of place.

The film is not only a treat for girl watchers but boy watchers as well. Clad in tight colorful ski pants, the guys and gals shake their buttocks to a number of groovy tunes performed by the musical guest stars. The good-looking cast also helps buoy the film. Roguish James Stacy and virile William Wellman, Jr., continue the successful pairing begun with *A Swingin' Summer*. Stacy's playfulness is a great contrast to Wellman's seriousness and the two perform well together. Stacy in particular is delicious looking in his ski attire. Dark-haired and boyish, Tom Nardini is cute as the naïve lad who is unlucky with the ladies. Beverly Adams makes a beautiful female lead and Jill Donohue an icy rich bitch bad girl. But naïve, busty blonde Nancy Czar, wisecracking dark-haired Julie Parrish and slinky redhead Linda Rogers upstage them. All three gals get to shake their bikini-clad behinds in an outdoor setting despite the freezing temperatures. As an added attraction, there are four additional lovelies billed as the Winter a-Go-Go girls who are in the film for no other reason than for exploitation purposes as their voluptuous scantily-clad bodies are on display.

Working with a larger budget than on *A Swingin' Summer*, Reno Carell provides a sleek production featuring a handsome cast, good music and excellent photography. It is pure, unadulterated, campy fun.

The Story

Jeff Forrester has just inherited a ski lodge called Snow Mountain and has become partners with his friend Danny Frazer to help him make a go of it. After hiring a crew of young guys and gals including loyal Jo, unlucky-in-love Frankie, strapping Bob, wisecracking Dee Dee, ditzy blonde Jonesy and titian-haired Penny, the gang drives up to the lodge. It turns out to be an eyesore inside and out, but the gang pitches in to help spruce it up. Bob plugs in his phonograph so they can listen to music as they clean. Danny leaves them to their chores and heads off to ski, encountering pro skier and instructor Peter Brinkman.

Later, Jeff thanks the gang for the great job they did. When he notices Danny getting cozy with Jonesy, Jeff declares that there will be no fraternization between the sexes in the upstairs bedrooms. Jeff confides to Jo that he hopes the lodge is a hit so he will finally have enough money to cut loose with different women. The disappointed, smitten gal advises Jeff to find a loyal girlfriend instead. While everyone is sleeping, an alarm sounds in the middle of the night—set off by Danny, trying to sneak into Jonesy's room.

The next day Danny gets an idea for a promotional gimmick to lure guests to the lodge. He convinces Jonesy to wear a fur coat at the side of the road and slip it off as cars come by, revealing herself in a bikini with a sign on her back plugging the lodge's vacancies. Soon she has a caravan of cars trailing her back to Snow Mountain. Later Danny entices a giggling cook named Cholly to come work at the lodge with promises of lots of nubile young women to ogle daily, including the scantily clad Winter a-Go-Go girls.

Burt and Will, ski bums hired by Jordan the mortgage holder on Snow Mountain, check into the lodge to sabotage business. Snooty rich girl Janine, who has had a past romantic relationship with Burt, arrives at the lodge with her friends Dori and Roger. Janine flirts with an uninterested Jeff. After rejecting Burt, the out-for-kicks heiress sets her sights on Danny. She hires him to be her private ski instructor even though she is a very experienced skier. After Danny rebuffs her, Janine flirts once again with Jeff. A jealous Jo decides to fight fire with fire and masquerades as a French blonde named Claudine to catch Jeff's interest, but he sees right through her ruse. Jo is hurt until Jeff confesses that she is his "Miss Ideal." They seal it with a kiss while eyed by a miffed Janine and her friends. Burt and his buddy show up and purposely spill a Coke on Roger. When Jeff and Danny ask the troublemakers to leave, they are sucker-punched. A fight breaks out and Jeff and Danny get the best of the troublesome duo, physically ejecting them from the lodge. A grateful Janine tries to seduce her hero Danny, who declines.

The next day Danny and Jeff learn that Burt and his pal have been roughing up some of the guests while skiing. They decide to take action before someone else gets hurt. Their chance comes when the two hoods return to the lodge and begin harassing Jo and Dee Dee. Burt challenges Jeff to a ski race the next day and he accepts.

After striking out with Jonesy, Dee Dee and Penny, Frankie is depressed but Jeff and Danny instill enough confidence in him that he gets up the gumption to ask Jo out. But she only has eyes for Jeff. Dori is the one smitten with Frankie but the naïve guy is oblivious to her feelings. The ever-persistent Danny (nicknamed "the night owl") makes his obligatory trek to the girls' wing of the lodge to rendezvous with Penny. When she discovers that he had previous dates with Jonesy and Dee Dee, the girls set him up to get caught by Jeff, and his amorous plans are foiled once again. Since everybody is awake, they throw an impromptu "Hip Square Dance."

That morning, Jeff and Danny meet Burt and Will on the slopes for a game of chicken on skis. It develops into fisticuffs with Jeff tumbling over a cliff. While Jeff clings for dear life, Burt grabs his ski pole and pulls Jeff to safety. Realizing he came close to killing a man, Burt confesses to Jeff that Jordan paid him to wreck business at the lodge so that Jeff would default on the loan payment and Jordan could claim ownership. After apologizing to Jeff, Burt reconciles with Janine. Back at the lodge, a jubilant Jeff and Jo announce their engagement. While the gang celebrates, Jordan shows up to spoil the festivities. However, Jeff makes the first payment on the note while Burt gives Jordan a farewell sock to the jaw. The film concludes with Danny giving away Jo as she is wed to Jeff. Dee Dee, Jonesy and Penny reach for the bouquet, shredding it into three while the garter lands in Danny's arms. The marriage-minded trio than chases the fun-loving bachelor around the grounds as the film comes to a close.

Behind-the-Scenes

When Columbia Pictures could not get the distribution rights to *A Swingin' Summer*, they offered Reno Carell a deal to produce another beach party-type film starring James Stacy and William Wellman, Jr. According to Wellman, "I wasn't the producer on this but I sort helped set it up with Mike Frankovich, who was the head of Columbia Pictures. He had seen *A Swingin' Summer* and wanted Jim and

Winter a-Go-Go producer Reno Carell on the town with actress Quinn O'Hara, c. 1965 (*courtesy Quinn O'Hara*).

me to star in another film." *Winter a-Go-Go* was envisioned as a companion film to *A Swingin' Summer* at one point and its working title was *A Swingin' Winter*.

Actor Bob Kanter, who played feature roles in such films as *The War Lover* (1962) and *The Thin Red Line* (1964), wrote the screenplay (his first and only) from a story by Reno Carell, and Richard Benedict was tapped to direct. As with Don Taylor of *Ride the Wild Surf*, Benedict was a former actor. He began working on television where he directed numerous episodes of *Hawaiian Eye*, *The Virginian*, *Twelve O'Clock High* and *Combat!* *Winter a-Go-Go* was the first movie directed by Benedict (whom Wellman describes as being "a real hard-nosed and macho kind of guy").

Quinn O'Hara of *A Swingin' Summer* was considered for one of the female lead roles but Columbia demanded that the roles be cast from its roster of studio contract players. "I was so mad that they got Dick Benedict to direct this movie," says O'Hara. "I would have loved to have appeared in this. But Benedict is the one director who would never hire me because I worked with him once before and he tried to put the make on me. I rebuffed him and Troy Donahue stood up for me. I vowed that I would never work for him again."

The female lead went to Columbia starlet Beverly Adams, who had just been loaned out to AIP for a role in *How to Stuff a Wild Bikini* (1965) where she had to wear a long red wig. Here her natural dark-haired beauty was on display. Jill Donohue was the daughter of director Jack Donohue but her mother raised her in Europe. *Winter a-Go-Go* was her first American movie. Tom Nardini had just come off

In *Winter a-Go-Go* (Columbia, 1965), lodge staff members William Wellman, Jr., Beverly Adams, Nancy Czar and James Stacy listen intently to guest Bob Kanter's complaints.

receiving rave reviews for his film debut in the Western comedy *Cat Ballou* (1965), which was also the first movie for Duke Hobbie (who played a very minor role).

Julie Parrish, Linda Rogers and Nancy Czar were not under contract to Columbia but were cast by Reno Carell. Brunette Parrish was a very busy television actress and had played small roles in *The Nutty Professor* (1963) and *Harlow* (1965). Raven-haired Rogers was a veteran of the *Beach Party* films playing a member of Eric Von Zipper's biker gang in three movies. Nancy Czar, a Carroll Baker look-alike, starred in the B-movie *Wild Guitar* (1962) and played a bikini-clad beach beauty in *Girl Happy* (1965).

The ski footage and outdoor scenes were shot on location in Heavenly Valley, on the south shore of Lake Tahoe, and the Eldorado National Forest. As with most lead actors cast in surf and ski movies, Wellman did not know how to ski. "They gave me two weeks of skiing lessons in Snow Valley with an Olympic ski instructor before filming began," he recalls. "Those were the days of the big long skis and snowplow turns. I practically took out an entire ski class coming down the hill one time—crashed right into them. Luckily no one including me got hurt. At that point we decided that I didn't have enough time to learn to ski so they hired Loren Janes, who was Steve McQueen's stunt man for 22 years, to double for me in those scenes and a portion of the fight scenes."

"I never even put a pair of skis on during the entire shoot," continues Wellman with a laugh. "It seemed that everybody who worked on this movie was a skier. When the filming was over for the day, everybody hit the slopes. I hit the cabin."

According to Wellman, it wasn't his lack of skiing ability that caused a problem with this movie but the antics of co-stars Nancy Czar and Linda Rogers. "They were two playgirls," reveals Bill. "When we were on location in Heavenly Valley, Eddie Fisher was appearing at Harvey's and he was crazy about both Linda and Nancy. He would send a limousine to pick one of them up each day. He was going to do a cameo in the film but it didn't pan out. I know that Nancy married this extremely wealthy guy who was about a hundred years old but I don't know what became of Linda Rogers."

Though there are no beach scenes in *Winter a-Go-Go*, the producers stuck in an obligatory bikini scene as the gals lounge around on a deck in their brief swimsuits despite the fact that is nary a pool or ocean in sight. The late Julie Parrish recalled in *Fantasy Femmes of Sixties Cinema*, "The only thing I didn't like about making this movie was that it was filmed during the winter in Lake Tahoe and we had outdoor bikini scenes. We would be shaking and turning blue with blankets draped on us waiting for the shot to be set up. But when the director yelled action, I'd forget I was freezing and really pretend it was warm. It was amazing!"

Regarding his thoughts if Bob Kanter's character was a homosexual, Wellman opines, "I don't know what Bob Kanter's sexual preference was in real life. He authored the screenplay and wanted to act so he wrote the part of Roger for himself. The character made no sense and I guess it does sort of come off like the gay best friend. I had to deal with the gay issue. There were rumors about me because I never partied with the girls on these films. But I was a happily married man and devoted to my wife."

Wellman's *A Swingin' Summer* co-star Quinn O'Hara says with a laugh, "I never thought that of Bill. He was just a straight arrow. I thought Martin West [of *A Swingin' Summer*] might be gay. I never tried to did find out if he was or not."

By all accounts the cast of *Winter a-Go-Go* got along quite well. Julie Parrish found everyone nice to work with but did mention that James Stacy was a bit insecure and could be difficult. Wellman remarks, "On this and *A Swingin' Summer* there really wasn't anybody who was a pain in the ass. Everybody was having a good time and doing the best they could."

"Julie Parrish was a wonderful gal," continues Bill. "So is Beverly Adams. Jill Donohue was also the child of a film director and I liked her a lot. She had a way about her that made a lot of people feel that she was stuck up. She really wasn't. Of the cast, she was my favorite person to work with."

The musical performers lined up for *Winter a-Go-Go* greatly paled compared to the groups that appeared in *A Swingin' Summer*. However, some of the songs are quite pleasant. The Hondells sing over the opening and end credits the title tune, which ranks with "Ride the Wild Surf" and "Beach Blanket Bingo" as one of the beach genre's best. The Nooney Rickett Four (now billed with the "4" spelled out unlike in *Pajama Party*) do two numbers, the better of which is "Do the Ski (with Me)" where the group is joined by vocalist Joni Lyman. She solos on "King of the Mountain" and is introduced in the film with the remark "This is her latest

Colpix recording." Colpix Records was a subsidiary of Columbia and Screen Gems. However, the soundtrack album was never released despite the chart success of the Hondells and the Reflections, a doo-wop–influenced group who scored a Top Ten hit in 1964 with "(Just Like) Romeo and Juliet."

Winter a-Go-Go was released in late 1965 as the beach party genre was beginning to wind down. Even so, the movie was profitable for Columbia. Wellman remarks, "*Winter a-Go-Go* was not as good a film as *A Swingin' Summer* though Columbia did put a little more money into it. The story was pretty much the same but I think flimsier. At that point of time, though it was released in a lot of theaters and I am sure Columbia didn't lose money on it, the jig was up on the beach party movies. It was all downhill for the few films that came after this."

The movie made money, but producer Reno Carell did not produce another film. Instead he formed a distribution company—the first of many enterprises he would be involved with. Per William Wellman, Jr., Reno Carell lived the life of a playboy and in his later years traveled the world on his savings. He died of cancer in 2003.

None of the actors in *Winter a-Go-Go* found super stardom, but the one who Wellman thought was most destined for it was James Stacy. "I think Jim was a pretty bad actor early in his career but all of a sudden in *A Swingin Summer* I thought he was damn good,' comments Bill. "It is extremely tough to be good in a low-budget film with silly dialogue and a rushed shooting schedule. You can't imagine how hard it is. But Jim was excellent. It jumpstarted his whole career. He told me that he began taking acting classes from this woman who taught with Sandy Meisner in New York. His acting style had really changed and he was doing very well with his part. I always thought Jim was on his way to become a huge movie star and I think he would have if not for his accident."

In 1967, Stacy starred with Wayne Maunder in the television Western series *Lancer*. His friendship with William Wellman, Jr., had dissipated by then due to Stacy's wild lifestyle, which did not sit with his happily married pal. Jim returned to the big screen opposite his *Swingin' Summer* co-star Raquel Welch in *Flareup* (1969). Tragically, in 1973 while riding his motorcycle with his girlfriend on back, a drunken driver hit them. Stacy lost an arm and leg and his passenger was killed. The good-natured actor persevered and was able to continue acting for a period of time playing supporting roles in *Posse* (1975) and *Double Exposure* (1982) and even giving Emmy-nominated performances in *Just a Little Inconvenience* (1977) and an episode of *Cagney and Lacey* in 1986. In 1995, Stacy was sentenced to six years in prison for molesting an 11-year-old girl.

Beverly Adams is best remembered as Dean Martin's amorous sexy assistant Lovey Kravezit in three of the Matt Helm spy spoofs beginning with *The Silencers* (1966). After reprising the role in *Murderers' Row* (1966) and *The Ambushers* (1967), Adams jetted to London to film another spy thriller *Hammerhead* (1968). There she met her husband-to-be, stylist Vidal Sassoon. After the two were wed in 1968, Adams retired from acting to become an active board member of his company and to raise their four children. When her marriage of 13 years came to an end, Adams, now using her married name of Sassoon, returned to acting and wrote a number of books on health and beauty. Currently she is the corporate spokesperson and head of product development for Beverly Sassoon and Co., which manufactures VitaOrganic Skin Care products.

Julie Parrish would go on to act beside Frankie Avalon and Annette Funicello in the racecar action flick *Fireball 500* (1966) and Elvis Presley in *Paradise, Hawaiian Style* (1966). On television she starred opposite Joby Baker in the sitcom *Good Morning, World* (1967–68). She remained very active in episodic television during the seventies and in 1982 she became a regular on the CBS daytime drama *Capitol* playing loyal secretary Maggie Brady for five years. Younger audiences may recall her recurring role as Joan Diamond, the girlfriend and then wife of Peach Pit owner Nat on *Beverly Hills, 90210.* She survived two bouts with ovarian cancer in the eighties and nineties. Though her illness slowed her down, she never gave up on life and continued with her job as a counselor for battered women. The outgoing actress, who received a Los Angeles Drama Critics Award for her performance in Arthur Miller's *After the Fall,* passed away on October 1, 2003.

William Wellman, Jr., dressed to hit the slopes in *Winter a-Go-Go* (Columbia, 1965) (*courtesy William Wellman, Jr.*)

Tom Nardini seemed destined to achieve major film stardom but by the seventies his career had fizzled out. He made his film debut as Jackson Two Bears, the whimsical Indian bronco rider, in *Cat Ballou* (1965), his acclaimed performance earning him Golden Globe and BAFTA nominations for Most Promising Newcomer. Nardini quickly became popular with the Clearasil set, which is why he may have gotten mired in such exploitation fare as *The Young Animals* (1968) and *The Devil's 8* (1969). He made only a few film appearances during the early seventies. His last known feature film credit is the Canadian action flick *Siege* (1983).

Memorable Lines

(Danny whispers something to the bikini-clad Jonesy and they begin to walk away from the gang.)

DEE DEE: We're you off to?

DANNY: Work time.

DEE DEE: Work, *I bet.*

Reviews

Boxoffice—"Full of swinging tunes, swinging snow beauties and handsome athletic young men who combine to create an interesting episode of events at a mountain ski lodge."

Loren G. Buchanan, *Motion Picture Herald*—"Fun and games at a ski lodge.... While short on marquee power, it is long on luscious girls in tight costumes."

Ann Guarino, *New York Daily News*—"*Winter a-Go-Go* features new names, new faces and new music accenting the go-go beat so popular with the discotheque crowd these days. The musical takes an old plot and dresses it up in modern trappings."

Frances Herridge, *New York Post*—"*Winter a-Go-Go* is strictly youth-formula as before, with a bunch of monkey-dancing chicks going to work at a ski lodge at California's Heavenly Valley."

Allan C. Lobsenz, *The Film Daily*—"Plot as usual is slim, but action, good production values and songs ... are all that kids could ask for."

James Powers, *The Hollywood Reporter*—"The action in *Winter a-Go-Go* is about equally divided between twisting at the hotel and ski action on the nearby slopes. Carell is ... addicted to what might be called the revolving butt shot, a close up, from the rear. It's kind of funny once, but gets tiresome the fourth or fifth time."

Robert Salmaggi, *New York Herald Tribune*—"All they seem to do is dance (in bathing suits or ski attire), flirt, sing, ski, listen to combos, and sit around gulping down Cokes and cocoa by the carload. Never saw so many Coked up kids—not a real drinker in the house."

Variety—"*Winter a-Go-Go* is a disappointing teenpic despite some occasional comic touches, good ski-country lensing, and talent glimmers among the younger players. Reno Carell production is not up to standards of his earlier *A Swingin' Summer....*"

Awards and Nominations

Photoplay Gold Medal Award nomination: "Favorite Male Star"—James Stacy

★ 25 ★

The Endless Summer (1966)

*A true motion picture about surfing. Filmed in Africa,
Australia, New Zealand, Tahiti, Hawaii and California.*

Fun: ★★★★
Surfing: ★★★★
Boy watching: ★★★★
Girl watching: ★★
Music: ★★★
Scenery: ★★★★

Release date: June 15, 1966. Running time: 95m. Box office gross: $5.0 million.
DVD release: Image Entertainment (August 14, 2002).
Mike Hynson (*Himself*), Robert August (*Himself*), Terence Bullen (*South African Guide*).
Not credited (in order of appearance): George Greenough, Robert "Nat" Young, Butch Van
Artsdalen, Paul Strauch, Gene Harris, Fred Hemmings, Wayne Miata, Lance Carson, Mickey
Dora, Charles "Corky" Carroll, John Whitmore, Jack Wilson, Max Wetteland, Harry Bold,
Phil Edwards, Bernie Ross, Lord "Tally Ho" Blears, Conrad Canha, Mick McMann, Bob
Casey, Rodney Sumpter, Greg Noll, Dick Brewer, Bob Pike.
Bruce Brown Films, a Cinema V release. *Photographed, Edited and Narrated by*: Bruce
Brown. *Assistant Photographers*: R. Paul Allen, Paul Witzig, Bob Bagley. "Endless Summer"
Musical Theme Written and Performed by: The Sandals.

Though not considered to be a Hollywood surf movie, *The Endless Summer*
was an independent documentary that stunned studio executives when it received
national distribution and became a worldwide box office hit, influencing the surfing
boom of the sixties even further. Filmmaker Barry Brown proved that you could
make an entertaining movie about real surfers without shimmying bikini-clad girls
or singing beach boys, and still attract the general public. The plot is simple as two
surfers traipse the globe following the summer season searching for the perfect
wave.

The Endless Summer opens with spectacular footage of silhouetted surfers riding the waves with the sun setting in the background. This is just a taste of what
is to come. Brown films his surfers from various angles as they ride small waves in
Tahiti to almost 40-foot swells at Pipeline. Some of the best footage includes Robert
August's long ride on a perfectly shaped wave in Cape St. Francis and some of the
thrilling wipeouts at Oahu.

But what really raises the movie above other surf movies is Brown's tongue-in-cheek narration. He delivers it with a laid-back California tone that gives the movie a comfortable, relaxed feeling. Knowing his audience is going to be mostly made up of non-surfers, he diligently explains surfing moves and terms in a witty enthusiastic manner that doesn't look down on the public but also keeps his core surfing audience entertained. His narration is consistently engaging, insightful and humorous. Brown also pays the utmost respect to the various cultures and its people, offering interesting facts about the different lands they visit.

The Endless Summer features a rollicking musical score highlighted by the Sandals' melodic, haunting opening title that rouses the feeling of surfing under the sun. If surfing is not your bag but boy watching is, just sit back and enjoy handsome, lean, dark-haired Robert August and blonde Mike Hynson looking very fine showing off their tight abs in swim trunks as they surf the globe. Other good-looking surfers join them at various surfing ports of call. Girl watchers will have to make do with some Australian babes in very low-rise bikinis. It's daytime and already there is a moon out tonight! However, be warned. These lasses are not stunning beach beauties, a la AIP's Mary Hughes or Salli Sachse. They are just semi-attractive gals who like to surf.

The Endless Summer serves up some of the finest surfing footage of the decade, excellent photography, gorgeous scenery, handsome surfers and witty narration, making it the definitive surf movie of the sixties and perhaps of all time.

The Story

The movie begins with narration extolling the joys of surfing as a number of top surfers demonstrate various maneuvers in popular surfing spots in California and Hawaii during the summer months. Big surf hits Southern California in the winter when the water temperature drops to 48 degrees. Only the diehards venture out into the ocean when it is that cold.

Leaving the brisk chill of California to follow summer around the world, surfers Mike Hynson, Robert August and Bruce Brown depart for Dakar, Senegal, on the African continent, the first stop on their 35,000-mile trip. Staying at a government-owned hotel for a whopping $30 per person a night (ridiculously expensive in 1963), the surfers discover great surf just outside the establishment's front door. A number of yards out in the ocean are two small islands that produce awesome waves on either side that had never been surfed before. Curious natives try to imitate Mike and Robert by riding the waves in their two-ton fishing canoes while youngsters watch mesmerized from the shoreline.

The surfers leave expensive Senegal and head for Accra, Ghana. Mike and Robert surf off a beach near a fishing village. The natives have never seen a white man before, let alone a surfboard, and they are fascinated with the sport; practically the whole village comes down to the shore to watch August and Hynson surf. The natives get so stoked by what they are seeing for the first time that they try to surf with their fishing canoe while the kids use wood from their huts as makeshift belly boards. Later Mike and Robert give surfing lessons to the village boys while their elders just take the guys' boards and attempt riding the waves. When the surf dies down, Mike and Robert say goodbye to their newfound friends and depart for Lagos, Nigeria.

In Lagos, the surfers find yet another beach where no one has ever surfed before. The waves are good but small. What amazes the duo is that the water temperature is an unheard of 91 degrees, melting the wax right off their surfboards, while the air temperature is a humid 100 degrees. It is so unbearably hot on the beach that Brown stands in waist-deep water as he films Mike and Robert riding the waves. To make matters worse, the trio has to traipse through a bug-infested jungle to find the main road back to town.

Leaving Nigeria, the boys cross the equator, flying to Cape Town, South Africa, where it is officially summertime. Before hitting the surf, the boys travel by cable car to the top of Table Mountain. Unlike the other places they previously visited in Africa, Mike and Robert are not the only wave riders in town. They are joined by "the father of South African surfing" John Whitmore and about 100 of his surfing buddies who are mostly in their late twenties and thirties. There are very few surfers close to Robert and Mike's age. Later the boys find a secluded stretch of sand called Long Beach. Due to the kelp beds, the conditions resemble Northern California with smooth but small waves.

Heading north to Durban, Mike and Robert hitch a ride from an African game hunter and prankster named Terrence Bullen. He was only journeying a few miles to take his young friend named James surfing but decides to be the boys' guide and driver for the remainder of their time in South Africa. Driving the 1,200 miles along the coast of the Indian Ocean, the group stops at various deserted beaches to surf or to just eye the wildlife.

Arriving in Durban, Mike and Robert hook up with local surfers Jack Wilson, Max Wetteland and Harry Bold and head out for some early morning surfing. At 4:30 A.M., both the air and water temperature is a balmy 80 degrees. Since the ocean water is that warm, the surfers have to keep an eye out for sharks. The guys aren't used to the skimpy swimsuits worn by some of their fellow surfers. Brown describes the foreign Speedo bathing suits as being "a G-string." Robert and Mike get a lift back to their hotel in a rickshaw pulled by a Zulu tribe member clad in native dress.

While journeying north to Johannesburg to catch an airplane to Hawaii, Terence and the guys pinpoint an interesting spot on the map called Cape St. Francis that has possible potential for good surfing conditions. The boys trek across three miles of barren white sand dunes that slope down into the green waters of the Indian Ocean. There they discover the most perfectly shaped three-to five-foot waves breaking parallel with the beach. Mike, Robert and their new friend James are totally stoked and whoop and holler after each ride. Some of their rides in the curl last so long that Brown cannot record it in one shot. Though the exhilarated surfers wish they could remain in Cape St. Francis longer, they know they have to travel on.

While Mike and Robert fly to Australia, Malibu surfers Phil Edwards, Butch Van Artsdalen and Mickey Dora are featured riding the big waves of Haleiwa Beach on the North Shore of Oahu, Hawaii. Edwards and Bob Casey sail a speedy catamaran in the ocean waters off Diamond Head.

Brown catches up with Mike and Robert in Perth, Australia, as they join a

Classic poster art for the surfing epic *The Endless Summer* (Cinema V, 1966).

group of locals on a surfing excursion, driving over 1,000 miles in four days seeking surf. The conditions at Ocean Beach are fair but the boys don't venture in due to shark sightings. Giving up on Western Australia, the trio jets to Melbourne on the East Coast of Australia. After landing, the surfers immediately drive out on "a dry, dusty dirt road" to Bell's Beach where they find no waves. Hanging out on the beach (infested with flies), British surfer Rodney Sumpter informs Mike and Robert that Bell's Beach has the best surf during the winter month of July as he flashes back to surfing it and Ocean Beach with Nat Young.

The last Australia stop for Robert and Mike is Sydney, where they strike out again. Surfing conditions are poor with one-foot waves and three inches of rain. The huge waves are in Hawaii at Waimea Bay, where surfers ride longer and more streamlined surfboards nicknamed the "big guns." Mickey Dora, Greg Noll and Dick Brewer are just some of the surfers who test their skills trying to ride 30-foot waves.

Back in Sydney, Robert and Mike pass on surfing until a bevy of uninhibited bikini-clad beauties hit the waves. Mike especially goes gaga as the girls' skimpy bikini bottoms slide down, exposing their shapely derrieres. The lucky blonde boy gets to drive one of the girls home, leaving a disappointed Robert alone on the beach.

The duo reunites and crosses the Tasman Sea to Aukland, New Zealand. They meet two local surfers, John and Tim, who drive the guys to the extreme northeast tip of the North Island. After spending the day surfing some fair-sized waves, the locals return home to spend the holidays with their families. Mike and Robert travel to the West Coast to a place called Ragland, stopping to do some trout fishing along the way. They arrive at a deserted cove on Christmas morning and spend the whole day riding the waves. As with Cape St. Francis, Mike and Robert get some very long rides on almost perfect waves.

In Tahiti, which was not supposed to have any good surf, the boys find three unnamed beaches with small but decent waves and at one of them they even ride waves *out* to sea. Leaving the South Sea paradise, the duo heads for their last port of call, Hawaii. There they and others tackle the mammoth waves at Pipeline. The danger of surfing these mammoth waves is demonstrated with some jaw-dropping wipeouts. Australian surfer Bob Pike is seen being led from the water with a broken collarbone and three broken ribs. Robert and Mike's journey ends here as they wait for the summer season to begin again in their home of Southern California. The final shot gives "special thanks to Old King Neptune for providing the waves."

Behind-the-Scenes

Clean-cut, all–American Bruce Brown was a little known filmmaker outside of the underground world of surf movies. He was born in San Francisco but spent most of his childhood growing up in Oakland. At around the age of ten, he and his family relocated to Long Beach, where the precocious blonde-haired lad learned to surf and became a big fan of filmmaker Bud Browne's early surf movies. In 1955, while in the Navy, Bruce made his first film, an 8mm short.

Returning to civilian life in 1957, Bruce was working as a lifeguard in Dana

Point, California, when a local surf entrepreneur, Dale Velzy, hired him to shoot a film promoting his surf team. The novice filmmaker was so green that he had to purchase a book on how to make movies. Brown's first official surf movie was *Slippery When Wet* (1959) a silent 16mm picture that he showed on the lecture circuit, providing live narration. He followed this with *Surf Crazy* (1959), *Barefoot Adventure* (1960), *Surfing Hollow Days* (1961), which spotlights surfer Phil Edwards with surfing footage shot in Australia and New Zealand, and *Waterlogged* (1962), among others.

In 1962, Brown got the idea to produce *The Endless Summer,* a surf movie that would appeal to non-surfers and as well as surfers. The search for a perfect wave during an endless summer came to Bruce when his travel agent informed him that an around-the-world plane ticket was $50 cheaper than a roundtrip one from LA to South Africa. Brown commented to writer Patrick McNulty in *The Los Angeles Times,* "I've always felt that an endless summer would be the ultimate for a surfer. It's really simple to cross the equator during our winter and find summer in the Southern Hemisphere. I thought how lovely just to travel slowly around the world following summer...."

Brown chose two local Southern California surfers who had appeared in some of his earlier films. Neither of them were to be paid to appear in the movie but Brown would cover their traveling expenses. Eighteen-year-old Robert August was from Seal Beach, California, and the son of Brown's friend Blackie August. A straight-A student, he was the president of his student body and he planned on a career in dentistry. But Robert was also a very competent surfer and had appeared in two Bruce Brown films while in his early teens. However, due to the embarrassing images of surfers from *Gidget* and *Beach Party*, August was a "closeted" hotdogger and none of his school chums knew that he was an expert surfer. When Brown first offered August the chance to travel around the world surfing, he declined because he was worried about skipping his first semester at college. So studious was the serious teenager that his parents had to convince him to accept Brown's once-in-a-lifetime offer.

Blonde Mike Hynson was the complete opposite of August. He was born in 1942 in Crescent City, California, and grew up in San Diego. He had a cocky attitude and a reputation as one of the bad boys of surfing. At 14 he was caught stealing nine surfboards at a Laguna Beach surf shop. Other surfers regarded Hynson's surfing skills very highly and he was one of the first to surf Pipeline on Oahu's North Shore. He became a surfboard shaper in 1959 and was working for Hobie Surfboards by 1963. His surfing prowess was captured on film in a few surf movies, including Bruce Brown's *Surfing Hollow Days*. When Bruce came calling a second time, handsome Hynson, nicknamed "helmet head" due to his trademark slicked-back blonde hair, agreed to participate to keep one step ahead of the pursuing draft board.

A number of big-name surfers are shown riding the waves and demonstrating various surfing maneuvers in *The Endless Summer*. One of them was Fred Hemmings. Among his many achievements in the surfing world was winning the 1968 World Surfing Championship and founding the Pipeline Masters and the International Professional Surfers world tour. Hemmings recalled in his autobiography that he was surfing at Ala Moana when Bruce Brown was shooting footage for his movie.

He was tired so he sat down as he was riding his board into shore. As Brown aimed the camera at him, "I stood up and turned 360 degrees, keeping my eyes on him as I surfed by." Kids into surfing today still remember Hemmings most from this moment. He joked, "All those years of surfing and I have been reduced to 'the guy sitting down in *Endless Summer*.'"

Brown and company departed on their idyllic trip in November 1963. The surfers had one suitcase each plus their surfboards. They crossed the equator five times and traveled to such exotic ports as Africa, New Zealand, Australia, Japan, Tahiti and Hawaii. Despite traveling around the world with two young surfers in foreign places that he had never been to, Brown reveals that they didn't encounter a single major problem—just "a hundred little ones." Kenya offered a beautiful beach by day and the start of a revolution by night so the surfers were escorted to the airport the next morning by security forces. In Senegal, the crew had to deal with a newly formed country with a high inflation rate. Brown was shocked that a gallon of gasoline cost a dollar and that the hotel rates were $30 per person. Though the locals were enraptured with Robert and Mike's surfing prowess, they did not make the least impression on the hotel's French tourists, who snubbed them. The native children were fascinated with Brown's cameras so he had to adopt an awkward stance to shoot his surfers on the waves while trying to protect his equipment from the prying hands of the curious kids. Minor complications arose at airports where some personnel were suspicious of Brown's camera equipment and dumbfounded by the two surfboards, which they had never seen before.

Some locations were chosen knowing that there were plenty of beaches with good surf while other places were a gamble. Brown was familiar with Australia and New Zealand and he received recommendations where to surf in South Africa. However, West Africa was totally alien to the filmmaker. In these places where the natives had never heard of the sport of surfing, Brown had to rely on the knowledge of the fishermen (who are reliant on the sea and cognizant of weather conditions) to find beaches conducive to surfing. Even with the known surfing hot spots, Brown was taking a chance shooting this movie. He commented, "It is always a big gamble taking a trip like this because the surf is like the weather, unpredictable."

To obtain the shots of the surfers from their boards, Brown designed a wind-up 16mm Bolex, which he described as being "the smallest underwater housing in the world. It's a very small, waterproof camera that only holds 50 feet of film and you have to spend most of your time reloading." This compact camera weighing approximately 20 pounds helped him achieve some spectacularly peculiar shots such as Hynson or August's feet walking up to the nose of the board.

Both August and Hynson agree that the highlight of their journey occurred in South Africa's Cape St. Francis, located approximately halfway between Cape Town and Durban along the Indian Ocean coastline. After trekking three miles over pristine, lofty sand dunes, the trio discovered the most perfectly shaped glassy waves imaginable. (In actuality, this scene was filmed *after* the guys surfed to make its discovery more dramatic.) Brown remarked in *Surfer*, "On some of the rides I timed Mike and Robert in the curl, crouching and driving, screaming at the top of their lungs, for 45 seconds! The thing that is almost impossible to show or describe is the feeling you had while riding these waves. It was unlike any other surfing spot."

August commented, "I was so damned excited that I threw up in the water. It was something I'd been dreaming about since I was a little kid."

In February 1964, Brown and August returned to Southern California while Hynson, who was still trying to duck the draft, remained in Hawaii. Brown's biggest regret is that he wound up with so much footage that he had to cut a lot of it to fit within a reasonable running time. He remarked, "I don't like to go to a place and just show a few waves. I think most people like to see a bit of the country and watch a story develop." It was for this reason that Brown did not include in *The Endless Summer* the segment shot in Japan. He had 30 minutes worth of first-rate footage but including it would have made the film too lengthy.

On their homecoming, Brown expressed pride in Mike Hynson and Robert August. They did not act like typical, vulgar, loud-mouthed American tourists throwing money around in any of the countries that they visited. The pair got along fine and made great traveling partners. They were very polite and respectful of the different cultures and even donned sports coats as they boarded their plane for Africa. August admitted in *People* that they were not only chasing the perfect wave but also a bikini-clad beauty or two. On film, the lads dispelled the stereotypical surf bum image, which the mainstream press loved to berate.

The Endless Summer was shot in 16mm like most 1960s surf movies, which were intended for the surfing crowd only. However, Brown and his associate R. Paul Allen had grander aspirations for the film. Brown imbued the movie with a mellow haunting theme instrumental by the Sandals. Surprisingly, the theme never charted and a soundtrack LP was not released until the mid-nineties. Brown also commissioned John Van Hammersveld to design a movie poster. He created one of the most memorable of the decade, using fluorescent orange, purple and yellow surrounding a silhouette shot of Brown, Hynson and August holding their surfboards

Comparing his picture to the surf movies of the day, Brown opined, "Too many films ... are like a newsreel. This is interesting to surfers but not to many other people. I think by integrating surfing with a story or some kind of theme ... makes it suddenly entertaining." *The Endless Summer* truly is entertaining so Brown wanted to reach an audience beyond local surfing enthusiasts. The movie recouped its cost playing auditoriums and small venues on the beach city surf and lecture circuit beginning in the summer of 1964 through the following year.

Brown and Allen shopped the film to distributors in Hollywood and New York who rejected it because they felt it wouldn't draw an audience "ten miles from the ocean." To see if *The Endless Summer* had an appeal to the mainstream, Brown and Allen tested it in one theater in Wichita, Kansas in November 1965. The day the film premiered, there was a freak blizzard and a local union projectionist strike. Surprisingly, the movie sold out during its entire two-week run and outgrossed the previous big-budget Hollywood features that played there, *The Great Race* and *My Fair Lady*. However, Brown still could not interest a distributor. He remarked in *Life* magazine that Hollywood executives felt that since "there was no sex and violence, it was therefore noncommercial."

Brown borrowed $50,000 to have the film blown up to 35mm and was able to convince the Kip's Bay Theater in New York City to run the film. To get the booking, Brown had to guarantee the art house a profit and a holdover clause. The

Surfers Mike Hynson and Robert August hike through the bush to find a main road in *The Endless Summer* **(Cinema V, 1966).**

movie opened on June 15, 1966, without a distributor and with limited promotion financed by Brown. Even though he had sunk almost $100,000 into *The Endless Summer*, Brown was not worried about the outcome. Days before the opening, the laid-back filmmaker commented in *The New York Times*, "I just can't get worked up. Either we'll clean up or we won't." The movie received rave reviews with Brown being dubbed the "Fellini of the Foam" by *The New York Times* and a "Bergman of the boards" by *Time Magazine*. The only one head-scratching bad notice came from the Harvard Lampoon, who inexplicably voted *The Endless Summer* the worst surfing movie of 1966.

Spurred on by the glowing critical notices, *The Endless Summer* was a smash hit, running for a record 48 weeks in New York City. Much of this was due to the estimated 20 percent repeat audience. Regarding the film's success, Brown opined in *Life*, "I think we stoked them with simplicity." Brown secured a distributor, Cinema V, and the movie began playing in all the major cities, setting attendance records nationwide. The film was a phenomenal success and grossed $5 million in the U.S. according to *Entertainment Weekly*. It remained the highest grossing documentary of all time until Michael Moore's *Roger & Me* was released in 1989. Though *The Endless Summer* received raves from the critics, it was snubbed by the Academy Awards and failed to receive a nomination for Best Documentary.

Commenting on the film's reception across the U.S., Robert August told the *Star Ledger* that the film "made people aware of what surfers really do. Before that, it was really 'Beach Blanket' films and silly Beach Boy music about going nuts in your own bedroom and stuff."

The Endless Summer brought Bruce Brown fame and fortune but the laid-back family man rejected all attempts to exploit the movie. He turned down all advertisers who wanted to incorporate the film into their ad campaigns as well as *Endless Summer* surfboards, t-shirts and hair bleach. Declining offers from Hollywood to direct fiction movies ("That would be a disaster," he remarked in *Newsday*), Brown announced plans to film a documentary about tuna fishing but it never materialized. Instead he made a tribute to motorcycling called *On Any Sunday* (1972). He got hooked on motorcycles while viewing the Steve McQueen movie *The Great Escape* while in Japan shooting *The Endless Summer*. He even got aficionado McQueen to finance the picture, which received a Best Documentary Academy Award nomination.

Hollywood producers hounded Brown to make a sequel and for the longest time he declined. He opined in *People*, "After I do something once, I begin to lose interest in it." He directed a few commercials for Kodak, dabbled in commercial fishing and real estate and restored old Hudson automobiles, but he mostly hung out with his buddies surfing. The wealth he accumulated from *The Endless Summer* gave him the luxury to be a man of leisure. In the eighties, he took up commodities trading.

In 1992, prodded by his son Dana Brown, Brown agreed to make *The Endless Summer II* for New Line Cinema with Dana as editor and co-writer. Released in 1994, *The Endless Summer II* was almost a carbon copy of the original right down to the laid-back narration provided by Brown and a modern version of the theme song by the Sandals. It followed surfers Robert "Wingnut" Weaver and Pat O'Connell as they surfed and traveled from California to Costa Rica, France, Australia, Indonesia, Fiji and Hawaii. The biggest difference between the two films is that the sequel used a team of cinematographers using sophisticated 35mm camera equipment to capture the surfers in their wave-riding glory. After the film was released, Brown commented in *Variety*, "I have a surfer mentality: You just work if you have to. I worked 2½ years, and I'll go surf 2½ years. Then I'll be even." Brown would come out of retirement to co-produce with Dana the videos *Endless Summer Revisited* (2000) and *On Any Sunday Revisited* (2001) as well as the highly acclaimed surf movie *Step into Liquid* (2003).

Mike Hynson beat the draft by pretending to be a nutcase. Upon his return to the U.S. after filming *The Endless Summer*, Gordon & Smith Surfboards hired Hynson, who designed for the company his signature board, the Hynson Model. He continued surfing but did not enjoy competitions though he entered the 1963 Malibu International and was chosen to participate in the 1965, 1966 and 1967 Duke Kahanamoku Invitational. In 1970, Mike attempted to launch his own surfboard company (Rainbow Surfboards in La Jolla) but its failure could be attributed to Hynson's drug and alcohol problems. A friendship with rock star Jimi Hendrix had previously introduced Hynson to the world of LSD. He hit rock bottom during the early seventies, spending time in jail and living on the streets. But by the end of the decade, he had turned his life around and was shaping and designing surfboards once again. In 1995, he filed a lawsuit against Brown for a share of *The Endless Summer* profits. The courts dismissed it in 2000. Mending his friendship with Brown, Hynson joined him and August for an *Endless Summer* reunion in 2001 at the San Diego County Fair.

The search for the endless summer had the most profound effect on Robert August. He returned to school and quickly became disenchanted with becoming a dentist. He dropped out and began working at a local surf shop. Like Hynson, August was also not into competing though he placed in the top three in the 1964 United States Invitational and the 1965 United States Surfing Championships. August worked as a surfboard shaper for a few years before opening a failed Huntington Beach restaurant called Endless Summer in 1971. He had better luck with the Robert August Surf Shop. When long boards came back into fashion in the early eighties, August saw his business boom. In 1992, the affable August made a guest appearance in *The Endless Summer II* and was inducted into the Huntington Beach Surfing Walk of Fame. He closed his retail shop in 1998 though his factory still keeps churning out surfboards.

Memorable Lines

(The surfers arrive at Cape St. Francis, South Africa, where for centuries the steady-breaking four-foot curls have never been surfed.)

BRUCE BROWN: Just think of all those waves that have gone to waste!

(The surfers arrive in Australia only to encounter flat surf.)

BROWN: Everywhere they went they were greeted with a familiar cry surfers have heard a thousand times each. Quote—You guys ree-ely missed it—you shoulda been here yesterday!

Reviews

Raley Benet, *The Villager*—"If we had our way *The Endless Summer* ... would be playing somewhere nearby all the time. There is an innocence about this film that is pleasant to come upon."

Vincent Canby, *The New York Times*—"Bruce Brown has compiled a visually fascinating feature length documentary. There are marvelous shots in color of surfers testing the waters ... particularly, off Oahu, where the waves are 40 feet high. There is hypnotic beauty and almost continuous excitement in these scenes."

Film Quarterly—"It has undeniable charms; lots of telephoto shots of surfers on them, and a curious *entre-nous* narration of such stupefyingly ethnocentric character that what in other mouths would be grotesque or even despicable takes on a genial naïveté."

Wanda Hale, *New York Daily News*—"An exciting color documentary on surfing ... Brown's photography is breathtakingly beautiful, clear and vibrant. The young producer also wrote and delivers the narration that is witty and complete both in information and description."

New Yorker—"A brilliant documentary ... Mr. Brown constructs an unanswerable argument for the surfer's dream world, where the summer sun always shines on long, well-shaped waves, breaking evenly on uncrowded beaches. Great background music. Great movie. Out of sight."

Time—"Audiences everywhere, surf-bored by the dry run of Hollywood's beach-party musicals, may relish the joys of *Summer*. From the shores of Ghana ... to Hawaii's perilous 'Pipeline' ... chills and spills crowd onto the screen."

Roger Vaughan, *Life*—"An imaginative 1 1/2-hour documentary on the art of surfing."

Variety—"Bruce Brown has successfully edited his nine miles of color film into a feature that will excite sports fans and should delight most other filmgoers."

Archer Winsten, *New York Post*—"There have been Hollywood films about surfing, and they've contained some memorable shots. There have been special films on surfing, and they've been pretty spectacular. But the *Endless Summer* makes them all seem mild. As a travelogue the picture is well photographed and pleasingly narrated."

Awards and Nominations

Harvard Lampoon Movie Worst Award: "The Bennett" (for the worst surfing movie)—*The Endless Summer*

Newsweek Top Ten Films of 1966

★ 26 ★

The Ghost in the Invisible Bikini (1966)

*There's something blood curdling for everyone ... when
a pretty GHOUL trades in her bed sheet for a BIKINI!*

Fun: ★★½
Surfing: ★
Boy watching: ★★
Girl watching: ★★★★
Music: ★★★
Scenery: ★

Release date: April 6, 1966. Running time: 82m. Box office gross: $1.5 million.

DVD release: Double bill with *Ghost of Dragstrip Hollow*, MGM Home Entertainment (August 2004).

Tommy Kirk (*Chuck Phillips*), Deborah Walley (*Lili Morton*), Aron Kincaid (*Bobby*), Quinn O'Hara (*Sinistra*), Jesse White (*J. Sinister Hulk*), Harvey Lembeck (*Eric Von Zipper*), Nancy Sinatra (*Vicki*), Claudia Martin (*Lulu*), Francis X. Bushman (*Malcolm*), Benny Rubin (*Chicken Feather*), Bobbi Shaw (*Princess Yolanda*), George Barrows (*Monstro*), Basil Rathbone (*Reginald Ripper*), Patsy Kelly (*Myrtle Forbush*), Boris Karloff (*Hiram Stokely*), Susan Hart (*Cecily*), Piccola Pupa (*Piccola*), Luree Holmes, Ed Garner, Frank Alesia, Mary Hughes, Salli Sachse, Patti Chandler, Sue Hamilton (*Boys and Girls*), Alberta Nelson (*Puss*), Andy Romano (*J.D.*), Myrna Ross, Jerry Brutsche, Bob Harvey, John Macchia, Alan Fife (*The Rat Pack*), Elena Andreas, Herb Andreas (*The Statues*). Not credited: Peter Sachse.

Guest Stars: The Bobby Fuller Four

American International Pictures. *Produced by*: James H. Nicholson and Samuel Z. Arkoff. *Directed by*: Don Weis. *Screenplay by*: Louis M. Heyward and Elwood Ullman. *Story*: Louis M. Heyward. *Co-Producer*: Anthony Carras. *Production Supervisor*: Jack Bohrer. *Director of Photography*: Stanley Cortez, A.S.C. *Art Director*: Daniel Haller. *Film Editors*: Fred Feitshans, Eve Newman. *Sound Effects*: Nelson-Corso. *Musical Supervisor*: Al Simms. *Musical Score by*: Les Baxter. *Choreography by*: Jack Baker. *Costumer*: Richard Bruno. *Titles and Photographic Special Effects*: Butler-Glouner. *Special Effects*: Roger George. *Ghost Sequences Produced by*: Ronald and Carol Sinclair. *Assistant Director*: Clark Paylow. *Properties*: Karl Brainard, Richard M. Rubin. *Mixer*: Wally Nogle. *Makeup*: Ted Coodley. *Hairstylist*: Ray Foreman. *Set Decorator*: Clarence Steensen. *Construction Coordinator*: Ross Hahn. *Production Assistant*: Jack Cash. *Sound by*: Ryder Sound Services, Inc. *Musical Instruments by*: Vox. Filmed in Panavision and Pathecolor.

"Geronimo" by Guy Hemric and Jerry Styner, performed by Nancy Sinatra. "Swing-a-Ma-Thang" and "Make the Music Pretty" by Guy Hemric and Jerry Styner, performed by the Bobby Fuller Four. "Don't Try to Fight It" by Guy Hemric and Jerry Styner, performed by Quinn O'Hara. "Stand Up and Fight" by Guy Hemric and Jerry Styner, performed by Piccola Pupa.

Financially the least successful of the *Beach Party* movies, *The Ghost in the Invisible Bikini* put the nail in the coffin for the genre at AIP. After six movies, seven if counting *Ski Party*, the beach films was getting tired. AIP tried to pump life into it by shifting the locale to a creepy mansion and mixing aspects of the beach party formula with the horror genre and populating it with fresh faces. Three heirs to a fortune gather at a dead man's mansion for the reading of his will, unaware that his crooked lawyer plans to off them so he can steal the inheritance. His plans go awry due to the interference of a beautiful ghost in an invisible bikini who is sent down to make sure the money winds up in the rightful hands. There's nary a beach or a surfboard in sight, which greatly hurts the movie. Instead all the action takes place at the spooky old estate with a fair number of scenes around an in-ground swimming pool with boys in bathing trunks and girls in bikinis twisting to the sounds of the Bobby Fuller Four and Nancy Sinatra.

Tommy Kirk and Deborah Walley are passable as the young romantic leads but they get overshadowed by the supporting cast who steal the film from them. Sexy redhead Quinn O'Hara delivers the best performance as the near-sighted Sinistra, whose attempts to kill Aron Kincaid's Bobby are constantly thwarted. O'Hara is very amusing either singing to a suit of armor thinking it is her intended victim or mistaking a statue for the surfer boy and rubbing its neck ("Ooh, aren't you built!") before pushing it over a cliff. Quinn also has the distinction of being the first actress clad in a bikini to sing a solo in a *Beach Party* movie. Amazing that it took seven films for it to finally happen.

Kincaid, saddled with an unflattering pageboy haircut, has some funny moments in the role of the dumb sidekick usually reserved for Jody McCrea. Nancy Sinatra sings well but proves once again that acting the ingenue was not her forte. Harvey Lembeck's schtick as the inept motorcycle leader has totally worn thin by now and the less said about singer Piccola Pupa the better. Suffice it to say the teenage public rightfully sent this Italian meatball, hired by AIP to replace Donna Loren, bouncing back to her native Italy.

Though most of the musical numbers have nothing to do with the film's plot some of the songs are quite catchy. The Bobby Fuller Four was the only rock act hired to perform. It is their sole film appearance before lead singer Bobby Fuller's untimely death almost a year later. Their version of "Make the Music Pretty" is very lively and they perform a rockin' instrumental. The group also backs the peppy Nancy Sinatra on the bouncy song "Geronimo." All these numbers are performed poolside with the beach gang gyrating wildly. For one number, every boy is attached to a girl by a "Thing-a-Ma-Jig," which is a sort of stick with two suction cups and a rotating ball on each end. The annoyingly precocious Piccola Pupa surprisingly delivers a good rendition of the perky number "Stand Up and Fight." But it is Quinn O'Hara who steals the spotlight, even though she is not a trained vocalist, with her sexy Marilyn Monroe–inspired bump-and-grind number "Don't Try to Fight It," which she sings to a suit of armor thinking it is Aron Kincaid's Bobby.

The Ghost in the Invisible Bikini also scores very highly in the girl-watching department. Guys should just sit back, ignore the dumb plot and enjoy the array of shapely starlets who parade by. The movie is packed with sexy blondes, sultry brunettes and scorching redheads including Deborah Walley, Susan Hart, Quinn O'Hara, Nancy Sinatra, Claudia Martin, Bobbi Shaw, Mary Hughes, Luree Holmes and Salli Sachse. Boy watchers lose out. Tommy Kirk and Aron Kincaid remain covered up for the most part and the only recognizable surfer boy in the crowd is blonde Ed Garner.

What *The Ghost in the Invisible Bikini* lacked in musical guest stars, it made up in the number of veteran actors hired to bring the thin plot alive. Unfortunately, even they do not fare well. Patsy Kelly is overbearing and bellows throughout the movie as Kincaid's Aunt Myrtle while Benny Rubin as Chicken Feather falls flat. Only Boris Karloff as the dear departed Hiram and Basil Rathbone as the villainous attorney bring a touch of class to this production. Rathbone especially is very good and you sense that his distaste for the teenagers' gyrating and running amok was not acting.

Though Rathbone, O'Hara, Kincaid, Sinatra and the Bobby Fuller Four perform valiantly, they cannot overcome the tired screenplay, making *The Ghost in the Invisible Bikini* one of the lesser AIP beach party movies.

The Story

The movie opens in a crypt with the lovely young blonde ghost Cecily welcoming her newly deceased husband Hiram Stokely into the afterlife. However, she informs her aged husband that to get into Heaven and attain eternal youth, he must perform a good deed. Cecily returns to Earth as a ghost to make sure Hiram's rightful heirs inherit his money so she and her spouse can be reunited for eternity. Crooked attorney Reginald Ripper has summoned the three heirs—nice guy Chuck Philips, independent-minded redhead Lili Morton and the feisty, older Myrtle Forbush—to Stokely's creepy mansion for the reading of his will, which reveals that his fortune is hidden somewhere in the house. Myrtle's nephew Bobby, his girlfriend Vicki and a gaggle of surfer boys and bikini girls crash the estate and frolic by the pool.

Ripper hatches a scheme to bump off the heirs but, unbeknownst to him, Cecily is there to make sure his plot backfires. Surprised by the existence of Bobby, the greedy lawyer instructs his curvaceous but nearsighted daughter Sinistra to eliminate the buff beach boy. The brainy bikini-clad beauty at first begins to flirt with the wrong boy. After her father makes her put on her eyeglasses, she entices the smitten Bobby away from his annoyed girlfriend ("I'm Vicky ... *I'm Vicky*") into her lab. When she coaxes the blonde surfer to drink one of her smoky concoctions, he realizes that she is out to kill him. Bobby uses her poor eyesight to his advantage and slips out as she searches for her misplaced glasses. After doing a sensuous song and dance, the nearsighted beauty winds up pouring the deadly cocktail down a suit of armor thinking it is Bobby.

A few miles away, motorcycle leader Eric Von Zipper and his Rat Pack follow carnival performers Princess Yolanda, her Indian partner Chicken Feather and Monstro the gorilla to the house. They have been hired by Ripper to work with J. Sinister Hulk to kill the heirs.

Poster art for *The Ghost in the Invisible Bikini* **(AIP, 1966).**

Sinistra tries again with Bobby, luring him to a bluff high above some jagged rocks and the sea. Bobby wisely removes Sinistra's glasses and she mistakes a statue for the surfer boy, rubbing its neck before pushing it over a cliff.

Chuck and Lili vow not to be scared off from the mansion. Hiram's trusted servant Malcolm tries to warn Chuck of the danger of staying at the estate but before he can reveal anything more, Ripper kills him. Eric Von Zipper and gang learn of the hidden loot and decide to stick around and claim it for themselves. At the midnight reading of the will, the heirs learn of their connection to Stokely and that they are to split the deceased carnival owner's million dollar fortune evenly if they can find it hidden somewhere in the house ("Look to the Prince of Love"). Soon after, Ripper berates his trio of inept hired assassins for not doing their job.

During the night, Bobby is terrorized by a hatchet-throwing mummy while Monstro carries Lili down into Stokely's secret Chamber of Horrors. Everybody descends into the basement and a melee ensues between the various groups in pursuit of the money. Cecily guides Chuck to the loot and, just as Ripper is about to shoot everybody, she plugs up the barrel of his gun, killing him. The rightful heirs inherit the fortune, Stokely gets into Heaven and achieves eternal youth (though in the body of a ten-year-old) and the film ends with the surfer crowd having a pajama party in the Chamber of Horrors.

Behind-the-Scenes

The Ghost in the Invisible Bikini began life as *Pajama Party in a Haunted House*, the title of the original screenplay. It was re-titled *Slumber Party in a Haunted House* and then *Bikini Party in a Haunted House* during production. With the box office receipts declining for their beach movies in 1965, this film was AIP's attempt to revive the genre. However, Frankie and Annette as well as Jody McCrea, John Ashley and Donna Loren were nowhere to be found. Frankie has remarked in many interviews that he was tiring of the beach party films, while Annette was enjoying motherhood and devoting time to her newborn. Though AIP couldn't or didn't try to coax them to star in this film, they were able to reunite the pair in the racing car drama *Fireball 500* (1966) co-starring Fabian and Julie Parrish with direction by William Asher.

Now left without leading players, the producers cast familiar faces Tommy Kirk and Deborah Walley with support from disappointed AIP contract player Aron Kincaid. Wanting to sing, and being a fan of the swashbucklers of the 30s, a jubilant Kincaid was cast as Sir Guy DeGisbourne in a musical version of *The Adventures of Robin Hood* with Frankie Avalon and Annette Funicello as Robin and Maid Marian. The film, however, was scrapped and Kincaid instead was given a supporting role in this movie along with Nancy Sinatra, Quinn O'Hara, Claudia Martin, Ed Garner and Piccola Pupa, who was discovered by Danny Thomas.

Recalling the original screenplay sent to him, Aron Kincaid says with a laugh, "It was the *worst* script that I ever read. It took place in a swamp in Florida with alligators. There were all these things in the screenplay about the swamp and this old house that was in the bayou. I was also reluctant to do the film because my character had too many scenes in the swamp and I did not want to injure myself.

AIP was never astute with safety precautions and it was well known that people were always getting hurt on its sets." In fact, on the first day of *Invisible Bikini* filming, a grip fell to his death from a catwalk. They couldn't get all the blood-stains off the carpet so it was just left there for the actors to traipse over.

Kincaid was contractually bound to appear in *Bikini Party in a Haunted House*. His disappointment with the script was quickly eclipsed by the fact that he would be working with Francis X. Bushman, Patsy Kelly, Benny Rubin (a last-minute replacement for the ailing Buster Keaton) and one of his idols, Basil Rathbone. "It was like my dreams came true tenfold," exclaims Kincaid. Quinn O'Hara, who was cast as Rathbone's seductive daughter Sinistra, was also overjoyed to be working with Rathbone. "He was delightful," gushed O'Hara in *Drive-in Dream Girls*. "When I first met him I was so afraid I'd say 'Rasil Bathbone' that I actually did! He was a charming man."

Though the younger players were thrilled to be working with the esteemed Rathbone, according to Aron Kincaid the feeling wasn't mutual. "My favorite line in the movie is when all the kids coming running in the house after the rain breaks at the pool party and Basil Rathbone says, 'Nah, nah, nah! Revolting little pip-squeaks.' He didn't need *any* acting lessons to say that line. He was pretty well dis-gusted with the whole thing. I could tell since he hid in his dressing room. I took in a book called *Stars of the Photoplay 1934* to show him. I asked him to sign the front cover. He was great to talk with and had so many stories. He was amazed that I knew all of his former co-stars—even the obscure ones. I had seen *The Garden of Allah* about 15 times. I knew all of his lines of dialogue in it. He said, 'A young fel-low like you knowing all this just amazes me!'"

Don Weis, who helmed *Pajama Party*, was hired to direct the film but revealed in *Filmfax* magazine that he was committed to AIP for a second film and could not get out of directing this. Though its budget was higher than the previous beach movies, the picture quickly ran into shooting problems. One reason was due to the artistry of cinematographer Stanley Cortez, who received Academy Award nomi-nations for *The Magnificent Ambersons* (1942) and *Since You Went Away* (1944). Quinn O'Hara recalled, "He really took a lot of time with the shots and the pro-ducers got mad at him because we were going over budget. I thought he was a fan-tastic cameraman and we got along wonderfully."

Counting pennies, the producers began trying to save money any way they could. Aron Kincaid was supposed to perform two musical numbers. "I was happy that I was going to be able to sing in this because I felt the audience would get the chance to hear my real singing voice," remarks Aron. But as with most everything at AIP, things did not go as planned. To save time and to keep the costs down, these scenes were dropped. Though Kincaid did perform with the cast the title tune, it was eventually cut from the movie while his version of "Make the Music Pretty" backed by the Bobby Fuller Four was recorded but never filmed. Instead, the group *sans* Kincaid sang it on screen.

Keeping with the tradition of the previous AIP beach party movies, *The Ghost in the Invisible Bikini* was filmed during the fall of 1965 for a spring release. Clad skimpily through out the movie, Quinn O'Hara resorted to desperate measures to keep warm. She recalls with a laugh, "I had done a *G.E. Theatre* with Ida Lupino where we were shooting a scene on the back lot and it was winter but we had to

Quinn O'Hara and Aron Kincaid listen intently to director Don Weis between takes on *The Ghost in the Invisible Bikini* (AIP, 1965) (*courtesy Quinn O'Hara*).

pretend it was summer. We were freezing our asses off. Ida gave me a couple of shots of vodka to keep me warm. When I learned that we had to film at night in Pasadena and I was going to be colder than hell since I had to wear a bikini, I remembered that night with Ida so I brought some cognac with me. It was a good thing to do. You don't keep going in and out so you don't catch a cold."

Filming went smoothly and O'Hara credits director Weis' professionalism. She says fondly, "Don was a really likable warm teddy bear type of guy. I think he just exuded that. He reminded me of a younger Edmund Gwenn from *Miracle on 34th Street*. You couldn't help but like him. Don was very sensitive and was tuned in to people, which made him an extremely good director." But not everyone was satisfied with Weis. Aron Kincaid insists that "I was the one who came up with half the ideas that I did in the comedy scenes such as tickling the gorilla while trapped in the bathroom. I also thought of putting candle wax on my heels so I could whip around after bumped by the actors running by. Don Weis was in no shape to give me acting direction."

For the most part, the cast of *The Ghost in the Invisible Bikini* seemed to get along. Ed Garner remarks, "Aron Kincaid is a fabulous guy. He was the most dedicated, serious guy I ever worked with who wanted to become a movie star. He actually lived, breathed and ate show business. I was amazed. He couldn't believe that I couldn't give a hoot about it." Quinn O'Hara too enjoyed working with Aron. She exclaims, "He is one of the nicest people you ever want to meet. He is cheerful, upbeat, considerate and very talented. He is a lot of fun to work with. I didn't interact much with Ed Garner or the other kids because I really only had two brief scenes with them when I walked through the pool area and the girls' bedroom."

Returning the compliments, Aron Kincaid says, "Nancy Sinatra was nice but I adored Quinn O'Hara. I had known her for a few years prior to this. She was a wonderful girl and an actual beauty queen—Miss Scotland. She had been at Universal when I was there. I had always said that once they put her in color, everything would change. She looked great in black and white but nothing like she did in person.

"Ed Garner and I shared a trailer," continues Aron. "He is a good friend to this day and we have lunch together about every five months or so. He was in more beach films than Frankie and Annette though to my knowledge he didn't have many speaking lines. But there he was getting billing and appearing in all the fan magazines. It didn't matter to him. He had no interest for the acting thing. He came from a long line of actors. H.B. Warner was his grandfather and Ed didn't care about his lineage. I would get so frustrated with him sometimes. Once on tour to promote the movie I told him to stop acting like a teenager when he started to get out of hand."

But it was not all wine and roses on this set. Harvey Lembeck, who played Eric Von Zipper, the leader of the motorcycle gang, did not take to the golden-haired Aron Kincaid, who became friendly with Myrna Ross and Alberta Nelson who were part of Lembeck's group. "The three of us (or sometimes just two of us) would have nice long talks," recalls Aron. "Harvey got wind of this and became jealous in his own nasty little way. I only had two brief scenes with him. That was it. But he began saying horrible things about me to everyone. I'd be walking off after finishing a scene and he'd be sitting over with Bobbi Shaw and his Rat Pack. He really thought he *was* Eric Von Zipper. The other people were very nice but they all stuck next to him because they probably knew their paycheck would depend upon it. I'd pass by, he'd make a comment, which I couldn't hear, and Bobbi and the rest would all appreciatively laugh while looking over at me. It was pretty obvious what he was doing. I was not fond of him or Bobbi Shaw in the least.

"Bobbi had a standoffish attitude," continues Aron. "She fancied herself some brilliant comedienne and thought the material was beneath her. I didn't really have a single scene with her so I never had to interact with her. Even still, she acted as if I didn't exist. In the morning, you go in and people would all be saying 'Hello.' Bobbi would come breezing through with a sort of get-out-of-my-way type attitude. I really didn't care for her at all."

After filming wrapped, some of the cast was sent to the Disney Ranch to film the opening number titled "Bikini Party in a Haunted House," which was heavily choreographed. Aron Kincaid and Piccola Pupa sang lead vocals and recorded the song while on screen they are supported by Nancy Sinatra, Claudia Martin, Ed Garner, Luree Holmes, Salli Sachse, Peter Sachse, Patti Chandler, Sue Hamilton and Mary Hughes, among others. The song is fun and features Kincaid's rich baritone that nicely complimented Pupa's lightly accented voice. However, the number and the song never saw the light of day due to the film's title change, though Kincaid does own a copy of the record.

When Don Weis delivered the finished film to James H. Nicholson and Samuel Z. Arkoff at AIP, the producers were dismayed and deemed the film unreleasable. Trying to salvage their investment, Nicholson came up with the idea to add a sexy ghost in an invisible bikini and to re-cut the movie.

The movie was re-titled *The Ghost in the Glass Bikini* before the more appropriate *The Ghost in the Invisible Bikini* was settled on. Susan Hart was cast as the ghost with Boris Karloff as the newly departed who has to perform a good deed to earn eternal youth. Neither actor worked with any of the original cast. Their scenes together were tacked onto the beginning and end of the film. During the interim, shots of Hart in her invisible bikini were inserted, as they would freeze-frame the action when she was supposed to be talking to Tommy Kirk or Aron Kincaid.

To create the effect of a girl in an invisible bikini, they filmed Susan Hart wearing a blonde wig and a black bathing suit against a dark background. "It was nothing like the special effects they have now but is was about as good as it got back then," remarks Hart. "The only direction I received were cues from Ronnie Sinclair, the film editor, saying things like, 'Okay, there is a hammer over your head, duck!' Or, 'You're sitting on a chandelier, pretend like you are swinging back and forth.'"

It took approximately two weeks to shoot Hart's scenes in the invisible bikini. To make her hair stand out and look shiny against the black backdrop, they would spray it heavily with Caryl Richard's hairspray. Hart remembers, "The day they sprayed the wig and turned the heavy-duty lights on for the scene, the makeup girl came over to powder me and she turned her head away as she did. Then the guy who measures the light readings came near me and let out a 'whoa!' I thought, 'My gosh, what is the matter?' Ronnie started to come over and he wouldn't get close to me. I started to get puzzled. Finally, somebody came over and asked me, 'What's the matter?' I answered, 'I don't know but something is wrong because everybody who comes over to me looks at me funny, turns around and walks away. Please, what is it?' As it turned out, the hairspray contained sheep oil, and when it got hot, it started to smell. I couldn't smell it because those big fans were blowing it away from me."

Boris Karloff's scenes were all shot in a day. Since he was ill, there were never shots of him standing. Susan Hart adored working with him and film buff Aron

Publicity photograph from *The Ghost in the Invisible Bikini* (AIP, 1966) with (in descending order) Aron Kincaid, Nancy Sinatra, Patti Chandler, unidentified actor, Claudia Martin and Ed Garner (*courtesy the Billy Rose Theatre Collection, The New York Public Library for the Performing Arts, Astor, Lenox and Tilden Foundations*).

Kincaid made sure he was on the set to meet him. "I got to take some pictures of him and get his autograph," remembers Aron fondly. "Boris was quite elderly by then. But he was so nice! He had dark, sad, 'Omar Sharif' kind of eyes that were very hypnotic and difficult to look away from. And his skin was brown mixed with a kind of greenish gold as if he'd been cast out of some strange alloy. I thought he may have been part Indian."

As with the two previous AIP beach party movies, the closing credits do not feature any bikini-clad beauties such as Mary Hughes or Salli Sachse. Instead, the Bobby Fuller Four perform an instrumental version of "Geronimo" while the pajama-wearing boys and girls dance in the Chamber of Horrors.

The Ghost in the Invisible Bikini was a major box office disappointment for AIP. But the innovative James Nicholson and Sam Arkoff were smart enough to realize that the cycle of beach movies had come to an end. With the times a-changing in 1966, they began producing biker and hippie movies aimed at the restless youth of the day. When filming wrapped, Tommy Kirk and Deborah Walley immediately began working in *It's a Bikini World* for Trans American but it would not see the light of day until the spring of 1967.

This was the last AIP movie for contract players Bobbi Shaw and Luree Holmes. Mary Hughes, Salli Sachse, Ed Garner, Sue Hamilton and Patti Chandler went on to appear with Frankie Avalon and Annette Funicello in *Fireball 500* (1966). It was the end at AIP for all of them except Sachse and Chandler, who appeared in the spy adventure *The Million Eyes of Su-Muru* (1967) with Frankie Avalon and Shirley Eaton. Chandler moved on to other television projects for awhile, but Sachse kept working at AIP in *The Devil's Angels, The Trip* (both 1967), and *Wild in the Streets* (1968) before abandoning acting for a modeling and photography career. She currently resides in San Diego and is a psychotherapist. Chandler married in the seventies and stopped acting to raise a family. Mary Hughes also quit acting. She became a very successful physical fitness trainer in Malibu, where she resides with her husband. Bobbi Shaw teaches acting under the name Bobbi Shaw-Chance while Luree Holmes, now back to Luree Nicholson, worked as a family counselor and educator, and co-authored the book *How to Fight Fair with Your Kids and Win*.

As for Sue Hamilton, after being let go from AIP with most of the other contract players, Sue returned to modeling and was the cover girl for *Sheer Magic* beginning in May 1966. It has been reported on the Internet that the perky beauty passed away on September 2, 1969, and is buried at Forest Lawn Memorial Park in Los Angeles. The grave is marked Karen Sue Hamilton and sources believe it is the former *Playboy* Playmate and AIP beach girl.

If it is Hamilton buried there, it would one of many tragedies that plagued *The Ghost in the Invisible Bikini* beginning with the crew member who plunged to his death off a catwalk. Within a year or two of its release, a number of cast members were deceased as well. Bobby Fuller of the Bobby Fuller Four was found dead in a hotel room, Peter Sachse was killed in a plane crash, and in quick succession Francis X. Bushman, Boris Karloff, Patsy Kelly and Basil Rathbone had all passed away.

Jim Nicholson lost controlling shares in AIP after he divorced his wife in 1965 to marry Susan Hart. He continued with the company (producing biker and hippie films and the first blaxpoitation movie) until 1972, when he signed a deal with 20th Century–Fox. He was the executive producer of *The Legend of Hell House* (1973) and was readying *Dirty Mary, Crazy Larry* (1974) for production when he was diagnosed with a brain tumor. He passed away on December 10, 1972. Sam Arkoff held on to the company until 1979. He then sold it to Filmways, which was bought by Orion. Today MGM-UA holds the rights to all of the AIP movies except the 42 films from a limited partnership that Nicholson and Arkoff formed during the fifties. Sam passed away on September 1, 2001, from natural causes.

After Jim Nicholson's sudden death, his widow Susan Hart and his daughters Luree and Laura became frustrated with the boastful Sam Arkoff for taking so much credit for Nicholson's ideas and AIP's success in his autobiography and the AMC documentary *It Conquered Hollywood! The Story of American International Pictures*. Luree quipped, "Sam had been re-writing history for years." She and her sisters are in the process of writing their own book about AIP. Most people agree that Jim as the creative force behind AIP was the show and Sam the business.

Louis Arkoff understands their feelings but defends his father and offers another point of view. "Here is the best way to look at this," he opines. "Twenty-five years after AIP started, the last thing my dad would have imagined was that the small, little, seemingly inconsequential movies he made in the fifties and sixties would achieve a bigger-than-life cult status. It's not as if Jim and Sam were like Sam Goldwyn who had a filmography of great movies. They made these teenage movies in order to make a buck. It's now almost 50 years and their movies still have a cult status! Part of that cult status was achieved through a very outgoing, forceful and very public personality that my dad had. AIP was known for Jim and Sam. They made mutual decisions creatively. As far as working with the directors and going to the set, Jim did more of that. Dad would come on the set when there was a problem. He ran the business side but everything creative was jointly decided. But my dad as a living being was bigger than life and an entertaining man. He was also an incredible public speaker. During the AIP era, at all of the film conventions he would speak out against the studios. He would give these incredible speeches and get front-page space in the trade papers with pictures of him always with a cigar in his mouth.

"With Sam being a bigger-than-life character, he wound up taking a great degree of the credit," continues Louis. "It was given to him and he was honored for it because he was alive and Jim wasn't. The interesting thing is that Jim was 56 years old when he died. He was never a public figure. He never was a public character. He was basically a studio head executive who silently did his work. I thoroughly believe that if Jim had not died, he would have become a very well-known, successful producer. But he didn't and he wasn't. As far as my dad taking any credit and saying 'I made 500 films,' yes he could have said 'Jim and I made 500 films' but Jim had been dead for over 30 years. Don't forget, my dad had quite a successful career after Jim left with films such as *Dressed to Kill* and *The Amityville Horror*."

Memorable Lines

(Ripper introduces his curvy, seductive bikini-clad daughter Sinistra to Myrtle's nephew Bobby who follows the girl, abandoning his girlfriend Vicki.)

RIPPER: Men do seem to like her for some reason.

MYRTLE: I can think of three reasons—38-24-36. Yii!

Reviews

Margaret Harford, *Los Angeles Times*—"Little to distinguish it from its predecessors...."

Glenn Hawkins, *Los Angeles Herald-Examiner*—"A ghostess who is the mostess turns a haunted house into a lair of laughter...."

Mandel Herbstman, *The Film Daily*—"A ghostly story is washed with wave upon wave of pop songs and spirited dances. The picture aims mainly at fun and frolic. The pace is wild and zany."

Sy Oshinsky, *Motion Picture Herald*—"A haunted house rocking and rolling from an invasion of bikini-clad teenage girls and their beach boys provides the setting for a bright 'fun' picture that should keep a youthful audience happy and smiling."

James Powers, *The Hollywood Reporter*—"The picture is as limp and pointless as an unfilled bikini."

Variety—"Another combination of comedy and spooks. Former 'beach' types compete with old-hand comedians for laughs. Disappointing are the waste of Susan Hart (who has earned a better vehicle by now than this carbon copy of more successful films). All in all, a good try but short on script and inspiration."

Awards and Nominations

Boxoffice: "Stars of the Future"—Nancy Sinatra, second place

Boxoffice "Stars of the Future"—Deborah Walley, fifth place

Photoplay Gold Medal Award nomination: "Most Promising New Star—Male"—Aron Kincaid

Teen Screen Award: "Most Promising New Female Personality"—Quinn O'Hara

★ *27* ★

Out of Sight (1966)

The way "in" plot to wipe out way out music!

Fun: ★★★
Surfing: ★
Boy watching: ★
Girl watching: ★★★★
Music: ★★★★
Scenery: ★★★

Release date: May 12, 1966. Running time: 87m. Box office gross: Not available. DVD release: Not as of January 2005.

Jonathan Daly (*Homer*), Karen Jensen (*Sandra*), Robert Pine (*Greg*), Carole Shelyne (*Marvin*), Wende Wagner (*Scuba*), Maggie Thrett (*Wipeout*), Deanna Lund (*Tuff Bod*), Rena Horten (*Girl from FLUSH*), John Lawrence (*Big Daddy*), Jimmy Murphy (*Mousie*), Norman Grabowski (*Huh!*), Forrest Lewis (*Mr. Carter*), Deon Douglas (*Mike*), Bob Eubanks (*M.C.*), Pamela Rodgers (*Madge*), Vicki Fee (*Janet*), Coby Denton (*Tom*), Billy Curtis (*Man from FLUSH*), John Lodge (*John Stamp*). Not credited: Richard Dawson, Teri Garr. Special Guest Stars: Gary Lewis and the Playboys, Freddie and the Dreamers, Dobie Gray, The Turtles, The Astronauts and The Knickerbockers.

Universal Pictures. *Produced by*: Bart Patton. *Directed by*: Lennie Weinrib. *Screenplay by*: Larry Hovis. *Story by*: Dave Asher and Larry Hovis. *Music*: Al de Lory, Fred Darian, Nick Venet. *Music Supervisor*: Nick Venet. *Director of Photography*: Jack Russell, A.S.C. *Art Director*: Loyd Papez. *Set Decorator*: Audrey A. Blasdel. *Sound*: Corson Jowett. *Unit Production Manager*: Abby Singer. *Title by*: Pacific Title. *Film Editor*: Jack Woods. *Makeup*: Bud Westmore. *Hair Stylist*: Larry Germain. *Costume Designer*: Helen Colvig. *Assistant Director*: Thomas J. Schmidt. The ZZR by: George Barris Custom Car. *Motorcycles*: Yamaha. *Sportswear by*: Catalina. Filmed in Techniscope. Color by Technicolor.

"Malibu Run" by Jim Karstein, Leon Russell, Gary Lewis and T. Leslie, performed by Gary Lewis and the Playboys. "It's Not Unusual" by Gordon Mills and Les Reed, performed by the Knickerbockers. "Funny Over You" by Freddie Garrity, performed by Freddie and the Dreamers. "Baby, Please Don't Go" by Joe Williams, performed by the Astronauts. "A Love Like You" by Quinn and Jones, performed by Freddie and the Dreamers. "She'll Come Back" by Nita Garfield and Howard Kaylan, performed by the Turtles. "(Out of Sight) Out on the Floor" by Fred Darian and Alfred V. de Lory, performed by Dobie Gray.

After wiping out with *Wild Wild Winter*, the team of producer Bart Patton and director Lennie Weinrib redeemed themselves with the enjoyable spy spoof a-go-go, *Out of Sight*. A pretty beach bunny discovers that a madman named Big D is planning to vaporize the rock acts hired to perform at the upcoming Teen Fair that he is sponsoring. She and her ditzy friend seek the help of secret agent John Stamp but it is actually his butler masquerading as the spy who agrees to take the assignment. The film's running joke is that Big D wants to rid the world of that "annoying, popular British group whose members each sport a mop of long hair." This tease leads the audience to believe that the Beatles will appear but instead we get Freddie and the Dreamers, one of the lesser Beatles imitators to invade the shores of the U.S.

Though the plot is inane, there are some amusing scenes in this entertaining film. Screenwriter Larry Hovis succeeds best with the witty lines written around the shapely assassins Wende Wagner as Scuba, Maggie Thrett as Wipeout and Deanna Lund as Tuff Bodd hired to stamp out Stamp. After revealing her name, Homer says to Scuba, "What do your friends call you?" She coos with a seductive look, "Easy." When Mousie asks, "Wipeout, did you come all the way from Hawaii on that board?" She replies drolly, "Sure. I caught a good wave." Wipeout then relaxes dancing to the sounds of the Astronauts on the shore, prompting one teenager to exclaim, "She must be at least 22!" When Tuff Bod is told her assignment is to kill special agent John Stamp, she remarks, "Groovy! I've always wondered— now I'll find out." Big D asks, "What is that?" Tuff Bod responds, "What makes him so special." Throw in the charming and curvy Karen Jensen as the bewildered beach bunny and you have a feast for girl watchers.

For boy watchers, though, the film is a washout. Resident shirtless surf movie hunks such as Aron Kincaid, Steve Rogers and Mike Nader are nowhere in sight. Instead the goofy-looking Jonathan Daly and virile Robert Pine hold center stage and are always covered up. (There are a few no-name beach boys to look at occasionally.) Daly has a boyish charm as the inept butler who desperately wants to emulate his boss and become a top-notch secret agent. His bungling is reminiscent of Jerry Lewis and it is to Daly's credit that he never makes his character annoyingly stupid but just naïve in the ways of spying. His pairing with Carole Shelyne as the boy-crazy Marvin works well.

All the musical acts deliver rockin' performances. Gary Lewis and the Playboys stand out with the opening number "Malibu Run" while the Turtles go psychedelic singing "She'll Come Back." The Knickerbockers' version of "She's Not Unusual" almost tops Tom Jones'. Though Freddie and the Dreamers and Dobie Gray seem out of place in a beach party movie, they offer catchy tunes that are performed at the end of the movie at the teenage fair.

Overall, *Out of Sight* is lots of fun, expertly photographed and nicely populated with a bevy of shapely bikini-clad lovelies and an impressive array of rock acts.

The Story

Beach babe Sandra accidentally overhears a conversation between maniacal Big D and his henchmen Mousie and Huh!, in which they plan to execute some nefarious scheme at the upcoming Teenage Fair. Urged by her boy-crazy girlfriend Marvin with the horn-rimmed glasses, Sandra goes to secret agent John Stamp for help, but on arriving at his home, mistakes his butler Homer for the renowned spy. Homer wants to be a secret agent so he masquerades as John Stamp while the real Stamp recuperates in the hospital from injuries sustained from a bomb explosion caused by the bungling Homer on a mission.

Homer drives Stamp's hot rod, the ZZR, to Sandra's home and sets up his base of operation. As they travel, two agents from FLUSH, a gorgeous blonde and a dwarf riding in a sidecar motorcycle, pursue them but Homer thwarts the duo. Making it safely back to Sandra's place, Homer is introduced to her inventor father Mr. Carter, who reveals that he has been hired by Big D to work on a secret project. Homer awakes the next day to the smitten Marvin sitting on his bed and she immediately sets her eyes for the agent, later admitting she "digs the weird ones."

At Big D's, the Knickerbockers audition to gain entrance as performers at the Teenage Fair. Mousie then announces to the teenagers that Big D has signed the most popular British group with the foppish long hair for the fair. As the kids play volleyball on the sand, Homer meets Sandra's suave car-crazy boyfriend Greg while continuing his investigation. Big D is on to Homer after Mousie overhears Marvin boast to the other kids about him and he sends for his top assassin Scuba. Clad in a bikini top and scuba wear, the seductive agent confronts Homer on the docks, where he learns of a secret underwater entrance to Big D's. The wily agent wannabe jumps into the water as Scuba aims her spear gun at him but she misses. Big D reprimands Scuba for missing her target and explains to Mousie and Huh! his master plan of wiping out the world's rock groups. He is secretly eavesdropped on by Homer.

Karate-chopping FLUSH agent Wipeout arrives in Malibu on a surfboard from Hawaii to finish off Homer. Huh! and Mousie meet her on the beach. After the curvaceous assassin with the long jet-black hair knocks Huh! out with a powerful karate chop to the neck, the behemoth becomes smitten. Before attending to her assignment, Wipeout dances on the shore to the sounds of the Astronauts before luring Homer to a private pad. The two fight and, just as Wipeout is about to finish Homer off with a karate chop, a jealous Huh! walks in and sees lipstick on Homer's cheek. He goes to karate chop Homer and knocks out Wipeout, thwarting her objective.

Frustrated by the ineptness of his agents, Big D unleashes his secret weapon, Tuff Bod. With flaming red hair, clad in a black leotard under a see-through dress, the agent is a knockout. Snooping around Big D's, Homer stumbles across Tuff Bod "selling Girl Scout cookies." While trading witty repartee, Big D's henchman Huh! sneaks up behind Homer and knocks him unconscious. He awakens shackled to a perpetual tape deck that plays the same song over and over. Big D leaves Tuff Bod to watch over Homer as a horrible 1920s tune plays incessantly. She tires of the song and puts on a groovy tune to dance to. When she releases Homer to do the Frug with her, he tricks her, straps her to Big D's device and escapes.

After foiling these three attempts on his life, Homer follows Big D and his gang to the Teenage Fair the next day. After a wild chase, the bad guys capture Homer. Freddie and the Dreamers perform on stage to open the fair. Tom finds Homer being held in a tool shed and, with the help of one of Mr. Carter's inventions, frees the agent. Big D's plan is foiled when Carter uses his laser device on him, Mousie and Huh! as they try to capture Freddie and the Dreamers. The gang thanks Homer and he tries to let down Marvin, who admits that she knew all along that he was not John Stamp but his butler. Homer is shocked but flattered that Marvin liked him anyway. As they are about to kiss, Homer is ejected from the ZZR and lands in the sidecar of the Girl from FLUSH, who is really secret agent John Stamp in disguise. He berates his butler for driving his ZZR.

Behind-the-Scenes

Out of Sight was the third beach party movie from producer Bart Patton and director Lennie Weinrib. It was also the first beach movie to spoof the spy genre, which was so prevalent during the mid-sixties due to the success of the James Bond films. AIP previously released *Dr. Goldfoot and the Bikini Machine* (1965); the cast was populated with actors from its *Beach Party* movies but the film was set in San Francisco with nary a shot on the beach.

When Patton's movie was announced in the trades, the title of the film was the ridiculous *Thunder Blunder* and Richard Dawson was attached as the star. The movie was eventually re-titled *Out of Sight* and Dawson only appeared in an unbilled cameo as the manager of a rock group. "Richard was never slated to star in this," reveals Bart Patton. "That was just planted by the studio publicist, I am sure. Dawson was friendly with Lennie so he did the bit at the end as a favor."

Comedian and actor Larry Hovis, another friend of Weinrib's, wrote the *Out of Sight* screenplay. He was better known for his year-long stint on *Rowan and Martin's Laugh-In* and for playing POW Sgt. Carter on the hit comedy series *Hogan's Heroes*, which also featured Richard Dawson.

Now ensconced on the lot at Universal Pictures, Bart Patton and Lennie Weinrib were obligated to cast actors contracted to the studio. "This old broad named Monique James was the head of the talent school at Universal," says Patton with a laugh. "She was powerful and went way back with the studio. You didn't want to cross her."

Jonathan Daly was an up-and-coming comedian making his film debut. He previously hit it big in Australia and co-starred on the television series *The Delo and Daly Show* before returning to the U.S. Carole Shelyne was a former dancer (billed as "The Girl with the Horn Rimmed Glasses" on *Shindig*) who was now trying to make it as an actress. Pretty blonde Karen Jensen, whom the studio was grooming for major movie stardom, played the female lead while Maggie Thrett, Deanna Lund and Wende Wagner appeared as the three shapely assassins hired to off Jonathan Daly.

The role of Jensen's boyfriend went to Robert Pine. Arriving in Hollywood in April of 1964, Pine began appearing in such television series as *Kraft Suspense Theatre*, *The Virginian* and *Convoy*. He made his film debut in the Western *Gunpoint* (1966) starring Audie Murphy and Joan Staley before landing the role in *Out of Sight*. "I can't remember if I had to audition for this or if I just got the part," says Pine. "But at that time anything I did, I was just grateful for getting a chance to act. But sure I would have liked to have been doing more of an A-picture than a B-picture.

"I thought *Out of Sight* had a cornball script," continues Pine with a laugh. "I

In *Out of Sight* (Universal, 1966) beach babe Karen Jensen tries to distract her car-crazy boyfriend Robert Pine from his hot rod (*courtesy the Billy Rose Theatre Collection, The New York Public Library for the Performing Arts, Astor, Lenox and Tilden Foundations*).

played up the pomposity of my character but I wouldn't say it was one of my finest hours. I thought it was a very underwritten part. I had to make my mark quickly in what I did because there was no extended scenes or anything. I would have loved to have Jonathan Daly's part. He seemed to have a lot of fun with it but he obviously was better suited for it than I was."

Big, brawny, blonde Norman Grabowski, who played Huh!, was a staple of teenage movies of the late fifties and sixties, usually playing threatening loudmouth tough guys or dopey big lunks. His credits include *High School Confidential!* (1958), *Girls Town* (1959), *College Confidential* (1960), *Roustabout* (1964), *Girl Happy, The Monkey's Uncle* and *Sergeant Deadhead* (all 1965).

"We were really forced by the studio to use almost everybody in this film," reveals Bart Patton. "Karen Jensen was not a strong leading lady. But Jonathan Daly and Robert Pine were fine and I thought Carole Shelyne was cute. There was a spy girl character named Scuba where we wanted to cast this wonderful black actress whose name escapes me. She did a lot of television and movies. Universal would not allow a black actress to appear opposite Jonathan Daly, which we found absolutely absurd. There was barely anything between the characters. Just a bit of a come-on and then she tries to shoot him. It was no big deal. We wound up having to hire Wende Wagner, who happened to be the wife of the chief casting director at Universal."

Though actors known to younger audiences were significant to the beach movies, the rock acts were equally or even more important to lure fickle teenagers into the theaters. Patton, once again following in the tradition he started with *Beach Ball* and *Wild Wild Winter*, hired another outstanding line-up of musical talent. However, he let one major group slip away. "Dennis Jakob was a filmmaker that I was friendly with from UCLA and contacted me in 1965 while we were prepping *Out of Sight*," recalls Patton. "Promoters were always coming to us with demo tapes to pitch their musical clients. Dennis came by our offices at Universal and played us their demo. I said, 'Nah, I don't think they'd work in our picture. Good luck, Dennis.' It was Jim Morrison and the Doors. I have the distinct honor of turning down the Doors for *Out of Sight*."

Gary Lewis and the Playboys, who had appeared previously in *A Swingin' Summer* before they hit it big, are top-billed here. They perform "Malibu Run," their only surf–hot rod-related recording other than "Little Miss Go-Go." Representing the British invasion was Freddie and the Dreamers, who by this time could see that their popularity in the U.S. had waned since hitting No.1 on the charts with "I'm Telling You Now" in 1965. Dobie Gray, who scored with "The In Crowd," was the third act who had chart success previous to his appearance. This was the third film for the Astronauts and although the Midwest group never had major chart success with their recordings they were a favorite of the teenage set due to their surfing sound. *Out of Sight* was rounded out with two up-and-coming groups, the Turtles and the Knickerbockers.

"We filmed the big musical finale on a set similar to the one they used on *Shindig*," says Bart. "But there was no audience. I couldn't afford to fill the set with screaming teenyboppers so we intercut stock footage. One of my major dancers in that was Teri Garr. We were friends and I had seen her on a lot of sets either as an extra or a dancer. I'm sitting there with her and all these other girls shimmying on the stage and Francis Coppola comes to visit. He says to me, 'Bart, I envy you. I need this. I want to direct these kinds of movies.' At that moment he was writing the screenplay for *Patton*. Needless to say, we know what he went on to."

Recalling the film's rock groups, Robert Pine says, "I never had anything to do with them. Quite honestly, I was never crazy about this music. I thought it was really goofy having us sit around listening to them play. They had every gimmick in the world going in this film. They had all these different rock groups to try to cover every base possible to get an audience."

Out of Sight was a two- to three-week shoot with beach scenes filmed at Zuma Beach in Malibu. "Lennie and I were paid $10,000 apiece provided we didn't go over budget," reveals Bart. "If we did, the amount was to be subtracted from our ten grand, so talk about pressure. We built a beach house set right at the end of Point Dume Beach. We shot Gary Lewis and the Playboys performing on the deck and other scenes with the actors around the house. Some of the interiors were also filmed there looking out onto the ocean."

Recalling the film, Karen Jensen remarked in *Fantasy Femmes of Sixties Cinema*, "I remember that I had never worked harder and got less sleep in my life while doing this film. There was no time off. Most of the exteriors were filmed on Zuma Beach. And we spent most of our time there. After doing a long day's work, the cast would sit around for awhile because we were so tired, and then we'd all race home to get four hours sleep before we had to show up again. It was most exhausting. But it was a nice experience working with other young actors and I made a lot of friends. My leading man was Jonathan Daly and I liked him a lot. He is very talented. Deanna Lund was very friendly and we worked together again on a film for television. Carole Shelyne and I became roommates and I became very close with an actress named Rena Horten. Even though it was a short shoot, the cast would hang out together and we became like a big family."

Robert Pine concurs, "It was quite pleasurable working on this. Bart Patton was a really nice guy. Jonathan Daly was a lot of fun and we had a good time. I think this was Jonathan's first big picture—if you can call it a big picture. I had done a few parts in films but we were all relatively new. Karen was a very, very delightful young lady. Norman Grabowski and Jimmy Murphy were nice guys too. I happened to run into Jimmy not too long ago. I reminded him that we worked on *Out of Sight* and he just rolled his eyes. Carole Shelyne was very pleasant. She became a very prominent casting lady in town. She cast a lot of commercials and taught acting for awhile.

"I have one funny story about Carole Shelyne," continues Pine. "Every Thanksgiving in Hollywood they had the Santa Claus Lane Parade as it was called then. I traveled in a car with Carole and they had our names on a banner alongside the car. I don't think anybody knew us from Adam. As we were getting closer to the reviewing stand, Carole complained that everybody always mispronounced her name. The correct way to say it is She-lynn. As we went by, the announcer said, 'Coming by us now are the stars of the upcoming Universal release *Out of Sight*—Carole She-lynn and Robert Pi-nay.' He pronounced her name correctly but all of a sudden I became this French actor. A lot of my friends to this day still jokingly call me that."

"Jonathan Daly was a funny guy," comments Bart Patton. "But he was probably too old for his part as well. He got away with it more than the other guys because he wasn't supposed to be in college. There's a funny story regarding the exterior of secret agent John Stamp's house. We couldn't get permission to shoot it so one night I sneaked a camera home from the studio and went up to where I lived in the Hollywood Hills. I zoomed in and shot that half-arched house you see in the movie."

Despite its cast of newcomers and roster of musical acts, what received the most publicity was the automobile named the ZZR, which was designed for the movie by George Barris at a cost of $22,000. Barris was famous for his outlandish automobiles such as the ones he built for the television shows *The Munsters* and *Batman.* Inspired by the Aston Martin from *Goldfinger,* the ZZR featured twin eight cylinder engines, flame-throwers in each fender, a parachute that disconnected to shroud chasing cars and a tar and feather feature. The car's nine-foot hood was removable, revealing two chrome-laden engines. The metalflake painted body was a replica of a Model T Ford. "George Barris had deep deals with people that we never knew about," remarks Bart Patton. "The cost for the car came from our budget but we didn't know how much. Of course, the studio felt George would give the movie so much publicity it was worth the money.

Behind the scenes on *Out of Sight* with (*left to right*) Jonathan Daly, unidentified actress, Robert Pine, Carole Shelyne, producer Bart Patton and Universal honcho David Hammond (*courtesy Bart Patton*).

"We went to George's shop and sat down with his drawings," continues Patton. "We approved the design and the car was definitely built for this movie."

The Barris-designed car at times was treated as the star of the movie. Karen Jensen says, "We shot the scenes with that car on this out-of-the-way road where we did a lot of the chase scenes. I never got to ride in the hot rod but I did get to sit in it and touch it and pose next to it. They babied that car. It was a big deal having it in the movie." Robert Pine adds in agreement, "At that time George Barris was a famous car guy so the auto was a very big deal indeed."

At one point Lennie Weinrib boasted to journalist Vernon Scott of the UPI that he and Patton were "the Borscht Belt of the motion-picture industry." This had to do with the team delivering quality films for the teenage audience with shooting schedules of no longer than 15 days and budgets under $500,000. Despite the fast-paced filmmaking, Weinrib treated his cast with the utmost respect. Karen Jensen said fondly, "Lennie always had a smile on his face. I never had any problems with him because he was easy to get along with. We had a very short shooting schedule and he managed to get it all done without anyone getting angry with him. That's a pretty good feat in this business."

As with Patton's previous film *Wild Wild Winter,* Universal also capitalized on the musical performances in *Out of Sight,* issuing a soundtrack LP through Decca Records. All the musical acts from the movie are included along with instrumentals from the Nick Venet Orchestra. "I didn't make a dime off of the soundtrack releases," says Patton with a laugh. "All I got was a credit."

Regarding his movies, Bart Patton commented to Vernon Scott in 1966, "Our pictures are farcical fun, adventure comedies. We never deal with teenage jokes or teenagers' problems. The kids are too hip and sophisticated to be talked down to. And they don't like to see a lot of downbeat stuff either."

Out of Sight was the last collaboration between producer Patton and director Lennie Weinrib, who were dropped from Universal. Patton went on to produce just one more movie, Francis Ford Coppola's *The Rain People* (1969) starring James Caan and Shirley Knight. Weinrib never directed a film again but became a mainstay of Saturday morning television. He wrote every episode of *H.R. Pufnstuf* and voiced a number of animated characters on such cartoons as *The Pink Panther Show, Scooby Doo, Where Are You!, Help! It's the Hair Bear Bunch, The Pebbles and Bamm Bamm Show, Inch High, Private Eye, Hong Kong Phooey, The New Adventures of Batman,* etc. He currently lives in South America.

None of the *Out of Sight* cast hit the big time but most of them kept acting for a period of time. Audiences remember Jonathan Daly best as Bobbie Jo Bradley's bungling suitor Orrin Pike on the last season of *Petticoat Junction.* In the seventies, he became a fixture in Walt Disney movies including *The $1,000,000 Duck* (1971), *Superdad* (1974) and *The Shaggy D.A.* (1976), his last known credit.

Pretty Karen Jensen should have appeared in more beach party movies but she arrived in Hollywood as the genre was fading. Instead she landed on television, playing an ambitious starlet in the underrated TV dramatic series *Bracken's World,* co-starring Laraine Stephens and Linda Harrison and set in a movie studio.

Blonde Carole Shelyne danced regularly on *Shindig* from 1964 to 1966. She became so popular on the show that she released a record capitalizing on her trademark look in 1965 entitled "Boys Do Make Passes At Girls Who Wear Glasses" but it failed to chart. Shelyne next tried acting and guest starred on a number of television series including *The Man from U.N.C.L.E., Star Trek* and *Here Come the Brides.* In 1976, she co-wrote and starred in the supernatural thriller *Dark August,* her last known credit. She married actor J.J. Barry and became a very successful casting director.

Two of the film's shapely assassins, Wende Wagner and Deanna Lund, would also find success on television. Wagner played the intrepid secretary Lenore "Casey" Case on *The Green Hornet* while Lund was cast as glamorous intergalactic castaway Valerie Scott on Irwin Allen's fourth sci-fi series, *Land of the Giants.*

Post–*Out of Sight,* statuesque beach girl Pamela Rodgers (with her strawberry–blonde hair and a Betty Boop–type voice) became a regular on the television sitcom *Hey, Landlord* starring Will Hutchins and Sandy Baron. More memorable was her one-season (1969–70) stint on *Rowan and Martin's Laugh-In.* She had previously worked with the comedy team in their unsuccessful horror movie spoof *The Maltese Bippy* (1969), playing a porn starlet.

Robert Pine reunited with Jonathan Daly in the war film *The Young Warriors* (1967) and then appeared in the western *Journey to Shiloh* (1967). After three years, Universal dropped Pine ("the handwriting was on the wall") and the young actor went freelance. He played a minor role in *The Graduate* (1967) and worked steadily on television doing guest stints and television movies. In 1969, he wed actress Gwynne Gilford, the daughter of actress Anne Gwynne, and they would go on to raise a son and a daughter. In 1975, Pine was handed a nice-sized role in John Schlesinger's *Day of the Locust* but most of his scenes were cut. He then went from the cult sci-fi flick *Empire of the Ants* (1977) to his best remembered role as Sgt. Getraer in the hit television series *CHiPs* (1977–83).

CHiPs became a huge hit, especially with the younger audiences. Most of the adulation went to the good-looking, well-built Erik Estrada. With his oh-so-tight uniform, the Latin heartthrob became one of the biggest sex symbols of the late seventies and early eighties. His soaring popularity sometimes wrecked havoc on the set. "Erik walked off twice," says Robert. "The one time I didn't agree with his decision was when he did it during the middle of the season. It delayed things and people had schedules. I thought that was in some way not the greatest thing to do. Erik and Larry Wilcox both had their moments but it was like any family where there are times when you disagree. But overall I enjoyed working on *CHiPs* very much." Daytime fans will recognize Pine for his recurring role as Stephen Logan, Jr., the father of grasping Brooke Logan Forrester, on *The Bold and the Beautiful*, a part he has played on and off since 1988. In 1993, Pine received good notices cast against type as a child molester in *Big Boys Don't Cry* on television's *CBS After School Break*. His most recent motion picture is *Confidence* (2003) with Edward Burns and Dustin Hoffman.

As for *Out of Sight*, Robert Pine concludes laughing, "I saw it a couple of years ago for the first time in decades. I watched it shaking my head the whole time because I couldn't believe how lame it was! But I did have fun making it."

Memorable Lines

(After overhearing Big D's plan to destroy the Teenage Fair, Sandra races to tell her girlfriend Marvin who is ogling a surfer from the deck of the beach house.)

SANDRA: Marvin, listen to me!

MARVIN: He's pretty and he's all alone.

SANDRA: Marvin!

MARVIN: He's just my type—*a boy*!

Reviews

Loren G. Buchanan, *Motion Picture Herald*—"Combining the features of a beach film ... rock-and-roll picture ... and a spy spoof ... producer Bart Patton and director Lennie Weinrib have come up with a wide-screen color mixture which should do well. Adults might be better advised to pass this one up...."

Edward Lipton, *The Film Daily*—"With a number of the top combos of the day ... sun, beach and surf, bright Technicolor photography and a gimmicked up plot providing a teen-age takeoff on the James Bond brand of picture, *Out of Sight* will have its devotees."

Motion Picture Exhibitor—"This combination of a beach girl picture and a spoof on secret agent films proves that American International has no copyright on such nonsense. It is fairly entertaining with its little known cast, including the bikini-clad bathing beauties, who perform their capers nicely. Jonathan Daly in the lead ... shows promise."

James Powers, *The Hollywood Reporter*—"*Out of Sight* is a teen-angled comedy with musical guest stars, but it is a weak entry even for this relatively undemanding field. The dialogue is trite and the characters vapid. There is no indication why it is called *Out of Sight*. It could more accurately be called *Out of Mind*."

Variety—"There's plenty to see—bikini-clad cuties, a souped-up jalopy and five top rock groups—for the teenage action market ... Pic moves along at go-go speed, serving as little more then a pegboard to display the rock 'n' roll groups, interspersed with the junior jet set continually dancing. Jonathan Daly is okay. Miss Jensen looks good in a bikini and is believable. Robert Pine is husky and handsome."

★ 28 ★

Wild Wild Winter (1966)

From the surf to the mountains ... The hot doggers and the surf bunnies have the sea sizzlin' and the ice meltin' with their singin', swingin' snow ball!

Fun: ★★
Surfing: ★
Boy watching: ★★
Girl watching: ★★
Music: ★★★★
Scenery: ★★★

Release date: January 5, 1966. Running time: 80m. Box office gross: Not available. DVD release: Not as of January 2005.

Gary Clarke (*Ronnie Duke*), Chris Noel (*Susan*), Steve Franken (*John*), Don Edmonds (*Burt*), Suzie Kaye (*Sandy*), Les Brown, Jr. (*Perry*), Vicky Albright (*Dot*), Jim Wellman (*Dean Carlson*), Steve Rogers (*Benton*), Val Avery (*Fox*), James Frawley (*Stone*), Dick Miller (*Rilk*), Mark Sturges (*Danny*), Anna Lavelle (*Bus Bit Girl*), Linda Rogers (*Trisha*), Fred Festinger (*Jake McCloskey*), Buck Holland (*McGee*), Darryl Vaughan (*Bob*) Loren Janes (*The Bear*), Paul Geary (*Larry*). Special Guest Stars: Jay and the Americans, The Beau Brummels, Dick and Dee Dee, The Astronauts and Jackie and Gayle

A Bart Patton—Lennie Weinrib Production. Universal Pictures release. *Produced by*: Bart Patton. Directed by: Lennie Weinrib. Written by: David Malcolm. Director of Photography: Frank Phillips, A.S.C. Film Editor: Jack Woods. Associate Producer and Unit Production Manager: Harry R. Sherman. Music: Jerry Long. Music Supervisor: Frank Wilson. Set Decorator: Victor Gangelin. Sound: Lambert Day. Costume Designer: Paula Giokaris. Men's Wardrobe: Walt Hoffman. Makeup: Rolf Miller. Hairstylist: Eve Newing. Assistant Director: Thomas J. Schmidt. Titles by Pacific Title. Surfboards by: Phil. Clothes for Beau Brummels by: Sy Devore. Filmed in Techniscope. Color by Technicolor.

"Wild Wild Winter" by Chester Pipkin, instrumental. "Heartbeats" by Al Capps and Mary Dean, performed by Dick and Dee Dee. "Our Love's Gonna Snowball" by Al Capps and Mary Dean, performed by Jackie and Gayle. "A Change of Heart" by Chester Pipkin and Mark Gordon, performed by the Astronauts. "Two of a Kind" by Victor Millrose and Tony Bruno, performed by Jay and the Americans. "Just Wait and See" by Ronald Elliot, performed by the Beau Brummels.

Wild Wild Winter is one of the lesser beach party movies released during the mid-sixties. Three college guys keep striking out with their coed girlfriends due to their prudish sorority leader, Susan. They coax ladies' man Ronnie away from the beach bunnies in Malibu to attend their school to melt the icy veneer from Susan.

To do that, he has to pretend to be a champion skier when in fact he is a surfer. All the ingredients are here to make a successful movie—nicely photographed ski footage, romantic misunderstandings, lots of pretty girls and good-looking guys, and an array of musical guest stars. But *Wild Wild Winter* is a letdown that is hampered by an unoriginal script with a weak subplot of some shadowy mobster-types who threaten to foreclose on the school. The movie's major assets are leading lady, Chris Noel, the energetic supporting cast and the peppy musical numbers.

Gary Clarke tries to lighten things up as Ronnie but he and Steve Franken as his rival are too long in the tooth to be believable as college students. Pretty Chris Noel gives her usual perky, agreeable performance and looks stunning against the snow-covered background. Handsome Steve Rogers as Benton stands out due to his charisma and movie star good looks, as does Don Edmonds for his clowning. Sexy redhead Linda Rogers has some good moments opposite Clarke on the beach in Malibu. Anna Lavelle, who was so good in *Beach Ball*, makes a cameo appearance as a bus passenger but she really should have had the part played by Vicky Albright, who gives a very bland and uninspired performance as one of the sorority girls. The bubbly Suzie Kaye, sporting dark hair just before she went blonde, plays the other.

The musical performers buoy *Wild Wild Winter* from being a total wipeout. Jay and the Americans rock on the rousing "Two of a Kind" as the entire cast dances. Another surreal musical highlight is Jackie and Gayle singing about their love snowballing while on the sandy shores of Malibu with swimsuit-clad boys and girls gyrating around them. The Beau Brummels and the Astronauts perform too but it is Dick and Dee Dee, looking like Sonny and Cher Lite, who stand out with their rendition of "Heartbeats."

The Story

Burt and Perry are transfer students newly arrived at Alpine College high up in the mountains where the student body seems to be majoring in skiing and romance. Two pretty coeds, dark-haired Sandy and blonde Dot, catch their eye on the slopes. Frat boy Benton tells the guys that the girls won't give them the time of day due to their Zeta Theta sorority leader "professional goodie-goodie" Susan Benchley, who thinks men should not be trusted or dated. When she is not doling out dating advice, Susan works as the assistant to Dean Carlson and is present when three shady characters from the mortgage company inform the Dean that he has a month to pay the outstanding debt or they will foreclose on the college.

Trying to impress the ski bunnies, Burt and Perry lie and tell them that their fathers are in the television and motion picture industry. They make a date for dinner but it is spoiled when Susan looks up their records and learns the truth—Burt's father owns a television repair shop and Perry's dad is a film projectionist. Burt and Perry are furious with Susan and come up with a plan to entice their fraternity brother Ronnie Duke to enroll in school and win over Susan even though she has a snooty fiancé named John.

In Malibu, Ronnie, the wave-riding lothario, has just completed another surfing lesson with red-haired Tricia and gives her one of his surfing medals to show that he cares about her. He gets the shapely girl to promise to keep it a secret but when her friend Sherry walks by after Ronnie leaves to take a phone call, the ecstatic beauty tells all. Ronnie at first refuses Burt's plea to come to Alpine as he has a good thing going in Malibu teaching surfing to 12 beautiful young women while romancing them on the side. However, things get pretty ugly for him when Tricia and Sherry gather all of Ronnie's other duped bikini-clad pupils and they read him the riot act. Needing to leave the sandy shores of California quickly, he takes Burt up on his offer.

Ronnie immediately impresses Benton and the other guys when he arrives by bus and is seen smooching with a dippy blonde whom he just met on the ride from LA. He starts his campaign to win Susan by pretending to be the son of a millionaire pineapple grower from Hawaii who has rejected his father's fortune to prove that he can make it on his own. Ronnie gets Susan to promise to keep his secret and to teach him to ski, cutting into the time she has to spend with her fiancé. A jealous John interrupts their idyllic first lesson on the slopes and scolds Susan for missing their ski date.

As the guys celebrate the headway Ronnie has made with the icy sorority leader, John stops by the frat house to let Ronnie know that he will be his new ski instructor in place of Susan. Foiled, Ronnie comes up with a new plan. Burt and Perry share a secret with Sandy and Dot that Ronnie is a ski champ feigning ignorance about the sport just to spend time with Susan. Ronnie's plot backfires again when Dean Carlson, seeing dollar signs, is delighted to learn that he is a champion of the slopes and the son of a millionaire. When he offers Ronnie the job of captain of the college ski team, John protests. Susan suggests that they compete to see who is the better skier. With the help of Benton and Burt, Ronnie wins the race by cheating. An outraged John accuses him of being a fraud. Disappointed in her fiancé's attitude, Ronnie wins Susan as well. But his good fortune quickly turns sour when Dean Carlson announces that Ronnie will lead the ski team in the next day's Intercollegiate Ski Championship.

To avoid skiing, Ronnie decides to lay low at a cabin just outside the campus. He makes a ski date with Susan and fakes twisting his ankle during his run. She takes him to the cabin to recuperate where she pledges her love to him. After finding two Malibu phone numbers in Ronnie's locker, a suspicious John hires a private detective to dig up dirt. The private dick heads to the beach where Trisha and the other girls give him an earful about Ronnie, which he shares with John. Susan happens by with supplies for the cabin and is shocked when she gets an earful about Ronnie. When she returns to the shack, a contrite Ronnie tries to confess to his charade since he has fallen in love with Susan. With vengeance in her heart, Susan doesn't give him a chance to speak and chloroforms him. She wraps him in bandages with a "I hate you, you rat!" attached and leaves him bound. A ravenous bear breaks into the cabin and chases Ronnie, who dons skis to escape from it. In the course of the chase, Ronnie wins the ski championship, getting Alpine College out of debt and winning the love of Susan as well.

Chris Noel as a frisky coed puts the romantic moves on a startled Gary Clarke, a college Romeo, in *Wild Wild Winter* (Universal, 1966).

Behind-the-Scenes

Impressed with footage of *Beach Ball*, Universal Pictures signed producer Bart Patton and director Lennie Weinrib to a seven-year contract. The studio was almost the last to get in on the teenage beach party craze and wanted the team to replicate their prior movie. Following the lead of AIP with *Ski Party*, they decided to set it in the snow. Sam Locke (still working under the pseudonym of David Malcolm) was recruited to write the screenplay. The film's working title was *Snow Ball* but it was changed at the last minute by Universal to *Wild Wild Winter* with the tag line "a surfin' snow ball." The film was budgeted at approximately $220,000 and finished under budget by $5,000.

"We shot this at Sam Goldwyn Studios and not on the Universal lot," reveals Bart Patton. "We were considered a sort of independent film so we were allowed to cast actors of our choosing and were not limited to Universal's contract players like we were with *Out of Sight*. Once the studio approved the leading actor, we had pretty much autonomy."

Patton and Weinrib cast *Beach Ball* actors Chris Noel ("She was great to work with and a good actress," remarks Bart Patton), Don Edmonds and Anna Lavelle

Wild Wild Winter's snow studs—Don Edmonds, Steve Rogers and Les Brown, Jr. (*courtesy the Billy Rose Theatre Collection, the New York Public Library for the Performing Arts, Astor, Lenox and Tilden Foundations*).

in this production. Edmonds says with a laugh, "Bart personally asked me to appear in this one too. He and Lennie *liked my style!*"

Steve Rogers, another friend of Bart Patton's, was hired to play Benton, the college guy who recruits his surfer friend Ronnie to come to school to romance Noel's Susan. "Steve Rogers was an old friend of mine for years," says Bart Patton. "His real name is Rick Rogers. He played Doc on the television series *Combat*. He was the heir to the American Linen Supply Company and independently wealthy. Rick was a bizarre actor. Some of these people were very strange but we had a sort of camaraderie amongst us though." Anna Lavelle, so perky and funny in *Beach Ball*, was unjustly reduced to a minor role and deserved better. Her broken romance with director Weinrib may have cost her a bigger part.

Noel once again was cast as the square coed who gets hip at the end. In virtually all of her movies, Chris played these virginal good girl roles—a sort of bikini-clad Doris Day. She remarks, "I didn't mind. I liked playing those innocent roles. It was fun. I loved Doris Day movies anyway."

What Chris did mind was the short hairstyle she sported in *Wild Wild Winter*. She explains, "I went to Gene Shacove who was one of the top celebrity hairstylists in Hollywood. It was his bright idea to cut my hair that short and I went along with it. I think he did the same thing with all the attractive girls when he first met them. '*Oh, come to my salon and I will give you a free haircut.*' Then he hit on you!

I think that movie *Shampoo* was based more on him than Jay Sebring, who was weird in his own way."

As with *Beach Ball*, when it came time to cast the leading man the producers turned to television for a recognizable name rather than someone better suited for the role. Gary Clarke, looking every bit his age if not older, was 29 years old when he landed the part of surfer stud Ronnie. Of Mexican and French descent, Clarke got his acting start at AIP playing the lead roles in such teenage exploitation fare as *How to Make a Monster* and *Dragstrip Riot* (both 1958). Fame came his way when he starred as cowpoke Steve Hill on the hit television western *The Virginian* from 1962 to 1964. After leaving the series, he could be seen in such obscure B-movies as *Strike Me Deadly* (1963) and *Passion Street, USA* (1964).

Clarke's rival for the pretty Chris Noel was Steve Franken as her preppy college boyfriend—who was 33 at the time! The role was basically a clone of prissy rich college boy Chatsworth Osborne, Jr., from television's *The Many Loves of Dobie Gillis*, a part Franken played from 1960 to 1963. When that series came to an end, he progressed to playing a high school teacher during the 1963–64 season on the drama series *Mr. Novak* starring James Franciscus. Though Franken had comedic talent, his being cast two years later as a college boy was absurd.

"Yes, Gary and Steve looked old," laughs Patton. "But all you had to do is look over at AIP. Who the hell were they starring? *Those people looked damn near 40!* I'm not sure how we came to settle on Gary. It might have had something to do with Universal but it escapes me now. But his age didn't matter because everybody in these beach movies was older than what they should have been. Gary had a dry sense of humor and had a subtlety that I loved. It may not have come across in the film but I thought he was wonderful."

Commenting on the casting, Don Edmonds says, "Gary Clarke (as well as Edd Byrnes in *Beach Ball*) were cast because the producers thought their name value would give the movie box office clout rather than because they were perfect for their roles. Yeah, they reached a little on the age with Gary and Steve Franken, who is a peach and a very funny guy. They stretched the age with me, too, if you want to know the truth. I was in my late twenties when we did this. We were *all* too old to be playing these roles. We weren't kids! But we all tried to act younger. I've been silly all my life, so has Aron Kincaid, so we were able to do it easier and believably compared to some of the other actors."

"Gary Clarke is a real *beauty*," continues Edmonds with a laugh. "He's a terrific guy and a really funny dude. Gary would put Chris Noel on the floor laughing in hysterics. But then he did that to *me* too. We were all staying in a hotel in Alpine Meadows. As with all location shoots, you have a tendency to bond with each other, and we absolutely did."

Chris agrees with Don and says, "Gary Clarke was a very funny guy. We got along very well. But I adored Steve Franken, who played my fiancé. I think he is just a superb actor. He was so humorous acting like a nerd and did the part so well. He never gave anyone any problems. There was no attitude with him at all."

Cast as a coed and the love interest of Don Edmonds, spunky brunette Suzie Kaye (whom Noel describes as being "a cutie") sang and danced as a Shark Girl in *West Side Story* (1961) and did a wild mambo on a spaceship in the low-budget *Women of the Prehistoric Planet* (1966). Fellow sorority sister Vicky Albright had appeared in a few television shows such as *Leave It to Beaver* before making her film debut in *Wild Wild Winter*. Les Brown, Jr., played Edmonds' buddy. The son of the famous bandleader, Brown previously co-starred in two unsuccessful television series, the sitcom *The Baileys of Balboa* and the daytime drama *The Young Married*.

Recalling his co-stars, Edmonds says, "Les Brown was a cool and very sweet guy. Steve Rogers and I became very friendly and formed a production company soon after this. Suzie Kaye is still my dear friend. She is terrific and a real pro. She came out of *West Side Story* and was a monster dancer in her day. Suzie went blonde after this and was in *Clambake* with Elvis and shaking her beads in some hippie movies. Those were really trippy days in Hollywood. It was the time of the riots on Sunset Strip and the Doors with Jim Morrison being the house band at the Whiskey a-Go-Go. It was great."

Bart Patton had a fairly large budget for musical talent and spent more than half of it on Jay and the Americans, who commanded a fee of $5,000. The Beau Brummels and the Astronauts received $1,500 per group, Dick and Dee Dee were paid $500, and Jackie and Gayle got $400. Motown Records later released the *Wild*

Wild Wild Winter producer Bart Patton (*left*) gives instructions to the film's lead, Gary Clarke (*courtesy Bart Patton*). That's Lennie Weinrib's reflection in the mirror.

Wild Winter soundtrack LP due to musical supervisor Frank Wilson's connection to the record company, where he sometimes worked as producer and recording artist.

A piece in *The Hollywood Reporter* announced that Universal was so pleased with the movie that it would be released to theaters in late October 1965. However, *Wild Wild Winter* was delayed until January 1966 but it proved to be another winner at the box office for producer Bart Patton and director Lennie Weinrib as it turned a profit for the studio. However, Patton never knew how much. He reveals, "I never got any of the gross figures. We were at the tail end of the whole era. Universal was lagging badly in terms of pop culture. When we started doing these pictures, AIP was beginning to wind down with the beach party films. We were competing with $1.5 million budgets."

Commenting on their winning formula, Patton said in *The Citizen-News* in 1966, "We believe kids are embarrassed by sex in the movies and they prefer cinema action. We especially stay away from shots of the anatomy. We don't hide it, but we don't accentuate this sort of stuff. We also play down love scenes and never let them get out of hand, so to speak. That's when you hear giggles at the wrong time, which can really louse up a movie. We put the emphasis on action—chases, races, dances, sight gags—because that's what we think the kids want to see." Weinrib commented further, "We're low-budget but never cheap. I think the number one reason for our success is that we don't play down to the young. You can't do that. Kids today are much too hip."

Chris Noel credits the lasting popularity of *Beach Ball* and *Wild Wild Winter* to the music. "The beach movies were great and a lot of that had to do with the rock 'n' roll stars," opines Chris. "It was very clever of producers like Bart Patton who put up-and-coming rock artists in the movies. Back then you didn't see popular artists on television like you do now."

Summing up his experience on *Wild Wild Winter*, Don Edmonds remarks, "That picture was a total blast and laughfest for the cast and crew from beginning to end. We all knew that we were just doing a piece of silliness and that's the way we acted off camera. I have very fond memories of this. Oh, if all the films I've been involved with had been that much fun. But alas they weren't and I've got the scars to prove it!"

Post–*Wild Wild Winter*, Gary Clarke starred in his second Western series, *Hondo*, but it was not a hit. Clarke had better luck writing scripts under his real name of Clarke F. L'Amoreaux for *Get Smart*. His most notable screen credit was the Don Murray–directed film *Childish Things* (1969), which was re-released as *Confessions of Tom Harris* in 1972. He worked intermittently during the seventies and eighties on television and returned to the big screen in the all-star Western *Tombstone* (1993). He last played a judge in the television-movie *My Son Is Innocent* (1996). Today he resides in Arizona and works in radio.

Some 35 years later, Don Edmonds attended (along with Gary Clarke) the celebrity-laden Chiller Theatre Convention on Halloween weekend 2003 in New Jersey. "Gary's still just as funny and nice a guy as you'll ever want to meet," says Don fondly. "We really enjoyed running into each other."

Memorable Lines

(After peeking at Burt and Perry's files, Susan reveals to Sandy and Dot that the guys' fathers were not in show business.)

SANDY: They were lying!

SUSAN: Look, I thought I drilled it into you. Most boys are not interested in love and marriage. It's just hi and goodbye.

Reviews

Boxoffice—"This fast-paced musical will please the audiences who tune in bouncy music for sound's sake and don't ask for too much in the way of story line to hang it on."

Loren G. Buchanan, *Motion Picture Herald*—"A rolling snowball, light and frothy but with very little substance...."

Kathleen Carroll, *New York Daily News*—"Don't be snowed by *Wild Wild Winter*. Under those ski clothes are just some beach party rejects."

James Powers, *The Hollywood Reporter*—"*Wild Wild Winter* is another of those beach party, ski-party pictures, with lots of pretty young things—male and female.... The Universal release occasionally shows a flicker of originality, of satire and sharp comment."

Robert Salmaggi, *New York Herald Tribune*—"*Wild Wild Winter* is another one of those rah-rah go go dum-dums with built-in pop rock 'n' roll groups, rosy-cheeked college girls, Jack Armstrong–type college boys, and a flimsy, silly plot to hang it all (or itself) on."

Howard Thompson, *The New York Times*—"Maybe *Wild Wild Winter* will make the teenagers tingle—the ones planning to attend a snow-draped college.... The picture is clean, at least and at most. Higher education? Swing, it, man!"

Variety—"*Wild Wild Winter* packs enough salable ingredients to be an okay entry for situations which like music with their entertainment. To whet eye appeal, a bevy of bikini-clad babes prance on the Malibu beach, and another set of youthful pulchritude supplants them for the snow and college sequences, where most of the action unfolds."

Archer Winsten, *New York Post*—"One of those surf-dance-sing-jive specialties that low-rate the youthful set by transferring their activities to a snow setting but providing lines and action too dismal to contemplate."

Awards and Nominations

Photoplay Gold Medal Award nomination: "Favorite Female Star"—Chris Noel

★ 29 ★

Catalina Caper (1967)

The nation's swinginest playground becomes the background for the most audacious crime of the century ... with the ocean's floor as a hideaway!

Fun: ★½
Surfing: ★
Boy watching: ★★
Girl watching: ★★★
Music: ★★
Scenery: ★★★

Release date: April 26, 1967. Running time: 84m. Box office gross: Not available.

DVD release: Part of *Mystery Science Theater 3000 Collection, Volume 1,* Wea Corp. (November 12, 2002)

Tommy Kirk (*Don Pringle*), Del Moore (*Arthur Duval*), Peter Duryea (*Tad Duval*), Robert Donner (*Fingers O'Toole*), Ulla Stromstedt (*Katrina*), Jim Begg (*Larry Colvis*), Sue Casey (*Anne Duval*), Venita Wolf (*Tina Moss*), Brian Cutler (*Charlie Moss*), Peter Mamakos (*Borman*), Lyle Waggoner (*Angelo*), Lee Deane (*Lakopolous*), Michael Blodgett (*Bob Draper*), Bonnie Lomann (*Redhead*), Britt Nilsson (*Brunette*), Donna Russell (*Blonde*), James Almanzar (*Sid*). Guest Stars: Carol Connors, Little Richard, The Cascades, Adrian Teen Models, Timothy Garland.

An Executive Pictures Corporation production. A Crown International release. *Produced by*: Bond Blackman, Jack Bartlett. *Directed by*: Lee Sholem. *Screenplay by*: Clyde Ware. *Story by*: Sam Pierce. *Executive Producer*: Sherman H. Dryer. *Associate Producers*: Willis Osborn, Salvatore Mungo. *Director of Photography*: Ted V. Mikels. *Camera*: Robert Caramico. *Film Editor*: Herman Freedman. *Music Composed by*: Jerry Long. *Music Supervisor*: John Caper, Jr. *Choreographer*: Michael Blodgett. *Sound Recording*: Rod Sutton. *Assistant Directors*: Dick Dixon, Wendell Franklin. *Production Manager*: Ron Terry. *Assistant to the Producer*: Bruce Clark. *Wardrobe*: Dorothy Worner. *Makeup*: Mark Snegoff. *Prop Master*: Earl Phillips. *Swimsuits by*: Anne Cole. Filmed in Eastman Color and Widescreen.

"Never Steal Anything Wet" by Jerry Long, performed by Mary Wells over the opening and end credits. "Scuba Party" by Jerry Long and Richard Penniman, performed by Little Richard. "There's a New World" by Ray Davies, performed by the Cascades. "Book of Love" by Carol Connors and Roger Christian, performed by Carol Connors.

A nice change in locale from the shores of Malibu to Santa Catalina is the only thing that makes *Catalina Caper* worth watching. Scuba diving college students on summer break get involved with art forgers, Greek mobsters and a stolen priceless Chinese artifact. Sticking to formula, there are the bikini-clad beauties, bare-chested beach boys, musical guest stars and silly comedy bits but the plot is convoluted and pointless. You really have to pay attention to follow the inane story but who wants to pay that close observance to a beach movie?

Ted V. Mikels' colorful photography is the best thing about the movie, as Santa Catalina looks very picturesque. Too bad the actors keep getting in the way of the scenery. His shots on the beach and in the ocean are also done well as are the underwater scuba diving scenes. Tommy Kirk looks better here than he does in *It's a Bikini World* but his body is no great shakes even for 1965. Forget him and nebbish-looking Peter Duryea and concentrate on blonde hunks Brian Cutler and Michael Blodgett. Girl watchers are treated to the luscious blonde Venita Wolf and a bevy of beauties that never leave Cutler's side, all wearing some of the coolest swimsuits of the time courtesy of designer Anne Cole. Ulla Stromstedt (hidden under an unflattering dark wig) definitively lives up to the nickname "Creepy Girl" bestowed upon her by the gang at *Mystery Science Theater 3000.*

As with most of the later Hollywood surf movies and beach party flicks, the musical guest stars are the reason to tune in. *Catalina Caper* offers an eclectic mix of performers. Mary Wells in her post–Motown years is not seen but belts out the catchy "Never Steal Anything Wet" over the opening and closing credits. Little Richard (wearing a gold lame suit) steals the show as he literally rocks the boat singing "Scuba Party." The bland Cascades are the resident house band while Carol Connors hardens her image and rocks on "Book of Love" leaving her good-girl Teddy Bear persona far behind.

Catalina Caper gets credit for trying to infuse the beach party formula with more of a plot but the execution of it, coupled with adult actors who are not funny in the least, makes this one of the genre's biggest stinkers.

The Story

College student Don Pringle from Arizona decides to spend his summer vacation scuba diving on Santa Catalina, the home of his buddy Charlie Moss. On the ferry ride over, he meets a mysterious, dark-haired beauty named Katrina. The two hit it off as they watch Little Richard perform. Don makes a date with Katrina but as they disembark her fiancé Angelo greets her on the dock while a trio of bathing beauties welcome home Charlie. Katrina says goodbye and leaves the smitten Don standing on the pier.

Charlie's pretty blonde sister Tina comes to pick up Charlie and Don via schooner and almost crashes into an anchored yacht owned by Arthur and Anne Duval. Their teenage son Tad has accompanied them and is attracted to the blundering Tina but she has eyes for Don. Arthur encourages his son to hang out with his new acquaintances. Tad obliges but knows his parents are up to something. He's right as Arthur and Anne are swindlers. Their latest scheme involves stealing a priceless Chou Dynasty scroll from a Los Angeles museum to sell to a shady Greek millionaire, Lakopolous. Once it is verified as the real thing by Lakopolous' art expert, Duval will replace it with a phony scroll forged by Anne and return the original to the museum before anyone notices it missing.

Duval's plan quickly goes awry due to his accomplice Larry. A rendezvous at

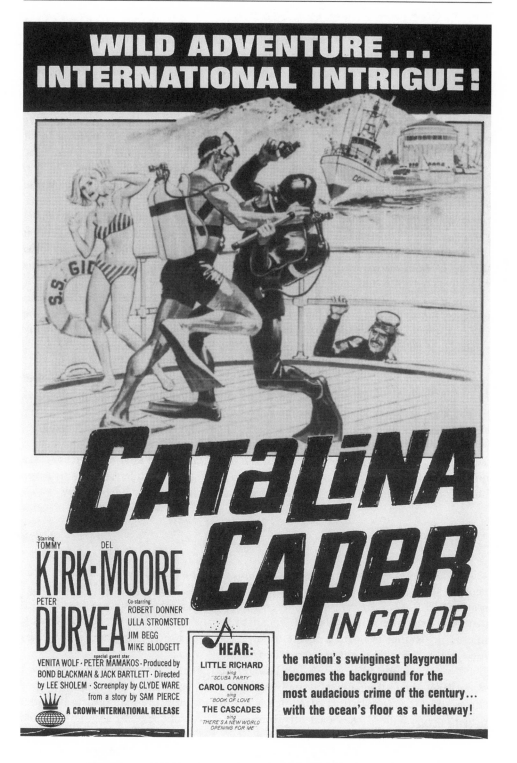

Poster art for *Catalina Caper* (Crown-International, 1967).

sea with the art expert Borman results in the loss of the genuine scroll overboard during a scuffle between Borman and Larry. Don, Charlie and the scuba gang become involved in the struggle and Don is almost drowned during an underwater fight with the escaping Borman. Duval knows he has to act quickly to recover the scroll before Borman's divers can.

On the beach, Tina dons a new white mesh swimsuit to attract Don's attention. She does briefly until he notices a bikini-clad Katrina sunbathing. All the guys go gaga over the Swedish bombshell, angering their girls. Tina decides not to sit back and pretends to be drowning to get Don to notice her again. Her stunt fails. Arthur and Anne stroll by, pretending to see if Tad is having a good time. The real reason they are there is that Duval noticed what expert scuba divers Don, Charlie and their friends were, and he proposes an undersea treasure hunt as a ruse to retrieve the scroll. The kids agree and prepare for the contest but first attend a yacht party with musical guests. Tina invites Don but he declines and remains on the beach. Katrina has gone swimming but catches Don's attention when she loses the top of her swimsuit in the surf. He does the gentlemanly thing and offers his windbreaker to the half-clad beauty and the two grow close.

When Don escorts Katrina to the party, an enraged Tina turns her attention towards Tad to make Don jealous. Don couldn't care less and is intrigued with the sultry Katrina. After Angelo threatens Don for being with his woman, Katrina reveals that he is being paid "to do nothing" by a Greek tycoon.

At the treasure hunt, Don and Tad become suspicious of Duval when Borman's divers show up. Don retrieves the scroll but holds it back. He realizes that Katrina's burly boyfriend is involved with the men after the scroll. Don proposes to Tad that they use it to smoke out Borman and to make his parents and Larry sweat their larceny scheme. Katrina agrees to help and to get the goods on Angelo. A chase ensues with Borman and his goons after Don and his friends, who outwit the thieves. The scroll is placed back in the museum before anyone notices it was missing. Don and Katrina and Tad and Tina get together while Arthur and Anne Duval promise their son that they will go straight, for a little while anyway.

Behind-the-Scenes

Catalina Caper was filmed on location in Catalina Island in 1965. Money woes kept the film sitting on the shelf until its release in the spring of 1967. It was originally titled *Scuba Party* and then *Never Steal Anything Wet*. This was the title until just before the movie was released. Vocalist Mary Wells even recorded a song with that name. Rather than drop it, the tune played over the opening and end credits though the film was re-titled.

Producers Bond Blackman and Jack Bartlett, deciding to cash in on the *Beach Party* films, made their film unique by setting it on Catalina Island and, instead of surfing, the teenagers' sport of choice was scuba diving (hence the original title, *Scuba Party*). Walt Disney cast-off Tommy Kirk was chosen to play the lead role as Don. He had previously starred for AIP in *Pajama Party* (1964) and had just wrapped shooting on *The Ghost in the Invisible Bikini* (1966). He not only had a fan following but he was an ace swimmer and scuba diver.

Veteran low-budget director Lee Sholem, who was nicknamed "Roll 'em" Sholem, was hired to direct. He had a reputation of being fast, efficient and always on or under budget. Between shooting hundreds of television shows, he was able to direct such low-budget features as *Tarzan and the Slave Girl* (1950), *Superman and the Mole Men* (1951), *Jungle-Man Eaters* (1954) and *Louisiana Hussy* (1959). Hired as director of photography was the prolific Ted V. Mikels. With his trademark handlebar mustache, the busy Mikels directed a number of documentaries and low-budget features beginning in 1955. His prior credits included the clever mystery *Strike Me Deadly* (1963) starring Gary Clarke of *Wild Wild Winter*, the bizarre sex comedy *Dr. Sex* (1964) and the adults-only feature *One Shocking Moment* (1965), all of which he produced, directed and photographed.

"I am a director but am also a trained cinematographer," says Mikels. "I was on the qualifying board along with Willy [Vilmos] Zsigmond interviewing prospective DPs. We'd certify anybody wanting to be upgraded to director of photography. Because of this, a lot of friends would ask me to help them out on their movies. I was meeting with Joseph Robertson and he introduced me to the producers of *Catalina Caper*. They asked me if I'd shoot for them and I accepted.

"However, the big problem that you have when you are a director and cinematographer is that other directors are a little bit afraid to have you around," continues Mikels. "They feel they you may take away from their thunder because you have knowledge. Knowing this, I agreed to work on this anyway to supplement my income and to keep working. We used my equipment to shoot this and I hired my crew whom I trusted to work on it with me."

For the female leads the producers chose two actresses who had never appeared in a movie before. During the mid-sixties, blonde Venita Wolf first achieved fame in a series of television commercials. She was the sparkling hair model for Lady Clairol. Casting directors quickly took notice and the acting offers came rolling in. She signed to play Tina in *Catalina Caper* without even an audition. According to the movie's pressbook, "So great a 'find' did the producers consider her, that Venita got the role without a screen test and without reading a line. They'd already seen for themselves how she looked and sounded on the commercial that told how much it was fun to be blonde!" Wolf received "and introducing" billing in the film's credits to bring attention to her.

The role of Wolf's rival went to another blonde, Swedish newcomer Ulla Stromstedt. Needing someone who was an expert swimmer and could learn to scuba dive plus look awesome in a bikini, the producers suspected that Stromstedt would be perfect for the role of Katrina. The only problem was that she was a blonde just like the previously cast Venita Wolf. Ulla agreed to don a dark wig to play the part. Regarding her new appearance, she commented in the film's pressbook that it made her look "more mature and fascinating."

Actor Dan Duryea's son Peter was cast as the naïve Tad. The flaxen-haired lad had some television credits under his belt as well as playing minor roles on the big screen in the Westerns *Taggart* (1964) and *The Bounty Killer* (1965) both starring his dad. Duryea grew up in Malibu, and it was his swimming and scuba diving skills that secured him the role in *Catalina Caper*. His parents were played by veterans Del Moore, a frequent comic foil for Jerry Lewis, and Sue Casey, the sexy stepmother from *The Beach Girls and the Monster* (1965).

Other roles went to strapping newcomer Lyle Waggoner as Katrina's muscular boyfriend; blonde, beefy Brian Cutler as Tommy Kirk's best friend; and lean Michael Blodgett, who did double duty as actor and choreographer as he did on *A Swingin' Summer* (1965).

According to the film's pressbook, a number of the actors were hired because they were skilled swimmers and could scuba dive. Ted V. Mikels thinks that was just publicity hype. "The underwater footage was jobbed out to a second unit crew. Most always the performers never do those stunts. Not wanting to take anything away from the actors but I would be surprised if they did the underwater scenes. But we did shoot in the ocean and one time I had my cameras on a barge. There were a number of scenes shot on boats and the water's edge so I am sure the producers wanted to make sure their actors knew at least how to swim."

To round out the cast, an eclectic array of musical performers were hired including the aforementioned ex–Motown vocalist, Mary Wells. Rock 'n' roll pioneer Little Richard, who hadn't had a Top 10 hit since 1958, is seen performing on the ferry to Catalina Island. The Cascades, whose "Rhythm of the Rain" climbed to No. 3 on the *Billboard* Pop Charts in 1963, were the movie's house band and perform an original Ray Davies song, "There's a New World." Songwriter Carol Connors, formerly of the Teddy Bears, rocked at the film's yacht party backed by the Cascades.

Filming began on *Catalina Caper* in August 1965 on location on Catalina Island and Malibu, California. Ted Mikels immediately sensed that Lee Sholem's style of directing was not the way he approached his own projects. "They called him 'Roll 'em' Sholem," says Ted with a big cheerful laugh. "I had a heart-to-heart talk with him before the end of the shoot because he never really gave anybody time to do *anything*. I said to him, 'You know, Lee, I direct my movies with love and kindness and I get a lot out of my people.' He replied, 'I don't. I direct my movies with hate. Hatred brings on anger, which brings on action. I get more out of my people by making them hate.' Can you believe that?"

Since the cast was made up of a number of newcomers, it was a good bet that they were terrified of Lee Sholem. "I can't confirm this," says Mikels. "But they probably were. He didn't give them time to rehearse and scenes were shot usually in one take. He was the driver and that's why they nicknamed him 'Roll 'em' Sholem. He was probably a nice enough guy in his private life but he was very aggressive, forceful and determined. He said he liked to run his movies like the military." Sholem wouldn't have disagreed with this statement and remarked in *Filmfax* magazine that he *was* a "tough guy, a rough man to work for." He was especially noted for shouting "Cut!" at the top of his lungs.

Despite Sholem's taskmaster ways, Ted Mikels enjoyed shooting on Catalina Island and had fun with the cast and crew. "Little Richard was a kick in the butt," laughs Ted Mikels. "We actually shot his scene as the ferry was taking us to Catalina. That was sort of tricky because the boat was never rock steady. We filmed a lot of stuff underway to the island." The film also contained many scenes on a boat supposedly at sea but in reality it was not. "I always had to watch for my camera not to shoot out through any port holes or windows showing we were on the dock. The one time Lee Sholem and I got into it, he yelled, '*Why didn't you move the camera?*' I said, 'I told you if I move the camera we'd be shooting through the window at the dock and we are supposed to be out in the middle of the ocean.

"I loved the scenes I shot on Catalina," continues Ted. "We had plenty of sunshine though we were always on the run with Sholem directing. I remember that he didn't give us time to put scrims over the sun boards. In other words, you had to put gauze over the sun boards or you could blind the actors. That bothered me a lot because I had to rush to get my crew to get the boards in so I could shoot and you had to put the boards in the actors' faces. They tried their best not to squint. If you look closely at the movie—at least on the 35mm print— the boards are actually reflecting in their eyeballs."

Despite the hectic pace, Mikels' crew (assistants, grips and cameramen) and the cast were professional and got along splendidly. "The actors were wonderful," remarks Mikels. "I had known Tommy Kirk because I shot a movie at his parents' place for my dear friend Rafael Campos. Del Moore was a really nice man—very congenial and easy to work with.

Catalina Caper co-star Michael Blodgett was never shy about showing off his body in beach movies or any other type of movie as he bathes in a barrel in this beefcake shot from *There Was a Crooked Man...* (Warner Bros., 1970).

Venita Wolf was a pretty little girl. At the end of the day, when the sun was gone and we had to retire to the hotel, we'd all have dinner together. It was a very enjoyable experience for me. I came back to Catalina a few years later to shoot *The Doll Squad.*"

When *Catalina Caper* was released, it sunk into the ocean—along with the acting careers of most of the cast. The trades ignored reviewing it as it played mostly drive-ins across the South and Midwest. But the film found cult status 23 years later when it was satirized on the hit television series *Mystery Science Theater 3000.* So popular was the episode that *Catalina Caper* was one of five films chosen for inclusion on the first *Mystery Science Theater 3000* DVD Collection. The funniest running gag is the nickname given to Ulla Stromstedt's character, "Creepy Girl," for which a song of the same name was composed.

The one aspect of the film that holds up quite well—rising above the *Mystery Science Theater*'s cast putdowns—is Mikels' expert cinematography. Santa Catalina never looked so inviting. "At one time a lot of people thought I was the best cinematographer in Hollywood," boasts Mikels. "I was paid enormous dollars because I had directing and cinematography as my mainstays. I would help new directors who had no idea where to put cameras and things like that. I would do literally everything for them except tell the actors how to perform."

As for the cast members of *Catalina Caper,* only Lyle Waggoner found fame, first co-starring in the hit variety series, *The Carol Burnett Show* (1967–74) and then as leading man opposite Lynda Carter in *Wonder Woman* (1975–77) and *The New Adventures of Wonder Woman* (1977–79). "Lyle dated my daughter during the filming," reveals Mikels. "I had to give him some sharp boundaries because my daughter was very pretty and had just won a beauty contest. I told him, 'You better have my daughter home by such-and-such a time or else.' That was funny."

Tommy Kirk managed to scrounge up a few more lead roles but in Grade Z productions while Sue Casey continued landing minor character parts. By 1970, Del Moore was dead as were the movie careers of leading players Peter Duryea, Venita Wolf and Ulla Stromstedt.

The supporting actors from the film fared a little better and kept working. Michael Blodgett essayed the role of Tad, a football player facing a career-ending injury on the youth-oriented daytime drama *Never Too Young* from 1965 to 1966. Blodgett made an impression and was picked to host a new syndicated variety series, *Groovy* (1966). This pop music beach party show was filmed at the beach with Blodgett usually shirtless, baring his fine physique while interviewing bikini-clad actresses or introducing musical performers singing their latest songs. In 1968, Blodgett was not happy with the direction his career was going. Reflecting on his acting roles in over 40 television shows and in beach films, Blodgett told *The Los Angeles Times*, "They were crummy ... terrible. I like to things I'm proud of. I'd rather make less money and be Michael Blodgett." He soon got his chance when he was hired to host his own local youth-oriented talk show, *The Michael Blodgett Show*, a 90-minute discussion-interview program airing on Sunday nights in LA.

When his series came to an end, Blodgett re-focused on his acting career. His later films include the cult classic *Beyond the Valley of the Dolls* (1970), *There Was a Crooked Man...*, *The Velvet Vampire* (both 1971) and *The Carey Treatment* (1973). During this time, Blodgett was battling a drug and alcohol problem. After kicking his habit, he authored his first work of fiction, *Captain Blood*. His other novels include *White Raven* and *Hero and the Terror*. In the eighties and nineties, Blodgett turned to screenwriting. Among his credits are the Tom Hanks comedy *Turner & Hooch* (1989) and the screen adaptations of his novels *Hero and the Terror* (1988) and *White Raven* (1998). Today, the successful novelist still resides in Southern California and recently attended an anniversary screening of *Beyond the Valley of the Dolls*.

Brian Cutler, who played a minor role in *Beach Ball* (1965), co-starred in the popular Saturday morning television series *Isis* in 1975 and the popular family film *The Further Adventures of the Wilderness Family* (1978). In 2002, he produced, directed, wrote and co-starred in the romantic comedy *My One and Only*. Today he is an acting instructor in Kansas City. Jim Begg could be seen playing minor roles in a number of teenage exploitation films including *Village of the Giants* (1965), *It's a Bikini World* (1967) and *The Cool Ones* (1967). In the seventies he turned to voiceover work and in the eighties and nineties produced a number of movies including *Leo and Loree* (1980), *On the Right Track* (1981), *Leprechaun* (1993) and *Children of the Corn III* (1995).

As for Ted V. Mikels, he went on to work again as director of photography for producers Blackman and Bartlett on *Agent for H.A.R.M.* (1965) when the original cinematographer quit. "The director was very apprehensive about me working on this," says Ted with a laugh. "He bellowed, 'There is only *one* director on the set!'" Mikels went on to become one of *the* notables of trash B-cinema and influenced a generation of movie fans with such films as *The Astro-Zombies* (1967), *Girl in Gold Boots* (1969), *The Corpse Grinders* (1972) and *Blood Orgy of the She-Devils* (1972). Among his seventies output was the action film *The Doll Squad* (1973), which Mikels claims was used as the basis for the television series *Charlie's Angels*. Leading lady Francine York commented in *Filmfax* magazine, "I love Ted Mikels. He is an incredible man—very talented—and a real filmmaker who loves his work. Everybody has their own little idiosyncrasies. One of Ted's was that he loved to do movies about women beating up guys. And he did too but he is a very good person. My mother and father met him and adored him. He would call my parents every year at Christmas. But he had a rough time on *The Doll Squad*. He was fighting with his girlfriend Sherri Vernon, who played one of the Doll Squad members during the picture, and she slugged him on the way to Catalina on this nine-passenger plane. And he was smarting all day. The poor guy had to direct 50 scenes and he was very angry."

Today, Mikels runs TVM Productions; "Everything I've done in the last 14 years I write, produce, direct, light, shoot and edit." His most recent output includes *Dimensions in Fear* (1998), *The Corpse Grinders 2* (2000), *Mark of the Astro-Zombies* (2002) and *Cauldron: Baptism of Blood* (2004). In between appearing at horror film conventions throughout the world and teaching a seminar on independent motion picture production, the busy filmmaker is working on his next movie sequel, *Doll Squad 2: Female Fury*.

Memorable Lines

(Don eyes a gaggle of bathing beauties on the beach.)

DON: I never saw so many trying to cover so much with so little success.

Reviews

Variety—"This is pretty insubstantial of its kind but even if it had been done better *The Catalina Caper* would face an unresponsive market. [It] takes on whole some aspects of the AIP formula ... but it is labored and boring because the kids themselves are all of the healthy, handsome variety and there are no character juveniles of the likes of Jody McCrea, who used to provide comic relief in the AIP productions. Everything's been under rehearsed and/or done in one take, with result that all lines are read with little inflection. The touch of William Asher, the (relatively) young director who created the 'beach party' series for AIP, is sorely missing."

∗ 30 ∗

Don't Make Waves (1967)

Fun: ∗∗½
Surfing: ∗∗
Boy watching: ∗∗∗
Girl watching: ∗∗∗
Music: ∗∗
Scenery: ∗∗∗∗

Release date: June 20, 1967. Running time: 97m. Box office gross: $1.25 million. DVD release: Not as of January 2005.

Tony Curtis (*Carlo Cofield*), Claudia Cardinale (*Laura Califatti*), Robert Webber (*Rod Prescott*), Joanna Barnes (*Diane Prescott*), Sharon Tate (*Malibu*), David Draper (*Harry Hollard*), Mort Sahl (*Sam Lingonberry*), Dub Taylor (*Electrician*), Ann Elder (*Millie Gunder*), Chester Yorton (*Ted Gunder*), Reg Lewis (*Monster*), Marc London (*Fred Barker*), Douglas Henderson (*Henderson*), Sarah Selby (*Ethyl*), Mary Grace Canfield (*Seamstress*), Julie Payne (*Helen*), Holly Haze (*Myrna*), Edgar Bergen (*Madame Lavinia*) Paul Barselow (*Pilot*), George Tyne, David Fresco, Gil Green (*Newspapermen*), Eduardo Tirella (*Decorator*), Henny Backus (*Herself*), Jim Backus (*Himself*). Uncredited: China Lee, Haji (*Topless Swimmers*), John Fain (*Surfer*).

A Martin Ransohoff production. A Filmways-Reynard Picture. An MGM release. *Produced by*: John Calley and Martin Ransohoff. *Directed by*: Alexander Mackendrick. *Screenplay by*: Ira Wallach and George Kirgo. *Adaptation by*: Maurice Richlin. Based on the novel *Muscle Beach by*: Ira Wallach. *Associate Producer*: Julian Bercovici. *Music Composed and Conducted by*: Vic Mizzy. *Director of Photography*: Philip H. Lathrop, A.S.C. *Art Directors*: George W. Davis, Edward Carfagno. *Set Decorators*: Henry Grace, Charles S. Thompson. *Recording Supervisor*: Franklin Milton. *Film Editors*: Rita Roland, Thomas Stanford. *Assistant Directors*: Carl Beringer, Erich von Stroheim, Jr. *Unit Production Manager*: Edward Woehler. *Makeup by*: William Tuttle. *Hairstyles by*: Sydney Guilaroff. *Costumes Designed by*: Donfeld. *Technical Advisor*: Eduardo Tirella. *Sky diving Sequence by*: Leigh Hunt. Filmed in Panavision and Metrocolor.

"Don't Make Waves" by Chris Hillman and Jim McGuinn, performed by the Byrds over the opening credits.

Don't Make Waves is the first of two surf movies from the major studios geared for adults shortly after the teenage beach party genre had died out. Carlo, a newly arrived salesman in Southern California, loses his automobile and worldly possessions due to the carelessness of a beautiful but self-absorbed foreign beauty. She invites him to stay the night with her and he learns that she is the mistress of a rich married guy who owns a pool company. He blackmails the boss into giving him a job and becomes involved with the wacky denizens of Malibu Beach. *Don't Make*

Waves is entertaining but it could have been better if it would have stuck to satirizing the Southern California lifestyle instead of turning into a typical romantic comedy. The movie succeeds most when poking fun at infidelity, cliffside houses, sky diving, publicity stunts, trampolines, salesmen, astrology and other traits of Southern California living. Its portrayal of all surfers and musclemen as vapid airheads, only interested in the quest of catching the perfect wave or developing the biggest biceps, is a bit unfair but hey, it's only a movie.

Tony Curtis is okay as the Malibu hustler but the role called for a younger actor. It is more pathetic than funny seeing a fortysomething guy con his way into a typical middle class salesman's job. Claudia Cardinale is a knockout but here she is more irritating than amusing in the stereotypical role of the hot-tempered foreigner. Bikini-clad Sharon Tate proves she was one of the screen's great beauties and she is especially stunning with her wet hair matted back à la Ursula Andress in *Dr. No* as she pulls an injured Curtis from the surf. She listlessly glides through most of the rest of the film though she has some funny moments after she hooks up with Curtis. Surprisingly, bodybuilder Dave Draper gives the most sincere performance as the lovelorn muscleman. He and the other bodybuilders sport awesome physiques, which they love to show off.

Despite some of the cast's shortcomings, the slick MGM production values make *Don't Make Waves* memorable. Cinematographer Philip H. Lathrop beautifully films the Malibu colony as it comes to life in the morning as surfers, bodybuilders and sun worshippers hit the shore. His beautiful vistas excellently capture the allure of Southern California for the masses and some of the shots of the shoreline from high up on the cliffs are breathtaking. The musical score is sprightly and adds a nice flavor to the movie, as does the theme song sung by the Byrds. And the special effects as Curtis' Malibu pad tumbles down the cliff during a mudslide are very impressive.

The Story

Carlo Cofield, newly arrived in Southern California, pulls his car over at a scenic bluff in Malibu to enjoy the view of the ocean. He notices a beautiful dark-haired woman painting below. Frustrated with her work, she hurls her canvas into the sea before going off in a huff up to her car. As she pulls out, the reckless girl's car bumper locks with Cofield's old Volkswagen, sending the unoccupied car careening down the hillside. Within minutes, Carlo's car tumbles down a cliff and then bursts into flames. He loses his life possessions despite the helpfulness of a group of bodybuilders on their way to Malibu.

The artist is Laura Califatti and she offers to take Carlo (left only with the boxer shorts he is wearing after his pants caught fire) home to give him the insurance information. He learns that she is a failed actress and that the car belongs to her patron, Rod Prescott, who has decided to pay a late night. Carlo tries to hide but reveals himself when the pompous Rod thinks he is a private eye hired by his wife Diane to follow him. When Laura explains what Carlo is doing there, Prescott believes her but tosses him out onto the sand anyway.

Carlo awakes to a beautiful Malibu morning as the beach comes alive with surfers, bathing beauties, bodybuilders and gymnasts. He decides to take a swim and, after diving into the waves, he is knocked unconscious by a surfboard belonging to a bikini-clad buxom blonde knockout named Malibu. The seductive surfer drags Carlo to the shore; as he comes to, he gets a glimpse of her shapely derriere as she pulls him onto the sand. Her beauty astounds and captivates Cofield. Laura arrives and has one of the bodybuilders help Carlo back to her place. When Prescott calls and informs Laura that he won't be putting in an insurance claim, Carlo gets an idea and decides to get his money another way. He borrows one of Prescott's suits and goes off with his briefcase, which Prescott left at Laura's the night before.

Pretending to be a pool salesman for Sea Spray, Carlo convinces Jim and Henny Backus to allow the company to build a demonstration pool on their grounds to be used for publicity purposes. After getting their consent, he heads straight for the company's headquarters. While driving over, Laura explains that though she and Rod are in love they cannot marry, as Rod is too decent a man to leave his invalid, bedridden wife. At the office, the first person Carlo meets is Mrs. Prescott, who is fit as a fiddle. Startled by his presence, Prescott reluctantly agrees to see Carlo and is forced to hire him.

Cofield heads back to the beach, where he is enthralled by the trampoline-jumping Malibu. He overhears some of the bodybuilders discussing astrology and debating if sex is bad for the physique. One of the musclemen's wives, Millie Gunther, tells Carlo that Malibu is the girlfriend of blonde bodybuilder Harry, who doused Carlo's pants when they were on fire on the mountain road.

Laura hooks Carlo up with a realtor who sells him a cliffside house overlooking Malibu Beach with a Rolls-Royce thrown in. Still intrigued with the pensive Malibu, Carlo hires Harry and his friends to move furniture into his new home. When Carlo gets Malibu alone, he hires her to sky dive into his pool as a publicity stunt. A worried Harry asks Carlo's advice about abstaining from sex. Carlo suggests that he have a session with astrologer Madame Lavinia and promises to set up an appointment. As a grateful Harry thanks him, Diana Prescott shows up at the house. She divulges that she knows all about her husband's affair with Laura and that she owns Sea Spray Pools. Diana thinks Cofield is the perfect man to replace her husband as the company's manager. An irate Laura questions Carlo about the identity of the blonde woman and also lets him know that she is wise to his plan of breaking up Harry and Malibu.

Carlo denies all, but pays a visit to Madame Lavinia (who is actually Zack Rosenkrantz) and bribes him with a pool at a very discounted rate if he will advise Harry to give up sex. The gullible lug runs into Laura on the beach but, seeing how the boy looks up to Carlo, she doesn't have the heart to tell him that Carlo has set him up. Cofield meanwhile has gone to pick up Malibu for her sky diving jump despite Prescott's nix on the publicity stunt for insurance reasons.

Malibu's jump goes awry when Cofield accidentally falls out of the plane. The ace sky diver not only saves his life but also makes the intended landing into his pool. Carlo is injured and, when he awakes in his bed, Malibu is there to comfort him. He surprises her with his confession of love. Harry has arrived to take Malibu home and the sensitive muscleman drives off alone in tears as Malibu has chosen to be with Carlo. Soon Cofield realizes that Malibu is not the girl he imagined as she sits in bed topless with her hair in curlers eating potato chips and intently watches a Spanish program on television though she doesn't speak a word of the language.

A torrential rainstorm hits the Southern California coast. Carlo, Laura, Malibu, Prescott and Diane get trapped in Cofield's house during a mudslide. The dwelling is knocked off its perch and begins to slide down the hill toward the Pacific Ocean. While trapped, Laura learns that Diane is Rod's wife and that the cad has been lying to her. The volatile Italian throws a fit and things go from bad to worse when the house begins to slide again and flips over. The rescue squad can't get to the house but Harry braves the rain and mud to save Malibu. The house makes one last slide before crashing onto the beach. Everyone crawls out alive and all the lovers are united. Carlo and Laura realize that they have been fighting their attraction to one another, Diane and Rod decide

Tony Curtis and Dave Draper played romantic rivals for Sharon Tate in *Don't Make Waves* (MGM, 1967).

to give their marriage another chance, and Harry proposes that Malibu come back to live with him in the bus.

Behind-the-Scenes

Don't Make Waves was based on the novel *Muscle Beach* by Ira Wallach, published in 1959. The book was touted as "the wildly spoofing story of a young Egghead from the East—and the wild, wild things that happen to him in Sunny California, the Land of the Palm and the Starlet, where they sleep out every night." Though this was a very American movie, producer Martin Ransohoff chose Alexander Mackendrick, an American raised in Scotland, to direct. Mackendrick's films included *The Man in the White Suit* (1951) and *The Ladykillers* (1955). His most notorious and ignored film (at the time) was *The Sweet Smell of Success* (1957), a no-holds-barred look at the world of ruthless New York City gossip columnists. It is probable that Ransohoff thought Mackendrick would be perfect to poke fun at the denizens of Malibu Beach in *Don't Make Waves* as he did with the characters in *The Sweet Smell of Success*.

Ransohoff used *Don't Make Waves* as a vehicle to launch the career of his contract player, Sharon Tate. Though she received "and introducing" credit, the beautiful blonde, a native of Texas, played major roles in *Eye of the Cat* (1966) and *The Fearless Vampire Killers* (1967) prior to this. Tony Curtis and Claudia Cardinale were offered the roles of Carlo and Laura while a number of actors, including Dave Draper, tested for the part of Harry.

The blonde bodybuilder relocated to Santa Monica from New Jersey in the spring of 1963 to work for a muscle magazine publisher called Weider, Inc. Draper began training at Joe Gold's original gym and working out at Muscle Beach. His perfectly sculpted body included a 56-inch chest and 21-inch arms and sported enough definition for him to win the Mr. America title in 1965. During this time he hosted a popular local Saturday night television program on KHJ-TV in Los Angeles dressed as a gladiator, which led to minor parts in films such as *Lord Love a Duck* (1966) and *Three on a Couch* (1966).

"I was busy training for Mr. Universe," recalls Draper. "It was amid that training that another cattle call echoed through the beaches and gyms in close proximity to Hollywood. Filmways of MGM needed one Harry Collard to lift weights on Muscle Beach in *Don't Make Waves*. The word got out fast around the gyms via agents, extras and bit-part players when the movie and television makers were looking for muscle. The herd gathered to pick up whatever there was to pick up. It was a ritual—a social event where old faces met to kill time, exchange stories and shoot the breeze while they collected their unemployment.

"I heard about the occasion on Wednesday night at the Muscle Beach Gym (a.k.a. the Dungeon) and appeared with the livestock on Thursday morning after my workout," continues Draper. "Varied assistants interviewed us and the gleaning began. In a day, eight finalists, including me, were chosen for outdoor screen tests before the bigwigs, and in another day I was chosen to be the brilliant and loquacious Harry 'Big Boy' Hollard of *Don't Make Waves*. I said, 'Yes.'"

Early in production, Alexander Mackendrick, nicknamed Sandy, asked Draper to lunch to get to know the inexperienced actor who was chosen to play a major role in his movie. They ate at the MGM cafeteria and discovered that they were both quiet, unassuming men. According to Dave, during filming, "He would point and I would go. He was looking for an image of a musclehead on screen and my incompetence as an actor portrayed that image rather well. I missed cues, looked naturally unsure of myself, forgot my lines and made up my own and I bet Sandy thought to himself, 'Why screw it up? Just let him be himself.'"

Making things a lot easier for Dave was a helpful cast. There were no ego problems on this set, according to Draper. Both Tony Curtis and Claudia Cardinale were big movie stars but they did not act like it in the least. "Tony is a prince," says Draper. "I liked him and felt equality with him, though I tended to kneel when he stood by my side. He was fun, honest and full of energy. He's a friend. Claudia Cardinale and I sat together in those folding director's chairs on a dark and deserted set as we waited wearily for some late pick-up shots. We talked about her sister who was a fashion photographer, Italy and her villa, and I listened to her wonderful accent. And then she winsomely walked toward a harsh cluster of lights and activity a world away after someone yelled, 'Camera's ready' and it was time for her to shoot. Wow!"

Another reason Draper felt comfortable working on *Don't Make Waves* was due to the graciousness of Sharon Tate. Though she was being groomed for major movie stardom and this film was specifically chosen for her as a vehicle to reach that plateau, Tate simply charmed the young bodybuilder. "Sharon was not unlike a female version of me," remarks Dave. "She was young and consumed by her attendees and guardians. She was a star in the making and I watched her from a distance. She was gutsy and willing and quiet and wanting to yell aloud, I think. We flew in a small aircraft over South Carolina and she held tightly onto my hand, yet she didn't hesitate to leap high from a trampoline and into my arms. We hung in the shade and talked about this or that or nothing with the rest of the crew till it was our turn to tumble in the forsaken house in Malibu. She was a friend and we hugged." Tony Curtis also adored Tate and remarked in the *Los Angeles Herald-Examiner* that "Sharon Tate is talented and is going places."

Despite the friendliness of the cast, the massive bodybuilder still felt intimidated by them and timid in their company. Always invited to have lunch with the lead actors and director at a big, long table, he chose to hang out with the other bodybuilders and extras. "I chickened out," admits Dave. "In reality, I felt it would be a disloyalty to my own—a snub, a dishonoring, false. I chose to relax among the few I knew. We lifted, sunned, had curling contests, did back flips in the sand, worked the trampoline, read, nodded and twitched, and scratched. A smarter person would have enjoyed the companionship of the cast and crew. They were terrific people, admirable and had a lot to offer a guy if he was half-awake and not so darn shy and unsure."

During the shoot, budget woes marred the production. The executives at MGM were getting worried that the film was going to go over-budget so some scenes were shot very quickly with not as many takes.

A number of newspaper columnists including Dorothy Manners and Sidney Skolsky were invited to play reporters covering the parachute jump of the Tony Curtis and Sharon Tate characters into a swimming pool. According to Skolsky, MGM rented the private hillside home of actor Elliott Lewis, who closed the main part of the house—denying the cast and crew access to bathrooms. To compensate, the studio provided transportation to two trailers with facilities set up halfway down the hill from the house. Manners reported that she arrived on location at 9:00 A.M. and the shooting of her scene did not commence until 1:00 P.M. The male extras seemed not to mind, as topless bathing beauties including China Lee and Haji were present as well as Sharon Tate (clad in a bikini) to keep cool in the 90-degree weather. Curtis and Tate had to do the leap into the pool five times. Each time they had to towel off and change into dry clothes. Dorothy Manners was supposed to return the following day but the monotony was too much for her and she declined.

Had Manners shown up the second day, she would have been witness to a tragic accident. According to Dave Draper, "While shooting one sunny afternoon in the late summer, a small crowd of crew, actors and extras watched in fascination as parachutists descended a half-mile off Malibu Beach, the location depicting the famed Muscle Beach. A daring team was shooting the sky diving sequence featured in *Don't Make Waves*. One chute fell quickly and there was alarm, fear. Small speedboats raced to the site, too late to rescue the cameraman who became entangled in the cords and sank into the sea. We all witnessed his death in cold, helpless disbe-

In *Don't Make Waves* (MGM, 1967), muscleman groupie Ann Elder and salesman Tony Curtis look on as bikini-clad surfer Sharon Tate leaps into the arms of her brawny lover, Dave Draper.

lief." The dead sky diver was Bob Buquor, who was photographing Leigh Hunt and Jim Dann (doubling for Sharon Tate and Tony Curtis) during their free fall from a plane. A second tragedy befell the production soon after when technical advisor Eduardo Tirella died suddenly.

Other visitors to the set included Terry Southern who, according to Gail Gerber, was hired by MGM to doctor the screenplay for *Don't Make Waves* without screen credit. Harrison Carroll of the *Los Angeles Herald-Examiner*, was present the day Curtis and Tate filmed their comic bedroom scene. When asked what kind of love scene this was, Curtis replied, "Sex on the screen has taken a strange turn these days. To see somebody do something straight and romantically just isn't enough."

The movie's most infamous scene is the mudslide as Curtis' cliff side home topples to the beach with the cast trapped inside. This took two weeks to film, prompting co-star Joanna Barnes to quip to Harrison Carroll, "I feel like a glorified prop."

While working on *Don't Make Waves* during the summer and fall of 1966, Dave Draper was simultaneously training for the Mr. Universe contest, which he won. Returning to the set, "I was awarded a hand-painted sketch by the MGM art department of an Oscar in a muscle pose, titled 'Super Oscar for Mr. Universe.' It's enclosed in an antique-gold frame and says above the statuette, 'We're Proud of You.' The cast and crew signed it and it hangs on my wall above a staircase."

When *Don't Make Waves* was released in 1967, it received mixed reviews. As a bodybuilder who really trained at Muscle Beach, Dave opines, "It was not entirely accurate nor was it a mindless spoof. The early bodybuilding scene, like a diamond, had many facets. It was dumb and innocent and lazy, and it was fast, sharp and visited by courageous and hard-working men and women. There were artists, mail carriers, airline pilots, cops, engineers, schoolteachers, heroes and bums. Some lived in the back of their cars or the old Muscle House on the beach or homes in Culver City and North Hollywood. One man's brush and palette of colors painted the movie. Hollywood highlighted it with bright tones and impressionist strokes. Yeah, the picture's worth framing and hanging on a favorite wall in your living room—better than another fading sunset or a still life of wilting flowers."

Two years after filming wrapped, Dave Draper ran into Sharon Tate at LAX airport. Tate, now Mrs. Roman Polanski, had achieved her goal of movie stardom due to her success in *Don't Make Waves* and *Valley of the Dolls*. Dave recalls, "A voice called 'Dave! Dave!' across the desolate late-night floor. I turned and it was Sharon dressed in black and wearing high heel boots. She ran and jumped into my arms, excitedly introduced me to her young friends and was off. That was the last I saw of the beautiful girl." A year later Sharon Tate was dead. She only made two more films (one of which was 1969's *The Wrecking Crew*) before her untimely death at the hands of Charles Manson's minions from hell. She was over eight months pregnant with Roman Polanski's son when she was slaughtered (along with four others) in her Hollywood Hills home.

Despite the good reviews Dave Draper received as the sensitive muscleman (Richard Davis in *Films and Filming* remarked that his performance contained "a spark of genuine pathos"), *Don't Make Waves* was his last film. A few television appearances followed, including an episode of *The Monkees* where the bodybuilder unintentionally clashed with the group's most diminutive member, Davy Jones, when he inadvertently called him a twerp. "The script called for the uncomplimentary designation 'Shrimp,' not the 'T' word, which evidently held an especially nasty connotation to Davy," says Draper. "He assumed a karate stance before me and called the action to a halt. It took me a full ten seconds to realize that the boy wanted revenge and the crew around him, assistant director, wardrobe, makeup and stagehands were holding him back." Draper quickly expressed regret. "My apology was awkward but I was sufficiently contrite. We went back to work and the sun shined on Burbank."

Returning to bodybuilding, Dave won one more title, Mr. World in 1970, before losing interest in competing. He made furniture for awhile and hung out with Arnold Schwarzenegger during the seventies. Today, Draper owns two World Gyms and continues to be a highly sought-after authority on weight training. With his wife Laree, he operates his own web site Iron Online (www.davedraper.com) where he doles out nutrition and weight training advice. His weekly newsletter to his subscribers motivates them to continue their respective paths of training. Visitors could also purchase products that Dave endorses as well as his publications, including *Your Body Revival* and *Brother Iron, Sister Steel*.

Memorable Lines

(Carlo watches as Malibu slips on her sky diving outfit over her bikini and tells him that Harry won't make love to her anymore.)

MALIBU: Mr. Cofield, do you find me attractive? I mean, if you were a man, would you be attracted to me?

Reviews

Judith Crist, *TV Guide*—"Based on a novel by Ira Wallach called *Muscle Beach* ... the muscles appear to be in the heads of all those involved. It's slapsticky as you could possibly want it ... a rather smutty, smirky would-be swingy movie. *Don't Make Waves* doesn't really make a ripple or a dent, not even on your funny bone."

Richard Davis, *Films and Filming*—"Almost abysmally unfunny: the plot meanders along from one half-developed situation to another without getting anywhere at all ... it seems to be an attempt ... to burlesque the beach society of Southern California."

Joseph Gelmis, *Newsday*—"*Don't Make Waves*, a beach bunny opus ... was a film I was prepared to hate. Maybe that's why I liked it so much.... It is a subdued slapstick satire ... [Alexander] Mackendrick has ... made an unambitious satire within the framework of a conventional, glossy MGM sex farce."

Andrew Sarris, *The Village Voice*—"*Don't Make Waves* is one of the more underrated comedies of the season. Alexander Mackendrick's direction is longer on quiet chuckles than noisy belly laughs, and Tony Curtis gives his most perceptive performance since *Sweet Smell of Success*. The biggest liability is Claudia Cardinale, who should never act in English until she can read lines as skillfully as Sophia Loren.... Claudia's troubles are compounded by the fact that she is out va-va-voomed by Sharon Tate...."

Howard Thompson, *The New York Times*—"*Don't Make Waves* is pretty awful. It's altogether a silly tired business.... About all Mr. Curtis can do here is pop his eyes and no wonder. The luscious Miss Cardinale screeches like a Sicilian pizza vendor."

Variety—"A mildly amusing film which never gets off the ground in its intended purpose of wacky comedy.... The script mixes romance, infidelity, beach antics and sky diving with utter confusion."

Archer Winsten, *New York Post*—"*Don't Make Waves* is billed as a satire on 'sex and status-symbolism,' whatever those things might be, but you might as easily think they were making fun of swimming pools at every home, the sun of California and California earth's tendency to slide. We are vouchsafed three muscle monsters.... The greatest of these, blond David Draper, is a beautiful creation. His abstention from sex ... is an act of noble beauty."

Awards and Nominations

Photoplay Gold Medal Award nomination: "Favorite Female Star"—Claudia Cardinale

Photoplay Gold Medal Award nomination: "Favorite Comedy Star"—Tony Curtis

★ *31* ★

It's a Bikini World (1967)

The Bikini-Bunnies are bustin' out all-over!

Fun: ★★½
Surfing: ★
Boy watching: ★★★
Girl watching: ★★★
Music: ★★★★
Scenery: ★★

Release date: April 19, 1967. Running time: 86m. Box office gross: Not available. DVD Release: Not as of January 2005.

Deborah Walley (*Delilah Dawes*), Tommy Kirk (*Mike Samson/Herbert Samson*), Robert Pickett (*Woody*), Suzie Kaye (*Pebbles*), Jack Bernardi (*Harvey Pulp*), William O'Connell (*McSnigg*), Sid Haig (*Daddy*), Jim Begg (*Boy*), Lori Williams (*Girl*), Pat McGee (*Cindy*). Guest Stars: The Animals, The Castaways, The Toys, The Gentrys and Pat and Lolly Vegas.

Trans American Films. *Produced by*: Charles S. Swartz. *Directed by*: Stephanie Rothman. *Written by*: Charles S. Swartz and Stephanie Rothman. *Director of Photography*: Alan Stensvold, A.S.C. *Second Unit Photographer*: Brick Marquard, A.S.C. *Set Decorator*: Harry Reif. *Film Editor*: Leo Shreve. *Music by*: Mike Curb, Bob Summers. *Music Production*: GP IV Productions. *Sound*: Wallace Nogle. *Assistant Director*: Larry Johnson. *Production Manager*: Paul Lewis. Filmed in Techniscope and Technicolor.

"Walk on (Right Out of My Life)" written and performed by Pat and Lolly Vegas. "Attack" by Sandy Linzer and Denny Randall, performed by the Toys. "Spread It on Thick" by Wilkins-Hurley-Cates, performed by the Gentrys. "We Gotta Get Out of This Place" by Barry Mann and Cynthia Weil, performed by the Animals. "Liar, Liar" by James Dona, performed by the Castaways.

It's a Bikini World features an interesting premise, a great lineup of musical talent and a spirited cast but the extremely low-budget production values hamper the movie. There's a new beach babe on the shore and when she rebukes the advances of the local Casanova, he masquerades as his nerdy brother to get even with her. Meanwhile he competes against her as his real persona in a serious of athletic competitions. It was very novel in 1965 to feature in a film aimed at teenagers a determined independent-thinking heroine. This was years before the Women's Liberation movement and this feminist slant shows that Stephanie Rothman was a director and screenwriter ahead of her time.

Deborah Walley, who by 1965 matured into a shapely young woman, plays the determined Delilah with spunk and vigor while Tommy Kirk makes for a good conceited foe in their battle of the sexes. However, Kirk's Casanova persona (surrounded by bikini-clad beach babes) quickly turns laughable every time he takes off his shirt. He is by far one of the skinniest runts on the beach, especially compared with blonde hunk Jim Begg, and should have been mandated to pump some iron at the gym before filming began. Bob Pickett plays the Jody McCrea–Deadhead best friend role with a big grin and a droll touch. Bikini-clad Suzie Kaye, now sporting blonde hair delivers some amusing lines with flair.

Stephanie Rothman keeps the pace moving briskly but lets the end competition sequences run on much too long dragging down the movie. Everything from skateboarding to camel racing is thrown in. Though hampered by the limited budget, she adds some surreal touches to the film. Whereas the expected gaggle of bikini-clad girls are present, Rothman throws in some unexpected titillation such as guy-girl wrestling on the beach and some boys stripping down from racing coveralls to Speedos for the swimming competition.

As with most of the later beach movies, the musical acts make this worth while viewing. The groups all perform their own hit records. Standing out are Eric Burdon with the Animals in their post–Alan Price lineup doing "We Gotta Get Out of This Place," which became an anthem for Vietnam War protestors, and garage rock band the Castaways singing their lone hit "Liar, Liar." The Gentrys, sounding like Paul Revere and the Raiders, sing "Spread It on Thick," which should have been a big hit but it never cracked the Top 40.

It's a Bikini World is not recommended for surfing buffs (the water is like glass and there is nary a surfer in sight) but if you are looking for something a bit different in a beach movie, check it out.

The Story

There's a new girl on the beach named Delilah Dawes. The curvaceous redhead is a friend of dippy blonde Pebbles, whose not-so-bright boyfriend Woody is best buddies with ladies' man Mike Samson. When he notices Delilah, Mike abandons his beach babes and tries to get a date with her. She flatly rejects him. Stunned, Mike promises Woody that he will get back at her for being the first gal to turn him down. To reach his goal, he and his friend eavesdrop on Delilah and Pebbles. They learn that Delilah thinks Mike is a braggart and that she prefers the quiet, brainy types. Mike then gets an idea to pose as his shy and bespectacled brother Herbert to teach her a lesson. Once she falls for Herbert, he'll then reveal his true identity.

Herbert meets Delilah, who is immediately attracted by the boy's sensitivity and shyness. Meanwhile, Daddy, the owner of the dance club the Dungeon, joins forces with publisher Harvey Pulp, who is launching *Pulp Magazine*, a new publication aimed at the college crowd. To arouse interest in the debut issue and Daddy's array of beach equipment, the pair organizes a series of contests. First up is skateboarding. Delilah practices and, after Herbert commends her prowess, she announces that she is entering the contest in hopes of beating Mike. Despite Herbert's protestations, the headstrong girl has made up her mind. She asks him to accompany her to the beach to challenge Mike in person but of course Herbert declines.

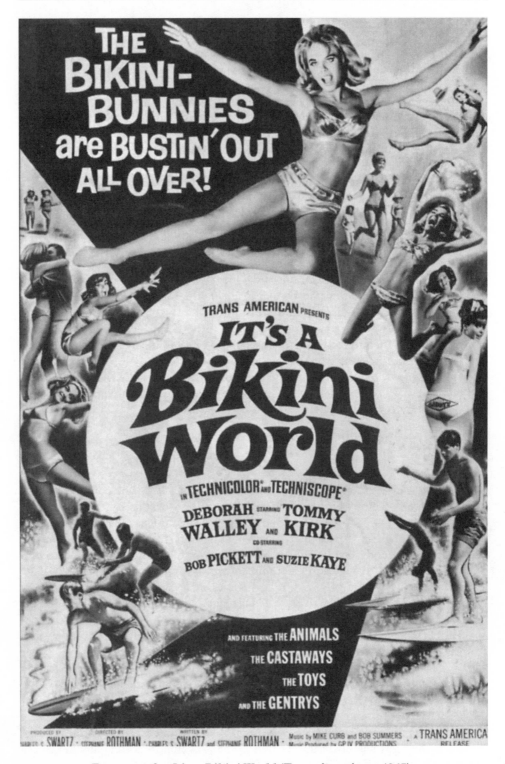

Poster art for *It's a Bikini World* (Trans American, 1967).

Rushing back to his pad, Mike finds the Gentrys performing in his living room while Woody, Pebbles and the gang are dancing along. Confused by Mike's nerdy appearance, Woody agrees to meet him on the beach. Mike has a plan to avoid the competition but Woody, boasting of his buddy's skills, accepts Delilah's challenge for him. Mike wins the event but Delilah will not concede that he is the best over-all athlete around.

The gang heads to the Dungeon to hear the Animals perform. Mike dances with Pebbles but he abandons her on the dance floor to change into Herbert. Harvey Pulp gets Delilah to dance with him but she leaves him twitching with his photographer while she goes off with Herbert. They try to be alone at Herbert's place. Just as Delilah offers to help Herbert overcome his shyness, an oblivious Woody interrupts, spoiling the moment. Not taking a hint, the big goofball even crashes their date to the movies and sits between them.

At the Dungeon, Daddy invites Mike to listen to the Castaways who are auditioning for a chance to play there. He also wants Mike to enter the next competition and to make sure Delilah signs up as well, to exploit the battle-of-the-sexes. On the beach, Delilah confides in Pebbles that she is falling in love with Herbert. Woody returns with food and asks Pebbles for money. His miserly ways finally get to the bikini-clad beauty and she smashes his face with a pie before breaking off with him.

The next competition is speedboat racing and Mike comes out on top again. After the race at the boat shop, Delilah is given a book belonging to Mike, *Famous Dirty Tricks in History*. She then secretly watches as Mike "changes" into Herbert. Realizing that he has been trying to make her look like a fool, Delilah decides to get even. She plays along with Mike's charade and reveals that she is entering Daddy's cross-country race. They agree to meet at Herbert's later.

At his apartment, Mike finds Woody with his entourage of girls. He lets his friend have them since he realizes that he has fallen for Delilah. Woody suggests that Mike tell Delilah the truth about his scheme. However, his plan goes awry when Delilah beats him to it and berates him for his lies. She vows to win the next day's big contest, which consists of ten parts including drag racing, skateboarding, swimming and running. The whole race is nip and tuck between Mike and Delilah. Mike heads for the finish line first but pulls a muscle and Delilah wins. While the gang celebrates her victory and Woody and Pebbles reconcile, Delilah notices that Mike isn't limping. Realizing he let her beat him, she kicks the guy in the shin before running off into the surf with Mike in pursuit. When he catches her, they kiss.

Behind-the-Scenes

Trans American's *It's a Bikini World* was shot in the late fall of 1965 but did not get released until the spring of 1967. According to *Boxoffice*, Trans American was a subsidiary of American International Pictures, set up to distribute art and specialty films. It is reasonable to conjecture that since AIP had no faith in this beach movie, they let it sit on the shelf for over a year and to cut their losses released it through Trans American.

The movie, which Sid Haig says was originally titled *The Girl in Daddy's Bikini*, was put together by the husband-and-wife team of Charles Swartz and Stephanie Rothman. They co-wrote the screenplay with Swartz producing and Rothman directing. This was his first movie but Rothman, a protégé of Roger Corman, had worked as an associate producer on *Beach Ball* (1965), *Queen of Blood* (1965) and *Voyage to the Prehistoric Planet* (1966). She also did second-unit work on *Beach Ball* and was responsible for the Keystone Kops–type footage with the police chasing two of the beach guys driving a hot rod. Producer Bart Patton remarks, "Stephanie did a great job incorporating those classic movie gags into the picture."

The first woman to receive a fellowship to the Directors Guild while studying cinema at USC, Rothman made her directorial debut with the horror opus *Blood Bath* (1966), replacing Jack Hill who was fired by executive producer Roger Corman. Corman did not receive screen credit for *Blood Bath* and according to Bob Pickett, "He was somehow involved with *It's a Bikini World*." This may explain Rothman and her husband's participation in the movie.

Tommy Kirk and Deborah Walley, fresh off their pairing in *The Ghost in the Invisible Bikini*, were tapped for the film's leading roles. The part of Kirk's best friend Woody was originally offered to Aron Kincaid, who turned it down. At the time he was involved in litigation with AIP and was frustrated with his build-up after appearing in four beach party type movies. "I had given statements that I would never appear in anything to do with salt water and sand for the rest of my life," says Aron with a laugh. "It was a bit dramatic but I was trying to make a complete break."

When Kincaid passed on the role, Swartz and Rothman opened it up for auditions. One of the actors who read was Bob Pickett, who as Bobby "Boris" Pickett had a No. 1 smash hit record with 1962's "Monster Mash," a Boris Karloff spoof he co-wrote with Cordials member Leonard Capizzi. Pickett recalls, "My agent called me about *It's a Bikini World*. I went to Beverly Hills to audition for Charles and Stephanie. I read for the role and they offered me the part. It was my first movie but I had done a little bit of television previously.

"I decided to be billed using the name Bob Pickett to escape the image of Bobby 'Boris' Pickett the guy who did 'Monster Mash,'" continues Pickett. "I was aspiring to be like Richard Chamberlain—someone people would take seriously as an actor."

Among the actors cast in supporting roles were Lori Williams, Sid Haig and Suzie Kaye. Buxom blonde Williams was a veteran dancer of a number of beach party films including *Pajama Party* (1964) and *A Swingin' Summer* (1965). Tall and menacing-looking, Haig had worked with Jack Hill previously on *Spider Baby* (1964) and made a career playing sleazy villains though here he played an enterprising club owner. Petite and perky Kaye danced on Broadway in *The Music Man* and on the big screen in *West Side Story* (1961). She knocked around Hollywood landing small roles including a part in *Wild Wild Winter* (1966). It was at this point that she decided to bleach her hair. She remarked in *Drive-in Dream Girls*, "I think I got typecast with the dark hair because of *West Side Story*. I thought I'd get more roles as a blonde, which I did, but I was always cast as a bit of a dopey blonde."

It's a Bikini World was produced on a shoestring budget, which shows. Sections of the movie looked as if they were shot without sound or dialogue, which was dubbed or looped in at a later date. According to Bob Pickett, "The shoot was only supposed to be about 10 or 12 days but it got stretched out a bit. This was because we shot at a lot of different locations including the beach at Malibu, a theater in the Palisades and on Hollywood Boulevard where most of the musical acts were filmed." The actual spot in Hollywood was a popular mid-sixties discotheque called the Haunted House.

To keep costs down, most of the cast is attired in bathing suits even in the interior scenes. A costumer commented in the film's pressbook, "At times we had 50 to 100 guys and gals working before the cameras in the elaborate beach scenes, but the entire wardrobe for the picture company could be carried around in a little laundry bag." Another crew member quipped, "With all this shapely talent around, who needs expensive costumes?"

Per Bob Pickett, producer Charles Swartz was around the sets and on location a good deal of the time, but this was Stephanie Rothman's show. Surprisingly, the cast and male crew members respected Rothman and nobody gave her trouble in her role as director, a position for the most part held exclusively by men. "Stephanie was very pleasant, easy to get along with and very smart," remarks Bob. "She was just a pleasure to work with. Everybody toed the line with her. She wore riding pants a lot and looked like a female Cecil B. DeMille."

"It was nice being directed by a woman," admits Suzie. "I felt more comfortable. I was awestruck because to me it was magical to have a female director. The film was still exploitation but Rothman did it in a more wholesome form—I didn't do anything embarrassing. She would let the scene play." Picket concurs with Kaye

In *It's a Bikini World* (Trans American, 1967), the beach gang, led by Bob Pickett (*second from right*), celebrates Deborah Walley's athletic competition victory.

and adds, "Stephanie took bikini beach movies to a higher level with Deborah Walley's character trying to best her male antagonist in a series of events."

The cast of *It's a Bikini World* seemed to get along well and there were no prima donnas amongst them. "Everybody was having a good time making this picture," professes Pickett. "Suzie Kaye was great and just wonderful to work with. Sid Haig was such a character! Deborah Walley was wonderful. Tommy Kirk was a nice guy, but he was moody and sometimes reclusive though I got along with him fine. Overall, this was a fabulous experience for me.

"At the time I wasn't really looking any social morays that Stephanie was trying to bring to the movie," continues Pickett. "I was just elated to be in a movie and it was a fun thing to do at the moment. That's how I approached all of it. I was concentrating more on stretching my acting chops. Everybody was interested in their own careers and worrying if your last acting job would be your *last* acting job."

Despite its low budget, Charles Swartz was able to assemble an eclectic array of musical talent to appear singing their own music. Credit needs to go to composer Mike Curb, who soon after the film wrapped worked as an executive at MGM records and later became the Lieutenant Governor of California from 1978 to 1982. The Animals, led by lead vocalist Eric Burdon, perform one of their biggest U.S. hits, "We Gotta Get Out of This Place." "Eric has become a friend of mine since then," reveals Pickett. "We laugh about this today because we were both in the same movie but we didn't meet each other at that time." The Castaways sang their lone hit, "Liar, Liar," which reached No. 12 on the *Billboard* Pop Charts in 1965.

By the time *It's a Bikini World* had been released, the Gentrys, who had a Top 20 record with "Keep on Dancing," had disbanded. Vocalist Jimmy Hart resurrected the group in 1969 with little success. He then went on to become a manager in the World Wrestling Federation now calling himself Jimmy "The Mouth of the South" Hart. Native Americans Pat and Lolly Vegas would find chart success during the seventies when they formed the group Redbone. Their biggest hit was "Come and Get Your Love" in 1974. Representing the Girl Group sound was the Toys, a trio of African-American girls whose biggest hit was "A Lover's Concerto" in 1965.

When asked if not getting a chance to vocalize in the movie disappointed him, Bob Pickett remarks, "I never saw myself as a singer. I considered myself a songwriter of novelty records and an aspiring actor. Not singing in the movie didn't bother me at all. But it was interesting that they didn't use 'Monster Mash' in it. I don't think they knew too much about it though I am sure my agent mentioned it to them. I guess they didn't think it was any big deal."

It's a Bikini World was released in the spring of 1967 but by then the teenage beach party movie craze had ebbed. The film found very limited release in the big cities and played mostly drive-ins in the South. In some markets it was the lower part of a double bill with the exploitative documentary *Teenage Rebellion*. Bob Pickett comments, "When they first screened the movie, it was like watching somebody you used to know. I liked the movie and thought it was pretty well done. I was proud of my work in it."

Stephanie Rothman was not so satisfied. She commented in *Scream Queens*, "I became very depressed after making *It's a Bikini World*. I had very ambivalent feelings about continuing to be a director if that was all I was going to be able to do."

Tommy Kirk detested the movie also and remarked to Kevin Minton of *Film-fax* magazine, "It was one of the worst pieces of shit that I've ever been in my life. I can't believe that I could be so stupid! Poor Deborah Walley, poor me."

Rothman didn't direct a movie again until *The Student Nurses* (1970), arguably her best-known film. She became well respected for instilling in her politically charged seventies exploitation movies strong female characters and comments on the social mores of the time while poking fun at the genre. In *The Velvet Vampire* (1971), Celeste Yarnall's female bloodsucker is portrayed sympathetically compared to the bikers and flower children that she encounters. Rothman, her husband and Larry Wollman founded Dimension Pictures in 1971 and she directed *Group Marriage* (1972), *Terminal Island* (1973) and *The Working Girls* (1974). The company disbanded in 1977 and Rothman's last credit was as screenwriter for *Starhops* (1978), about four buxom carhops out to save the drive-in restaurant they work at.

Tommy Kirk and beach boy Jim Begg would appear together again in *Catalina Caper* (1967) but the beach party came to an end for Deborah Walley after *It's a Bikini World*. She hung up her swimsuit and became a regular on the underrated sitcom *The Mothers-in-Law* starring Eve Arden and Kaye Ballard in 1968.

Perky Suzie Kaye sang and danced in two more youth-oriented musicals, *Clambake* (1967) with Elvis Presley and *C'mon, Let's Live a Little* (1967) with Bobby Vee and Jackie DeShannon. After playing a biker chick in *The Angry Breed* (1968), Kaye found steady work on daytime television playing devious Angel Allison Chernak on *Love Is a Many-Splendored Thing* from 1969 through the show's cancellation in March of 1973. "Angel Chernak was an absolute villainess until she got cancer and then atoned," laughs Suzie. When the series came to an end, so did Kaye's show business career as a burnt-out Kaye went through a period of drug and alcohol abuse. Clean and sober for 23 years, she and her ex-husband run a successful computer supply company.

Bob Pickett's acting career picked up after *It's a Bikini World*. He played roles in the Oscar-nominated *The Baby Maker* (1970), written and directed by James Bridges, and the biker film *Chrome and Hot Leather* (1971) with another beach movie veteran, Peter Brown. Pickett saw his "Monster Mash" enter the *Billboard* Pop Charts in 1970 and then re-enter in 1973, climbing up to No. 10—making it the only song in history to chart on three separate occasions. The eighties kept Bob busy appearing in low-budget films including *Strange Invaders* (1983) and *Frankenstein General Hospital* (1988). With Sheldon Allman, who wrote the theme song to *George of the Jungle* and many other Saturday morning kids shows, he co-authored a musical called *I'm Sorry the Bridge Is Out, You'll Have to Spend the Night*, which has been performed in high schools and colleges around the world. It was turned into a movie called *Frankenstein Sings* in 1995 with Pickett starring as Dr. Frankenstein. When it was released to video, the title was changed to *Monster Mash: The Movie*. Today, Pickett is still very active in show business making personal appearances across the country.

Memorable Lines

(On the beach, Delilah and Mike begin another argument but Woody interjects.)

WOODY: Here we go again! Hey, look—before this turns into the 100 Years War, let's meet at the Dungeon for a peace conference.

PEBBLES: *The 100 Years War!* Where did you ever learn about that?

WOODY: I'm a math major!

★ 32 ★

The Sweet Ride (1968)

The Cycles ... the Surf ... and the Swingers That Make It All Go!

Fun: ★★★
Surfing: ★★
Boy watching: ★★★
Girl watching: ★★★
Music: ★★
Scenery: ★★★

Release date: May 22, 1968. Running time: 110m. Box office gross: $1.5 million. DVD release: Not as of January 2005.

Tony Franciosa (*Collie*), Michael Sarrazin (*Denny*), Jacqueline Bisset (*Vickie*), Bob Denver (*Choo-Choo*), Michael Wilding (*Mr. Cartwright*), Michele Carey (*Thumper*), Lara Lindsay (*Martha*), Norma Crane (*Mrs. Cartwright*), Percy Rodriguez (*Lt. Atkins*), Warren Stevens (*Brady Caswell*), Pat Buttram (*Texan*), Michael Forest (*Barry Green*), Lloyd Gough (*Parker*), Stacy King (*Big Jane*), Corinna Tsopei (*Tennis Girl*), Charless Dierkop (*Mr. Clean*), Arthur Franz (*Psychiatrist*), Seymour Cassel (*Surfer/Cyclist*), Paul Condylis (*Sgt. Solomon*), Ralph Lee (*Scratch*), Lou Procopio (*Diablo*). Not credited: Linda Gamble, Sam Chew, Jr.

20th Century–Fox. *Produced by*: Joe Pasternak. *Directed by*: Harvey Hart. *Screenplay by*: Tom Mankiewicz. *Based on the novel by*: William Murray. *Music*: Pete Rugolo. *Director of Photography*: Robert B. Hauser, A.S.C. *Art Directors*: Jack Martin Smith, Richard Day. *Set Decorators*: Walter M. Scott, Stuart A. Reiss. *Special Photographic Effects*: L. B. Abbott, A.S.C., Art Cruickshank, Emil Kosa, Jr. *Film Editor*: Philip W. Anderson, A.C.E. *Unit Production Manager*: Francisco Day. *Assistant Director*: Eli Dunn. *Surfing Sequences Staged by*: MacGillivray/Freeman Films. *Sound*: Harry M. Lindgren, David Dockendorf. *Makeup by*: Dan Striepeke, S.M.A. *Hairstyling by*: Edith Lindon. *Titles by*: Richard Kuhn and National Screen Service. Filmed in Panavision. Color by DeLuxe.

"Sweet Ride" by Lee Hazelwood, performed by Dusty Springfield over the opening credits. "Never Again" by and performed by the Moby Grape.

While *Don't Make Waves* took a light-hearted look at the denizens of Malibu, *The Sweet Ride* is much more serious and melodramatic in its treatment of the aimless youths who could be found living in that part of Southern California. The film is interesting and realistically captures a certain lifestyle from that time in history. What weakens the film is the head-scratching motivation of the two lead characters. But as the last gasp in the sixties' surfing sagas, *The Sweet Ride* offers an absorbing glimpse into the world of surfer boys, tennis bums and bikini girls who want to keep the beach party going forever and never grow up.

The Sweet Ride was the springboard for handsome newcomers Michael Sarrazin and Jacqueline Bisset, who both showed great promise. There is real chemistry between their characters—he an aimless surfer who believes in absolute honesty and she an aspiring actress with a secret. However, their characters' actions weaken the film. It is never made clear why a swinging chick like Vickie who has sex with a guy she just met would be so ashamed of sleeping with her producer to get a leading role in a television series. Or why a pot-smoking, womanizing surfer all of a sudden gets a case of jealousy and possessiveness.

Tall, tan and muscular, Tony Franciosa puts a lot of the younger guys on the beach to shame. Acting-wise, he is excellent as an arrogant and flippant tennis hustler who refuses to grow up. His last scene, where he desperately pleads with Sarrazin's Denny to stick around instead of moving to Santa Monica for a job, is both sad and pathetic. Franciosa truly captures a man who wants to stay carefree and single for the rest of his life. Bob Denver gives a surprisingly easygoing performance playing Choo-Choo while busty Michele Carey is very amusing as his volatile girlfriend Thumper, an adult film star. But it is Bisset who provides the near-nudity as she loses her top in the ocean and is too embarrassed to emerge from the surf at the beginning of the movie.

The film's flashback technique keeps the story interesting; the shots of Malibu are nice but nearly as breathtaking as in *Don't Make Waves*. The surfing scenes are expertly filmed and feature impressive small wave riding. The producers wisely left that footage to surf filmmakers Greg MacGillivray and Jim Freeman. They expertly captured the crowded surfing scene at Malibu, which top surfer Mickey Dora constantly griped about in interviews. Dusty Springfield sings the title song in her usual expert fashion; it should have been a hit for her but it never charted.

The Story

The nearly dead body of a brutally beaten and molested young woman is dumped on a highway in the Malibu Beach area peopled by surfers, drifters and bikers. A police investigation reveals that the victim is actress Vickie Cartwright. She was dating surfer Denny McGuire, who shares a beach pad with Collie Ransom, an aging tennis hustler who won the use of the house for eight months by winning a bet, and Choo-Choo Burns, a temperamental jazz pianist. Choo-Choo's girlfriend Thumper awakens a passed-out Collie with the news after reading it in the morning paper. After another run-in with his neighbor Parker who threatens to shoot Collie the next time he steals his newspaper, Collie sends his previous night's date Martha home and heads down to the beach. He finds Denny surfing and the two race to the hospital only to be met by Vickie's hostile father and acerbic stepmother. While questioned by Lt. Atkins, Denny explains how he first met Vickie on the beach and how their love affair was rocky from the start.

Denny came to Vickie's aid with a towel after she lost her bikini top while swimming in the ocean. He brings her back to his beach pad and his housemates flip over the beautiful woman, who agrees to stay for a drink. Collie tries to entice

Vickie with tennis lessons but she prefers Denny. The two make love and the next day he drives her home. Agreeing to meet for dinner, Denny asks Collie for money while Choo-Choo has to stand by and allow Thumper to make another adult movie to earn some cash. Collie hustles a tennis match and wins enough for Denny to take out Vickie. She refuses to make love with him at her home, leading Denny to believe that she is either kept or turning tricks. He leaves and catches up with Collie and Martha at a dive bar where Choo-Choo is playing piano. Trouble follows when a degenerate biker gang enters. Collie's fast-talking gets him and his friends out of the bar without getting hurt.

The next day, Vickie shows up on Denny's door with a suitcase. He is elated to have her stay despite Collie's protestations. She later confides to Collie that she has not told Denny that she is going to be starring in a new television series. He takes her down to the beach to watch Denny surf. Later they all head to a nightclub to hear the Moby Grape perform. The next morning, Vickie lies to the young surfer and tells him that she has to leave town for a few days to see her father and ailing stepmother. When she goes to say goodbye to him, the leader of the motorcycle gang Mr. Clean along with bikers Scratch and Big Jane are on the beach. When Parker threatens to shoot them, Collie invites them up to the deck where Mr. Clean makes an unwanted pass at Vickie.

Choo-Choo gets a two-week gig playing at a lounge in Las Vegas but his good

Poster art for *The Sweet Ride* (20th Century–Fox, 1967).

luck quickly changes for the worse when Thumper admits to stealing his draft notice that arrived in the mail. To get out of the service, Choo-Choo pretends to be extremely eccentric and overly attached to his pink dog. His act gets him a 90-day extension. While driving home, he spots Vickie on the street and Denny comes to the studio to confront her regarding her whereabouts. There he runs into producer Brady Caswell and then notices a bruise on Vickie's arm but she claims it is a burn caused by her negligence. He invites her to Choo-Choo's opening but she doesn't respond. After he leaves, Vickie goes to Caswell's office and announces that she is leaving the television show to go to Vegas with Denny. Caswell threatens to sue her for breach of contract and expose her for being a whore.

In Las Vegas, Thumper gets lucky at the craps table with a rich Texan while Denny is not happy to see Vickie. When Denny demands the truth about Caswell, Vickie only tells him that it is over and she is happy to be with him. Denny rejects her and, frustrated with her lies, slaps her. When the Texan gets fresh with Thumper, an irate Choo-Choo attacks him, which starts a melee. Hiding under the craps table, Thumper announces to her beau that she is pregnant. Collie goes to find Denny and Vickie and discovers an upset Vickie, who tells him that Denny is missing. The cad then makes a romantic move on the distraught actress, who tells him off. This is the last anyone saw of Vickie before she is found on the side of the road.

Once the police questioning is over and Denny and Collie are released, they head over to Mr. Clean's hangout, thinking he was responsible for beating Vickie. He at first lies that he never saw her again after the time on the deck and splits. But after being jumped by Collie and Denny, he confesses that saw her on the beach one night after she had an argument with some older guy. After she had slipped out of her dress and offered herself to him, he wrapped her in a blanket and split without touching her. Caswell turns out to be the culprit who savagely beat her and left her for dead. In revenge, Denny attacks Caswell at his home, leaving him bloody and unconscious.

Denny tries to reconcile with a recuperating Vickie but she sends him away. At last recognizing that there must be more to life than the endless "sweet ride" that he has been on, Denny abandons Collie and the still-single Choo-Choo (Thumper lied about being pregnant) and leaves to take a job at a Santa Monica hardware store.

Behind-the-Scenes

When 20th Century–Fox decided to make a film version of William Murray's *The Sweet Ride*, they turned to producer Joe Pasternak and director Harvey Hart, both of whom had experience in youth movies. Veteran Pasternak had numerous credits going back to the late twenties. In the sixties, he produced one of the first beach movies, *Where the Boys Are* (1960), and worked with vocalists Connie Francis on *Looking for Love* (1964) and Elvis Presley on *Girl Happy* (1965) and *Spinout* (1966). Hart had much less experience. He worked steadily in television beginning in 1961 before making his directorial bow on the big screen with *Bus Riley's Back in Town* (1965), screenwriter Willim Inge's tale of disillusioned youth starring Michael Parks and Ann-Margret.

20th Century–Fox contract player Jacqueline Bisset was given the lead role of Vickie in *The Sweet Ride*. The stunning actress started out as a model before landing a bit role in *The Knack ... And How to Get It* (1965). In 1967, she delivered two performances that got the critics and Hollywood talking. In *Two for the Road* she played a vacationing schoolgirl who comes down with the measles. The other role was that of Giovanna Goodthighs in the ornate, overdone James Bond spoof *Casino Royale*. Impressed with her talent and beauty, Fox signed her to a contract. Her first starring role for the studio was in the barely noticed spy thriller *The Cape Town Affair* (1967) with James Brolin. She was back to a supporting role in *The Detective*

(1968) starring Frank Sinatra and Lee Remick before being handed the role of the put-upon actress left for dead in *The Sweet Ride.*

Canadian Michael Sarrazin was a struggling New York actor before returning to his home country where he began appearing on CBC teledramas. A talent scout spotted him and brought the young actor to Hollywood where he signed a "cast-iron contract" with Universal Pictures. The studio was big in television production during the mid-sixties so Sarrazin began appearing on such series as *The Virginian* and *The Bob Hope Chrysler Theatre.* His first movie was *The Doomsday Flight,* which was produced for television. His official movie debut was in the Bobby Darin Western *Gunfight in Abilene* (1967) where the tall, good-looking Sarrazin went unnoticed by everyone except Irvin Kerschner. That director wanted the newcomer to play George C. Scott's young partner in *The Flim-Flam Man* (1967) but 20th Century–Fox wanted their contract player Christopher Jones in the role. Kerschner won out and Sarrazin was loaned to the studio; he received very good reviews for his performance. Universal wasted him in another Western, *Journey to Shiloh* (1968), before Fox came calling again, requesting the lanky actor to play the aimless surfer Denny in *The Sweet Ride.*

Forty-year-old Tony Franciosa was the perfect actor to play the aging tennis bum. He had an auspicious first year in films when he received an Academy Award nomination for Best Actor for his performance as a drug addict in *A Hatful of Rain* (1957). In 1959, he received a Golden Globe Award for Best Actor in a Motion Picture Drama for playing a grasping actor in *Career* (1959) and big things were expected from this Italian New York native. However, due to his strapping good looks and talent for light comedy, Franciosa got typecast playing philandering rogues or international playboys in such frothy, forgettable films as *The Pleasure Seekers* (1964), *The Swinger* (1966), *A Man Could Get Killed* (1966) and *Fathom* (1967).

Bob Denver, who had one beach movie on his résumé, *For Those Who Think Young* (1964), returned to the shore after *Gilligan's Island* came to an end in the spring of 1968 after three successful seasons. Texas native Michele Carey was cast as Denver's on-again, off-again girlfriend Thumper. She made her film debut (receiving very good notices) the year before in the popular Western *El Dorado* (1967) starring John Wayne and Robert Mitchum. The executives at Fox were impressed enough to cast her in *The Sweet Ride* though she never made another film for the studio in the sixties.

Interiors for *The Sweet Ride* were filmed on the Fox lot. Exteriors were shot on location near Malibu at Point Dume in Los Angeles County. In his autobiography, Bob Denver described working on *The Sweet Ride* as "a treat." Recalling the scene where his character is stoned while playing the piano, he recalled that a jazz pianist was supposed to stand-in for him to play the music. "For the heck of it he taught me a few chords to rehearse with. In the take I played them and they used that version. Luckily, I was supposed to be high."

According to Denver, the only problem that occurred while making the movie was that the actors hired to play members of the motorcycle gang looked too real and scary for their own good. The cast would sometimes eat lunch at a Mexican restaurant near the studio. As Denver pulled out of the studio's gates, a bunch of police cars whizzed by him. When he arrived at the Mexican joint, "The 'motor-

Michael Sarrazin, Jacqueline Bisset and Tony Francios as aimless Malibu beach denizens in *The Sweet Ride* (20th Century–Fox, 1968).

cycle gang' was lined up on the sidewalk surrounded by very nervous policemen. No guns were drawn, but hands were hovering. One by one the gang showed their SAG cards and were allowed to go into the restaurant."

Castmates Michael Sarrazin and Jacqueline Bisset got along so well that they became romantically involved off-screen. With life imitating art, the couple moved into a beach shack together. Bisset commented in *The New York Times*, "When I first met him [Sarrazin] I thought he was a strange guy, quiet and moody. There was something kind of animal about him ... I couldn't see his face. He had lots of hair, and he wouldn't take off his sunglasses so I could see his eyes. I thought, 'God, is this the guy I'm going to fall in love with in the movie?'" Sarrazin and Bisset starred in one more film together, *Believe in Me* (1971), which was originally titled *Speed Is the Essence*, about drug addiction, before they broke up in the mid-seventies.

The Sweet Ride grossed only $1.5 million at the boxoffice and it was the death knell for sixties surfing epics. Producers and studios realized that the genre had played itself out and they turned to motorcycle dramas and hippie and college protest flicks to draw that elusive teenage audience into theaters.

Memorable Lines

(Clad in only a pair of boxer shorts, a desperate Collie tries to change Denny's mind about leaving. Pressured, Denny bluntly tells the aging tennis bum why.)

DENNY: Look, I'm tired of looking at myself at 40! I'm sorry.

COLLIE: Don't ever be sorry for anything kid—nothing.

Reviews

Judith Crist, *New York Magazine*—"For the current 'youth' film, *The Sweet Ride* wallows in near-moronic cavortings of surfers and cyclists, with a heroine who would rather have her surfing sweetie think she worked in a brothel than in a television series...."

Ann Guarino, *New York Daily News*—"*The Sweet Ride* ... tries to cover too many facets of the new generation—alienated young adults, beach drifters, hippies and a scummy-looking crew of motorcycle riders. But the plot is forced, the dialogue commonplace and the motivation of the characters beyond belief."

Arthur Knight, *Saturday Review*—"A sure directorial hand does a great deal to lift *The Sweet Ride* well above the ranks of most of the beatnik films that have been crowding the screen lately."

David Rider, *Films and Filming*—"It's back to Malibu again, everyone, so polish up your surfboards, dig out the bleached beach shorts and off to sunny California, 20th Century–Fox style. Once again we are invited to drop in on the dropouts and enjoy sun, sand, surf and sex in roughly equal proportions."

Variety—"*The Sweet Ride* could sum up as 'Hell's Angels' Bikini Beach Party in Valley of the Dolls near Peyton Place.' Though well mounted and interesting in the spotlighting of Michael Sarrazin and Jacqueline Bisset, the overall result is a flat programmer."

Archer Winsten, *New York Post*—"*The Sweet Ride* ... is a Joe Pasternak grab-bag of youth kicks that have come up in the southern California-Hollywood-beach culture of the past few years. It is ... a remarkably dull view of second-hand characters assembled from everything in the Hollywood youth file."

William Wolf, *Cue*—"There is a sadness about overgrown juveniles cavorting aimlessly through empty lives. But without a penetrating script and artistry to touch us, spending time with such characters can be as boring as the overgrown juveniles themselves."

Awards and Nominations

Golden Globe Award nomination: "New Star of the Year—Male"—Michael Sarrazin

Golden Globe Award nomination: "New Star of the Year—Female"—Jacqueline Bisset

Golden Laurel Award: "Top Male New Face"—Michael Sarrazin, fourth place

Golden Laurel Award: "Top Female New Face"—Jacqueline Bisset, fifth place

Photoplay Gold Medal Award nomination: "Favorite Male Star"—Tony Franciosa

Photoplay Gold Medal Award nomination: "Favorite Male Star"—Michael Sarrazin

Photoplay Gold Medal Award nomination: "Most Promising New Star—Female"—Jacqueline Bisset

Screen World Award: "Most Promising Personalities of 1968"—Jacqueline Bisset

Screen World Award: "Most Promising Personalities of 1968"—Michael Sarrazin

PART II

The Players

★ *John Ashley* ★

Being in the right place at the right time is a cliché but it particularly applies to the career of John Ashley. Dark-haired and handsome, the baby-faced Ashley was the only actor at American International Pictures who was able to make the leap from its juvenile delinquent films of the late fifties to the beach party movies in the sixties. He played Frankie Avalon's best buddy in *Beach Party* (1963) and most of the sequels. However, in *Beach Blanket Bingo* (1965) Ashley played Avalon's rival, who steams while his sky diving girlfriend (Deborah Walley) puts the romantic moves on Frankie.

John Ashley was born in Kansas City, Missouri, on December 25, 1934. A student at Oklahoma State University where he earned a B. A. in economics, he was visiting a friend in California and accompanied him to the set of the 1956 movie *The Conqueror* starring John Wayne. The Duke was impressed with the good-looking Ashley and guided him to a role on television's *Men from Annapolis*. Ashley's film career began when he was spotted in the reception area of American International Pictures while waiting for his girlfriend to audition. She left without a role while he copped the male lead as a juvenile delinquent hot rodder in *Dragstrip Girl* (1957). He immediately became a favorite of studio head James H. Nicholson's daughters Laura and Luree so more lead roles followed in *Motorcycle Gang* (1957) and *Hot Rod Gang* (1958), which featured Ashley's singing talents.

During this period, Ashley lost out to Michael Landon for the lead in *I Was a Teenage Werewolf* (1957). He played a bit as a television singer in his first big studio film *Zero Hour!* (1957), but appeared in such exploitation fare as *Frankenstein's Daughter* (1958) and *High School Caesar* (1960). In 1961, he and Brian Kelly starred as racing car designers who own a garage in the television adventure show *Straight-away*. At the time Ashley remarked to columnist Kay Gardella, "I don't want to be a fad like some television stars." He got his wish as the series lasted only 26 episodes.

In 1962, Ashley married Gidget #2, Deborah Walley, and they had a son in 1963. After playing a small role in *Hud* (1963) starring Paul Newman, AIP came calling again with an offer to play a supporting role as a surfer in their new comedy with music. Based on his popularity with the teenage audience, that was not surprising; the fact that he was not offered the lead *was*, since he could sing (he had recording contracts with a few labels) and he had a fan following. Nevertheless, Ashley accepted the role of Ken, best buddy of surfer Frankie Avalon in *Beach Party*. After the film became a huge hit, he went on to reprise his role, though the name was changed to Johnny, in *Muscle Beach Party* (1964) and *Bikini Beach* (1964).

None of these movies gave the 30-year old Ashley much to do other than to play confidante to Avalon's lovelorn character. Still, Ashley was extremely popular with teenagers, especially females. He toured the country promoting the hell out of these films. He remarked in *The Saturday Evening Post*, "Anytime I get depressed and feel I'm not doing as well as I should, I go on the road for a week. I come back to my wife thinking I'm Rock Hudson." However, these films did have a downside to them. Ashley also bemoaned that he was afraid of being typecast, but on the other hand he also spoke frankly about the financial rewards the movies brought him.

In *Beach Blanket Bingo*, Ashley was cast in the change-of-pace role of a pilot named Steve who becomes jealous when his neglected girlfriend Bonnie (Deborah Walley) starts paying more attention to surfer boy Frankie. Steve makes a half-hearted attempt to make Bonnie jealous by flirting with Frankie's girl Dee Dee

Beach movie actor John Ashley frolics on the shore with his then-wife, Deborah Walley (*courtesy the General Research Division, The New York Public Library, Astor, Lenox and Tilden Foundations*).

(Annette Funicello). Ashley was back to his good guy role as Johnny in *How to Stuff a Wild Bikini* (1965) and finally was able to show off his singing talents as Avalon's character was away on naval reserve duty. In between beach party movies, Ashley returned to his earlier punk roles when cast as Baby Face Nelson in the violent crime drama *Young Dillinger* (1965) starring Nick Adams and Mary Ann Mobley.

How to Stuff a Wild Bikini was the end of the beach party for John Ashley. When his days on the sand came to an end, so did his marriage to beach cutie Walley. With two sons to support, Ashley journeyed to the Philippines to play leading roles in a string of Eddie Romero–produced grade-Z horror movies for Hemisphere—*Brides of Blood* (1968), *The Mad Doctor of Blood Island* (1968) and *Beast of Blood* (1971). When the head of Hemisphere became ill, Ashley partnered with Romero to produce and co-star in *Beast of the Yellow Night* (1971), *The Twilight People* (1972) and *Beyond Atlantis* (1973). He also began working for Roger Corman in production on such Philippines–lensed films as *The Big Doll House*

(1971) and *Black Mama/White Mama* (1973) while still accepting supporting roles in various types of B-movies.

Ashley's Philippines moviemaking experience led him to work coordinating production for director Francis Ford Coppola on the Academy Award–winning *Apocalypse Now* (1978). Branching out into television production during the eighties, Ashley teamed with Frank Lupo and had a huge success with the vastly popular action series *The A-Team*. He co-produced two other mindless television adventure shows: *Walker, Texas Ranger* starring Chuck Norris during the 1993-94 season and *Marker* in 1995. Ashley died of a heart attack in New York on October 3, 1997, on the set of his new movie *Scarred City*. He was 62.

Film credits: 1957: *Dragstrip Girl; Motorcycle Gang; Zero Hour!*; 1958: *Hot Rod Gang; Frankenstein's Daughter; Suicide Battalion*; 1960: *High School Caesar*; 1963: *Hud; Beach Party*; 1964: *Muscle Beach Party; Bikini Beach*; 1965: *Beach Blanket Bingo; Young Dillinger; How to Stuff a Wild Bikini; Sergeant Deadhead*; 1967: *Hell on Wheels*; 1968: *Manila, Open City; The Mad Doctor of Blood Island; Brides of Blood*; 1971: *Beast of Blood; Beast of the Yellow Night*; 1972: *Woman Hunt; The Twilight People*; 1973: *Beyond Atlantis*; 1974: *Savage Sisters; Black Mamba*; 1975: *Smoke in the Wind*; 1997: *Invisible Mom* (video).

★ *Frankie Avalon* ★

Frankie Avalon's name has become synonymous with the beach due to his co-starring stint with Annette Funicello in a string of movies for AIP beginning with *Beach Party* (1963) and continuing with *Muscle Beach Party* (1964), *Bikini Beach* (1964) and *Beach Blanket Bingo* (1965). It is ironic that Hollywood's ultimate big screen surfer was a dark-haired Italian-American from Philadelphia who had never encountered the sport in his life.

Frankie Avalon was born Francis Thomas Avallone in Philadelphia on September 18, 1940. As a child he began playing the trumpet and was spotted by a talent scout while he played at a neighborhood party hosted by Al Martino. He appeared on *The Jackie Gleason Show* and then joined a local dance band called Rocco and the Saints. Avalon's musical career skyrocketed after local songwriters Peter De Angelis and Robert Marucci formed Chancellor Records. They signed and began managing Avalon along with another local boy, Fabian Forte. His managers got the 17-year-old singer a cameo in the film *Jamboree* (1957) singing "Teacher's Pet" and then a guest stint on a new national dance show called *American Bandstand*. Avalon performed a song he disliked called "De De Dinah" but his one appearance on the program propelled the song to sell over one million copies.

Avalon quickly became one of the era's most popular teen idols, filling the void left by Elvis Presley who was drafted into the Army. Between 1958 and 1959 he placed eight songs in the Top 40. Two of his records, "Venus" and "Why," climbed to the top of the charts. However, by 1960 Avalon's popularity began to wane and none of his recordings were able to break into the Top 20. His managers then steered the handsome youth into a movie career. He made his film debut in *Guns of the Timberland* (1960) starring Alan Ladd. Then he and Joan O'Brien were the only adult survivors in John Wayne's epic Western *The Alamo* (1960). He impressed the Duke, who said of Avalon, "He's a born pro who took his great part without any difficulty whatsoever."

Avalon's association with American International Pictures began when he was cast as Ray Milland and Jean Hagen's resourceful son in *Panic in Year Zero!* (1962), about a family who survives a nuclear attack that destroys Los Angeles. That same year he married Kay Diebel, a former Miss Rheingold contestant, and they would go on to have eight children.

In his next two films Avalon was miscast, playing a bumbling adventurer in the low-budget *Hatari* rip-off *Drums of Africa* (1963) and a Spanish warrior fighting the Moors in *The Castilian* (1963). When AIP heads James H. Nicholson and Samuel Z. Arkoff could not get Fabian to star in their new movie *Beach Party* (1963), they remembered Avalon and signed him to play the surfing sweetheart of Annette Funicello. While Frankie tries to make Annette jealous by feigning a romantic interest in a Hungarian sexpot, she spends time with an older professor— unaware that he is studying the mating habits of teenagers.

Beach Party was an enormous hit by AIP standards and sequels reuniting Frankie and Annette were immediately planned. According to *The Saturday Evening Post*, Frankie signed a ten-picture deal with the studio for a salary of roughly $35,000 a film. His agreement also granted him a percentage of the profits and associate-producer billing on five of them. Avalon boasted rather prematurely to the *Post*, "I don't doubt that I will become one of the great matinee idols."

In *Muscle Beach Party* (1964), Avalon and his surfer friends tangle with an army of musclemen while Annette vies for his attentions with a spicy Italian heiress. *Bikini Beach* (1964) gave Avalon his most challenging acting assignment playing the dual role of Frankie the surfer and the Potato Bug, a British pop singer. He received his some of his finest notices. For instance, the critic in the *Los Angeles Herald-Examiner* raved, "Avalon is a top-notch performer throughout" and the reviewer in *The Hollywood Reporter* remarked, "Frankie Avalon does very well in a dual role." A number of well-deserved accolades came the young actor's way, including being named one of *Film Daily*'s Famous Fives for Best Juvenile Actor and being selected a Star of the Future by *Boxoffice* magazine.

During this time, Avalon continued with his recording career and released two LPs. New recordings of the songs he sang in the beach movies were featured but the albums never caught on with the teenage audience who were by then immersed in the British Invasion. He bemoaned that fact to the UPI in 1965 and vowed that, even though he hadn't had a hit record in three or four years, a la Frank Sinatra and Dean Martin he would rise to the top of the charts again.

AIP kept Avalon working non-stop in 1965. The busy young actor who proved he had a flair for comedy teamed once again with Annette Funicello in *Beach Blanket Bingo*, where the beach gang gets involved with sky diving, a mermaid and a girl singer. After filming wrapped, Avalon commented in *Seventeen*, "I think the 'beach' pictures have pretty much run out of sand for me. Somebody said Annette Funicello and I were becoming the Ma and Pa Kettle of the teenagers, but I don't believe it. In any case, they've been fun to make, but I think we need something new."

Sans Annette, Frankie co-starred with Dwayne Hickman, playing college students who dress in drag as British lasses to learn what girls want in a boy in *Ski Party*, a beach party in the snow. Regarding this change of pace role far from the

shores of Malibu, Avalon remarked
to the UPI, "I was getting typed.
People are beginning to think of
me as the Beach Party Kid." Sticking to his convictions, he agreed to
only make a guest appearance in
How to Stuff a Wild Bikini as his
character was away on Naval
reserve duty in the Pacific.

AIP allowed Avalon to stretch
his acting muscles playing another
dual role in the service comedy
Sergeant Deadhead and an inept
secret agent in the spy spoof *Dr.
Goldfoot and the Bikini Ma*chine. He
even found the time to play Tuesday Weld'a all–American boyfriend
in the Bob Hope comedy *I'll Take
Sweden* (United Artists).

Though the beach party had
come to an end by 1966, Avalon
remained under contract to AIP. In
Fireball 500 (1966) he and Annette
were paired one last time; Avalon
and Fabian played racecar drivers
who were rivals on and off the
track. He journeyed to Hong Kong,
along with AIP regulars Patti Chandler and Salli Sachse, to co-star

In this publicity photograph, Annette Funicello seems more interested in her sunglasses
than her cute co-star, Frankie Avalon.

with George Nader and Shirley Eaton in the spy adventure *The Million Eyes of Su-
Muru* (1967). In his last AIP movie he and Jill Haworth played swinging London
college students in the thriller *Horror House* (1969).

During the seventies, Avalon concentrated on television, making appearances
on numerous variety programs and in his own short-lived series *Easy Does It* with
Annette Funicello (1976). On the big screen, he cameoed as the Teen Angel singing
"Beauty School Dropout" in *Grease* (1978) and then almost ten years later reunited
with Annette for the feature film *Back to the Beach* (1987). Unfortunately, except for
Dick Dale none of the other AIP regulars appear. Instead we get the always-annoy-
ing Connie Stevens and cameos from Edd Byrnes and Jerry Mathers from *Leave It
to Beaver*. This hurts the film and was disappointing to fans of Deborah Walley, Jody
McCrea, Aron Kincaid, etc., especially since two years prior the entire AIP *Beach
Party* contingent gathered for a twentieth reunion. In an interview with *The New York
Post*, Avalon blamed the film's mediocre box office receipts on a "poor release date
[late summer], poor marketing, targeting the wrong age group." But the film still
made money once it went to video and a sequel entitle *Surfing Safari* was planned
but never filmed. Frankie and Annette reunited most recently in 1990 when they
toured the country together for the first time, performing their hit songs live on stage.

Avalon's endeavors have not been limited to entertainment. In 1992 he became the National Ambassador for the National Arthritis foundation and in 1993 and 1994 he hosted the New York TV Center Jerry Lewis Muscular Dystrophy Telethon. Soon after he began his own manufacturing and distribution of health products as President and CEO of Frankie Avalon Products Incorporated, appearing on the Home Shopping Network monthly.

Today, Frankie Avalon, who still looks great, concentrates on his company, performing live in nightclubs and concert venues throughout the world either as a solo headliner or part of Dick Clark's Golden Boys of Rock with a lineup that includes Fabian and Bobby Rydell. And he also manages to find the time to reprise his role as the Teen Angel in stage productions of the popular musical *Grease* throughout the U.S.

Film credits: 1957: *Jamboree*; 1960: *Guns of the Timberland*; *The Alamo*; 1961: *Alakazam the Great* [voice only]; *Voyage to the Bottom of the Sea*; *Sail a Crooked Ship*; 1962: *Panic in Year Zero!*; 1963: *Operation Bikini*; *Drums of Africa*; *Beach Party*; *The Castilian*; 1964: *Muscle Beach Party*; *Bikini Beach*; *Pajama Party* [cameo]; 1965: *Beach Blanket Bingo*; *I'll Take Sweden*; *Ski Party*; *How to Stuff a Wild Bikini* [uncredited]; *Sergeant Deadhead*; *Dr. Goldfoot and the Bikini Machine*; 1966: *Fireball 500*; 1967: *The Million Eyes of Su-Muru*; 1968: *Skidoo*; 1969: *The Haunted House of Horror/Horror House*; 1973: *Saga of Sonora* (television); 1974: *The Take*; 1978: *Grease*; 1982: *Blood Song*; 1987: *Back to the Beach*. 1994: *The Stoned Age* (video) [cameo as himself]; 1995: *Casino* [cameo as himself].

★ *Peter Brown* ★

Dark-haired Peter Brown was the heartthrob of the television series *Lawman* for four years before he accepted the role of uptight, staid Chase Colton in the surf movie *Ride the Wild Surf* (1964) co-starring Fabian and Tab Hunter. The handsome actor had to bleach his brown hair blonde for the role, causing quite a stir among his loyal female fans. Happily, the flaxen-haired Brown and the film were a hit but Peter never ventured into the surf movie genre again. Instead, it was back to television Westerns for this cowboy-at-heart.

Peter Brown was born Pierre de Lappe on October 5, 1935, in New York City. His family relocated to Spokane, Washington, where the now strapping six-footer graduated high school from North Central High. He began acting as an adult when he was stationed in Alaska as a member of the Army's Second Infantry Division. To "get the hell out of the cold," he organized a base theater group to put on shows for the men stationed there. After his tour of duty was over, he headed for Southern California and studied acting at UCLA. Among his mentors were actor James Edwards and legendary acting coach Jeff Corey.

Jack L. Warner discovered Brown while the young actor was pumping gas. He was put under contract at Warner Bros. and made his film debut in *Darby's Rangers* (1958). He received co-star billing for his next film *Onionhead* (1958) but most of his scenes ended up on the cutting room floor. Still, he impressed the film's producer Jules Schermer, who cast the young actor as Deputy Johnny McKay opposite John Russell in the very successful television Western series *Lawman*, which ran for four seasons beginning in 1958. Commenting on the popularity of Westerns, Brown opined to columnist Ben Gross, "The Western is successful because it sells sex. This is so, even though in the old movies the hero would rather kiss a horse than a girl. The strong, virile hero provides it [the sex]. He's usually a handsome guy dressed in a manner to bowl over the women."

When *Lawman* ended its run in 1962, Brown was cast in the war movie *Merrill's Marauders* (1962) for Warner Bros. before going freelance. Possibly feeling that he was being typecast as cowboys and soldiers, Brown tried to change his image by appearing in two films for Walt Disney—the musical *Summer Magic* (1963) with Hayley Mills and the family drama *A Tiger Walks* (1964) with Pamela Franklin. He signed a contract with Universal and was immediately loaned out to Columbia for *Ride the Wild Surf* (1964), replacing Dean Torrence of the singing sensation Jan and Dean. With his bleached hair and muscular torso, Brown was the perfect choice to bring surfer Chase alive on the big screen and he received fine notices. He was described as being "an accomplished actor on his way up" in *The Los Angeles Times* and "surprisingly agreeable" by *The New York Times*. He was extremely popular during this period and was nominated for *Photoplay*'s Gold Medal Award for Favorite Actor three years in a row from 1963 to 1965.

One year after playing a psycho-babbling juvenile delinquent out for kicks in the trash classic *Kitten with a Whip* (1964) starring Ann-Margret, Brown was cast in the lighthearted television Western series *Laredo* co-starring Neville Brand, William Smith and Phil Carey. After years of playing cowboys Brown became so adept as a horseman and marksman that he and his *Laredo* co-stars would appear at rodeos and state fairs throughout the country. He boasted in 1967 that he could handle a gun better than anyone in Hollywood except Sammy Davis, Jr.! According to Peter, "Sammy is superb."

During the run of *Laredo*, Brown (who had a short-lived marriage to actress Diane Jergens in 1958) married former model Sandra Edmundson; their son Matthew Peter was born in 1966. After *Laredo* was cancelled in 1967, Brown went the guest star route and also appeared in made-for-television movies. On the big screen, he did the motorcycle flick *Chrome and Hot Leather* (1971) playing a soldier rather than a biker, reunited with *Laredo* co-star William Smith for *Piranha, Piranha!* (1972) and co-starred in a few cult B-movies including *Rape Squad* (1974) and the blaxploitation classic *Foxy Brown* (1974). Starring with Pam Grier, Brown played the twisted, sexy leader of a dope ring who gets his comeuppance in the most dreaded way any male could imagine. He would go on to play another drug dealer in the violent women's prison flick *The Concrete Jungle* (1982) starring Jill St. John and Barbara Luna.

While his sixties contemporaries saw their careers sputter during the seventies and eighties, talented Brown reinvented himself and carved out a whole new career. In 1972 he was cast as the good Dr. Greg Peters on *Days of Our Lives* and stayed in the part until 1979. Brown was able to continue in soaps due to his talent and professionalism as well as having the perfect features to play very distinguished-looking heroes or villains. He roles included attorney Robert Laurence on *The Young and the Restless* (1981-82; 1989-91), philandering politician Roger Forbes on *Loving* (1983-84) and Charles Sanders III on *One Life to Live* (1985-86), where he reunited with *Laredo* co-star Phil Carey. Brown remarked to writer Jennifer

Bialow in *Soap Opera Digest* that *Loving* stands out for him because of the brawl he had to do on his first day of shooting. "The actor I was fighting was a college boxer, and he threw one that really laid me down. That was my introduction to *Loving*; it was more like *hating*."

His last soap role was scheming, self-made Texas millionaire Blake Hayes on *The Bold and the Beautiful* from 1991 to 1992. The character was not from Texas or a millionaire when it was offered to Brown by producer Bill Bell, whom he previously worked for on *The Young and the Restless*. Peter commented in *Soap Opera Digest*, "When Bill told me about the character, Blake was a commodities broker. This is what they had on paper, and I didn't accept it on the phone. I wanted it, but only under certain conditions." It is a testament to Brown's talent and professionalism that the producers and writers tailored the character to Brown's characteristics and traits.

In 2002, Brown was the recipient of the Golden Boot Award for his contribution over the years to the Western genre. Nowadays Peter spends his free time in the mountains, playing tennis or just visiting with his adult sons Matthew and Joshua between acting in such films as *Land of the Free?* (2004) and *Big Chuck, Little Chuck* (2004) and running his production company, Handshake Films, where he produced and narrated the instructional video *The Penning Tape*. According to Peter, "Team penning is when three riders enter an arena, gallop across a start line and separate three same-numbered steers from a herd of 30, then drive them over the start line to the opposite end of the arena into a holding pen under a two-minute time limit. The fastest time wins."

Intense-looking James Darren, who gained immense popularity as Gidget's surfer guy, Moondoggie.

Looking back at his time in the water on *Ride the Wild Surf*, Brown reflects, "I'm glad I made it and I'm glad for the experience that I had there in Hawaii. I met a lot of nice folks—some of whom I still know. I always enjoyed working. Every actor likes to work. But there are different qualities of work. I've gone to the Philippines to make war movies in the jungles and swamps with leeches and I've ridden horses playing cowboys and Indians. I've lots of different kinds of work and I am grateful for all of it."

Film credits: 1958: *Darby's Rangers*; *Marjorie Morningstar* [uncredited]; *Onionhead*; 1959: *Westbound* [voice only]; 1962: *Merrill's Marauders*; *Red Nightmare* (short); 1963: *Summer Magic*; 1964: *A Tiger Walks*; *Ride the Wild Surf*; *Kitten with a Whip*; 1970: *Hunters Are for Killing* (television); *The Big Escape/ Eagles Attack at Dawn*; 1971: *Chrome and Hot Leather*; 1972: *Piranha, Piranha!*; 1974: *Memory of Us*; *Rape Squad*; *Foxy Brown*; 1975: *Slashed Dreams/Sunburst*; 1979: *Salvage* (television); 1980: *Top of the Hill* (television); *The Girl, the Gold Watch & Everything* (television); 1982: *The Concrete Jungle*; 1984: *Cover Up* (television); 1986: *The Aurora Encounter*; 1989: *Demonstone*; 1995: *Fists of Iron*; 1997: *Asylum* (video); 1999: *Wasteland Justice*; 2002: *Y.M.I.*; 2004: *Big Chuck, Little Chuck*; *Land of the Free?*

★ *James Darren* ★

Before Frankie Avalon hit the surf in *Beach Party*, there was James Darren as Moondoggie, Gidget's true love in the surf movies *Gidget* (1959) and *Gidget Goes Hawaiian* (1961). Darren immediately became one of the top teen idols of the period for his portrayal of the surfer boy. He rode the waves one last time as a rich playboy out to win poor but proud coed Pamela Tiffin in *For Those Who Think Young* (1964) before heading for the shore.

James Darren was born James William Ercolani on June 8, 1936, in Philadelphia, Pennsylvania. As a teenager he began commuting from South Philly to New York to attend drama classes with the Stella Adler Group. A trip to Hollywood in 1954 with the hope of being discovered failed. Darren returned home and (purportedly) while waiting for an elevator in the Brill Building he was spotted by talent scout Joyce Selznick of Columbia Pictures, who brought the young actor to the attention of Harry Romm, Columbia's eastern talent representative. He was soon signed to a contract and flown to Hollywood to star in the low-budget Sam Katzman potboiler *Rumble on the Docks* (1956), playing a gang leader, and *The Tijuana Story* (1957), as a teenager addicted to narcotics. "James Ercolani" was not a marquee name so Jimmy chose his new moniker, Darren, "as a homage to the Kaiser-Darrin sports car."

Darren continued landing movie roles at Columbia. He played the crooked younger brother of Richard Conte in *The Brothers Rico* (1957), a buddy of G.I. Jack Lemmon in the comedy *Operation Mad Ball* (1957) and one of the sons of evil land baron Van Heflin in *Gunman's Walk* (1958).

Now with a strong résumé, the good-looking young actor should have been an obvious choice to play Moondoggie, the surfer boy whom Sandra Dee's Gidget goes gaga over in the first Hollywood surf movie, *Gidget*. However, the studio inserted two songs to be sung by the character and, as Darren had not demonstrated singing ability to them, he was not considered for the part even though he was performing from the time he was 15. Sensing this movie was going to become a big hit, the enterprising lad cut a single with the studio's recording subsidiary Colpix Records. Seeing that the record charted, Columbia acquiesced and Darren got the part despite the hindering facts that the Philadelphia native could not surf and was a very weak swimmer.

Darren acquits himself well in *Gidget* and is especially effective playing a hot dogger torn between the surf bum lifestyle and the reality of growing up. He received some of his finest notices for this role. The critic in the *Los Angeles Examiner* remarked "Both Sandra and Darren imbue the story with refreshing liveliness" while the reviewer for *The Los Angeles Times* commented, "Darren and [Cliff] Robertson play ingratiatingly."

Gidget's success brought Darren enormous popularity with the teenage audience (mostly female) but it also had its drawbacks. Before his teen idol persona overshadowed his acting ability, Darren was able to land dramatic roles in *The Gene Krupa Story* (1959) starring Sal Mineo, the Korean war drama *All the Young Men* (1960) starring Alan Ladd and *Let No Man Write My Epitaph* (1960). In the latter, he arguably gives his finest performance as the problem-plagued son of Shelley Winters, trying to rise out of a life of crime and drug dependency. Though all three films received positive notices, none was a major box office hit. In 1960, Darren, who had a child named Jimmy from a previous short-lived marriage to his childhood sweetheart Gloria Terlitsky, wed Evy Norlund, the former Miss Denmark 1958. They would go on to have two sons, Christian and Anthony.

Nineteen sixty-one turned out to be a banner year for James Darren. He played the important role of Pvt. Spyros Pappadimos in the Academy Award–winning *The Guns of Navarone* and critics took notice of how he held his own as a Greek soldier against such acting stalwarts as Gregory Peck, David Niven and Anthony Quinn. His teenage fans, however, wanted to see him playing the all–American boy next door and flocked to see him reprise his Moondoggie role in *Gidget Goes Hawaiian* co-starring newcomer Deborah Walley in place of Sandra Dee. They also began buying up his single "Goodbye Cruel World" despite the fact that, of all the teen idols of the day (including Frankie Avalon, Fabian and Bobby Rydell), Darren's musical talent was the most tenuous.

Darren's teen idol image immediately had its drawbacks for the actor, who did not relish the spotlight. The family man who liked spending time at home bemoaned about his popularity in *TV Guide*, "At times it was Chinese torture." In San Francisco a crowd of teenage girls broke into a television studio and literally ripped the clothes off Darren's back. In New England, the police rescued him from a gang of rowdy fans, and in Hollywood amorous female followers vandalized his car.

In 1962, Darren was ridiculously cast as a full-bred Hawaiian native boy in love with white girl Yvette Mimieux, the sister of bigoted land baron Charlton Heston, in *Diamond Head* (1962). He then reluctantly reprised his Moondoggie role for a third time opposite yet another new Gidget. With Deborah Walley pregnant, actress Cindy Carol took over as the surfing sweetie abandons the sunny shores of California for romantic Italy in *Gidget Goes to Rome* (1963). It was back to the beach for Jimmy Darren when he was paired with Pamela Tiffin in the *Beach Party* knockoff *For Those Who Think Young*.

Darren hung up his surfboard after *For Those Who Think Young*. He reunited with Pamela Tiffin in the college hot rod flick *The Lively Set* (1964), his last teenage movie. Regarding the film, he remarked in *Seventeen*, "This is a role I can get my teeth into. I play a cocky driver who designs a gas turbine engine and builds an experimental car." Many years later, Darren also lamented making this film and commented in *Starlog*, "I was probably guilty of letting other people guide my career. I should have taken control ... after *The Guns of Navarone*. I would not have done movies like *The Lively Set* or *For Those Who Think Young*." Even still, these films were popular enough for Darren to be nominated for the Photoplay Gold Medal Award for Favorite Actor.

To shake the Moondoggie persona, Darren took some time off from acting. In *TV Guide* he admitted to becoming moody during this period because "it's from not being able to do the things I want to do. Forget *Gidget*. I want a chance to do other things." In 1966, a matured Darren got his opportunity and co-starred with Robert Colbert in Irwin Allen's science-fiction series *The Time Tunnel*. At first Darren turned the part down because he didn't want to do television but Allen's enthusiasm for the series swayed the actor. When the show ended after only one season, he concentrated on his singing career for the next ten years, touring the country with comedian Buddy Hackett while accepting intermittent acting roles. Most notably he played a jazz musician who witnesses a murder in *Venus in Furs* (1969), Jess Franco's cult movie featuring the director's familiar elements of sex and sadism. Darren also turned up in the television-movies *City Beneath the Sea* (1971) from producer Irwin Allen and *The Lives of Jenny Dolan* (1975).

In 1983, Darren returned to series television playing Officer James Corrigan in the popular police show *T.J. Hooker* (1983–86). He directed the series' final episode, which led to a very successful television directing career for him. Among his credits are episodes of *The A-Team, Hunter, Walker, Texas Ranger, Savannah* and *Melrose Place*.

Darren returned to acting in the late nineties as Vic Fontaine, a holographic swinging sixties lounge singer, which he played as a parody of his younger days, on several episodes of *Star Trek: Deep Space Nine* during its final season. Silver-haired and still extremely attractive, Darren continues to direct and to perform live across the country.

Film credits: 1956: *Rumble on the Docks*; 1957: *Operation Mad Ball*; *The Brothers Rico*; *The Tijuana Story*; 1958: *Gunman's Walk*; 1959: *Gidget*; *The Gene Krupa Story*; 1960: *Because They're Young* [cameo as himself]; *All the Young Men*; *Let No Man Write My Epitaph*; 1961: *Gidget Goes Hawaiian*; *The Guns of Navarone*; 1962: *Diamond Head*; 1963: *Gidget Goes to Rome*; 1964: *For Those Who Think Young*; *The Lively Set*; 1970: *Paroxismus/Venus in Furs*; 1971: *City Beneath the Sea* (television); *Mooch Goes to Hollywood* [cameo as himself]; 1975: *The Lives of Jenny Dolan* (television); 1978: *The Boss' Son*; 1980: *Turnover Smith* (television); 1981: *Scruples* (television); 1986: *Blood Sport* (television); 2001: *Random Acts*.

★ *Sandra Dee* ★

Petite and blonde with penetrating brown eyes, Sandra Dee rode the crest of the wave into Hollywood movie history as Gidget in the film that started the surfing craze on celluloid, *Gidget* (1959). She should have continued playing the role in the sequels but the studio she was contracted to instead cast her as Tammy and as a junior Doris Day in a series of forgettable but profitable comedies such as *Come September* (1961), *If a Man Answers* (1962), *Take Her, She's Mine* (1963) and *I'd Rather Be Rich* (1964). Despite the mediocrity of her movies, Dee was extremely popular and her love affair with singer Bobby Darin kept her in the gossip columns for years. By the time she was 26 in 1970, her once promising movie career had fizzled out.

Sandra Dee was born Alexandra Zuck on April 23, 1944, in Bayonne, New Jersey. When she was five, her mother divorced her drunken father and Dee never saw him again. A few years later she took a new husband, Eugene Douvan, a real estate developer, and the family moved to Manhattan where Sandra was enrolled in the Professional Children's School. She participated in a Girls Scout fashion show, which led to a contract with the Conover Modeling Agency. Dee became one of the most sought-after teen models of the fifties, earning over $70,000 a year. She also became so worried about her weight that she was anorexic before anyone had a word for it.

Douvan passed away in 1956 and during the wake Dee was contacted by producer Ross Hunter. Refusing to meet Natalie Wood's outrageous salary demands, he decided to find another teenage actress to star in *The Restless Years* (1958). Impressed with her fragile beauty, Hunter signed Sandra to a contract with Universal Studios. Her mother lied about her daughter's age and changed her birth year to 1942 so she could attain more film work without having to adhere to the child labor laws. Before filming began on the movie, Hunter loaned her out to MGM for a role in *Until They Sail* (1957) starring Paul Newman. Though she didn't display any distinctive acting prowess, Dee had an affable charm that shone through. It was enough for her to win a Golden Globe Award that year (along with Carolyn Jones and Diane Varsi) as the Most Promising Female Newcomers.

After appearing in *The Reluctant Debutante* (1958), whose title sums up her role, Sandra Dee had a banner year in 1959. She gave a wonderfully perky performance as the petite surfer in *Gidget* co-starring Cliff Robertson and James Darren, who (Dee admitted in *People*) she had a secret crush on. After playing Lana Turner's neglected daughter in *Imitation of Life* (1959), she portrayed a good girl drawn to the strikingly handsome Troy Donahue as they bond over their parents' philandering on an island off the Maine coast in *A Summer Place*, featuring Max Steiner's lush score. Her question to Donahue once they returned to the mainland ("Johnny, have you've been bad with girls?") sums up her character's naïveté and clinched her the award for Worst Supporting Actress from the *Harvard Lampoon*.

These roles typecast Dee as the virginal ingénue. They also made her one of the most popular actresses of the day. Ross Hunter opined in *Dream Lovers* that her star quality "was so unusual in that she was so natural. You never felt that she was acting. She really was above the average girl, and yet she was very down to earth with it all." Dee won the Photoplay Gold Medal Award in 1959 for Favorite Actress and was voted the No. 1 Star of Tomorrow by theater owners in *The Motion Picture Exhibitor*. Dee commented in *People*, "It was fun. But it was my mother who really loved all my acclaim." The other studios fell over themselves trying to discover the new Sandra Dee and soon Tuesday Weld, Carol Lynley, Yvette Mimieux, Diane McBain and Connie Stevens were making the Hollywood scene.

Fans couldn't get enough of Sandra Dee. She adorned the cover of every movie magazine at least once. Audiences flocked to her pictures, which on a whole were a dismal lot though a few stood out. Beautifully shot in Italy, the Rock Hudson-Gina Lollabrigida comedy *Come September* (1962) is where she met future husband Bobby Darin. In the James Stewart family comedy *Take Her, She's Mine* (1963), Dee is rather amusing as an rambunctious college coed.

Despite critical barbs for her performances in most of her other films such as *Tammy and the Doctor* (1963) and *I'd Rather Be Rich* (1964), Dee scored where it counted most—at the box office. Practically every one of her movies made money and she was voted one of the year's Top Box Office Stars, placing in the top ten from 1960 to 1964. Dee should have been enormously happy but behind that Hollywood cotton candy façade as America's Sweetheart was a young girl in turmoil. She was chain smoking at age twelve and was hooked on pills and booze by the time she was 19. In 1963, she was quoted as saying, "There should be a law against martinis. Yesterday I had my first one and I didn't think it did anything. Then someone said have another. And wow, I got looped." Sadly, this wasn't the last martini Dee would sip. That same year Darin filed for divorce, which devastated the starlet and new mother. They reconciled in 1965 after Darin got her off the speed and liquor but the marriage disintegrated by 1967.

Dee was supposed to co-star with Warren Beatty in the fluffy comedy *That Funny Feeling* but the pairing fell through when Dee wouldn't concede top billing. She defended her stance in an interview with *Seventeen* and remarked, "I've worked hard for seven years making one picture after another and I didn't think it was fair to take second billing under Warren, who's been around such a short time. My pride hurt." Dee offered to split the billing but was rebuffed by Beatty's agents, so Bobby Darin stepped in as his substitute. She signed to co-star with Beatty in the British thriller *Kaleidoscope* but was replaced by Susannah York.

After appearing as the innocent in the spy spoof *A Man Could Get Killed* (1966) with James Garner, Dee firmly stated in *Seventeen*, "They can't keep me in Peter Pan collars for the rest of my life. I've got to move on, I've got to grow up. I want to do drama, sex, pictures with real substance."

In the lame sex comedy *Doctor, You've Got to Be Kidding!* (1967), Dee played a single aspiring singer who learns she is pregnant. She hit a new low playing a

The big screen's original Gidget, Sandra Dee, shows off her assets.

blonde Cajun girl in *The Manhunter*, a debacle that didn't see the light of day until it was televised in 1976. This was Dee's last film for Universal in 1968 before she acrimoniously split with the studio and went freelance. Though Sandra praised Universal in the past to *Photoplay* and *Modern Screen*, she bemoaned the typecasting she suffered under them and exclaimed to columnist Sidney Skolsky, "I have a chance to play a variety of roles. A freedom of choice—something as a studio contractee I never had." Alas, Dee left the comfy confines of Universal during a time in Hollywood (the late sixties) when younger audiences were rebelling against the fifties ideals of their parents. Dee was so much a part of that with her icky-sweet Tammy image that she and others such as Shelley Fabares, Troy Donahue and Annette Funicello were deemed out of fashion at a time when bikers ruled the drive-ins and LSD was the recreational drug of choice.

After starring in the gothic thriller *The Dunwich Horror* (1970) where she does well as a virginal librarian who falls under the spell of a demented stranger, Dee took a respite from acting. She resumed her career in 1972 due to the prodding of her ten-year-old son. She remarked to columnist Sidney Skolsky that when Dodd asked if she was going to return to work, she asked why and he replied, "If you don't hurry up you'll be a has-been." Unfortunately, his words were prophetic as Dee found it nearly impossible to shake her ingénue image (her name was used as a parody in the song "Look at Me, I'm Sandra Dee" in the Broadway musical *Grease*) and she could only conjure up roles on *Night Gallery, Love, American Style* and a few made-for-television movies. Her true love Bobby Darin died in 1973, sending Dee into a further depression. Audiences were used to seeing a slender Dee but she looked extremely gaunt and pale playing the lost love of service man Bill Bixby in *Fantasy Island* (1977).

In the eighties, Dee returned to the big screen in the low-budget Al Adamson-directed film *Lost* (1983) before disappearing once again from the public eye after the death of her mother. Dee became a recluse, only finding solace in a bottle of scotch, and didn't even bother attending her own son's wedding.

In 1991, Dee shared with the world the traumas of her life—including being sexually abused by her stepfather. The exposure led to a number of television talk show appearances, the lead in a local stage production of *Love Letters* with John Saxon, a television commercial for Captain D's Restaurant and the chance to provide the voice of a radio call-in listener on an episode of *Frasier*. But her comeback was short-lived. Her son Dodd, who authored the book *Dream Lovers: The Magnificent Shattered Lives of Bobby Darin and Sandra Dee*, remarked to the *New York Daily News* in 1994 that Dee "lives alone, eats sparingly, reads voluminously and drinks heavily."

Dee finally conquered her demons after her granddaughter Alexa was born in 1996. She returned to the stage in a 1998 production of *Grease* in Detroit and participated in the making of a documentary on her life for *A&E Biography* in 2000. Despite the years of hard drinking, Sandra Dee was surprisingly still a beautiful woman, and the proud grandmother strived to stay happy and sober. She exclaimed to *The National Enquirer*, "I've gone through a nightmare. And thank God I'm out of it!"

Sandra Dee died on February 20, 2005, from kidney disease.

Film credits: 1957: *Until They Sail;* 1958: *The Reluctant Debutante; The Restless Years;* 1959: *A Stranger in My Arms; Gidget; Imitation of Life; The Wild and the Innocent; The Snow Queen* [voice only]; *A Summer Place;* 1960: *Portrait in Black;* 1961: *Romanoff and Juliet; Tammy Tell Me True; Come September;* 1962: *If a Man Answers;* 1963: *Tammy and the Doctor; Take Her, She's Mine;* 1964: *I'd Rather Be Rich;* 1965: *That Funny Feeling;* 1966: *A Man Could Get Killed;* 1967: *Doctor, You've Got to Be Kidding; Rosie!;* 1970: *The Dunwich Horror;* 1972: *The Daughters of Joshua Cabe* (television); 1974: *Houston, We've Got a Problem* (television); 1976: *The Manhunter* (television) [completed in 1968]; 1977: *Fantasy Island* (television); 1983: *Lost.*

⋆ *Mickey Dora* ⋆

Mickey "Da Cat" Dora (a.k.a. Mickey Chapin Dora, a.k.a. Miki Dora) is considered to be one of the best surfers of the sixties. Nicknamed the Master of Malibu, Dora's surfing expertise was sometimes overshadowed by his outrageous behavior on and off the beach. He is credited with inventing the myth of the rebel surfer. The angry, outspoken young man remarked in the pages of *Surfer* that "I'm a freak of nature and don't fit in with anybody."

Born in Budapest, Hungary, on August 11, 1934, Miklos S. Dora III was the son of Miklos and Ramona Dora. His parents divorced when he was very young and his mother married surfer Gard Chapin, who introduced the young, dark-haired lad to the sport of surfing and the beach. He became a regular surfing the Malibu area and with his great agility and maneuvering expertise was one of the dominant surfers of the period. In late June 1956, he was surfing with buddies Mickey Munoz and Terry "Tubesteak" Tracey when petite Kathy Kohner joined their crowd as the newly nicknamed Gidget. Kathy remarks, "Mickey definitely had a personality and an original sense of style. People copied his use of hand language. He was probably the greatest surfer I've ever seen on a surfboard. He was a bit of a rogue but I had fun with him and he never stepped over the boundaries of propriety with me. He played a wicked game of ping-pong and he was the only guy to take me surfing at Rincon. We also went skiing together but he wouldn't pay for the lift tickets so we'd have to hike up the mountain." Seems only natural then, due to his connection to Gidget, that Dora was hired to surf in the film, where he doubled for James Darren.

Before Dora parlayed his experience in *Gidget* into getting hired for a number of Hollywood surf movies, he appeared in a number of surfing documentaries including *Search for Surf* (1958), *Surfing Hollow Days* (1961) and *Gun Ho!* (1963). His friendship with the younger Malibu surfer Ed Garner led to his association with AIP. He was hired to surf double and to do background work in *Beach Party* (1963).

Director William Asher took a shine to the offbeat Dora despite his unorthodox behavior off-camera and employed him in subsequent films, *Muscle Beach Party* (1963), *Bikini Beach* (1964), *Beach Blanket Bingo* (1965) and *How to Stuff a Wild Bikini* (1965). He also freelanced for other film companies, turning up in *Surf Party* (1964), which gave him his most screen time, *For Those Who Think Young* (1964) and most notably *Ride the Wild Surf* (1964), where Dora tackled for the first time the big waves of Hawaii. Unlike fellow Malibu surfers such as Johnny Fain and Mike Nader, Dora had no interest in acting and usually hid in the background when he was on land. He remarked, "I'm usually not seen because I don't believe in looking over someone's shoulder and grinning in the camera."

Commenting on his film work, the candid Dora remarked in *Surfer*, "I've done some very difficult things like surfing through a pier with a camera strapped to my back. Surfing stunts depend on the vivid imagination the director has and, naturally, what the storyboard calls for. Some pansy directors dream up situations not even Clark Kent could survive. The great aggravation is trying to communicate with these people on what is possible and what isn't." But Dora kept stunt surfing as he needed the money.

While working in Hollywood, Dora (the "Black Knight of Malibu") let it be known that he hated the establishment, and he always had a scheme or scam going. "Mickey was always Mickey," laughs Ed Garner. "He was probably the biggest prankster you could imagine. He would come up with a handful of tricks no matter what time of the day or where we were or what we were doing. There was always something mischievous going on in the back of his mind. I don't think he totally meant to be malicious but I think it was more to see what he could get away with.

"He had a friend named George who was the maitre d' at a restaurant called La Scala in Beverly Hills," continues Ed. "It was one of *the* top celebrity hangouts during the sixties. Whenever they were going to cater a major event for any of the big movie stars such as Robert Wagner, Frank Sinatra or Dean Martin, George would call Mickey and tell him about it. Mickey would dress up in a waiter's uniform and crash the party. *But he wouldn't take any orders!* He'd just walk around pretending to be a waiter and enjoy the food and drink while ingratiating himself with as many people as possible before leaving the party."

How to Stuff a Wild Bikini was Dora's Hollywood swan song. After *Gidget* brought surfing to the masses, Dora's Malibu surfing milieu was invaded by "kooks" from the Valley and other outsiders. This displeased him to no end and he made sure the surfing world knew it in the pages of all the surf publications. In 1968 he even authored his own article for *Surfer*, a diatribe against the magazine's associate editor Bill Cleary, surf contest judges and the invading surfers of his beloved Malibu.

Though he was inducted into the International Surfing Hall of Fame in 1966, competition had soured for Dora, who felt that contests were controlling surfers in a "fascist" way. Regarding his infamous war (and shoving match) with Johnny Fain during the 1965 Malibu International, Dora shrugged it off and remarked, "[The judges] told me to go out and surf like I always do ... so I did. Nothing happened. Just one little push...."

On the big screen, Dora could be seen briefly in the surf movies *The Endless Summer* (1966) and *Golden Breed* (1968). At the height of his popularity the "Angry Young Man of Surfing" fled the U.S. in 1970 after a warrant had been issued for his arrest for credit card and check fraud. He traveled the world surfing.

When Mickey Dora returned to California in 1973, he was sentenced to probation, which he broke. For the next decade, Dora was in and out of jail twice and spent much time in France. Dora resurfaced in the documentary *Surfers: The Movie* (1990) and his appearance is one of the film's many highlights. Dora also became the subject of his own film, *In Search of da Cat* (1998).

Forty years after she last saw him, Kathy Kohner ran into Dora at a Southern California shopping mall. Kathy recalls, "I said, 'Mickey!' He replied, 'You recognize me, Gidget?'" Soon after, Malibu's bad boy passed away from pancreatic cancer on January 3, 2002, in Montecito, California.

Film credits: 1959: *Gidget*; 1963: *Beach Party*; 1964: *Surf Party*; *Muscle Beach Party*; *For Those Who Think Young*; *Bikini Beach*; *Ride the Wild Surf*; 1965: *Beach Blanket Bingo*; *Ski Party*; *How to Stuff a Wild Bikini*.

⋆ *Don Edmonds* ⋆

Tall with sandy blonde hair, Don Edmonds was attractive with fine features but he lacked that leading man look. Consequently, he was saddled playing the goofy sidekick, most notably in three beach movies. Edmonds made his film debut as Larry in *Gidget Goes Hawaiian* (1961) after knocking around Hollywood since 1958. Friendly with actor-turned-producer Bart Patton, Don was cast in two of his beach movies. He went from the shores of Malibu in *Beach Ball* (1965) to the slopes of Sun Valley in *Wild Wild Winter* (1966).

Don Edmonds was born in Kansas City, Missouri. His father relocated the family to Long Beach, California, in the thirties and got work as a timekeeper at the shipyards. Soon the elder Edmonds' entrepreneurial son began offering to shine shoes for military men at the Pike, a Long Beach amusement park, earning more money than his father. The cute-looking youngster also had a talent for singing and appeared in local USO shows singing "Mammy" in blackface.

As a teenager, Edmonds spent his time hanging out on the beach. "The first surfboard I ever saw was in 1950 when my friend Terry McGelrand, who was this wild guy, brought one back from Hawaii," recalls Edmonds. "This board must have been 50 feet long and it had no fin on it. We loaded it up on his Woodie and took

Publicity shot of Don Edmonds in *Gidget Goes Hawaiian* (Columbia, 1961) (*courtesy the Billy Rose Theatre Collection, The New York Public Library for the Performing Arts, Astor, Lenox and Tilden Foundations*).

it down to the beach. We had always been belly floppers before that. He took it out into the water and stood up on it. We gasped, 'Whoa, check that out!'

"We all began surfing after that," continues Don. "A couple of legends came from our group. Hobie Alter had this shack out there where he was experimenting with different kinds of weights and woods. He began designing surfboards. Later he was famous for the Hobie Cat [which Matt Warshaw described as being 'an easy-to-use 14-foot catamaran designed to launch from the beach and ride over the surf']. The other guy who I really grew up with was about three or four years younger than us and he'd plead, 'Can I hang around with you guys?' We'd say, 'No, go away! We're going to look for girls.' He was always the kid we'd chase away. His name was Bruce Brown who went on to make *The Endless Summer*."

Though he was surfing around the same time as Mickey Dora, Terry "Tubesteak" Tracey, Mickey "Mongoose" Muñoz and Kathy "Gidget" Kohner, Edmonds did not encounter them in the ocean. "We never went up to Malibu because we'd end up in a fight," states Don emphatically. He revealed that turf wars were common between the surfers from various beaches. You were expected to stay on your own beach and not invade anybody else's.

After graduating high school, Edmonds joined the service and became a paratrooper with the 82nd Airborne. While stationed at Fort Bragg in North Carolina, he joined the Spielhaus Players and appeared in works by such renowned playwrights as Tennessee Williams and William Inge. Returning to Long Beach, he was cast in several local theater productions before joining the Estelle Harmon Actor's Workshop where his classmates included Barbara Luna, Bill Bixby, Millie Perkins and Ty Hardin. From there Edmonds was able to finagle an agent to represent him and began landing work on television, most notably in five episodes of *Playhouse 90*.

While working on *Playhouse 90*, Edmonds became fascinated with directing. "I'd sit and just watch the director," reveals Don. "I just knew I wanted to direct. I never just hung out in my dressing room. Instead I would come out on the set and observe gentlemen like Ralph Nelson and John Frankenheimer work. They were young guys back then making their bones too. This was the only schooling that I had. I was just so interested in the directing process."

Edmonds made his film debut in *Gidget Goes Hawaiian* (1961), playing a college guy who (along with Joby Baker and Bart Patton) befriend Deborah Walley's Gidget on her island vacation. He landed a much smaller role as a doctor in his next movie *The Interns* (1962). In a wild New Year's Eve party scene, he does the twist with dancer Carroll Harrison. A photographer shot stills of it and they appeared in most of the popular fan magazines to publicize the movie. This and Edmonds' friendship with a club reporter named Rona Barrett kept his name alive in the movie rags for years despite his small number of film credits. Though he was being cast on television in such series as *Combat* and *McHale's Navy*, Don was only able to land minor roles on the big screen in two Walt Disney features, *Son of Flubber* (1963) and *The Misadventures of Merlin Jones* (1964).

Television offered more opportunity for the struggling actor and he landed a regular role on the sitcom *Broadside* (the female version of *McHale's Navy*) in 1964. But halfway through the season his character was phased out because they had nothing for him to do. He recalls, "I really liked working with Joan Staley. She was neat and a very sexy girl. Sheila James was one of the brightest people I ever met. She graduated from one of the Ivy League schools and is now part of the Legislature in California."

Edmonds' friendship with *Gidget Goes Hawaiian* co-star Bart Patton came in handy when Patton became a producer and hired the young actor for lead roles in *Beach Ball* (1965) and *Wild Wild Winter* (1966). Though he worked with some heavyweight talent on *Playhouse 90* in his early days in Hollywood, acting in beach movies did not diminish the work ethic Edmonds learned from them. He says, "When you are starting out in show business, there are certain ethics you must learn. If you worked with people who had those ethics, you either picked them up or got out. I was taught that you always show up on time and you know your lines. You're a pro and never come in with a B-game. If you do that, you are never going to make it in this town. No matter if it is one line of dialogue or the lead, you act like a pro. So by the time that I worked in the beach movies, that ethic had been ingrained in me. Also I was never an actor who had so many choices—I took what was there and did my best."

Edmonds post–*Wild Wild Winter* acting career trailed off with appearances on the television series *Green Acres* and a return to the beach in *Gidget*. "I did a few of episodes of *Gidget* with Sally Field," recalls Edmonds. "She was only about 15 years old. The first time I ever stepped on set with this little girl, I had the lame idea that I was just going to work with another kid star. *Well, I was never so wrong in my whole life!* The camera rolled and suddenly I was saying lines to a *consummate* pro. Her eyes popped into mine and I could feel the connection, which I've only felt with very few actors I've ever worked with in my entire career. She absolutely blew me away. I knew right that second that she was going to be huge. Not just because of the *Gidget* series but because I was working with an *ultimate* actor. It was absolutely *thrilling* to get that feeling. I've worked with actors from Boris Karloff to Andy Garcia and as great as they were I *never* have worked with anyone that outdistanced her. That time proved me right and that she took the Oscar absolutely didn't surprise me. It thrilled me but it didn't surprise me. She's as good as they get in movies. I just wish she'd work more."

In the late sixties, Edmonds stopped acting for a period of time. "I gave it up because of my desire to get onto the other side of the camera," reveals Edmonds. "I'd been around it a lot. I liked directing but nobody was going to hire me. Who was going to give me a chance? They just considered me a dumb actor. So that's when Rick Rogers and I paired up." Rick Rogers used the stage name Steve Rogers and had worked with Don Edmonds in *Wild Wild Winter*.

"Rick and I had these great offices on Brighton Way in Beverly Hills and we wore suits to lunch at La Scala. But we weren't making any movies. We walked around with business cards convincing ourselves that we were producers for about a year and a half. Finally, I said, 'Rick, we're bullshit! We're looking good and doing nothing!' He didn't care because he was wealthy and living up on Stone Canyon in a Colonial mansion with his wife and two children. His family owned American Linen Supply Company and Steiner Products. But I'm over there on Orchid Avenue in an $85-a-month pad and I can't make the rent. I told him we were going to go out and make a tits-and-ass movie. He said, 'My wife would never allow me to make a tits-and-ass movie.' I said, 'Yes, she will.' And that's how we made *Wild Honey*

[1971]." Edmonds directed and wrote the sexy comedy about a country girl who comes to the big city and gets in all sorts of trouble. But he and Rogers had a falling out due to "creative differences" and have never spoken since. "I don't bear him any ill will but I think he does me," says Don with a sigh.

Wild Honey made money at the box office and the film's success led to more behind-the-scenes work for Edmonds during the seventies in soft-core sex films. He wrote *Saddle Tramp Women* (1972) starring porn actress Rene Bond, directed *Southern Double Cross* (1973) and wrote, produced and directed *Tender Loving Care* (1974) starring Donna Desmond as a nurse investigating the mysterious death of a boxer. Edmonds' most infamous movies were the cult film favorites *Ilsa, She Wolf of the SS* (1974) and *Ilsa, Harem Keeper of the Oil Sheiks* (1976) starring Dyanne Thorne as Ilsa, a sadistic Nazi warden. These low-budget, violent exploitation movies are talked about to this day and have been called everything from "sleazy," "tasteless" and "dreadful" to "amazing," "superior" and "legendary."

Regarding *Ilsa*, Edmonds says, "I appeared at the Chiller Theatre Convention in the fall of 2003 and people would walk up to me and tell me that I was the god-father of all the trash films that they love. I'd never gone to a cult movie convention before and the reaction I received from the fans literally stunned me. These guys were practically kissing my ring. You wouldn't believe how many websites are dedicated to *Ilsa, She Wolf of the SS*—hundreds! It's amazing!"

Edmonds returned as a triple threat with the violent bounty hunter film *Bare Knuckles* (1978) starring Robert Viharo and Sherry Jackson. During the eighties he was vice-president at Producers Sales Organization where he was involved in getting such big-budget movies as *Short Circuit* (1986) and *Clan of the Cave Bear* (1986) produced. More recently Edmonds (who described himself in a recent interview as being "a film doctor") worked in production on more mainstream films such as *True Romance* (1993) with Christian Slater, Val Kilmer and Brad Pitt, *Fast Money* (1995) and the direct-to-video *Larceny* (2004). "I was one of the producers of *True Romance*," states Don. "Quentin Tarantino wrote it but I didn't know who he was. He came to lunch with the director, four suits and me. We all introduced ourselves, shook hands and sat down. Quentin whispered to me, 'What's your name again?' I said, 'Don Edmonds.' He said, '*The* Don Edmonds?' I replied, 'I'm the only one I know.' He asked, 'Did you direct *Ilsa, She Wolf of the SS*?' I hesitantly admitted that I did and he proceeded to list all the movies that I directed including the ones that I had forgotten about. He just floored me!"

In 2003, Edmonds returned to acting playing Uncle A in *Killer Drag Queens on Dope* starring Alexis Arquette and Omar Alexis in the title roles. "I'm brilliant in this, by the way," jokes Don with a laugh. "I played the head of a family of mobsters. I can't put two thoughts together. The character is confined to a wheelchair and I wear a patch over one eye. This is a silly, dumb movie that will probably never see the light of day." Today Don Edmonds is working with producer David Friedman on a new *Ilsa* movie about her daughter. Fans have been clamoring for another sequel for years.

Looking back on his beach movie days, Edmonds remarks, "I am not embarrassed to have worked in these films but when I see them now I groan, 'Oh, man!' But it was a wonderful part of my life. I would not trade that experience for all the money in the world. It was a terrific time and era—the tenor of the country was much different then. Hollywood meant everything to me. I was in the movies. I was successful. Those times were the best. It was just fun. I would wake up each morning and think, 'What's next for me?'"

Film credits: 1961: *Gidget Goes Hawaiian*; 1962: *The Interns*; 1963: *Son of Flubber*; 1964: *The Misadventures of Merlin Jones*; 1965: *Beach Ball*; 1966: *Wild Wild Winter*; 1980: *Getting Over*; 1986: *8 Million Ways to Die*; 1995: *Last Gasp*; 2003: *Killer Drag Queens on Dope*.

★ *Shelley Fabares* ★

Shelley Fabares truly transcends the decades. During the fifties she made movies with John Saxon and Natalie Wood and became a teen idol when she was cast as Mary Stone in the hit comedy series *The Donna Reed Show*. In the sixties, Shelley's popularity extended to the recording industry with a million-selling record "Johnny Angel" and to the big screen with *Ride the Wild Surf* (1964) and Elvis Presley's *Girl Happy* (1965), *Spinout* (1966) and *Clambake* (1967). During the seven-

Shelley Fabares leaves her teen queen persona far behind in this publicity pose.

ties and eighties, Fabares kept busy on television with the classic made-for-television movie *Brian's Song* (1971) and as a regular on the series *Forever Fernwood*, *The Practice* and *One Day at a Time*. Always exuding a warm, sparkling quality, Shelley attracts new fans with each passing decade. Her comedic timing became flawless, culminating with her most impressive work as television anchorwoman Christine Armstrong in the hit nineties sitcom *Coach*.

Shelley Fabares (pronounced Fah-bah-ray) was born Michelle Marie Fabares on January 19, 1944, in Santa Monica, California. The niece of comedienne Nanette Fabray, Shelley followed her aunt into a very successful career in show business. She began taking tap dance lessons at age three. A year later, Shelley began modeling and at age nine Frank Sinatra sang to her on one of his television specials. Appearances on such early television shows such as *Matinee Theatre, Captain Midnight* and *Annie Oakley* followed. She made her film debut in 1956 playing Rock Hudson's daughter in the weeper *Never Say Goodbye*. Regarding her performance, Shelley remarked in *Outré* magazine, "I was awful." Nevertheless, she was good enough to land the role of John Saxon's younger sister Twinky in one of the earliest rock 'n' roll films *Rock, Pretty Baby* (1956) and its sequel *Summer Love* (1958).

Shelley's big break came at age 14 when she was cast as Donna Reed's precocious teenage daughter Mary in the sitcom *The Donna Reed Show* co-starring Carl Betz and Paul Petersen. The show was an immediate hit and ran for eight seasons. During the run of the show, the producers asked Shelley to cut a record to try to draw more of a younger audience. Despite her limited singing ability, Shelley agreed and the Colpix release "Johnny Angel" hit No. 1 on the *Billboard* charts on April 7, 1962, after she warbled it on the show. Shelley attributes its popularity not to her vocal ability but to the "great production of the song by Tony Owen and Stu Phillips." Her success catapulted her to the highest echelon of teen idols.

In 1964, Shelley left *The Donna Reed Show* after five seasons ("It was the hardest decision of my life") to concentrate on a movie career. Audiences who saw her in the boss surfer film *Ride the Wild Surf* (1964) were pleasantly surprised to behold a new Shelley—bikini-clad and blonde—cavorting on the shores of Oahu with Fabian. However, not to completely tarnish her wholesome image, Fabares remained chaste through the film's exciting climax.

Fabares' agent negotiated for her a three-picture deal with MGM. The first film sent her back to the beach for *Girl Happy* (1965) as the good girl being secretly chaperoned by combo leader Elvis Presley while on spring break in Fort Lauderdale. Also in the movie were Joby Baker, Gary Crosby and Jimmy Hawkins as Elvis' band mates, Mary Ann Mobley as a Southern vixen, Fabrizio Mioni as an amorous Italian playboy with eyes on Fabares, Chris Noel and Lyn Edgington as Fabares' college friends and Nita Talbot as a stripper.

After co-starring with Peter Noone of Herman's Hermits in *Hold On!* (1966), Fabares worked with the King two more times. *Spinout* (1966) cast her as a pampered rich brat who sets her sights on racecar driver Elvis. In *Clambake* (1967), Fabares was a golddigger trying to avoid her feelings for Elvis (who she thinks is a poor water ski instructor) while lasciviously pursuing rich playboy Bill Bixby. Fabares says, "[*Clambake*] is the one Elvis and I had the most fun on. We just literally laughed from beginning to end. I think Elvis was very happy at that time because he and Priscilla were planning to get married as soon as the film was finished. Nobody knew this then. Also it was our third film together so I knew him and his guys really well. And the man who directed this was a sweet, sweet man by the name of Arthur Nadel. It was one of those magical times the cast and crew just jelled."

Shelley was adored by audiences and the critics who used such words as "talented" and "perky" to describe her, so it is surprising to learn that beginning in 1967 she didn't work for four years. "Nobody would hire me," recalls Shelley. "I did get a guest shot here and there but I was used to working *constantly*." Since Shelley was so identified with the moralistic fifties and early sixties, she was not cool in the eyes of teenagers who were now into Janis Joplin, the Doors and hippie and biker films. In 1971 she landed a *Mannix* episode which led to her being cast in the beloved made-for-television movie *Brian's Song* starring James Caan. Her sensitive portrayal of the wife of dying football player Brian Piccolo received kudos. Shelley never had to worry about a lack of work again.

During the seventies, Shelley could be found as a series regular on the forgettable sitcoms *The Little People* (1972–73), *The Brian Keith Show* (1973–74), *The Practice* (1976–77) and *Highcliff Manor* (1979). In 1975, she joined the cast of the late night soap *Forever Fernwood* as crippled tennis star Eleanor Majors, whom Shelley describes as being "a completely evil, manipulative, total bitch of a person hiding behind a sweet façade." Playing against type, Shelley impressed the critics with her excellent portrayal. In the early eighties, Fabares landed the role of Bonnie Franklin's self-absorbed business rival Francine on the sitcom *One Day at a Time.* "This was a wonderfully, villainous role," says Shelley. "Francine's selfishness could be summed up in just one scene from the episode where Valerie Bertinelli's character got married. Francine gets to the church late and her high heels go clickety-clack as she walked down the aisle. When the people turn to look at her, she says, 'No, don't get up.' It was my only line in that show but it is one of my favorites."

However wonderful Shelley was playing these deliciously devious women, it is for her role as the strong, independent Christine on the hit comedy series *Coach* (1989–97) that she will be most remembered. Her fiery relationship with Craig T. Nelson as blustery college football coach Hayden Fox was acted to perfection, earning Shelley two Emmy nominations. "At the beginning of the show, one of the great difficulties we had was that the audience didn't like Hayden—they liked Craig—but felt Hayden was a jerk," recalls Fabares. "So it was important for the audience to like and respect Christine because if she loved Hayden it would help them to get to love him too. Hayden was an infuriating, fascinating man who couldn't discuss his feelings. Christine demanded he do and that's one reason the romance was so rocky." After a slow start in the ratings, the show became hugely popular, finishing in the Nielsen Top 10 for most of its run.

Post–*Coach*, Shelley starred in the 1998 made-for television movie *Playing to Win: A Moment of Truth Movie.* That same year, Fabares was diagnosed with an auto-immune form of hepatitis, which resulted in a liver transplant in 2000. It sidelined her for a few years but in 2004 a recovered Shelley Fabares returned to work as one of the producers of *The 10th Annual Screen Actors Guild Awards.*

Film credits: 1956: *Never Say Goodbye*; *Rock, Pretty Baby*; 1958: *Summer Love*; *Marjorie Morningstar* [uncredited]; 1964: *Ride the Wild Surf*; 1965: *Girl Happy*; 1966: *Hold On!*; *Spinout*; 1967: *Clambake*; 1968: *A Time to Sing*; 1969: *U.M.C.* (television); 1971: *Brian's Song* (television); 1972: *Two for the Money* (television); 1975: *Sky Heist* (television); 1979: *Pleasure Cove* (television); *Donovan's Kid* (television); *Friendships, Secrets and Lies* (television); 1980: *Gridlock* (television); 1983: *Memorial Day* (television); 1985: *The Canterville Ghost* (television); 1987: *Hot Pursuit*; 1988: *Run Till You Fall* (television); 1989: *Class Cruise* (television); 1990: *Love or Money*; 1993: *Deadly Relations* (television); 1995: *The Great Mom Swap* (television); *A Dream Is a Wish Your Heart Makes: The Annette Funicello Story* (television) [cameo as herself]; 1997: *A Nightmare Come True* (television); 1998: *Playing to Win: A Moment of Truth Movie* (television).

⋆ *Johnny Fain* ⋆

Blonde, boyishly cute and powerfully built, Johnny Fain was able to parlay his surfing expertise into a brief movie career. One of the legendary Malibu surfers of the late fifties and early sixties, he surf-doubled in *Gidget* (1959) and *Beach Party* (1963). Despite his diminutive stature (Fain was just under 5'5"), he was able to land lots of screen time in the remaining Frankie and Annette beach films including *Bikini Beach* (1964) and *Beach Blanket Bingo* (1965). He concentrated solely on surfing during the later part of the sixties and then gave acting a second try during the seventies.

John Fain was born in 1943. His family was extremely wealthy and he grew up in the exclusive Malibu Colony. Johnny began surfing at 13 years old and quickly fell in with the Malibu surfing crowd of the time including Lance Carson, Dewey Weber and Mickey Dora. Fain became especially close with Dora and according to friends he just idolized Malibu's bad boy of surfing. Though overshadowed by Dora, Fain was one of the top surfers at Malibu and his fellow surfers nicknamed him "The Malibu Lizard." Writing in *The Encyclopedia of Surfing*, Matt Warshaw described Fain as "an agile, quick, flamboyant surfer." When the producers hired Fain to double for Sandra Dee in the kelp scene in *Gidget*, the young surfer made sure that his mentor and friend Dora was also included.

After *Gidget*, Fain continued to ride the waves at Malibu right alongside Mickey Dora. They were featured in such early classic surf movies as Dale Davis' *Walk on the Wet Side* (1961) and seen competing against each other at the Malibu Invitational in *Strictly Hot* (1963).

In 1963, Fain and Dora were hired to surf-double and to do background work in *Beach Party*, the first Frankie and Annette beach bash, due to their friend surfer Ed Garner who recommended the duo to director William Asher. While Dora just wanted to surf and had no interest in an acting career, Fain was immediately drawn to the world of filmmaking. Due to his size, Fain doubled in the surfing scenes for Frankie Avalon. He also let it be known that he wanted to act and to have lines. Though he gets lots of screen time in *Muscle Beach Party* (1964), *Bikini Beach* (1964) and *Pajama Party* (1964), he is seen but not heard (unlike fellow Malibu surfer Mike Nader, whose role got bigger in each subsequent movie). But Fain didn't seem to care and remarked in an interview that he was elated to earn a tidy sum of $400 a week to do what he loved most—surf.

Ed Garner comments, "Johnny Fain was a bit apprehensive about his stature. He idolized Mickey Dora and tried to ape everything he did. But Johnny didn't have Mickey's personality—nobody did."

Between working in Hollywood surf movies, Fain was surfing professionally. In 1965, during the finals at the Malibu International surfing contest, former friends and now rivals Johnny Fain and Mickey Dora got into a shouting, pushing and shoving match on the waves. Johnny remarked in *Surfer*, "I've never been in a place where there was so much tension ... but I didn't try any pranks. Not me. I just rode the waves." Dora feigned innocence too. The result was that a 17-year-old named Buzz Sutphin won the contest with Fain placing second and Dora third. But the real winner was the surfing press, which had a field day reporting on their legendary feud.

Surfers John Calvin (*left*) and Johnny Fain (*center*) come to the aid of novice wave raider Dennis Christopher, who has just wiped out in *California Dreaming* (AIP, 1979).

Back on the big screen, Fain was featured dancing with Linda Opie on a surf-board held up on the shoulders of his fellow surfers during the opening of *Beach Blanket Bingo* (1965) and later being fed a hot dog by his pal Mike Nader as Donna Loren warbles a love song. His next movie, *How to Stuff a Wild Bikini* (1965), was his swan song for AIP. Fain still had a desire to act but he was only able to land a minor bit as a surfer in *Don't Make Waves* (1967). He's the guy on the right when Sharon Tate drags Tony Curtis in from the surf.

In 1968, Fain was back competing and he advanced to the World Surfing Championship held in Puerto Rico. According to author Matt Warshaw, "Unlike most of his Malibu contemporaries, Fain made the transition to the short surfboard in 1968, and the Fain Formula model, produced by Greg Noll Surfboards, sold well in the late sixties." Fain turned up in such surf movies as Dale Davis' *Inside Out* (1966) and Hal Jepsen's *The Cosmic Children* (1970).

In 1972, Fain gave up surfing due to the unruly crowds of surfers that descended on Malibu and the erection of a sewage treatment plant nearby. He decided to try to become a serious actor and was cast as Shorty Shea a ranch hand purportedly killed by some of Charlie Manson's followers in the made-for-television movie *Helter Skelter* (1976). Fain was excited to get cast in the surf epic *Big Wednesday* (1978) but he expected to get a bigger part and was further disappointed that he didn't do as many surf stunts as he anticipated.

Fain was then cast as one of the three main supporting actors in *California Dreaming* (1979), which he was hoping would finally exploit his acting ability. He played hotshot Malibu surfer Tenner, who befriends Dennis Christopher's awkward T.T. and teaches the Ohio native how to surf. However, more bad luck came Johnny's way. During the shooting of the film's surfing climax, one of Fain's co-stars lost his footing on his board, which shot out and sliced the nearby Fain's cheekbone. It required 55 stitches. As a result, his remaining screen time was reduced though Fain pleaded with the director to shoot him from the opposite side.

Fain's last movie appearance was as a biker in the comedy spoof *Loose Shoes* a.k.a. *Coming Attractions* (1980). He then went into real estate where he made a very good living for over a decade. Still residing in the Malibu area, Fain became very active with the Surfrider Malibu Chapter, an ecological preservation group. A hip replacement in 1992 left the once-agile surfer depressed. For a short period, booze and pills were his escape. Happily, Fain beat his substance abuse and is surfing the waves at Malibu once again.

Film credits: 1959: *Gidget*; 1963: *Beach Party*; 1964: *Surf Party*; *Muscle Beach Party*; *Bikini Beach*; *Pajama Party*; 1965: *Beach Blanket Bingo*; *How to Stuff a Wild Bikini*; 1967: *Don't Make Waves* [uncredited]; 1976: *Helter Skelter* (television); 1978: *Big Wednesday*; 1979: *California Dreaming*; 1980: *Loose Shoes*.

★ *Annette Funicello* ★

To the surprise of Hollywood, this former Mouseketeer blossomed into a beauty who became the queen of the beach. It's ironic as Annette Funicello was a dark-haired Italian Catholic from Utica, New York, who hated the sand and sea air, wouldn't wear a bikini and refused to get her hair wet. She was as far from being a true Southern California beach girl as you could get. But Annette had a charm to her and when paired with Frankie Avalon the two struck a chord with teenagers across the country. When the buxom knockout strolled on to the sand in her form-fitting one-piece swimsuit in *Beach Party* (1963), she left her Disney image far behind.

Annette Joanne Funicello was born on October 22, 1942. Her family relocated to Los Angeles from Utica when Annette was just a child and her mother enrolled her timid daughter in dance classes to help her overcome her shyness. Producer Walt Disney happened to see her dance the lead role in *Swan Lake* at her school's year-end recital in the spring of 1955 and had an associate contact her to audition to become a Mouseketeer. *The Mickey Mouse Club* debuted in October 1955 and Annette quickly became one of the show's most popular cast members. Part of this had to do with her talent and the sweetness that she just radiated—but the fact that the 12-year-old was maturing into womanhood far faster than her peers certainly played a big factor. Due to her growing bosom, she quickly became the fantasy girl of pubescent boys around the country.

The Mickey Mouse Club was excellent training for the newcomer as she sang and danced, and also acted in a number of its serials including her own entitled "Annette." When the series came to an end in 1959, Funicello was the only Mouseketeer who remained under contract at Disney. Though her singing voice was thin, it was perfect for the undiscriminating teenage rock 'n' roll fan. Annette cut a few singles, the most popular being "Tall Paul," which climbed to No. 7 on the *Billboard* charts in 1959. She had another Top 10 hit the following year with "O Dio Mio."

Walt Disney knew she had acting talent and cast her in the hit comedy *The Shaggy Dog* (1959) starring Fred MacMurray and Tommy Kirk. Annette went on to *The Horsemasters* (1960), one of her three starring films that were broadcast in two parts on *Walt Disney's Wonderful World of Color* but released theatrically in Europe and other parts of the world. Annette could be seen on the big screens in the U.S. as Mary Contrary in the disappointing musical *Babes in Toyland* (1961).

In 1962, Annette turned 20 and Disney was having trouble finding parts for the well-developed actress. When AIP offered her a lead role in the swinging new surfing epic *Beach Party* (1963), Disney strongly advised Annette to take the role but not to wear a bikini. She was paired with Frankie Avalon as teenage lovers Frankie and Dolores, and *Beach Party* was the sleeper of the year; AIP immediately commissioned a sequel. After starring with Tommy Kirk in Disney's *The Misadventures of Merlin Jones* (1964), Annette reprised her *Beach Party* character (renamed Dee Dee) in that same year's *Muscle Beach Party* and *Bikini Beach*. *Pajama Party* (1964) was an offshoot as Annette co-starred with Disney alumni Tommy Kirk playing a Martian.

All four of Annette's movies were box office hits and she delivered charming performances, especially in *Muscle Beach Party*. She was voted a Star of Tomorrow, placing second in the *Motion Pictures Exhibitor*'s poll, and was named a Star of the Future by *Boxoffice* magazine. That same year she was also nominated for the Photoplay Gold Medal Award for Favorite Actress. But Annette was not liked by all. She became a favorite target of the *Harvard Lampoon*, which bestowed three of their Movie Worst Awards on her, including back-to-back "wins" as the least promising newcomer of 1963 and '64.

Though Annette became synonymous with surfing and beach movies, she rarely ventured into the ocean with her surfboard or even got her hair wet. She explained in *Interview*, "The surfboards were so big and heavy. A couple of times we tried to get a shot of me grabbing a board, running down to the water and diving in. But every time we'd rehearse it I'd grab this huge board and say something like, 'Hey kids! Surf's up!' and then I'd have to drag this heavy, ungainly board down to the water. By the time I got to the ocean I'd be totally out of breath." Needless to say, director William Asher gave up and used the old reliable blue screen to show Annette "surfing" the waves.

Annette had a very busy year in 1965. She married her agent Jack Gilardi and then re-teamed with Tommy Kirk in the Disney comedy *The Monkey's Uncle*, whose title tune was sung by Annette and the Beach Boys on-screen. After co-starring with Frankie Avalon in *Beach Blanket Bingo* and making a very funny cameo appearance as an amorous college professor in *Ski Party*, Annette became pregnant with her first child. She was a few months along when she had to head back to the beach for *How to Stuff a Wild Bikini*. To hide the fact that she was expecting, the producers ridiculously had her wear slacks and oversize blouses even on the beach! This was one of Annette's worst performances as you could tell that the expectant young woman wanted to be anywhere but on the sands of Malibu.

Though *How to Stuff a Wild Bikini* was the end of the beach party for Frankie and Annette, AIP would team the popular duo one last time. *Fireball 500* (1966) featured Avalon and Fabian as rival stock car racers who battled over the charms of Annette while embroiled in a moonshine smuggling operation. Funicello would co-star again with Fabian in *Thunder Alley* (1967) playing the good girl vying with Diane McBain (a golddigging vixen) for stunt driver Fabian. It was her final movie for AIP.

After leaving AIP in 1967, Funicello did a cameo as Davy Jones' girlfriend in the Monkees' madcap musical *Head* (1968) before limiting her acting career to spend more time with her children. She made sporadic television guest appearances during the seventies and co-hosted with Frankie Avalon the variety series *Easy Does It* in 1976. But she is best remembered as the spokeswoman for Skippy Peanut Butter in a string of commercials that ran into the eighties. Annette was more active during the Reagan years and donned a swimsuit for her return with Avalon to the sandy shores of Malibu in *Back to the Beach* (1987) and did a cameo playing herself in *Troop Beverly Hills* (1989) starring Shelley Long.

Annette was diagnosed with multiple sclerosis in 1988. At first the devastating nerve disorder just affected her balance but it has gotten progressively worse. According to *The National Examiner*, "She's nearly blind, she can barely speak and she can't walk." She recently underwent brain surgery to relieve the tremors that had wracked her body. It was successful, so Annette now lives a more comfortable and normal life. Though her eyesight is too poor for her to read, Annette talks by telephone to her family, watches the big screen television her husband Glen Holt purchased for her and still has close ties with friends such as Shelley Fabares, Frankie Avalon, Luree Nicholson and ex–Mouseketeer Sharon Baird. Annette also devotes as much time and money as possible to the Annette Funicello Research Fund for Neurological Diseases, an organization she founded to help other MS victims.

Film credits: 1959: *The Shaggy Dog*; 1961: *Babes in Toyland*; 1963: *Beach Party*; 1964: *The Misadventures of Merlin Jones*; *Muscle Beach Party*; *Bikini Beach*; *Pajama Party*; 1965: *Beach Blanket Bingo*; *The Monkey's Uncle*; *Ski Party* [cameo]; *How to Stuff a Wild Bikini*; *Dr. Goldfoot and the Bikini Machine* [cameo]; 1966: *Fireball 500*; 1967: *Thunder Alley*; 1968: *Head*; 1985: *Lots of Luck*; 1987: *Back to the Beach*; 1989: *Troop Beverly Hills* [cameo as herself]; 1995: *A Dream Is a Wish Your Heart Makes: The Annette Funicello Story* (television) [herself].

★ *Ed Garner* ★

Lanky Ed Garner with his mop of bushy blond hair was literally plucked from the shores of Malibu to appear in the first AIP beach movie, *Beach Party* (1963).

The surfer then went on to appear in every movie from *Muscle Beach Party* (1964) to *Fireball 500* (1966). Though he never had many lines, Ed Garner saw his face plastered across the teen movie fan magazines and he became part of that AIP stable of contract players which included Mike Nader, Salli Sachse, Patti Chandler, Mary Hughes and Luree Holmes. He never considered himself an actor, and when the beach party came to an end this surfer went on to other endeavors.

Ed Garner, the grandson of esteemed actor H.B. Warner, was born in 1944. His parents were friendly with the Wilson family who owned Wilson's House of Suede and Leather. While on vacation in Hawaii, Eugenia Wilson began teaching Ed and her son Brian how to surf. Back in California, the teenagers would head to Malibu almost every weekend to ride the waves. "I went to Beverly Hills High School with some of my surfing buddies," recalls Garner. "We didn't fall into the normal crowd. We were dying our hair and T-shirts and causing a kind of surfing momentum at our school. We were driving Hearsts and Woodys, which became our transportation to the beach. Mike Nader was the first one to purchase a Hearst. We all basically hung out and surfed together. We'd drive from State Beach to Huntington Beach to San Onofre to the caves. When we became a little more adventurous we'd drive down to Copas San Lucas. In those days we were like a little family. It was thumbs up or thumbs down if there were any good waves. It was a real tight community and we got along very well."

Beach boy Ed Garner models surfers' swim trunks called Baggies to help promote *Muscle Beach Party* in 1964 (*courtesy Aron Kincaid*).

At Malibu, Garner and his high school buddies became friendly with such surfers as Mickey Dora, Johnny Fain and Butch Van Artsdalen. However, Garner never ranked his surfing skill on par with them. "On a scale of one to ten I was about a six," remarks Ed. "I felt relaxed surfing at certain places but there were spots that were just too hairy for me. I liked surfing at Topanga Canyon, Malibu and San Onofre where there were easy waves and it was comfortable to know I could get out of trouble if I got into any. Some of the spots with big shore breaks and big waves I was not ballsy enough to surf."

A family friend knowing that Garner could surf led him to being cast in *Beach Party* (1963) starring Frankie Avalon and Annette Funicello. Director William Asher was so taken with the blonde surfer that he asked him to select some of his surfing buddies to be in the movie. Mickey Dora, Johnny Fain, Mike Nader and Duane King were just some of the surfers who got their start at AIP due to Garner. *Beach Party* became such a big hit for AIP that a sequel was immediately rushed into production. Garner was back as a beach boy in *Muscle Beach Party* (1964) as the surfers tangled with a group of bodybuilders. Impressed with Garner's screen presence and all–American California good looks, AIP signed him to a contract though he had no interest in pursuing an acting career.

In between his next two AIP beach movies, *Bikini Beach* and *Pajama Party* (both 1964), Garner, along with Mickey Dora and Mike Nader, were loaned to United Artists for their beach party–type movie *For Those Who Think Young* (1964) starring James Darren and Pamela Tiffin. Garner also made an appearance on television's *Dr. Kildare* in the two-part episode "Tyger, Tyger" where Richard Chamberlain falls in love with Yvette Mimieux as an ill-fated surfer. "They had a make-out scene wearing bathing suits where he had the biggest erection that I had ever seen in my life," exclaims Garner with a laugh. "I am probably the only guy in Hollywood who had no clue that Richard Chamberlain was gay."

In 1965, it was a return to the background for Ed in *Beach Blanket Bingo* and *How to Stuff a Wild Bikini*. His next movie *The Ghost in the Invisible Bikini* (1966) tried to breathe new life into the beach party shenanigans by moving it to a haunted house setting. Garner played Ed, best friend to Aron Kincaid's Bobby, who brings his beach friends (including Nancy Sinatra, Claudia Martin, Piccola Pupa, Luree Holmes and Mary Hughes) to the spooky mansion where his aunt (Patsy Kelly) is waiting the reading of the will of Hiram Stokley. The absence of the sand and surf, not to mention Frankie and Annette, put the nail in the coffin to the AIP beach party movies.

In *Fireball 500* (1966) the action was switched from the beach to the race car circuit, as Frankie Avalon and Fabian played rival drivers who, when not competing on the track, were vying for the lovely Annette Funicello. Garner, in his last role, played a hillbilly track hand named Herman who is married to a very old woman.

Commenting on the success of the beach party movies, Ed Garner says ruefully, "You know, it never affected me one way or the other. I didn't appreciate what I had. For me it was just a great gig, making great money and basically introducing myself to a totally different lifestyle. I went from being a carpenter's apprentice and surfing to making movies and dating in a whole different circle. I was having the time of my life." He sure was as the ladies' man was romantically linked at one time or another to such beauties as Dany Saval, Jennifer Billingsley and Claudia Martin.

Proving there is life once the beach party stops, Garner began working with Doris Day's son Terry Melcher, who was in the music industry and did promotion for the Beach Boys and Jan and Dean. Garner then went into business with a disc jockey from KFWB-FM and started a production company.

In 1974, Ed left the music business and relocated to Santa Barbara where he became a successful restaurateur. Then the successful entrepreneur segued to a career in retail clothing. After selling his chain of stores, Garner began creating cartoon characters including Camp California, which became the mascot for the Beach Boys in 1982. A lucrative licensing deal led to stores in Japan selling everything imaginable with these characters on it. On the brink of a U.S. launch, one of the partners at Weintraub Entertainment Group died and his stock reverted to Mike Love of the Beach Boys, who pulled the plug on Camp California.

Today, Ed Garner is semi-retired and assists his wife Kelly J. Green with her clothing accessory business. Though he has more free time on his hands, he no longer surfs. "I broke my neck about eight years ago surfing in Malibu," says Garner with a sigh. "I absolutely miss surfing. It is a great sport—no doubt about it!"

Film Credits: 1963: *Beach Party*; 1964: *Muscle Beach Party*; *For Those Who Think Young*; *Bikini Beach*; *Pajama Party*; 1965: *Beach Blanket Bingo*; *How to Stuff a Wild Bikini*; *Sergeant Deadhead*; 1966: *The Ghost in the Invisible Bikini*; *Fireball 500*.

* *Susan Hart* *

Dark haired and sultry, Susan Hart displayed her shapely bikini-clad body in a string of popular surf and beach movies. It is no wonder considering her measurements were usually touted as 37-23-36 as she was being groomed to become

Sexy Susan Hart relaxes on the shore in this publicity photograph.

Hollywood's newest sex symbol. After playing one of Pamela Tiffin's sorority sisters in *For Those Who Think Young* (1964), Hart frolicked on the sand as a hula-swaying half–Hawaiian who falls for surfer Tab Hunter despite her mother's vehement objections in *Ride the Wild Surf* (1964). She snagged a contract at American International Pictures where her roles included a hip-swiveling beach girl in *Pajama Party* (1964) and the title role in *The Ghost in the Invisible Bikini* (1966).

Susan Hart was born on June 2, 1941, in Wenatchaee, Washington, the apple capital of the world. When she was in the second grade her family began spending the winters in Palm Springs, California, and the summers in Washington because her mother had contracted tuberculosis. As a student in Palm Springs High School, she was extremely active in the school's drama department and also played a few roles at the famed Herb Rogers' Theatre-in-the-Round.

After graduating high school, Hart vacationed in Hawaii twice. On her second visit, manager Morton Smith discovered her and she looked him up when she went to Hollywood. He helped her get an agent and she was cast in several roles on television in such series as *The Joey Bishop Show* and *The Alfred Hitchcock Hour*. Hart then landed the female lead opposite Robert Hutton in the B monster movie *The Slime People* (1963) about subterranean creatures who menace stragglers in an evacuated Los Angeles.

After playing a bit role in the Bob Hope comedy *A Global Affair* (1964), Hart joined Nancy Sinatra and Claudia Martin as one of Pamela Tiffin's classmates in the beach film *For Those Who Think Young* (1964). She finally landed a film role worthy of her beauty and talent when she was cast as a half–Hawaiian girl who falls in love with a visiting surfer (Tab Hunter), much to her mother's chagrin in *Ride the Wild Surf* (1964). Susan received fine notices for her role and lots of publicity. She even caught the eye of AIP co-founder James H. Nicholson, who had access to the film's dailies.

Despite interest from Columbia Pictures, Hart signed a contract with American International and soon after married the boss. First up for Hart at her new home was the small role of hip-swaying Jilda in *Pajama Party* (1964), starring Tommy Kirk and Annette Funicello. AIP was always touting the voluptuous Susan Hart's measurements, rather than her comedic ability, in press releases and publicity material hoping she would ascend to the top of the sex symbol heap.

Back on the big screen, Hart starred as the damsel in distress in the Jules Verne–inspired fantasy film *War-Gods of the Deep* (1965) with Vincent Price as the villain and her *Ride the Wild Surf* co-star Tab Hunter as the hero. She then switched gears to give an amusing, well-received performance as a bikini-clad robot in *Dr. Goldfoot and the Bikini Machine* (1965), a goofy take-off on the James Bond film *Goldfinger*. It co-starred Vincent Price, Frankie Avalon and Dwayne Hickman. This spy spoof proved to be quite popular and grossed $2.5 million, a smash hit by AIP standards.

To promote *Dr. Goldfoot and the Bikini Machine*, an hour-long musical special entitled *The Wild, Weird World of Dr. Goldfoot* was produced and aired in place of *Shindig*. Price, Hart, Tommy Kirk and Aron Kincaid starred. After garnering much praise for *Dr. Goldfoot and the Bikini Machine*, the red hot Susan Hart was much in demand. But her marriage to Jim Nicholson and subsequent pregnancy sidelined her. After the birth of her son, there was much talk of Hart appearing in the

Italian production *Planet of the Vampires* and a proposed sequel to *Dr. Goldfoot and the Bikini Machine* to be titled *Dr. Goldfoot and the S Bombs,* but neither panned out for her.

Hart was next cast as *The Ghost in the Invisible Bikini* (1966) after the finished film, originally titled *Bikini Party in a Haunted House,* was deemed not releasable by AIP. Dependable Hart and Boris Karloff appeared in added scenes that gave the film some life. Neither of them worked with the movie's original cast members.

The Ghost in the Invisible Bikini turned out to be Susan's last feature. A number of things contributed to that including the upbringing of her son and problems that arose between her husband and Sam Arkoff, who gained the controlling shares of AIP due to Nicholson's divorce from his first wife. Not wanting to get involved with AIP politics, Hart focused on singing. She cut several songs for MGM and went on the road to promote them.

Though Susan left AIP, Jim Nicholson continued with the company until 1972, when he signed a deal with 20th Century–Fox. He was the executive producer of *The Legend of Hell House* (1973) and was readying *Dirty Mary, Crazy Larry* (1974) for production when he was diagnosed with a brain tumor. He passed away on December 10, 1972. After his death, Susan became involved in a lawsuit that dragged on for years with the two men who were hoping to take over his company, Academy Pictures Corp. Susan became president of the company in 1973 and has remained so ever since. She acquired ten AIP films that her late husband helmed, including *I Was a Teenage Werewolf, Invasion of the Saucer Men* and *It Conquered the World.*

As for her feelings regarding Jim Nicholson's contribution to AIP, Hart proudly comments, "He was the creative genius and essence behind American International Pictures. Jim was the show and Sam was the business. Jim created every trend AIP ever had from the biker pictures to the Poe-inspired pictures to the beach pictures to the blaxpoitation pictures. He was not only a title genius but his marketing skills were beyond reproach. The two films he slated for Fox were huge financial successes for that company. *Dirty Mary, Crazy Larry* was one of 20th's top grossers in 1974."

Today, the still beautiful Susan Hart resides year-round in the Palm Springs area. She remarried in the early eighties and has become a champion precision ice skater. In early 2004, she was awarded a "Star" on the Palm Springs Walk of Stars. It is a fitting tribute to this talented and charming lady.

Film Credits: 1963: *The Slime People*; 1964: *A Global Affair; For Those Who Think Young; Ride the Wild Surf; Pajama Party*; 1965: *War-Gods of the Deep; Dr. Goldfoot and the Bikini Machine*; 1966: *The Ghost in the Invisible Bikini.*

★ *Aron Kincaid* ★

With his sun-drenched blonde hair, all–American good looks and quirky charm, actor Aron Kincaid epitomized the surfer boy image so prevalent during the mid-sixties. Unjustly considered a Troy Donahue clone by casting directors,

Kincaid could more than hold his own (looks and acting-wise) against fellow golden boys Donahue and Tab Hunter who were popular at that time. Kincaid's beach persona easily transferred to the screen as he could be seen frolicking on the sandy shores of Santa Monica in 1965's *The Girls on the Beach* and *Beach Ball*. He swapped his surfboard for skis in *Ski Party* (1965) and then abandoned the beach for a haunted house in *The Ghost in the Invisible Bikini* (1966).

Aron Kincaid (born Norman Neale Williams III on June 15, 1940) grew up in Southern California as the only child of an Air Force pilot and his wife. His father was killed in the service when Williams was just a child. Perhaps feeling lonely and abandoned, the youngster found solace in drawing and spending hours in darkened movie theaters. He sold his first oil painting at ten years of age and won his first national contest at 14. An avid film buff and autograph collector, the fanatical young lad swam out to Humphrey Bogart and Lauren Bacall's yacht, climbed aboard and innocently asked for an autograph. His other Lucy Ricardo–like schemes in Hollywood included sneaking onto the Universal lot where he was befriended by buxom sex bomb Mamie Van Doren and charming the secretary of Cecil B. DeMille so he could spend his summer vacation on the set of *The Ten Commandments*.

After graduating high school it was off to film school at UCLA where his classmates included Francis Coppola, Jim Morrison, actor-producer Bart Patton and future beach movie co-star Mary Mitchel. During a semester break, the young Williams played a beekeeper in scenes added to *The Wasp Woman* to extend its running length for television broadcast. "They asked me if I was afraid of bees and I lied saying, 'No, no.' I was actually deadly allergic to them and have to be hospitalized if I get stung by one—but that's show biz." The aspiring cinematographer then ditched six months of school to jet off to Rome where he found work as an extra on *Spartacus*.

Returning to California, Kincaid landed a small role on television's *Thriller* and decided acting was his true vocation. "I was 21 and I had a definite plan of what I wanted to do," says Kincaid. "I wanted to be a *movie star*—not a great actor—but a movie star. I wanted my picture in *Photoplay*. I wanted to get fan mail. I wanted to wear costumes and fight with long swords. I think I just really wanted to be a kid." Feeling that he needed a more marquee-type moniker, he enlisted the help of his fraternity brothers and thusly Aron Kincaid was born. The newly named actor was signed to a contract with Universal and landed a regular gig as Noreen Corcoran's boyfriend during the last season of *Bachelor Father*. The studio dropped his option and when roles became scarce in 1963, the frustrated Kincaid enrolled in the U.S. Coast Guard. His movie career began in 1965 when he co-starred in three *Beach Party*–type movies.

First up for Kincaid was *The Girls on the Beach*. He was one a trio of surfer boys (along with Martin West and Steve Rogers) who lie to coed Noreen Corcoran and her gaggle of sorority sisters (Linda Marshall, Gail Gerber and Lana Wood) that they know the Beatles. Kincaid fared even better in his next movie, *Beach Ball*. He played a college dropout and member (along with Robert Logan and Don Edmonds) of a band called the Wigglers who reside in a beach shack in Malibu and try to con four brainy coeds to grant a student loan (with which they intend to pay off the money owed on their instruments).

Kincaid's talent and dedication impressed Gene Corman, who produced *The Girls on the Beach* and *Beach Ball*. When AIP recruited Corman to produce *Ski Party*, he insisted that Kincaid be cast as suave Freddie Carter, the handsome comic foil to Frankie Avalon and Dwayne Hickman as the beach gang hits Sun Valley for a ski vacation. Kincaid received positive reviews for his performance with the most flattering coming from *Variety*—"Kincaid stands out as the lightweight heavy who fights off femmes but goes after Hickman's 'Nora.'" *Screen World* voted him one of the year's Most Promising Personalities and he was Louella Parsons' first choice for stardom in her monthly column for *Modern Screen* in January 1966.

Aron Kincaid was one of Hollywood's most popular surfer boys on the beach during the mid-sixties (*courtesy Aron Kincaid*).

After *Ski Party* was released, Sam Arkoff's son Louis, who was working in the AIP mail room, reported to his father that Kincaid was receiving more fan mail than Frankie and Annette combined. The shrewd producer and his partner James Nicholson immediately offered Kincaid a contract. Though the excited newcomer was eager to sign, his manager almost spoiled the deal. "At that time, I had a very manipulative manager who caused many, many problems with [AIP] for me," reveals a perturbed Kincaid. "I said I wanted the contract. My manager didn't want me to sign it because he felt we could do much better elsewhere. I said, 'No. This is the studio that gave me a chance and I want to work for them. That's it. It's my career.'"

Kincaid's first assignment at AIP was a cameo role in the spy spoof *Dr. Goldfoot and the Bikini Machine* (1965) starring Vincent Price, Frankie Avalon and Dwayne Hickman (he didn't work with any of them). AIP's founder James Nicholson brought Aron over to the MGM lot where the movie was filming to introduce him to director Norman Taurog. "Jim introduced me to Taurog and said [*lowers voice*], 'Norman, I would like you to meet Aron Kincaid. He is under contract. I thought that Aron might be suitable for the part of the young sports car driver who hits Miss Hart with his car.' Norman said, 'Yeah, yeah, that's fine.' Norman could have cared less. He had no choice in the matter, really. But I thought it was nice of him anyway to agree."

In his next film for AIP, *The Ghost in the Invisible Bikini* (1966) starring Tommy Kirk and Deborah Walley, Kincaid was upped to the second male lead. This was AIP's attempt to pump new life into the beach party formula but it was not a success. The film's working title was *Bikini Party in a Haunted House* when it was offered to Kincaid. "It was the *worst* script that I ever read," laughs Aron. "It took place in a swamp in Florida with alligators. There were all these things in the screenplay about the swamp and this old house that was in the bayou." *The Ghost in the Invisible Bikini* put the nail in the coffin as far as AIP beach movies went though Kincaid received some nice notices. The *Los Angeles Herald-Examiner* critic said he "comes on strong" while *The Hollywood Reporter* reviewer remarked that he "delivers favorably."

When *The Ghost in the Invisible Bikini* wrapped, Kincaid began the second year of his contract with AIP and was surprised to be getting paid the same as during the first year. "I was supposed to get an increase of $200 a week," says Aron. "My manager called them and they said, 'We will go on to the second year but we want him to accept the salary of the last year.' My manager told them that they couldn't do that because we had a contract. They said we didn't because I never signed it. I did but my manager, who was a devious son of a bitch, kept it and never gave it to AIP. The next thing I knew—I had very little choice in the matter—I was suing American International Pictures."

While his lawsuit dragged on, Kincaid landed a supporting role as one of Lesley Ann Warren's many suitors in the snappy Walt Disney musical *The Happiest Millionaire* (1967). What was supposed to be a two-week gig dragged on for weeks due to the ill health of Warren. "She was overworked and got sick so she was hospitalized," explains Kincaid. "I was kept on salary through her entire convalescence. I was sending flowers to the hospital saying, 'Please, stay sick. I'm making more money than I ever have!' Not too gentlemanly but honest."

Before filming ended on *The Happiest Millionaire*, Kincaid's claim versus AIP was settled out of court. "I was so relieved to see an end to the ordeal that the studio's request for two more 'play or pay' films from me seemed a small concession, considering that I was becoming physically ill from this seemingly endless army of people fighting over bits of meat," reveals Aron. "My manager did not want me to do the movies because at this point I was working at Disney."

Kincaid was next offered a role in *It's a Bikini World* (1967) but passed on it, explaining, "What I wanted was to be in adult pictures and not do any more beach films. I was auditioning for a lot of movies I didn't get. I came real close to getting a part in *Divorce, American Style* [Dick Gautier got the role]. They had me in at least four times to read for the lead in *The Graduate*. Mike Nichols told me that they wanted to screen test me when he came back from New York. I was really excited because *The Graduate* was originally written for Robert Redford but he had moved on. I was close to his look and persona. It was in New York that Mike Nichols saw Dustin Hoffman in a play and *that was the end of Aron Kincaid*! There was some talk about me doing a silent part as Katharine Ross' groom. My agent said no way. My friend Brian Avery did it and I don't think he ever had a film that brought him as much fame as that."

Kincaid's last film for AIP was the abysmal made-for-television horror opus *Creature of Destruction* (1968), directed by Larry Buchanan, whom Kincaid describes as being "huge in stature and minuscule in the areas of charm and talent."

He ended the decade back where his film career began—in the water and on the beach with close friend Lana Wood. ("Though I vowed no more beach movies, I didn't consider working on a boat in the Bahamas the beach"): In the made-for-television movie *Black Water Gold* (1969), Kincaid played a scuba bum enlisted by marine archaeologist Keir Dullea and historian Ricardo Montalban to find a sunken galleon off the coast of Nassau in the Bahamas before fortune hunters Bradford Dillman and France Nuyen do. Wood was the shapely and scantily clad love interest whose steamier moments were cut from the U.S. print but showed in Europe. But it seems what went on behind the camera was more sensational than what appeared on film as Wood was bedding co-star Dullea while his wife was dating Kincaid! "The Bible Belt would have condemned all of us to the fires of hell," laughs Aron. "But when you are young and in movies, none of it all seems to matter."

Kincaid next journeyed to scenic Colombia for the low-budget Western *The Proud and the Damned* (1970) co-starring Chuck Connors and Cesar Romero. Kincaid played one of a handful of Confederate soldiers who wander into a local Colombian revolution. As the sensitive one who falls in love with the cloistered fiancée of the mayor's nephew, Aron received some of his finest notices. John Mahoney in *The Hollywood Reporter* remarked, "Kincaid manages the most sympathetic and credible performance of the film."

After playing a male slave in the Gene Roddenberry–produced television-movie *Planet Earth* (1974) with John Saxon, Kincaid became disenchanted with Hollywood and moved north. "At the time I thought, 'Here I am—all of a sudden 30 years old—and the films I've done are never going to be seen again. They are off in a vault somewhere rotting. It's all been for nothing and that I'm wasting my life.' I then leased my house, took my possessions and moved to San Francisco. I left no forwarding address and stayed there for ten years."

Not in town more than a week, Kincaid was offered several modeling jobs and within two months he became San Francisco's top male model even though he was over 30. "There was nobody up there who had the experience that I had," boasts Kincaid. "People who were good in modeling went to New York. The guys who stayed were amateur night in Dixieland. I had my pick of everything. I made more money modeling in the seventies than I made in a decade and a half in Hollywood." His success propelled him to the modeling world of New York, where he appeared in *GQ* and on the cover of *New York* magazine.

When he could find the time, Kincaid still accepted an occasional movie role, including playing one of the lovers of Carole Lombard (Jill Clayburgh) in *Gable and Lombard* (1976) and a state trooper in *Cannonball* (1976). While living in the City by the Bay, he became friendly with writer Armistead Maupin. "One night Armistead said to me, 'Would you care if I used your real name for one of my characters in my newspaper serial *Tales of the City*?' I replied, 'No, you have my full permission. I'm honored.' Ha! Norman Neal Williams turned out to be a child molester. *Tales of the City* has been published in like 37 languages and turned into a miniseries. I thought, 'Oh, God! I've destroyed my name!'"

In the eighties, Kincaid made a brief return to acting but, disillusioned with the new Hollywood, he limits his talents to voiceovers only. Cartoon fans may recognize Kincaid's baritone from a number of animated characters including Sky

Lynx on *Transformers*, Killer Croc on *Batman: The Animated Series* and the Iron Sheik on *Rock 'n' Wrestling*.

It also must be noted that throughout his acting and modeling careers, Kincaid never gave up artistic endeavors. His Hollywood caricatures became legendary among show people. This led to him designing posters for a number of films during the seventies and eighties including *Going Berserk*, *The Treasure of the Four Crowns* and *Herbie Goes Bananas*. In 1988, he began painting California landscapes. Today, his artwork is displayed at Gallery Grace in Laguna Beach where he paints under his legal name of N. N. Williams II. Among his collectors are Berry Gordy (the founder of Motown), Lana Wood, Senator Barry Goldwater and Mrs. Dean Martin. He also does his famed oil caricatures of Hollywood stars under his stage name of Aron Kincaid.

Asked why he felt these surf and beach movies are as popular as ever, Kincaid opines, "As corny as they all were, they really captured an era."

Film Credits: 1959: *The Wasp Woman* [new scenes for television]; 1960: *Spartacus* [uncredited]; 1965: *The Girls on the Beach*; *Ski Party*; *Beach Ball*; *Dr. Goldfoot and the Bikini Machine* (television) [cameo]; 1966: *The Ghost in the Invisible Bikini*; 1967: *The Happiest Millionaire*; 1968: *Creature of Destruction*; 1969: *Black Water Gold* (television); 1970: *A Storm in Summer* (television); 1971: *The Secret Sharer* [not released]; 1972: *The Proud and the Damned* [completed in 1969]; 1974: *Planet Earth* (television); 1976: *Gable and Lombard*; *Cannonball/Carquake*; 1980: *Brave New World* (television); 1984: *Silent Night, Deadly Night* [voice only]; 1986: *The Golden Child* [voice only]; 1991: *Fire! Trapped on the 37th Floor* (television).

★ *Tommy Kirk* ★

Popular teenage actor Tommy Kirk was the second contract player from Walt Disney recruited by AIP to star in its beach movies. Kirk teamed with fellow Disney cast-off Annette Funicello in the handsomely produced *Pajama Party* (1964) playing a Martian who crashes the beach party to lead an invasion. He worked again for AIP opposite Deborah Walley in the problem-plagued production *The Ghost in the Invisible Bikini* (1966). After that, Kirk starred in two low-budget beach movies, *Catalina Caper* and *It's a Bikini World*, both of which sat on the shelf until the spring of 1967.

Tommy Kirk was born on December 10, 1941, in Louisville, Kentucky. His father relocated the family to California when Tommy was two years old to obtain work in the aircraft industry. They settled in Downey and the Kirk children attended school in Los Angeles. The acting bug bit Tommy's older brother Joe in 1954, and Tommy accompanied Joe on an audition for *Ah, Wilderness!* at the Pasadena Playhouse. Bobby Driscoll got the part his brother wanted while the director hired Tommy for the role of a young boy. A talent agent saw Kirk in the play and took him on as a client.

Guest shots on such series as *Matinee Theatre*, *Gunsmoke* and *The Loretta Young Show* led Kirk to being cast as Joe Hardy in "The Adventures of the Hardy Boys," which was serialized on *The Mickey Mouse Club*. Walt Disney was very impressed with the teenaged Kirk and signed him to a contract. Kirk won kudos for his poignant performance in the popular sentimental weeper *Old Yeller* (1957) playing Travis Coates, the 16-year-old boy who adopts a dog nicknamed Old Yeller and who has to put the dog down when it contracts rabies.

Despite his dramatic capabilities, Disney co-starred Kirk in a string of profitable family comedies such as *The Shaggy Dog* (1959), *The Absent Minded Professor* (1961), *Bon Voyage!* (1962) and *Son of Flubber* (1963). Though none of these films stretched Kirk's acting muscles, he displayed a natural charm, usually cast as the scrappy teenager. He also got the opportunity to work with some very famous actors some of which he did not particularly care for. In a candid interview in *Scarlet Street* magazine, Kirk described Fred MacMurray as being "a very cold person off the screen" and Jane Wyman as "a mean, mean bitch" whom he hated by the time he was through working with. Though Kirk liked MacMurray, he admitted that his relentless quest for a father figure might have pushed the actor away.

Kirk was also wrestling with his own demons during the sixties. He began drinking at age 14 and became addicted to amphetamines in 1962. At this point he was also dealing with his sexuality. While for publicity purposes he was giving interviews in newspapers and the fan magazines describing what his ideal wife would be or going on arranged dates, he was concealing his homosexuality. However, it came to light in 1964 after Kirk wrapped production on *The Misadventures of Merlin Jones* with Annette Funicello. The young actor picked up a teenager at the Burbank Pool and they had sex. The boy squealed to his parents, who went directly to Walt Disney. The studio immediately released Kirk from his contract.

Now a freelancer, AIP paired Kirk with his frequent Disney co-star Annette Funicello in *Pajama Party* (1964). That year he was up for the Photoplay Gold Medal Award for Favorite Actor. AIP wanted to re-team Kirk and Annette in *How to Stuff a Wild Bikini* (1965) but just before filming began the troubled young man was busted for possession of marijuana. Kirk spent Christmas Day 1964 in jail but the charges were dismissed. The bad press not only lost him this role but also a co-starring part in the John Wayne Western *The Sons of Katie Elder* (1965). Kirk remarked, "From 1964 to 1974, it was pretty much of a nightmare. I was still drinking heavily; I didn't really get off drugs ... till the end of the 60s. I was never quite in my right mind."

Though he admits to being unemployable during this period, Kirk kept getting work due to his continuing popularity with the teenage set. In 1965, Disney hired him for one last movie, *The Monkey's Uncle*, and he starred in two *Beach Party* clones, *Catalina Caper* and *It's a Bikini World*. Neither was released until 1967. Kirk commented in *StoryboarD*, "With the exception of ... *Pajama Party*, which I thought was kind of cute, I made a series of 'B' and 'C' grade beach movies after I left Disney studios." He was the good teen battling Beau Bridges as the leader of the bad teens in Bert I. Gordon's *Village of the Giants* (1965) and was back at AIP for *The Ghost in the Invisible Bikini* (1966), a step up from his previous movies. Though the movie paled next to *Pajama Party*, Kirk enjoyed working with co-star Basil Rathbone immensely.

Kirk's downward slide into oblivion continued with the bizarre sex comedy *Mother Goose a-Go-Go* (1966) with Anne Helm and the cult sci-fi made-for-television movie *Mars Needs Women* (1966) with Yvonne Craig. The later was directed by Larry Buchanan, as was Kirk's next movie, *It's Alive!* (1968). Kirk was especially

Tommy Kirk played an arrogant Casanova always surrounded by beach girls in *It's a Bikini World* (Trans American, 1967).

outraged by Buchanan's cheapness in hiring a stuntman to play the monster wearing a scuba suit with ping-pong balls for eyes. He railed in *Scarlet Street*, "I feel very great anger that I even consented to be in it; it was just disgusting."

Kirk knew he had hit rock bottom after accepting a role as a cop in schlockmeister Al Adamson's zombie movie *Blood of Ghastly Horror* (1972). Kirk takes full responsibility for his bad career choices but he also blames the misguided advice he received at the time. He commented in *Filmfax*, "I got involved with a manager who said it didn't matter what you did as long as you kept working. He put me in every piece of shit that anybody offered. I did a series of terrible things, but it was only to get the money."

Kirk eventually dried out after kicking the drug habit in the late sixties. Disgusted with acting, he dropped out of show business in the early seventies and opened his own very successful carpet and upholstery cleaning business. Kirk holds no grudges against Walt Disney or any other studio for firing him and has completely forgiven himself for his mistakes. What upsets him more is listening to other ex–child actors who go on television to bemoan their sorry fates. He candidly remarked in *Filmfax*, "It gives me a distinct pain in my ass. I've never been like that. I richly deserved to be fired from the studios because of my irresponsibility. A person on drugs is not fit for work."

In the nineties, Kirk was lured out of retirement to do a cameo in *Attack of the 60 Foot Centerfold* (1995) and went on to appear in a few more direct-to-video movies including *Billy Frankenstein* (1998) and *The Education of a Vampire* (2001).

Film credits: 1957: *Old Yeller;* 1959: *The Shaggy Dog; The Snow Queen* [voice only]; 1960: *Swiss Family Robinson;* 1961: *The Absent Minded Professor; Babes in Toyland;* 1962: *Bon Voyage;* 1963: *Son of Flubber; Savage Sam;* 1964: *The Misadventures of Merlin Jones; Pajama Party;* 1965: *The Monkey's Uncle; Village of the Giants;* 1966: *The Ghost in the Invisible Bikini; Mother Goose a-Go-Go/The Unkissed Bride;* 1967: *It's a Bikini World; Catalina Caper; Mars Needs Women* (television); 1968: *Track of Thunder;* 1969: *It's Alive!* (television); 1971: *Ride the Hot Wind* [unreleased]; 1972: *Blood of Ghastly Horror;* 1976: *My Name Is Legend;* 1987: *Streets of Death* (video); 1995: *Attack of the 60 Foot Centerfold* (video); 1997: *Little Miss Magic/Kidwitch;* 1998: *Billy Frankenstein* (video); 2000: *Club Dead* (video); 2001: *The Education of a Vampire.*

★ *Jody McCrea* ★

Tall, strapping, square-jawed Jody McCrea became a favorite of the teenage audience for his amusing performances as Deadhead in *Beach Party* (1963) and its sequels. As the dumb surfer in the bunch, Deadhead could be counted on to say something idiotic in his slow drawl. Though McCrea was always assured a laugh based on how the role was written, it is to his credit that Deadhead came off as sweetly naïve rather than a complete moron.

Jody McCrea was born on September 6, 1934, in Los Angeles. His father was movie star Joel McCrea and his mother was the underrated actress Frances Dee. As a child, Jody and his brother David worked the 2300 acres of ranch that his father bought in the San Fernando Valley. The boys toiled in the bean fields; per his interview with *TV Guide,* it was Jody's early ambition to become "the greatest bean-hoer in the State of California." While attending the New Mexico Military Institute, Jody visited his dad on the set of the movie *Lone Hand.* Though surrounded by show business his whole young life, it was on this set that the acting bug finally bit him. He told *TV Guide,* "I found I had some creative instincts. This was something where I could put my athletic ability to use and also my ability with horses."

McCrea studied drama at UCLA and began taking acting lessons on the side. He made an uncredited appearance in *Lucy Gallant* (1955) but his official debut was playing Lt. Baker in the Western *The First Texan* (1956) starring his father Joel McCrea as Sam Houston. Jody would go on to work with his dad in other Westerns including *Trooper Hook* (1957) and *Gunsight Ridge* (1957). McCrea's first significant part was playing Tim Hitchcock in the William Wellman–directed biopic *Lafayette Escadrille* (1958) starring Tab Hunter in a story of the famous French flying legion of WWI. "I had known William Wellman and his son [William Wellman, Jr.] for years," recalls Jody. "They were great friends. Wellman, Sr., cast Bill and me in *Lafayette Escadrille* along with David Janssen and Tom Laughlin. Clint Eastwood played a part that I was supposed to play but I was bumped up to a bigger role and he took my place."

Television fans discovered Jody McCrea when he teamed up with his dad to star in the Western series *Wichita Town* during the 1959–60 season. Joel played the town marshal and his son was cast as his deputy. The series unfortunately was saddled with a bad time slot (following the weepy *This Is Your Life*) so when the show's sponsor pulled out, the series was cancelled. He returned to the big screen playing supporting roles in low-budget comedies and Westerns including *Young Guns of Texas* (1963) featuring other second generation actors (such as James Mitchum and Alana Ladd) in leading roles.

The WWII adventure *Operation Bikini* (1963) was Jody's first pairing with Frankie Avalon and his first movie for American International Pictures. He was cast next as Deadhead in *Beach Party* the same year. When that movie broke box office records for the independent company, McCrea was coaxed back to reprise the role of the dumb surfer supporting Frankie and Annette in *Muscle Beach Party* and *Bikini Beach* (both 1964). Due to his popularity with the

Strapping Jody McCrea, best known for playing the moronic surfer Deadhead in the *Beach Party* movies.

teenage audience, McCrea progressed to second lead in *Pajama Party* (1964) playing Annette Funicello's boyfriend who prefers volleyball to romance. McCrea was finally able to shine and received good reviews for his performance. *Variety* said McCrea "hams it up the way he should for such a part."

Beach Blanket Bingo (1965) also gave McCrea a chance to do some real emoting as his character Bonehead falls in love with a mermaid. He received positive reviews such as in *The Los Angeles Times*, whose critic remarked, "Jody McCrea … handles the comedy as a kooky beach bum on whom the sun really shines." Regarding his popularity playing a doltish surfer, McCrea told *Newsday*, "It took me four pictures to figure it out—the kids liked Deadhead because they felt superior to me, to him." However, McCrea was getting disillusioned with the beach movies due to the fact he was afraid that he would be typecast. After *How to Stuff a Wild Bikini* (1965) wrapped, affable Jody McCrea was determined to shake his Bonehead persona.

The Western *Stagecoach to Nowhere* (based on *Oedipus Rex*) was supposed to be McCrea's next movie but it was never produced. Instead, the tall, broad-shouldered actor was perfectly cast as a rambunctious race car driver in *The Girls from Thunder Strip* (1966) and a hardened biker in *The Glory Stompers* (1967) co-starring

Dennis Hopper and Chris Noel. The latter was co-produced by McCrea. "I remember that Chris Noel was reluctant to do the movie," says McCrea. "I said to her, 'What do you want to be, the Tokyo Rose of your time?' Chris had her own radio show broadcast to the GIs in Vietnam. I think she was happy to have done the movie because she had a big part and the movie was a hit. She also got paid a pretty good salary.

"Dennis Hopper was an enfant terrible at times," continues McCrea. "I don't want to say anything too negative but he wanted to direct and it worked out for him but it was hard on the rest of us. You're not supposed to take the wheel from the guy who is the captain of the ship but our director [Anthony Lanza] was more of an editor and he wasn't strong. Dennis was very tenacious and had a good background. I think Dennis is a very good actor but a better director. He worked with me on a scene and he was awfully skilled coaxing a good performance from me. Dennis was excellent but at times I was sorry that I hired him because he was so hard to deal with. He did extremely well directing his next movie, *Easy Rider*."

In 1970, McCrea returned to the Western genre playing a mysterious gun-slinger a la Clint Eastwood in *Cry Blood, Apache*, which was his show business swan song. "I co-produced this movie as well," remarks McCrea. "I did not think it was going to be my last and had plans to produce two sequels. I got married to a Native American woman named Rosebud from Great Family and she didn't want me working in the industry. I couldn't even help promote *Cry Blood, Apache*. She was very restrictive of my working in Hollywood and for very good reason. She kept me to herself and it was wonderful to learn about the world of Native Americans."

McCrea abandoned show business in 1971 to run a cattle and elk ranch in Hondo, New Mexico. He says, "I had 13 years of struggle with it but I did well and made more money in ranching then I would have probably made acting. That life gave me a lot more privacy and anonymity, which I enjoyed. Growing up with famous parents, I was in the spotlight a lot. We'd go out to dinner as a family and you really couldn't be yourself with the fans and photographers around. I didn't miss that aspect of show business at all."

Today, Jody McCrea has retired from ranching. His wife passed away but he is still full of life and very energetic. He is also pleased that the *Beach Party* movies have been released on DVD. "I'm delighted and happy that the beach movies have been rediscovered," exclaims McCrea. "They are considered cult classics now. It is like getting on a big wave and riding it. I didn't like being typecast but I was happy to make people laugh."

Film credits: 1955: *Lucy Gallant* [uncredited]; 1956: *The First Texan*; *Naked Gun/The Hanging Judge*; 1957: *The Monster That Challenged the World*; *Trooper Hook*; *Gunsight Ridge*; 1958: *Lafayette Escadrille*; *The Restless Years*; 1961: *All Hands on Deck*; *Force of Impulse*; 1962: *The Broken Land*; 1963: *Young Guns of Texas*; *Operation Bikini*; *Beach Party*; 1964: *Muscle Beach Party*; *Law of the Lawless*; *Bikini Beach*; *Pajama Party*; 1965: *Young Fury*; *Beach Blanket Bingo*; *How to Stuff a Wild Bikini*; 1966: *The Girls from Thunder Strip*; 1967: *The Glory Stompers*; *Sam/The Hottest Fourth of July in the History of Brewster County* [unreleased]; 1969: *Free Grass/Scream Free!* 1970: *Cry Blood, Apache*.

⋆ *Yvette Mimieux* ⋆

A talented leading lady, wispy blonde Yvette Mimieux was very popular during the early sixties. With her angelic looks, Mimieux excelled playing blank-faced waifs such as Weena in the classic H.G. Wells sci-fi tale *The Time Machine* (1960). In *Where the Boys Are* (1960), Mimieux holds the distinction of playing the first gal in a sixties beach movie to go all the way with a boy. She was also the only member of the cast to return to the shore. In 1964, she portrayed a bikini-clad surfer in a two-part episode of television's *Dr. Kildare* starring Richard Chamberlain.

Yvette Mimieux was born on January 8, 1941 (though some sources list the year as 1939), to a Mexican father named Rene Mimieux and a French mother, Carmen. Mimieux grew up in Hollywood so it is not too surprising that she became an actress. The intelligent and talented blonde who was fluent in English, French and Spanish was interested in art and joined a local theater group to work on set designs but wound up on stage playing an ingenue in *Liliom* and was spotted by director Vincente Minnelli. He cast her in a small role in *Home from the Hill* (1960) but all her scenes were excised from the final print.

Undeterred, Mimieux's manager Jim Byron made sure to get her as much press as possible. She began modeling and entering local beauty contests; she was crowned Los Angeles Boat Queen and Miss Harbor Day, among others. Her big publicity build-up was noticed by MGM, who signed her to a seven-year contract in 1959 beginning at $250 a week. The untrained blonde, who was married at age 17 and had to keep her husband under wraps, was quickly enrolled in the studio's acting, dance and speech training classes.

Mimieux made her film debut in B-movie producer Albert Zugsmith's exploitation film *Platinum High School* playing a sexy tease who is the only girl on campus at an all-boys military school for delinquents. The MGM publicity machine went full throttle promoting the studio's rising new star and their efforts resulted in Mimieux

Yvette Mimieux was one of the sexiest gals on the beach during the sixties.

receiving a Golden Globe Award nomination (Most Promising Newcomer—Female) though her performance was not very impressive.

Yvette was much better suited to play the beautiful Weena, one of the gentle Eloi that Rod Taylor's Time Traveler encounters in the year 802,701 in *The Time Machine* (1960), directed by George Pal and featuring Oscar-winning special effects. She then joined Dolores Hart, Paula Prentiss and Connie Francis on a trek to Fort Lauderdale during spring break in the pleasant beach movie *Where the Boys Are* (1960). While Hart's character talked and talked about having sex before marriage, Mimieux's Melanie was the one to act on it. This being the prudish early sixties, of course her character had to pay for her sins and the wanton young woman gets raped at the end to send a message to the teenage girls in the audience. Mimieux received fair notices for her dramatics and raves for her ethereal beauty. For instance, the reviewer in *Variety* remarked, "Visually she is a knockout, and has a misty quality." *Where the Boys Are* was an enormous hit and paved the way for the beach party films to come.

During the early sixties, baby doll blondes were in vogue and, along with Sandra Dee, Connie Stevens and Carol Lynley, Mimieux was a favorite of adolescent girls. However, unlike her counterparts, Mimieux was equally popular amongst teenage boys due to the sexiness she brought to her ingenue roles. So it was surprising that MGM did not choose her to be their representative in the Hollywood Deb Star Ball of 1960. Enraged, the ambitious starlet applied as an independent and was chosen to participate but she refused to pose with any of the other Deb Stars. Instead, she swathed herself in a number of white fox stoles and literally stole the spotlight as her picture appeared in newspapers across the country.

MGM then rushed her into the role of a storybook princess in *The Wonderful World of the Brothers Grimm* (1962). Director George Pal described Mimieux in *Look* magazine as being "a cross between a little princess and Brigitte Bardot." She was a part of the all-star cast in the disastrous flop *The Four Horsemen of the Apocalypse* (1962) and then played the spoiled rich girl who flaunts her Hawaiian boyfriend James Darren in the faces of her disapproving family with tragic results in the lush soaper *Diamond Head* (1962). Though she wasn't used as much more than scenery in her previous films, Mimieux was out of her depth playing the challenging role of Olivia de Havilland's mentally handicapped daughter in *The Light in the Piazza* (1962). That year, she was voted a Star of Tomorrow in the *Motion Picture Herald* and unsuccessfully tried to stretch her acting muscles again the following year playing Dean Martin's child-like bride in *Toys in the Attic* (1963).

In January 1964, Mimieux portrayed an ill-fated surfer diagnosed with epilepsy but still determined to surf professionally in the two-part episode entitled, "Tyger, Tyger" on the hit television medical series *Dr. Kildare* starring Richard Chamberlain. To prepare for her role, Mimieux trained at San Onofre Beach with Rick Grigg, one of the top big wave riders from Hawaii, who remarked in *Life* that her natural surfing skill was "amazing." Yvette took to the sport quickly and revealed that during her first ride "I was hooked. I want to go on riding." The willowy blonde's performance was so well received that she received a Golden Globe nomination for Best Actress in a Television Series. It also brought her reams of publicity including a *Life* cover story where the sexy actress posed in a revealing bikini holding a surfboard.

All the accolades and publicity began to go to Mimieux's head. In an interview with *The Saturday Evening Post* Mimieux refused to talk about her male co-stars because she found most of them to be "egotistical, conceited and have no minds." She then added, "I like stories about me, just me." When her manager was quoted as saying that he was confident that Mimieux would be a legend in three or four years, the blonde replied confidently, "I feel it is my destiny." Alas, she became a legend in her own mind only.

The critics weren't kind to Mimieux regarding her performance in the lifeless love story *Joy in the Morning* (1965); *The New Yorker*'s reviewer insultingly described her as "the poor man's Carol Lynley." Trying to shake off her earlier ingenue roles, which she described as "frightened fawns," Mimieux starred in the Western *The Reward* (1965), *The Caper of the Golden Bulls* (1967) and the Disney comedy *Monkeys, Go Home!* (1967) but they did nothing for her career. The exciting African adventure *Dark of the Sun* (1968) reunited Mimieux with her *Time Machine* co-star Rod Taylor but the movie was not a box office hit. More popular was the exploitative *Three in the Attic* (1968) where she played a vengeful coed who ties up her former lover Christopher Jones to drain him of his sexual potency.

Yvette next turned up in the low-budget spy movie *The Delta Factor* (1969) co-starring Christopher George and Diane McBain. In *Fantasy Femmes of Sixties Cinema*, McBain stated that Mimieux caused many problems for director Tay Garnett, who wished that he hired Diane for the lead because she was a "much more professional actress."

With her once-promising movie career floundering, Mimieux began branching out. A student archaeologist, Mimieux traipsed the world between film roles, going on expeditions and writing about them for journal articles. Also a trained vocalist, she recorded an LP of poetry entitled *Baudelaire's Flowers of Evil* that featured a raga accompaniment by Indian musician Ali Akbar Khan.

Mimieux's extracurricular activities had to be put on hold when she was asked to replace the recently deceased Inger Stevens as the female lead in the television show *The Most Deadly Game* in 1970. This mystery series co-starring George Maharis had some interesting episodes but it never caught on with the viewing audience and was cancelled after only one season. Despite her lone excursion into television on *Dr. Kildare*, Mimieux agreed to star in the series because most of the movie scripts offered her contained nude scenes, which she refused to do. Mimieux did well in her role as a criminologist and received her third Golden Globe nomination this time for Best Actress in a Leading Role—Drama Series.

Back on the big screen, Mimieux played a heroic stewardess in the popular *Airport* rip-off *Skyjacked* (1972) and then sank to the bottom of the ocean with the rest of the cast in the tiresome *The Neptune Factor* (1973). Fed up with the roles that were being offered to her, Mimieux authored the teleplay and played the title role in the television-movie *Hit Lady* (1974). She then starred in her most infamous film *Jackson County Jail* (1976) as a rape victim who turns the tables on her assailants. Too graphic for television broadcast, the movie instead was remade as a toned-down version entitled *Outside Chance* (1978). Her newfound notoriety and good reviews were helpful in her snaring the female lead in the big-budget Walt Disney science-fiction film *The Black Hole* (1979). Though the movie featured Oscar-nominated special effects, it was not well-received by either critics or fans.

The film's spaceship was not the only thing that disappeared into the black hole—Mimieux's big screen movie career went with it.

The eighties found her relegated to the small screen in a series of forgettable television movies and as the star of the failed primetime soap *Berrenger's* (1985), about a family dynasty that owns a high-end department store. Her last known credit was a supporting role in the made-for-television movie *Lady Boss* (1992), based upon the novel by Jackie Collins.

Mimieux gave up acting in the nineties to concentrate on her business endeavors including her own line of clothing and jewelry. A practitioner of yoga since 1966, she released the video entitled *Harper Bazaar's Yoga Workout with Yvette Mimieux* in 1995. Mimieux currently lives in Beverly Hills and shuns all interviews regarding her acting career, though she did pose for a short piece about herself in *Vanity Fair* in 2001.

Film credits: 1960: *Platinum High School; The Time Machine; Where the Boys Are;* 1962: *Light in the Piazza; The Four Horsemen of the Apocalypse; The Wonderful World of the Brothers Grimm; Diamond Head;* 1963: *Toys in the Attic;* 1964: *Looking for Love* [cameo as herself]; 1965: *Joy in the Morning; The Reward;* 1967: *Monkeys, Go Home!; The Caper of the Golden Bulls;* 1968: *Dark of the Sun/The Mercenaries; Three in the Attic;* 1969: *The Picasso Summer;* 1970: *The Delta Factor;* 1971: *Death Takes a Holiday* (television); *Black Noon* (television); 1972: *Skyjacked;* 1973: *The Neptune Factor;* 1974: *Hit Lady* (television); 1975: *Journey into Fear; The Legend of Valentino* (television); 1976: *Jackson County Jail;* 1977: *Snowbeast* (television); *Ransom for Alice!* (television); 1978: *Devil Dog: The Hound of Hell* (television); *Outside Chance* (television); 1979: *Disaster on the Coastliner* (television); *The Black Hole;* 1982: *Forbidden Love* (television); 1983: *Circle of Power; Night Partners* (television); 1984: *Obsessive Love* (television); 1986: *The Fifth Missile* (television); 1990: *Perry Mason: The Case of the Desperate Deception* (television); 1992: *Lady Boss* (television).

★ *Mike Nader* ★

Of all the Malibu surfers who were recruited to appear in the AIP beach party movies, none had as much acting success as Mike Nader. Tall, slim, athletic, with dark haunting features, he immediately took to acting and the camera took to him. Nader was just a part of the beach crowd in *Beach Party* (1963) and the first few sequels. He graduated to featured player status with roles in *Beach Blanket Bingo, Ski Party* and *How to Stuff a Wild Bikini* (all 1965), and on television opposite Sally Field in the sitcom *Gidget.*

Michael Nader was born in St. Louis, Missouri, on February 18, 1945. When he was a small child his family relocated to Beverly Hills, California. He attended Vista Grammar School and Beverly Hills High School where he became friendly with Ed Garner. However, Nader was not part of that Beverly Hills crowd of mansions and Porsches. His family lived in an apartment and he drove an old Woody. At school, his rebellious demeanor was forever getting him into trouble. Surfing was his only escape. He remarked in *TV Guide,* "You got a pair of trunks, the ocean, a board under you—and no regulations." Nader began hanging out with that legendary Malibu surfer crowd that included Mickey Dora and Johnny Fain.

Nader was apart of the group of friends that Ed Garner introduced to direc-

Frankie Avalon, Annette Funicello, Mike Nader and Mary Hughes in *Beach Blanket Bingo* (AIP, 1965).

tor William Asher to surf-double and populate the background in *Beach Party*. Asher was immediately impressed with the young surfer and gave him lots of screen time. Though he didn't have many lines, Nader had a charisma that came across on the screen and made him a standout from the rest of the crowd.

Nader remained part of the contingent of surfer boys in *Muscle Beach Party*, *Bikini Beach* and *Pajama Party* (all 1964) and he began studying acting with guidance from Harvey Lembeck. He finally broke free from the surfer boy pack in *Beach Blanket Bingo* (1965). With John Ashley playing Frankie Avalon's rival, this left the best friend role vacant. Nader was then cast as Butch, loyal buddy to Frankie and boyfriend of the amorous Animal (Donna Michelle). In *Ski Party* (1965) Mike played college guy Bobby, who with pal Steve Rogers try to make time with Bobbi Shaw's Swedish ski instructor. In *How to Stuff a Wild Bikini* (1965) he was once again the boyfriend of Animal, now played by Marianne Gaba, though his character was named Mike. With Frankie away on Naval reserve duty, Mike's loyalty switched to Frankie's best friend, Johnny.

One of Nader's co-stars in *Ski Party* was Aron Kincaid, who remarked, "Mike Nader is a very good actor. He had that great speaking voice that he still has today. I remember at the time he was in an effort to bring the spotlight on himself so he was telling everyone that he was the nephew of George Nader."

In the fall of 1965, Nader began playing the recurring role of Peter Stone on the *Gidget* series starring Sally Field. After finishing out his contract with AIP by playing Joey in the stock car action film *Fireball 500* (1966), Nader headed for New York. He was accepted into Lee Strasberg's Actors Studio and for the next ten years he studied and performed in Off-Broadway plays. To earn money he waited tables and (like other beach movie veterans such as Aron Kincaid and Salli Sachse) he began modeling.

In 1976, Nader was cast as Kevin Thompson, a proposed love interest for the daytime drama *As the World Turns*' resident bad girl Susan Stewart (Marie Masters). He described the character as "a mysterious unknown entity." When his contract ended in 1978 (his character died from liver failure), Nader abandoned New York for Hawaii to surf and to re-evaluate his life.

Instead of returning to the Big Apple, he decided to move back to Los Angeles in 1981. He landed the role of handsome Greek Alexi Theophilus in *Bare Essence* (1983) but it was cancelled after only a handful of episodes aired. He then beat out Dean Paul Martin and Jon-Erik Hexum, among others, for the role of sexy, suave Dex Dexter who stole the heart of Joan Collins' Alexis Colby on *Dynasty* (1983–89). Nader commented in *Hollywood Drama-Logue*, "I didn't have the look they wanted. I was the only one with a dark Mediterranean look. But Joan and I clicked with the spirit they wanted." His love scenes with Collins smoldered across the small screens of America. The role made Mike Nader an international television star. He was voted one of the sexiest men of the decade and he was chosen to play Susan Lucci's leading man in the television-movie *Lady Mobster* (1988).

After *Dynasty* ended, Nader appeared in a few forgettable television movies, including *Nick Knight* (1989) and *The Flash* (1990), and the miniseries *Lucky/Chances* (1990). In 1991 he joined *All My Children* as the mysterious Count Dimitri Marick and had another long run playing the part until 1999 when his role was written out. The fans were outraged and flooded the network with complaints. The soap rehired Nader in 2000 only to fire him a year later due to his arrest for possession of and selling cocaine at a social club. The charges were reduced to misdemeanor possession and Nader entered a treatment program admitting to his drug and alcohol abuse. Despite his taking responsibility for his actions, the producers of *All My Children* still refused to take him back after a nine-month recovery period. Nader remarked to *The New York Post*, "And I was shocked because, you know, it hurts." He filed a $32 million lawsuit against ABC for being wrongfully dismissed, violating his contract and the Americans with Disabilities Act. His suit was dismissed in August 2004.

Film credits: 1963: *Beach Party*; 1964: *Muscle Beach Party*; *Bikini Beach*; *Pajama Party*; 1965: *Beach Blanket Bingo*; *Ski Party*; *How to Stuff a Wild Bikini*; *Sergeant Deadhead*; 1966: *The Ghost in the Invisible Bikini*; *Fireball 500*. 1967: *The Trip*; 1988: *Lady Mobster* (television); *The Great Escape II: The Untold Story* (television); 1989: *Nick Knight* (television); 1990: *The Flash* (television); 1991: *Perry Mason: The Case of the Maligned Mobster* (television); 1992: *The Finishing Touch* (video); 1996: *Fled*.

★ Chris Noel ★

After Annette Funicello and Deborah Walley, the actress most associated with beach and teenage movies of the sixties is Chris Noel. The perky curvaceous blonde only made two official beach movie appearances, as uptight college coeds who learn to swing in *Beach Ball* (1965) and *Wild Wild Winter* (1966), but she was bikini-clad in most of her other roles as well. Unlike other actresses who didn't want to be known just for their bodies, Chris loved all the attention and donned her skimpy swimsuits with pride. In 1966, Noel's career took a serious turn when she became a disc jockey on Armed Forces Radio and soon after began visiting Vietnam on her own at the request of the U.S. Army.

Born Sandra Louise Noel in West Palm Beach, Florida, Chris began modeling at age 15 and had her own modeling school a few years later. During high school, her best friend at the time was dating Errol Flynn's son Sean Flynn. "My modeling agent told me one day that Errol Flynn wanted to meet me," recalls Chris. "I went over to his house. He had a tape recorder and began talking into it. He then asked me to do the same. After I did, he handed me ten cents and said, 'When you reach 18 I want you to call me.' You know his story!"

After being crowned Miss Palm Beach, Chris became a cheerleader for the New York Giants football team. She turned down an offer to be a *Playboy* Playmate and became a finalist in the Miss Rheingold contest. Her boyfriend, actor Hugh O'Brian, recommended her for a small role in the play *Mister Roberts* that he was touring in, and she was discovered one night by an MGM talent scout. Her film debut was on loanout to Allied Artists in the underrated comedy-drama *Soldier in the Rain* (1963) starring Steve McQueen and Jackie Gleason. Fetching Chris got noticed and was MGM's Hollywood Deb Star for 1963.

On television, Noel co-

MGM cheesecake photograph of contract player Chris Noel.

starred with Gary Lockwood and Robert Vaughn in *The Lieutenant,* which Gene Roddenberry created before *Star Trek* blasted off. The 1963–64 series depicted the adventures of a young career officer in the Marines during peacetime. Though a regular, Chris played a different role in each episode. When the show came to an end after only one season, Noel began popping up all over the television dial in episodes of such popular sixties series as *Dr. Kildare, Burke's Law, Perry Mason, My Three Sons, Bewitched* and *My Mother, the Car.*

Returning to the big screen, Chris had small decorative roles in *Looking for Love* (1964) with Connie Francis and Jim Hutton and *Honeymoon Hotel* (1964) with Robert Morse and Robert Goulet. A bigger part followed, playing a bikini-clad coed on a ski vacation in *Get Yourself a College Girl* (1964) with Mary Ann Mobley, Joan O'Brien, Chad Everett and Nancy Sinatra. This was Noel's first of three movie appearances with former Miss America Mobley, whom the actress did not care for.

Chris had a very busy 1965 appearing in three motion pictures. First up was *Girl Happy,* one of Elvis Presley's best and highest grossing films of the mid-sixties. She played the friend of Shelley Fabares, whose overprotective father sends Elvis and his musical combo to Fort Lauderdale during spring break to babysit the vacationing coeds. Of course, romantic entanglements ensue.

Noel was cast as a college student once again in *Joy in the Morning* starring Richard Chamberlain as a struggling law student newly married to Yvette Mimieux. There were no bikinis for Chris to wear as the film was set during the late 1920s. Noel finally landed her first starring role, opposite Edd Byrnes in the Hollywood surf movie *Beach Ball*—but she had to leave MGM to get it, which she later felt was a mistake.

Then came the war in Vietnam. A visit to a veteran's hospital in San Francisco with comics Dan Rowan and Dick Martin and starlets Beverly Adams and Eileen O'Neill would change Noel's life forever. Seeing the devastation of war up close made her want to go to Vietnam to show her support of the GIs. She was turned down by Bob Hope's people because she "wasn't a big enough star" and never thought she'd get there. However, her then-boyfriend, singer Jack Jones, who had just accompanied Hope to Vietnam, informed her that Armed Forces Radio was auditioning for a disc jockey. Chris tried out and became the military's first female to spin records during the Vietnam conflict. Her program, *A Date with Chris,* was broadcast to the servicemen in the war-torn country and around the world from 1966 through 1971. She became the Unites States' answer to Hanoi Hannah.

The dedicated blonde starlet soon began visiting Vietnam to entertain the troops. But unlike the stars who were part of Bob Hope's entourage, Chris traveled on her own to hospitals, firebases and remote outposts. Twice, the helicopter she was riding in was shot down. Clad in the shortest of mini-skirts ("I was only allowed one suitcase and they were easy to pack"), Noel performed and brought comfort to many servicemen. During her sojourns to Vietnam, Chris encountered various military personnel from grunts in the field to majors and generals. She also became friendly with some of the photojournalists including Tim Page, whose exploits was the basis for the Dennis Hopper character in *Apocalypse Now* (1979). "I love Tim Page," says Chris fondly. "He really is a fascinating man."

The Vietcong did not take too kindly to Chris and put a bounty of $10,000 on her head. (Bob Hope's head was worth $25,000.) Because of her involvement with the Vietnam War, Noel received a backlash from the liberal (anti-war) Hollywood community and found it more difficult to obtain acting roles.

In between doing her radio show and trips to Vietnam, Noel continued making films but of the B-movie kind aimed at younger audiences. Due to her professionalism, Bart Patton hired her again, this time to play a stuffy sorority gal in the snow-covered beach party film *Wild Wild Winter* (1966). "I was never one of the party girls in Hollywood," reflects Chris. "I was into just my work and wanted to be as good as I possibly could be. I guess that is why I wound up being the one who went to Vietnam. I've always had that serious side of me." After being kidnapped by biker Dennis Hopper in *The Glory Stompers* (1967), Chris was back to bikinis in the swinging comedy-drama *For Singles Only* (1968) starring John Saxon and Mary Ann Mobley.

Of her beach party films, Chris prefers *Beach Ball* to *Wild Wild Winter* because "I got to wear a bikini and I looked good in it! On *Wild Wild Winter* I had that short hairstyle and had to wear all those ski clothes and it was cold. I liked filming on the beach much better than in the snow."

Noel's last visit to Vietnam was in 1969. She stopped going after her first husband, Cpt. Ty Herrington, a Green Beret who proposed to her in a helicopter, committed suicide during Christmas of that year. They were married for only 11 months.

Though her involvement in Vietnam seriously hurt her career and she suffered from depression, which turned out to be Post-Traumatic Stress Syndrome (PTSS), Chris persevered. Returning to Hollywood in 1978, she guest starred on a few television series and landed small roles in the television movies *Wild Times* (1980), *Detour to Terror* (1980) and *Fly Away Home* (1981). She even cut a number of CDs, the latest being *Nashville Impact,* released in 1999. Her last theatrical film was the powerful *Cease Fire* (1985) with Don Johnson, who played a Vietnam veteran struggling with the effect of PTSS. She was cast as the wife of a Vietnam vet who committed suicide. The role hit very close to home for her but she gave it her all and delivers a very heartfelt portrayal.

In 1987, Noel's book *Matter of Survival: The "War" Jane Never Saw* was published detailing her experiences in Vietnam. Today Chris spends most of her time in Florida directing Vetsville Cease Fire House, Inc., which she founded in 1993. Her wonderful non-profit organization consists of two halfway houses in West Palm Beach and Boynton Beach and provides shelter, food, clothing and counseling for homeless Vietnam veterans. An advocate for Vietnam veterans, Chris continues making personal appearances around the country in support of them. In 2004, she was the subject of the DVD documentary *Blonde Bombshell: The Incredible True Story of Chris Noel.*

Film credits: 1963: *Soldier in the Rain*; 1964: *Honeymoon Hotel*; *Diary of a Bachelor*; *Looking for Love*; *Get Yourself a College Girl*; 1965: *Girl Happy*; *Joy in the Morning*; *Beach Ball*; 1966: *Wild Wild Winter*; 1967: *The Glory Stompers*; 1968: *For Singles Only*; 1971: *The Tormentors/Terminators*; 1980: *Wild Times* (television); *Detour to Terror* (television); 1981: *Fly Away Home* (television); 1985: *Cease Fire*; 1986: *Sin of Innocence* (television).

⋆ *Quinn O'Hara* ⋆

A "red-headed gasser," Quinn O'Hara certainly lived up to that description and became very popular with teenage audiences during the sixties. A former Miss Scotland, this titian-haired beauty began on television before appearing in minor film roles with major stars such as Jerry Lewis and Jack Lemmon. Younger audiences remembered her best for her back-to-back starring roles in two beach party movies. O'Hara exuded a natural sex appeal that had every boy's heart racing, either playing the good girl as in *A Swingin' Summer* (1965) or the vixen as in *The Ghost in the Invisible Bikini* (1966). She should have become a major star; however, disenchanted with the roles being offered her, Quinn fled to England in the late sixties where she worked on stage, television and an occasional film.

O'Hara was dramatically born in a hospital's elevator going up in Edinburgh, Scotland, January 3, 1941 to a Welsh father and a Scottish-Irish mother who named the impatient newborn Alice Jones. Most of her childhood was spent in a convent boarding school in Wales. When she turned 14, she and her mother moved to Quebec, Canada, where the blossoming teenager learned to speak French. After three

You know it's going to be a swingin' summer when the girls on the beach include sexy Quinn O'Hara (*courtesy Quinn O'Hara*).

years, they upped and moved to Long Beach, California, where the red-haired beauty stood out from the myriad of California blondes. Her European origins prevented her from competing in the Miss California contest but she was dubbed Miss Scotland by the Royal Order of her home country.

With all the newfound attention she was receiving and with the acting offers coming in, Alice Jones was dropped in favor of a more appropriate name for a Scottish lass, Quinn O'Hara. Her big screen debut was in a bit part in *The Errand Boy* (1961) starring Jerry Lewis. O'Hara would go on to work with Lewis again in *The Patsy* (1964, playing the minor role of a cigarette girl) and in *Who's Minding the Store?* (1963), though her scenes were cut from the latter.

O'Hara's first taste of

fame came when she was selected to appear with Vic Damone in his 1962 Emmy-nominated summer series *The Lively Ones*. The popular show brought O'Hara notoriety and she became very much in demand on television but she wasn't having much luck with films. Only her hand was on display in *The Caretakers* (1963) where she played a nurse. *Good Neighbor, Sam* (1964) featured all of Quinn in the small role of a curvy secretary to recently promoted ad man Jack Lemmon. O'Hara kept persevering. She began getting press in all the movie rags of the time and she was chosen by *Photoplay* to be photographed on a pre-arranged "date" with teen idol Fabian. But surprisingly, the duo hit it off and it developed into a relationship that lasted a year.

In 1965, Quinn co-starred in one of the better *Beach Party* knockoffs, *A Swingin' Summer* with William Wellman, Jr., and James Stacy, her first lead role. She looked terrific in her revealing swimsuits and more than held her own with rising super-star Raquel Welch.

Quinn next auditioned at AIP for the role of the sexy though bumbling Sinistra in what was then titled *Bikini Party in a Haunted House*. It was not her first encounter with the company. The producers and director Don Weis originally wanted her for a role in *Pajama Party* (1964) but she declined because "I didn't want to be just one of the beach girls so I turned it down." AIP decided they needed to pump new life into their beach party genre so they came up with an idea of combining it with a horror angle, which had worked so well for them with the series of Edgar Allan Poe films. *Bikini Party in a Haunted House* featured Tommy Kirk, Deborah Walley and Patsy Kelly as heirs to a fortune who gather at the creepy mansion of dead millionaire Hiram Stokely, to hear the reading of his will. O'Hara plays the bumbling daughter of crooked attorney Basil Rathbone, who instructs the vixen to off Kelly's interfering nephew Aron Kincaid. But her nearsightedness keeps getting in her way.

The head honchos at AIP decreed that *Bikini Party in a Haunted House* was not releasable. To salvage the film, scenes with Boris Karloff as the recently departed Hiram Stokely and Susan Hart as his long-dead wife Cecily were added and the film was re-titled *The Ghost in the Invisible Bikini*. Though the film was not a big moneymaker, AIP was so impressed with O'Hara that they offered her another film. However, it was the laughable low-budget sci-fi flick *In the Year 2889* (1967), co-starring Paul Petersen of *The Donna Reed Show* and directed by self-described "schlockmeister" Larry Buchanan. Much better was the Academy Award–nominated short film *Prelude* (1968), starring O'Hara as the bitchy wife of meek John Astin, who meets his fantasy girl Karen Jensen in a supermarket.

It was shortly thereafter that Quinn O'Hara departed Hollywood for London to do theater. One of the films Quinn O'Hara did while in Europe was a small role as a "witch wench" in the AIP horror film *Cry of the Banshee* (1970) starring Vincent Price. Another was *Rubia's Jungle* (1971), which was shot in the Netherlands.

During her time in England, O'Hara made periodical trips back to Hollywood to maintain her working status. She could be seen on television in *To Rome with Love*, *The Smith Family* and *Ironside*, and on the big screen in the cult sex comedy *The Teacher* (1974). Then Quinn disappeared from show business. On a trip to Africa to visit her father who was working there, she met an Italian man. She accompanied him back to Italy where they were supposed to marry but didn't. When she returned to Hollywood in the late seventies, she found it surprisingly difficult to get work. Her friend, director Don Weis, gave her a part in an episode of *CHiPs* and she landed two small roles on *One Day at a Time*. Unfortunately, that was all she could muster.

Like a number of her contemporaries, O'Hara took up real estate to make ends meet. After a short-lived marriage, Quinn met Bill Kirk, who is 20 years her junior, in 1981. They married, divorced and have since reconciled. Today she works as a nurse and has reactivated her acting career. She still has her va-va-voom looks and wants another chance at the big time. "I wanted then and still might get an Academy Award," says Quinn defiantly. "I haven't given up and will put my face out there and let people know that I am alive. I have set up a website and have started attending acting workshops and Tai Chi classes." Quinn can be seen in the independent feature *Me, Miami and Nancy* (2004) starring Ringo Starr, Steven Tyler and Cloris Leachman.

Looking back at her beach partying days, Quinn says, "Beach movies reflected the times. I think that is important that people look back on these films and remember them for what they were. It was good clean fun, not like the smut you see today on the Internet. I am proud to have been a part of it."

Film credits: 1961: *The Errand Boy* [uncredited]; 1963: *The Caretakers*; 1964: *Good Neighbor, Sam*; *The Patsy*; 1965: *A Swingin' Summer*; 1966: *The Ghost in the Invisible Bikini*; 1967: *In the Year 2889* (television); 1968: *Prelude* (short); 1970: *Cry of the Banshee*; 1971: *Rubia's Jungle*; 1974: *The Teacher*; 2004: *Me, Miami and Nancy*.

★ *Bart Patton* ★

Tall and lanky, handsome Bart Patton played a surfing college boy on vacation in Waikiki in *Gidget Goes Hawaiian* (1961) but it is his work behind the camera that he is best remembered for. An association with Roger Corman led the actor to become a 24-year-old producer of the beach movies *Beach Ball* (1965), *Wild Wild Winter* (1966) and *Out of Sight* (1966).

Bart Patton was born in 1939. At ten he played Scampy the Clown for four years on the ABC children's program *Super Circus*. While attending UCLA in the late fifties, he met his future wife, pretty blonde actress Mary Mitchel, and became close friends with an aspiring filmmaker named Francis Coppola. His other classmates at the time included actor Aron Kincaid, singer Jim Morrison and Dennis Jakob. "I was friends with Bart Patton and his wife Mary Mitchel since our college days at UCLA," says Aron fondly. "Bart was handsome, friendly and a great guy. Mary was gorgeous, talented and seemed destined for stardom. In my eyes they were the perfect couple. I visited them at their house at the end of Malibu Road many times."

Patton made his film debut playing a high school student in *Because They're Young* (1960), which began his four-year relationship with Columbia Pictures. "I was never signed to a contract," reveals Bart. "But they liked me and hired me for a few films. I worked for weeks on *Strangers When We Meet* [1960] and I am only on screen for five minutes. I played the boyfriend of Roberta Shore whose parents were portrayed by Kirk Douglas and Barbara Rush. This film was so star-packed that I couldn't believe it." He would go on to work for the studio joining Joby Baker and Don Edmonds as partying college boys in *Gidget Goes Hawaiian* (1961) starring Deborah Walley in the title role and in the juvenile comedy *Zotz!* (1962) starring Tom Poston as an average Joe who finds a coin with super powers.

Bart also began working on television and guest starred on such varied series as *77 Sunset Strip, Father Knows Best, Thriller* and *General Electric Theatre*. His next film role was as an axe murderer in *Dementia 13* (1963), directed by Francis Coppola. This eerie black-and-white horror movie is set (and actually shot) in an Irish castle and also starred William Campbell, Luana Anders, Mary Mitchel and Patrick Magee. "Francis Coppola was the sound mixer on *The Young Racers*, which was directed by Roger Corman," says Bart. "Menacham Golan was the grip on the film. Roger said to them that since he had all these sets in Europe, that he would ship them to Ireland and whomever could come up with a script for a horror film first can direct it. By the next morning, Francis had written a 35-page treatment while Menacham was on page two. Francis got the gig.

"I was living in Malibu with my wife at the time," continues Bart. "Francis called me and said, 'I want you to come to Ireland to play William Campbell's younger brother. There is a role for Mary too as his fiancée.' He wanted me to produce it as well but I told him, 'I'm an actor, not a producer.' He needed an art director so Mary and I recommended our friend Eleanor Neil. We asked her and she took the job. Eleanor is Francis' wife today."

It was on *Dementia 13* that Patton began to get involved with the production side of making movies. "We all did everything to help each other out," remarks Bart. "At one point during the shoot I operated the camera and lit myself for a close-up while Francis watched because we missed the shot when a pub closed us down. We were all such total filmmakers that, whenever someone needed a hand, you'd go help them."

Producer Roger Corman was impressed with Patton and he began working as a production manager for his company. He helped put the cult horror movie *Spider Baby* (1964) together before Corman offered him a chance to produce *Beach Ball* (1965), one of the most blatant and successful knockoffs of AIP's *Beach Party*. This began his short partner-

The boyishly handsome Bart Patton, who went from co-starring in *Gidget Goes Hawaiian* to producing *Beach Ball, Wild Wild Winter* and *Out of Sight* (courtesy Bart Patton).

ship with director Lennie Weinrib. The success of *Beach Ball* landed the duo a seven-year contract at Universal Pictures. First up was *Wild Wild Winter* (1966), a beach party in the snow starring Gary Clarke and Chris Noel, and then the combination beach and spy spoof *Out of Sight* (1966) with Jonathan Daly and Karen Jensen.

Patton's films were successful because he knew what teenagers wanted to see on screen and followed the necessary formula. Though his leading actors were a bit long in the tooth for their roles, they all had fan followings from television to draw the kids into the theaters. Patton made sure to surround them with shapely young actresses not afraid to exploit their figures in the skimpiest of bikinis, actors who looked good shirtless and could deliver a funny line, and an eclectic roster of rock groups. Though the plots were thin and the dialogue usually corny, Patton kept the pace brisk and the production values high despite his limited budgets.

In between producing assignments, Patton continued accepting roles on such television sitcoms as *Petticoat Junction* and *Hank*. At Universal, he and Weinrib had a number of projects in development including *Over the Fairway and Into the Trees*, an adult satire on golfing, and *Rancho Bikini*, among others. "The studio didn't put much money to promote *Out of Sight* as a release," remarks Patton. "It wasn't a huge hit, I don't believe. Lennie and I then started writing *Rancho Bikini*, which was sort of like *Risky Business* with Tom Cruise. We never got too far with it. One day we had a meeting with Ned Tanen, an executive at the studio and our mentor. We pitched *Rancho Bikini* and he said, 'Sounds good, boys. Hope everything goes fine.' We went back to work. The next morning I drove to the studio on my motorcycle wearing a sports coat because you had to at Universal. I arrive on the lot and find that my name had been taken off my parking space. So had Lennie's. I go to my office and my typewriter is gone. I called Ned and asked him what was going on. He said, 'I thought you guys were working from home.' He had just been in our office the day before. I thought, 'This is it. The handwriting is on the wall.' This was a major studio adios-motherfucker-deal. They kept saying however, 'No, no. We're going to pick up your option in August when it is due.' Lennie was positive that they would but I knew better. I told him to find a job.

"I went to England with my wife Mary to try and sell our projects that Universal did not own," continues Patton. "We just left the country because I knew it was the end for us at Universal. Lennie kept holding on but eventually we were dropped like hot potatoes. It was sad ending to a nice era."

Patton went on to produce the trouble-plagued production *The Rain People* (1969), directed by his friend Francis Coppola. The movie starred Shirley Knight as a pregnant Long Island housewife who abandons her husband, hits the road and picks up hitchhiker James Caan, a mentally challenged former football star. "This was a great film," exclaims Patton. "It was one of the first movies to show a woman leaving her husband and becoming an independent person. It was an early woman's rights movie, basically. But Shirley Knight caused so much trouble on it. She and Francis were at odds from day one of shooting. Shirley was a Method actress and didn't agree with anything that Francis wanted to do. He had a theatrical background and the project started off as a love fest, or so we thought. It quickly went sour and at one point he threatened to fire her. I had to help him keep it together.

Shirley was very good in the film but her name meant nothing at the box office, that's for sure, and the movie never made a nickel."

Another interesting fact about *The Rain People* was that Rip Torn was supposed to play the role of the cop that went to Robert Duvall. "Rip was very influential in Francis' early career and got everybody including his wife Geraldine Page to agree to work for scale on *You're a Big Boy Now*," reveals Bart. "His deal on *The Rain People* was for scale but it also included giving him a brand new Harley-Davidson motorcycle. My producing partner Ron Colby got him a used one that was stolen the first day Rip parked it outside his home in New York City. When he demanded another one, Francis balked and Rip refused to do the film. We hired Robert Duvall, who made such an impression on Francis that he cast him as the attorney in *The Godfather*. That role would have probably gone to Rip if he didn't walk off this film." After *Easy Rider* (where he had good reasons to turn down the Jack Nicholson part), this was probably the biggest mistake of Torn's career.

Patton began making commercials for John Urie and Associates. "I couldn't get any films off the ground even though I optioned a couple of books," admits Patton. "I was never good at selling. In the sixties, those films were offered to me. I didn't have to pitch them. I started acting again and did a play in LA called *The Star and the Buttercup Tree*. I kept writing screenplays but never could sell any of them." The one film that Patton produced was *The Further Adventures of the Wilderness Family* (1978) starring Robert Logan of *Beach Ball*. Patton also began working steadily as an assistant director on a number of projects.

Today Patton lives in Georgia with his second wife and family. His son Tyler Patton from his first marriage to Mary Mitchel has worked in the art direction departments on a number of films including *Fight Club* (1999), *Frailty* (2001), *Looney Tunes: Back in Action* (2003), in which his mother played a bit, and *Hostage* (2004) starring Bruce Willis. Bart is still very active in show business despite living miles from Hollywood. "In 1999 I was called in to budget and produce an independent feature called *Unshackled* starring Stacy Keach and Morgan Fairchild," says Bart proudly. "I ended up hiring myself as director and it turned out very well. The movie was released in Georgia but it had no money behind it for promotion so it disappeared after two weeks. It was finally released on DVD in March 2004."

When asked which of his beach party movies he thought was best, Patton remarks, "I haven't seen *Wild Wild Winter* in a long time but I think *Beach Ball* was the best of the three. It had more spirit, more heart and much cleverer gags. *Out of Sight* did not work for me at all. I saw it on television not too long ago and I was almost embarrassed by some of the gags."

Film credits: 1960: *Because They're Young*; *Strangers When We Meet*; 1961: *Gidget Goes Hawaiian*; 1962: *Zotz!*; 1963: *Dementia 13*; 1965: *Beach Ball* [uncredited]; 1966: *Wild Wild Winter* [uncredited]; *Out of Sight* [uncredited]; 1971: *THX 1138*; 1993: *Silent Victim/Hothouse* (television).

★ *Pamela Tiffin* ★

A sulty brunette, this former *Vogue* cover girl became one of the early sixties' most popular actresses. She won critical raves for her first two performances, in

Summer and Smoke (1961) and *One, Two, Three* (1961). But Hollywood typed Pamela as the virginal ingenue a la Sandra Dee in a string of teenage films—*State Fair* (1962), *Come Fly with Me* (1963) and *The Pleasure Seekers* (1964). Tiffin also hit the beach as a surfboard-riding coed opposite James Darren in *For Those Who Think Young* (1964). The popular pair were re-teamed as college students in the lightweight hot rod drama *The Lively Set* (1964).

Pamela Tiffin was born Pamela Tiffin Wonso on Oct. 13, 1942, in Oklahoma City. She is the only child of retired architect Stanley Wonso and his wife Grace. She began modeling at age 13 and after graduating from high school she relocated

Sultry Pamela Tiffin, the star of *For Those Who Think Young*, strikes a very provocative pose.

to New York to pursue her modeling career. Soon she became one of New York's top fashion models, earning up to $1,500 a week. A chance encounter with producer Hal B. Wallis led to a role of the young woman who steals the heart of Dr. Laurence Harvey from spinster Geraldine Page in *Summer and Smoke*. But it was her superior performance that same year (1961) in Billy Wilder's frenetic comedy *One, Two, Three* that brought her real attention. Pamela won raves as the impetuous, scatterbrained Scarlett Hazeltine who, while on vacation in West Berlin, meets and marries a Communist (Horst Buchholz) to the consternation of her guardian (James Cagney). Pamela's performance earned her a Best Supporting Actress Golden Globe nomination from the Hollywood Foreign Press.

In 1962, Tiffin married Clay Felker, the publisher of *Esquire*. Despite her marital status, Hollywood typed her as the innocent virgin role in a series of popular though forgettable films aimed at the youth market. To Tiffin's credit she injected in each of roles a comedic touch that made these characters much more interesting than expected. She stood out in *Come Fly with Me* (1963) as one of three stewardesses out to land rich husbands while working the New York-to-Paris and -Vienna routes. The surf movie *For Those Who Think Young* (1964) starred Tiffin in ("the Annette Funicello role" as the poor but proud good girl fighting off the advances of rich playboy James Darren from the campus to the beach. In *The Lively Set* (1964) Pamela did the chasing as a persistent coed who pursues James Darren, who prefers his hot rods to babes.

The most lavish of Tiffin's youth-oriented movies was *The Pleasure Seekers* (1964), a remake of *Three Coins in the Fountain* (1954) by the same director, Jean Negulesco. Pamela, Ann-Margret and Carol Lynley are swinging chicks looking for fun and romance in Madrid. As usual, Pamela played the naïve virginal one. Even though she was extremely popular with younger movie fans and received a Gold Medal Award nomination for Favorite Actress from *Photoplay*, Pamela was tired of teenage films. She bemoaned in *Fantasy Femmes of Sixties Cinema*, "I didn't want to do these type of movies. I wanted to do Tennessee Williams and work with Billy Wilder again." It wasn't until she co-starred with Paul Newman in the hard-boiled detective drama *Harper* (1966) that Pamela was able to shake her ingenue image. In *Harper* she played a sex-starved heiress who unsuccessfully tried to seduce the gumshoe.

Soon after completing *Harper*, Pamela went to Italy to play the wife of Marcello Mastroianni in *Oggi, Domani, Dopodomani* (1965), which was released in the U. S. as *Kiss the Other Sheik* in 1968. She went blonde for the part and loved her new look so much that she did not go back to brunette after filming wrapped. Her sexy persona helped land her the Jean Harlow role in the 1966 Broadway revival of *Dinner at Eight*, for which she received a Theatre World Award. However, Tiffin missed her opportunity for major stardom. Shortly after the play closed in 1967, Pamela relocated to Italy to escape an unhappy marriage.

Though Tiffin cavorted on screen with Italy's most popular leading men including Vittorio Gassman, Nino Manfredi, Ugo Tognazzi and Lou Castel, her films were rarely released in the U.S. with the exception of *Deaf Smith and Johnny Ears* (1973) a Western co-starring Anthony Quinn and Franco Nero. Pamela did sneak in one Hollywood film, the hilarious *Viva Max!* (1969) starring Peter Ustinov as a Mexican general who retakes the Alamo complete with wacky American tourists as hostages (including Tiffin as a sympathizing coed).

After her 1969 divorce from Clay Felker, Pamela married Edmondo Danon (the son of film producer Marcello Danon of *La Cage au Folles* fame) in 1974. She retired shortly thereafter to raise her two daughters Echo and Aurora though she was lured out of retirement in 1986 to appear in *Rose* starring Valerie Perrine and Brett Halsey for Italian television. Tiffin faced the cameras again recently, appearing as herself in Iranian director Rafi Pitts' documentary *Abel Ferrara: Not Guilty* (2003), a look at the quirky director through the eyes of Tiffin's actress-daughter Echo Danon.

Looking back on *For Those Who Think Young*, which she did not want to appear in, Pamela Tiffin remarked, "When you're young you have definite tastes and predilections. Now I find this and my other teenage movies adorable and innocent. We were *all* innocent back then."

Film credits: 1961: *Summer and Smoke*; *One, Two, Three*; 1962: *State Fair*; 1963: *Come Fly with Me*; 1964: *For Those Who Think Young*; *The Lively Set*; *The Pleasure Seekers*; 1965: *The Hallelujah Trail*; 1966: *Harper*; *Delitto Quasi Perfetto/An Almost Perfect Crime*; 1968: *Kiss the Other Sheik* (completed in 1965 as *Oggi, Domani, Dopodomani*); *I Protagonisti/The Protagonists*; *Straziami, ma di Baci Saxiami/Kill Me with Kisses*; 1969: *Viva Max!*; *L'Archangelo/The*

Archangel; 1971: *Cose di Cosa Nostra/Gang War*; *Il Vichingo Venuto dal Sud/The Viking Who Came from the South*; *Giornata Nera per l'Ariete/The Fifth Cord*; 1972: *Prelude to Taurus*; *I Giorni del Sole*; 1973: *Los Amigos/Deaf Smith and Johnny Ears*; 1974: *La Signora e Stata Violentata/The Lady Has Been Raped*; *E se per Caso una Mattina*; 1986: *Rose* (television-Italy); 2003: *Abel Ferrara: Not Guilty* (doc) [herself].

* *Deborah Walley* *

Red-haired knockout Deborah Walley's first film role was Gidget the teenage surfer in *Gidget Goes Hawaiian* (1961) and no matter how hard she tried to shake that bikini-clad image, the sand-and-surf would always be associated with Walley. Remarkably popular with younger audiences, the perky Walley would go on to appear in such beachy-keen films as *Beach Blanket Bingo* (1965), *Ski Party* (1965), *The Ghost in the Invisible Bikini* (1966) and *It's a Bikini World* (1967).

Deborah Walley was born on August 12, 1943, in Bridgeport, Connecticut. Her parents, Nathan and Edith Walley, were figure skaters and choreographers with the Ice Capades so Walley spent most of her childhood on the road. Settling in New York when a teenager, she began modeling and taking acting classes at the New York Academy of Dramatic Arts. She was playing Irina in an Off-Broadway production of Chekhov's *Three Sisters* when Columbia talent scout Joyce Selznick spotted her. The talented redhead was brought to Hollywood and beat out numerous other actresses to succeed Sandra Dee as Gidget in *Gidget Goes Hawaiian*. The film was a hit and made Walley a star. Her energetic performance won her the Photoplay Gold Medal Award for "Favorite Female Newcomer." She was receiving 500-600 fan letters a day and with the help of her mother answered every single one. But Walley did not want to be typecast as Gidget and had to fight hard to get varied roles.

Walley then made two films (*Bon Voyage* [1962] and *Summer Magic* [1963]) for Walt Disney and gave a fine performance as a flaky coed in *The Young Lovers* (1964) starring Peter Fonda, winning the best reviews of her career. Howard Thompson of *The New York Times* exclaimed that Walley and co-star Nick Adams "steal the picture" from the film's leads, Fonda and Sharon Hugueny. With encouraging notices like this, Walley strove mightily to win challenging roles such as Susan Hayward's wayward teenage daughter in *Where Love Has Gone* (1964). Purportedly, it came down to Walley, Laurel Goodwin, Lana Wood and Joey Heatherton for the part, which went to Heatherton.

Perhaps out of frustration for not being taken seriously as an actress, Walley signed a contract with AIP in 1964 and her name would forever become synonymous with beach movies. In *Beach Blanket Bingo* (1965) Walley unsuccessfully vied with Annette Funicello for the charms of Frankie Avalon. She had to settle for John Ashley (whom she was married to in real life) instead. Walley, however, did win Frankie in that same year's dumb military comedy *Sergeant Deadhead* and in *Ski Party* co-starring Dwayne Hickman, Yvonne Craig and Aron Kincaid. The popularity of these films earned Walley a third straight Photoplay Gold Medal nomination for Favorite Actress. In the last beach party movie, *The Ghost in the Invisible*

Bikini (1966), Walley had to survive a night in a haunted mansion along with heir Tommy Kirk and the rest of the beach gang to collect their inheritance. Though these roles were beneath her, Walley could be counted on to give a lively performance no matter how lame the script.

In between beach movies, Walley found the time to appear in the sci-fi cheapie *The Bubble* (1966) and compete with Shelley Fabares and Diane McBain for the charms of Elvis Presley in *Spinout* (1966). Regarding the King, Walley gushed to Sharyn Peacocke, "Elvis and I became really close friends. He was like a brother to me. There was no affair, no love thing, but we became very, very close friends and … I knew him for 11 years afterwards. I really enjoyed working with him and we had a really tight relationship while we were working."

During the later part of the decade, Walley became a regular on the sitcom *The Mothers-in-Law* starring Eve Arden and Kaye Ballard, which ran from 1967 to 1969. She also made her last beach movie appearance in the appropriately titled *It's a Bikini World* (1967). Released by Trans America, it reunited Walley with Tommy Kirk, this time playing rivals in a multi-event athletic contest. Deborah didn't return to the big screen until 1973's horror opus *The Severed Arm* but her role as an inept thief in the low-budget comedy *Benji* (1974) was much more memorable and the movie became one of that year's biggest surprise hits. Soon after Walley retired because she discovered it was too difficult as a single mother to juggle raising her two sons and an acting career. Instead she shifted focus to writing and producing.

She co-founded with actress Diane McBain Pied Piper Productions, a non-profit theater company for children, and worked for a number of production companies including Disney Animation, Animation Camera and Rick Kear Productions. In 1991, she relocated to Arizona and wrote her first children's book, *Grandfather's Good Medicine* (1993). Walley also became immersed in the Native American culture and started the Swiftwind Theater Company, coaching Native Americans in writing and acting. During this time she produced the award-winning short film *The Vision of Seeks-to-Hunt Great*. She returned to Hollywood in the late nineties and immediately snagged a guest shot on *Baywatch*—an appropriate comeback vehicle for the sixties' ultimate beach babe. While pursuing acting roles "as a hobby," she continued working with children, setting up acting workshops in the United States and Australia through her *Imagination Playshops*.

When asked by Sharyn Peacocke why she felt that the sixties surf and beach party movies are still popular with audiences, even teenagers, to this day, Walley replied, "It's so different from what's going on today. Maybe that's the appeal. It is so diametrically different. It's so clean and fresh and fun-filled, as opposed to the movies they make for teenagers today. Horror films are probably number one—and they're so full of sex. It's amazing to me that these kids from today would find appeal in the films of that era, but of course it's delightful to me."

To the shock of her fans, old and new, Deborah Walley passed away on May 10, 2001, of esophageal cancer at her home in Sedona, Arizona. The former Gidget was only 57.

Film credits: 1961: *Gidget Goes Hawaiian*; 1962: *Bon Voyage!*: 1963: *Summer Magic*: 1964: *The Young Lovers*; 1965: *Beach Blanket Bingo*; *Ski Party*: *Sergeant Deadhead*; *Dr. Goldfoot and the Bikini Machine* [cameo]; 1966: *The Ghost in the Invisible Bikini*; *Spinout*; *The Bubble*; 1967: *It's a Bikini World*; 1973: *The Severed Arm*; 1974: *Benji*.

★ *William Wellman, Jr.* ★

With his dark hair, slim physique and handsome looks, William Wellman, Jr., played straight man to wisecracking, fun-loving James Stacy in two sixties beach party movies. Though Stacy was the charming rogue every sixties teenage girl wanted to date, William Wellman, Jr., was the all–American boy you brought home to meet Daddy. *A Swingin' Summer* (1965) sent the duo to Lake Arrowhead as managers of the resort's summer teenage dance pavilion, where they find romance while fighting off interlopers who want to ruin their gig. They donned skis for their next film together *Winter a-Go-Go*, a beach party in the snow, as new owners of a ski resort for young hipsters and their girls. Though Stacy got all the laughs and flirted with all the bikini-clad babes in these films, Wellman's earnest performances as the serious-minded lad with eyes for only one girl—Quinn O'Hara in *A Swingin' Summer* and Beverly Adams in *Winter a-Go-Go*—stops Stacy from walking off with the films.

William Wellman, Jr., was born on January 20, 1937. He is the son of former Busby Berkeley dancer Dorothy Coonan and esteemed director William Wellman, whose films included *Wings, Public Enemy, A Star Is Born, Nothing Sacred, Beau Geste, The Ox-Bow Incident, Battleground* and *The High and the Mighty.* "Wild Bill," as he was nicknamed, was notorious for his temper and for telling off studio chiefs.

Extremely athletic, the younger Wellman excelled in baseball and dreamed of playing in the major leagues. In his junior year of high school, the "hot shot high school ballplayer" got his chance when he was invited to try out for the New York Giants then managed by Leo Durocher. "I went to the Giants' training camp in Arizona," recalls Bill. "I was an outfielder so I hid out there with the other guys. When Durocher called me in to take my swats at the plate, I did well against the batting practice pitcher. Durocher then started to bring in his best hurlers, which he always did for the wannabes. I did okay against Big Jim Hearn but he threw a fast ball that I had not seen in high school. Then he brought it their ace left-hander, Johnny Antonelli. The first pitch he threw me sat me down on my butt and it was a strike. The catcher laughed. I was able to only muster a foul tip against the curve balls he threw me. I was really out of my element."

As his desire of being a professional ballplayer dissipated partly due to injuries he suffered playing football, the versatile Wellman joined the golf team and majored in business administration while attending Duke University. He also began boxing as an amateur for a period of time before going pro. However, Wellman remained disenchanted in the way his life was progressing. While home for the summer break after his freshman year, Wellman, Sr., prodded by the head of publicity at Warner Bros., asked his son to test for the role of Wellman, Sr.(!), in his movie *Lafayette Escadrille* (1958) as he needed younger actors to surround the film's star Tab Hunter. The movie was originally slated for James Dean, who had been killed, and Paul Newman, who was suspended from the studio.

"Though I tried out for the major leagues, my screen test was the hardest thing I ever did in my whole life—47 years in this business," admits Wellman, Jr. "I had to audition in front of Jack Warner, the big executives at the studios, my father and all the actors—they put us all in one room like a big classroom. I tested with Tab

Hunter. He was the kind of person who was nervous and his uneasiness showed. Mine didn't even though I was nervous as hell and felt like I had volcanic eruptions going off inside of me. I think he made me look better. Not that the role was real demanding but it was an important part. They said, 'You know, the kid's okay.' I got the role in *Lafayette Escadrille* and on the second day of shooting on location, I thought, 'This is it. This is what I want to do.' I've spent my whole career in show business and nothing else."

Though *Lafayette Escadrille* was the newcomer's first movie, it was released after his second film, *Sayonara* (1957). With his combination of macho good looks and athletic prowess, Wellman, Jr., began being cast as soldiers or cowboys in such male-oriented films as *Darby's Rangers* (1958), *Pork Chop Hill* (1959) and *The Horse Soldiers* (1959), the latter directed by his father. He was offered

The brooding William Wellman, Jr., star of *A Swingin' Summer* and *Winter a-Go-Go* (*courtesy William Wellman, Jr.*).

a contract by Warner Bros. but passed on it, afraid that he was going to be drafted into military service. Instead Wellman, Jr., joined the reserves. During the six months he was away he had to turn down a number of films, including a co-starring role in *The Deep Six* (1958) with Alan Ladd.

During the sixties, William Wellman, Jr., seemed to alternate playing leads and supporting roles in an array of B-movies. He co-starred with blonde bombshells Mamie Van Doren in *College Confidential* (1960) and June Wilkinson in the cult voodoo movie *Macumba Love* (1960). His boxing skills led to the lead role as a college boy who secretly spars under the name Kid Gallant to earn extra cash for his fraternity in *A Swingin' Affair* (1962) featuring Dick Dale and His Del-Tones. Wellman, Jr., also became a favorite of Jerry Lewis, who cast him in the unsold television pilot *Permanent Waves*. So impressed was Lewis with the young actor that he hired him to play minor roles in a number of his subsequent movies including *The Ladies Man* (1961), *The Errand Boy* (1961) and *The Patsy* (1964).

In *A Swingin' Summer*, Wellman, Jr., not only starred but he also co-produced without credit. He played the staid Rick who along with James Stacy as his pal and Quinn O'Hara as his girlfriend gets the chance to run the Lake Arrowhead Dance Pavillion. Though the reviewer in *Variety* found Wellman "somewhat wooden and mechanical," he conceded that the actor "had good potential." Other reviewers remarked that the up-and-coming actor "shows promise," "is gifted" and "gives a nice performance."

In *Winter a-Go-Go*, Wellman inherits a ski lodge and with his enterprising friend (James Stacy) and a gaggle of college students (including Beverly Adams, Tom Nardini, Julie Parrish, Duke Hobbie, Linda Rogers and Nancy Czar) tries to make a go of it.

Playing literally straight man to Stacy's charming, roguish characters in both movies, Wellman gives sincere performances in each. "I had been taking acting classes for years and then switched acting teachers during the filming of *Winter a-Go-Go*. It is very hard to compare but I think if you look at my work in *A Swingin' Summer* and *Winter a-Go-Go*, which is the weaker film, you'll see that I am doing a better job in the latter. I took myself too seriously in *A Swingin' Summer*, which is the worst thing you can do in a picture like that."

Unlike many beach movie actors, Wellman was able due to his talent and versatility to cross over into biker movies with *The Born Losers* (1967) starring Tom Laughlin in his first appearance as Billy Jack. Trailing *The Wild Angels* (1966) into theaters across the nation, the film was a huge hit and helped kick-start the biker movie genre. "Actually, *The Born Losers* would have been the first biker movie released but Tom had financial problems which took him a long time to get the film in the can," says Wellman.

Bill made such a convincing biker as the bearded Child in *The Born Losers* that he was offered and turned down roles in other motorcycle dramas. "I was offered two or three more biker movies right after completing *The Born Losers* including the biggest mistake that I ever made in my career," reveals Wellman. "I was trying to develop projects to get them produced. One was a Western where I wanted every part played by a second-generation son or daughter of a famous person. I was having trouble getting the film off the ground. One day I was having lunch with Peter Fonda at Cyrano's on the Sunset Strip and he said, 'Don't worry about it, Bill. Look, I'm going to do a movie where they promised to give me a Harley. Dennis Hopper and I are putting it together. Why don't you work in this film with us?' Because of his reputation, I didn't want to have anything to do with Dennis Hopper. I gave Peter an excuse and said, 'I just did a biker movie and turned down another one called *The Glory Stompers* [coincidentally Dennis Hopper took the role he passed on]. I quickly got out of it and they went on to make *Easy Rider*!'"

Wellman's boxing skills came into play when he was cast as a prizefighter in the big-budget Disney musical *The Happiest Millionaire* (1967). "When I met Walt Disney I called him Mr. Disney but he told me to call him Uncle Walt," says Wellman, laughing. "I thought it was a joke. But it was true. He was a fabulous guy and on the set all of the time." Jerry Lewis kept the young actor busy as well, offering cameo roles in *The Big Mouth* (1967), *Hook, Line & Sinker* (1968) and *Which Way to the Front?* (1970). This was a good thing since he had a family to support.

By the end of the decade, it was clear that superstardom had passed Wellman by. But the talented actor continued working at a consistent pace. Just as in the sixties, the seventies found Wellman playing small roles in studio productions and lead or featured roles in exploitation movies. After playing "honkies" in the blaxploitation films *Black Caesar* (1973) and *Hell Up in Harlem* (1973), the handsome actor copped the important role of Lt. John Duncan Bulkely in *MacArthur* (1977) starring Gregory Peck. Wellman also maintained relationships with director Larry Cohen and Tom Laughlin, working with them on a number of their movies includ-

418   Part II : The Players

ing Cohen's classic cult horror film *It's Alive!* (1974) (about a mutant baby that goes on a killing spree) and Laughlin's sequel to *Billy Jack* entitled *The Trial of Billy Jack* (1974). He also remained very active on television, guest starring on numerous series including *The FBI, The Brady Bunch, Adam-12, Marcus Welby, M.D.* and *Charlie's Angels.*

While continuing acting, the multi-faceted Wellman returned to producing beginning with *Billy Jack Goes to Washington* (1977) and *It Lives Again* (1978) and working in production for a number of television movies and mini-series at Lorimar. In the early eighties, he landed the lead role in *Image of the Beast,* which was produced by Mark IV Pictures, a company of Christian filmmakers. He went on to star in two more movies, *Prodigal Planet* (which he co-wrote) and *Brother Enemy* (1981) as a puppeteer who takes in the young hoodlums who destroyed his life's work and teaches them his craft. For that film, he won the Christian Film Distributors Best Actor of the Year award. "Two of the three films were based on the Book of Revelations," says Bill. "Mainstream Hollywood has no idea about these films. They shot them in 16mm as rentals for churches. They then became available on home video later in the decade. I did them between 1980 and 1983 and they still play worldwide in over 40 countries in many different languages. You wouldn't believe the fan mail I get for these films—tons of letters."

In the late eighties and nineties, acting on such hit television shows as *Dallas, Beverly Hills 90210, Star Trek: Deep Space Nine* and *The Practice* kept Wellman very busy. In 1996, he executive-produced and created the award-winning documentary *Wild Bill Hollywood Maverick* (1996), exploring the career of his father, William A. Wellman. Among the many accolades the film received were prizes from the Sundance Film Festival, the National Board of Review, the Houston International Film Festival, the San Luis Obispo International Film Festival, the Newport Beach International Film Festival and the Hong Kong International Film Festival. Acting-wise, Wellman recently guest starred on the television series *Alias, Jag* and *Watching Ellie.* He currently has in development a screenplay entitled *C'est La Guerre* and a biography that should be published in 2005 about his father's life and times.

Film credits: 1957: *Sayonara;* 1958: *Darby's Rangers; Lafayette Escadrille; High School Confidential!;* 1959: *Pork Chop Hill; The Horse Soldiers;* 1960: *Sergeant Rutledge; Macumba Love; College Confidential;* 1961: *Dondi; The Ladies' Man; The Errand Boy;* 1962: *How the West Was Won;* 1963: *A Swingin' Affair; Gunfight at Comanche Creek;* 1964: *The Patsy; The Disorderly Orderly;* 1965: *Young Fury; A Swingin' Summer; The Family Jewels; The Young Sinner* [completed in 1960]; *Winter a-Go-Go;* 1967: *The Happiest Millionaire; The Big Mouth; The Born Losers; The Private Navy of Sgt. O'Farrell; Blue;* 1969: *Hook, Line and Sinker;* 1970: *Which Way to the Front?;* 1973: *Black Caesar; Hell Up in Harlem;* 1974: *It's Alive!; The Trial of Billy Jack;* 1975: *The Master Gunfighter* [voice only]; 1976: *Midway* [television version only]; 1977: *Billy Jack Goes to Washington; MacArthur; The Amazing World of Psychic Phenomenon* [himself]; *Private Files of J. Edgar Hoover;* 1978: *A Love Affair: The Eleanor and Lou Gehrig Story* (television); *Fire in the Sky* (television) [voice only]; 1981: *Image of the Beast; Brother Enemy;* 1983: *Prodigal Planet;* 1986: *Crown World Airlines;* 1988: *Curfew;* 1994: *Lies of the Heart: The Story of Laurie Kellogg* (television); *The Puppet Masters; Blood Run/Outside the Law* (television); 1996: *Wild Bill Hollywood Maverick* (doc) [himself].

Bibliography

General

Arkoff, Samuel Z. *Flying Through Hollywood by the Seat of My Pants: From the Man Who Brought You "I Was a Teenage Werewolf" and "Muscle Beach Party."* Secaucus, NJ: Carol, 1992.

Armstrong, Richard B., and Mary Willems Armstrong. *Encyclopedia of Film Themes, Settings and Series.* Jefferson, NC: McFarland, 2001.

Barilotti, Steve. "Celluloid Sacrament: Reviving the Surf Film Ritual in the New Millennium." *Surfer,* July 2004: 110–27.

Barrett, Michael. "AMC Spotlighting Campy, Teen Films the Critics Hated." *San Antonio Express News,* April 30, 2001: 4D.

Bart, Peter. "Hollywood Beach Bonanza." *New York Times,* December 1964.

Betrock, Alan. *The I Was a Teenage Juvenile Delinquent Rock 'n' Roll Horror Beach Party Movie Book.* New York: St. Martin's Press, 1986.

Beyette, Beverly. "Riding That Wave Again: The Original Gidget Revisits Her Past, Which Differed from the Beach Party That Ignited the Malibu Coast." *Los Angeles Times,* October 14, 2001: E1, E4.

Blum, Daniel, ed. *Daniel Blum's Screen World: 1960.* Philadelphia: Chilton Company—Book Division, 1960.

_____. *Daniel Blum's Screen World: 1961.* Philadelphia: Chilton Company—Book Division, 1961.

_____. *Daniel Blum's Screen World: 1962.* Philadelphia: Chilton Company—Book Division, 1962.

_____. *Daniel Blum's Screen World: 1964.* Philadelphia: Chilton Books, 1964.

_____. *Daniel Blum's Screen World: 1965.* Philadelphia: Chilton Books, 1965.

_____. *Daniel Blum's Screen World: 1966.* New York: Crown, 1966.

Caine, Andrew. "The A.I.P. Beach Movies—Cult Films Depicting Subcultural Activities." *Scope: An Online Journal of Film Studies* (December 2001), http://www.nottingham.ac.uk/film/journal/articles/aip-beach-movies.htm.

Craig, Yvonne. *From Ballet to the Batcave and Beyond.* Venice, CA: Kudu Press, 2000.

Cralle, Trevor. *The Surfin'ary: A Dictionary of Surfing Terms and Surfspeak.* Berkeley, CA: Ten Speed Press, 1991.

Crenshaw, Marshall. *Hollywood Rock.* New York: HarperPerennial, 1994.

Darin, Dodd, and Maxine Paetro. *Dream Lovers: The Magnificent Shattered Lives of Bobby Darin and Sandra Dee.* New York: Warner Books, 1994.

Denver, Bob. *Gilligan, Maynard & Me.* Secaucus, NJ: Carol, 1993.

Dufoe, Terry, Tiffany Dufoe, Becky Dufoe, and Meredith Asher. "That Bewitched, Lucy Lovin', Beach Party Movie Guy! An Interview with Film and Television Director William Asher." *Filmfax Plus,* April/June 2004: 88–93, 138.

Edelstein, Andrew J. *The Pop Sixties.* New York: World Almanac Publications, 1985.

Ehrlich, Henry. "Hollywood's Teen-age Gold Mine." *Look,* November 3, 1964: 60–64, 66.

Funicello, Annette, and Patricia Romanowski. *A Dream Is What You Make It: My Story.* New York: Hyperion, 1994.

Gabbard, Andrea. *Girl in the Curl: A Century of Women in Surfing.* Seattle, WA: Seal Press, 2000.

Gardner, Christopher. "Up from the Beach." *New York Sunday News,* August 1, 1965.

Gault-Williams, Maxwell. "1963." *Legendary Surfers: A Definitive History of Surfing's Culture and Heroes* 3, no. 17, http://www.legendarysurfers.com/surf/legends/lsc215.html.

_____. "1964: The Year of the Endless Summer." *Legendary Surfers: A Definitive History of Surfing's Culture and Heroes* 3, no. 21, http://www.legendarysurfers.com/surf/legends/lsc217_1964.html.

Greene, Ray. "Sam Arkoff: The Last Interview." *Cult Movies,* No. 36, 2002: 10–14.

Harmetz, Aljean. "Samuel Z. Arkoff, Maker of Drive-In Thrillers, Dies at 83." *New York Times,* September 19, 2001: C14.

Harris, Leonard. "Beach Films Figure to Make Money." *New York World-Telegram and Sun,* January 25, 1965: 15.

Headrick, Robert J., Jr. "Beach Blanket Babylon: The Rise and Fall of Surf City Cinema." *Filmfax,* August/September, 1994: 50–55.

Henderson, Jennifer. "Fun in the Sun Cinema." *Big Reel,* August 2002: 69–75.

Hickman, Dwayne. *Forever Dobie: The Many Lives of Dwayne Hickman.* Secaucus, NJ: Carol, 1994.

Hughes, Kathleen A. "Riding the Wave: Variety of Businesses Seek to Cash in on Surge in Surfing Chic." *Wall Street Journal,* May 11, 1987.

King, Susan. "Documentary Hails the Conquering B-Movie Machine." *Los Angeles Times,* May 1, 2001: F3.

Krafsur, Richard P., ed. *The American Film Institute Catalog of Motion Pictures: Feature Films 1961–1970.* New York & London: R.R. Bowker, 1976.

Lewis, Richard Warren. "Those Swinging Beach Movies." *Saturday Evening Post,* July 31, 1965: 83–87.

Lisanti, Tom. *Drive-in Dream Girls: A Galaxy of B-Movie Starlets of the Sixties.* Jefferson, NC: McFarland, 2003.

_____. *Fantasy Femmes of Sixties Cinema: Interviews with 20 Actresses from Biker, Beach, and Elvis Movies.* Jefferson, NC: McFarland, 2001.

Lopez, Daniel. *Films by Genre: 775 Categories, Styles, Trends and Movements Defined, with a Filmography for Each.* Jefferson, NC: McFarland, 1993.

Lueras, Leonard. *Surfing: The Ultimate Pleasure.* New York: Workman, 1984.

McCrohan, Donna. *Prime Time, Our Time: America's Life and Times Through the Prism of Television.* Rockin, CA: Prima Publishing & Communications, 1990.

McParland, Stephen J. *It's Party Time: A Musical Appreciation of the Beach Party Film Genre.* Southern California: PTB Productions, 1992.

Maltin, Leonard. *Leonard Maltin's Movie and Video Guide 1995.* New York: Penguin Books USA, 1994.

Marcus, Ben. *The Price of Gas: Watermen as Stuntmen, from Duke to Dora to Doerner,* http://www.cinemasanfrancisco.com/priceofgas.html.

_____. "The Surfer Interview with Stacy Peralta." *Surfer,* July 2004: 86–96.

Mars, Mikey. "The Music of the Beach Party Clones." *The Music of the Beach Party Movies.* http://beachpartymoviemusic.com/The BeachPartyClones.html.

_____. "The Musical Scores." *The Music of the Beach Party Movies.* http://beachpartymoviemusic.com/MusicalScoring.html.

Modern Screen. "Two on a Beach Blanket," July 1965: 40–43.

Monush, Barry. *Screen World Presents the Encyclopedia of Hollywood Film Actors: From the Silent Era to 1965.* New York: Applause Theatre & Cinema Books, 2003.

Nott, Robert. "Weis Guy, Huh! Comedy in the Trenches with Don Weis." *Filmfax,* May/June 1995: 71–75.

O'Neill, James. *Terror on Tape: A Complete Guide to Over 2,000 Horror Movies on Video.* New York: Billboard Books, 1994.

Ormrod, Joan. "Issues of Gender in *Muscle Beach Party.*" *Scope: An Online Journal of Film Studies* (December 2002), http://www.nottingham.ac.uk/film/journal/articles/muscle-beach.htm.

Photoplay. "The Beach Gang Goes Formal," December 1965: 64–66.

Saint Louis, Catherine. "Surfing Gauguin." *New York Times Magazine,* July 4, 2004: 40.

Steinberg, Cobbett S. *Film Facts.* New York: Facts on File, 1980.

Stillman, Deanne. "The Real Gidget." In *Surf Culture: The Art History of Surfing,* by Bolton Colburn, Ben Finney, Tyler Stallings, C. R. Stecyk, Deanne Stillman, and Tom Wolfe, 116–29. Laguna Beach, CA: Laguna Art Museum in association with Gingko Press, 2002.

Teen Screen. "First Annual TS Awards & Models Graduation," June 1965: 20–23.

_____. "TS Awards—The Story Behind a Star-Studded Night," July 1967: 20–25.

Variety Film Reviews 1907– 1980. 16 vols. New York: Garland, 1983.

Viharo, Robert. "James Nicholson: From Rags to Riches in the Low-Budget B-Movie Business." *Filmfax,* Aug./Sept. 1999: 44–49, 86.

Voger, Mark. "Call Me Sam (Arkoff, That Is)." *Filmfax,* Feb./Mar. 1991: 73–79, 87–89.

Walker, Brian J. "Beach Party Movies at Brian's Drive-in Theater." *Brian's Drive-in Theater.* http://briansdriveintheater.com/beach.html

Warshaw, Matt. *The Encyclopedia of Surfing.* Orlando, Florida: Harcourt, 2003.

Weldon, Michael. *The Psychotronic Encyclopedia of Film.* New York: Ballantine, 1983.

_____. *The Psychotronic Video Guide.* New York: St. Martin's Griffin, 1996.

Willis, John, ed. *Screen World: 1967.* New York: Crown, 1967.

_____. *Screen World: 1968.* New York: Crown, 1968.

_____. *Screen World: 1969.* New York: Crown, 1969.

Wynn, Ned. *We Will Always Live in Beverly Hills: Growing Up Crazy in Hollywood.* New York: W. Morrow, 1990.

Individual Films

Beach Ball

Bernstein, Stan. "Tide Rolls In on Latest Beach Epic." *Los Angeles Times,* October 22, 1965.

Boxoffice. Review of *Beach Ball,* October 4, 1965.

Buchanan, Loren G. Review of *Beach Ball. Motion Picture Herald,* October 13, 1965.

Byrnes, Edward. *Edd Byrnes "Kookie" No More.* New York: Barricade Books, 1996.

Carroll, Kathleen. "*Beach Ball* Lacks Bounce." *New York Daily News,* December 9, 1965.

Herbstman, Mandel. Review of *Beach Ball. Film Daily,* September 28, 1965.

Molleson, John. Review of *Beach Ball. New York Herald Tribune,* December 9, 1965.

Munroe, Dale. "*Ball* Bounces for Contemporary Teen." *Citizen-News,* October 22, 1965.

Photoplay. "Be a Beach Bunny," June 1965.

Rider, David. Review of *Beach Ball. Films and Filming,* May 1966: 11.

Beach Blanket Bingo

Asher, Jerry. "Behind the Scenes: *Beach Blanket Bingo.*" *Screen Stories,* May 1965.

Carroll, Kathleen. "*Beach Blanket Bingo* Is More Fun in the Sun." *New York Daily News,* June 3, 1965.

Harford, Margaret. "*Blanket Bingo* Wins with Teens." *Los Angeles Times,* April 9, 1965.

Herbstman, Mandel. Review of *Beach Blanket Bingo. Film Daily,* June 3, 1965.

Houser, John G. "*Beach Blanket Bingo* Good Fun." *Los Angeles Herald-Examiner,* April 8, 1965.

Kane, Chris. "*Beach Blanket Bingo.*" *Screen Stories,* May 1965.

Lovece, Frank. "Beach Party Buster." *Video,* February 1987: 20.

Salmaggi, Robert. Review of *Beach Blanket Bingo. New York Herald Tribune,* June 3, 1965.

Variety. Review of *Beach Blanket Bingo,* April 7, 1965.

The Beach Girls and the Monster

The Astounding B Monster. "Sand Blast: Cahuna Jon Hall Makes a Monster from the Surf." *The Astounding B Monster.* http://www.bmonster.com/scifi3.html.

Boxoffice. Review of *The Beach Girls and the Monster,* November 15, 1965.

Edwards, Nadine M. "No Appetite for the Monster Mash." *Citizen-News,* September 17, 1965.

Thomas, Kevin. "*Beach Girls and the Monster* a Perfectly Frightful Movie." *Los Angeles Times*, September 17, 1965.

Variety. Review of *The Beach Girls and the Monster*, September 16, 1965.

Weaver, Tom. "The B-Girl and the Monsters." *Fangoria*, November 2000: 67–70, 82.

Beach Party

Atwell, Lee. Review of *Beach Party*. *Film Quarterly*, Spring 1964: 61.

Flynn, Hazel. "*Beach Party* Bows with Surf Fest." *Citizen-News*, August 30, 1963.

Greater Amusement. Review of *Beach Party*, August 16, 1963.

Masters, Dorothy. "*Beach Party* Opens Saturation Booking." *New York Daily News*, September 26, 1963.

Motion Picture Herald. Review of *Beach Party*, July 24, 1963.

New York Post. "*Beach Party* Romps at 3 Theaters," September 26, 1963.

New York Post. Review of *Beach Party*, 1963.

Newsweek. "The King at 24: Dick Dale," August 26, 1963: 71.

Powers, James. "*Beach Party* Summer: Comedy with Music Has Youth Appeal." *Hollywood Reporter*, July 15, 1963.

Thompson, Howard. "Screen: 'Beach Party': Musical Opens Here and in Brooklyn." *New York Times*, September 26, 1963.

Time. Review of *Beach Party*, August 16, 1963.

Variety. Review of *Beach Party*, July 17, 1963.

Zunser, Jesse. Review of *Beach Party*. *Cue*, August 31, 1963.

Bikini Beach

Archer, Eugene. Review of *Bikini Beach*. *New York Times*, September 17, 1964.

Ehrlich, Henry. "Success Overtakes Patti Chandler." *Look*, June 29, 1965: 33–37.

Graves, Janet. Review of *Bikini Beach*. *Photoplay*, 1964.

Herbstman, Mandel. Review of *Bikini Beach*. *Film Daily*, July 7, 1964.

Houser, John G. "Lusty, Busty Film Fun: *Bikini Beach* Buoyant." *Los Angeles Herald-Examiner*, August 21, 1964.

Powers, James. "*Bikini Beach* Ready for Good B. O. Swim." *Hollywood Reporter*, July 15, 1964.

Salmaggi, Robert. Review of *Bikini Beach*. *New York Herald Tribune*, September 17, 1964.

Thomas, Kevin. "Younger Set Frolics Again in *Bikini Beach*." *Los Angeles Times*, August 21, 1964.

Variety. Review of *Bikini Beach*, July 8, 1964.

Blue Hawaii

Bean, Robin. Review of *Blue Hawaii*. *Films and Filming*, January 1962.

Brown, Peter Harry, and Pat H. Broeske. *Down at the End of Lonely Street: The Life and Death of Elvis Presley*. New York: Dutton, 1997.

Clayton, Rose, and Dick Heard, eds. *Elvis Up Close: In the Words of Those Who Knew Him Best*. Atlanta: Turner, 1994.

Douglass, Greg. "From Ed Wood to Elvis! The Incredible Saga of Dolores Fuller: Part Two." *Outré: The World of Ultra Media*, No. 17: 42–48.

Ivers, James D. Review of *Blue Hawaii*. *Motion Picture Herald*, November 24, 1961.

Masters, Dorothy. "Elvis Shares Billing with Asiatic Rebels." *New York Daily News*, February 1, 1962.

McLafferty, Gerry. *Elvis Presley in Hollywood: Celluloid Sell-Out*. London: Hale, 1989.

Miller, Edwin. Review of *Blue Hawaii*. *Seventeen*, 1961.

Newsweek. Review of *Blue Hawaii*, February 19, 1962.

Powers, James. "*Blue Hawaii*: Wallis-Taurog Pic Packs Youth Appeal." *Hollywood Reporter*, November 24, 1961.

Rockin' Robin. "Jean Blackman Interview." *Elvis Presley News*, http: www.elvispresleynews.com/article2002.html.

Show Business Illustrated. Review of *Blue Hawaii*, November 28, 1961.

Thompson, Howard. "*Blue Hawaii* Opens." *New York Times*, February 23, 1962.

Variety. Review of *Blue Hawaii,* November 29, 1961.
Variety. "Wallis Replaces Prowse in 'Hawaii'; Next Move Now Up to 20th–Fox," March 14, 1961.
Wallis-Paramount. *Blue Hawaii* Exhibitor's Campaign Manual, 1961.
Webb, Jean Francis. *"Blue Hawaii." Screen Stories,* January 1962: 28–32, 67–69.

Catalina Caper

Beaulieu, Trace, Paul Chaplin, Jim Mallon, Kevin Murphy, Michael J. Nelson and Mary Jo Pehl. *The Mystery Science Theater 3000 Amazing Colossal Episode Guide.* New York: Bantam Books, 1996.
Crown International. *Catalina Caper* Exhibitor's Campaign Manual, 1967.
Galligan, David. "The Party's Over: Michael Blodgett Writes." *Hollywood Drama-Logue,* May 22, 1980.
Henderson, Jan Alan. "Director Lee Sholem Interviewed: Superman Director Takes the Hard-Nosed Path to Insure the Transition from Feature Films to TV Series." *Filmfax,* December 1988: 53–55.
MacMinn, Aleene. "Michael Blodgett: Serious Show for Ex-Groovy Host." *Los Angeles Times,* February 23, 1968.

Daytona Beach Weekend

Dominant Films. *Daytona Beach Weekend* Pressbook, 1965.

Don't Make Waves

Carroll, Harrison. "Directed Approach." *Los Angeles Herald-Examiner,* September 18, 1966.
_____. "Plot Fairly Oozes Tilting at Mud Slides." *Los Angeles Herald-Examiner,* October 2, 1966.
Davis, Richard. Review of *Don't Make Waves. Films and Filming,* October 1967.
Gelmis, Joseph. *"Waves* Makes a Joyful Splash." *Newsday,* June 22, 1967: 2A.
Manners, Dorothy. "Acting No Joke." *Los Angeles Herald-Examiner,* August 24, 1966.
Sarris, Andrew. Review of *Don't Make Waves. Village Voice,* June 29, 1967.
Skolsky, Sidney. Hollywood Week. *Citizen-News,* August 22, 1966.
Thompson, Howard. "Circuit Houses Offer *Don't Make Waves." New York Times,* June 21, 1967.
Variety. Review of *Don't Make Waves,* June 31, 1967.
Winsten, Archer. Review of *Don't Make Waves. New York Post,* June 21, 1967.

The Endless Summer

Alexander, Max. "Surf, Sand, Cinema." *Variety,* June 13, 1994: 2.
Bart, Peter. "Fellini of the Foam." *New York Times,* June 12, 1966.
Benet, Raley. Review of *The Endless Summer. (NY) Villager,* June 22, 1967: 12.
Brown, Bruce. "Africa—The Perfect Wave." *Surfer,* November 1964: 48–55.
Canby, Vincent. "It Surfs Them Right." *New York Times,* August 21, 1966.
_____. Review of *The Endless Summer. New York Times,* June 16, 1966.
_____. "Surfing Film Earns Its First Million." *New York Times,* June 13, 1967.
Film Quarterly. Review of *The Endless Summer,* Fall 1967.
Galbraith, Jane. "Surf's Up for Sequel to '66 Classic: A New-Wave Follow to *Endless Summer." Newsday,* June 2, 1994: B3, B19.
Geeslin, Ned, and Dirk Mathison. "The Surf's Still Up for the Men Who Made *The Endless Summer." People,* August 25, 1986: 56–58.
Gelmis, Joseph. "He's Riding Out Sudden Success Smoothly." *Newsday,* c. 1967.
Goodman, Mark, and Johnny Dodd. "Reshooting the Curl." *People,* May 30, 1994: 101–102.
Hale, Wanda. "Surfing Film for Dad, Son." *New York Daily News,* June 16, 1966.
Hemmings, Fred. *The Soul of Surfing.* New York: Thunder's Mouth Press, 1997.
Koch, John. "Brown's Myth-Killing: Bikeys Without Swastikas." *Boston After Dark,* July 27, 1971: 14.
Kung, Michelle. "Moore the Merrier: The *Fahrenheit 9/11* Director Brings on a Nonfiction Revolution." *Entertainment Weekly,* July 16, 2004: 10, 11.

McLellan, Dennis. "Cult Movie *Endless Summer* Follows Surfers in Search of the 'Perfect Wave.'" *Star Ledger (Newark, NJ)*, August 4, 1991: 11.

Moore, Gilbert. "The Endless Summer of Film-Maker Bruce Brown: A Happy Tycoon Takes Off." *Life*, August 25, 1967: 37–42.

Ryan, Wayne. 2004. *Line Up Surf Australia: Robert August Interview* [online]. Available from World Wide Web: 〈http://www.lineup.com.au〉

Sciaky. "Riding High." *Women's Wear Daily*, July 22, 1971: 8.

Strauss, Neil. "Surf's Up Dude. Hang On to Your Couch." *New York Times*, August 4, 2002: Section 13, 4–5.

Time. Review of *The Endless Summer*, July 8, 1966.

Variety. Review of *The Endless Summer*, June 22, 1966.

Variety. "Surfer a Sleeper in First Playoff," September 28, 1966.

Vaughan, Roger. "A Splashy, Surf-Soaked Sleeper: *The Endless Summer*." *Life*, November 25, 1966: 19.

Winsten, Archer. "*Endless Summer* Follows Surfers Around the World." *New York Post*, June 16, 1966.

_____. Rages and Outrages. *New York Post*, December 12, 1966: 42.

For Those Who Think Young

Crist, Judith. *Judith Crist's TV Guide to the Movies*. Toronto: Popular Library, 1974.

Eyles, Allen. Review of *For Those Who Think Young*. *Films and Filming*, January 1965: 37.

Hale, Wanda. "Youthful Ado About Nothing." *New York Daily News*, July 9, 1964.

Harford, Margaret. "Think Young Fare for Teeners." *Los Angeles Times*, July 18, 1964.

Keller, Frank. "My Adventures with Two Sprocket Holes." *Cinemeditor* (Winter 1964): 4.

Powers, James. Review of *For Those Who Think Young*. *Hollywood Reporter*, May 19, 1964.

Seidenbaum, Art. "*For Those Who Think Young* Going All Out with Tie-Ins." *Los Angeles Times*, October 25, 1963: Part V, 13.

Thompson, Howard. "Collegians' Frolic." *New York Times*, July 9, 1964.

Time. Review of *For Those Who Think Young*, July 24, 1964.

United Artists. *For Those Who Think Young* Exhibitor's Campaign Manual, 1964.

Variety. "Paul Winchell Sues, Charges UA Used His TV Character," August 5, 1965.

Winsten, Archer. "*Those Who Think Young* Bows Here." *New York Post*, July 10, 1964.

Wolf, William. Review of *For Those Who Think Young*. *Cue*, July 11, 1964.

The Ghost in the Invisible Bikini

Harford, Margaret. "*The Ghost* a Romp at Beach." *Los Angeles Times*, April 22, 1966.

Hawkins, Glenn. "*Bikini* Skimpy Comedy." *Los Angeles Herald-Examiner*, April 21, 1966.

Herbstman, Mandel. Review of *The Ghost in the Invisible Bikini*. *Film Daily*, April 27, 1966.

Oshinsky, Sy. Review of *The Ghost in the Invisible Bikini*. *Motion Picture Herald*, April 13, 1966.

Powers, James. "Offbeat Ghost Yarn Lacks Story Point." *Hollywood Reporter* April 7, 1966.

Variety. Review of *The Ghost in the Invisible Bikini*, April 6, 1966.

Gidget

Carpinone, George. "Legendary Sandra Dee." *Celebrity Collector Magazine*: 1995.

Hollywood Reporter. Review of *Gidget*, March 16, 1959.

Knutzen, Erik. "Darren Doesn't Gun for Trouble." *Los Angeles Herald-Examiner*, c. 1961.

Miller, Edwin. Review of *Gidget*. *Seventeen*, April 1959: 46.

Petersen's Surfing Yearbook. "Interviews with the Greats," No. 3, 1966.

Ribakove, Barbara. "*Gidget*." *Screen Stories*, May 1959: 29–32, 80–82.

Scheuer, Philip K. "*Gidget* Invigorating as Sandra Rides Surf." *Los Angeles Times*, March 26, 1959.

Surfing Yearbook. "Interviews with the Greats," 1963.

Thirer, Irene. "Joby Doesn't Want to Be Handsome." *New York Post*, September 18, 1959: 70.

Thompson, Howard. "Sun and Surf: 'Gidget' the Story of a Teen-Age Girl, Opens." *New York Times* April 23, 1959.

Variety. Review of *Gidget*, March 18, 1959.

Gidget Goes Hawaiian

Associated Press. "Actress' Marriage Is Over." *New York Daily News*, October 5, 1963.
Columbia Pictures. *Gidget Goes Hawaiian* Exhibitor's Campaign Manual, 1961.
Hamilton, Sara. Review of *Gidget Goes Hawaiian. Los Angeles Herald-Examiner*, June 22, 1961.
Herbstman, Mandel. Review of *Gidget Goes Hawaiian. Film Daily*, June 1, 1961.
Hurley, Joseph. "The Name Change." *Newsday*, June 9, 1987.
Kane, Chris. "*Gidget Goes Hawaiian.*" *Screen Stories*, July 1961: 32–37, 66–68.
Look. "Vicki Trickett: Omaha Girl Breezes Through Hollywood," March 14, 1961: 72, 74.
Manners, Dorothy. "About James Darren." *Los Angeles Herald-Examiner*, May 31, 1964.
Powers, James. "Bresler, Wendkos Pic Highly Pleasing." *Hollywood Reporter*, May 31, 1961.
Salmaggi, Bob. Review of *Gidget Goes Hawaiian. New York Herald Tribune*, August 10, 1961.
Scott, John L. "Gidget's Problems Beached at Waikiki: Film Story of Puppy Love Has Exotic Island Setting." *Los Angeles Times*, June 22, 1961.
Thompson, Howard. "Strange Mates: Sequel to *Gidget* and 'Historical' Film Open." *New York Times*, August 10, 1961.

Girl Happy

Graves, Janet. Review of *Girl Happy. Photoplay*, May 1965: 12.
Harford, Margaret. "*Girl Happy* Promises More Box Office Joy for Elvis." *Los Angeles Times*, April 6, 1965.
Herbstman, Mandel. Review of *Girl Happy. Film Daily*, January 22, 1965.
Herridge, Frances. "Presley Goes to Fort Lauderdale." *New York Post*, May 27, 1965.
Houser, John G. "*Girl Happy* Kind of Sad." *Los Angeles Herald-Examiner*, April 16, 1965: D-4.
MGM. *Girl Happy* Exhibitors Campaign Manual, 1965.
Powers, James. "Presley's *Girl Happy* Will Do His Usual Good Business." *Hollywood Reporter*, January 21, 1965.
Thompson, Howard. "*Girl Happy* at Forum Has Elvis Presley Singing Again." *New York Times*, May 27, 1965.
Weaver, William R. Review of *Girl Happy. Motion Picture Herald*, February 5, 1965.
Webb, Jean Francis. "*Girl Happy.*" *Screen Stories*, May 1965: 60–62, 66–69.

The Girls on the Beach

Harford, Margaret. "A Beach Gang in Same Old Formula." *Los Angeles Times*, June 21, 1965.
Herbstman, Mandel. Review of *The Girls on the Beach. Film Daily*, May 10, 1965.
Paramount Pictures. *The Girls on the Beach* Pressbook, 1965.
Powers, James. "Jacobson-Witney Pic Aimed at Juveniles." *Hollywood Reporter*, May 10, 1965.
Redelings, Lowell E. "*Girls on Beach* Bright, Bouncy." *Los Angeles Herald-Examiner*, June 18, 1965.
Salmaggi, Robert. Review of *The Girls on the Beach. New York Herald Tribune*, June 17, 1965.
Sanders, Coyne Steven. "Noreen Corcoran." *Emmy*, July/August 1984: 66.
Variety. "Exhib Who B.R.'d Corman's *Girl* Will Premiere Pic," May 14, 1964: 4.
Variety. Review of *The Girls on the Beach*, May 19, 1965.

The Horror of Party Beach

Archer, Eugene. "Two Horror Films." *New York Times*, April 20, 1964.
The Astounding B Monster. "Greetings from Party Beach: The Story of Del Tenney's Shore Thing." *The Astounding B Monster.* http://www.bmonster.com/profile9.html.
Durgnat, Raymond. Review of *The Horror of Party Beach. Films and Filming*, January 1965.
Herridge, Frances. "Teenage Appeal in Fright Films at the Paramount." *New York Post*, April 29, 1964.
Medved, Harry, and Michael Medved. *The Golden Turkey Awards: Nominees and Winners, the Worst Achievements in Hollywood History.* New York: Putnam, 1980.
Munroe, Dale. "Monsters Await *Beach* Visitors." *Citizen-News*, June 4, 1964.
Salmaggi, Robert. Review of *The Horror of Party Beach. New York Herald Tribune*, April 29, 1964.

20th Century–Fox Film Corp. *The Horror of Party Beach* Pressbook, 1964.

Walker, Brian J. "Del Tenney." *Brian's Drive-in Theater.* http://briansdriveintheater.com/beach.html

Weaver, Tom. "He Came from Party Beach: The Life and Times of That Favorite Low-Budget Director, Del Tenney, the Man Who Gave You Roy Scheider's First Movie and the World's Greatest Surf Monster." *Fangoria,* August 1984: 53–57, 64.

Wood, Wallace. *The Horror of Party Beach.* New York: Warren, 1964.

How to Stuff a Wild Bikini

Boxoffice. Review of *How to Stuff a Wild Bikini,* July 26, 1965.

Herbstman, Mandel. Review of *How to Stuff a Wild Bikini. Film Daily,* July 16, 1965.

Miller, Edwin. "I Was a Teenager for 10 Years (Dwayne Hickman)." *Seventeen,* June 1965: 94, 175, 176.

Munroe, Dale. "Beach Party Gang Flips Over Witch." *Citizen-News,* August 5, 1965.

Playboy.com. "Playmates: Sue Williams, April 1965." *Playboy.com.* http://playboy.com/playmates/directory/196504.html

Porter, Reed. "AIP Production Has Boxoffice Appeal." *Hollywood Reporter,* July 23, 1965.

Redelings, Lowell E. "Rooney's Shenanigans Enliven *Wild Bikini.*" *Los Angeles Herald-Examiner,* August 5, 1965.

Rotter, C. Robert. "Sue Hamilton." *Glamour Girls of the Silver Screen.* http://www.glamourgirlsofthesilverscreen.com/hamilton_s/.

Variety. Review of *How to Stuff a Wild Bikini,* July 28, 1965.

It's a Bikini World

Beck, Calvin Thomas. *Scream Queens: Heroines of the Horrors.* New York: Collier Books, 1978.

Trans American Films. *It's a Bikini World* Pressbook, 1967.

Muscle Beach Party

Boxoffice. Review of *Muscle Beach Party,* March 30, 1964.

Graves, Janet. Review of *Muscle Beach Party. Photoplay,* 1964.

Miller, Edwin. Review of *Muscle Beach Party. Seventeen,* 1964.

New York Post. Review of *Muscle Beach Party,* May 28, 1964.

Powers, James. "*Muscle Beach Party* Ace Comedy-Musical Picture." *Hollywood Reporter,* March 25, 1964.

Salmaggi, Robert. Review of *Muscle Beach Party. New York Herald Tribune,* May 28, 1964.

Thompson, Howard. Review of *Muscle Beach Party. New York Times,* May 28, 1964.

Variety. Review of *Muscle Beach Party,* July 28, 1965.

One Way Wahine

United Screen Arts, Inc. *One Way Wahine* Exhibitor's Campaign Folder, 1965.

Variety. Review of *One Way Wahine,* October 6, 1965.

Out of Sight

Buchanan, Loren G. Review of *Out of Sight. Motion Picture Herald,* May 25, 1966.

Buck, Jerry. "When the *CHiPs* Are Up." *New York Post,* August 4, 1981: 62.

Davidson, Bill. "Mr. No-Name's in the Chips: Robert Pine Philosophically Settles for Being Third Banana." *TV Guide,* January 30, 1982: 20, 22, 23.

Lipton, Edward. Review of *Out of Sight. Film Daily,* May 19, 1966.

Motion Picture Exhibitor. Review of *Out of Sight,* May 11, 1966.

Powers, James. "Universal Entry Banks on Groups." *Hollywood Reporter,* May 12, 1966.

Universal Pictures. *Out of Sight* Pressbook, 1966.

UPI. "New Role Brings New Life Style." *New York Daily News,* November 2, 1977: 56.

Variety. Review of *Out of Sight,* May 18, 1966.

Pajama Party

Boxoffice. Review of *Pajama Party*, November 23, 1964.

Herbstman, Mandel. Review of *Pajama Party*. *Film Daily*, November 12, 1964.

Munroe, Dale. "Teen Funsters Go on *Pajama Party*." *Citizen-News*, December 5, 1964.

Powers, James. "Another Pic for Younger Patrons." *Hollywood Reporter*, November 12, 1964.

Scott, John L. "*Pajama Party* Slanted for Younger Audiences." *Los Angeles Times*, December 4, 1964.

Variety. Review of *Pajama Party*, November 18, 1964.

Ride the Wild Surf

Carroll, Kathleen. "New Surf Film Zooms All Out for Sea Sport." *New York Daily News*, December 24, 1964.

Columbia Pictures. *Ride the Wild Surf* Exhibitor's Campaign Manual, 1964.

Motion Picture Exhibitor. Review of *Ride the Wild Surf*, August 5, 1964.

Munroe, Dale. "*Wild Surf* Offers Thrills and Spills." *Citizen-News*, August 27, 1964.

Powers, James. "*Ride the Wild Surf* Has Excellent Marquee Value." *Hollywood Reporter*, July 29, 1964.

Salmaggi, Robert. Review of *Ride the Wild Surf*. *New York Herald Tribune*, December 24, 1964.

Thomas, Kevin. "Younger Cinema Set Frolics in *Wild Surf*." *Los Angeles Times*, August 28, 1964.

Tusher, William. "My Love for Fabian by Quinn O'Hara." *Photoplay*, March 1964: 44, 84–87.

Variety. Review of *Ride the Wild Surf*, July 29, 1964.

Ski Party

Arceneaux, Noah. "A Talk with TV's Favorite High School Hipster: Dwayne Hickman." *Filmfax*, Nov./Dec. 1995: 65–69.

Carroll, Harrison. "Dwayne Hickman: Celebs Suffer." *Los Angeles Herald-Examiner*, March 5, 1965.

Gilroy, Harry. Review of *Ski Party*. *New York Times*, October 23, 1965.

Harford, Margaret. "Humor in Ski Film Is an Uphill Battle All the Way." *Los Angeles Times*, August 13, 1965.

Herbstman, Mandel. Review of *Ski Party*. *Film Daily*, June 17, 1965.

Motion Picture Exhibitor. Review of *Ski Party*, June 23, 1965.

Okuda, Ted. "Yvonne 'Batgirl' Craig: From Ballet to Batcycle, This Curvaceous Costumed Crimefighter Had to Keep on Her Toes." *Filmfax*, August 1989: 42–47.

Oshinsky, Sy. Review of *Ski Party*. *Motion Picture Herald*, July 7, 1965.

Variety. Review of *Ski Party*, June 16, 1965.

Surf Party

Boxoffice. Review of *Surf Party*, March 16, 1964.

Carroll, Kathleen. "Beach Hijinks in *Surf Party*." *New York Daily News*, March 13, 1964.

Levy, Alan. "So Who Is This Bobby Vinton?" *Life*, March 12, 1965: 76–91.

Miller, Kenny, and Donald Vaughan. *Kenny Miller: Surviving Teenage Werewolves, Puppet People and Hollywood*. Jefferson, NC: McFarland, 1999.

New York Post. Review of *Surf Party*, March 12, 1964.

Rider, David. Review of *Surf Party*. *Films and Filming*, May 1964: 25.

Salmaggi, Robert. Review of *Surf Party*. *New York Herald Tribune*, March 12, 1964.

Seventeen. Teens Are Listening to…, April 1964: 217.

20th Century–Fox Film Corp. *Surf Party* Exhibitor's Campaign Manual, 1964.

Widem, Allen M. Review of *Surf Party*. *Motion Picture Herald*, March 4, 1964.

The Sweet Ride

Crist, Judith. Review of *The Sweet Ride*. *New York Magazine*, July 8, 1968.

Guarino, Ann. "Sweet Ride Trip in All Directions." *New York Daily News*, June 13, 1968: 95.

Klemesrud, Judy. "A Good Roommate Is Hard to Find." *New York Times*, December 20, 1970.

Knight, Arthur. Review of *The Sweet Ride*. *Saturday Review*, June 1, 1968.

MacDonough, Scott. "The Public and Private Life of an Enigma: Michael Sarrazin." *Show*, April 1971: 19–21.

Rider, David. Review of *The Sweet Ride*. *Films and Filming*, February 1969: 47.

Skolsky, Sidney. Tintypes. *New York Post*, May 23, 1970.

20th Century–Fox Film Corp. *The Sweet Ride* Pressbook, 1968.

Variety. Review of *The Sweet Ride*, May 8, 1968.

Winsten, Archer. Review of *The Sweet Ride*. *New York Post*, June 13, 1968.

Wolf, William. Review of *The Sweet Ride*. *Cue*, June 15, 1968.

A Swingin' Summer

Boxoffice. Review of *A Swingin' Summer*, March 22, 1965.

Powers, James. "*Swingin' Summer* aimed at Teenage B.O. Business." *Hollywood Reporter*, March 3, 1965.

United Screen Arts Inc. *A Swingin' Summer* Exhibitor's Campaign Folder, 1965.

Variety. Review of *A Swingin' Summer*, March 3, 1965.

Weaver, William. Review of *A Swingin' Summer*. *Motion Picture Herald*, March 17, 1965.

Where the Boys Are

Angell, Roger. Review of *Where the Boys Are*. *New Yorker*, January 28, 1961.

Christian Science Monitor. "Dunces on the Dunes," January 25, 1961.

Colacello, Bob. "Charm Kills: The George Hamilton Story." *Vanity Fair*, January 1991: 99–102, 104, 118–20.

Cue. "Teenage Shenanigans," January 21, 1961.

Faas, Horst, and Tim Page, eds. *Requiem: By the Photographers Who Died in Vietnam and Indochina*. London: Jonathan Cape, 1997.

Graves, Janet. Review of *Where the Boys Are*. *Photoplay*, February 1961.

Meyers, Jeffrey. *Inherited Risk: Errol and Sean Flynn in Hollywood and Vietnam*. New York: Simon & Schuster, 2002.

MGM. *Where the Boys Are* Pressbook, 1960.

Miller, Edwin. "Connie Francis Talks About Boys, Music, Movies from the Heart." *Seventeen*, February 1961: 130, 178, 179.

———. Review of *Where the Boys Are*. *Seventeen*, February 1961.

Powers, James. Review of *Where the Boys Are*. *Hollywood Reporter*, November 30, 1960.

Rechetnik, Sidney. Review of *Where the Boys Are*. *Motion Picture Daily*, November 30, 1960.

Roman, Robert C. Review of *Where the Boys Are*, February 1961.

Time. Review of *Where the Boys Are*, January 20, 1961: 72.

TV Guide. "The Girl with 65,000 Greeting Cards: Dolores Hart, a Sometimes Caricaturist, Discusses Her Full-time Acting Career." November 5, 1960: 12–14.

Variety. "Pasternak Sees His *Where Boys Are* First Big-Budget Pic Sans Names." 1960.

———. Review of *Where the Boys Are*, November 30, 1960.

Walker, Brian J. "Sean Flynn." *Brian's Drive-in Theater*. http://briansdriveintheater.com/beach.html

Winsten, Archer. Review of *Where the Boys Are*. *New York Post*, January 20, 1961.

Wild on the Beach

Carroll, Kathleen. "*Wild Beach* Dull as Sand." *New York Daily News*, August 26, 1966.

New York Post. Review of *Wild on the Beach*, August 26, 1965.

Pattison, Barry. "Where Credit Is Due: The Work of Producer/Director Maury Dexter." *Big Reel*, November 1997: 136, 137.

Salmaggi, Robert. Review of *Wild on the Beach*. *New York Herald Tribune*, August 26, 1965.

20th Century–Fox Film Corp. *Wild on the Beach* Exhibitor's Campaign Manual, 1965.

Wild Wild Winter

Boxoffice. Review of *Wild Wild Winter*, February 1966.
Buchanan, Loren G. Review of *Wild Wild Winter*. *Motion Picture Herald*, February 6, 1966.
Carroll, Kathleen. "*Wild Wild Winter* Leaves Viewer Cold." *New York Daily News*, January 6, 1966.
Greenberg, Abe. "Patton-Weinrib on Sex and Good Films." *Citizen-News*, January 14, 1966.
Hollywood Reporter. "Patton-Weinrib Moves Onto Universal Lot for 4 Pix Plus Options," August 2, 1965.
Powers, James. "Wild Wild Youth: Patton-Weinrib Pic Has Nice Touches." *Hollywood Reporter*, January 5, 1966.
Salmaggi, Robert. Review of *Wild Wild Winter*. *New York Herald Tribune*, January 6, 1966.
Thompson, Howard. Review of *Wild Wild Winter*. *New York Times*, January 6, 1966.
Universal Pictures. *Wild Wild Winter* Exhibitor's Campaign Manual, 1966.
Variety. Review of *Wild Wild Winter*, January 12 1966.
Weaver, Tom. "I, Too, Was a Teenage Werewolf: Gary Clarke Clues Everyone in on Ways to *Get Smart* (or Not) in Hollywood and *How to Make a Monster*." *Starlog*, June 2003: 80–85.
Winsten, Archer. Review of *Wild Wild Winter*. *New York Post*, January 6, 1966: 16.

Winter a-Go-Go

Associated Press. "Actor Wins $1.9M in Cycle Accident." *New York Post*, May 5, 1976: 8.
Boxoffice. Review of *Winter a-Go-Go*, November 8, 1965.
Buchanan, Loren G. Review of *Winter a-Go-Go*. *Motion Picture Herald*, November 10, 1965.
Columbia Pictures. *Winter a-Go-Go* Exhibitor's Campaign Manual, 1965.
Guarino, Ann. "New Names, Faces, Music But Old Plot." *New York Daily News*, December 9, 1965: 92.
Herridge, Frances. Review of *Winter a-Go-Go*. *New York Post*, December 9, 1965.
Lobsenz, Allan C. Review of *Winter a-Go-Go*. *Film Daily*, October 29, 1965.
Los Angeles Times. "Passings: Julie Parrish," October 8, 2003.
Post Wire Services. "Tragic '60s Star Gets Jail." *New York Post*, March 7, 1996: 85.
Powers, James. Review of *Winter a-Go-Go*. *Hollywood Reporter*, October 28, 1965.
Salmaggi, Robert. Review of *Winter a-Go-Go*. *New York Herald Tribune*, December 9, 1965.
Variety. Review of *Winter a-Go-Go*, November 3, 1965.

Actors

John Ashley

Gardella, Kay. "New ABC Star Nixes Television Fad Billing." *New York Daily News*, July 9, 1961: 12.
Olson, Eric. "John Ashley: Obituary." *Variety*, November 24, 1997: 77.
Weaver, Tom, and John Brunas. "From B-Movies to the *A-Team*." *Fangoria*, March 1985: 56–60, 64.

Frankie Avalon

Burden, Martin. "Of Mice and Them! Funicello & Avalon Take Fans Down Memory Lane." *New York Post*, July 28, 1990: 17.
Miller, Edwin. The Hollywood Scene. *Seventeen*, July 1965: 40.
Scott, Vernon. "Reign's End? Frankie Avalon Calls Halt to Beach Party Movies." *Newark Evening News*, April 7, 1965.
Skolsky, Sidney. Hollywood Is My Beat. *New York Post Magazine*, November 13, 1960: 3.

Peter Brown

Antell, Tish. "I'd Like You to Meet My Son." *Photoplay*, May 1966.
Archer, Eugene. Review of *Ride the Wild Surf*. *New York Times*, December 24, 1964.

Bialow, Jennifer. "You Can Lead a Horse to Water ... but You Can't Make an Actor Do Something He Doesn't Want To." *Soap Opera Digest*, September 17, 1991: 120–123.
Gross, Ben. "The Western Is Every Man's Dream." *New York Daily News*, January 22, 1967: S23.
Rizzo, Tony. "Peter Brown: He's Found His Place in the Sun." *Soap Opera Digest*, May 11, 1982: 29–35.

James Darren

Counts, Kyle. "A Time to Remember." *Starlog*, July 1992: 32, 33, 35, 66.
Films and Filming. "The Good Old Moondoggie Days," November 1973: 8.
Miller, Edwin. The Hollywood Scene. *Seventeen*, September 1964: 26.
TV Guide. "A Teen-age Idol Passes 30," June 24, 1967: 14–16, 18.

Sandra Dee

Beigal, Jerry. "Sandra Dee & Universal End Long, Warm (As in Affection) Contract on Hot (As in Temper) Farewell." *Variety*, June 26, 1968: 4, 16.
Connelly, Sherryl. "Sandra Dee's Son Reveals All the Family Skeletons." *New York Daily News,* October 9, 1994: 24.
Connolly, Mike. Star of the Month. *Screen Stories*, February 1959: 52, 53.
Dee, Sandra. "Learning to Live Again." *People*, March 13, 1991: 87–94.
Jennings, C. Robert. "The Odd Odyssey of Sandra Dee." *Saturday Evening Post*, June 22, 1963: 22, 23.
Miller, Edwin. "Peter Pan Is Out! (Sandra Dee)." *Seventeen*, March 1966: 159, 176.
Morning Telegraph (NY). "Sandra Dee Wants Back in Films in Adult Roles," August 19, 1970.
Rodack, Jeffrey. "Sandra Dee: Anorexia and Alcohol Drove Me to the Brink of Death." *National Enquirer*, July 14, 1998.
Skolsky, Sidney. Tintypes. *New York Daily News,* 1972.
Willens, Michele. "Gidget Grows Up and Likes It." *Sunday Record*, January 28, 1973: B-16.

Mickey Dora

Dora, Mickey. "Mickey on Malibu." *Surfer,* January 1968: 37–42.
Gault-Williams, Maxwell. "Miki 'Da' Cat." *Legendary Surfers: A Definitive History of Surfing's Culture and Heroes* 3, no. 18, http://www.legendarysurfers.com/
Surfer. "Mickey Chapin Dora—Surf Stuntman," July 1965: 28–31.

Don Edmonds

Bearden, Keith. "Edmonds: Director of the SS." *Fangoria* (No. 155) 1996.
Gaita, Paul. "Father of Ilsa! A Conversation with Don Edmonds." *Worldly Remains,* (no. 8) 2003: 12–20.

Shelley Fabares

Lisanti, Tom. "Swingin' with Shelley Fabares: From Donna Reed to Elvis to Coach." *Outré: The World of Ultra Media*, No. 16: 34–37, 76, 77.
People. "Gift of Hope." November 13, 2000: 239.

Johnny Fain

Cleary, Bill. "The Day War Came to Malibu." *Surfer,* January 1966: 63–73.
Inside Surfin'. "Legendary Surfers: Johnny Fain." http://www.firehorse.com.au/insidesurfin/nviews-fain.html (site now discontinued).

Annette Funicello

Loud, Lance. "Annette Funicello." *Interview,* August 1987: 142.
National Examiner. "Annette Funicello's Future Grim as MS Steals Her Sight and Voice ... Pray for a Miracle, January 2, 2001: 29.

Aron Kincaid

Kincaid, Aron. "*Creature of Destruction*: Another 'Worst Movie Ever Made'?" *Scarlet Street*, Winter 1994: 93–95.
Mahoney, John. "*Proud, Damned & Dead* Only Lives Up to Last." *Hollywood Reporter*, June 11, 1969: 16.
Neeley, Jerry. "Aron Kincaid Interviewed." *Cult Movies & Video*, No. 5, 1992: 20–24.
Parsons, Louella. I Nominate for Stardom. *Modern Screen*, January 1966.
Shinnick, Kevin G. "Aron in Wonderland." *Scarlet Street*, Fall 1993: 80–85.
_____. "Aron in Wonderland, Part Two." *Scarlet Street*, Winter 1994: 89–92.

Tommy Kirk

Brown, Vivian. "Mr. Kirk Dreams: Seeking Beauty and Brains." *Newark Evening News*, June 8, 1963.
Minton, Kevin. "Sex, Lies and Disney Tape: Walt's Fallen Star." *Filmfax*, April/May 1993: 67–71.
Valley, Richard. "Just an Average Joe (Hardy): An Interview with Tommy Kirk." *Scarlet Street*, Spring 1993: 60–69, 97.

Jody McCrea

Gelmis, Joseph. "Jody Hopes Oedipus Ends Bikini Complex." *Newsday*, February 8, 1965.
TV Guide. "A Family Affair: On Paper Joel and Jody McCrea Were the Perfect Combination," January 9, 1960.

Yvette Mimieux

Fields, Sidney. Faces the Music. *New York Daily News*, July 6, 1966: 64.
Garfield, Kim. "Yvette Mimieux." *Hollywood Drama-Logue*, October 14–20, 1982: 15.
Guarino, Ann. "Off Camera: Yvette Mimieux." *Sunday Daily News (NY)*, October 13, 1974: leisure section, 9.
Hamilton, Jack. "Yvette Mimieux: Hollywood's Little Princess." *Look*, February 16, 1960: 78–81.
Hoffmann, Bill. "Yvette Mimieux's a Yoga Bearer." *New York Post*, January 19, 1996: 17.
Lewis, Richard Warren. "The Fair Young Hollywood Girls." *Saturday Evening Post*, September 7, 1963: 22–27.
Life. "A Blonde Called Me-Me-Oh," May 9, 1960: 85–88.
_____. "LIFE Pays a Call on Dr. Kildare's Pretty TV Patient: She Sure Doesn't Look Sick," October 25, 1963: 119–121.
Mackin, Tom. "Flees Nudity Into TV." *Newark Evening News*, June 29, 1970: 29.
Musto, Michael. "Where the Holes Are." *Soho Weekly News*, December 20, 1979: 59.
New Yorker. Review of *Joy in the Morning*, June 19, 1965: 114.
Smith, Bea. "Starlet on Screen Now: Yvette Mimiuex's Scenes Clipped from First Film." *Newark Sunday News*, June 19, 1960: section 3, E4.
Variety. Review of *Where the Boys Are*, November 30, 1960: 6.

Michael Nader

Ballard, Gary. "Michael Nader." *Hollywood Drama-Logue*, June 13, 1985: 11.
Goodwin, Betty. "I Still Do Foolish Things." *TV Guide*, November 10, 1984: 45–49.
Mangan, Dan. "Fired Soap Hunk: I'm Not a Junkie—Just Disabled." *New York Post*, December 31, 2002.
Starr, Michael. "Druggie Soap Star Shocked by Firing." *New York Post*, January 23, 2003.

Bart Patton

Champlin, Charles. "Film Team Young, Foolish and Funny." *Los Angeles Times*, September 24, 1965.
Scott, Vernon. "Mystery Men of Teen-Age Films No Mystery." *Courier-Journal (Louisville, KY)*, March 20, 1966.

Pamela Tiffin

Lisanti, Tom. "Pamela Tiffin: From Hollywood Ingenue to Italian Bombshell." *Outré: The World of Ultra Media*, No. 19: 68–72.

Deborah Walley

Cleaves, Henderson. "Gidget Gets a Heap of Mail." *New York World-Telegraph & Sun*, August 1, 1961: 10.
Variety. Obituary, May 21, 2001.

Web Sites

All Movie Guide [www.allmovie.com]
All Music Guide [www.allmusic.com]
The Astounding B-Monster [www.bmonster.com]
Bad Movie Planet [www.badmovieplanet.com]
Boxoffice Online [www.boxoffice.com]
Brett Cullen—Official Web Site [www.brettcullen.com]
Brian's Drive-In Theater [www.briansdriveintheater.com]
Chris Noel—The Starlet Who Became a Soldier [www.chrisnoel.com]
CultCuts: Films for the Rest of Us Magazine [www.cultcuts.net]
DaveDraper.com [www.davedraper.com]
Dick Dale's Official Worldwide Web Site [www.dickdale.com]
Don Edmonds Mustang Film Co. [www.donedmonds.com]
DVD Talk [www.dvdtalk.com]
Frankie Avalon Products [www.frankieavalon.com]
Frankie Randall Web Site [www.frankierandall.com]
Glamour Girls of the Silver Screen [www.glamourgirlsofthesilverscreen.com]
Hollywood Teen Movies [www.hollywoodteenmovies.com]
Internet Movie Database [www.imdb.com]
James Darren: An Unofficial Web Site [www.celebhost.net/jamesdarren]
Legendary Surfers by Malcolm Gault-Williams [www.legendarysurfers.com]
Leonard Maltin's Movie Crazy [www.leonardmaltin.com]
Line Up Surf Australia [www.lineup.com.au]
The Lively Set [www.encore4.net/livelyset]
Marta Kristen—The Official Web Site [www.martakristen.com]
MichaelNader.Com [www.michaelnader.com]
Music of the Beach Party Movies [www.beachpartymoviemusic.com]
The Official Peter Brown Fan Site [www.peterbrown.tv/]
The Official Site of Fabian Forte [www.fabianforte.com]
Quinn O'Hara's Official Web Site [www.quinnohara.com]
The Science Fiction, Horror and Fantasy Film Review [www.roogulator.esmartweb.com]
Sixties Cinema: The Books of Tom Lisanti [www.sixtiescinema.com]
SurfArt.com [www.surfart.com]
Surfline [www.surfline.com]
Ted V. Mikels Web Site [www.tedvmikels.com]
TheMonsterMash.Com Featuring Bobby "Boris" Pickett [www.themonstermash.com]
The Ultimate Sandra Dee [www.sandradeefans.com]
The Unofficial Shelley Fabares Homepage [www.geocities.com/Shelleyfan/]
Wild Bill: Hollywood Maverick [www.wildbillfilms.com]
William Wellman, Jr.'s Official Web Space [www.williamwellmanjr.com]

Index